PUBLIC BORROWING

Critical Concepts in Finance

PUBLIC BORROWING

Critical Concepts in Finance

Edited by
Tehreem Husain and D'Maris Coffman

Volume I
The Advent of Modern Public Borrowing

Routledge
Taylor & Francis Group

LONDON AND NEW YORK

First published 2022
by Routledge
2 Park Square, Milton Park, Abingdon, Oxon OX14 4RN

and by Routledge
52 Vanderbilt Avenue, New York, NY 10017

Routledge is an imprint of the Taylor & Francis Group, an informa business

British Library Cataloguing-in-Publication Data
A catalogue record for this book is available from the British Library

Library of Congress Cataloging-in-Publication Data
A catalog record has been requested for this book

ISBN: 978-1-138-90553-5 (set)
ISBN: 978-1-138-90554-2 (volume I)

Typeset in Times New Roman
by Deanta Global Publishing Services, Chennai, India

Publisher's Note
References within each chapter are as they appear in the original complete work

CONTENTS

CONTENTS

CONTENTS

CONTENTS

VOLUME IV   MARKET MICROSTRUCTURE, CREDITOR ACTION, AND CONTAGION

CONTENTS

EDITORS' ACKNOWLEDGEMENTS

The editors would like to thank Simon Alexander, Senior Development Editor of Major Works at Routledge, for commissioning this volume back in late 2014 and then for remaining patient through the vicissitudes of the intervening half decade. The selection of contributors and contributions presented a challenging task with the consequence that many readers will notice inevitable oversights. We tried to balance classical texts with those that might be otherwise difficult to obtain. We hope that readers will, in the process of perusing the volume, discover scholarly interventions they may have otherwise overlooked.

Professor Coffman would like to thank Dr Roberto Cardinale, who at the time was working mainly as a research assistant on the companion *Infrastructure Finance* volume, for useful discussions about the contents. Conversations at the Centre for Financial History (then at Newnham College, now at Darwin College) in Cambridge were also helpful for refining the topics to be covered, with special thanks due to Dr Anthony Hotson, Professor Larry Neal, and Professor Roberto Scazzieri. Any errors or omissions nevertheless remain her responsibility, not theirs.

Tehreem Husain would like to extend thanks to Dr Nadeem Aftab for useful conversations on topics covered in these volumes. She would also like to thank Sahar Z Babar, Corporate Secretary at the State Bank of Pakistan, for encouraging the exploration of the role of public borrowing in economic growth from a financial stability perspective. Special thanks are also due to Dr Ali Coşkun Tunçer for many beneficial conversations on public borrowing in a historical perspective. Any errors or omissions nevertheless remain her responsibility, not theirs.

Finally, Professor Coffman would like to thank Gerard De Valence at the University of Technology Sydney and Professor Giuseppe De Luca at the University of Milan (Statale) for impressing upon her the importance of these compendia for scholars working in the Global South. It is a great honour to be part of a series that aims to make foundational scholarship available to academics and students working and studying at institutions that do not have the library budgets that more privileged institutions enjoy.

VOLUME I ACKNOWLEDGEMENTS

The publishers would like to thank the following for permission to reprint their material:

The Latin American Studies Association for permission to reprint Werner Baer, 'Import Substitution and Industrialization in Latin America: Experiences and Interpretations', *Latin American Research Review* 7, 1, 1972, 95–122.

Elsevier for permission to reprint Robert J. Barro and David B. Gordon, 'Rules, Discretion, and Reputation in a Model of Monetary Policy', *Journal of Monetary Economics* 12, 1983, 101–121.

Oxford University Press for permission to reprint A. Drazen and P. R. Masson, 'Credibility of Policies Versus Credibility of Policy Makers', *Quarterly Journal of Economics* 109, 1994, 735–754.

John Wiley & Sons for permission to reprint S. Feuerstein and O. Grimm, 'On the Credibility of Currency Boards', *Review of International Economics* 14, 2006, 818–835.

Cambridge University Press for permission to reprint D. North and B. Weingast, 'Constitutions and Commitment: The Evolution of Institutional Governing Public Choice in Seventeenth-Century England', *Journal of Economic History* December 1989, pp. 803–832.

The Federal Reserve Bank of St. Louis for permission to reprint L. D. Neal, 'The Bank of England's First Return to Gold and the Stock Market Crash of 1825,' *Federal Reserve Bank of St. Louis Review*, 79 (May/June), 1998, 53–76.

The American Economic Association for permission to reprint Ross Levine and Sara Zervos, 'Stock Markets, Banks, and Growth', *American Economic Review* 88, 3, 1998, 537–558.

The authors for permission to reprint Nathan Sussman and Yishay Yafeh, 'Contagion and Capital Market Integration in Asia: Historical and Contemporary Evidence', *Seoul Journal of Economics* XII, 1999, 391–417.

Cambridge University Press for permission to reprint Marc Flandreau, '*Caveat Emptor*: Coping with Sovereign Risk Under the International Gold Standard, 1871–1913', in Marc Flandreau, Carl-Ludwig Holtfrerich and Harold James, (eds), *International Financial History in the Twentieth Century: System and Anarchy* (Cambridge: Cambridge University Press, 2003).

The American Economic Association for permission to reprint S. Edwards, 'LDC Foreign Borrowing and Default Risk: An Empirical Investigation, 1976–80', *American Economic Review* 74, 4, 1984, 726–734.

Cambridge University Press for permission to reprint Marc Flandreau, 'The French Crime of 1873: An Essay in the Emergence of the International Gold Standard, 1870–1880', *Journal of Economic History* 56, 4, 1996, 862–897.

Cambridge University Press for permission to reprint Michael Bordo and Hugh Rockoff, 'The Gold Standard as a Good Housekeeping Seal of Approval', *Journal of Economic History*, LVI, 1996, 389–428.

Cambridge University Press for permission to reprint Niall Ferguson and Moritz Schularick, 'The Empire Effect: The Determinants of Country Risk in the First Age of Globalization, 1880-1913', *Journal of Economic History* 66, 2, 2006, 283–312.

John Wiley & Sons for permission to reprint A. Tooze and M. Ivanov, 'Disciplining the Black Sheep of the Balkans: Financial Supervision and Sovereignty in Bulgaria, 1902–1938', *Economic History Review* 64, 2011, 30–51.

Disclaimer

VOLUME I INTRODUCTION
The Advent of Modern Public Borrowing

As we write the introduction to this volume, national and local governments across the globe have undertaken costly relief measures to fight the COVID-19 pandemic and its sequelae. Debt levels globally have burgeoned. The IMF projects that average 2021 debt ratios will rise by 20 percent of gross domestic product (GDP) in advanced economies, 10 percent of GDP in emerging market economies, and about 7 percent in low-income countries (Georgieva, Pazarbasioglu & Weeks-Brown, 2020). This has made public debt management imperative. Debt management policies create leverage for monetary and fiscal policies to play their balancing role effectively, hence reducing economy-wide vulnerabilities (Missale, 2012). Debt sustainability, a measure of effective debt management, hinges on how credible a government's strategy is to reduce excess debt levels. Credibility enables governments to stabilize market expectations in order to avoid rising long-term interest rates, thus reducing the risks of insolvency (de Medonça & Machado, 2013). Sovereign credibility rests on three pillars: past performance of generating primary surpluses, institutional frameworks ensuring achievement of debt targets, and, lastly, a credible reform programme to dynamically absorb changes in domestic and global economic cycles and shocks. This volume covers all three themes and offers insight into how historical precedents can be instructive for the present. It surveys in detail a distinct period of public borrowing from 1873–1913 which the editors see as one of four discrete periods of public borrowing using different instruments, institutions, and international contexts. The volume also explores the 'credible commitment' thesis emphasizing the need for 'commitment mechanisms' to protect a sovereign's creditors from default.

We start the volume with Baer (1972), who describes the nature of Import Substitution Industrialization (ISI) in Latin America, its development in the 1950s and 60s, and the problems that emerged as it reached maturity. This policy, adopted to reduce foreign dependency through the local production of industrialized products, was ultimately unsustainable and led to accelerating inflation and stagnant economic growth during the 1970s. Such problems give rise to dynamic or time inconsistency. Dynamic inconsistency reflects a misalignment somewhere in the decision makers' preference continuum (Moloi & Marwala, 2020). This is illustrated in a simple framework pioneered by Barro and Gordon (1983), studying the policy responses of welfare-maximizing governments who cannot pre-commit to their future behaviour and thus retain policy discretion in every period. The authors note that if unanticipated inflation increases the level of output and distortionary policies make the 'natural' level of output high, policymakers are tempted to generate 'surprise' inflation in every period to move the output closer to its optimal level. Institutions that can enforce commitments on monetary policy behaviour eliminate the potential for ex post surprises and hence result in lower equilibrium rates of inflation and monetary growth.

Discretionary policies, a manifestation of dynamic inconsistency, pose a significant impediment to achieving policy credibility and are thus non-optimal, resulting in the social objective function not being maximized (Kydland & Prescott, 1977). Time inconsistency is either the result of the changing preferences of decision makers over time or of the effect of external shocks. Drazen and Masson (1994) find that time inconsistency in policy might arise from the state of the economy, thereby creating perverse outcomes. They show that if there is persistent unemployment, economic agents observing a 'tough policy in a given period may *lower* rather than raise the credibility of a no-devaluation pledge in subsequent periods'. Feuerstein and Grimm (2006) evaluate policy credibility when the economy is subject to shocks by examining currency pegs and currency boards. Studying the institutional mechanisms of currency boards, they argue that a currency board solves the time-inconsistency problem of monetary policy. However, policy can only react to unexpected shocks with a time lag, which can increase the likelihood of departure from the monetary rule. Overall, their results show that currency boards are more credible than standard pegs if the time-inconsistency problem dominates. In contrast, standard pegs are more credible if exogenous shocks are highly volatile and constitute the dominant problem. It is important to note that time-inconsistency problems can be minimized in three possible ways. First, as mentioned above, institutional mechanisms such as currency boards prevent governments from creating surprise inflation (Alesina, Barro & Tenreyro, 2002; Feuerstein and Grimm, 2006). Second, through long-run reputational considerations which, as Barro and Gordon (1983) showed, could substitute for formal rules if policymakers and private agents interact repeatedly. Lastly, through constitutional constraints (Dixit & Londregan, 2000), discussed in the following paragraph (Montiel, 2005).

Constitutional constraints ensuring credible commitment are extensively studied in the literature and some seminal pieces are covered in this volume. In 'Constitutions and Commitment: The Evolution of Institutions Governing Public Choice in Seventeenth-Century England', North and Weingast study the new political institutions emerging out of the Glorious Revolution of 1688. They emphasize the evolution of institutions of representative government consisting of the primacy of Parliament ruling in conjunction with the monarchy. This arrangement was alongside a judiciary that was *independent* of monarchical authority. The authors argue that the emergence of the new institutions ensured for the first time a 'credible commitment' that the sovereign would not default on its debt.

As a result, not only did the sovereign become financially solvent but also enjoyed unprecedented access to funds on the capital market. Stasavage (2002) corroborates this by arguing that in political systems with multiple veto players, private economic agents will be less fearful of governments enacting opportunistic policy changes such as repudiation of debt or changes to investment regulations.

The emergence of new political institutions and separations of power in the aftermath of the Glorious Revolution also trickled down to the financial sector and had two major effects. First, as Neal (1998) argues, the new institutional environment helped reduce informational uncertainties and improved the efficiency of information gathering by the government, the Bank of England, the banking system, and the stock market. All this was undertaken while maintaining the separation of functions among them. Neal concludes that this separation enabled them to become increasingly effective over time and laid the basis for Britain's dominance in the world financial system until the outbreak of World War I.

Second, the new institutional environment deepened the financial market as evidenced by the dramatic increase in sovereign debt. Investors' growing demand for sovereign securities suggests that governments, working within constitutional constraints, convinced investors of their willingness to commit credibly to honour the agreements. In the early modern period (sixteenth–eighteenth centuries), sovereign debt became the dominant form of collateral for short-term credit in Europe, contributing to the development of financial markets, expansion of trade, and acceleration of growth (Eichengreen et al., 2019). However, it was the late-nineteenth century (1873–1913), known as the *Belle Époque*, that reached the zenith of 'financialization'. This period closely resembles the late-twentieth-century globalization experience (1989–2008). London was the world's financial capital, giving investors wide access to domestic and foreign securities. Financialization during this period contributed to economic growth (Schularick & Steger, 2010). Modern studies investigating the impact of financialization on economic growth yield similar results. Levine and Zervos (1998) investigate the role of stock markets and banks in promoting long-term economic growth. They find that stock market liquidity and banking development positively predict economic 'growth, capital accumulation and productivity improvements even after controlling for economic and political factors'.

Episodic financialization, both in the past and in the present, shows that the credibility of political commitments plays a crucial role in overall economic outcomes. There is a consensus that credible commitment mechanisms are necessary to keep political authorities from making time-inconsistent policy decisions, and institutions are the most important device for ensuring 'credible commitments' are made and honoured. In a globalized world, international institutions provide an important mechanism through which countries can credibly signal their commitment to open economic policies (Fang & Owen, 2011). In the absence of multilateral institutions and credit ratings in the period 1873–1913 ensuring credible commitment, how did investors perceive country risk? Key macroeconomic indicators were used in the historical and contemporary period to form perceptions on country creditworthiness. Sussman and Yafeh (1999) compare yields on nine-teenth-century Japanese sovereign bonds with modern-day Korean sovereign debt and show that foreign investors in both periods use summary indicators to evalu-ate country risk. Flandreau (2003) corroborates this finding by investigating the evolution of the Service des Etudes Financières (SEF), a research department of Credit Lyonnais, which developed techniques to analyse sovereign risks. Given the prominence of Credit Lyonnais, the department's analysis played a critical role in influencing investors' perceptions on the size and direction of capital flows. Edwards (1984) studies public and publicly guaranteed Eurodollar loans granted to Less Developed Countries (LDCs) between 1976 and 1980, and finds that lenders take into account structural (macroeconomic) factors such as debt/ gross national product (GNP) and the debt-servicing ratio to gauge default risk. A combination of market infrastructure (existence of international financial insti-tutions) and availability of information about risks (macroeconomic, political) allows government borrowers to signal their capacity, thereby building their repu-tation to commit in a credible manner to honour their obligations.

The institutional arrangement leading to the development of capital markets over the past 150 years would not have been sufficient had there not been a mon-etary environment ensuring the credibility of economic policies. As noted above, economic policies are more effective if they are credible to private economic agents (Blackburn & Christensen, 1989). Rule-based monetary policy affects the agents' expectations and therefore economic performance. The gold standard widely used in the nineteenth and early part of the twentieth century offers an example of a credible monetary system. Flandreau (1996) examines the origins of the international gold standard to argue that political and historical factors con-tributed to precipitating the uncoordinated emergence of the international gold standard. He argues that the gold standard did not emerge out of the structural contradictions of bimetallism or from the adoption of constitutions, but rather through a change in central bank policies. Bordo and Rockoff (1996) argue that long-term adherence to the gold standard served as a 'good housekeeping seal of approval', facilitating access by peripheral countries to foreign capital from the core countries of western Europe. Capital markets gave significance to gold standard adherence and charged countries with poor adherence records consider-able penalties. By contrast, Ferguson and Schularick (2006) challenge the impor-tance of the gold standard and highlight the importance of the 'empire effect' in British colonies borrowing in London at significantly lower rates of interest than non-colonies. They argue that the 'empire effect' mattered more than either gold standard adherence or the sustainability of fiscal policies.

An important element of maintaining the credibility of financial controls is the tension between national sovereignty and access to capital markets. Tooze and Ivanov (2011) highlight this with respect to the experience of peripheral debtors in the late nineteenth and early twentieth centuries. Taking the case of Bulgaria, the authors show that the country's politics were destabilized prior to 1914 by the demands of its creditors. Post-World War I, Bulgaria was forced to submit to an even tighter system of creditor control. The country received substantial debt relief during the 1930s, but these concessions came at the price of even closer supervision. Similar to the experience of Bulgaria, the 1980s debt crisis in many Latin American countries led to an agreement between the International Monetary Fund, the World Bank, and the US Department of Treasury on ten economic policy recommendations called the Washington Consensus. To a certain degree, adherence to these recommendations did determine access to bank financing and to international capital markets. Yet there remains considerable disagreement about how far any or all of these were of key importance to markets. These debates are covered in detail in Volume II.

References

Alesina, A., Barro, R. J., & Tenreyro, S. (2002). Optimal currency areas. *NBER Macroeconomics Annual, 17*, 301–345.

Blackburn, K., & Christensen, M. (1989). Monetary policy and policy credibility: theories and evidence. *Journal of Economic literature, 27*(1), 1–45.

Coffman, D. M., Leonard, A., & Neal, L. (Eds.). (2013). *Questioning credible commitment: perspectives on the rise of financial capitalism.* Cambridge: Cambridge University Press.

de Mendonça, H. F., & Machado, M. R. (2013). Public debt management and credibility: evidence from an emerging economy. *Economic Modelling, 30*, 10–21.

Dixit, A., & Londregan, J. (2000). Political power and the credibility of government debt. *Journal of Economic Theory, 94*(1), 80–105.

Eichengreen, B., El-Ganainy, A., Esteves, R., & Mitchener, K. J. (2019). *Public debt through the ages* (No. w25494). National Bureau of Economic Research.

Fang, S., & Owen, E. (2011). International institutions and credible commitment of non-democracies. *The Review of International Organizations, 6*(2), 141–162.

Georgieva, K., Pazarbasioglu, C., & Weeks-Brown, R. (2020). Reform of the international debt architecture is urgently needed. IMF Blog. https://blogs.imf.org/2020/10/01/reform-of-the-international-debt-architecture-is-urgently-needed.

Kydland, F. E., & Prescott, E. C. (1977). Rules rather than discretion: the inconsistency of optimal plans. *Journal of Political Economy, 85*(3), 473–491.

Missale, A. (2012). Sovereign debt management and fiscal vulnerabilities. BIS Paper (65j).

Moloi, T., & Marwala, T. (2020). Dynamic Inconsistency Theory. In *Artificial intelligence in economics and finance theories* (pp. 43–52). Cham: Springer.

Montiel, P. J. (2005). Public debt management and macroeconomic stability: an overview. *The World Bank Research Observer, 20*(2), 259–281.

Schularick, M., & Steger, T. M. (2010). Financial integration, investment, and economic growth: evidence from two eras of financial globalization. *The Review of Economics and Statistics, 92*(4), 756–768.

Stasavage, D. (2002). Credible commitment in early modern Europe: North and Weingast revisited. *Journal of Law, Economics, and Organization, 18*(1), 155–186.

1

IMPORT SUBSTITUTION AND INDUSTRIALIZATION IN LATIN AMERICA

Experiences and Interpretations*

Werner Baer

Source: *Latin American Research Review* 7, 1, 1972, 95–122.

THROUGHOUT MOST OF THE FIFTIES AND SIXTIES MANY LATIN AMERICAN GOVERNMENTS adopted Import Substitution Industrialization (ISI) as their principal method to achieve economic growth and socio-economic modernization. By the opening of the Seventies, however, there is considerable doubt about ISI's success in solving the region's development problems. In many countries the possibilities for further import-substitution had disappeared. Industrial growth had slowed, job opportunities in industry for Latin America's rapidly growing urban population were scarce, income distribution had in many countries either remained unchanged or had become more concentrated than in the early post-World War II years, and most industrial goods produced within the region were priced so high that export possibilities were severely limited.

Considerable debate has taken place among economists and policymakers over the merits of ISI as a strategy for economic development, the performance of ISI in various countries, over the nature of post-ISI problems which these countries have faced, and over policies to deal with these post-ISI problems.

In this review article I shall first describe the nature of ISI in Latin America, its occurrence prior to World War II, and its development in the decades of the Fifties and Sixties. I shall then review the problems which developed as ISI reached maturity and review various analyses developed to explain these problems. Finally, I shall examine various strategies which have been suggested for the post-ISI period.

THE NATURE OF ISI IN LATIN AMERICA

ISI is an attempt by economically less-developed countries to break out of the world division of labor which had emerged in the nineteenth century and the early part of the twentieth century. Under this division, Latin America (and most areas of Asia and Africa) specialized in the export of food and raw materials, while importing manufactured goods from Europe and the United States. Import substitution consists of establishing domestic production facilities to manufacture goods which were formerly imported. It follows that all countries which industrialized after Great Britain, went through a stage of ISI; that is, all passed through a stage where the larger part of investment in industries was undertaken to replace imports. ISI would come to a close when most investment was channeled towards the construction of capacity to produce for new incremental demand.

The ISI wave in Europe and the United States occurred in the middle and second half of the nineteenth century.[1] It is a well-known fact that in this early ISI process governments played an active role in encouraging and protecting the development of infant industries. Another characteristic of nineteenth century ISI is its "national" character. Although in some countries finance for infrastructure investment was obtained from abroad, industries were for the most part in domestic hands, while the design of machines and skilled manpower to run them were often imported from England in the early industrialization period.

Once Western Europe and the United States had undergone their initial industrializations, import substitution did not come entirely to an end. However, it ceased being mainly a mechanism of industrialization, and became in the twentieth century part of a continuing process of growth and of a changing pattern of industrial specialization among economically advanced countries.[2]

There are various historical reasons why the countries of Africa, Asia and Latin America did not undergo ISI at the time of, or right after, the European ISIs. Colonial policies of European countries provide much of the explanation for the former two cases, while socio-economic structure helps explain the Latin American case. The presence of attractive external markets for the region's primary exports, which benefited the elites, meant that there was little political desire to change the structure of the economies. Also in the nineteenth century and early part of the twentieth century, Latin American countries did not have the entrepreneurial classes, labor force, infrastructure, market size, or administrative capacity to cope with an extensive industrialization process. Also in the case of some countries, like Brazil, European powers had enough leverage to force governments to maintain free trade policies, thus in effect blocking any possibility of ISI.[3]

ISI BEFORE AND DURING THE SECOND WORLD WAR

Latin America was not completely devoid of manufacturing activities prior to World War I. It has by now been well documented that in the latter part of the nineteenth century workshops and small factories in textiles and food products industries had developed in some parts of Argentina, Brazil, Mexico and other larger countries. Also, machine tools and spare parts workshops developed to service railroads, sugar refining mills, etc.[4] These activities were usually started by importers of equipment. There were some isolated attempts to raise tariffs both to protect incipient industries and to stimulate the creation of new ones.[5] It would be mistaken, however, to speak of "industrialization" prior to World War I. The bulk of manufactured goods consumed in Latin America were either imported or produced by small domestic workshops, while exports consisted almost entirely of primary products.[6] Except for Argentina, the population was primarily rural, and the primary export sector was the pacesetter of economic activity, while workshops and small industries were appendages to general economic activity.

It should be noted, however, that on the eve of World War I the primary export sector with its complementary activities in services (banking, merchandizing, government) and social infrastructure (communication, transportation, etc.) had in many Latin American countries created a fairly substantial middle class which consumed large quantities of imported manufactured consumer goods.

ISI INDUCED FROM ABROAD

World War I, the Great Depression of the Thirties and World War II induced pronounced spurts of ISI in most larger Latin American countries.[7] The interruption of shipping and the decline of non-military production in Europe and the United States during World War I created severe shortages of imported manufactured goods in Latin America, raised relative prices of such goods, and increased profitability of ISI investment. Textiles, food products, and various other light consumer goods industries were the principal fields of ISI in that period. In the Twenties many of these newly created ISI industries stagnated because of renewed U. S. and European competition and the general refusal of policy makers to protect infant industries of recent vintage. It was generally thought that World War I had been an aberration from the natural order of things, which was reflected in the world division of labor of the nineteenth century. Hence policy makers were reluctant to tamper with a movement back to "normalcy."[8]

The depression of the Thirties resulted in renewed shortages of imported goods. The fall of foreign exchange receipts from exports forced most countries of the region drastically to curtail imports. The decline resulted at first in increased use of productive capacity which had been underutilized in the Twenties, and later in the creation of new industrial capacity.[9] As in World War I, the depression-induced ISI occurred primarily in light consumer goods industries, although in some cases, especially Brazil,[10] steel and capital goods industries were developed on a relatively small scale.

World War II had a stimulating effect on ISI industries: shortages of foreign manufactured goods led to full utilization of industrial capacity;[11] some investment in new capacity occurred when capital goods could be imported; and even some textile products were exported by Argentina, Brazil, and Mexico.

ISI IN THE FIFTIES AND SIXTIES

But it was only after World War II that ISI became a deliberate policy tool for economic development. Most of the larger countries of Latin America implicitly or

3

explicitly accepted the ECLA analysis of the hopelessness of gearing their economies towards the traditional world division of labor.[12] Continued reliance on the
export of food and primary products was thought to be precarious because of the
instability of such exports, which would not be conducive to long term development because of the relatively slow growth of world demand for such products.[13] It
was thought that ISI would introduce a dynamic element into the Latin American
economies and increase their rates of growth. The latter were deemed essential to
deal with the population explosion of the region and to meet the demands of the
increasingly urban population for the ways of life of the masses in more advanced
countries. It was also thought that ISI would bring greater economic independence to Latin American countries: self-sufficiency in manufactured goods would
place Latin American economies less at the mercy of the world economy.

The principal policy instruments used to promote and intensify ISI were: protective tariffs and/or exchange controls; special preferences for domestic and
foreign firms importing capital goods for new industries; preferential import
exchange rates for industrial raw materials, fuels and intermediate goods; cheap
loans by government development banks for favored industries; the construction
by governments of infrastructure especially designed to complement industries;
and the direct participation of government in certain industries, especially the
heavier industries, such as steel, where neither domestic nor foreign private capital was willing or able to invest.[14]

The promotion of ISI industries was indiscriminate, that is, there were not
attempts to concentrate on industrial sectors which might have had a potential
comparative advantage. In some countries ISI occurred for considerable periods
of time in consumer goods industries only. A concise summary is given by David
Felix: "... the initial industries are generally consumer goods or building materials producers with a relatively simple technology and a low capital requirement
per worker and per unit of output. They are then followed by consumer goods
industries requiring a more sophisticated technology and larger capital outlay,
shading subsequently into industries producing relatively complex consumer
durables, steel, engineering and chemical products"[15] This description is especially relevant in the cases of countries such as Argentina, Chile, Venezuela. In
other countries, especially Brazil, the government was anxious to promote maximum vertical integration, i.e., to promote both final consumer goods industries
and intermediate and capital goods sectors.

In some cases, where the initial thrust of ISI was on final consumer goods
industries, a built-in resistance to backward vertical integration developed.[16] That
is, firms which established themselves in the first ISI period pressured governments not to develop domestic intermediate and capital goods industries, since
these would produce inputs at substantially higher prices than imported inputs.
However, as the areas for further ISI declined, most countries pressed on with
backward integration efforts.

An important feature of Latin American ISI in the Fifties and Sixties was the
participation of foreign capital. Although its proportion of total savings was often

4

substantially below 10 per cent, it was instrumental in setting up key manufacturing industries by transferring know-how and organizational capabilities. This was also true in infrastructure investments and heavy industries owned by governments, which depended on foreign financing and technical aid.[17]

THE RESULTS OF ISI

Tables 1 through 5 present a summary of the impact of ISI on the principal economies of the region and on the Latin American economy as a whole. In Table 1 we have various measures of the changes in the percentage distribution of the Gross Domestic Product. It should be noted that for countries where the data are available, industry already represented a significant proportion of GDP in the earlier decades of the century.[18] However, as mentioned earlier, these industries consisted to a large extent of small workshops; in 1950 still over half of the work force in manufacturing was engaged in artisan-type of activities (see Table 2a). By the Sixties, industry had become the dominant sector in Argentina, Brazil, Mexico, and Chile. The annual rates of growth of various sectors shown in Table 1 indicate the extent to which industry was the pace setter in the post-World War II decades. We shall comment later on the other tables.

CRITIQUES OF ISI

Let us now turn to the various critiques which have been made of Latin American ISI. The critics can be divided into two groups which I shall designate as the "market critics" and the "structural critics." Although some arguments are common to both sets of critics, there is a certain philosophic-analytical similarity of the views within each camp which seem to justify the division I have made.

a) The Market Critics

Many economists in this category view Latin America's ISI as an inefficient way of using resources to develop the region's countries.[19] The more conservative economists believe that since world production can be best be maximized by having each country (or area of the world) specialize in the sectors where it has the greatest comparative advantage, Latin America should have continued to specialize in the production of primary products. This specialization would have maximized world output and made possible a higher income level in all parts of the world.

Because of the declining share of food and primary products in world trade, more moderate critics recognize the need for some ISI.[20] But they criticize the indiscriminate way in which ISI was carried on, that is, by across-the-board promotion of industries without regard even to potential comparative advantage. The Latin American ISI strategies are seen as drives towards national self-sufficiency in total disregard of the advantages of an international division of labor along

Table 1 Changes in the Structure of the Economies of Selected Countries (Percentage Distribution of Gross Domestic Product According to Principal Sectors)

ARGENTINA

	1960 Prices		1937 Prices	
	1927–9	*1963–5*	*1927–9*	*1963–5*
Agriculture	27.4	17.1	30.5	18.4
Oil & Mining	0.3	1.5	0.6	3.5
Manufacturing	23.6	33.7	13.4	18.6
Construction	4.2	3.6	3.1	2.6

Source: Díaz-Alejandro, *Essays.*

BRAZIL

	Current Prices					1953 Prices			
	1939	*1947*	*1953*	*1960*	*1968*	*1947*	*1953*	*1960*	*1968*
Agriculture	25.8	27.6	26.1	22.6	17.9	30.0	26.1	22.2	20.5
Industry	19.4	19.8	23.7	25.2	28.0	20.6	23.7	28.0	29.3
Other	54.8	52.6	50.2	52.2	54.1	49.4	50.2	49.8	50.2

Source: Fundação Getulio Vargas, Centro de Contas Nacionais.

MEXICO

	Current Prices					
	1900	*1910*	*1930*	*1940*	*1950*	*1960*
Rural	34.6	27.9	25.9	24.3	22.5	18.9
Extractive	6.4	9.1	13.5	8.5	5.7	5.4
Commerce & Transp.	23.4	23.4	23.4	28.5	31.0	30.6
Mfg., Construc. & Elec.	13.2	13.7	16.7	22.6	24.5	27.7

Source: Reynolds, *Mexican Economy.*

LATIN AMERICA

	Current Prices		Annual Rates of Growth		
	1950	*1967*	*1950–60*	*1960–67*	*1950–67*
Produc. of Goods	52.4	52.3	4.9	4.6	4.8
Agriculture	25.2	20.5	3.5	3.5	3.5
Mining	4.1	4.4	6.1	4.1	5.3
Manufacturing	19.6	24.1	6.2	5.8	6.0
Construction	3.5	3.3	4.6	4.1	4.4
Basic Services	7.2	8.3	5.5	5.7	5.6
Other Services	40.4	39.4	4.8	4.4	4.6
Commerce & Finance	18.0	18.8	5.1	4.9	5.0
Misc. Services	22.4	20.6	4.5	3.9	4.2
Total	100.0	100.0	4.9	4.6	4.8

Source: Naciones Unidas, CEPAL, *Estudio económico de América Latina, 1968* (New York, 1969), p. 18.

Table 2

a) Distribution of Economically Active Population *(per cent distribution)*

ARGENTINA

	1925–9	1960–1
Rural Sector	35.7	21.7
Oil and Mining	0.3	0.6
Manufacturing	22.0	26.0
Construction	5.5	6.0
Public Utilities	0.5	0.8
Transport	4.6	5.7
Communications	0.5	1.0
Commerce, Finance and Housing	13.6	14.3
Government Services	4.6	10.4
Other Services	12.6	13.6

Source: Díaz-Alejandro, *Essay.*

BRAZIL

	1940	1950	1960
Primary	71.0	64.4	58.5
Secondary	8.9	12.9	12.7
Tertiary	20.1	22.7	28.8
Total	100.0	100.0	100.0

Source: Various Brazilian Demographic Censuses.

MEXICO

	1910	1940	1950	1960
Agriculture	67.1	65.4	58.3	54.1
Mining	1.9	1.7	1.2	1.2
Mfg., Construc. & Power	13.1	11.0	14.8	17.7
Services	17.8	21.9	25.7	27.0
Total	100.0	100.0	100.0	100.0

Source: Reynolds, *Mexican Economy.*

LATIN AMERICA

	1950	1960	1965	1969
Agriculture	53.4	47.2	44.5	42.2
Mining	1.1	1.0	1.0	1.0
Manufacturing	14.4	14.4	14.0	13.8
(artisan)	(7.5)	(6.8)	(6.4)	(6.1)
Construction	3.8	4.1	3.9	4.5
Basic Services	4.2	5.1	5.3	5.5
Other Services	23.1	28.2	31.3	33.0
(commerce & finance)	(7.8)	(9.0)	(9.5)	(10.1)
Total	100.0	100.0	100.0	100.0

Source: CEPAL, 1969.

(*Continued*)

Table 2 Continued

b) *Growth of Employment by Sectors and Population Growth (yearly rates of growth)*

	Employment Growth		Population Growth		
	1950–60	*1960–69*		*1950–60*	*1960–69*
Agriculture	1.3	1.5	Total	2.8	2.9
Manufacturing	2.6	2.3	Urban	4.8	4.4
(artisan)	(1.5)	(1.6)	Rural	1.4	1.4
Mining	2.0	2.2			
Construction	3.2	4.0			
Basic Services	4.6	3.4			
Other Services	4.7	4.6			

Source: CEPAL, 1968.

Table 3

a) Real Rate of Growth (annual) by Sectors for Latin America and Selected Countries

	1955–60	*1960–65*	*1955–60*	*1960–65*	*1955–60*	*1960–65*
	Latin America		*Argentina*		*Brazil*	
Agriculture	2.7	4.8	—0.4	2.1	3.7	6.9
Manufacturing	6.6	5.6	3.8	4.1	10.3	4.9
Construction	4.2	5.9	4.3	2.0	7.2	2.8
	Chile		*Mexico*		*Colombia*	
Agriculture	2.3	3.1	3.0	3.9	3.5	3.0
Manufacturing	3.2	6.7	8.1	8.0	6.1	5.9
Construction	1.4	4.6	8.1	5.9	—0.2	1.9

Source: Naciones Unidas, *Estudio económico de América Latina,* 1965.

b) Latin America: Growth Rates of the Total Gross Domestic Product and of Industrial Product (Annual Cumulative Rates)

	Total Product	*Industrial Product*
1940–50	5.0	6.8
1950–60	4.7	6.3
1960–68	4.5	5.4

Source: United Nations, *Economic Bulletin for Latin America,* Second Half of 1969.

newer lines. This emphasis on autarky is seen as prejudicial to rapid economic growth for a number of reasons.

Given small markets, limited capital, and a dearth of skilled manpower, autarkic industrial growth leads to the development of inefficient and high-cost industries. The situation becomes especially pronounced in industries having high fixed costs.

Table 4

a) Growth of Urban Population and Industrial Employment *(Average Annual Rates of Growth: 1950–60)*

	Urban Population	Industrial Employment
Argentina	3.0	1.7
Brazil	6.5	2.6
Mexico	5.6	4.8

Source: Table in Little, Scitovsky, and Scott, *Industry and Trade*, p. 84.

b) Growth of Industrial Product and Industrial Employment *(Annual Growth Rates: 1950–68)*

	Industrial Product	Industrial Employment
Argentina	4.5	2.2
Brazil	7.3	2.2
Colombia	6.2	2.4
Chile	4.6	2.2
Peru	7.8	3.4
Mexico	6.7	4.7
Latin America	6.0	2.8

Source: Raúl Prebisch, *Transformación y desarrollo: la gran tarea de América Latina,* (Washington, D.C., 1970), p. 45.

These industries require large-scale output in order to bring costs down to levels prevailing in more advanced industrial countries. Outstanding examples are the steel and automobile industries which have been established in most of the larger Latin American countries. In the case of automobiles, the situation was worsened because a large number of these countries permitted the establishment of many firms, thus completely eliminating the possibilities of economies of large scale production. In the late Sixties, the annual output of cars and trucks in eight Latin American countries was 600,000, which was produced by ninety firms (an average of 6,700 per firm).[21] The situation is well summarized by Scitovsky: "Protection usually confines the protected manufacturer to the domestic market and so inhibits the exploitation of economies of scale, especially in small countries and in industries where scale economies are important and call for very large-scale operations. Moreover, governments anxious to secure the benefits of competition often encourage many firms to enter industry in order to create domestic competition where protectionist policies have suspended foreign competition."

The result, however, is contrary to what is aimed for, since such government policy "… restricts the scope for economies of scale yet further and often leads to the emergence of too many firms, each with too small an output capacity, and frequently with too small a market to utilize fully even that capacity."[22]

Table 5

---

a) Latin America's Participation in World Trade
(Latin America's Exports as a Per Cent of World Exports)

1948—10.9%	1960—7.0%
1950—10.6%	1964—6.4%
1957—7.8%	1968—5.0%

Source: *Regional Integration and the Trade of Latin America,* Committee for Economic Development, Jan. 1968; and *International Trade, 1968*, GATT.

---

b) Changes in Latin America's Import Coefficients
(Value of Imports of Goods and Services as a Per Cent of GDP)

	1928	1938	1948–9	1957–8	1962	1960*	1967*
Argentina	17.8	12.1	11.2	5.8	7.1	8.0	6.6
Brazil	11.3	6.2	6.6	5.8	4.5	7.8	5.6
Chile	31.2	14.9	11.5	9.5	11.3	15.7	15.7
Colombia	18.0	11.0	10.6	8.2	8.8	12.2	8.8
Mexico	14.2	7.0	8.5	7.8	6.8	7.8	7.8
Peru			9.6	16.1	13.6	19.0	28.1
Latin America			10.2	9.9	8.7	10.0	9.9

Source: Joseph Grunwald and Philip Musgrove, *Natural Resources in Latin American Development* (Baltimore, 1970), p. 20.
* CEPAL, 1968.

---

c) Imports as a Percentage of Total Supplies by Categories

	Consumers' Goods	Intermediate Goods	Capital Goods
Brazil			
1949	9.0	25.9	63.7
1955	2.9	17.9	43.2
1959	1.9	11.7	32.9
1964	1.3	6.6	9.8
Mexico			
1950	2.4	13.2	66.5
1955	2.3	n.a.	63.4
1960	1.3	10.4	54.9
1965	n.a.	9.9	59.8

Source: Little, Scitovsky, and Scott, *Industry and Trade*, p. 60.

In the last few years the concept of "effective protection" has been used by numerous economists to analyze distortions which have arisen during the ISI process. Nominal tariff rates measure only the percentage by which prices of protected goods exceed their world prices. This amount is also the difference by which domestic substitutes can exceed the international price. The "effective" tariff or rate of protection "... shows the percentage by which the value added at a stage of fabrication in domestic industry can exceed what this would be in the absence of protection; in other words, it shows by what percentage the sum of wages, profits, and depreciation allowances, payable by domestic firms can, thanks to protection, exceed what this sum would be if the same firms were fully exposed to foreign competition."[23] Thus, if a product uses a considerable amount of imported inputs on which there is no tariff or on which the tariff rate is lower than the tariff on the finished product, protection is higher than is indicated by the nominal tariff, since the margin available for domestic value added is larger than the difference indicated by the tariff. In a number of Latin American countries the effective tariff on consumer goods was found to be much higher than for intermediate or capital goods.[24] Such high levels of effective protection eliminate incentives to increase production efficiency and make it difficult to bring the cost of production to international levels.

The stress on autarky—on maximizing internal vertical industrial integration (promoting not only final goods production, but also intermediate and capital goods)—impedes growth because resources are not used in sectors where they will produce the highest possible output. Had Latin American countries specialized in only a few products with the greatest potential comparative advantage, and exported a large surplus while importing other goods, total output available would have been higher and these nations would have grown more rapidly than they actually did. As it happened, autarky was practiced in each country, and no attempt was made until the late Sixties to at least promote ISI on a regional basis; in other words, to promote a complementary industrial structure within Latin America.

A study by Baranson of automobile industries in developing countries (which includes information on Argentina, Brazil, and Mexico) illustrates many of the problems of autarkic development. He contrasts the proliferation of automobile firms in developing countries with the quest by European producers for increased exports and consolidation with competitors, both inside and outside their countries, in order to keep down unit cost.[25] He finds that among the main deficiencies are "... underdeveloped supplier capacities, inadequate quality control systems, and a dearth of qualified technicians and managers. By creating a 'sellers' market', protection and import substitution tend to undermine quality."[26] Thus, Baranson found that many "... basic materials that are considered standard stock in open economies often must be procured locally or specially ordered in small batches at considerably higher cost or at inferior quality... . Lack of uniformity in raw materials and semi-finished goods such as castings and forgings creates special problems in milling and machining to required specifications. In

11

high-volume production, precision and uniformity are built into automated equipment. Developing countries with limited markets are much more dependent upon the very machine labor skills in which they are deficient." Also, considering the many parts which go into an automobile, Baranson found that outside plant procurement averages about 60 per cent by value in advanced economies, while in countries like Mexico and Brazil this factor amounts to only 40 per cent. Such a condition further reduces the possibility of economies of large scale production.[27] As a result, Baranson found that factory costs in Argentina, Brazil, and Mexico were about 60 per cent to 150 per cent higher than in the United States.[28]

Similar problems were found in many other industries. A study of the manufacture of heavy electrical equipment in developing countries found that in Argentina '... excessive diversification, unused capacity, large inventories because of import controls, and difficulties in obtaining outside finance explain the high price level... .'[29] ECLA has also provided numerous illustrations of the problems discussed above. It found that in 1964, "... the paper industry (excluding newsprint) had 292 plants of which only 25 had a capacity of 100 tons daily, which is considered the minimum economic size. In the chemical industry, too, there are a great many instances in which there is a wide gap between the plant sizes most frequently found in the region and the sizes constructed in the industrialized countries."[30]

Some economists have been concerned about the domestic resource cost involved in the type of ISI which has been promoted in Latin America. They have stressed the need to calculate for various industries the value of domestic resources required to save a unit of foreign exchange. The rate of transformation between domestic and foreign resources thus obtained should be compared to the appropriate exchange rate.[31] The higher the former is over the latter, the greater presumably is the "waste" of resources; that is, if domestic resources had been used for export purposes, the foreign exchange earned would have fetched more goods than the goods produced by using the resources domestically.[32]

Policies employed to stimulate industries have often been prejudicial to the functioning of the more traditional agricultural sector. The allocation of investment resources (credit) to new industries has often meant that a few resources were available to increase agricultural efficiency. Overvalued exchange rates, which favored industries by providing cheap imported inputs, hurt agriculture by making its goods less competitive on the international market and/or by making it less profitable to export agricultural products. Finally, the combination of higher industrial prices caused by protection and by price control of agricultural goods, turned the internal terms of trade against agriculture. All these factors hurt agricultural production and exports. Argentina is probably the outstanding example of ISI occurring to the detriment of agriculture and agricultural exports.[33]

Critics have also pointed to the detrimental results of neglecting exports during the heyday of ISI. Some stress the negative effects of ISI policies on the production and exportation of traditional goods, while others emphasize the failure to diversify the export structure in accordance with the changing internal economic structure which ISI brought about. While, as was mentioned earlier, the contribution of industry to GDP became dominant in the years after World War II, the commodity composition of Latin America's exports remained almost unchanged. For example, in the late Sixties, over 90 per cent of Argentina and Brazil's exports still consisted of traditional primary and food products, while about three-quarters of Mexico's exports consisted of such products. Until the Sixties, little efforts were made by Latin American countries to stimulate non-traditional exports. And while in the early Sixties the development of the Latin American Common Market, the Central American Common Market, the introduction of drawbacks and rebates on domestic taxes for export efforts in some countries (Argentina, Mexico, Colombia) represented attempts to stimulate non-traditional exports, the net effects by the late Sixties were still slight.

The neglect of exports during the ISI period in Latin America, that is, the failure to stimulate traditional exports and to diversify the export structure, could have serious consequences. The original advocates of ISI had hoped that their policy would lead Latin American countries to greater self-sufficiency and would make their economies more independent of the vicissitudes of international trade. It appears, however, that there is a lower limit to the import coefficient (import/GDP ratio) for most economies, as becomes clear by examining Table 5(b). While ISI was taking place, not only was the import coefficient reduced,[34] but the commodity composition of imports changed. An increasingly larger proportion of imports consisted of raw materials, semi-finished products, and capital goods. These represented the inputs of the ISI industries which were not available domestically, and were thus the principal reason for the increasing downward stickiness of the import coefficient.[35]

It is thus ironic that the net result of ISI has been to place Latin American countries in a new and more dangerous dependency relationship with the more advanced industrial countries than ever before. In former times, a decline in export receipts acted as a stimulus to ISI. Under the circumstances, a decline in export receipts not counterbalanced by capital inflows can result in forced import curtailments which, in turn, could cause an industrial recession. Such results have been experienced by Argentina and Colombia, and other countries face the same danger.[36]

To guard against such a situation, Latin American countries would have to make increasing efforts to diversify exports. Such actions, however, assume that they are able to compete in the international market. Considering the high cost structure of many Latin American ISI industries, the many bureaucratic obstacles exporters have faced, and the lack of an adequate credit mechanism to export manufactured goods, export diversification is not an easy task.[37]

b) Structural Critics

Since World War II, most Latin American countries have experienced a population explosion. Annual population growth for the entire region increased from 1.9

per cent to over 2.8 per cent in the late Fifties and Sixties. During the same period, migration from the countryside to the cities increased dramatically. One may see in Table 2 (b) that the urban population growth rate in the post-World War II period was over three times as large as the rural growth rate. The same table also shows that the rate of labor absorption in industry was substantially smaller than the rate of growth of urban population. In Table 2(a), it is clear that after two decades of industrialization, the proportion of the labor force employed in manufacturing industry in Latin America as a whole actually declined somewhat, and that almost half of these workers were still engaged in artisan workshops. In some of the individual countries shown, the proportion rose a few points, but very modestly compared to the changes in the contribution of industry to GDP. The failure of ISI to create direct employment opportunities has worried both "structural" and "market" critics.[38]

The latter blame the low labor absorption rate on price distortions. Most countries used certain types of subsidies to capital in order to stimulate industrialization. In a number of countries, domestic and foreign firms were given special exchange rate privileges to import capital equipment. Development banks gave cheap credit (often at negative real rates of interest) to help finance investment in favored industries. At the same time, wages in industry were relatively high because of labor legislation which had been introduced in the Thirties and Forties in such countries as Argentina, Brazil, and Chile. Thus, there were no incentives to adopt labor-intensive techniques of production. On the contrary, the relative price structure of capital and labor was such as to actually stimulate the search for and adoption of capital-intensive techniques.[39]

The structural critics of ISI worry about low labor absorption rates not only because of the severe social problems of urban unemployment or underemployment which result, but also because of their implication for income distribution. With an unequal distribution of income, a fiscal system which does not redistribute income, and a leading growth sector (industry) whose incremental capital/labor ratio is high (usually substantially higher than the economy's average capital/labor ratio), the tendency will be for income to become even more concentrated than before. The evidence available for Latin American countries tends to confirm this trend.[40]

Because of the concentration of income, the growth of demand for industrial products may not be sufficient to maintain the initial ISI momentum. What makes this situation worse is the lumpiness of many ISI industries. Because of indivisibilities, many industries were forced to build substantially ahead of demand. Thus, the existence of excess capacity which is not being rapidly filled by growing demand dampens the incentive to invest.[41]

This situation could, of course, be avoided by various types of redistributive policies of governments—redistribution by income groups, by sectors of the economy, and by regions. Progressive tax measures and/or appropriate wage policies could be used to redistribute incomes among social groups; government credit and fiscal policies could redirect resources to neglected sectors (such as agriculture, housing, road building) and geographical regions.

Potential domestic demand for industrial products exists in most Latin American countries because the ISI process occurred in an unbalanced fashion. We have already mentioned the trends towards the concentration of income which could be reversed by appropriate policies and thus result in considerable demand expansion. However, there were other imbalances. As ISI proceeded, such sectors as agriculture, low income housing, transportation, and other infrastructure facilities were often neglected, threatening countries with severe bottlenecks. In the larger countries, ISI resulted in a strong regional concentration of industry and income, especially in Brazil, Mexico, and Argentina. Although such regional concentration made sense when taking into account external economies to firms settling close to suppliers, to decent infrastructure facilities, and to skilled labor supplies, etc.,[42] it was of a self-reinforcing nature. Increasing regional concentration of wealth presented many countries with the political need to redistribute income on a regional basis. All these forces make it possible to generate new demand through government policies.[43]

Georgescu-Roegen, however, called attention to a problem which might arise from post-ISI redistribution efforts.[44] The profile of the productive structure which resulted from the ISI process reflects the demand profile which existed at the time when the process was started. This demand profile was based on a distribution of income which, in most cases, was quite unequal. Efforts to change the distribution of income in the post-ISI era in order to achieve greater social justice, increase aggregate demand, diminish inter-sectoral and/or inter-regional imbalances, will change the demand profile. Such changes could result in a substantial amount of imbalance or lack of synchronization between the country's productive and demand profiles. The degree of such imbalance depends, of course, on the flexibility of various productive sectors. For example, to what extent can the productive facilities of the consumer goods and capital goods industries be converted from producing luxury goods to producing mass consumption goods?

The greater the inflexibility of the country's productive structure, the greater the "structural-lock" dilemma of the country. Thus, the full use of the existing productive capacity would imply the necessity for the type of income distribution which would produce the requisite demand profile, i.e., a very unequal distribution of income.[45] The alternative, a more egalitarian distribution of income, might imply considerable capacity in a number of industries.[46]

This "structural lock" dilemma should be set off, however, against the import constraint problem. It has been claimed that high income inequality encourages a more import-intensive demand profile. That is, higher income groups consume technically more sophisticated goods which have relatively high direct and indirect import requirements. Thus, although a greater degree of income concentration could avoid a "structural lock" problem, it could lead to stagnation caused by import constraints.[47]

EVALUATION AND OUTLOOK FOR THE FUTURE

In my general attitude towards the critiques which I have summarized, I fully subscribe to the views of Bergsman and Candal in their evaluation of the Brazilian ISI experience: "Hindsight makes it easy to point out specific mistakes, even to suggest some modifications in policy that clearly would have avoided the greatest inefficiencies. It is much harder to compare actual results with those that might have come from some totally different policy that would not have included industrialization.[48]

It is clear that in most, if not all, Latin American countries, industrialization was carried out on too wide a spectrum, given limited capital and human resources and very narrow markets. Also, excessively high effective production did not lead resources into fields which would have the highest possible potential comparative advantage, and protection gave a comfortable enough profit margin to all inside the market to neglect the search for greater efficiency. However, outright condemnation of inefficiencies has to be qualified. For political reasons, ISI within the context of a larger Latin American Common Market was not feasible in the immediate postwar period. A more specialized export-oriented ISI not only depended on the possibilities of Latin American economic integration, but also on the willingness of the United States and Europe to accept Latin American manufactured imports. If one admits that an international division of labor can no longer be based on nineteenth century lines (given the relative decline of primary products in world trade), one has to expect structural changes in both the developing and the developed parts of the world. For example, one would expect the United States and Europe to accept a decline in the textile industry in order to make room for such imports from the Third World. Given the unwillingness to do this, one should temper one's condemnation of Latin American countries for not being more selective in their choice of industries.[49] This does not excuse the proliferation of many firms in small markets (e.g., automobiles) which produced unnecessary high costs.

Many economists have the bad habit of generalizing from limited experience and evidence. This is especially true in the ISI discussions. The development of an integrated industrial structure might not make much sense in a small country like Chile, while it does make some sense in a country like Brazil. Although an elegant argument about industrialization having been promoted at the expense of agriculture can be made with empirical evidence from Argentina, it would be difficult to apply this argument to the Brazilian case. Coffee output was not sacrificed for the sake of industrialization.[50]

The explanation of the labor-absorption problem in terms of factor price distortion is based on good deductive reasoning in economic theory, but there is little empirical evidence to back the explanation. In some industries the technological choices are limited.[51] In most Latin American automobile industries the equipment installed was second hand and thus the assembly line operations are technologically substantially behind the more automated plants in Europe and the

United States. The equipment in most of Latin America's textile industries is so old that various missions have recommended a thoroughgoing modernization in order to make these industries profitable and competitive. There exists, of course, the possibility of placing greater efforts in discovering more labor-intensive techniques, which might be achieved if Latin American countries would increase the resources earmarked for scientific and technological research. Only 0.5 per cent of Latin America's GNP goes into such efforts, as compared to over 3 per cent for the United States.[52] It remains doubtful, however, whether price distortions explain Latin America's labor absorption problem.

Although the argument about the necessity for export diversification is well taken, the pontification of many economists concerning the past neglect of industrial exports is open to some criticisms. It seems that many forget that a large number of the key manufacturing industries of Latin America were constructed by or with the aid of foreign capital. The chief attraction of the latter was the promise of a growing protected market. It might have been rather difficult to convince firms to establish themselves in Brazil, Argentina, and other countries on the condition that from the beginning 40 to 50 per cent of the output should be exported. Had there been a genuine interest by domestic and foreign firms to export manufactured goods, I suspect that the bureaucratic and exchange rate obstacles to such exports might have fallen earlier.

It could also be asserted that the high-cost structure of Latin America's industries makes export diversification difficult. Here, of course, there might be a dilemma. If the high-cost structure is in large part caused by the narrow market which raises unit costs, only increased sales could reduce the latter. And thus we might face an interesting chicken-egg problem. But even if this could be resolved through subsidies, exports of manufactured goods would still have to face non-price competitive factors such as credit terms, brand names, delivery terms, marketing organizations, etc. Since the importance of price vs. non-price competition in the international trade of manufactured and capital goods has never been firmly established, it is difficult to claim that the high cost structure is one of the principal barriers to export diversification. We have already mentioned the political problem of penetrating European and American markets.

Since most economists' intellectual energies in the last few decades have been spent worrying about the efficient allocation of resources, it is natural that those economists who have devoted their attention to developing countries should have spent most of their time examining and recommending how factors of production are or should be allocated. Relatively little thought was given to the fact that concern about development should include concern about the development of factors of production, not just their allocation. The many "inefficiencies" might prevent a developing country undergoing ISI from realizing its maximum crude growth rate in the short-run. This cost has to be weighed against the modernization or development which ISI brings about.[53] Little work along these lines, that is, on the measurement of changes in the quality of factors of production, has been done in Latin America or in other parts of the developing world.

FUTURE POLICIES

By the late Sixties many Latin American countries were taking measures to eliminate some of the grosser distortions which ISI had brought along. In a number of countries the tariff level was brought down (e.g., Brazil, Argentina). This was not done to encourage more imports, but to decrease the level of effective protection and monopoly profits and thus give an incentive to firms to rationalize their operations. Measures were taken in such countries as Brazil, Argentina, and Peru to reduce the number of automobile firms and thus encourage lower cost production by scale economies.

There has been a constant effort by ECLA and the Inter-American Development Bank to push for greater economic integration via the Latin American Common Market. It is hoped that such integration would increase and diversify the exports of individual countries and that there would also result a rationalization of production throughout the continent by making the Latin American economies more complementary to each other. Besides trade in finished goods, attempts have been made to encourage "complementation agreements," in which there would be a division of labor along vertical lines (for example, the Chilean automobile industry specializing in the production of certain parts which would be assembled in Brazil).[54] Unfortunately this process has not made as much progress as its advocates had hoped. It seems that a division of labor within Latin America would not necessarily result in national economic structures which would be to the liking of individual countries.[55]

The problem of post-ISI stagnation, i.e., the finding of a new dynamic source of growth, has preoccupied many Latin American governments as the decade of the Seventies opened. In Brazil the government of President Emilio Medici has stated that its principal aim would be to develop a "program of social integration" which would increase the labor force participation in the national product, to develop the internal frontier of Amazonia, and to begin a gigantic road building program which would more effectively link various regions of the country and better link farming areas to markets. Peru is currently experiencing some drastic social reforms—land reform, programs of worker profit-sharing schemes, etc. The new Mexican president has also emphasized the need for income redistribution.

It remains to be seen if a redistribution of income and a growth of industrial exports will provide the same dynamism to the Latin American economies as the period of ISI.[56] Turning from the demand to the supply side, one should also consider the effects of high population growth rates and social equity policies on the capital/output ratio. The latter will probably be much higher than in the past, which means that the growth produced by each unit of investment will be lower than in the past. Thus many economies in the future might have to balance the conflicting claims arising from the need for higher saving to attain growth rates similar to those in the ISI days, and the pressures for more egalitarian socioeconomic policies which tend to depress the capacity to save.

The employment problem will probably be the most difficult to cope with. At this writing it is doubtful that industry will be able to absorb a substantially larger proportion of the economically active population. Can the service sector effectively make use of the burgeoning urban masses? Can agrarian reforms be instituted in such a manner as to absorb manpower, or will agricultural modernization of necessity have to result in an increased expulsion of labor from the countryside? Even if there is no food problem, is there any possible economic structure in Latin America which will effectively employ all those who are employable? Or is the only solution to the dilemma the development of a population policy? These are probably the most interesting questions which economists doing relevant work in Latin America will have to struggle with in the Seventies.

*The author wishes to thank David Felix, Andrea Maneschi, Carlos M. Pelaez, William Steel, and William O. Thweatt for many useful suggestions.

Notes

1 For an interesting analysis of continental Europe's emulation of England's industrial development during the nineteenth century, see David S. Landes, "Technological Change and Development in Western Europe, 1750–1914," In: *The Cambridge Economic History of Europe,* H. J. Habakkuk and M. Postan, eds., VI: 274–601 (Cambridge, England, 1966). The description Landes gives of the effects of the Napoleonic wars sounds quite familiar to contemporary students of import substitution: "To be sure, war and isolation had some favourable effects... . Technology, for example, was stimulated by the need to create substitutes for overseas imports... . The trouble was that not all of these wartime anomalies were ready to disappear once peace returned. For every substitute that died quietly ... another remained as a vested interest... . Thus mechanized textile manufacture in central Europe, essentially a product of wartime shortages, made a strong effort to convert monetary advantage into permanent privilege, with some success ..." (373).

2 The importance of trade relations, i.e., division of labor, among industrialized countries is demonstrated by the following data on trade among these countries as a proportion of world trade:

   1953—31.7%   1960—42.3%   1965—46.8%   1968—49.3%
       (Source: Annual Reports of GATT—*International Trade.*)

   For perceptive explanations of changes in trade specialization among developed countries, see Raymond Vernon, "International Investment and International Trade in the Product Cycle," *The Quarterly Journal of Economics* (QJE) (May 1966); Albert O. Hirschman, *National Power and the Structure of Foreign Trade* (Berkeley and Los Angeles, 1945; reprinted 1969).

3 Stanley Stein and Barbara Stein, *The Colonial Heritage of Latin America* (New York, 1970), have succinctly summarized the main obstacles to earlier industrialization in Latin America:

   Ex-colonies, then and now, cannot readily shed the economic legacy of centuries of colonialism, they cannot rapidly close the gap between backwardness and modernity, between primitive and advanced technology, between low and high levels of income, saving, and investment, between literacy and illiteracy, between obscurantism and enlightenment, between closed and open society.... It is not surprising, then, that Latin America did not begin to modernize its economy through industrialization until a century after independence. Under these circumstances the major consequence of the anticolonial movements in Latin America between 1810 and 1824, the crushing of the ties of the transatlantic empire led ... to neo-colonialism... . We can see how the economic growth of Latin America through diversification and industrialization could not occur while colonial patterns of production, capital accumulation and investment, income distribution and expenditure survived (136).

The backwardness of the Iberian metropolises in capital and technology opened the way to English entrepreneurs. Their textiles and hardware undersold those of their competitors; their capital resources facilitated long-term operations including the payment of high import duties; they extended their credits to Latin American merchants at half the interest rate of their competitors ... (154).

In his research on the economic history of Brazil, Carlos M. Pelaez has found substantial evidence to show that in the period 1898–1945 the effects of coffee and monetary policies were more to blame for the retardation of industrialization than the neo-colonial influence of European countries and the U.S.

4 Warren Dean, *The Industrialization of São Paulo, 1880–1945* (Austin, Texas, 1969); Carlos F. Díaz-Alejandro, *Essays on the Economic History of the Argentine Republic*, chs. 1–3 (New Haven, 1970); Clark W. Reynolds, *The Mexican Economy: Twentieth Century Structure and Growth*, ch. 5 (New Haven, 1970).

5 Dean, *Industrialization*, ch. 5; Díaz-Alejandro, *Essays*, ch. 4.

6 Comisión Económica para la América Latina de los Naciones Unidas (CEPAL), *El proceso de industrializatión en América Latina,* 14–17 (New York, 1965).

7 For some case studies, see: Díaz-Alejandro, *Essays,* chs. 1–3; Celso Furtado, *The Economic Growth of Brazil,* chs. 30 and 31 (Berkeley and Los Angeles, 1963); Werner Baer, *Industrialization and Economic Development in Brazil,* ch. 2 (Homewood, Illinois, 1965); Carlos M. Pelaez, "Acêrca de politica governamental, da grande depressão e da industrialização do Brasil," *Revista Brasileira de Economia* (RBE) (1969); Markos Mamalakis, *Growth and Structure of the Chilean Economy: 1840–1968,* chs. 2 and 6 (forthcoming); Oscar E. Muñoz, "An Essay on the Process of Industrialization in Chile since 1914," *Yale Economic Essays* (1968); CEPAL, *El proceso de industrialization* ..., 17–37.

8 Reviewing the experience of Argentina during the first three decades of the twentieth century, Díaz-Alejandro, *Essays*, ch. 3, states that, "... contrasted with later periods, the growth of manufacturing during 1900–29 may be explained primarily by the expansion of exports and domestic demand, with a relatively small contribution by import substitution."

9 In the case of Brazil this alteration has been documented in two studies: Annibal V. Villela, *Fontes de crescimento da economia Brasileira* (mimeographed, 1970) I: 406 and II: 218; Carlos M. Pelaez, "A balança comercial, a grande depressão e a industrialização Brasileira," RBE (1968), 15–47.

10 Baer, *The Development of the Brazilian Steel Industry, ch.* 4 (Nashville, Tennessee, 1969); Pelaez, "O desenvolvimento da industria do aço no Brasil," RBE (1970) 191–217; Nathaniel H. Leff, *The Brazilian Capital Goods Industry, 1929–1964,* 8–20 (Cambridge, Mass., 1968). According to Don Huddle's calculations, "Postwar Brazilian Industrialization: Growth Patterns, Inflation, and Sources of Stagnation," In: *The Shaping of Modern Brazil,* Eric N. Baklanoff, ed., 96 (Baton Rouge, Louisiana,

1969), ISI in Brazil "... had already been carried very far by 1939. Thus continued across the board import substitution between 1939 and 1963 was necessarily somewhat limited."

11 In a quantitative analysis of five Latin American countries, Henry J. Bruton "Productivity Growth in Latin America," *American Economic Review* (AER), 57: 1110 (1967), found that as a result of being forced to use domestic capacity to the fullest extent, firms had to "... find ways to use their existing capital stock with increasing effectiveness. Improvisation and adaptation of existing equipment were common, and one can find many examples of ingeniously and indigenously devised machines producing various items for household and business use... . The war then not only provided 'protection' from foreign competition, but also helped to create an environment within which entrepreneurs had incentives to use available resources with increasing effectiveness."

12 The initial position of the Economic Commission for Latin America (ECLA) was contained in *The Economic Development of Latin America and its Principal Problems* (United Nations, 1950); and an elaboration of these views appeared in Raul Prebisch's "Commercial Policy in the Underdeveloped Countries," AER, 49: 251–273 (1959). There exists a vast literature attacking and defending the Prebisch-ECLA position. See, for instance: Baer, "The Economics of Prebisch and ECLA," *Economic Development and Cultural Change* (EDCC) 10: 169–182 (1962); June Flanders, "Prebisch on Protectionism: An Evaluation," *Economic Journal* (EJ) 74: 305–326 (1964); Gottfried Haberler, "Terms of Trade and Economic Development," In: *Economic Development for Latin America,* Howard S. Ellis and Henry C. Wallich, eds., 275–297 (New York, 1961). An ECLA-type model which avoids the controversial terms of trade arguments, yet builds a similar case for industrialization can be found in Dudley Seers, "A Model of Comparative Rates of Growth in the World Economy," EJ 62: 45–78 (1962).

13 See, for example, the projections for world trade found in Bela Belassa, *Trade Prospects for Developing Countries* (Homewood, Ill., 1964) and UNCTAD, *Trade Prospects and Capital Needs of Developing Countries* (New York, 1968).

14 For policies followed in individual countries, see Díaz-Alejandro, *Essays;* Baer, *Industrialization,* ch. 3; Joel Bergsman, *Brazil, Industrialization and Trade Policies,* chs. 3 and 4 (New York, 1970); Reynolds, *The Mexican Economy,* ch. 7; Timothy King, *Mexico: Industrialization and Trade Policies Since 1940,* chs. 3–5 (New York, 1970); Mamalakis, *Growth and Structure,* chs. 6 and 7 (forthcoming); CEPAL, *El proceso de industrializacion ... ,* ch. III.

15 David Felix, "Monetarists, Structuralists, and Import-Substituting Industrialization: A Critical Appraisal," In: *Inflation and Growth in Latin America,* Werner Baer and Isaac Kerstenetzky, eds., 383 (Homewood, 1964; 2nd printing, New Haven, 1970).

16 Albert O. Hirschman, "The Political Economy of Import-Substituting Industrialization in Latin America," QJE, 82: 17–24 (1968).

17 For example, all automobile plants were built and run by foreign firms. Almost all government steel mills in Latin America were built with foreign financing and planned and constructed under the supervision of foreign consulting firms. For some interesting comparative data on the macroeconomic impact of foreign financing, see I. Little, T. Scitovsky, and M. Scott, *Industry and Trade in Some Developing Countries: A Comparative Study,* 47–59 (New York, 1970).

18 It has been argued by a number of economists that even if measured in constant prices, taking a base year where relative prices of manufactured goods were not at their highest, the contribution of manufacturing is exaggerated. Some have tried to measure the contribution of the sector by valuing manufactured products at world prices. But even such deflation of industry's contributions do not erase the basic trends. Little, Scitovsky, and Scott, *Industry and Trade,* 7.

19 The region's countries vary substantially as to potential for ISI. However, most of the market critics whose views are summarized here have dealt with the larger Latin American countries.

20 The growth of manufactures as a proportion of world trade was quite spectacular in the forty years, 1928–68, as shown by the following data:

1928—39%; 1938—40%; 1953—45%; 1960—54%; 1968—67%.

Richard N. Cooper, *The Economics of Interdependence* (New York, 1968); GATT, *International Trade 1968.*

It should also be noted that in the post-World War II period, Third World countries have drastically lost their shares in world trade. Their share of world exports declined from 34 per cent in 1950 to 19 per cent in 1968; see various annual reports of GATT, *International Trade.* Finally, it should be noted in Table 5(a) that in the twenty year period 1948–68, Latin America's share in world trade declined from 10.9 per cent to 5.0 per cent.

21 Tibor Scitovsky, "Prospects for Latin American Industrialization within the Framework of Economic Integration," In: *The Process of Industrialization in Latin America,* 43 (Washington, D.C., 1969). The average number might be somewhat misleading. For example, in Brazil, Volkswagen produces more than half the passenger cars, thus benefitting more from scale economies than most other plants. See Bergsman, *Brazil,* 120–130. For an interesting case study of the Chilean automobile industry, which was characterized by a small market being served by twenty firms operating more than one thousand miles away from the principal market, see Leland J. Johnson, "Problems of Import Substitution: The Chilean Automobile Industry," EDCC 15: 202–216 (1967).

22 Scitovsky, "Prospects," 42.

23 Little, Scitovsky, and Scott, *Industry and Trade,* 39.

24 It has been estimated that effective protection for manufactured products in Brazil in 1966 was 254 percent as compared with product protection of 99 percent. Bergsman, *Brazil,* 42; for other countries see Little, Scitovsky, and Scott, *Industry and Trade,* 174.

25 Jack Baranson, *Automotive Industries in Developing Countries,* 15 (Baltimore, 1969).

26 Baranson, *Automotive Industries,* 22.

27 Baranson, *Automotive Industries,* 25–26.

28 Baranson, *Automotive Industries,* 28. He also found that Brazil's costs as compared to those of Argentina are lower because the former's market is larger, the industry is older, and many producers have written off capital costs for machines which are still in good working order, and Brazilians have had a longer period to develop suppliers, improve quality, and reduce costs (39). It is of interest to mention some specific numbers cited by Baranson: he found that in Argentina materials and parts averaged 3.3 times the U.S. cost level; administrative and selling costs are twice as high in Mexico as in the U.S.; special tooling amortization is almost three times as expensive per vehicle in Brazil and Mexico as in the U.S. (39). A yet unpublished study of the Brazilian automobile industry by José Almeida, of the Fundação Getúlio Vargas, presents similar conclusions. One of the principal reasons for the high cost of Brazilian automobiles was found to be the extreme autarky of the industry. The domestic content of Brazilian vehicles amounts to 98 percent. Decreasing this content to a level of 50 percent to 60 percent would substantially lower costs.

29 Ayhan Cilingiroglu, *Manufacture of Heavy Electrical Equipment in Developing Countries,* 31 (Baltimore, 1969).

30 "Industrial Development in Latin America," *Economic Bulletin for Latin America,* 13 (1969).

31 For a thorough discussion of problems in defining the appropriate exchange rate and the domestic resource cost, see William F. Steel, "Import Substitution Policy in Ghana in the 1960's," 53–80 (unpublished Ph.D. dissertation, MIT, 1970).

32 The theoretical literature on this topic is rather lengthy. See, for instance, Bela Balassa and Daniel M. Schydlowsky, "Effective Tariffs, Domestic Cost of Foreign Exchange, and the Equilibrium Exchange Rate," *The Journal of Political Economy* (JPE), 76: 348–360 (1968). For an application of such a criterion to measure the efficiency of an industry in Latin America, see Baer, *Brazilian Steel Industry,* 146–151.

33 See Díaz-Alejandro, *Essays,* ch. 6; also, "An Interpretation of Argentine Economic Growth Since 1930," Part I, *Journal of Development Studies* (JDS), 3: 25–28 (1966).

34 A recent article by Samuel A. Morley and Gordon W. Smith, "On the Measurement of Import Substitution," AER, 60: 728–735 (1970), challenges the usual measurements of import substitution. These underestimate ISI if imports are replaced without induced rises in imported inputs. The authors develop a formula for appropriate corrections.

35 This situation has been well described by David Felix, "The Dilemma of Import Substitution—Argentina," In: *Development Policy: Theory and Practice,* Gustav F. Papanek, ed., 60–61 (Cambridge, Mass., 1968): "As the consumer-goods phase of ISI is succeeded by a predominantly capital- and intermediate-goods phase, three sets of forces close in on the strategy. The import mix shifts predominantly to one of fuels, industrial materials, essential food-stuffs, and capital goods required by the industrial sector. The capital intensity of import-substituting projects rises, resulting in a rising import content of investment and causing the level of investment to be more severely constrained by the capacity to import. The projects tend to require increasingly large markets in order to reach minimum efficient scale, so that the ability of ISI to induce investment is progressively weakened by the thin domestic markets of even the larger Latin American countries." See also Díaz-Alejandro, "On the Import Intensity of Import Substitution," *Kyklos,* 18: 495–511 (1965), who stresses the fact that rapid ISI raises income before investments mature, resulting in an increase in imports. See also Maria Conceição Tavares, "Auge y declinación del proceso de substitución de importaciones en el Brasil," *Boletín Económico de America Latina,* 9: 1–59 (1964).

36 John Sheahan, "Imports, Investment, and Growth——Colombia," In: *Development Policy: Theory and Practice,* 97–99. See also Jaroslav Vanek, *Estimating Foreign Resource Needs for Economic Development* (New York, 1967). For Argentina, see Díaz-Alejandro, *Essays,* ch. 7.

37 Leff, "Export Stagnation and Autarkic Development in Brazil," QJE, 81: 286–301 (1967); Little, Scitovsky, and Scott, *Industry and Trade,* ch. 7.

38 One should, of course, take into account the fact that the industrial growth stimulates both direct and indirect employment. Thus, not all employment growth in the service sector can be looked upon as residual; i.e., a sector into which people go if they cannot find employment in industry. Many government financial and commercial services grow in a fashion complementary to industry. It is obvious, however, that the extremely high rates of growth of employment in services in Latin America reflects a large proportion of residual labor absorption. Interesting analyses and data on employment in Latin America can be found in Raúl Prebisch, *Transformación y desarrollo: la gran tarea de América Latina* (Washington, D.C., 1970); also in ILO, *Hacia el pleno empleo: un programa para Colombia* (Geneva, 1970).

39 Little, Scitovsky, and Scott, *Industry and Trade,* ch. 3; Henry J. Bruton, "The Import Substitution Strategy of Economic Development: A Survey of Findings," 17 (Mimeographed Research Memorandum No. 27, Williams College, Williamstown, Mass., 1969); Baer and Michel Hervé, "Employment and Industrialization in Developing Countries," QJE, 80: 88–107 (1966); Benjamin Cohen and Nathaniel Leff, "Employment and Industrialization: Comment," QJE, 81: 162–164 (1967); Baer and Hervé, "Employment and Industrialization: Reply," QJE, 81: 532–533 (1967).

40 Little, Scitovsky, and Scott, *Industry and Trade,* 41–47; W. Baer and Andrea Maneschi, "Import-Substitution, Stagnation and Structural Change: An Interpretation of the

Brazilian Case," JDA, 5: 177–192 (1971); King, *Mexico: Industrialization,* 26–32; Naciones Unidas, *El desarrollo económico y la distribución del ingreso en la Argentina* (New York, 1968); ILO, *Hacia el pleno empleo,* ch. 10.

41 Although capacity utilization data are rare because of capacity measurement difficulties, some evidence of underutilization can be found in the following sources: Baer and Maneschi, "Import Substitution," and "Industrial Development in Latin America," *Economic Bulletin for Latin America,* 14: 2: 14–15 (1969); Little, Scitovsky, and Scott, *Industry and Trade,* 93–99; Baer, *The Development of the Brazilian Steel Industry,* 89.

42 For a discussion of regional imbalances in the Brazilian context, see Baer, *Industrialization,* 163–185.

43 For a thorough survey and analysis of the potential effect of income redistribution in Latin America, see William R. Cline, *The Potential Effect of Income Redistribution on Economic Growth in Six Latin American Countries* (mimeographed; Discussion Paper No. 13, Research Program in Economic Development, Princeton, N.J., 1970).

44 Nicholas Georgescu-Roegen first raised this question in an article published in Brazil, "Inflação estrutural e o crescimento economico," RBE, 22: 5–14 (1968); since then he has published an expanded version in English: "Structural Inflation-Lock and Balanced Growth," *Economies et Sociétés,* Cahier de L'T.S.E.A., Tome IV: 3 (Geneva, 1970). An interesting model of growth and stagnation based on Georgescu-Roegen's original idea is contained in Francisco Lopes, "Subsidios a formulação de um modelo de desenvolvimento e estagnação no Brasil," RBE, 23: 59–78 (1969).

45 An alternative might be a change in the demand profile of lower income groups. A good example of this was the boom in automobile sales in Brazil in the late Sixties. This boom was mainly due to the rise of "consorcios." This is an ingenious device which was invented to create credit for buying cars. Under a typical scheme, a group of, say, 24 people get together to buy a Volkswagen. Each member of the consorcio agrees to pay every month 1/24th of the price of a VW into a kitty and every month a VW is bought. Payments are readjustable for inflationary rates. Thus, each month one member gets a VW, but everyone continues to pay for 24 months, until everyone has received his VW. The doubt which can be raised about this scheme is whether the opportunity cost to the economy is not too great. People buying cars will forego buying many other goods (often wage goods) and many will forego saving.

46 It could be claimed that the "structural lock" problem is not important since imbalances between the demand and productive profiles are eliminated over time as investment takes place in shortage areas. However, given the huge amounts of excess productive capacity which was referred to earlier, this problem cannot be disregarded on the basis of long-run adjustments.

47 I would like to thank David Felix for pointing this out. Also see his article "The Dilemma of Import Substitution—Argentina," 65–70.

48 Joel Bergsman and Arthur Candal, "Industrialization: Past Success and Future Problems," In: *The Economy of Brazil,* Howard S. Ellis, ed., 47 (Berkeley and Los Angeles, 1969).

49 Given their many special economic and political circumstances, it is doubtful whether the examples of Taiwan, Korea, or Hong Kong can be taken as proofs that the Latin American economies were not in a dilemma.

50 Erroneous price policies in the late Forties when Brazil still dominated the world coffee market had nothing to do with the argument that agriculture was sacrificed. A valid argument might be that Brazil neglected the use of resources to invest in a new type of agriculture which would diversify agricultural exports. Although this would have been a correct policy to follow, it would not have been a substitute for ISI.

51 Baer, *The Development of the Brazilian Steel Industry,* ch. 2.

52 "Industrial Development in Latin America," *Economic Bulletin for Latin America*, 14: 12 (1969). In an interesting study of Peruvian industries, Christopher Clague found that labor intensive industries are less efficient than capital intensive ones. He finds this discouraging since labor intensive industries produce more easily exportable products. "The Determinants of Efficiency in Manufacturing Industries in an Underdeveloped Country," EDCC, 18: 188–205 (1970).

53 I have developed this point in "Sobre os usos e abusos da teoria economica," RBE, 22: 7283 (1968).

54 For a discussion of such "complementation agreements" in Latin America, see GATT, *International Trade 1968*, 63–74 (Geneva, 1969).

55 A good critical appraisal of Latin American integration possibilities can be found in Keith Griffin, *Underdevelopment in Spanish America*, ch. VI (Cambridge, Mass., 1970). The best and most extensive empirical work on specialization possibilities within a Latin American common market has been done by a group of Latin American research institutes (collectively known as ECIEL) led by Joseph Grunwald of The Brookings Institution. Results were presented at a Conference on Research in Income and Wealth of the National Bureau of Economic Research by Joseph Grunwald and Jorge Salazar under the title, "Economic Integration, and Price and Value Comparisons in Latin America" and published in *International Comparisons of Prices and Real Income: Studies in Income and Wealth,* D. J. Daley, ed. (N.Y., 1972).

56 In his interesting study, "The Potential Effect of Income Redistribution on Economic Growth in Six Latin American Countries" 95 (mimeographed, Discussion Paper No. 13, Princeton, 1970), William Cline found that "Using the estimated income distributions and consumption function estimates from family budget studies, simulation exercises suggested that for Argentina, Brazil, Mexico and Venezuela income redistributions toward equality of the level found in Britain would cost on the order of 1% annual growth in GNP ..."

Bibliography

BAER, WERNER
    1962   The Puerto Rican Economy and U.S. Economic Fluctuations. Río Piedras.
    1965   Industrialization and Economic Development in Brazil. Homewood, Ill.
    1969   The Development of the Brazilian Steel Industry. Nashville, Tenn.
BAER, WERNER AND I. KERSTENETZKY
    1971   The Brazilian Economy in the Sixties. In: Brazil in the Sixties. Riordan Roett, ed. Nashville, Tenn.
BAER, WERNER AND A. MANESCHI
    1971   Import-Substitution, Stagnation and Structural Change: An Interpretation of the Brazilian Case. The Journal of Developing Areas (JDE). Jan.
BARANSON, JACK
    1969   Automotive Industries in Developing Countries. Baltimore. (Includes analysis of Argentinian, Brazilian, and Mexican Industries.)
BERGSMAN, JOEL
    1970   Brazil: Industrialization and Trade Policies. N.Y.
BRUTON, HENRY J.
    1967   Productivity Growth in Latin America. American Economic Review (AER). Dec.
    1968   Import Substitution and Productivity Growth. Journal of Development Studies (JDS). April.

1968   Export Growth and Import Substitution. Research Memorandum No. 22. Williams College, Center for Development Economics. Williamstown, Mass.

1969   The Import Substitution Strategy of Economic Development: A Survey of Findings. Research Memorandum No. 27. Williamstown. (This is a survey of the findings of Williams College economists studying ISI in various parts of the world, including Latin America. The inclination of this survey and most Williams College researchers is more towards what I have called the "market critics.")

BRODERSOHN, MARIO S., ed.

1970   Estrategias de industrialización para la Argentina. Buenos Aires. (This volume contains articles both on ISI problems of Argentina and also on the general nature of ISI and its related problems.)

CILINGIROGLU, AYHAN

1969   Manufacture of Heavy Electrical Equipment in Developing Countries. Baltimore. (Includes considerable information on Brazil, Argentina, and Mexico.)

CLAGUE, CHRISTOPHER

1970   The Determinants of Efficiency in Manufacturing Industries in an Underdeveloped Country. Economic Development and Cultural Change (EDCC). Jan. (Efficiency in Peruvian industries.)

CLARK, PAUL G.

1967   Brazilian Import Liberalization. Research Memorandum No. 14. Williamstown, Mass. Sept.

1967   Import Demand Functions for Brazil. Research Memorandum No. 15. Williamstown, Mass.

CLARK, PAUL G. AND RICHARD WEISSKOFF

1967   Import Demands and Import Policies in Brazil. Research Memorandum No. 8. Williamstown, Mass. Feb.

CLINE, WILLIAM R.

1970   The Potential Effect of Income Redistribution on Economic Growth in Six Latin American Countries. Mimeographed Discussion Paper No. 13. Princeton.

DEAN, WARREN

1969   The Industrialization of São Paulo, 1880–1945. Austin, Tex.

DEVRIES, BAREND A.

1967   The Export Experience of Developing Countries. Baltimore. (DeVries' statistical analysis also covers most Latin American countries.)

DÍAZ-ALEJANDRO, CARLOS F.

1965   On the Import Intensity of Import Substitution. Kyklos. 18: 495–511.

1966–67   An Interpretation of Argentine Economic Growth Since 1930. JDS. Oct. and Jan.

1970   Essays on the Economic History of the Argentine Republic. New Haven.

DORFMAN, ADOLFO

1967   La industrialización en la América Latina y las políticas de fomento. México.

ELLIS, HOWARD S., ed.

1969   The Economy of Brazil. Berkeley and Los Angeles. (See especially articles by Bergsman and Candal, "Industrialization: Past Success and Future Problems"; and by Samuel A. Morley, "Import Demand and Import Substitution in Brazil.")

FELIX, DAVID

1968   The Dilemma of Import Substitution—Argentina. In: Development Policy: Theory and Practice. Cambridge, Mass.

1969   Economic Development: Take Offs into Unsustained Growth. Social Research: 36: 2.

1970   Monetarists, Structuralists, and Import-Substituting Industrialization: A Critical Appraisal. In: Inflation and Growth in Latin America. Baer and Kerstenetzky, eds. Homewood, 111. New printing, Cambridge, Mass.

FERRER, ALDO

1963   La economía Argentina. México/Buenos Aires.

FURTADO, CELSO

1963   The Economic Growth of Brazil. Berkeley and Los Angeles.

1966   Subdesenvolvimento e estagnação na America Latina. Rio de Janeiro.

1968   Um projeto para o Brasil. Rio de Janeiro.

        (For a summary of Furtado's ideas on growth and stagnation in Latin America which are elaborated in various publications of his, see W. Baer, "Furtado on Development: A Review Essay," JDA, Jan. 1969.)

FURTADO, CELSO AND A. MANESCHI

1968   Um modelo de simulação de desenvolvimento e estagnação na America Latina. RBE. June.

GENERAL AGREEMENT ON TARIFFS AND TRADE (GATT)

        International Trade. (Annual volumes which contain excellent information on the performance of less developed countries in world markets.)

GEORGESCU-ROEGEN, NICHOLAS

1970   Structural Inflation-Lock and Balanced Growth. Economies e Sociétés. 4: 3. Geneva.

GRIFFIN, KEITH

1970   Underdevelopment in Spanish America. Cambridge, Mass.

GRUNWALD, JOSEPH

1970   Some Reflections on Latin American Industrialization Policies. Journal of Political Economy (JPE). 78: 4: 826–856.

GRUNWALD, JOSEPH AND JORGE SALAZAR

1972   "Economic Integration, and Price and Value Comparisons in Latin America." In: International Comparisons of Prices and Real Income: Studies in Income and Wealth. D. J. Daly, ed. N.Y.

GRUNWALD, JOSEPH AND PHILIP MUSGROVE

1970   Natural Resources in Latin American Development. Baltimore.

HARBERGER, A. C.

1970   Economic Policy Problems in Latin America: A Review. JPE. July/Aug., Part II.

HIRSCHMAN, ALBERT O.

1958   The Strategy of Economic Development. New Haven.

1968   The Political Economy of Import-Substituting Industrialization. QJE. Feb.

HUDDLE, DONNALD

1969   Postwar Brazilian Industrialization: Growth Patterns, Inflation, and Sources of Stagnation. In: The Shaping of Modern Brazil. Eric N. Baklanoff, ed. Baton Rouge.

HUNT, SHANE J.

1969   Distribution, Growth, and Government Economic Behavior in Peru. (Mimeographed). Princeton.

INTERNATIONAL LABOR ORGANIZATION

1970   Hacia el pleno empleo: Un programa para Colombia preparado por una misión internacional organizada por la Oficina Intenacional del Trabajo. Geneva.

INTER-AMERICAN DEVELOPMENT BANK
1970   Socio-Economic Progress in Latin America. Ninth Annual Report, 1969. Washington, D.C.
        (This issue contains a general review of Latin American economies in the Sixties.)
JOHNSON, LELAND J.
1967   Problems of Import Substitution: The Chilean Automobile Industry. EDCC. Jan.
KAFKA, ALEXANDRE
1961   The Theoretical Interpretation of Latin American Economic Development. In: Economic Development for Latin America. Howard Ellis and Henry Wallich, eds. N.Y.
KING, TIMOTHY
1970   Mexico: Industrialization and Trade Policies Since 1940. N.Y.
LEFF, NATHANIEL
1968   The Brazilian Capital Goods Industry, 1929–1964. Cambridge, Mass.
1967   Export Stagnation and Autarkic Development in Brazil. QJE. May.
LITTLE, IAN, TIBOR SCITOVSKY AND MAURICE SCOTT
1970   Industry Trade in Some Developing Countries. N.Y.
LOPES, FRANCISCO
1969   Subsidios a formulação de um modelo de desenvolvimento e estagnação no Brasil. RBE. June.
MAMALAKIS, MARKOS
        Growth and Structure of the Chilean Economy: 1840–1968.
        (Mimeographed; soon to be published by Yale University Press).
MAMALAKIS, MARKOS AND CLARK W. REYNOLDS
1965   Essays on the Chilean Economy. Homewood, Ill.
MACARIO, SANTIAGO
1965   Protectionism and Industrialization in Latin America. Economic Bulletin for Latin America. March.
MORLEY, SAMUEL A. AND GORDON W. SMITH
1970   On the Measurement of Import Substitution. AER. Sept.
MOSK, SANFORD A.
1954   Industrial Revolution in Mexico. Berkeley and Los Angeles.
MUÑOZ, OSCAR
1968   An Essay on the Process of Industrialization in Chile Since 1914. Yale Economic Essays. Fall.
PELAEZ, CARLOS M.
1968   The State, the Great Depression and the Industrialization of Brazil. (Unpublished Ph.D. dissertation, Columbia University). N.Y.
1968   A balança comercial, a grande depressão e a industralização Brasileira. RBE. Mar.
1969   Açerca de politica governamental, da grande depressão e da industrialização no Brasil. RBE. Jul./Set.
1970   O desenvolvimento da industria do aço no Brasil. RBE. Abr./Jun.
PREBISCH, RAUL
1970   Transformación y desarrollo: la gran tarea de América Latina. Banco Interamericano de Desarrollo. Washington, D.C.

REYNOLDS, CLARK W.
1970   The Mexican Economy: Twentieth Century Structure and Growth. New Haven.
ROBOCK, STEFAN H.
1970   Industrialization through Import-Substitution or Export Industries: A False Dichotomy. In: Industrial Organization and Economic Development. J. W. Markham and G. F. Papanek, eds. Boston.
SHEAHAN, JOHN
1968   Imports, Investment, and Growth. In: Development Policy: Theory and Practice. Gustav F. Papanek, ed. Cambridge, Mass.
1969   Criteria for Investment Allocation in Colombia. Center for Development Economics Research Memorandum No. 33. Williamstown. Nov.
SCHYDLOWSKY, DANIEL M.
1967   From Import Substitution to Export Promotion for Semi-Grown-Up Industries: A Policy Proposal. JDS. July.
SCITOVSKY, TIBOR
1969   Prospects for Latin American Industrialization within the Framework of Economic Integration: Bases for Analysis. In: The Process of Industrialization in Latin America. Inter-American Development Bank, Washington, D.C.
STEIN, STANLEY AND BARBARA H. STEIN
1970   The Colonial Heritage of Latin America. N.Y.
STRASSMANN, W. Paul.
1968   Technological Change and Economic Development: The Manufacturing Experience of Mexico and Puerto Rico. Ithaca, N.Y.
TAVARES, MARIA CONÇEICÁO
1964   Auge y declinación del proceso de sustitución de importaciones en el Brasil. Boletín Económico de América Latina. Mar.
TENDLER, JUDITH
1968   Electric Power in Brazil: Entrepreneurship in the Public Sector. Cambridge, Mass.
UNITED NATIONS ECONOMIC COMMISSION FOR LATIN AMERICA (ECLA)
1965   The Process of Industrialization in Latin America. N.Y.
1969   Industrial Development in Latin America. Economic Bulletin for Latin America. 14: 2: 1–77.
UNCTAD
1968   Trade Prospects and Capital Needs of Developing Countries. N.Y.
VANEK, JAROSLAV
1967   Estimating Foreign Resource Needs for Economic Development. N.Y. (Case Study of Colombia.)
VERNON, RAYMOND
1963   The Dilemma of Mexico's Development. Cambridge, Mass.
1964   (editor) Public Policy and Private Enterprise in Mexico. Cambridge, Mass.
VILLELA, ANIBAL V.
1971   Fontes de crescimento da economia Brasileira. (Mimeographed.)

2

RULES, DISCRETION AND REPUTATION IN A MODEL OF MONETARY POLICY*

Robert J. Barro and David B. Gordon

Source: *Journal of Monetary Economics* 12, 1983, 101–121.

In a discretionary regime the monetary authority can print more money and create more inflation than people expect. But, although these inflation surprises can have some benefits, they cannot arise systematically in equilibrium when people understand the policymaker's incentives and form their expectations accordingly. Because the policymaker has the power to create inflation shocks ex post, the equilibrium growth rates of money and prices turn out to be higher than otherwise. Therefore, enforced commitments (rules) for monetary behavior can improve matters. Given the repeated interaction between the policymaker and the private agents, it is possible that reputational forces can substitute for formal rules. Here, we develop an example of a reputational equilibrium where the outcomes turn out to be weighted averages of those from discretion and those from the ideal rule. In particular, the rates of inflation and monetary growth look more like those under discretion when the discount rate is high.

1. Introduction

In a discretionary regime the monetary authority can print more money and create more inflation than people expect. The benefits from this surprise inflation may include expansions of economic activity and reductions in the real value of the government's nominal liabilities. However, because people understand the policymaker's incentives, these types of surprises — and their resulting benefits — cannot arise systematically in equilibrium. People adjust their inflationary expectations in order to eliminate a consistent pattern of surprises. In this case the potential for creating inflation shocks, ex post, means that, in equilibrium, the average rates of inflation and monetary growth — and the corresponding costs of inflation — will be higher than otherwise. Enforced commitments on monetary behavior, as embodied in monetary or price rules, eliminate the potential for ex post surprises. Therefore, the equilibrium rates of inflation and monetary growth can be lowered by shifts from monetary institutions that allow discretion to ones that enforce rules.

When monetary rules are in place, the policymaker has the temptation each period to 'cheat' in order to secure the benefits from inflation shocks. (Because of existing distortions in the economy, these benefits can accrue generally to private agents, rather than merely to the policymaker.) However, this tendency to cheat threatens the viability of the rules equilibrium and tends to move the economy toward the inferior equilibrium under discretion. Because of the repeated interactions between the policymaker and the private agents, it is possible that reputational forces can support the rule. That is, the potential loss of reputation — or credibility — motivates the policymaker to abide by the rule. Then, the policymaker foregoes the short-term benefits from inflation shocks in order to secure the gain from low average inflation over the long term.

We extend the positive theory of monetary policy from our previous paper [Barro and Gordon (1983)] to allow for reputational forces. Some monetary rules, but generally not the ideal one, can be enforced by the policymaker's potential loss of reputation. We find that the resulting equilibrium looks like a weighted average of that under discretion and that under the ideal rule. Specifically, the outcomes are superior to those under discretion — where no commitments are pertinent — but inferior to those under the ideal rule (which cannot be enforced in our model by the potential loss of reputation). The results look more like discretion when the policymaker's discount rate is high, but more like the ideal rule when the discount rate is low. Otherwise, we generate predictions about the behavior of monetary growth and inflation that resemble those from our previous analysis of discretionary policy. Namely, any change that raises the benefits of inflation shocks — such as a supply shock or a war — leads to a higher growth rate of money and prices.

2. The policymaker's objective

As in our earlier analysis, we think of the monetary authority's objective as reflecting the preferences of the 'representative' private agent. Ultimately, we express this objective as a function of actual and expected rates of inflation. Specifically, benefits derive from positive inflation shocks (at least over some range), but costs attach to higher rates of inflation.

2.1. The benefits from surprise inflation

We assume that some benefits arise when the inflation rate for period t, π_t exceeds the anticipated amount, π_t^e. One source of benefits — discussed in Barro and Gordon (1983) and in an example from Kydland and Prescott (1977, p. 477) — derives from the expectational Phillips curve. Here, unanticipated monetary expansions, reflected in positive values for $\pi_t - \pi_t^e$, lead to increases in real economic activity. Equivalently, these nominal shocks lower the unemployment rate below the natural rate. By the natural rate, we mean here the value that would be ground out by the private sector in the absence of monetary disturbances. This natural rate can shift over time because of supply shocks, demographic changes, shifts in governmental tax and transfer programs, and so on. The natural rate also need not be optimal. In fact, the benefits from surprise inflation arise when the policymaker views the natural rate as excessive. This can occur, for example, if the distortions from income taxation, unemployment compensation, and the like make the average level of privately-chosen work and production too low. Because of the externalities from these distortions, the government (and the private agents) would value stimulative policy actions that lower the unemployment rate below its natural value.

Other sources of benefits from surprise inflation involve governmental revenues. Barro (1983) focuses on the proceeds from inflationary finance. The expectation of inflation (formed the previous period), π_t^e, determines people's holdings of real cash, M_{t-1}/P_{t-1}. Surprise inflation, $\pi_t - \pi_t^e$, depreciates the real value of these holdings, which allows the government to issue more new money in real terms, $(M_t - M_{t-1})/P_t$, as a replacement. The policymaker values this inflationary finance if alternative methods of raising revenue — such as an income tax — entail distortions. Hence, the benefit from surprise inflation depends again on some existing externality. Calvo (1978) discusses the necessity of existing distortions in this type of model.

The revenue incentive for surprise inflation relates to governmental liabilities that are fixed in nominal terms, rather than to money, *per se*. Thus, the same argument applies to nominally-denominated, interest-bearing public debt. Suppose that people held last period the real amount of government bonds, B_{t-1}/P_{t-1}. These bonds carry the nominal yield, R_{t-i}, which is satisfactory given people's inflationary expectations over the pertinent horizon, π_t^e. Surprise inflation $\pi_t - \pi_t^e$, depreciates part of the real value of these bonds, which lowers the government's future real expenditures for interest and repayment of principal. In effect, surprise inflation is again a source of revenue to the government. Quantitatively this channel from public debt is likely to be more significant than the usually discussed mechanism, which involves revenue from printing high-powered money. For example, the outstanding public debt for the U.S. in 1981 is around $1 trillion.[1] Therefore, a surprise inflation of 1% lowers the real value of this debt by about $10 billion. Hence, this channel produces an effective lump amount of revenue of about $10 billion for each extra 1% of surprise inflation. By contrast, the entire annual flow of revenue through the Federal Reserve from the creation of high-powered money is about the same magnitude ($8 billion in 1981, $13 billion in 1980).

The attractions of generating revenue from surprise inflation are clear if we view the depreciation of real cash or real bonds as an unexpected capital levy. As with a tax on existing capital, surprise inflation provides for a method of raising funds that is essentially non-distorting, ex post. Once people have built up the capital or held the real cash or real bonds, the government can extract revenue without disincentive effects. Of course, the distortions arise — for capital, money or bonds — when people anticipate, ex ante, the possibility of these capital levies, ex post. That's why these forms of raising revenue will not end up being so desirable in a full equilibrium where people form expectations rationally. But, for the moment, we are just listing the benefits that attach, ex post, to surprise inflation.

2.2. *The costs of inflation*

The second major element in our model is the cost of inflation. Costs are assumed to rise, and at an increasing rate, with the realized inflation rate, π_t. Although people generally regard inflation as very costly, economists have not presented very convincing arguments to explain these costs. Further, the present type of cost refers to the actual amount of inflation for the period, rather than to the variance of inflation, which could more easily be seen as costly. Direct costs of changing prices fit reasonably well into the model, although the quantitative role of these costs is doubtful. In any event the analysis has some interesting conclusions for the case where the actual amount of inflation for each period is not perceived as costly. Then, the model predicts a lot of inflation!

3. The setup of our example

We focus our discussion on the simplest possible example, which illustrates the main points about discretion, rules and reputation. Along the way, we indicate how the results generalize beyond this example.

The policymaker's objective involves a cost for each period, z_t, which is given by

$$z_t = (a/2)(\pi_t)^2 - b_t(\pi_t - \pi_t^e) \quad \text{where} \quad a, b_t > 0. \tag{1}$$

The first term, $(a/2)(\pi_t)^2$, is the cost of inflation. Notice that our use of a quadratic form means that these costs rise at an increasing rate with the rate of inflation, π_t. The second term, $b_t(\pi_t - \pi_t^e)$, is the benefit from inflation shocks. Here, we use a linear form for convenience.[2] Given that the benefit parameter, b_t, is positive, an increase in unexpected inflation, $\pi_t - \pi_t^e$, reduces costs. We can think of these benefits as reflecting reductions in unemployment or increases in governmental revenue.

We allow the benefit parameter, b_t, to move around over time. For example, a supply shock — which raises the natural rate of unemployment — may increase the value of reducing unemployment through aggressive monetary policy. Alternatively, a sharp rise in government spending increases the incentives to raise revenue via inflationary finance. In our example, b_t is distributed randomly with a fixed mean, $\bar{b}$, and variance, σ_b^2.[3] (Hence, we neglect serial correlation in the natural unemployment rate, government expenditures, etc.)

The policymaker's objective at date t entails minimization of the expected present value of costs.

$$Z_t = E\left[z_t + \left(1/(1+r_t)\right)\cdot z_{t+1} + \left(1/(1+r_t)(1+r_{t+1})\right)Z_{t+2} + \ldots\right], \tag{2}$$

where r_t is the discount rate that applies between periods t and $t+1$. We assume that r_t is generated from a stationary probability distribution. (Therefore, we again neglect any serial dependence.) Also, the discount rate is generated independently of the benefit parameter, b_t For the first period ahead, the distribution of r_t implies a distribution for the discount factor, $q_t = 1/(1+r_t)$. We denote the mean and variance for q_t, by $\bar{q}$ and σ_q^2, respectively.

The policymaker controls a monetary instrument, which enables him to select the rate of inflation, π_t, in each period. The main points of our analysis do not change materially if we introduce random discrepancies between inflation and changes in the monetary instrument. For example, we could have shifts in velocity or control errors for the money supply. Also, the policymaker has no incentive to randomize choices of inflation in the model.

We begin with a symmetric case where no one knows the benefit parameter, b_t, or the discount factor for the next period, q_1, when they act for period t. Hence, the policymaker chooses the inflation rate, π_t, without observing either b_t or q_t. Similarly, people form their expectations, π_t^e, of the policymaker's choice without knowing these parameters. Later on we modify this informaticnal structure.

4. Discretionary policy

Our previous paper [Barro and Gordon (1983)] discusses discretionary policy in the present context as a non-cooperative game between the policymaker and the private agents. In particular, the policymaker treats the current inflationary expectation, π_t^e, and all future expectations, π_{t+i}^e, for $i > 0$, as given when choosing the current inflation rate, π_t Therefore, π_t is chosen to minimize the expected cost for the current period, Ez_t, while treating π_t^e and all future costs as fixed. Since future costs and expectations are independent of the policymaker's current actions, the discount factor does not enter into the results. The solution from minimizing Ez_t where z_t is given in eq. (1), is

$$\hat{\pi}_t = \bar{b}/a \quad (\text{discretion}). \tag{3}$$

We use carets to denote the solution under discretion. (With other cost functions, π_t would depend also on π_t^e.)

Given rational expectations, people predict inflation by solving out the policymaker's optimization problem and forecasting the solution for $\hat{\pi}_t$, as well as possible. In the present case they can calculate exactly the choice of inflation from eq. (3) — hence, the expectations are

$$\pi_t^e = \hat{\pi}_t = \bar{b}/a \tag{4}$$

34

Since inflation shocks are zero in equilibrium — that is, $\hat{\pi}_t - \pi_t^e = 0$ — the cost from eq. (1) ends up depending only on $\hat{\pi}_t$. In particular, the cost is

$$\hat{z}_t = (1/2)(\bar{b})^2/a \quad (\text{discretion}). \tag{5}$$

5. Policy under a rule

Suppose now that the policymaker can commit himself in advance to a rule for determining inflation. This rule can relate π_t to variables that the policymaker knows at date t. In the present case no one knows the parameters, b_t and q_t, at date t. But, everyone knows all previous values of these parameters. Therefore, the policymaker can condition the inflation rate, π_t, only on variables that are known also to the private agents. (The policymaker could randomize his choices, but he turns out not to have this incentive.) Therefore, the policymaker effectively chooses π_t and π_t^e together, subject to the condition that $\pi_t^e = \pi_t$. Then, the term that involves the inflation shock, $\pi_t - \pi_t^e$, drops out of the cost function in eq. (1). Given the way that we modeled the costs of inflation — namely, as $(a/2)(\pi_t)^2$ — it follows immediately that the best rule prescribes zero inflation at all dates,

$$\pi_t^* = 0 \quad (\text{rule}). \tag{6}$$

We use are asterisk to denote the results from a rule. Eq. (6) amounts to a con-stant-growth-rate-rule, where the rate of growth happens to be zero.

Finally, we can calculate the costs under a rule from eq. (1) as

$$z_t^* = 0 \quad (\text{rule}). \tag{7}$$

The general point is that the costs under the rule z_t^*, are lower than those under discretion, $\hat{z}_t$ from eq. (5). The lower cost reflects the value of being able to make commitments — that is, contractual agreements between the policymaker and the private agents. Without these commitments, inflation ends up being excessive — specifically, $\hat{\pi}_t > 0$ — but, no benefits from higher inflation result.

6. Cheating and temptation

As noted by others [e.g., Taylor (1975), B. Friedman (1979)], the policymaker is tempted to renege on commitments. In particular, if people expect zero infla-tion — as occurs under the rule — then the policymaker would like to implement a positive inflation rate in order to secure some benefits from an inflation shock. Further, this desire does not stem from a peculiarity in the policymaker's tastes. Rather, it reflects the distortions that make inflation shocks desirable in the first place.

35

How much can the policymaker gain in period t by cheating? Assume that people have the inflationary expectation, $\pi_0^e = 0$, which they formed at the start of period t. If the policymaker treats this expectation as a given, the choice of π_t that minimizes z_t is the one that we found before under discretion[4] — namely,

$$\tilde{\pi}_t = \bar{b}/a \quad \text{(cheating)}. \tag{8}$$

We use tildes to denote values associated with cheating. The expected cost follows from eq. (1) as

$$E\tilde{z}_t = -(1/2)\bar{b})^2/a \quad \text{(cheating)}. \tag{9}$$

The general point is that this expected cost is lower than that, $z_t^* = 0$ from following the rule. We refer to the difference between these expected costs as the temptation to renege on the rule — or simply as the temptation. In the present case we have

$$\text{temptation} = E\left(z_i^* - \tilde{z}_t\right) = (1/2)(\bar{b})^2/a > 0 \tag{10}$$

At the present stage we have three types of outcomes. Ranging from low costs to high, these are

(1) cheating (with people expecting the rule), $E\tilde{z}_t = -(1/2)(\bar{b})^2/a$,
(2) rule, $z_t^* = 0$,
(3) discretion, $\tilde{z}_t = (1/2)(\bar{b})^2/a$.

Discretion is worse than the rule because first, no inflation shocks arise in either case, but second, the commitment under the rule avoids excessive inflation. However, the rule is only a second-best solution. Cheating — *when people anticipate the rule* — delivers better results. That's because the inflation shock eliminates part of the existing distortion in the economy (which is worth the extra inflation). But, the cheating outcome is feasible only when people can be systematically deceived into maintaining low inflationary expectations. In our subsequent analysis this cannot happen in equilibrium. However, the incentive to cheat determines which rules are sustainable without legal or institutional mechanisms to enforce them. There is a tendency for the pursuit of the first best — that is, the cheating outcome — to generate results that are poorer than the second best (rules) and closer to the third best (discretion).

7. Enforcement of rules

Generally, a credible rule comes with some enforcement power that at least balances the temptation to cheat. We consider here only the enforcement that arises from the potential loss of reputation or credibility. This mechanism can apply here because of the repeated interaction between the policymaker and the private agents.[5] Specifically, if the policymaker engineers today a higher rate of inflation than people expect, then everyone raises their expectations of future inflation in some manner. Hence, in a general way, the cost of cheating today involves the increase in inflationary expectations for the future.

Consider a rule that specifies the inflation rate, π_t^*, for period t. The rule might prescribe $\pi_t^* = 0$, as before, or it might dictate some non-zero rate of inflation. Generally, the rule can specify some dependence of π_t^* on the realizations of all variables through date $t-1$ — that is, the values for date t are still not observed when π_t^* is set.

We postulate the following form of expectations mechanism, which we eventually show to be rational:

(1) $\quad \pi_t^e = \pi_t^*$ if $\pi_{t-1} = \pi_{t-1}^e$, and

(2) $\quad \pi_t^e = \hat{\pi}_t$ if $\pi_{t-1} \neq \pi_{t-1}^e$.

$$(11)$$

In other words if the previous inflation rate, π_{t-1}, accords with expectations, π_{t-1}^e, then people trust the government to perform in line with its announced rule for period t — that is, $\pi_t^e = \pi_t^*$. But, if the actual value departs from expectations last period, $\pi_{t-1} \neq \pi_{t-1}^e$, then people do not expect the government to follow its rule this period — hence, $\pi_t^e \neq \pi_t^*$. Rather, private agents anticipate that the policymaker will optimize subject to given expectations, which defines a discretionary situation. Hence, expectations are $\pi_t^e = \hat{\pi}_t$, where $\hat{\pi}_t$ is again the discretionary outcome.

If the government follows its rule in every period, then it also validates expectations each period. Then, the first part of eq. (11) says that the government maintains its reputation (or credibility) in each period. On the other hand, if the government cheats during period t, then the second part of eq. (11) says that the next period's expectations are the ones associated with discretion, $\hat{\pi}_{t+1}$. Then, if in period $t+1$ the government chooses the discretionary inflation rate, $\hat{\pi}_{t+1}$ (which is optimal given that expectations are $\hat{\pi}_{t+1}$), the actual and expected inflation rates coincide, although at the discretionary levels. Accordingly, the first part of eq. (11) says that people anticipate the rules outcome, π_{t+2}^*, for the following period. In other words the 'punishment' from violating the rule during period t is that the discretionary (non-cooperative) solution obtains during period $t+1$. But credibility is restored as of period $t+2$ — that is, things carry on as of date $t+2$ as though no previous violation had occurred. Therefore, the mechanism in eq. (11) specifies only one period's worth of punishment for each 'crime'[6]. Other equilibria exist that have punishment intervals of different length, as we discuss later on.

Consider our previous rule where $\pi_t^* = 0$. Suppose that the policymaker has credibility in period t, so that $\pi_t^e = 0$. If the policymaker cheats during period

t, then his best choice of inflation is $\pi_t = \bar{b}/a$ from eq. (8). [Note that eq. (11) says that the size and length of the punishment do not depend on the size of the crime.] Then, the policymaker gains the temptation, $E(z_t^* - \tilde{z}_t) = (1/2)(\bar{b})^2/a$, from eq. (10).

The cost of this violation is that discretion, rather than the rule, applies for period $t+1$. Hence, the policymaker realizes next period the cost, $\tilde{z}_{t+1} = (1/2)(\bar{b})^2/a$, from eq. (5), rather than that, $z_{t+1}^* = 0$. from eq. (7). Since costs for period $t+1$ are discounted by the factor $q_t = 1(1+r_t)$ in eq. (2), the expected present value of the loss is

$$\text{enforcement} = E\left[q\left(\tilde{z}_{t+1} - z_{t+1}^*\right)\right] = \tilde{q}(1/2)(\bar{b})^2/a. \tag{12}$$

We use the term, enforcement, to refer to the expected present value of the loss from transgressions.

The policymaker abides by the rule during period t — that is, sets $\pi_t = \pi_t^*$ — if the enforcement is at least as great as the temptation. Otherwise, he opts for the cheating solution. $\pi_t = \tilde{\pi}_t$ (and suffers the consequences next period). But, when forming expectations for period t, π_t^e people know whether the policymaker will find it worthwhile to cheat. Hence, if the cheating solution is preferable to this rule, then the expectation, $\pi_t^e = \pi_t^* = 0$, is irrational. Therefore, people would not stick with the expectation mechanism from eq. (11). The rules that can apply in equilibrium are those that have enough enforcement to motivate the policymaker to abide by them, given the expectations mechanism in eq. (11). Then, the equilibrium satisfies two properties. First, the expectations are rational. In particular, each individual's projection, π_t^e, is the best possible forecast of the policymaker's actual choice, π_t, given the way the policymaker behaves and given the way others form their expectations. Second, the policymaker's choice π_t, maximizes his objective, given the way people form their expectations.[7]

In equilibrium rules satisfy the enforceability restriction,

$$\text{temptation} = E\left(z_t^* - \tilde{z}_t\right) \leq \text{enforcement} = E\left[q_t\left(\hat{z}_{t+1} - z_{i+1}^*\right)\right]. \tag{13}$$

This condition says that the costs incurred today by following the rule, rather than cheating, are not greater than the expected value of having the cooperative (rules) outcome next period, rather than discretion. Consider now whether the proposed rule, $\pi_t^* = 0$, satisfies the enforceability restriction. From eq. (10), the temptation is $(1/2)(\bar{b})^2/a$, while from eq. (12), the enforcement is $\bar{q} \cdot (1/2)(\bar{b})^2/a$.[8] Since $\bar{q} < 1$, the temptation is strictly greater than the enforcement. Hence, the ideal rule, $\pi_t^* = 0$, is not enforceable, at least given the expectations mechanism from eq. (11). Therefore zero inflation is not an equilibrium in our model. [With a different form of cost function, rather than eq. (1), the ideal rule may or may not be enforceable.]

8. The best enforceable rule

We look here for the best enforceable rule — that is, the one that minimizes expected costs, subject to the constraint that the enforcement be at least as great as the temptation. In the present setting, where the parameters, b_t and q_t, are unobservable at date t, the best rule has the simple form,

$$\pi_t^* = \pi. \tag{14}$$

That is, the rule specifies constant inflation (a 'constant-growth-rate rule'). But, we already know that the ideal rule, $\pi = 0$, is not enforceable Given this, the enforceability restriction turns out to hold with equality for the best enforceable rule.

Using the procedures described before, we can calculate the temptation and enforcement associated with the rule, $\pi_t^* = \pi$. (Note that $\pi_t^e = \pi$ also applies here.) The results are

$$\text{temptation} = E\left(z_t^* - \hat{z}_t\right) = \left(a/2\right)\left(\overline{b}/u - \pi\right)^2, \text{ and} \tag{15}$$

$$\text{enforcement} = \overline{q} \cdot E\left(\hat{z}_{t+1} - z_{t+1}^*\right) = \overline{q} \cdot \left(a/2\right)\left[\left(\overline{b}/a\right)^2 - \pi^2\right]. \tag{16}$$

We graph the temptation and enforcement versus the inflation rate, π, in fig. 1. (This figure was suggested to us by John Taylor.) At $\pi = 0$, the temptation follows from eq. (10) as $(\overline{b})^2/2a$. Then, as π rises, the gain from cheating diminishes — hence, the temptation falls. Finally, when π equals the discretionary value, $\overline{b}/a$, the temptation equals zero. That's because the cheating solution and the rule prescribe the same inflation rate, $\overline{b}/a$ at this point (As π increases further, the temptation increases, because — for given expectations — the policymaker prefers the discretionary inflation rate $\overline{b}/a$ to higher rates of inflation.)

The enforcement equals $\overline{q}(\overline{b})^2/2a$ when $\pi = 0$, from eq. (12). Then, as π rises, the enforcement declines. That's because the cost from losing reputation becomes smaller when the rule prescribes a higher rate of inflation. As with the temptation, the enforcement equals zero when π equals the discretionary value, $\overline{b}/a$. Here, when the policymaker cheats, people expect the same rate of inflation — namely, the discretionary amount $\overline{b}/a$ — as when the policymaker abides by the rule. Consequently, there is no enforcement. (When π increases further, the enforcement becomes negative — that is. the policymaker prefers the punishment, where people anticipate the inflation rate $\overline{b}/a$, to the maintenance of the rule, where people expect an inflation rate that exceeds $\overline{b}/a$.)

Notice that fig. 1 determines a range of announced inflation rates that can be equilibria. Specifically, the enforcement is at least as large as the temptation for values of π in the interval, $(\overline{b}/a)(1-\overline{q})/(1+\overline{q}) \leq \pi \leq \overline{b}/a$. Among these, we focus on the value of π that delivers the best results in the sense of minimizing the

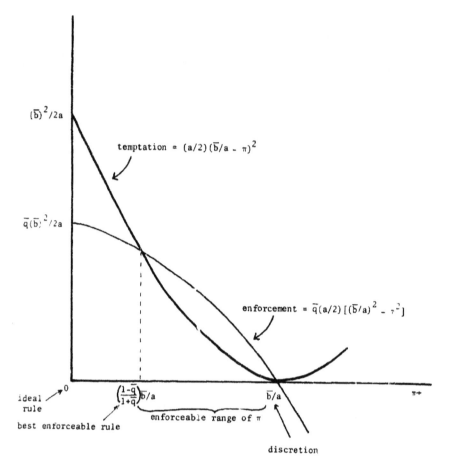

Figure 1 Temptation and enforcement.

expected costs from eq. (2). We can rationalize this focus on one of the possible equilibria by allowing the policymaker to choose which value of π to announce in some initial period. Then, as long as this value is m the enforceable range, we assume that the private agents follow along. That is, they all use the announced value of π as the basis for assessing the policymaker's performance [in accordance with eq. (11)].[9] Within this setup, the policymaker will, in fact, announce the value of π that leads to a minimum of expected costs.

The best of the enforceable rules occurs where the curves for temptation and enforcement intersect in the interior of fig. 1. (The curves also intersect at the discretionary value, $\pi = \bar{b}/a$, but expected costs are higher at this point.)

Hence, the announced infhtion rate is

$$\pi^* = (\bar{q}/a)(1-\bar{q})/(1+\bar{q}) \quad (\text{best enforceable rule}), \tag{17}$$

40

for which the expected cost in each period is

$$Ez_t^* = \left[(1/2)(\bar{b})^2/a\right]\left[(1-\bar{q})/(1+\bar{q})\right]^2. \tag{18}$$

Notice that, with $0 < \bar{q} < 1$, the inflation rate, π^*, is intermediate between the ideal rule, 0, and discretion, $\bar{b}/a$. In fact, the best enforceable rule is a weighted average of the ideal rule and discretion, with the weights depending on the mean discount factor, $\bar{q}$. A relatively small value of $\bar{q}$, which means a high rate of discount on future costs, implies a relatively high weight on discretion — that is, a high value of π^*. That's because a decrease in q weakens the enforcement [eq. (16)], which requires π^* to increase in order to maintain the equality between the enforcement and the temptation.

Generally, an increase in the mean discount factor, $\bar{q}$, reduces π^* with π^*. tending toward zero (the ideal rule) as $\bar{q}$ tends to one.[10] On the other hand, π^* tends to $\bar{b}/a$ — the discretionary result — as q tends to zero. (A zero discount factor means zero enforcement, so that only discretion is credible.) Notice that any force that influences the mean discount factor, $\bar{q}$, has a corresponding effect on inflation. For example, during a war we anticipate that $\bar{q}$ will be low, which triggers high inflation (via high monetary growth).

The expected cost from eq. (18) is also intermediate between that from the ideal rule, which is zero, and that for discretion, which is $(1/2)(\bar{b})^2/a$. Remember that the ideal rule is itself a second-best solution, which is inferior to cheating when people anticipate the ideal rule. But, cheating cannot occur systematically when people understand the policymaker's incentives and form their expectations accordingly. Rather, the lure of the better outcome from cheating creates the temptation, which makes the ideal rule non-enforceable. Hence, the attraction of the first best makes the second best unattainable. We end up with a cost that exceeds the second best (the ideal rule), but which is still lower than the third best (discretion).

The other feature of our results is the dependence of the inflation rate, π^* on the ratio of cost parameters, $\bar{b}/a$. This ratio pertains to the benefit from inflation shocks, which depends on b, relative to the costs of inflation, which depends on the parameter a. An increase in the ratio, $\bar{b}/a$, raises the temptation, relative to the enforcement, which requires π^* to increase. In particular, if inflation is not very costly, so that the parameter a is small, then we end up with a lot of inflation. Also, anything that raises the mean benefit attached to an inflation shock, b, leads to higher inflation (but, not to more benefits from inflation shocks). In our previous paper [Barro and Gordon (1983)], which focused on the results under discretion, we discussed some changes in the economy that can affect the benefits from inflation shocks. For example, the parameter $\bar{b}$ tends to be high in the following cases:

- when the natural unemployment rate is high,
- during a recession,
- during a war or other period where government expenditures rise sharply,

- when the deadweight losses from conventional taxes are high, and
- when the outstanding real stock of nominally-denominated public debt is large.

In each case we predict that the high value of $\bar{b}$ triggers a high value of π^*—that is, a high rate of monetary expansion by the policymaker. This view accounts for[11]

- a rise in the mean inflation rate along with a rise in the natural unemployment rate (as in the U.S. over the last 10–15 years),
- countercyclical response of monetary policy,
- high rates of monetary expansion during wartime,
- high rates of monetary growth in some less developed countries, and
- an inflationary effect from the outstanding real stock of public debt.

9. Contingent rules

We get some new results when we modify the informational structure in ways that motivate the policymaker to employ a contingent rule. Then, the inflation rate varies each period in accordance with the state of the economy.

Suppose that the policymaker knows the values of the benefit parameter, b_t, and the discount factor, q_t, when choosing the inflation rate, π_t. If people also condition their expectations, π_t^*, on b_t, and q_t, then the results change little from those already presented. So, we focus on the case where π_t^* is still generated without knowledge of the contemporaneous variables, b_t and q_t.

One possibility is that the policymaker receives information more quickly than private agents. However, our setup does not require this informational asymmetry. For example, when setting demands for real money balances or holdings of real government bonds, people have to forecast rates of inflation. Once people hold the government's nominal liabilities, their real wealth changes when subsequent inflation shocks occur. Therefore, although the government and private agents may have the same information at any point in time, the agents' decisions (on how much real money and bonds to hold) depend on expectations of inflation that were formed earlier. Therefore, we can think of π_t^* as not being conditioned on the realizations, b_t, and q_t. However, these realizations can influence the actual inflation rate, π_t.

The situation is less clear for the example of the Phillips curve. In models where only unperceived nominal disturbances matter for real variables — as in Lucas (1972, 1973) and Barro (1976) — the pertinent value for π_t^e is the one based on contemporaneously available information. However, some models with long-term nominal contracting [Gray (1976), Fischer (1977), Taylor (1980)] suggest that inflationary expectations formed at earlier dates will matter for today's choices of employment, production, etc. Then, the situation resembles that from above where people choose their holdings of money and bonds based on forecasts of inflation. However, the rationality of the Gray-Fischer-Taylor contracts has been questioned [Barro (1977)].

9.1 Discretion

We find the results under discretion in the same way as before. Specifically, we get

$$\hat{\pi}_t = b_t/a \tag{19}$$

Now, the policymaker reacts to the actual value of the benefit parameter, b_t rather than to its mean, $\bar{b}$. However, people's expectations — not conditioned on b_t — are $\pi_t^e = \bar{b}/a$. Therefore, although $\pi_t^e = E\hat{\pi}_r$, the realizations for b_t, generate departures of inflation from its expectation. Therefore, the inflation shocks — and the corresponding benefits from them — are sometimes positive and sometimes negative.

The costs under discretion are now

$$\hat{z}_t = (1/2)(b_t)^2/a - (b_t/a)(b_t - \bar{b}). \tag{20}$$

The results correspond to those from before [eq. (5)] if $b_t = \bar{b}$. Looking one period ahead, we can calculate

$$E\hat{z}_{t+1} = (1/2a)\left[(\bar{b})^2 - \sigma_b^2\right] \tag{21}$$

The new term is the variance of the benefit parameter, σ_b^2.

9.2 The ideal contingent rule

When b_t is observed, the ideal rule no longer prescribes zero (or constant) inflation at all times. Rather, the policymaker conditions the inflation rate on the realizations for the benefit parameter. The present example is simple enough to write out the ideal contingent rule in closed form. Specifically — abstracting from enforcement problems — the best rule turns out (after a large amount of algebra) to be

$$\pi_t^* = (1/a)(b_t - \bar{b}) \tag{22}$$

As before, the prior mean of inflation, $\pi_t^e = E\pi_t^*$, is zero. But, realized inflation exceeds its expectation — and benefit from inflation shocks arise — when b_t exceeds its mean, $\bar{b}$. Conversely, inflation is below its expectation — so that costs from unexpectedly low inflation occur — when b_t is below its mean.

Note that inflationary expectations are always zero, but the policymaker creates surprisingly low inflation (i.e., deflation) when the benefits parameter takes on relatively low values. These realizations may show up as a recession or as other costs from a negative inflation shock. Yet, ex post, it would clearly be preferable to have zero, rather than negative, inflation. Then, we avoid the negative inflation shock and also have less costs due to inflation [which are $(a/2)(\pi_1)^2$]. So, the negative inflation shocks may appear pointless. Yet, the ideal rule says that the policymaker should 'bite the bullet.' — that is, cause a recession through contractionary monetary policy — under some circumstances. That's because the surprisingly low rule of inflation when the benefit parameter, b_t is low is the counterpart of the surprisingly high rate of inflation when the benefit parameter is high. Choosing zero, rather than negative, inflation for the low states means that the prior expectation of inflation is higher than otherwise. Then, the policymaker achieves lower benefits in the states where b_t is relatively high. In fact, it is worthwhile to incur some costs in the low states — namely, bite the bullet through unexpectedly low inflation — in order to 'buy' the unexpectedly high inflation and the corresponding benefits in the high states. In effect the policymaker invests in credibility when it is relatively cheap to do so — namely, when b_t is low — in order to cash in on this investment when it is most important — that is, when b_t is high.

The costs associated with the ideal rule turn out to be

$$z_t^* = -\left(1/2a\right)\left[\left(b_1\right)^2 - \left(\bar{b}\right)^2\right] \tag{23}$$

Again, we get our previous results [eq. (7)] if $b_1 = \bar{b}$. Looking ahead one period, the expectation of these costs is

$$Ez_{t+1}^* = -\left(1/2a\right)\sigma_b^2 \tag{24}$$

Because the policymaker can match the variations in b_t with appropriate responses in π_t, the expected costs fall with an increase in the variance of the benefit parameter, σ_b^2.[12]

As before, we can show that the ideal rule is not enforceable in our model.[13] Therefore, we go on now to examine the best enforceable, contingent rule.

9.3 Enforceable contingent rules

We look at rules that express the inflation rate, π_t^*, as a stationary function of the state, which specifies the values of the two variables, b_t and q_t. Given that the ideal rule is unattainable, the best enforceable rule in our model turns out to equate the temptation to the enforcement *for all realizations of b_t and q_t*.[14] The temptation cannot exceed the enforcement for any of these realizations in order for the rule to be credible. Further, if the enforcement exceeds the temptation in some state, then we can do better by changing the inflation rate for that state. That is, we bear more costs than necessary by having excessive enforcement.

The present example is sufficiently simple to work out the results in closed form. The solution for inflation turns out to be a linear function of b_t and of $\sqrt{q_t}$, — that is,[15]

$$\pi_t^* = c_1 + c_2 b_t + c_3 \sqrt{q_t}, \tag{25}$$

where the c's are constants, which have to be determined. If we conjecture that the rule for inflation takes the form of eq. (25), then we can work out the temptation and enforcement as functions of the parameters, c_1, c_2, c_3 and the realizations for b_t and q. Then, we determine the value of the c-coefficients in order to equate the temptation to the enforcement for all values of (b_t, q_t). Since eq. (25) has the correct form, this operation turns out to be feasible. The results are

$$c_1 = 0, \quad c_2 = 1/a, \quad c_3 = -2\left(\overline{b}/a\right)\sqrt{q}\left(1+\overline{q}\right) \tag{26}$$

where $\sqrt{q}$ is the mean of $\sqrt{q_1}$. Hence, the best enforceable contingent rule for inflation is[16]

$$\pi_t^* = \left(b_t/a\right) - 2\left(\overline{b}/a\right)\sqrt{q} \cdot \sqrt{q_t}\left(1+\overline{q}\right) \tag{27}$$

The enforceable rule can again be viewed as a weighted average of the ideal rule — eq. (22) — and discretion — eq. (19). In particular, the mean rate of inflation is positive, but lower than that associated with discretion, which is $\overline{b}/a$. The relative weights depend on the discount factor — both on the parameters of the probability distribution for q_t and on the realized value. Given the parameters of the distribution, a higher realization for q_t means a lower inflation rate, π_t^*.[17]

Note that the realization of the discount factor does not affect current benefits and costs from inflation, but does influence the amount of enforcement. Thus, the ideal rule does not depend on q_t, in eq. (22). But, for low realizations of q_t, low inflation rates are not credible, because the temptation would exceed the enforcement. Therefore, the best enforceable rule does depend on q_t, in eq. (27).

The inflation rate now moves around with fluctuations in the benefit parameter, b_t, or in the discount factor, q_t. In particular, relatively high realizations for b_t and relatively low ones for q_t lead to unexpectedly high inflation. Conversely, the policymaker 'bites the bullet' — that is, creates negative inflation shocks — when the benefit parameter is lower than normal or the discount factor is higher than normal. The reasoning here is similar to that from before. It is worthwhile to suffer negative inflation shocks in some cases — that is, for low values of b_t or high values of q_t — in order to sustain low prior expectations of inflation. Then, large gains are attained in the cases where the benefit parameter, b_t, is high or the discount factor, q_t, is low. These last cases are likely to be emergencies — such as wars or other times where economic activity or government revenues are valued especially highly. In effect, the policymaker bites the bullet during the non-emergencies in order to invest in credibility — an investment that yields returns during the emergencies.

10. The length of the punishment interval

So far, our results apply when the length of the punishment interval is fixed at one period. That is, the length of time for which the discretionary outcome obtains, conditional on cheating, equals the length of time over which the policymaker can enjoy the results of his cheating. (The last interval essentially defines the length of the period.) Given the length of the punishment interval, we obtained a unique reputational equilibrium by allowing the policymaker to announce the best one. But, if we look at different punishment intervals (which can be either greater or smaller than one period), then we find an array of reputational equilibria. At this point, we have no satisfactory way to resolve this problem of multiple equilibria. However, we have some observations.

First, we know that the length of the punishment interval cannot be zero. That is, the policymaker cannot instantly restore a lost reputation. If he could, there would be no enforcement, which means that the only equilibrium is the discretionary one.

We can calculate the effect of longer punishment intervals on expected costs. In the present model the punishments — that is, discretionay outcomes — never occur as part of a reputational equilibrium. Hence, we always do at least as well if we increase enforcement, which corresponds here to raising the length of the punishment interval. In particular, it always looks desirable in this model to have an infinite interval, which amounts to a form of 'capital punishment'.

We can modify the model so that punishments take place occasionally.[18] For example, suppose that inflation depends partly on the policymaker's actions and partly on uncontrollable events. Further, assume that people cannot fully sort out these two influences on inflation, even ex post. Then, people adopt a form of control rule where the policymaker loses reputation if the observed inflation rate exceeds some critical value. But, because of the uncontrollable element, this loss of reputation — and hence, the punishment — actually occurs from time to time. Then, in contemplating a more severe form of punishment, we have to weigh the losses when punishments occur against the benefits from greater enforcement. Thus, it is likely that the optimal punishment interval would be finite. (However, from a positive standpoint, it does not necessarily follow that the equilibrium with this punishment interval will be selected.)

Finally, another possibility is to introduce uncertainty about the policymaker's preferences. Then, people try to learn about these preferences by observing behavior. Further, the policymaker knows that people learn from his actions, and acts accordingly. Kreps and Wilson (1980) and Milgrom and Roberts (1980), who uses this general type of model, show that unique equilibria sometimes obtain.[19] But, we have not yet pursued this route in our context, because it relies on differences in tastes among potential policymakers. Unfortunately, we have nothing interesting to say about the sources of these differences. But possibly, this idea would become meaningful if we identified policymakers with shifting interest groups, each of which were affected differently by variations in inflation.

11. Concluding observations

Our analysis provides an example of a reputational equilibrium for monetary policy. The results amount to a combination of the outcomes from discretion with those from the ideal rule. Previously, we analyzed discretion and rules as distinct possible equilibria. Now, the relative weights attached to the discretionary and rules solutions depend on the policymaker's discount rate and some other factors. From a predictive standpoint for monetary growth and inflation, the results modify and extend those that we discussed previously.

In some environments the rules take a contingent form, where inflation depends on the realization of the benefit parameter or the discount factor. Here, the policymaker sometimes engineers surprisingly low inflation, which is costly at a point in time. Thus, the monetary authority 'bites the bullet' and pursues a contractionary policy, given some states of the world. By acting this way, the policymaker sustains a reputation that permits surprisingly high inflation in other states of the world.

We have difficulties with multiplicity of equilibria, which show up also in the related game-theory literature. Here, the problem arises in determining how long a loss of reputation persists. In an extended version of the model, we can figure out the optimal length for this interval of punishment. But, from a positive standpoint, it is unclear which equilibrium will prevail.

*We have benefited from discussion at the conference and from seminars at Chicago, Northwestern and Iowa. We are particularly grateful for comments from Gary Fethke, Roger Myerson, José Scheinkman, and John Taylor. Part of this research is supported by the National Science Foundation.

Notes

1 For this purpose we should actually look at the privately-held component of the funded national debt, which is about $700 billion in 1981.

2 Our previous paper [Barro and Gordon (1983)] uses a term of the form, $\left[\phi_t - z(\pi_t - \pi^2)\right]^2$, here $\phi_t > 0$ depends on the natural unemployment rate for the period. Then, the policymaker values inflation shocks — that is, $\pi_t > \pi_t^e$—only over some range. But, the general nature of the results does not change if we substitute this more complicated form. Also, we could modify the cost of inflation to depend on $(\pi_t - \bar{\pi}_t)^2$ where $\bar{\pi}_t$ is the optimal inflation tax on cash balances.

3 In some models, such as Lucas (1973) and Barro (1976), the coefficient b_t depends on the forecast variance of inflation. Most of our results would not be affected if we allowed for this type of dependence. However, this element matters when we compare across regimes that have different forecast variances for inflation.

4 With a different cost function, the result for $\tilde{\pi}_t$ generally differs from that under discretion, $\hat{\pi}_t$.

5 This type of repeated game is discussed in J. Friedman (1971).

6 Green and Porter (1981) use an analogous model for oligopoly pricing. There, the observation of a low price triggers $(T-1)$ periods of punishment, during which firms behave in a Cournot manner.

7 The expectations mechanism from eq. (11) cannot be rational if the game has a known, finite endpoint. Then, no punishment arises for crimes in the last period. Working backward, the solution unravels period by period. Our framework assumes no known termination date for the game, although the game may end probabilistically. Then, a higher probability of termination shows up as a higher discount rate — that is, as a lower mean discount factor, $\bar{q}$. For some related game-theory literature, see Selten (1978), Kreps and Wilson (1980), and Milgrom and Roberts (1980).

8 The two terms are equal when $\bar{q} = 1$ only because of the specific cost function from eq. (1). Generally, equality would arise for a value of $\bar{q}$ that is either above or below one.

9 But, recall that the equilibrium is itself non-cooperative. In particular, each agent calculates the best forecast, π_t^e of the policymaker's actions, while taking as given the way the policymaker behaves and the way other agents form their expectations.

10 This last condition depends on the specifics of our example. However, the direction of effect for $\bar{q}$ on π^* applies generally.

11 Some of these results can also be explained by changes in the optimal tax rate on cash balances, which applies to the systematic part of inflation. For example, this effect is probably important for monetary growth during wartime and in less developed countries.

12 However, we did not enter the variance of inflation directly into the cost function of eq. (1). If we had, this result could change.

13 When considering the ideal rule, the temptation and enforcement turn out to be independent of the realization for b_t. Further, the temptation exceeds the enforcement for all discount factors, q_t that. are less than one.

14 With other cost functions, the enforcement may exceed the temptation for some realizations. In particular, we then find that the inflation rate does not react to variations in q_t in some regions.

15 The enforcement is linear in q_t. But. the temptation involves the square of the inflation rate. Therefore, if π is linear in $\sqrt{q_t}$ then the temptation also involves terms that are linear in q_t.

16 The solution reduces to the previous one in eq. (17) if there is no random variation in b_t and q_t. Then, $b_t = \bar{b}$, $q_t = \bar{q}$ and $\sqrt{q} = \sqrt{q}$.

17 Given the variance for $\sqrt{q}_t$ d the realized value of $\sqrt{q}_t$ a higher value of $\sqrt{q}$ also lowers π_t^*. This follows by using the formula, $\bar{q} = \mathrm{var}(\sqrt{c}_t) + (\sqrt{q})$.

18 Green and Porter (1981) have this feature in their model of oligopoly pricing.

19 Also, the solution does not necessarily degenerate to the discretionary equilibrium when the game has a known, finite endpoint. See footnote 7 above.

References

Barro, RJ., 1976, Rational expectations and the role of monetary policy, Journal of Monetary Economics 2, Jan., 1-32.

Barro, RJ., 1977, Long-term contracts, sticky prices, and monetary policy, Journal of Monetary Economics 3, July, 305-316

Barro, R.J., 1983, Inflationary finance under discretion and rules, Canadian Journal of Economics, Jan.

Barro, RJ. and D.B. Gordon, 1983, A positive theory of monetary policy in a natural-rate model, Journal of Political Economy 91, Aug.

Calvo, G., 1978, On the time consistency of optimal policy in a monetary economy, Econometrica 46, Nov., 1411-1428.

Fischeir, S., '977, Long-term contracts, rational expectations and the optimal money supply rule, Journal of Political Economy 85, Feb., 191-205.

Friedman, B., 1979, Optimal expectations and the extreme information assumptions of 'rational expectations' macromodels, Journal of Monetary Economics 5, Jan., 23-42.

Friedman, J.W., 1971, A non-cooperative equilibrium for supergames, Review of Economic Studies, 38, Jan., 861-874.

Gray, J.A., 1976. Wage indexation: A macroeconomic approach, Journal of Monetary Economics 2, April, 221-236.

Green, E.J. and R.H. Porter, 1981, Noncooperative collusion under imperfect price information, unpublished, California Institute of Technology, Pasadena, CA, Jan.

Kreps, D.M. and R. Wilson, 1980, On the chain-store paradox and predation: Reputation for toughness, unpublished, Stanford University, Stanford, CA, July.

Kydland, F.E. and E.C. Prescott, 1977, Rules rather than discretion: The inconsistency of optimal plans. Journal of Political Economy 83, June, 473-491.

Lucas, R.E., 1972, Expectations and the neutrality of money. Journal of Economic Theory 4, April, 103-124.

Lucas, R.E., 1973, Some international evidence on output-inflation tradeoffs, American Economic Review 63, June. 326-334.

Milgrom, P. and J. Roberts, 1980, Predation, reputation and entry deterrence, unpublished. Northwestern University, Evanston, IL.

Selten, R., 1978, The chain-store paradox, Theory and Decision 9, 127-159.

Taylor, J., 1975, Monetary policy during a transition to rational expectations. Journal of Political Economy 83, Oct., 1009-1022.

Taylor, J., 1980, Aggregate dynamics and staggered contracts. Journal of Political Economy 88, Jan., 1-23.

3

CREDIBILITY OF POLICIES VERSUS CREDIBILITY OF POLICYMAKERS*

Allan Drazen and Paul R. Masson

Source: *Quarterly Journal of Economics* 109, 3, 1994, 735–754.

Standard models of policy credibility, defined as the expectation that an announced policy will be carried out, emphasize the preferences of the policymaker and the role of tough policies in signaling toughness and raising credibility. Whether a policy is carried out, however, will also reflect the state of the economy. We present a model in which a policymaker maintains a fixed parity in good times, but devalues if the unemployment rate gets too high. Our main conclusion is that if there is persistence in unemployment, observing a tough policy in a given period may *lower* rather than raise the credibility of a no-devaluation pledge in subsequent periods. We test this implication on EMS interest rates and find support for our hypothesis.

I. Introduction

There is now an extensive literature on policy credibility, credibility being defined as the expectation that an announced policy will be carried out. Much of this literature has emphasized the role of a government's "type" (for example, the relative weights it puts on the losses from inflation versus unemployment) in determining the credibility of a policy. In this approach, introduced into the macroeconomics literature by Backus and Driffill [1985a, 1985b], a policymaker who assigns a relatively low cost to inflation may find it optimal to mimic the actions of a more inflation-averse policymaker to build "reputation." Observed monetary policy choices are thus taken to provide information about the government's (unobserved) inflation preferences, and they can therefore affect expectations about future policy. More specifically, when a policymaker delivers on an announced commitment to low inflation, this strengthens the belief that he really is inflation averse. Hence, a government that follows tough policies will see its reputation and the credibility of its commitment to anti-inflationary policies increase over time.[1]

Whether or not an announced policy is carried out, however, reflects more than the policymaker's intentions. The situation in which he finds himself can be as important. Since even a "tough" policymaker cannot ignore the cost of very high unemployment, he may renege on an anti-inflation commitment in sufficiently adverse circumstances, that is, in times of weak activity, when pressures to restore high employment are strong.[2] In short, the credibility the public assigns to an announced policy should therefore reflect external circumstances as well.

In assessing the effect of observed policy choices on credibility, the role of external circumstances may be especially important when policies have persistent effects on the economic environment. The purpose of this paper is to investigate the effect of such *persistence* and to demonstrate that if tough policies constrain the room to maneuver in the future, then following a tough policy may actually harm rather than enhance credibility. For example, a tough anti-inflation policy today may raise unemployment well into the future, making the commitment to future anti-inflation policy less credible. Similarly, monetary tightening may increase government debt accumulation, making it more likely that an adverse shock will lead to a monetary easing in the future.

Our result may be illustrated by a simple story. One afternoon, a colleague announces to you that he is serious about losing weight and plans to skip dinner. He adds that he has not eaten for two days. Does this information make it more or less credible that he really will skip dinner? The model of types outlined in the first paragraph would imply that with each meal he skips, the "tough policy" of skipping the next meal becomes *more* credible, as each observation of playing tough raises the probability we assign to his being a fanatical dieter. Once we realize that his skipping one meal makes him hungrier at the next mealtime (i.e., that policy has persistent effects), we are led to the opposite conclusion, namely, that it becomes less likely he will stick to his diet the more meals he has skipped. We apply this point to the credibility of fixed parities in the European Monetary System. In the early years of the EMS, the willingness to accept the costs of unemployment in order to avoid realignments gave the system credibility by signaling the toughness of governments. More recently, however, mounting unemployment made it more likely that a further unfavorable shock would lead to a devaluation. Under these circumstances, the absence of a realignment, and the resultant further upward pressures on unemployment, were seen as lowering the credibility of fixed parities.[3] This reasoning suggests that credibility need not monotonically increase with the length of time there has been no devaluation, as it would if uncertainty about the "type" of government were the only factor affecting credibility.[4] Furthermore, interest differentials (taken as a measure of the credibility of the policy of fixed parities) should be interpreted as reflecting not only signaling, but also the perception that in certain circumstances, devaluation will be viewed as being desirable, even by a tough government.

In the next sections we consider the issue of signaling when effects of policy on employment are persistent. We show formally how persistent unemployment effects of a tough policy (maintaining a fixed parity), may lower rather than raise the credibility of a pledge of no devaluations in subsequent periods. In the final section we apply the theory to France. Regression results suggest that while the signaling model may apply in a period in the mid-1980s in which the stated priorities of the authorities changed, the alternative notion of credibility set out in the paper may help explain devaluation expectations and interest differentials in the late 1980s and early 1990s.

51

II. A Basic Model

To illustrate our points, we use a two-period open-economy version of the simple Barro-Gordon [1983a, 1983b] model, in which surprise devaluations decrease unemployment, but expected devaluations have no effect. (Modeling persistence requires a multiperiod model; a two-period version is sufficient.) We use the Barro-Gordon model to facilitate comparison of our results with the existing macroeconomic literature on credibility, in which this model has been used extensively. To model the importance of external circumstances, we add a stochastic unemployment shock to the Barro-Gordon model, so that the government's choice of policy will depend on the realization of the shock, as well as the cost it assigns to inflation relative to unemployment. Our modeling of policy conditioned on the realization of shocks is based on Obstfeld's [1991] model of escape clauses, a model also used by Flood and Isard [1989] and Lohmann [1990].[5] In these models the government chooses between following a no-devaluation rule and following a discretionary policy: in the latter case it optimally chooses the magnitude of devaluation as a function of the realized state of the world.[6]

We depart from the basic escape-clause model by assuming that the choice is between the rule of a fixed parity, and the alternative of a devaluation of a fixed size. Formally, this is a state-contingent, two-part rule, so that devaluation at the preannounced trigger could be characterized as carrying out the "announced," or at least implicit, policy. In our opinion, this view, though semantically correct, misses the point—that even a tough policymaker who plans ex ante to keep the fixed parity (and makes public statements to that effect) will devalue in adverse circumstances. We therefore take devaluation to represent departing from the announced (no-devaluation) policy.

For EMS countries it is probably reasonable to consider a devaluation of an exogenously fixed size as representing the alternative to no realignment, since the EMS puts constraints on the realignments that are possible.[7] The problem of discretion always dominating does not arise here, since for small enough shocks, maintaining the existing parity will be preferred to a discrete devaluation. Moreover, limiting ourselves to two options does not change the qualitative nature of the results, and allowing other size realignments will leave our basic point intact.

We begin by supposing that unanticipated inflation reduces unemployment u_t relative to the natural rate u_N, where u_t is also subject to a stochastic shock η_t and is affected by its lagged value:

$$u_t = u_N + \eta_t - \sqrt{a}\left[\left(\pi_t - \pi_t^E\right) - \delta\left(u_{t-1} - u_N\right)\right] \tag{1}$$

where $\delta \geq 0$ is a measure of persistence in unemployment fluctuations ($\Delta = \delta\sqrt{a}$ is the autoregressive coefficient). (In the initial period $t = 1$ of the two-period model, the inherited unemployment gap $u_0 - u_N$ is assumed to be zero, so that persistence only affects unemployment in the second period.)[8]

The government's objective is to minimize an expected discounted loss function, where each period's loss is quadratic in the deviation of unemployment from a target level below the natural rate, $u_N - K$ (where K captures distortions leading to too high a natural rate), as well as in actual inflation. We assume that there can be different types of governments, implying possible uncertainty about the government's objective function.[9]

The tough government (with superscript T) cares about inflation with a weight θ^T, while the weak government (with superscript W) gives a lower weight θ^w to inflation in its objective function. The i-type government's objective function conditioned on information available at $t = 1$ is

$$\Lambda^i = L_1^i + \beta E L_2^i = \left(u_1 - u_N + K\right)^2 + \theta^i \left(\pi_1\right)^2$$

$$+ \beta E_1 \left[\left(u_2 - u_N + K\right)^2 + \theta^i \left(\pi_2\right)^2\right]. \tag{2}$$

Assume that the exchange rate is the policy instrument to influence the price level. For simplicity of exposition we suppose that the price level equals the exchange rate, so that if e_t is the *log* of the exchange rate at t, the inflation terms in (1) and (2) can be written as

$$\pi_t = e_t - e_{t-1}$$

$$\pi_t - \pi_t^E = \left(e_t - e_{t-1}\right) - \left(E_{t-1}e_t - e_{t-1}\right)$$

$$= e_t - E_{t-1}e_t.$$

We also define the transformed variables $\kappa = K/\sqrt{a}$ and $\epsilon_t = \eta_t/\sqrt{a}$. It is assumed that wages are set before the shock ϵ_t is realized; $E_{t-1}e_t$ is conditioned on information available at the end of the previous period.

III. Will a History of Tough Policy Necessarily Raise Credibility?

The basic question is how the probability of a devaluation in the second period, denoted μ_2, depends on the action of the government in the first period, once we consider not only the standard signaling of unknown government type, but also the effect of persistence. With uncertainty about types, we may write μ_2 as

$$\mu_2(j) = p_2(j)\rho_2^w(j) + \left(1 - p_2(j)\right)\rho_2^T(j). \tag{3}$$

where
p_2 = probability the government is of type w,
ρ_2^w = probability a government of type w will devalue (given the distribution of ϵ_2),
ρ_2^T = probability a government of type T will devalue.

The argument j (= D or F) indicates whether the government devalued (D) or kept the exchange rate fixed (F) in period 1.

To calculate ρ_2^i, we start by solving the government's second-period problem for given expectations of a devaluation $\mu_2(j)$. By substituting ρ_2^i into (3), we can then solve for $\mu_2(j)$. The functional relation between policy choice and the realization of ϵ, will become clear from this calculation. The public is assumed to know the values θ^T and θ^W. We shall consider the case where the public does not observe the shock ϵ_1. Let us denote the single-period loss function of a type i government if it (for example) devalues in the second period by $L_2^{i,D}(j)$, (where j was the first period action). Then the government will devalue in period 2 if $L_2^{i,D}(j) - L_2^{i,F}(j) < 0$. This defines a critical value of the shock $\hat{\epsilon}_2^i(j)$:

$$\hat{\epsilon}_2^i(j) = \frac{(a+\theta^i)s}{2a} - \kappa - \mu_2(j)s - \delta(u_1 - u_N),$$

where s is the fixed devaluation size and where the critical value is dependent both on the type of government (via θ^i) and on previously observed policy. If the realization of ϵ_2 is below this critical value $\hat{\epsilon}_2^i(j)$, a policy of maintaining the fixed parity is optimal; if it is above, a devaluation is optimal. If the distribution of e is uniform between $-v$ and $+v$, we have (for an interior solution)

$$\rho_2^i(j) = \text{prob}(\epsilon_2 > \hat{\epsilon}_2^i(j)) = (v - \hat{\epsilon}_2^i(j))/2v.$$

To calculate the probability of government type, we assume that the public uses a Bayesian approach, starting from uniform priors over the two types of governments. Expectations are conditioned on whether the government devalued or not in period 1, but not on the shock ϵ_1, which we assume that the public does not observe.[10] The probability that the government is weak conditional on its first-period action may then be written as

$$p_2(D) = \frac{\rho_1^w}{\rho_1^w + \rho_1^T}, \quad p_2(F) = \frac{1 - \rho_1^w}{2 - \rho_1^w - \rho_1^T},$$

when we start with uniform priors. Note that $p_2(D) > p_2(F)$ as long as $\rho_1^w > \rho_1^T$, that is, as long as the probability that a weak government will devalue in the first period is greater than the probability that a tough government will devalue.

The probability that a given type would devalue in the first period is derived in an analogous way to the above calculation for ρ_2^i. We calculate a critical value of the shock in the first period, namely $\hat{\epsilon}_1^i$, such that $\Lambda^i(D) = \Lambda^i(F)$. In the Appendix details of this calculation are shown, ρ_1^i, the probability that $\epsilon_1 > \hat{\epsilon}_1^i$, can then be calculated, assuming the same uniform distribution as above.

To calculate $\mu_2(D) - \mu_2(F)$, we combine equations (3), (5), and (6) to obtain, after some manipulation,

$$\mu_2(D) - \mu_2(F) = \frac{1}{1 - s/2v} \times \left[-\frac{\sqrt{a}\delta s}{2v} + \frac{\left(\rho_1^w - \rho_1^T\right)\left(\theta^T - \theta^w\right)(s/4av)}{\left(\rho_1^w + \rho_1^T\right)\left(2 - \rho_1^w - \rho_1^T\right)} \right], \quad (7)$$

where we have used $u_1(D) - u_1(F) = -\sqrt{as}$ (Note that $1 - s/2v > 0$, for otherwise, the devaluation size would exceed twice the maximum size of the shock it was aimed to offset.)

The persistence parameter δ will affect both terms inside the brackets. The effect on ρ_1^i ($i = T, W$) arises because the critical level $\hat{c}_1^i$ of the first-period shock depends on welfare in both periods and hence on 8. In the case of *no persistence* of unemployment effects across periods ($\delta = 0$), so that there is only a signaling effect, the first term in brackets disappears, and the expression in (7) is unambiguously positive. The standard result on signaling of types will then hold: observing a tough policy (no devaluation) in the first period will raise the probability of no devaluation in the second. That is, in this case we see from (7) that $\mu_2(D)$ is greater than $\mu_2(F)$ as long as $\rho_1^w > \rho_1^T$ that is, as long as a weak government is more likely to devalue in the first period. This will be true since $\theta^T > \theta^w$. Hence absence of persistence and different preferences over inflation imply that the signaling motive alone contributes to the credibility of the fixed exchange rate, which is therefore enhanced in the second period if no devaluation was observed in the first.

To add persistence back in, set $\delta > 0$. The dependence of $\mu_2(D) - \mu_2(F)$ on δ is complicated, reflecting the contribution of both terms. Solving (7) with MATHEMATICA, one can show that for δ sufficiently large, the persistence effect will tend to dominate the signaling effect, and (7) will become negative. This result is illustrated in Figure I for two sets of parameter values. In the two cases, the following values were imposed: $\kappa = 0.02$, $s = 0.1$, $a = 0.25$, $v = 0.15$, $\beta = 0.95$, $\theta^T = 1$, and either $\theta^w = 0$ or $0^w = 0.5$. Figure I then plots $\mu_2(D) - \mu_2(F)$ as a function of $\Delta = 8\sqrt{a}$ in the interval $[0, 1]$. It can be seen that at about $\Delta = 0.8$ (when $\theta^w = 0$) or $\Delta = 0.45$ (when $\theta^w = 0.5$), $\mu_2(D) = \mu_2(F)$, and for higher values of Δ, not devaluing in the first period *lowers* credibility in the second.

To summarize, positive persistence of unemployment implies that no devaluation in the first period may raise rather than lower the public's expectation of a devaluation in the second period. Shocks that are not offset through a devaluation in period 1 have further unfavorable effects in period 2, increasing the probability that a government of either type will devalue. If these persistence effects are sufficiently strong (δ large), not devaluing in the first period will raise the probability of a devaluation in the second. Thus, credibility will not necessarily be enhanced by "playing tough" in period 1.[11]

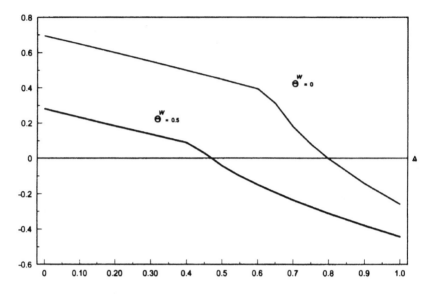

Figure 1 Effect of Persistence on the Likelihood of Devaluation.

V. Empirical Evidence

We now turn to how one can empirically distinguish the two influences of tough policy on credibility—its role in signaling type versus its effect in constraining future room to maneuver due to persistence. The model we have developed above implies that the correlation between changes in unemployment rates and the expectation of a devaluation will be quite different depending on whether the signaling factor or the "external circumstances" factor in policymaking dominates. If there is great uncertainty about the government's type, then high unemployment may convincingly signal that the government is tough and determined to carry through on its policy commitment; therefore, policy credibility should improve. However, if the government's type is known (or if the difference in types is small), then increased unemployment reduces credibility, since it makes it less likely that either type of government will deliver on its policy commitments in the future.

The EMS provides a good application of the model, and interest rate differentials relative to Germany, the anchor for EMS monetary policy, provide a good proxy for expected devaluation, and hence for the lack of credibility of fixed parities.[12] Received wisdom suggests that the EMS went from an initial stage of low credibility, lack of policy convergence, and relatively frequent realignments, to a later stage in which there was considerable policy convergence and realignments were infrequent or did not occur at all. Giavazzi and Spaventa [1990], for instance, refer to the latter period as the "New EMS." If there is a change in behavior along those lines, our model suggests that the partial effect of unemployment on the interest rate differential should be quite different in the different periods.

France may be an especially good case for examining alternative models of credibility. Between the formation of the EMS in March 1979 and the present, France has had six realignments relative to the deutsche mark (September 24, 1979; October 5, 1981; June 14, 1982; March 21, 1983; April 7, 1986; and January 12, 1987). While in the early part of the period the long-term interest differential between the franc and the DM rose, since the end of 1982, the interest differential has been falling steadily and, at the end of 1991, stood at less than half of a percentage point (Figure II).[13]

In the early part of the EMS period, the socialist government which came to power in May 1981 followed strongly expansionary policies, making it clear that it had little commitment to fixed parities. Higher unemployment would signal the need to stimulate aggregate demand, and hence make a realignment more likely. It should therefore have been associated with higher long-term interest rate differentials vis-à-vis Germany. However, there was an important change in behavior in June 1982, reinforced in March 1983, when France shifted to far tighter fiscal and monetary policies, the *politique de rigueur*. We would argue that this shift in policy was not immediately perceived as a long-term shift; that is, that it took time for policymakers to convince investors. They did so by showing that

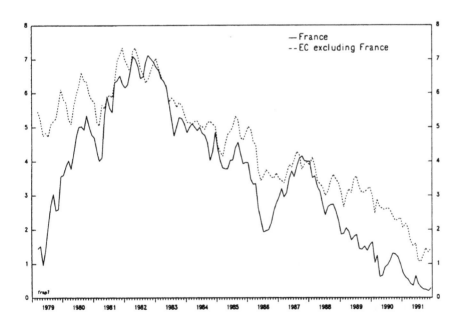

Figure II Long-Term Interest Differentials Against Germany.

they accepted the unemployment costs without devaluing, and there were in fact no realignments for a three-year period, despite high unemployment, which rose above 10 percent (Figure III). The commitment to a strong franc made by the socialist government was reaffirmed by the conservatives, who were in power between 1986 and 1988.[14] After returning to power in May 1988, socialist finance minister Bérégovoy further asserted that the franc would not be realigned against the deutsche mark in the future. The consistency in French policy no doubt helped to establish a reputation for toughness. However, unemployment remained a problem; after declining to about 9 percent, it rose once again to 10 percent as the economy slowed in 1990–1991. Though the reputation for toughness was established (so that p was close to zero), there may have been legitimate concerns that restrictive policies could not be maintained. In these circumstances, higher unemployment should once again tend to raise interest differentials, since even a tough government might devalue if the unemployment costs became too high.

Our theory therefore implies that the relationship between unemployment and long-term interest differentials should change over time, perhaps going through three phases. In the initial period following the election of François Mitterand as President and the formation of a socialist government, the authorities were perceived as being neither tough with respect to inflation nor committed to resisting realignments. They were willing to devalue, and the higher was the unemployment rate, the more likely was a realignment. After the 1982–1983 switch to a *politique de rigueur*, however, the absence of devaluations in spite of high unemployment helped signal to the public the change in the *type* of government,

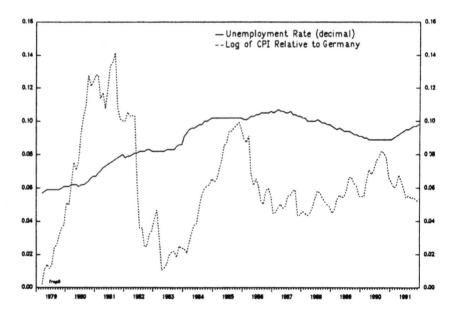

Figure III France: Unemployment and Relative Prices.

so that higher unemployment should have raised credibility (by lowering p) and hence led to declining interest differentials relative to Germany. Once a reputation for toughness was established, devaluation in the face of an adverse shock or accumulated loss of competitiveness (as occurred in January 1987) should not have significantly damaged the credibility of the strong franc policy. However, despite this favorable effect on credibility, increases in unemployment would be associated with fears of an eventual devaluation (raising both ρ^T and ρ^w) and hence would lead to higher interest differentials than would otherwise have prevailed.

This characterization of the difference in the relation between unemployment and interest differentials depending on which factor influencing credibility dominates suggests the following sort of empirical investigation: one can regress the long-term interest differential with Germany on variables which measure the policy stance to see how the relation changed over time. One can then ask whether such changes reflect political changes taking place in France which would operate in the direction predicted above.

Long-term interest differentials between France and Germany were regressed (using ordinary least squares in the first instance) on the unemployment rate and some other plausible measures of expected devaluation (see Panel A of Table I). These other indicators are a measure of competitiveness (the ratio of the CPI in France relative to that in Germany); the EC-wide interest differential (excluding France) with respect to Germany, which is intended to capture the overall credibility of the EMS commitment to fixed parities; and the lagged dependent variable, which can be expected to enter because the accumulation (or loss) of credibility can be expected to occur gradually.[15] (More general lag structures were tried, but in general other lagged dependent or independent variables were not significant.)

Changes in the relationship between the unemployment rate and interest differentials were examined in two ways. First, natural breaks in the series that correspond to the dating discussed above were imposed in estimation, using appropriately specified dummy variables. The discussion suggests an initial period ending in late 1982 or early 1983, a middle period extending to the most recent devaluation, in January 1987, and a final period since then. Second, tests of structural stability were performed, splitting the whole sample into two subperiods by successively trying different break points. If breaks are significant at several dates, the one that gives the maximum value of the likelihood ratio is chosen. Then, each of the two subsamples is further tested for break points in the same fashion. In doing these tests, the coefficients of both the unemployment rate and the constant term were allowed to vary, but the remaining coefficients were assumed constant over the whole sample.[16]

Using the first approach, the unemployment rate and the constant are entered with separate coefficients for the three subperiods discussed above (1979:05–1982:12, 1983:01–1986:12, and 1987:01–1991:12). The likelihood ratio test indicates that there is a significant difference in the regression coefficients on the unemployment rate and the constant across the three subperiods.[17] In the first and third subperiods, higher unemployment is associated with *higher* interest

Table I Regressions for the French Long-Term Interest Differential Against Germany (ID), May 1979–December 1991 (STANDARD ERRORS IN PARENTHESES)

$$ID = a_1 LRP + a_2 IDEC + a_3 ID_{-1} + DUM1(a_4 UR + a_5) + DUM2(a_6 UR + a_7) + DUM3(a_8 UR + a_9)$$

A. Ordinary least squares

Independent variables[a]									Statistics[b]					
LRP	IDEC	ID_{-1}	DUM1	DUM1.UR	DUM2	DUM2.UR	DUM3	DUM3.UR	R^2	SER	ARCH	LM(1,8)	Q(1,20)	LR(4)

Whole sample

| 0.492 | 0.265* | 0.801* | −0.892* | 0.043 | — | — | — | — | 0.979 | 0.279 | 0.83 | 12.20 | 26.3 | — |
| (0.789) | (0.050) | (0.037) | (0.311) | (0.024) | | | | | | | | | | |

Subperiods: May 1979–Dec. 1982, Jan. 1983–Dec. 1986, Jan 1987–Dec. 1991

| 0.985 | 0.316* | 0.703* | −2.125* | 0.242* | 0.309 | −0.074 | −3.269* | 0.294* | 0.981 | 0.267 | 1.18 | 8.21 | 25.7 | 17.9* |
| (0.956) | (0.059) | (0.047) | (0.522) | (0.072) | (0.778) | (0.070) | (0.804) | (0.084) | | | | | | |

Subperiods: May 1979–Sept. 1981, Oct. 1981–Oct. 1986, Nov. 1986–Dec. 1991

| −0.670 | 0.359* | 0.717* | −3.449* | 0.425* | −0.333 | −0.026 | −2.486* | 0.207* | 0.982 | 0.262 | 0.96 | 9.40 | 29.3 | 23.5* |
| (1.044) | (0.060) | (0.043) | (0.828) | (0.120) | (0.694) | (0.057) | (0.707) | (0.075) | | | | | | |

60

B. Instrumental variables

	Independent variables[a]									Statistics[b]	
	LRP	$IDEC$	ID_{-1}	$DUM1$	$DUM1.UR$	$DUM2$	$DUM2.UR$	$DUM3$	$DUM3.UR$	R^2	SER
Whole sample											
	0.491	0.264*	0.802*	−0.883*	0.042	—			—	0.979	0.279
	(0.789)	(0.050)	(0.037)	(0.312)	(0.024)						
Subperiods: May 1979–Dec. 1982, Jan. 1983–Dec. 1986, Jan. 1987–Dec. 1991											
	1.138	0.319*	0.691*	−2.248*	0.263*	0.568	−0.097	−3.482*	0.317*	0.980	0.267
	(0.962)	(0.059)	(0.048)	(0.526)	(0.073)	(0.793)	(0.072)	(0.821)	(0.085)		
Subperiods: May 1979–Sept. 1981, Oct. 1981–Oct. 1986, Nov. 1986–Dec. 1991											
	−0.832	0.365*	0.707*	−3.756*	0.476*	−0.221	−0.035	−2.549*	0.215*	0.982	0.261
	(1.052)	(0.060)	(0.043)	(0.838)	(0.122)	(0.705)	(0.058)	(0.719)	(0.076)		

[a]Variables names: LRP = log of French CPI relative to Germany's; $IDEC$ = EC interest differential with Germany (excluding France); ID_{-1} = lagged dependent variable; $DUM1$, $DUM2$, $DUM3$ = dummy variables, equal to unity within the relevant subperiods, zero otherwise; UR = French unemployment rate.
[b]Statistics: R^2 = explained sum of squares as a ratio to total sum of squares; SER = standard error of regression; $ARCH$ – autoregressive conditional heteroskedasticity test, distributed as $F(1,150)$; $LM(1,8)$ = Lagrange multiplier test for serial correlation, lags 1 to 8, distributed as $\chi^2(8)$; $Q(1,20)$ = Ljung-Box test for serial correlation, lags 1 to 20, distributed $\chi^2(20)$; $LR(4)$ = likelihood ratio test of structural break, distributed $\chi^2(4)$, *assuming that break points are known.*
* Significant at 5 percent level.

61

differentials, reflecting increasing concern with the possibility of realignment. In the second subperiod, when the authorities were attempting to signal a change in the priorities of the government and gaining credibility for a "hard currency" policy, a higher unemployment rate is associated with lower interest differentials, as the discussion above suggested that it should. However, the coefficient is not strongly significant.

The size of the coefficients in the first and third subperiods is also of interest. If a government is considered to be less concerned about the exchange rate and inflation (i.e., weak), then it is expected to resist movements away from a lower target for the unemployment rate. In the model the target unemployment rate is given by the ratio of the coefficients on the dummy variable and the product of the latter with the unemployment rate. That is, grouping the terms multiplied by each of the dummy variables as $a_4 DUM1$ $(UR + \alpha_5/\alpha_4)$, etc., then $-\alpha_5/\alpha_4$ is the level of unemployment rate in the first subperiod above which there is a positive effect on the interest differential, and similarly for the other subperiods. The values for the transformed constant term are, respectively, 8.78 and 11.2 for the first and third subperiods.

Thus, the target rate of unemployment is higher in the third subperiod, confirming the reasoning described above. As for the relative *size* of the unemployment rate effects (i.e., a_8 versus a_4), there is no unambiguous prediction: a tough government could conceivably be just as concerned about deviations of unemployment from its (much higher) target, and in fact, the estimates give a somewhat higher value for the third subperiod than the first.

The second approach identified the break points on the basis of the values of the likelihood ratio at the different dates (allowing for different coefficients on the unemployment rate and the constant before and after that date). The critical values of the likelihood ratio when the break point is not known have recently been tabulated by Andrews [1990]. For two degrees of freedom, they are 11.7 at the 5 percent level and 10.1 at the 10 percent level. Starting with the whole sample, the maximum likelihood ratio statistic (a value of 11.0) occurred when the sample was broken at 1986:9, and this is significant at the 10 percent level. If we then treat the first subperiod as a separate sample, the maximum likelihood ratio statistic (a value of 13.5) occurs when a further break is made at 1981:9. Using the second subperiod as a separate sample, the likelihood ratio has a maximum value of 8.1, well below the 10 percent critical value, suggesting no break point in this period. Therefore, the coefficients on unemployment and the constant were estimated over three subperiods: 1979:5–1981:9, 1981:101986:10, and 1986:11–1991:12. Interestingly, the second break point is very close to that suggested by our historical discussion.

Again the unemployment coefficients evolve over time as our model would suggest. Unemployment has a strongly significant, positive coefficient in the early and late periods. In contrast, in the middle period, when unemployment was rising strongly and the government was trying to establish credibility for greater exchange-rate stability and for limiting inflation, the coefficient is negative, though insignificant. Again, the target unemployment rate is higher in the third subperiod than in the first (12.0 percent versus 8.1 percent), though now the coefficient on unemployment is in fact lower in the later period than in the earlier one.

In order to correct for the possibility that the unemployment rate and the interest differential were jointly endogenous, instrumental variables estimation was also performed (see Panel B of Table I). Instruments used were the other regressors, plus time and the lagged unemployment rate. The results are very similar to the OLS results, and confirm the qualitative conclusions discussed above.

VI. Conclusions

The initial work on modeling credibility stressed a policymaker's intentions as summarized by his "type." It enabled macroeconomists to understand better how a "tough" policy could yield benefits well into the future via enhanced reputation. We were always uneasy, as were others, with the picture of a tough policymaker who would adhere to his anti-inflation policy no matter what was happening to the economy.

A more realistic picture is that of a policymaker who will renege on his commitment if circumstances are bad enough. Credibility, namely the expectation that an announced policy will be carried out, then reflects not only the policymaker's intentions, but also the state of the economy, where stochastic shocks will be important. The purpose of this paper was to show that this view of policymaking and credibility implies that tough policies may have adverse effects on credibility in the future if they severely constrain the choices of future policymakers. Policies that raise unemployment into the future, for example, will lower the "threshold" level of the random shock at which a future policymaker will find it optimal to devalue.

Using interest differentials relative to Germany as a measure of the perceived credibility of a country's pledge to maintain a fixed parity in the EMS, we found support for this alternative view in the effect of unemployment on credibility in France. In fact, though there was some weak evidence of the signaling role of unemployment in a period in the mid-1980s in which the priorities of the authorities had changed, in the earlier and later subperiods there seems to be clear evidence of a negative association between credibility and the unemployment rate. This suggests that *both* a policymaker's reputation for pursuing a hard-currency peg *and* durably lower unemployment are necessary to convince investors of the credibility of policy. The results are far from conclusive. But they indicate that modeling credibility solely in terms of a policymaker's preferences or intentions is seriously incomplete.

Appendix: The First-Period Decision Problem

The first-period decision for a government of type i is to choose a critical value $\hat{\epsilon}_1^i$ such that $\Lambda^i(D) = \Lambda^i(F)$, where $\Lambda^i(\ )$ is defined by (2) in the text. Using (2), one finds that

$$\hat{\epsilon}_1^i = -\kappa - \mu_1 s + \frac{a + \theta^i}{2a} s + \frac{\beta}{2as}\left[EL_2^i(D) - EL_2^i(F)\right], \tag{A1}$$

where μ_1 is the probability of a devaluation in the first period, which depends on ρ_1^w, ρ_1^T, and the uniform priors. To evaluate the terms in brackets, we use

$$EL_2^i(j) = \frac{1}{2v}\int_{\epsilon_2 = -v}^{\epsilon_2 = \hat{\epsilon}_2^i(j)} a\left[-\mu_2(j)s - \epsilon_2 - \kappa - \delta\left(u_1(j) - u_N\right)\right]^2 d\epsilon_2$$

$$+ \frac{1}{2v}\int_{\epsilon_2 = \hat{\epsilon}_2^i(j)}^{\epsilon_2 = v}\left(a\left[s - \mu_2(j)s - \epsilon_2 - \kappa - \delta\left(u_1(j) - u_n\right)\right]^2 + \theta^i s^2\right)d\epsilon_2 \tag{A2}$$

For ease of notation, define $m(j) = \mu_2(j)s + \kappa + \delta(u_1(j) - u_N)$. Using the fact that $\hat{\epsilon}_2^i(j) = -m(j) + (a + \theta^i)s/2a$, the integral (A2) may, after some manipulation, be evaluated as

$$EL_2^i(j) = a\left(m(j) + \kappa\right)^2 + \frac{av^2}{3} - \frac{as}{2v}\left(v - \hat{\epsilon}_2^i(j)\right)^2 \tag{A3}$$

The term in brackets in (A1), $EL_2^i(D) - EL_2^i(F)$ then becomes

$$\frac{a(2v - s)}{2v}\left[(m(D))^2 - (m(F))^2\right] + \left(\frac{(a + \theta^i)s^2}{2}v - as + 2a\kappa\right)$$

$$\times\left(m(D) - m(F)\right)$$

$$= \left(\left(\mu_2(D) - \mu_2(F)\right)s + \delta\left(u_1(D) - u_1(F)\right)\right) \tag{A4}$$

$$\times\left(\left(1 - \frac{s}{2v}\right)\left[\left(\mu_2(D) + \mu_2(F)\right)s + 2\left(\kappa - \delta u_N\right)\right.\right.$$

$$\left.\left. + \delta\left(u_1(D) + u_1(F)\right) - s\right] + \frac{\theta^i s^2}{2av}\right).$$

ρ_1^w and ρ_1^T may then be calculated from (A1), using (A4) and the uniform distribution.

University of Maryland and NBER
International Monetary Fund

*The authors would like to thank Robert Flood, Peter Isard, Peter Kenen, Donald Mathieson, and Bennett McCallum for helpful comments, as well as seminar participants at Boston University; the Hebrew University of Jerusalem; the

International Monetary Fund; the University of Maryland; the University of California, Los Angeles; and the NBER Seminar on Monetary Economics. The views expressed are those of the authors and do not necessarily represent those of the International Monetary Fund.

Notes

1 The basic approach of Backus and Driffill has been extended in several directions. Whereas they considered the case where the "tough" policymaker cares only about inflation, Vickers [1986] showed that if both tough and "weak" types care about unemployment, tough governments tend to be even more restrictive. Persson [1988] and Rogoff [1987, 1989] provide excellent surveys of models of credibility and reputation. An alternative approach is to define strength in terms of ability to precommit to a particular policy, as in Cukierman and Liviatan [1991].

2 A related point, made by Flood [1983] and Blanchard [1985], among others, is that if policies are too tough then current policymakers may be removed from power, leading to an easing of policies.

3 The paper was initially drafted in mid-1992. Events of September 1992 provide strong support for our contention that credibility is never definitively established because in some circumstances governments will choose to devalue.

4 Froot and Rogoff [1991] suggest a number of reasons why the credibility of the EMS may not be increasing monotonically over time. A recent paper by Chen and Giovannini [1992] presents empirical evidence which suggests that tough policy and lack of realignments have not enhanced the credibility of fixed exchange rates in the EMS. Klein and Marion [1992] use duration analysis to study the credibility of a fixed exchange rate as a function of the length of time since the last devaluation. They do not consider a persistence effect, however, and their model has the credibility of the no-devaluation policy rising over time the longer there has been no devaluation.

5 For a general discussion of this type of model, one may refer to Persson and Tabellini [1989].

6 The policymaker is modeled as choosing between a rule and discretion on the basis of the realized state of the world, rather than as using a two-part rule, in order to capture the notion that all states of the world cannot be foreseen ex ante. Hence, a fully state-contingent rule cannot be specified. To avoid problems of time-consistency, it is assumed that the policymaker must pay a private fixed cost when choosing discretion. Otherwise a benevolent policymaker would always choose discretion ex post.

7 Throughout, references to the EMS should be taken to refer to the countries participating in the exchange rate mechanism of the EMS.

8 We model persistent effects of policy in the equation summarizing the *structure* of the economy. Alternatively, one could model the effects of persistence in the *preference* equation, by putting lagged unemployment in the loss function (2). Much of the policy discussion in Europe which takes past policy choices as constraining current choices implicitly takes this second route. Our results would be the same under this alternative specification, the key point being that the probability of a devaluation in the second period may depend positively on first-period unemployment.

9 An alternative approach is to use a trigger-strategy model of expectations with uncertainty, along the lines of Canzoneri [1985]. Though this allows the government to depart from tough monetary policy in response to observable adverse shocks without losing credibility and may be simpler than the Kreps-Wilson [1982] framework for some purposes, it does not allow a simple comparison with the signaling-of-type

motive for tough policy, which we feel is important in understanding devaluation expectations.

10 One can do an analogous calculation in the case where the shock ϵ_1 is observed (or can be inferred). For θ^w not close to θ^T, there will be a separating equilibrium for some realizations of ϵ_1: action would be fully revealing, with a weak government finding it optimal to devalue and a strong government not to devalue at those realizations. For other realizations of ϵ_1, there would be pooling, with both types choosing the same policy, as would also be the case for all realizations of ϵ_1 for θ^w close to θ^T. $p_2(j)$ would equal zero or one in the relevant regions of separation and would equal the prior in the region of pooling.

11 In the case where the shock is observed (see footnote 10), we shall see the same effect: if persistence effects are strong enough, playing tough in the first period will lower the credibility of the no-devaluation policy in the second.

12 Recent empirical analyses of EMS credibility include Bartolini and Bodnar [1992], Koen [1991], and Weber [1991, 1992]. Koen calculates credibility bands around interest differentials which take into account the freedom for exchange rates to change without realignments being necessary. For long-term interest rates, which we use in our empirical work, the bands are quite narrow, however.

13 It subsequently widened, in large part because of the considerations discussed in this paper.

14 The fact that Mitterand was still President guaranteed some continuity in exchange rate policy. Besides, the conservatives already had a reputation of support for a strong currency.

15 The variables included, in particular the interest differentials, competitiveness, and unemployment, are nonstationary, 1(1), variables in our sample, but they are cointegrated. Our dynamic equation can thus be interpreted as an error- correction model.

16 Tests that allowed *all* of the coefficients to vary gave similar break points and test statistics.

17 On the assumption that the break points are known—see discussion on p62.

References

Andrews, Donald W. K., "Tests for Parameter Instability and Structural Change with Unknown Change Point," Cowles Foundation Discussion Paper No. 943: Yale University, 1990.

Backus, David, and E. John Driffill, "Inflation and Reputation," *American Economic Review*, LXXV (1985a), 530–38.

Backus, David, and E. John Driffill, "Rational Expectations and Policy Credibility Following a Change in Regime," *Review of Economic Studies*, LII (1985b), 211–21.

Barro, Robert J., and David B. Gordon, "Rules, Discretion, and Reputation in a Model of Monetary Policy," *Journal of Monetary Economics*, XII (1983a), 101–21.

Barro, Robert J., and David B. Gordon, "A Positive Theory of Monetary Policy in a Natural Rate Model," *Journal of Political Economy*, XCI (1983b), 589–610.

Bartolini, Leonardo, and Gordon Bodnar, "Target Zones and Forward Rates in a Model with Repeated Realignments," *Journal of Monetary Economics*, XXX (1992), 373–408.

Blanchard, Olivier J., "Credibility, Disinflation, and Gradualism," *Economics Letters*, XVII (1985), 211–17.

Canzoneri, Matthew, "Monetary Policy Games and the Role of Private Information," *American Economic Review*, LXXV (1985), 1056–70.

Chen, Zhaohui, and Alberto Giovannini, "The Credibility of Adjustable Parities: The Experience of the European Monetary System," mimeo, Columbia University, 1992.

Cukierman, Alex, and Nissan Liviatan, "Optimal Accommodation by Strong Policymakers Under Incomplete Information," *Journal of Monetary Economics,* XXVII (1991), 99–127.

Flood, Robert P., "Comment on Buiter and Miller," in Jacob A. Frenkel, ed., *Exchange Rates and International Macroeconomics* (Chicago: University of Chicago Press, 1983), pp. 359–65.

Flood, Robert P., and Peter Isard, "Monetary Policy Strategies," *IMF Staff Papers,* (1989), 612–32.

Froot, Kenneth A., and Kenneth Rogoff, "The EMS, the EMU, and the Transition to a Common Currency," in Olivier J. Blanchard and Stanley Fischer, eds., *NBER Macroeconomics Annual 1991* (Cambridge MA: MIT Press, 1991). pp. 269–317.

Giavazzi, Francesco, and Luigi Spaventa, "The New EMS," CEPR Discussion Paper No. 369, 1990.

Klein, Michael, and Nancy Marion, "The Duration of Fixed Exchange Rate Regimes," mimeo, Dartmouth College, 1992.

Koen, Vincent R., "Testing the Credibility of the Belgian Hard Currency Policy," IMF Working Paper WP/91/79, 1991.

Kreps, David, and Robert Wilson, "Reputation and Imperfect Information," *Journal of Economic Theory,* XXVII (1982), 253–79.

Lohmann, Susanne, "Monetary Policy Strategies-A Correction," *IMF Staff Papers,* XXXVI (1990), 440–45.

Obstfeld, Maurice, "Destabilizing Effects of Exchange Rate Escape Clauses," NBER Working Paper No. 3603, 1991.

Persson, Torsten, "Credibility of Macroeconomic Policy: An Introduction and Broad Survey," *European Economic Review,* XXXII (1988), 519–32.

Persson, Torsten, and Guido Tabellini, *Macroeconomic Policy, Credibility and Politics* (London: Harwood, 1989).

Rogoff, Kenneth, "Reputational Constraints on Monetary Policy," in K. Brunner and A. Meltzer, eds. *Carnegie-Rochester Series on Public Policy* 26 (Amsterdam: North-Holland, 1987), pp. 141–82.

_____, "Reputation, Coordination, and Monetary Policy," in R. Barro, ed., *Modern Business Cycle Theory* (Cambridge, MA: Harvard University Press, 1989), pp. 236–64.

van Wijnbergen, Sweder, "Intertemporal Speculation, Shortages and the Political Economy of Price Reform: A Case Against Gradualism," mimeo, World Bank, 1990.

Vickers, John, "Signalling in a Model of Monetary Policy with Incomplete Information," *Oxford Economic Papers,* XXXVIII (1986), 443–55.

Weber, Axel, "Reputation and Credibility in the European Monetary System," *European Policy,* XII (1991), 57–102.

_____, "The Role of Policymakers' Reputation in the EMS Disinflations: An Empirical Evaluation," *European Economic Review,* XXXVI (1992), 1473–92.

4

ON THE CREDIBILITY OF CURRENCY BOARDS*

Switgard Feuerstein and Oliver Grimm

Source: *Review of International Economics* 14, 5, 2006, 818–835.

Abstract

The paper compares the credibility of currency boards and (standard) pegs. Abandoning a currency board requires a time-consuming legislative process and an abolition will thus be well-anticipated. Therefore, a currency board solves the time-inconsistency problem of monetary policy. However, policy can react to unexpected shocks only with a time lag, thus the threat of large shocks makes the abolition more likely. Currency boards are more credible than standard pegs if the time-inconsistency problem dominates. In contrast, standard pegs, that can be left at short notice, are more credible if exogenous shocks are highly volatile and constitute the dominant problem.

1. Introduction

During the crisis-prone decade of the 1990s, currency boards proved to be remarkably robust. Even in the case of the 2002 Argentinean currency board collapse, both the event itself and the durability of the arrangement in the face of such large strains require an explanation. In this context, the question arises as to what constitutes the difference between a currency board and a standard peg system and under what circumstances does a currency board possess a credibility advantage.[1]

A currency board is characterized by a fixed exchange rate to a stable anchor currency and full coverage of the monetary base by foreign reserves. It requires a long-term commitment by policymakers and is usually introduced by law (which also specifies the fixed exchange rate). The main advantage of a currency board is the gain in credibility. The monetary base is changed only through buying and selling the anchor currency at the fixed rate. Thus, the trilemma that it is not possible to maintain a fixed exchange rate, free movement of capital, and an independent monetary policy at the same time is solved by clearly abstaining from monetary independence. Moreover, the time-inconsistency problem of monetary policy is solved, as it is not possible for the monetary authorities to create surprise inflation.

The anti-inflationary effects of currency boards have been confirmed empirically. Ghosh et al. (2000) find that countries with a currency board experienced lower inflation compared both with floating regimes and with simple pegs. Other econometric studies that investigate the relevance of exchange rate regimes for economic performance pool currency boards and countries with a shared currency into the group of hard pegs. The result that countries with hard pegs have lower inflation rates than countries with soft pegs or other regimes is found unequivocally (Levy-Yeyati and Sturzenegger, 2001; Ghosh et al., 2003; Bleaney and Francisco, 2005). There is, however, mixed evidence whether soft pegs are also associated with lower inflation than floating regimes and whether the gain in stability comes at the cost of lower growth.[2]

Obviously, the gain in credibility of monetary policy relies on the credibility of the currency board itself, which is, of course, not complete. Following the seminal work of Drazen and Masson (1994), the credibility of an exchange rate regime is defined as the probability that it is maintained. A currency board does not break down because it runs out of reserves necessary to intervene on the foreign exchange market, as may be the case in a standard peg system. Nevertheless, it can be abolished if the costs of maintaining it—for example, in case of a recession, a debt crisis, or problems within the banking sector—exceed its advantages.

Although currency boards have been discussed thoroughly, there is little literature that analyzes the difference between a currency board and a standard fixed exchange rate regime from a theoretical point of view.[3] One of the few papers that try to model this difference is Chang and Velasco (2000). They characterize a currency board by the full coverage of the monetary base, which excludes a run on the central bank's reserves that is possible in a standard peg. As Chang and Velasco consider opportunity costs of holding reserves, but do not model any possible disadvantages of flexible exchange rates, their conclusion that a flexible exchange rate is the optimal regime comes as no surprise. A different approach to capture the difference between a currency board and a standard peg is used by Oliva et al. (2001), who analyze whether monetary authorities can signal their preferences on price stability by choosing between these two exchange rate systems. They emphasize that a currency board constitutes a long-term commitment and assume that it can only be abolished in the second period of their two-period model, whereas with a standard peg, a realignment in response to a supply shock is possible in either period. In contrast, Irwin (2004) assumes that the policymaker can abolish a currency board without any time lag, and he characterizes a currency board only by its high exit costs. The central result is that "the combination of incomplete information and persistence of unemployment can lead to a build up of pressure on a currency board system to the extent that it does collapse, even where the true devaluation cost is very high."

In this paper, we take up the idea of Oliva et al. (2001) that a currency board cannot be abolished overnight, but we model this feature more consequently. A currency board is established by law, and leaving it requires a political process including preceding public discussion. While Oliva et al. (2001) allow for a *sudden exit* out of the system in the *second* period, our paper captures that it is hardly possible to generate a surprise, as repealing a currency board takes time.[4] When Argentina finally left its currency board, this had been largely expected.

Therefore in our model, the currency board is characterized by the assumption that—in contrast to the case of a standard peg—it can only be abandoned with a one-period delay. The currency board can only be left if this was—at least implicitly—announced earlier.[5] Thus, when expectations on inflation are formed, it is public information whether the currency board will still be in place in the next period. Hence, the currency board completely solves the time-inconsistency problem of monetary policy. Nevertheless, announcing the abolition of the currency board may make sense in case of a lasting misalignment. Pressure to change the exchange rate emerges from asymmetric shocks that require an adjustment of the real exchange rate, i.e. from stochastic shocks on the purchasing power parity (PPP) (Berger et al., 2001). These shocks may, for example, arise from differing business cycles. They may also reflect exchange rate movements between the anchor currency and third countries. Although the Argentinean currency board ultimately collapsed because of unresolved budgetary problems, the sharp devaluation of the Brazilian real in 1999 and the strength of the US dollar in the years 2000 until mid-2002 contributed to Argentina's difficulties and help to explain the timing of the breakdown.

The PPP shocks are assumed to be autocorrelated, meaning that a shock has lasting effects. After observing the shock of the first period, the policymaker will decide whether to initiate the process of repealing the currency board. If the shock is large, he knows that the misalignment will continue with a high probability in the following period. However, if the currency board is abolished, the time-inconsistency problem of monetary policy re-emerges. In contrast, in a standard peg regime the policymaker can make use of an escape clause after observing the shock in each period. He can respond to a large shock, but he is also tempted to create surprise inflation. As a result, a currency board arrangement is more credible than a standard-peg regime if the time-inconsistency problem is dominant, whereas the peg is maintained with a higher probability, if the ability to react to future shocks is more important.

This paper is organized as follows. In the next section we develop our two-period model. Section 3 considers the regime of a floating exchange rate, which will be in operation if the fixed exchange rate is abolished. Section 4 analyzes the policy options under a currency board. We derive conditions under which the currency board will be maintained and show in which situations it will be abandoned. In section 5 the behavior of the policymaker in a standard fixed exchange rate system is considered. Section 6 compares the credibility of the two fixed exchange rate regimes considered. Section 7 concludes the paper.

2. The Model

We consider a two-period model of a small open economy that has a time-inconsistency problem of monetary policy modeled as in Kydland and Prescott (1977) and in Barro and Gordon (1983). In each period t, output y_t is given by a standard *Lucas supply function*:

$$y_t = \gamma\left(\pi_t - \pi_t^e\right), \quad \gamma > 0. \tag{1}$$

Output depends on unanticipated inflation $(\pi_t - \pi_t^e)$, where π_t denotes inflation in period t and π_t^e is the inflation rate expected by the private sector. Expectations are formed rationally. Strictly speaking y_t denotes the deviation of output from its natural level, i.e. the natural output level is normalized to zero. The inflation rate and the exchange rate are linked by the *stochastic purchasing power parity (PPP)*:

$$\pi_i = \pi_i^* + e_t + \phi_t, \tag{2}$$

where π_i^* denotes foreign inflation, e_t the percentage change of the nominal exchange rate in period t, and ϕ_t is a random shock (Berger et al., 2001).

The shock ϕ_t is autocorrelated:[6]

$$\phi_t = \eta\phi_{t-1} + u_t, \quad \eta \in (0,1), \tag{3}$$

and it is assumed that initially there is no inherited shock, i.e. $\phi_1 = u_1$.

ϕ_t represents an asymmetric shock that changes the equilibrium real exchange rate reflecting for example differing business cycles or exchange rate movements between the anchor currency and third countries. A positive ϕ_t corresponds to the necessity of a real appreciation, which can either be realized by an inflation rate exceeding foreign inflation or by a falling exchange rate. New shocks u_t are i.i.d. with $E(u_t) = 0$ and $var(u_t) = \sigma_u^2$ for all t. In sections 5 and 6, we will assume in addition that u_t is uniformly distributed on the interval $[-A, A]$.

Normalizing the foreign inflation π^* to zero, equation (2) can be rewritten as

$$\pi_t = e_t + \phi_t. \tag{4}$$

The monetary authorities' loss in period t is given by the function

$$L_t = \left(y_t - k\right)^2 + \theta\pi_i^2 + \delta c, \tag{5}$$

and depends on the deviation of output from its target level $k>0$ and the actual inflation rate. The assumption that the policymaker's target output k is above the natural level can be interpreted as capturing distortions on goods and factor markets that lead to too low a natural level. The relative weight on inflation in the loss function is given by θ. In addition, there are political costs c that arise when the fixed exchange rate is given up under a peg regime or when the currency board arrangement is abandoned. These political costs can either be interpreted as reputation costs or as costs caused by political institutions in society (Lohmann, 1992). δ is a dummy variable, which equals one when leaving the peg or the currency board and equals zero otherwise. Inserting the supply function and the PPP (equations (1) and (4)) into the loss function (5) yields:[7]

$$L_t = \left(\gamma\left(\pi_t - \pi_t^e\right) - k\right)^2 + \theta\pi_t^2 + \delta c$$

$$= \left(\gamma\left(e_t + \phi_t - \pi_t^e\right) - k\right)^2 + \theta\left(e_t + \phi_t\right)^2 + \delta c. \tag{6}$$

The first term shows that the positive k leads to an incentive to create surprise inflation in order to push output above its natural level. According to the assumption of rational expectations, the private sector will take this incentive into account when forming its expectations. Therefore, the policymaker cannot generate a surprise, and a time-inconsistency problem of monetary policy arises, i.e. the larger the target output k is. A high weight on inflation in the loss function θ, i.e. a high preference for price stability, mitigates the time-inconsistency problem. The effect of these two parameters on the time-inconsistency problem will be discussed again in section 3, where the results for a free float, ie. for the case of unrestricted discretion of monetary policy, are derived.

In our model, the essential difference between a currency board and a standard peg lies in the procedure of abolishing the particular system. A currency board, characterized by its establishment by law and the complete renunciation of individual monetary policy, can only be repealed if this was announced one period in advance, i.e. before the private sector made its expectations on inflation. In contrast, monetary authorities can leave the fixed exchange rate in a far more flexible way after the shock was observed. The sequence of the model is depicted in Figure 1.

Expectations π_i^e have to be formed before the shock ϕ_t is observed. Actual inflation is determined by the purchasing power parity (equation (4)) if the exchange rate is fixed, and it is optimally set by the policymaker in response to the shock if the exchange rate is flexible or the fixed exchange rate is abandoned. In our two-period model, the decision whether to repeal the currency board in the second period or not is announced in the first period at time $\Diamond$ before the private sector forms expectations π_2^e. In the case of a standard peg, the fixed exchange rate can

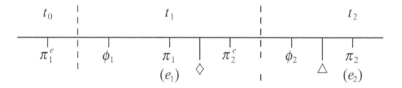

Figure 1 Sequence of the Model.

be abandoned after observing the shock which would actually be possible in the first as well as in the second period. However, we assume that the fixed exchange rate is maintained in the first period and the decision whether to defend it or not is considered at time Δ in the second period. This could be justified by the fact that a standard peg has some commitment value too, and cannot be abolished immediately after its adoption. The more important reason for making the assumption is, however, that a meaningful comparison of the credibility of a currency board and a standard peg has to be based on a *single* decision whether to give up the fixed exchange rate or not in both systems. If the currency board can only be abolished at one point of time, but for the standard peg abolition is considered both in period 1 and period 2, a statement that an abolition of the standard peg is more probable will be irrelevant.

3. Free-float Regime

In our model the process of repealing a currency board system takes time and has to be announced one period in advance. In this case, the policymaker will set the inflation rate (and thus the exchange rate) in period 2 optimally, and this policy will be taken into account when expectations are formed. This regime amounts to a free float in period 2 that will briefly be analyzed in this section.

Consider the loss in period 2 (equation (6)):

$$L_2 = \left(\gamma\left(\pi_2 - \pi_2^e\right) - k\right)^2 + \theta\pi_2^2.$$

The monetary authorities can freely choose inflation. By minimizing L_2, inflation in period 2 equals

$$\pi_2 = \frac{\gamma\left(\gamma\pi_2^e + k\right)}{\gamma^2 + \theta}. \tag{7}$$

As the private sector's expectations are rational, it follows that

$$\pi_2^e = \mathrm{E}\left(\pi_2\right) = \frac{\gamma^2\pi_2^e + \gamma k}{\gamma^2 + \theta},$$

and thus

$$\pi_2^e = \gamma\frac{k}{\theta}. \tag{8}$$

Using equations (1), (4), and (7) yields the equilibrium values for period t:

$$\pi_2^f = \gamma\frac{k}{\theta}, \ e_2^f = \gamma\frac{k}{\theta} - \phi_2, \ y_2^f = 0. \tag{9}$$

The superscript f denotes "free float." With flexible exchange rates, the PPP shock ϕ_2 is fully absorbed by the change of the exchange rate e_2, and the inflation rate π_2^f is independent of ϕ_2. The actual inflation rate is proportional to k, which is the difference between the target and the natural output level. Although the policymaker wants to push output above its natural level, output y_2 is not affected. Obviously, the loss would be smaller if actual and expected inflation equaled zero. However, a zero-inflation policy would be time inconsistent, as with $\pi^e = 0$ a higher inflation rate would actually be chosen. Thus in case of a free float, when there is unrestricted discretion of monetary policy, the inflation rate will be inefficiently high, and this problem is larger, the larger the parameter k. In contrast, a high weight θ on inflation in the policymaker's loss function makes the time-inconsistency problem of monetary policy smaller. The two parameters k and θ will therefore be interpreted as determining the size of the time-inconsistency problem in the remainder of the paper.[8] The resulting loss in period 2 is given by:

$$L_2^f = \frac{1}{\theta} k^2 \left(\gamma^2 + \theta \right).$$

(10)

Note that L_2^f does not depend on the shock ϕ_2, but only on k, hence $\mathrm{E}\left(L_2^f\right) = L_2^f$.

4. Policy Options under a Currency Board

The policymaker has to announce one period in advance (at time $\lozenge$ in Figure 1) whether to maintain or to abolish the currency board in the next period. Thus, the decision depends on the expected second-period loss of the two cases, which are compared to each other in the following analysis.

Currency Board Maintained over Both Periods

First, we consider the case of a currency board regime that is kept over both periods; i.e. the monetary authorities do not announce the abolition of the currency board in period 1, implying that $e_2 = 0$ irrespective of the shock in period 2. Using equations (3) and (4), the second period's inflation rate is given by

$$\pi_2 = \phi_2 = \eta \phi_1 + u_2,$$

(11)

meaning that inflation depends only on the shock ϕ_2. Thus the expected inflation π_2^e equals[9]

$$\pi_2^e = \mathrm{E}_1\left(\phi_2\right) = \eta \phi_1.$$

(12)

Expected and actual inflation differ by the new shock u_2. Substituting $\eta \phi_1$ for π_2^e in equation (6) yields a second-period loss of:[10]

$$L_1^{cc} = \left(\gamma \left(\phi_2 - \eta \phi_1 \right) - k \right)^2 + \theta \phi_2^2. \tag{13}$$

Equilibrium values are given by

$$e_2^{cc} = 0$$

$$\pi_2^{cc} = \phi_2 = \eta \phi_1 + u_2 \tag{14}$$

$$y_2^{cc} = \gamma \left(\pi_2^{cc} - \pi_2^e \right) = \gamma \left(\eta \phi_1 + u_2 - \eta \phi_1 \right) = \gamma u_2.$$

As the exchange rate cannot be changed, e_2^α equals zero. Thus, π_2^{cc} is independent of k and the time-inconsistency problem of monetary policy is solved at the cost of having no policy option to counteract ϕ_2. Equilibrium output depends on the realization of the unexpected part of ϕ_2, the new shock u_2. The expectation of period 2 loss, contingent on first-period information, is given by

$$E_1 \left(L_2^{cc} \right) = E_1 \left(\left(\gamma u_2 - k \right)^2 + \theta \phi_2^2 \right)$$

$$= \left(\gamma^2 + \theta \right) \sigma_u^2 + k^2 + \theta \left(\eta \phi_1 \right)^2. \tag{15}$$

The threat of a large expected second-period shock, represented by a high variance σ_u^2 and a high inherited shock ϕ_1, leads to a high expected second-period loss, as the policymaker has no options to counteract the shock. This effect is reinforced by a large time-inconsistency problem of monetary policy, represented by a high level of k.

Currency Board being Abolished after the First Period

In this subsection, we consider the case that the government has adopted a currency board regime, but announces its abolition at the end of the first period and introduces a free-float system for period 2. Note that e_1 equals zero and the monetary authorities can set π_2 (and therefore e_2) optimally after observing ϕ_2.

The monetary authorities optimize the period 2 social loss according to the flexible exchange rate case. The equilibrium values of e_2^{cf}, y_2^d, and π_2^{cf} are identical to those of a flexible exchange rate system. Hence, L_2^{cf} and also $E_1(L_2^{cf})$ are given by equation (10) plus the political costs c^{cf} of abandoning the currency board, yielding:

$$E_1 \left(L_2^{cf} \right) = L_2^{cf} = \frac{1}{\theta} k^2 \left(\gamma^2 + \theta \right) + c^{cf}. \tag{16}$$

Maintaining or Leaving the Currency Board Arrangement

The decision whether to maintain or abandon the currency board takes place in the first period before the private sector forms its inflation expectations for the second period. The policymaker will decide to maintain the currency board, if the expected second-period loss of leaving it exceeds the expected second-period loss of perpetuating the currency board, i.e. if

$$E_1\left(L_2^{cf}\right) - E_1\left(L_2^{cc}\right) > 0. \tag{17}$$

Using equations (15) and (16), this condition is equivalent to:

$$\phi_1^2 < \frac{1}{\theta\eta^2}\left(\frac{1}{\theta}k^2\gamma^2 - \left(\gamma^2 + \theta\right)\sigma_u^2 + c^{cf}\right). \tag{18}$$

The inequality shows that the decision whether to keep the currency board after the first period or not depends on the absolute value of the shock realization ϕ_1. The currency board is maintained for small shocks, whereas a large shock ϕ_1 prompts the policymaker to announce its abolition. A high target output k and a low weight θ of inflation in the loss function—both reflecting a large time-inconsistency problem of monetary policy—make the inequality more likely to hold.[11] The policymaker will continue the currency board in spite of a large shock requiring an adjustment of the real exchange rate, as an abolition of the currency board will revive a huge inflation bias. This effect is reinforced by the political costs c^d of abolishing the currency board.

In contrast, a high variance σ_u^2 of the PPP shock makes the interval in which the fixed exchange rate is defended smaller, and it is possible that the right-hand side of inequality (18) becomes negative which would mean that the currency board would be abolished irrespective of the shock (or it would not be a suitable system from the very beginning and would never be introduced). The higher σ_u^2, the more important it is for the policymaker to be able to react to a large possible shock ϕ_2. A high autocorrelation of the shocks ϕ_t, represented by a large η, decreases the range of shock realizations for which the currency board is maintained. In this case, the first-period shock contains much information about the second-period shock, implying that a large first-period shock makes the need for large further adjustments in the second period more likely. If η is interpreted as a degree of price stickiness (see note 6), a currency board is more likely to be maintained in case of a high price flexibility, whereas a relatively large η increases the probability of announcing its abolition.

5. Standard Peg

To ensure an unbiased comparison of a standard peg and a currency board, only the policymaker's decision of the second period is considered (see section 2).

After observing the shock ϕ_2, monetary authorities decide whether to maintain or to abandon the peg. In this section, the range of realizations of ϕ_2 in which monetary authorities would defend the peg is derived. Multiple equilibria for π_2^e may occur in this case. However, we will derive conditions sufficient for the uniqueness of the equilibrium.

Policy Decisions under a Peg

The second-period loss when leaving the peg L_2^f is given by the term[12]

$$L_2^{pf} = \theta \frac{\left(\gamma\pi_2^e + k\right)^2}{\gamma^2 + \theta} + c^{pf}, \tag{19}$$

which equals the second-period loss in a free-float system (equation (10)) plus the political costs c^{nf}. If the monetary authorities decide to maintain the peg after observing ϕ_2, L_2^{pp} equals

$$L_2^{pp} = \left(\gamma\left(\phi_2 - \pi_2^e\right) - k\right)^2 + \theta\phi_2^2. \tag{20}$$

The fixed exchange rate is defended if the second-period loss in case of leaving exceeds the loss in case of maintaining the peg, i.e. if

$$L_2^{pf} - L_2^{pp} = \left(\theta \frac{\left(\gamma\pi_2^e + k\right)^2}{\gamma^2 + \theta} + c^{pf}\right) - \left(\gamma\left(\phi_2 - \pi_2^e\right) - k\right)^2 - \theta\left(\phi_2\right)^2 > 0. \tag{21}$$

Isolating ϕ_2 in the above equation yields the result that the exchange rate remains fixed if and only if

$$\underbrace{\Gamma\left(\pi_2^e, k\right) - \sqrt{\frac{c^{pf}}{\gamma^2 + \theta}}}_{\phi_2^l} < \phi_2 < \underbrace{\Gamma\left(\pi_2^e, k\right) + \sqrt{\frac{c^{pf}}{\gamma^2 + \theta}}}_{\phi_2^u}, \tag{22}$$

where

$$\Gamma\left(\pi_2^e, k\right) = \gamma \frac{\left(\gamma\pi_2^e + k\right)}{\gamma^2 + \theta}.$$

The peg is maintained if the shock ϕ_2 lies in an interval of length $2\sqrt{c^{pf} / (\gamma^2 + \theta)}$, which is increasing in the political costs c^{pf}. Without political costs, this interval vanishes and monetary authorities will always abandon the fixed exchange rate and respond optimally to shocks If $\phi_2 < \phi_2^l$, the monetary authorities will devalue;

if $\phi_2 > \phi_2^u$ they will revalue. Using equation (3), the lower and upper boundary of the interval in which the peg is defended can be expressed in terms of the new shock u_2:

$$u_2^l = -\eta\phi_1 + \Gamma\left(\pi_2^e, k\right) - \sqrt{\frac{c^{pf}}{\gamma^2 + \theta}} \tag{23}$$

$$u_2^u = -\eta\phi_1 + \Gamma\left(\pi_2^e, k\right) + \sqrt{\frac{c^{pf}}{\gamma^2 + \theta}}. \tag{24}$$

The policymaker devalues, if the new shock u_2 is below u_2^l and revalues the currency if $u_2 > u_2^u$. In the following, it is assumed that the new shock u_t is uniformly distributed with $u_t - U[-A, A]$. Note that for certain parameter values, the boundaries u_2^π and u_2^l may lie outside the support of u_2.

It is assumed that political costs c^{pf} are small enough to ensure that $\sqrt{c^{pf}/(\gamma^2 + \theta)} \leq A$, i.e. the (maximum) length of the interval in which the policymaker maintains the fixed exchange rate is smaller than the length of the support of u_1. Thus, independent of the realization of ϕ_1, the probability of abandoning the peg is always positive. The probability of defending the fixed exchange rate is a measure of the credibility of the exchange rate system. In case that the whole interval $[u_2^l, u_2^\pi]$ is contained in the support $[-A, A]$, the probability of maintaining the peg equals $(1/A) \cdot \sqrt{c^{pf}/(\gamma^2 + \theta)}$, which is an upper boundary of the credibility of the fixed exchange rate system in all cases.

We use this upper boundary for the comparison of the credibility of a currency board and a standard peg in section 6. This way, the standard peg appears in a favorable light, and the credibility gains of a currency board can only be underestimated. Therefore, when pointing out situations in which a currency board has a credibility advantage, we will remain on the safe side.

Unique and Multiple Equilibria

The focus of this subsection is the position of the interval in which the peg is defended. The center of that interval depends on π_2^e, which is determined by rational expectations, i.e. $\pi_2^e = E_1(\pi_2)$.

The expected value of π_2 is given by

$$\begin{aligned}
E_1\left(\pi_2\right) = {} & P\left(u_2 < u_2^l\right) E_1\left(\pi_2 \middle| u_2 < u_2^l\right) \\
& + P\left(u_2^l < u_2 < u_2^u\right) E_1\left(\pi_2 \middle| u_2^l < u_2 < u_2^u\right) \\
& + P\left(u_2 > u_2^u\right) E_1\left(\pi_2 \middle| u_2 > u_2^u\right),
\end{aligned} \tag{25}$$

which is of course a function of the expected inflation π_2^e.

As in Obstfeld (1996), the existence of an equilibrium is ensured, but multiple equilibria may occur when determining π_2^e from equation (25).[13] However, multiplicities can be excluded for certain parameter sets (see the Appendix). The condition $\theta > \gamma^2 / 2$, which means that the weight on inflation θ in the policymaker's loss function is high relative to γ, the parameter in the Lucas supply function, is sufficient for a unique equilibrium to exist. Moreover, if there is a solution for equation (25) for which $[u_2^u, u_2^l] \subset [-A, A]$ (corresponding to case (iii) in the Appendix), the equilibrium is unique.

In this case

$$\pi_2^e = E_1\left(\pi_2 \middle| u_2^l > -A \wedge u_2^u < A\right) = \Gamma\left(\pi_2^e, k\right), \tag{26}$$

implying that[14]

$$\pi_2^e = \frac{\gamma k}{\theta}. \tag{27}$$

The same expected inflation $\pi_2^e = \gamma k / \theta$ would result, if the interval $[u_2^l, u_2^u]$ lay completely outside the support of $[-A, A]$, meaning that the peg would be abolished in any case (cases (i) and (v) in the Appendix). If the interval $\left[u_2^l, u_2^u\right]$ lies partly in the support of u_2 and partly outside on the left-hand side (case (ii)), it follows that $\pi_2^e > \gamma k / \theta$, whereas $\pi_2^e < \gamma k / \theta$ if a part of $[u_2^l, u_2^u]$ lies outside $[-A, A]$ on the right-hand side (case (iv)). In the latter case it is not excluded that expected inflation π_2^e is negative. However, a non-negative inherited shock $\eta\phi_1$ continues to ensure that the expected inflation rate is positive. A negative π_2^e may occur if ϕ_1 is sufficiently negative, the persistence parameter η is high, the target output k is small, and case (iv) is the relevant one. In this situation the conditional expectation on the inflation rate given that the peg is defended may be negative (reflecting that, on average, a real depreciation is required), and due to the small k, inflation will be low if the peg is abandoned.

If π_2^e is negative, $\Gamma(\pi_2^e, k)$, the center of the interval of period 2's shocks ϕ_2 in which the peg is defended (equation (22)) may also be negative.[15] Nevertheless, a positive $\Gamma(\pi_2^e, k)$ may be considered as the normal case.

6. Comparison of Peg and Currency Board

In the previous sections, we derived the ranges of the PPP shock in which the particular regimes are maintained. In section 4 (see equation (18)), the condition to keep the currency board was derived as

$$\phi_1^2 < \frac{1}{\theta\eta^2}\left(\frac{1}{\theta}k^2\gamma^2 - \left(\gamma^2 + \theta\right)\sigma_u^2 + c^{pf}\right).$$

Assuming as in section 5, that the new shock u_t is uniformly distributed on $[-A, A]$ the length of the interval is proportional to the probability of maintaining the currency board and can also be interpreted as a measure of credibility. This probability is given by[16]

$$P(\text{maintain CB}) = \frac{1}{A}\sqrt{\frac{1}{\theta\eta^2}\left(\frac{1}{\theta}k^2\gamma^2 - \left(\gamma^2 + \theta\right)\sigma_u^2 + c^{cf}\right)}. \tag{28}$$

From section 5 (equations (22) and (27)), we know that the fixed exchange rate is defended in the second period, if

$$\Gamma\left(\pi_2^e, k\right) - \sqrt{\frac{c^{pf}}{\gamma^2 + \theta}} < \phi_2 < \Gamma\left(\pi_2^e, k\right) + \sqrt{\frac{c^{pf}}{\gamma^2 + \theta}},$$

leading to the upper boundary for the probability of defending the peg given by

$$P(\text{maintain peg}) \leq \frac{1}{A}\sqrt{\frac{c^{pf}}{\gamma^2 + \theta}}, \tag{29}$$

where equality holds for $[u_2^l, u_2^u] \subset [-A, A]$.

A comparison of the intervals in which the particular exchange rate system is maintained shows that the interval is symmetric around zero in case of a currency board but shifted by

$$\Gamma\left(\pi_2^e, k\right) = \frac{\gamma^2\pi_2^e + \gamma k}{\gamma^2 + \theta}$$

in case of a peg. When $\Gamma(\pi_2^e, k)$ is positive, which can be considered as the normal case,[17] this shift amounts to an inflation bias under a standard peg that does not exist in a currency board system. A standard peg will rather be abolished in case of a negative ϕ_2, requiring a real depreciation than in case of $\phi_2 > 0$ which leads to a positive inflation when the exchange rate remains fixed.

Moreover, the credibility of the peg hinges on the political costs c^{pf} of abandoning it, as without these costs, the probability of maintaining the peg shrinks to zero (equation (29)). In contrast, the credibility of a currency board system is not exclusively based on the political cost c^{cf} (equation (28)). A large target output k (or a low degree of inflation aversion θ), reflecting a large time-inconsistency problem that would lead to a high future inflation in case of leaving the currency board system, may prevent the policymaker from announcing its abolition even if $c^{cf} = 0$. Conversely, the probability of maintaining the currency board may be zero in spite of positive political costs c^{cf} of abolishing it if σ_u^2 is large and the expression under the square root in equation (28) becomes negative. In this case, the ability to offset shocks promptly is more important for the policymakers than avoiding the inflation that results from the time inconsistency problem.

In addition, the credibility of the currency board depends negatively on η, the parameter representing the autocorrelation of the PPP shocks as the decision of abolishing the currency board is based on the expectation on the second-period shock $E_1(\phi_2) = \eta\phi_1$. In contrast, the credibility of a standard peg does not depend on η, as the decision whether to abolish the peg is made after observing ϕ_2 and does not depend on the degree of shock persistence.

For further comparison of the credibility of the two exchange rate regimes, it is assumed that the political costs are equal in both regimes,[18] which means that $c = c^{cf} = c^{pf}$.

A currency board system is more credible, if $P(\text{maintain CB}) > P(\text{maintain peg})$ which is the case if

$$\frac{1}{A}\sqrt{\frac{1}{\eta^2\theta}\left(\frac{1}{\theta}(\gamma k)^2 - \left(\gamma^2+\theta\right)\sigma_u^2 + c\right)} > \frac{1}{A}\sqrt{\frac{c}{\gamma^2+\theta}}, \tag{30}$$

i.e. if the length of the interval of maintenance is larger in the case of a currency board than under a fixed exchange rate regime.[19] The expression can be rewritten as

$$\frac{\gamma^2 k^2}{\theta} - \sigma_u^2\left(\gamma^2+\theta\right) + c\left(1 - \frac{\theta\eta^2}{\gamma^2+\theta}\right) > 0. \tag{31}$$

This inequality shows that a currency board is more credible than a standard peg regime when the time-inconsistency problem of monetary policy is large (as represented by a high k or a low θ). In the case of a currency board arrangement, the monetary authorities are tied by law to keep the fixed parity, when its abolition was not announced in the previous period and it is not possible to create surprise inflation. Thus, the time-inconsistency problem of monetary policy is solved, which is not the case in a standard peg system. High political costs c also increase the credibility of a currency board relative to a standard peg, as

$$1 - \frac{\theta\eta^2}{\gamma^2+\theta} > 0.$$

The peg regime achieves a credibility advantage vis-à-vis a currency board, when σ_u^2 becomes so high that the ability to react to shocks is more relevant than solving the time-inconsistency problem of monetary policy—higher shock variances lead to a higher probability that large shocks may hit the economy, and hence it can be important to be able to react immediately to the shock by choosing an optimal e_2 (and thus π_2), instead of having to keep a misalignment over one period.

81

7. Conclusion

In this paper we have addressed the issue of whether a currency board arrangement is indeed more credible than a standard peg system, and what exactly may make it more credible. The essential feature of a currency board captured in our model is its longer-term nature. The currency board can only be abolished if this has been announced one period in advance—reflecting the fact that a currency board can only be abandoned after a time-consuming political process. As a result, it is not possible to create surprise inflation, and the time-inconsistency problem of monetary policy is solved completely. In contrast, a standard peg does not solve the time-inconsistency problem, because of the permanently existing escape clause from the fixed exchange rate. The policymaker can abandon the peg overnight, and he is only deterred from doing so by the political costs of exiting the exchange rate system.

The comparison of both exchange rate regimes in section 6 shows that the currency board is more credible—in the sense of having a higher probability of being maintained—if the time-inconsistency problem is the dominant one in the economy considered. The threat of high future inflation will prevent the policymaker from starting the process of abolishing the currency board unless there is a large persisting misalignment. In contrast, the currency board is more likely to be abandoned than a standard peg if shocks with a high volatility constitute the dominant problem, i.e. if the flexibility to be able to react immediately to future shocks is of paramount importance. Summarizing, its capability of solving the time-inconsistency problem makes the currency board credible, but only as long as this advantage is not outweighed by the need for stabilization of shocks occurring with a high volatility.

Appendix

In the following analysis, we investigate thoroughly the expected inflation rate in the case of a fixed exchange rate system and derive sufficient conditions under which multiple equilibria can be excluded.

As mentioned in section 5 (second subsection), for certain parameter values the boundaries u_2^u or u_2^l may lie outside the support of the new shock u_2 which is uniformly distributed. In that case, we can replace the boundaries by $-A$ or A, respectively. To determine π_2^e, we thus define $\tilde{u}_2^l$ and $\tilde{u}_2^u$ as

$$
\begin{aligned}
\tilde{u}_2^l &= \min\left\{\max\left\{u_2^l, -A\right\}, A\right\} \\
\tilde{u}_2^u &= \min\left\{\max\left\{u_2^u, -A\right\}, A\right\}.
\end{aligned}
\tag{A1}
$$

For instance, $u_2^u > A$ implies $\tilde{u}_2^u = A$.

Using (A1), we can rewrite (25) as

$$E_1\left(\pi_2\right)=\frac{\tilde{u}_2^l+A}{2A}\cdot\Gamma\left(\pi_2^e,k\right)+\frac{A-\tilde{u}_2^u}{2A}\cdot\Gamma\left(\pi_2^e,k\right)+\left(\eta\phi_1+\frac{\tilde{u}_2^u-\tilde{u}_2^l}{2A}\right)\frac{\tilde{u}_2^u-\tilde{u}_2^l}{2A}$$

$$=\left(\eta\phi_1+\frac{\tilde{u}_2^u-\tilde{u}_2^l}{2}\right)\frac{\tilde{u}_2^u-\tilde{u}_2^l}{2A}+\left(1-\frac{\tilde{u}_2^u-\tilde{u}_2^l}{2A}\right)\Gamma\left(\pi_2^e,k\right)$$

(A2)

$E_1(\pi_2)$ is a continuous function of π_2^e. The equilibrium condition is given by $\pi_2^e=E_1(\pi_2)$. To solve for the expected inflation π_2^e, we consider the following five different cases:

- **Case (i):** $u_2^u<-A$, i.e. the interval $[u_2^l,u_2^u]$ lies outside the support of u_2.

$$E_1\left(\pi_2\left|\tilde{u}_2^u=-A\right.\right)=\frac{\eta\phi_1-2A}{2}\cdot\frac{-A+A}{2A}+\frac{1-\left(-A+A\right)}{2A}\cdot\Gamma\left(\pi_2^e,k\right)$$

$$=\Gamma\left(\pi_2^e,k\right).$$

(A3)

The solution equals the free-float equilibrium rate, as monetary authorities will always revalue.

- **Case (ii):** $u_2^u>-A$ and $u_2^l<-A$, i.e. $[u_2^l,u_2^u]$ lies partly in the support of u_2. In this case the expected value of π_2 is given by:

$$E_1\left(\pi_2\left|u_2^u>-A\wedge u_2^l<-A\right.\right)$$

$$=\left(\eta\phi_1+\frac{u_2^u-A}{2}\right)\frac{u_2^u+A}{2A}+\left(1-\frac{u_2^u-A}{2A}\right)\cdot\Gamma\left(\pi_2^e,k\right)$$

$$=\Gamma\left(\pi_2^e,k\right)+\frac{u_2^u+A}{2A}\left[\eta\phi_1+\frac{u_2^u-A}{2}-\Gamma\left(\pi_2^e,k\right)\right]$$

(A4)

$$=\Gamma\left(\pi_2^e,k\right)-\frac{1}{4A}\left(-\eta\phi_1+\Gamma\left(\pi_2^e,k\right)+\sqrt{\frac{c}{\gamma^2+\theta}}+A\right)$$

$$\cdot\left[-\eta\phi_1+\Gamma\left(\pi_2^e,k\right)-\sqrt{\frac{c}{\gamma^2+\theta}}+A\right].$$

- **Case (iii):** $-A \leq u_2^l < u_2^u \leq A$, i.e. $[u_2^l, u_2^u]$ is a subset of the support interval $[-A, A]$. This leads to

$$E_1\left(\pi_2 \middle| u_2^l > -A \wedge u_2^u < A\right) = \left(\eta\phi_1 + \frac{u_2^u + u_2^l}{2}\right)\frac{u_2^u - u_2^l}{2A}$$

$$+ \left(1 - \frac{u_2^u - u_2^l}{2A}\right) \cdot \Gamma\left(\pi_2^e, k\right)$$

$$= \left(\eta\phi_1 - \eta\phi_1 + \Gamma\left(\pi_2^e, k\right)\right)\frac{1}{A}\sqrt{\frac{c}{\gamma^2 + \theta}} \qquad (A5)$$

$$+ \left(1 - \frac{1}{A}\sqrt{\frac{c}{\gamma^2 + \theta}}\right)\Gamma\left(\pi_2^e, k\right)$$

$$= \Gamma\left(\pi_2^e, k\right)$$

- **Case (iv):** $u_2^l < A$ and $u_2^u > A$, i.e. the interval $[u_2^l, u_2^u]$ lies partly in $[-A, A]$

$$E_1\left(\pi \middle| u_2^l < A \wedge u_2^u > A\right) = \frac{\left(\eta\phi_1 + \frac{1}{2}A + \frac{1}{2}u_2^l\right)\left(A - u_2^l\right)}{2A}$$

$$+ \left(1 - \frac{A - u_2^l}{2A}\right) \cdot \Gamma\left(\pi_2^e, k\right)$$

$$= \Gamma\left(\pi_2^e, k\right) + \frac{1}{4A}\left[A + \eta\phi_1 - \Gamma\left(\pi_2^e, k\right) + \sqrt{\frac{c}{\gamma^2 + \theta}}\right] \qquad (A6)$$

$$\cdot \left(A + \eta\phi_1 - \Gamma\left(\pi_2^e, k\right) + \sqrt{\frac{c}{\gamma^2 + \theta}}\right).$$

- **Case (v):** If $u_2^l > A$, i.e. the interval $[u_2^l, u_2^u]$ also lies outside of the support interval of u_2, the policymaker will always devalue.

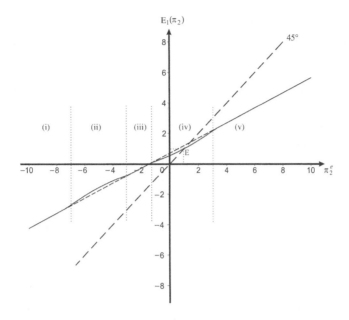

Figure A1 Expected Value of Second-period Inflation under a Peg.

Using $C := \sqrt{c(\gamma^2 + \theta)}$, we can rewrite the results for the different cases as:

$$E_1\left(\pi_2 | \text{case (i)}\right) = \Gamma\left(\pi_2^e, k\right)$$

$$E_1\left(\pi_2 | \text{case (ii)}\right) = \Gamma\left(\pi_2^e, k\right) - \frac{1}{4A}\left(-\eta\phi_1 + \Gamma\left(\pi_2^e, k\right) + C + A\right)$$

$$\left[-\eta\phi_1 + \Gamma\left(\pi_2^e, k\right) - C + A\right]$$

$$E_1\left(\pi_2 | \text{case (iii)}\right) = \Gamma\left(\pi_2^e, k\right)$$

$$E_1\left(\pi_2 | \text{case (iv)}\right) = \Gamma\left(\pi_2^e, k\right) + \frac{1}{4A}\left(-\eta\phi_1 + \Gamma\left(\pi_2^e, k\right) + C - A\right)$$

$$\left[-\eta\phi_1 + \Gamma\left(\pi_2^e, k\right) - C - A\right]$$

$$E_1\left(\pi_2 | \text{case (v)}\right) = \Gamma\left(\pi_2^e, k\right).$$

Graph of $E_1(\pi_2)$ as a Function of π_2^e

The function $E_1(\pi_2)$ is defined by cases. As u_2^l and u_2^u depend positively on π_2^e (equations (23) and (24)), the sequence of the respective intervals corresponds to the numbering of cases (i) to (v).

The graph of $E_1(\pi_2)$ lies on the straight line $\Gamma(\pi_2^e, k)$ with the slope $\gamma^2/(\gamma^2+\theta) < 1$ in the three cases (i), (iii), and (iv). By investigating the second derivative of $E_1(\pi_2)$, it follows that the function is concave in case (ii) and convex in case (iv). Thus $E_1(\pi_2)$ is a straight line with two convexities - one above (case (ii)) and one below (case (iv)) the line as illustrated in Figure A1. The position of the line and the convexities depend on the parameters, in particular on k and $\eta\phi_1$.

Conditions for a Unique Equilibrium under a Peg

In the following subsection, we derive two conditions excluding the possibility of multiple equilibria under a peg.

(A) From the description of the graph of $E_1(\pi_2)$ it is clear that the equilibrium is unique, if the function $E_1(\pi_2)$ cuts the bisecting line in the range of case (iii).

(B) Moreover, we can exclude the existence of multiplicities if the slope of $E_1(\pi_2)$ does not exceed one in the two cases (ii) and (iv), too. We take up case (iv) for further examination, the argument in case (ii) is analogous.

The first derivative of $E_1(\pi_2 \mid \text{case(iv)})$ is given by

$$\frac{dE_1\left(\pi_2 \middle| \text{case (iv)}\right)}{d\pi_2^e} = \frac{1}{2}\frac{\gamma^2\left(\gamma^2\pi_2^e + \gamma k + A\gamma^2 + A\theta - \eta\phi_1\theta - \eta\phi_1\gamma^2\right)}{A\left(\gamma^2+\theta\right)^2}$$

$$= \frac{1}{2A}\frac{\gamma^2}{\gamma^2+\theta}\left[\Gamma\left(\pi_2^e, k\right) - \eta\phi_1 + A\right].$$

The expression in equation (A7) equals one if:[20]

$$\pi_2^e = A + \eta\phi_1 + \frac{2A\theta^2 + 3\gamma^2 A\theta - \gamma^3 k + \gamma^2\eta\phi_1\theta}{\gamma^4}. \tag{A8}$$

The boundary between the ranges of cases (iv) and (v) is given by:

$$\pi_2^e = \left(A + \eta\phi_1 + \sqrt{\frac{c}{\gamma^2+\theta}}\right)\frac{\gamma^2+\theta}{\gamma^2} - \frac{k}{\gamma}. \tag{A9}$$

If that boundary lies left of the point where $dE_1(\pi_2)/d\pi_2^e = 1$, the slope of $E_1(\pi_2)$ is smaller than one also in the range of case (iv) because the function is convex in that interval. Thus, the following condition excludes multiplicities:

$$A + \eta\phi_1 + \frac{2A\theta^2 + 3\gamma^2 A\theta - \gamma^3 k + \gamma^2 \eta\phi_1\theta}{\gamma^4}$$

$$-\left[\left(A + \eta\phi_1 + \sqrt{\frac{c}{\gamma^2 + \theta}}\right)\frac{\gamma^2 + \theta}{\gamma^2} - \frac{k}{\gamma}\right] > 0$$

$$\Leftrightarrow \frac{1}{\gamma^4}\cdot\left(2A\theta^2 + 2\gamma^2 A\theta - \gamma^4 \sqrt{\frac{c}{g^2 + \theta}} - \gamma^2\theta\sqrt{\frac{c}{g^2 + \theta}}\right) > 0 \qquad (A10)$$

$$\Leftrightarrow 2A\theta\left(\gamma^2 + \theta\right) - \gamma^2\sqrt{\frac{c}{\gamma^2 + \theta}}\left(\gamma^2 + \theta\right) > 0$$

$$\Leftrightarrow 2A\theta - \gamma^2\sqrt{\frac{c}{\gamma^2 + \theta}} > 0.$$

As by assumption $\sqrt{c(\gamma^2 + \theta)} \leq A$:

$$2A\theta - \gamma^2 A > 0 \qquad (A11)$$

is sufficient for (A10). Thus, multiplicities can be excluded, if $\theta > \gamma^2/2$.

Figure A1 depicts $E(\pi_2)$ as a function of π_2^e for a set of parameters satisfying this condition (ie. $\gamma = 0.7, k = 1, c^{pf} = 1.2, A = 1.5, \eta = 0.5, \phi_1 = (-2/5)A$, and $\theta = 0.5$). The unique equilibrium is denoted by E.

*We thank Helge Berger, Hans Gersbach, Jochen Michaelis, and an anonymous referee for helpful comments. We also benefited from discussions at conferences in Göttingen (Workshop for International Economics), Warsaw (Spring Meeting of Young Economists), Madrid (European Economic Association), Strasbourg (Symposium on Banking and Monetary Policy), and Bonn (German Economic Association).

Notes

1 A thorough discussion of currency boards can be found in Williamson (1995) and Ho (2002). On Argentina's experience with the currency board see De la Torre et al. (2003) and Gurtner (2004).
2 While Ghosh et al. (2000) find that countries with a currency board experienced a higher growth, Levy-Yeyati and Sturzenegger (2001) conclude that there is a tradeoff between inflation and growth also for hard pegs. In the study of Bleaney and Francisco

(2005), the result of a lower growth of hard peg countries vanishes when regional dummies are introduced. The reason is that a large share of the hard peg countries is located in sub-Saharan Africa, the region with the lowest growth. The cited studies do not only vary in the period and the countries covered in the sample, but also in the exact classification of soft pegs and so-called intermediate regimes.

A new strand of the literature considers the transition between different exchange rate regimes—see Masson (2001), Husain et al. (2005), and Masson and Ruge-Murcia (2005).

3 Spiegel and Valderrama (2003) and Chan and Chen (2003) theoretically discuss specific aspects of currency boards. However, they do not distinguish between a normal peg and a currency board system. Spiegel and Valderrama (2003) characterize a currency board system by assuming that the costs of abandoning the fixed exchange rate decrease over time, being high in the first period, whereas the system is always abolished in the second period. In this framework, they study the effect of dollarized liabilities on monetary policy and compare the results to the case of a free float. Chan and Chen (2003) consider the possibility of increasing the credibility of a currency board by introducing irrevocable commitments to sell foreign currency at the prespecified exchange rate up to its commitment level even if the currency board is abandoned. Such a commitment could be achieved by depositing part of the currency board's foreign reserves with a third party.

4 The models also differ in the assumption on the exchange rate regime in case of abandoning the system. While Oliva et al. (2001) assume that the currency will devalue by an exogenously given amount after giving up the fixed exchange rate, in our paper the exchange rate will become flexible.

5 Of course, this is not to be understood literally in the sense that in the real world the exact date of the abolition will be announced. The point is, that the breakdown of the currency board will be expected and no surprise inflation can be created.

6 Equivalently, we could assume that shocks ϕ_t are uncorrelated, but prices are sticky instead. This would mean that inflation reflects the current shock only partially, leaving some of the required adjustment for future periods. In this sense, the parameter η can be interpreted as a degree of price stickiness.

7 This type of loss function, i.e. the policymaker's objective to create a certain amount of surprise inflation although he dislikes inflation itself, can also be derived from public finance considerations. In Sachs et al. (1996), the policymaker is tempted to create unanticipated inflation to deflate the real value of outstanding government debt. An alternative interpretation given by Sachs et al. (1996) is that the inflation tax increases with actual but falls with anticipated inflation, again giving rise to aiming at surprise inflation.

8 Of course, the size of the time-inconsistency problem also depends on γ. But it is natural to focus the interpretation on the parameters occuring in the policymaker's loss function in this context. The aim to increase output above its natural level—reflected in $k > 0$—is the basic cause for the time-inconsistency problem, and 0 measures the degree of inflation aversion.

9 In the following analysis, we use E_1 as the abbreviation for the expectation contingent on available information in the first period I_1, i.e. $E_1 = E(\cdot | I_1)$.

10 The superscript cc stands for the case in which the currency board is maintained over both periods and cf denotes the situation of abolishing the currency board in the second period.

11 If the right-hand side of equation (18) is positive, it depends negatively on 0. If it is negative, the inequality does not hold anyway.

12 The superscript pf denotes the situation of leaving the peg in the second period and pp stands for the case of maintaining the peg in both periods.

13 Obstfeld (1996) discusses the possibility of multiple equilibria in the private sector's expectations under fixed exchange rate regimes. In contrast to our model, the random shock occurs in the Lucas supply curve.

14 The inflation rate expected by the private sector is the same as in the free-float system. This result is a consequence of the assumption of a uniform distribution.

15 The case of $\pi_2^e < 0$ and $\Gamma(\pi_2^e, k) < 0$ occurs for example for the parameter values $A = 1$, $\eta = -0.3$, $\phi_1 = 0.9$, $k = 0.05$, $\gamma = 0.3$, $c = 0.5$, and $\theta = 0.6$.

16 Of course, the probability must be contained in $[0,1]$. If the expression exceeds one, the probability equals one; if the term under the square root is negative, the probability equals zero. Note that $\sigma_u^2 = A^2$.

17 See the discussion at the end of the second subsection in section 5. In particular, $\Gamma(\pi_2^e, k)$ is always positive if there is no inherited shock or if ϕ_1 is positive. The case $\Gamma(\pi_2^e, k) < 0$ may occur only if ϕ_1 is sufficiently negative.

18 Intuitively, the political costs of giving up the fixed exchange rate are higher under a currency board than under a standard peg as assumed by Irwin (2004). Higher political costs would give the currency board an additional credibility advantage.

19 As discussed at the end of the first subsection in section 5, we use the upper boundary of P. maintain peg) for the comparison of the two regimes Therefore, the credibility of the standard peg appears in a favorable light.

20 Note, that we first determine the point where the slope equals one and check afterwards if the point is in the range of case (iv).

References

Barro, Robert J. and David B. Gordon, "A Positive Theory of Monetary Policy in a Natural Rate Model," *Journal of Political Economy* 91 (1983):589–610.

Berger, Helge, Henrik Jensen, and Guttorm Schjelderup,"To Peg or Not to Peg? A Simple Model of Exchange Rate Regime Choice in Small Economies," *Economics Letters* 73 (2001):161–7.

Bleaney, Michael and Manuela Francisco, "Exchange Rate Regimes and Inflation: Only Hard Pegs Make a Difference," *Canadian Journal of Economics* 38 (2005):1453–71.

Chan, Alex and Nai-Fu Chen, "A Theory of Currency Board with Irrevocable Commitments," *International Review of Finance* 4 (2003):125–70.

Chang, Roberto and Andrés Velasco, "Financial Fragility and the Exchange Rate Regime," *Journal of Economic Theory* 92 (2000):1–34.

De la Torre, Augusto, Eduardo Levy-Yeyati, and Sergio L. Schmukler, "Living and Dying with Hard Pegs: the Rise and Fall of Argentina's Currency Board," *Economia* 5 (2003):43–99.

Drazen, Allan and Paul R. Masson, "Credibility of Policies versus Credibility of Policymakers," *Quarterly Journal of Economics* 109 (1994):735–54.

Ghosh, Atish R., Anne-Marie Gulde, and Holger C. Wolf, "Currency Boards: More than a Quick Fix?" *Economic Policy* 31 (2000):269–335.

———, *Exchange Rate Regimes,* Cambridge, MA: MIT Press (2003).

Gurtner, Francois J., "Why Did Argentina's Currency Board Collapse?" *The World Economy* 27 (2004):679–97.

Ho, Corinne, "A Survey of the Institutional and Operational Aspects of Modern-day Currency Boards," BIS working paper 110 (2002).

Husain, Aasim M., Ashoka Mody, and Kenneth S. Rogoff, "Exchange Rate Regime Durability and Performance in Developing versus Advanced Economies," *Journal of Monetary Economics* 52 (2005):35–64.

Irwin, Gregor, "Currency Boards and Currency Crises," *Oxford Economic Papers* 56 (2004): 64–87.

Kydland, Finn E. and Edward C. Prescott, "Rules Rather than Discretion: the Inconsistency of Optimal Plans," *Journal of Political Economy* 85 (1977):473–91.

Levy-Yeyati, Eduardo and Frederico Sturzenegger, "Exchange Rate Regimes and Economic Performance," *IMF Staff Papers* 47 (2001):62–98.

Lohmann, Susanne, "Optimal Commitment in Monetary Policy: Credibility versus Flexibility," *American Economic Review* 82 (1992):274–86.

Masson, Paul R., "Exchange Rate Regime Transitions," *Journal of Development Economics* 64 (2001):571–86.

Masson, Paul and Francisco J. Ruge-Murcia, "Explaining the Transition between Exchange Rate Regimes," *Scandinavian Journal of Economics* 107 (2005):261–78.

Obstfeld, Maurice, "Models of Currency Crises with Self-fulfilling Features," *European Economic Review* 40 (1996):1037–47.

Oliva, Maria-Angels, Luis A. Rivera-Batiz, and Amadou N. R. Sy, "Discipline, Signaling, and Currency Boards," *Review of International Economics* 9 (2001):608–25.

Sachs, Jeffrey, Aaron Tornell, and Andres Velasco, "The Mexican Peso Crisis: Sudden Death or Death Foretold," *Journal of International Economics* 41 (1996):265–83.

Spiegel, Mark M. and Diego Valderrama, "Currency Boards, Dollarized Liabilities, and Monetary Policy Credibility," *Journal of International Money and Finance* 22 (2003):1065–87.

Williamson, John, "What Role for Currency Boards?" *Policy Analyses in International Economics* 40 (1995).

5

CONSTITUTIONS AND COMMITMENT

The Evolution of Institutions Governing Public Choice in Seventeenth-Century England

Douglass C. North and Barry R. Weingast

Source: *Journal of Economic History 49*, 4, 1989, 803–832.

The article studies the evolution of the constitutional arrangements in seventeenth-century England following the Glorious Revolution of 1688. It focuses on the relationship between institutions and the behavior of the government and interprets the institutional changes on the basis of the goals of the winners— secure property rights, protection of their wealth, and the elimination of confiscatory government. We argue that the new institutions allowed the government to commit credibly to upholding property rights. Their success was remarkable, as the evidence from capital markets shows.

This article focuses on the political factors underpinning economic growth and the development of markets—not simply the rules governing economic exchange, but also the institutions governing how these rules are enforced and how they may be changed. A critical political factor is the degree to which the regime or sovereign is committed to or bound by these rules. Rules the sovereign can readily revise differ significantly in their implications for performance from exactly the same rules when not subject to revision. The more likely it is that the sovereign will alter property rights for his or her own benefit, the lower the expected returns from investment and the lower in turn the incentive to invest. For economic growth to occur the sovereign or government must not merely establish the relevant set of rights, but must make a credible commitment to them.

A ruler can establish such commitment in two ways. One is by setting a precedent of "responsible behavior," appearing to be committed to a set of rules that he or she will consistently enforce. The second is by being constrained to obey a set of rules that do not permit leeway for violating commitments. We have very seldom observed the former, in good part because the pressures and continual strain of fiscal necessity eventually led rulers to "irresponsible behavior" and the violation of agreements. The latter story is, however, the one we tell.

We attempt to explain the evolution of political institutions in seventeenth-century England, focusing on the fundamental institutions of representative government emerging out of the Glorious Revolution of 1688—a Parliament with a central role alongside the Crown and a judiciary independent of the Crown. In the early seventeenth century fiscal needs led to increased levels of "arbitrary" government, that is, to expropriation of wealth through redefinition of rights in the sovereign's favor. This led, ultimately, to civil war. Several failed experiments with alternative political institutions in turn ushered in the restoration of the monarchy in 1660. This too failed, resulting in the Glorious Revolution of 1688 and its fundamental redesign of the fiscal and governmental institutions.

To explain the changes following the Glorious Revolution we first characterize the problem that the designers of the new institutions sought to solve, namely, control over the exercise of arbitrary and confiscatory power by the Crown.[1] We then show how, given the means, motives, and behavior of the king during this century, the institutional changes altered the incentives of governmental actors in a manner desired by the winners of the Revolution. These changes reflected an explicit attempt to make credible the government's ability to honor its commitments. Explicit limits on the Crown's ability *unilaterally* to alter the terms of its agreements played a key role here, for after the Glorious Revolution the Crown had to obtain Parliamentary assent to changes in its agreements. As Parliament represented wealth holders, its increased role markedly reduced the king's ability to renege. Moreover, the institutional structure that evolved after 1688 did not provide incentives for Parliament to replace the Crown and itself engage in similar "irresponsible" behavior. As a consequence the new institutions produced a marked increase in the security of private rights.

As evidence in favor of our thesis, we study the remarkable changes in capital markets over this period. After the first few years of the Stuarts' reign, the Crown was not able systematically to raise funds. By the second decade of the seventeenth century, under mounting fiscal pressure, the Crown resorted to a series of "forced loans," indicating that it could not raise funds at rates it was willing to pay. Following the Glorious Revolution, however, not only did the government become financially solvent, but it gained access to an unprecedented level of funds. In just nine years (from 1688 to 1697), government borrowing increased by more than an order of magnitude. This sharp change in the willingness of lenders to supply funds must reflect a substantial increase in the perceived commitment by the government to honor its agreements. The evidence shows that these expectations were borne out, and that this pattern extends well into the next century.

Since we focus on the evolution and impact of the political institutions, of necessity we slight the larger economic and religious context, even though in many specific instances these larger religious and economic issues were proximate sources of actions and policies that we describe. Indeed, no history of the seventeenth century is complete that does not describe both the growing markets and the evolving organizations that accompanied economic expansion as well as the persistent religious tensions, particularly between Catholic and Protestant. A more thorough study, one far too big for this essay, would attempt to integrate the change in opportunity costs of both the economic and *religious* actors as they intermingled with the immediate political issues on which we concentrate. But having said that, it is important to stress that our central thesis is a key part of the whole process by which an institutional framework evolved in England. We contend that while the English economy had been expanding and its markets growing, in order for economic development to continue the constraints described below had to be altered.

This essay proceeds as follows. Section I develops the importance of political institutions and the constitution and their relevance for the sections that follow. Sections II and III develop the narrative of the period, focusing respectively on England under the Stuarts and on the evolution of new institutions and secure rights following the Glorious Revolution. Section IV contains the central part of our analysis and reveals why these institutions made *credible* the government's commitment to honoring its agreements. Sections V and VI present our evidence from public and private capital markets.

I. THE ROLE OF POLITICAL INSTITUTIONS AND THE CONSTITUTION

The control of coercive power by the state for social ends has been a central dilemma throughout history. A critical role of the constitution and other political institutions is to place restrictions on the state or sovereign. These institutions in part determine whether the state produces rules and regulations that benefit a small elite and so provide little prospect for long-run growth, or whether it produces rules that foster long-term growth. Put simply, successful long-run economic performance requires appropriate incentives not only for economic actors but for political actors as well.

Because the state has a comparative advantage in coercion, what prevents it from using violence to extract all the surplus?[2] Clearly it is not always in the ruler's interests to use power arbitrarily or indiscriminately; by striking a bargain with constituents that provides them some security, the state can often increase its revenue. But this alone is insufficient to guarantee consistent behavior on the part of the ruler.

The literature on transactions costs and institutions emphasizes that while parties may have strong incentives to strike a bargain, their incentives after the fact are not always compatible with maintaining the agreement: compliance is always a potential problem. This literature also notes that when ex post problems are anticipated ex ante, parties will attempt to alter incentives, devising institutions or constitutions that promote compliance with bargains after the fact. Oliver Williamson says:

> Transactions that are subject to ex post opportunism will benefit if appropriate actions can be devised ex ante. Rather than reply to opportunism in kind, the wise [bargaining party] is one who seeks both to give and receive "credible commitments." Incentives may be realigned and/

93

or superior governance structures within which to organize transactions may be devised.[3]

Problems of compliance can be reduced or eliminated when the institutions are carefully chosen so as to match the anticipated incentive problems. Under these circumstances, parties are more likely to enter into and maintain complex bargains that prevent abuse of political control by the state.

To succeed in this role, a constitution must arise from the bargaining context between the state and constituents such that its provisions carefully match the potential enforcement problems among the relevant parties. The constitution must be *self-enforcing* in the sense that the major parties to the bargain must have an incentive to abide by the bargain after it is made.[4]

Consider a loan to a sovereign in which the ruler promises to return the principal along with interest at a specified date. What prevents the sovereign from simply ignoring the agreement and keeping the money? Reputation has long been noted as an important factor in limiting a sovereign's incentive to renege, and this approach has recently been formalized in the elegant models of modern game theory. The "long arm of the future" provides incentives to honor the loan agreement today so as to retain the opportunity for funds tomorrow. In many of the simple repeated games studied in the literature, this incentive alone is sufficient to prevent reneging.

Yet it is also well known that there are circumstances where this mechanism alone fails to prevent reneging.[5] In the context of current Third World debt, Jeremy Bullow and Kenneth Rogoff show that repeat play alone is insufficient to police reneging, and that more complex institutional arrangements are necessary. Similarly, in the medieval context, John Veitch has recently shown that medieval states had strong but not unambiguous incentives to develop reputations for honoring debt commitments, and that by and large they did so. Nonetheless, a series of major repudiations occurred when a second and typically more plentiful source of funds emerged. Edward I confiscated the wealth of the Jews in the late thirteenth century once the Italian merchants began operating on a larger scale; Phillip IV confiscated the wealth of the Templars under similar circumstances.

One important context in which repeat play alone is insufficient to police repudiation concerns variations in the sovereign's time preference or discount rate. States in early modern Europe were frequently at war. Since wars became increasingly expensive over the period, putting increasingly larger fiscal demands on the sovereign, the survival of the sovereign and regime was placed at risk. When survival was at stake, the sovereign would heavily discount the future, making the one-time gain of reneging more attractive relative to the future opportunities forgone. Indeed, there is a long history of reneging under the fiscal strain accompanying major wars.[6]

The insufficiency of repeat play and reputation to prevent reneging provides for the role of political institutions. If the problem of variable discount rates is sufficiently important, individuals have an incentive to devise institutions to protect against reneging. It is important to observe that these institutions do not substitute for reputation-building and associated punishment strategies, but complement them.[7] Appropriately chosen institutions can improve the efficacy of the reputation mechanism by acting as a constraint in precisely those circumstances where reputation alone is insufficient to prevent reneging. The literature on the theory of the firm is replete with illustrations of how specific institutional features of the firm are necessary to mitigate an incentive problem that is insufficiently policed by reputation.[8]

This view provides an endogenous role for political institutions. Restrictions on the ex post behavior of the state improve the state's ability to maintain its part of bargains with constituents, for example, not to expropriate their wealth.[9] As we show below, this logic can be used to interpret the institutional changes at the time of the Glorious Revolution.

Our view also implies that the development of free markets must be accompanied by some credible restrictions on the state's ability to manipulate economic rules to the advantage of itself and its constituents. Successful economic performance, therefore, must be accompanied by institutions that limit economic intervention and allow private rights and markets to prevail in large segments of the economy. Put another way, because constitutional restrictions must be self-enforcing, they must serve to establish a credible commitment by the state to abide by them. Absolutist states which faced no such constraint, such as early modern Spain, created economic conditions that retarded long-run economic growth.

The ability of a government to commit to private rights and exchange is thus an essential condition for growth. It is also, as we shall see, a central issue in the constitutional debate in seventeenth-century England.

II. ENGLAND UNDER THE STUARTS: LIMITED CREDIBLE COMMITMENT TO RIGHTS

After the Crown passed from the Tudors to the Stuarts in 1603, revenue problems and their consequences become increasingly important. At this time the king was expected to "live on his own," that is, to fund the government in the manner of an extended household. The execution of public laws and expenditures was not subject to a public budgetary process, and Parliament played only a small role in the decisions over expenditure and investment. The Crown therefore had considerable discretionary power over how and on what the money was spent. Parliament's main source of influence over policy resulted from its power to provide the Crown with tax revenue, typically for extraordinary purposes such as various wars. Parliament was also responsible for granting the Crown its revenue from other sources, such as customs, but in practice, the Stuarts, particularly Charles I, continued to collect the revenue without parliamentary consent.

Throughout the Stuart period revenue from traditional sources did not match expenditures. While figures for government expenditures during the Stuart period have not been collected as systematically as for the period following the Glorious Revolution, the following picture emerges.

At the beginning of the Stuarts' reign, Crown lands produced roughly half the annual revenue. To make up annual shortfalls, the Crown regularly resorted to sale of these lands.[10] Following the war with Spain in 1588, Elizabeth had sold 25 percent of the lands, raising £750,000. Still, James I inherited sizable debts from Elizabeth's war. Over his reign (1603–1624), another 25 percent of Crown lands were sold, and the remainder went during the reign of his son, Charles I (1625–1641). Sale of a major portion of a revenue-producing asset for annual expenses indicates the revenue problem was endemic. It also implies that over time the revenue problem had to get worse, for with every sale the expected future revenue declined. And, indeed, as Table 1 shows, for the year 1617 total revenue did not match expenditures, leaving a deficit of £36,000 or of just under 10 percent of expenditures.

Under the Stuarts, therefore, the search for new sources of revenue became a major priority. An important new source which produced conflict between the Crown and Parliament was the raising of customs revenues through new "impositions." Indeed, in the 1630s such increases almost brought financial solvency, and with it the ability of the Crown to survive without calling Parliament.

Another method used by the Crown to raise revenue was to demand loans. The Crown did not, however, develop a systematic, regular relationship with moneyed interests, negotiating a series of loans in which it honored today's agreements because it wanted to avail itself of future loan opportunities. Indeed, just the opposite occurred. The Stuarts secured most of their loans under threat; hence they are known as "forced loans," of which more later. Repayment was highly unpredictable and never on the terms of the original agreement. In the forced loan of 1604/5 the Crown borrowed £111,891, nominally for one year; "although ... ultimately repaid, £20,363 ... was still due as late as December 1609."[11] The forced loan of 1617 (just under £100,000) was not repaid until 1628. The Crown behaved similarly on loans from 1611 and 1625. As time went on, such loans came to look

Table 1 REVENUE SOURCES AND EXPENDITURE LEVELS, 1617

Revenue Source	Amount (£/year)
Crown Lands	£80,000
Customs and "new impositions"	190,000
Wards, and so forth (besides purveyance)	180,000
Total Revenue	450,000
Total Expenditures	486,000
Deficit	36,000

Source: David Hume, *The History of England* (Indianapolis, 1983), appendix to "The Reign of James I."

more and more like taxes, but because these were nominally loans the Crown did not need parliamentary assent.[12]

The Crown's inability to honor its contractual agreements for borrowed funds is a visible indicator of its readiness to alter the rights of private parties in its own favor. Despite the significant incentive provided by the desire to raise funds in the future, the Crown followed its short-run interests, reneging on the terms to which it had agreed. As noted above, this type of behavior was not unique to England.

A second revenue-raising method was the sale of monopolies. While not the most important source of new revenue, it is particularly instructive because of its economic consequences.[13] In order to raise revenue in this manner, the Crown used patents in a new way. Originally designed to protect and promote the invention of new processes, patents came to be used to "reduce settled industries to monopolies under cover of technical improvements."[14] From a revenue standpoint, the best sources of new monopoly rights involved an economic activity that was profitable and whose participants were not part of the king's constituency. This led to a systematic search for and expropriation of quasi-rents in the economy. Moreover, as we will see in the next section, the Crown utilized a different system for enforcing these grants than that used for the older mercantilist controls, and one that was considerably more responsive to the Crown's interests. The system involved circumventing existing rights and the institutions designed to protect these rights.

Grants of monopoly clearly disrupted both existing economic interests in the targeted activity and those who depended on it (for example, suppliers and consumers). Monopoly grants thus acted as a tax that, since it expropriated the value of existing investment as well as future profits, was considerably greater at the margin than a 100 percent tax on profits. This risk lowered the rewards from all such new investments and hence discouraged their undertaking.

Beyond grants of monopoly, James, and especially Charles, used a variety of other, more subtle forms of expropriation of wealth. Because so many dimensions of public policy were involved, the political risk to citizens increased substantially over previous times. One important example was expansion of the peerage by the Crown, again in exchange for revenue.[15] While this expansion had broad social, cultural, and ideological implications, it also had significantly negative effects on existing peers. Expansion of the size of the House of Lords altered the value of an existing seat since it limited the ability of existing lords to protect themselves against the Crown.[16] Between the coronation of James I and the outbreak of the Civil War, the Stuarts' sale of peerages doubled the number of lay peers.

Governmental power was used in other ways to raise revenue. Employing the ancient power of purveyance, agents of the Crown seized various goods for "public purposes," paying prices well below market. Purveyance brought in an annual "unvoted" tax of £40,000 in the 1620s.[17] James also put hereditary titles up for sale: for example, offering to sell the title of baronet for £1,095 and promising that only a fixed number would be sold. This brought in £90,000 by 1614. But James soon reneged on this, lowering the price and selling more than the promised number. By 1622 the price had fallen to £220.[18] Through the court of wards, the Crown managed the estates which had passed to minors. These were often openly run for the advantage of the Crown, not infrequently extracting the full value of the estate.[19] The Crown put "dispensations" up for sale, that is, the use of its powers to allow specific individuals to dispense with a specific law or restriction. "Sale" of this power was often used in conjunction with the enforcement or threat of enforcement of regulations that had not been enforced for years. At times the Crown simply seized the property of citizens. An especially egregious example occurred in 1640 when "the government seized £130,000 of bullion which private merchants had placed in the Tower for safety, causing numerous bankruptcies."[20]

This clash of interests between the king on the one hand and wealth holders and tax payers on the other was a major reason why the Crown failed to obtain grants from Parliament. In exchange for grants, Parliament demanded conditions and limits on the king's power that he was unwilling to accept. Parliamentary interests thereby exacerbated the problem they were attempting to eliminate. Withholding funds worsened the Crown's fiscal problems and intensified its search for alternative sources of revenue.

Institutional Basis of Stuart Policymaking

Both Parliament and the common law courts fought the Crown's use of monopolies and other changes in rights in its search for revenue. Parliament regularly presented the king with "grievances," lists of problems caused by the king that it wanted addressed.[21] Grievances were part of a larger bargaining process in which Parliament attempted, in exchange for revenue, to limit the Crown's power and its use of policymaking to expropriate wealth. Because of ever-present revenue problems, the Stuarts often called on Parliament for additional revenue. Parliamentary interests regularly demanded that in exchange for revenue the Crown respect traditional property rights and institutions: for example, that it cease declaring new monopolies. The Crown, in turn, was evidently unwilling to accept these restrictions and hence Parliament was often dissolved without having come to an agreement with the Crown.[22]

Attempts were also made to prevent the Crown's using the law to further its objectives. In 1624 Parliament passed the much-noted Statute of Monopolies prohibiting the use of patents to grant monopolies to existing businesses in exchange for revenue. In this manner it attempted to assert the traditional rights of secure property. In addition common law courts handed down the famous "Case of Monopolies" in 1601, making the Crown's use of monopolies illegal in common law. The Crown, however, was able to evade these restrictions. While these evasions often took forms of questionable legality, so long as the Crown did not depend on Parliament for revenue, it was able to use them in practice.

Understanding the subsequent institutional reaction to these royal policies requires that we study the institutional means by which the Crown ran the government. For our purposes three elements of the royal powers and institutions were central to the Crown's success. First, a major source of power for the Crown was the royal prerogative, by which the Crown issued proclamations or royal ordinances. By this means it could issue new rules; that is, it had quasi-legislative powers without recourse to Parliament. Crown rules were enforced, not through the common law court system, but through the prerogative courts and included the power to suspend laws and to dispense with laws for specific individuals.[23]

Second, the Star Chamber, combining legislative, executive, and judicial powers, played a key role. On issues concerning prerogative, the Star Chamber had come to have final say, and could in certain circumstances reverse judgments against the Crown.[24]

Finally, since the Crown was personally responsible for day-to-day government operations, it paid the judges, who served at its pleasure. Increasingly the Stuarts used their power over judges to influence their judgments. Judges—Chief Justices Coke (1616/17) and Crew (1627)— were openly fired for ruling against the Crown. Ultimately this tactic produced judges who by and large supported the Crown.[25]

The effect of these institutions was to combine in the Crown executive, legislative, and judicial powers, limiting external institutional checks. While royal proclamations did not have the same legal status as an act of Parliament, they were enforced directly through the common law courts. While these courts did not have to go along with the king—and often did not—ultimately he won through the higher court, the Star Chamber. Thus, while the common law was often against the king, the king could alter the jurisdiction of a dispute by issuing proclamations. The expanded use of the Star Chamber and the successful running of the government for substantial periods without Parliament limited the ability of traditional institutions to constrain the Crown. Effective possession of legislative and judicial powers also gave the Crown the ability to alter economic and political rights when it was convenient to do so. In comparison with the previous century, the rights that Parliament and other institutions were designed to protect were considerably less secure.

In response, a coalition formed against the Crown, seeking to preserve personal liberties, rights, and wealth. This raised the stakes of the political game to the various economic interests—in particular the value of opposing the king rose. Moreover, because the Crown attempted to extract from its own constituents a major portion of the advantages it had bestowed on them, the value of supporting the king declined. It is clear, however, that the opposition would have been unlikely to succeed, had the English Crown, like its French or Spanish counterpart, had a standing army with which to quell the initial uprising.

Civil War to Glorious Revolution

Eventually the opposition openly challenged the king, leading the country into civil war. But the ultimate opposition victory was not inevitable.

After seizing power, the opposition modified the institutions underpinning the Crown's most egregious behavior. Not surprisingly, the Star Chamber was abolished in 1641 by an act requiring that all cases involving property be tried at common law, thus adding another milestone along the route toward supremacy of the common law, so favorable to property rights. Restrictions against monopolies were now enforced. In an attempt to prevent the Crown from ruling for substantial periods without calling a Parliament, Parliament passed the Triennial legislation, which called for regular standing of the Parliament. The royal administrative apparatus was dismantled, and with it the royal ability to impose regulatory restrictions on the economy in conflict with the rights enforced by the common law courts.

Important changes reduced restrictions on labor mobility. Land tenure modifications simultaneously favored the development of private rights and markets and reduced the Crown's political hold over this once-important part of its constituency.[26] New and profitable opportunities resulted from lifting restrictions on land use and improving markets.

After the Civil War a number of political innovations occurred, including the abolition of the monarchy and the House of Lords. Their failure led to pressure to bring back the king. With the Restoration of the monarchy in 1660, England was once again ruled by the Stuarts. It is critical for understanding the next series of events to notice a striking limitation of the institutional changes prior to the Restoration. While the details differ considerably, the next twenty-five years repeated the events of the earlier Stuarts' reign in one important respect. Political struggle with constituents resulted in the king's arbitrary encroachment. By far the most important instance of this—indeed, the one resulting in a nation united against the Crown—concerned the rechartering of local governments and political power. Rechartering came in reaction to the Whig-led "Exclusion Crisis"; it allowed the Crown to disenfranchise much of the opposition and thereby reduce impediments to its exercise of power. Of the 104 members of Parliament returned in the mid-1680s by the boroughs receiving new charters, only one Whig was elected. This converted "what had been a formidable, aggressive and highly organized opposition party into an impotent collection of a few individuals."[27]

Had the Crown succeeded in this political maneuver, there would be few checks on its powers, because it allowed the Crown to disenfranchise *any* opposition. But between 1686 and 1688, James II, having disenfranchised the Whig opposition, turned on his own supporters, causing his own constituents to join the opposition to remove him in the Glorious Revolution of 1688.

III. INSTITUTIONAL CHANGES FOLLOWING THE GLORIOUS REVOLUTION

At the same time it extended the Crown to William and Mary, Parliament restructured the society's political institutions in the Revolution Settlement. To understand the new institutions it is necessary to see clearly the problem the parliamentary interests sought to solve. The early Stuarts' use of the Star Chamber and the rechartering of the later Stuarts threatened the liberties and wealth of citizens, leaving them with little protection against Crown attempts to appropriate their wealth. But experience showed that simply removing the powers underpinning arbitrary behavior was insufficient to prevent abuse. Controlling Crown behavior required the solving of financial problems as well as appropriate constraints on the Crown. So the Glorious Revolution also ushered in a fiscal revolution.[28] The main features of the institutional revolution are as follows.

First and foremost, the Revolution initiated the era of parliamentary "supremacy." This settled for the near future the issue of sovereignty: it was now the "king in Parliament," not the king alone.[29] No longer would the Crown, arguing the "divine rights of kings," claim to be above the law. Parliamentary supremacy established a permanent role for Parliament in the on-going management of the government and hence placed a direct check on the Crown. The Crown no longer called or disbanded Parliament at its discretion alone.

Parliament also gained a central role in financial matters. Its exclusive authority to raise new taxes was firmly reestablished; at the same time the Crown's independent sources of revenue were also limited. For the Crown to achieve its own goals this meant it had to establish successful relations with Parliament. Shortly thereafter, Parliament gained the never-before-held right to audit how the government had expended its funds. Parliamentary veto over expenditures, combined with the right to monitor how the funds they had voted were spent, placed important constraints over the Crown.

Another important institutional change focused on the royal prerogative powers. These were substantially curtailed and subordinated to common law, and the prerogative courts (which allowed the Crown to enforce its proclamations) were abolished. At the same time the independence of the judiciary from the Crown was assured. Judges now served subject to good behavior (they could only be removed if convicted for a criminal offense or by action of both houses of Parliament) instead of at the king's pleasure. The supremacy of the common law courts, so favorable to private rights, was thereby assured.

Because the Stuarts had violated the personal liberties of their opponents (excessive bail, no writ of Habeas Corpus) as a means of raising the cost of opposition, reducing the arbitrary powers of the Crown resulted not only in more secure economic liberties and property rights, but in political liberties and rights as well. Political rights were seen as a key element of protection against arbitrary violations of economic rights.

Two final points are worth emphasizing. First, part of the glue that held these institutional changes together was the successful dethroning of Charles I and, later, James II. This established a credible threat to the Crown regarding future irresponsible behavior. The conditions which would "trigger" this threat were laid out in the Revolution Settlement, and shortly thereafter in the Declaration of Rights. Second, although parliamentary supremacy meant that Parliament dictated the form of the new political institutions, it did not assume the sole position of power within the government, as it did after the Civil War or in the nineteenth century. While substantial constraints were placed on the king, these did not reduce him to a figurehead.

IV. THE GLORIOUS REVOLUTION AND ENGLAND'S CREDIBLE COMMITMENT TO SECURE RIGHTS

The institutional innovations increased dramatically the control of wealth holders over the government. Since fiscal crises inevitably produced pressure on the Crown to break its agreements, eliminating unilateral control by the Crown over key decisions was a necessary component of the new institutions. As previously described, this occurred in two ways. First, by requiring Parliament's assent to major changes in policies (such as changing the terms of loans or taxes), the representatives of wealth holders could veto such moves unless they were also in their interest. This allowed action in times of crisis but eliminated the Crown's unilateral action. Second, several other ways for the Crown to renege on promises were eliminated, notably its ability to legislate unilaterally (through the prerogative), to by-pass Parliament (because it had an independent source of funds), or to fire judges who did not conform to Crown desires.

Two factors made the new arrangements self-enforcing. First, the credible threat of removal limited the Crown's ability to ignore the new arrangements. Second, in exchange for the greater say in government, parliamentary interests agreed to put the government on a sound financial footing, that is, they agreed to provide sufficient tax revenue. Not only did this remove a major motive underlying the exercise of arbitrary power, but for the new King William it meant he could launch a major war against France. The arrangement proved so satisfactory for the king that a host of precedents were set putting the new division of powers on a solid footing. As a consequence of these institutional changes, private rights became fundamentally more secure.[30]

Institutional and Political Constraints on Parliament

The triumph of Parliament raises the issue of why it would not then proceed to act just like the king? Its motives were no more lofty than those of the Crown. But the institutional outcome effectively deterred Parliament from similar behavior. Robert Ekelund and Robert Tollison provide the following general analysis:

> Higher costs due to uncertainty and growing private returns reduced industry demands for regulation and control in England. All this strengthened the emergent constitutional democracy, which created conditions making rent-seeking activity on the part of both monarch and merchants more costly. When the locus of power to rent-seeking shifted from the monarch to Parliament ... the costs of supply of regulation through legislative enactment rose.[31]

They suggest that the natural diversity of views in a legislature raises the cost of supplying private benefits in the form of favorable regulation.

The framework of institutional evolution we have described complements their story. The embedding of economic and political freedoms in the law, the interests of principals (for example, merchants) in a greater measure of freedom, and the ideological considerations that swept England in the late seventeenth century combined to play a role in institutional change. The new constitutional settlement endowed several actors with veto power, and thus created the beginnings of a division or separation of powers.[32] Supplying private benefits at public expense now required the cooperation of the Crown, Parliament, and the courts. Only the Crown could propose an expenditure, but only Parliament could authorize and appropriate funds for the proposal, and it could do so solely for purposes proposed by the Crown. Erskin May summed up this procedure as, "The crown demands, the Commons grants, and the Lords assent to the grant." A balance of power between the Crown and Parliament significantly limited publicly supplied private benefits.[33]

Three other political factors help explain why the new era of parliamentary supremacy did not simply transfer power from the Crown to Parliament. In 1641 the centralized administrative apparatus which enforced royal attempts to alter rights and property was destroyed. The absence of such a structure prevented either the Crown or Parliament from similar encroachment. Because a new apparatus—even one that was initially quite limited—would allow its future expansion, many interests could be counted upon to oppose its initiation.

Second, the commercially minded ruling Whig coalition preferred limited government and especially limited political interference with the common law courts. Parliament was thus *politically* constrained from intervention in the courts. As R. Braun observes:

> the Whig oligarchy was anxious to avoid encroachment upon the privacy of the business of those groups from which it drew its support. Not only the constitutional and institutional framework, but also the prevailing ideological basis of the [Whigs and their constituents] prevented the central administrative apparatus of the British government from developing [a major regulatory and control function].[34]

Widespread regulation of markets by Parliament along the line of Colbert in France (or the Stuarts) would have led to a clash with the common law courts. Thus the political independence of the courts limited potential abuses by Parliament. Combined with the explicit institutional limits on Crown intervention, this assured the courts important and unchallenged authority in large areas of economic activity.

Third, the creation of a politically independent judiciary greatly expanded the government's ability credibly to promise to honor its agreements, that is, to bond itself. By limiting the ability of the government to renege on its agreements, the courts played a central role in assuring a commitment to secure rights. As we will see, this commitment substantially improved the government's ability to raise money through loans.

Thus the institutional and political changes accompanying the Glorious Revolution significantly raised the predictability of the government. By putting the government on a sound financial basis and regularizing taxation, it removed the random component of expropriation associated with royal attempts to garner revenue. Any interest group seeking private gain had now to get approval from both the Crown and the Parliament.

V. THE FISCAL REVOLUTION

To see the profound effects of the Glorious Revolution, we focus on one important element of public finance, government borrowing. Since capital markets are especially sensitive to the security of property rights, they provide a unique and highly visible indicator of the economic and political revolution that took place. Indeed, they are one of the few means for empirically evaluating the effects of the Glorious Revolution.

Prior to the Glorious Revolution, payments on loans were subject to manipulation by the Crown; rescheduling and delays in payments were common. As indicated in Table 2, money was raised through forced loans in 1604/5, 1611/2, 1617, and 1625. In each instance the Crown did not honor its terms. In the loan of 1617, for example, James I raised £100,000 in London at 10 percent for the period of one year. At the end of the year, although James paid the interest, he refused to repay the principal and demanded that the loan be renewed. No interest was paid over the next several years, and each year another renewal was "agreed" to. In 1624 Charles I lowered the interest rate to 8 percent; however, he did not pay any interest, nor did he repay the principal until 1628. Such behavior was hardly designed to gain the confidence of potential sources of loans. As Robert Ashton concludes, the "cavalier treatment which the Crown meted out to its creditors, and more especially to those most unwilling lenders who made more or less compulsory contributions through the medium of the Corporation of London" helps

Table 2 FORCED LOANS BY THE EARLY STUARTS, 1603–1625

Year	Amount	Rate (percent per year)	Repayment
1604/5	£111,891	10%	£20,362 unpaid as of Dec. 1609
1611/2	116,381	10	£112,000 unpaid as of Jul. 1616
1617[a]	96,466	10[b]	Unpaid until 1628
1625[c]	60,000	8	Unpaid until 1628

[a] Extension in 1624 secured by Crown lands.
[b] Unilaterally lowered by Charles I in 1624 to 8%.
[c] Secured by Crown lands.

Source: Robert Ashton, *The Crown and the Money Market, 1603–1640* (Oxford, 1960), chaps. 2 and 5.

explain why London and the money interests supported the parliamentary cause.[35] Nor did the Stuarts attempt to develop a major international source of loans.[36]

Several financial innovations occurred under the late Stuarts, including some that were to play a key role in the "financial revolution" after 1688, for example, making notes "assignable," thus allowing them to be sold. The recent work of Glenn Nichols suggests that financial arrangements under the late Stuarts were far superior to those under the early Stuarts. Nonetheless, fiscal stress pressed the system to its limits, and led to a partial repudiation in the famous "stop the exchequer" in 1672. The debt in question, over a million pounds, shows that the late Stuarts—until that time, at least—could raise substantial sums.[37]

Institutional Innovations

A series of institutional innovations during the war with France (1689–1697) changed the way the government sought credit, facilitating the regularization of public finance. First, the government began as a regular practice to earmark new taxes, authorized by statute for each new loan issue, to pay the interest on all new long-term loans. By earmarking taxes beforehand, parliamentary interests limited the king's discretion each year over whether to pay bondholders their interest.

Second, the first large, long-term loan (£1,000,000) secured by new taxes took place in 1693. By 1694, however, these funds were exhausted. When the government sought a new large loan, it invited the subscribers to incorporate as the Bank of England. The Bank was responsible for handling the loan accounts of the government and for assuring the continuity of promised distributions. Certain restrictions were also imposed: the Bank could not lend the Crown money or purchase any Crown lands without the explicit consent of Parliament. As Macaulay observed over a century ago, this created a strong instrument of the Whig party (and hence of commercial interests). Since loans to the Crown went through the Bank, "it must have instantly stopped payment if it had ceased to receive the interest on the sum which it had advanced to the government."[38] The government had thus created an additional, private constraint on its future behavior by making it difficult to utilize funds of a current loan if it failed to honor its previous obligations.

Two other changes are worth noting. In 1698 the government created a separate fund to make up deficiencies in the event that the revenue earmarked for specific loans was insufficient to cover the required distributions (as was the case for several loans). This explicitly removed the component of risk associated with each loan due to its ties to a specific tax.[39] Second, during this period the milling of coins began, reducing the debasement of the currency due to shaving of coins.

Government Loans, 1688–1740

Thus were the institutional foundations of modern capital markets laid in England. These institutional changes were more successful than their originators had hoped.

The original subscription to the Bank of England, for instance, was expected to be slow and possibly unsuccessful. In actuality, one-third of the loan was subscribed on the first day and another third during the next two days. Ten days later the loan was fully subscribed.

To see the dramatic results of the fiscal revolution, we turn to the public finances during this period. Table 3 provides information on governmental expenditures and debt. On the eve of the Revolution governmental expenditures were about £1.8 million, reflecting a slow but steady increase over two decades.[40] Government debt was limited to about £1 million, or between 2 and 3 percent of GNP (estimated to be £41 million). Moreover, at a time when Holland was borrowing £5 million long term at 4 percent per year, the English Crown could only borrow small amounts at short term, paying between 6 and 30 percent per year.[41]

Table 3 GROWTH OF GOVERNMENT DEBT, 1618–1740 (£ million)

Year	Governmental Expenditure[1]	Debt[2]	Prices[3] (1701 = 100)
Stuart England			
1618[4]	£0.5	£0.8	
mid-1630s[5]	1.0	1.0	
1680[6]	1.4		113
1688[6]	1.8	1.0[7]	99
Post Glorious Revolution			
1695	6.2	8.4	116
1697	7.9	16.7	122
1700	3.2	14.2	115
1710	9.8	21.4	122
1714	6.2	36.2	103
1720	6.0	54.0	102
1730	5.6	51.4	95
1740	6.2	47.4	100
1750	7.2	78.0	95

Note: Because these figures are obtained from a variety of sources, they are intended solely to provide an indication of underlying trends. Figures for expenditures and debt after the Glorious Revolution are most reliable.

Sources:
1. Government Expenditure, post-1688: B. R. Mitchell, **British Historical Statistics** (Cambridge, 1988), chap. 11, table 2.
2. Debt, post-1688: Mitchell, *British Historical Statistics,* chap. 11, table 7.
3. Prices: Mitchell, *British Historical Statistics,* chap. 14: 1680–97, table 1, part A, "consumer goods"; 1697–1750, part B, "consumer goods."
4. Government Expenditure and Debt, 1618: David Hume, *The History of England* (Indianapolis, 1983), "Appendix to the Reign of James I."
5. Government Expenditure and Debt, mid-1630s: Derek Hirst, *Authority and Conflict: England, 1603–1658* (Cambridge, MA, 1986), p. 174.
6. Government Expenditure, 1680 and 1688: C. D. Chandaman, *The English Public Revenue, 1660–1688* (Oxford, 1975), appendix 2, table 7, "Total Available for Ordinary Purposes."
7. Debt, 1688: H. Fisk, *English Public Finance* (New York, 1920), p. 93.

The Revolution radically altered this pattern. In 1697, just nine years later, governmental expenditures had grown fourfold, to £7.9 million. The immediate reason for the rise was the new war with France. But importantly, the government's ability to tap the resources of society increased. This is evidenced by the increase in the size of government debt, which grew during the nine years of war from £1 million to nearly £17 million. This level of debt—approximately 40 percent of GNP—was previously unattainable. Moreover, the ability of the new government to finance a war at unprecedented levels played a critical role in defeating France. To put these figures in modern perspective, a trillion-dollar economy would have begun the period with $25 billion of debt, which in just nine years would grow to almost $400 billion.

Following the war, both government expenditures and the amount financed through debt were substantially higher than previous levels. By 1720 government debt was over fifty times the 1688 level and on the order of GNP. Financing wars by borrowing had another remarkable benefit. Previous instances of unexpected large wars were nearly always accompanied by large fiscal demands, the search for sources of revenue, and consequently unfavorable demands on wealth holders. Such demands were virtually eliminated by the new methods of finance. Another evidence of the new regime's increased predictability is indicated by the series of price changes. Despite sustained deficits resulting in the enormous increase in debt, government policy did not result in inflationary finance.[42]

At the same time that the scope of governmental borrowing increased, however, the market rate charged the government fell. Its initial long-term loans in the early 1690s were at 14 percent (see Table 4). By the end of the 1690s the rate was about half, between 6 and 8 percent. The rate continued to fall over the next two decades so that, by the 1730s, interest rates were 3 percent.

Table 4 GOVERNMENT LONG-TERM BORROWING: INTEREST RATES, 1693–1739 (selected loans)

Date[a]	Amount	Interest	How Funded
Jan 1693	£723,394	14.0%	Additional excise
Mar 1694	1,000,000	14.0	Duties on imports
Mar 1694	1,200,000	8.0	Additional customs and duties
Apr 1697	1,400,000	6.3	Excise and duties
Jul 1698	2,000,000	8.0	Additional excise duties
Mar 1707	1,155,000	6.25	Surplus from funds of five loans from 1690s; duties
Jul 1721	500,000	5.0	Hereditary revenue of Crown
Mar 1728	1,750,000	4.0	Coal duties
May 1731	800,000	3.0	Duties
Jun 1739	300,000	3.0	Sinking fund

[a] Date of royal assent to loan act.

Source: P. G. M. Dickson, *The Financial Revolution in England* (New York, 1967), tables 2, 3, and 22.

These numbers are impressive in two ways. First, the amount of wealth now available for use by others increased tremendously. Second, at the same time as governmental borrowing increased, the interest rate fell. Sharp increases in demand accompanied by decline in rates indicate that the overall risk associated with governmental behavior decreased considerably despite the enormous increase in the size of the debt. As the society gained experience with its new institutions, particularly their predictability and commitment to secure rights, expectations over future actions began to reflect the new order.

These changing expectations were directly reflected in the capital market response. The new institutional underpinnings of public finance provided a clear and dramatic credible commitment that the government would honor its promises and maintain the existing pattern of rights. While underlying economic conditions were surely an important component of the large increase in debt, they alone can not explain the *suddenness* with which the debt increased, nor its magnitude. Even though the later Stuarts were more financially successful than their predecessors, nothing that came before the Glorious Revolution suggests the dramatic change in capital markets that it unleashed.

VI. IMPLICATIONS FOR PRIVATE CAPITAL MARKETS

Our thesis is that the credible commitment by the government to honor its financial agreements was part of a larger commitment to secure private rights. The latter was clearly a major factor for the institutional changes at the time of the Glorious Revolution. Data on general economic activity are sparse, so we cannot perform a major test of our thesis, but we can provide some support. As evidence we turn to the development of private capital markets and the necessary evolution of the financial foundation of long-run economic success.

While it is clear that the institutions underlying private capital markets go back at least several centuries, it is widely agreed among economic historians that private capital markets date from the early eighteenth century.[43] The rise of banks and an increasingly differentiated set of securities, providing a relatively secure means of saving, brought individual savings into the financial system. Ashton reports that this "meant that men were less concerned than their fathers ... to keep quantities of coin, bullion, and plate locked up in safes or buried in their orchards and gardens."[44]

The institutions leading to the growth of a stable market for public debt provided a large and positive externality for the parallel development of a market for private debt. Shortly after its formation for intermediating public debt, the Bank of England began private operations. Numerous other banks also began operations at this time. This development provided the institutional structure for pooling the savings of many individuals and for intermediation between borrowers and lenders. A wide range of securities and negotiable instruments emerged in the early eighteenth century and these were used to finance a large range of activities.[45]

Phyllis Deane summarizes the development of private capital markets along-side that for public capital:

> The secondary effects of the Bank's financial transactions on behalf of the government stemmed from the new financial instruments which were thus created ... and because [the instruments] issued by a credit-worthy borrower are themselves readily saleable, the effect was further to lubricate the channels linking savings and investment by creating a large stock of negotiable paper assets which new savers could buy. Similarly, the deposits from private sources could also be used as a basis for further credit to the private sector.[46]

As a consequence, private capital markets flourished.

Several sources of evidence support our claims. First, research on interest rates for various forms of private credit reveals that these roughly parallel rates on public credit.[47] Falling private rates increased the range of projects and enterprises that were economically feasible, thus promoting the accumulation of capital. As L. S. Pressnell concludes, the "accumulation of capital in the 18th century, which the declining trend of interest rates ... clearly indicates, appears in this light as a major social and economic achievement."[48] Unfortunately the data from the first half of the eighteenth century, in contrast to those from the second half, are sketchy, and for the period prior to the Glorious Revolution, almost nonexistent.

Second, large-scale trading in private securities dates from this period.[49] Figure 1 shows the growth of one component of the market, short-dated securities. In the early 1690s the volume of these securities averaged £300,000 per year. Ten years later, volume averaged £3,400,000 per year, and by the early 1710s, £11,000,000 per year. While growth trailed off after the collapse of the South Sea Bubble, the market from 1715 to 1750 was far larger than that prior to the Revolution.

Third, the period saw the growth and development of banks. The Bank of England was followed shortly by numerous other banks in London. By the 1720s these numbered about 25. By 1750 there were 30; by 1770, 50; and by 1800, 70. While banks in areas outside London began to appear in large numbers only after 1750, Ashton argues that many of these areas were integrated into a national capital market much earlier.[50] "Inland bills and promissory notes played a considerable part in the trade of all parts of England and Wales. But nowhere had their use extended so far as in the north-west. The ubiquity of the bill was probably the reason why in this area formal banking made its appearance relatively late."[51]

The final set of evidence centers on the Bank of England's private activities in three areas. (1) Discounted bills. Systematic data on the Bank's discounting operations apparently do not survive. Nonetheless, sporadic reports are available and indicate a considerable growth of activity during the first few decades of the Bank's operations. For 1699 data reveal the following volume of notes

Figure 1 GROWTH OF THE STOCK MARKET: 1690–1750. *Source*: P. G. M. Dickson, *The Financial Revolution in England* (Landon, 1967), Appendix C.

discounted: 13–31 June, £8,534; 27 June-4 July, £14,000. By 1730 the *median* day's volume was over £10,000, and by 1760 days over £100,000 were common.[52] (2) Notes in circulation. During the eighteenth century the Bank's notes became a major medium of exchange, first in London, and then throughout England.[53] In the first two years of the Bank's operations the volume of notes grew to about £760,000 (see Table 5). By 1720 they numbered £2,900,000, and they were above £4,500,000 by 1730 and for the next few decades. (3) Drawing accounts. This early form of demand deposit seems to have become systematized about twenty years after the Bank's founding.[54] As shown in Table 5, drawing accounts were quite modest in the late 1690s. By 1720 they numbered more than a million pounds, growing to over two million by 1730. To summarize, the Bank expanded operations over several types of private credit. By 1720, a little over 25 years after the Bank's establishment, these sums reached substantial levels, showing the steady growth in financial services for private economic activity.

Thus it appears that the growth of private capital markets paralleled that of public capital markets. This development mobilized the savings of large numbers of individuals and, by mid-century, provided financial services in an integrated, national market. These funds appear to have financed a large variety of business activities and played a necessary role in the economic expansion throughout this

Table 5 THE BANK OF ENGLAND'S NOTES AND
DRAWING ACCOUNTS, 1698–1750 (£ thousands)

Year	Notes in Circulation	Drawing Accounts
1698	£1,340	£100
1720	2,900	1,300
1730	4,700	2,200
1740	4,400	2,900
1750	4,600	1,900

Note: Figures for 1720–1750 are averages for the five-year period beginning with the year listed. *Source*: John Clapham, *The Bank of England: A History* (New York, 1945), vol. 1: *1694–1797*.

century.[55] While these activities have not been studied in detail as they have for the period following 1750, 1688 appears to be a more abrupt break with the past than 1750. Returning to our main thesis, this growth indicates that the attempts to maintain secure private rights were largely successful. Although the evidence cannot be used to discern the precise level of security, it shows that it was substantial. A more systematic test awaits future research on these markets.

CONCLUSION

In this essay we have provided a brief account of the successful evolution of institutional forms that permitted economic growth to take place in early modern England. It is clear from this discussion of a century of civil war and revolution, however, that these institutional innovations did not arise naturally. Rather they were forced, often violently, upon the Crown. The Crown, however, nearly won the struggle. Had a standing army existed in England, it would have been under the control of the Crown, and the political and economic future of England would very likely have been different, potentially more in keeping with that of France and Spain.

We have shown how the political institutions governing society can be considered endogenously. Fiscal constraints and a revenue-seeking Crown, problems exacerbated by an uncooperative Parliament, created a situation of insecure rights in which the wealth and welfare of individual citizens were at risk. Prior to the Glorious Revolution, institutions such as the Star Chamber enabled the Crown to alter rights in its favor in a manner that parliamentary interests were hard pressed to resist.

Given their means and motives, the triumph of parliamentary interests in the Glorious Revolution led to five significant institutional changes. First, it removed the underlying source of the expediency, an archaic fiscal system and its attendant fiscal crises. Second, by limiting the Crown's legislative and judicial powers, it limited the Crown's ability to alter rules after the fact without parliamentary consent. Third, parliamentary interests reasserted their dominance of taxation issues, removing the ability of the Crown to alter tax levels unilaterally. Fourth, they assured their own role in allocating funds and monitoring their expenditure. The Crown now had to deal with the Parliament on an equal footing—indeed, the latter clearly had the advantage with its now credible threat of dethroning a sovereign who stepped too far out of line. Fifth, by creating a balance between Parliament and the monarchy— rather than eliminating the latter as occurred after the Civil War— parliamentary interests insured limits on their own tendencies toward arbitrary actions. In combination, these changes greatly enhanced the predictability of governmental decisions.

What established the government's commitment to honoring its agreements— notably the promise not to appropriate wealth or repudiate debt—was that the wealth holders gained a say in each of these decisions through their representatives in Parliament. This meant that only if such changes were in their own interests would they be made. Increasing the number of veto players implied that a larger set of constituencies could protect themselves against political assault, thus markedly reducing the circumstances under which opportunistic behavior by the government could take place.

In the story we have told, the emergence of political and civil liberties was inextricably linked with economic freedom. Opportunistic behavior on the part of the Crown was often accompanied by abuse of the opposition's political rights. The Crown had jailed people without charge or for lengthy periods prior to trial, and had required excessive bail to raise the costs of opposition. Hence protection of political liberties emerged as a component of the political protection of economic rights.

The principal lesson of our article is that the fundamental institutions of representative government—an explicit set of multiple veto points along with the primacy of the common law courts over economic affairs—are intimately related to the struggle for control over governmental power. The success of the propertied and commercially minded interests led to institutions that simultaneously mitigated the motive underlying the Crown's drive to find new sources of revenue and also greatly constrained the behavior of the government (now the "king in Parliament" rather than the king alone). Though these institutional innovations failed to anticipate the decline of the power of the Crown and ascendancy of Parliament in the latter half of the eighteenth century, the system successfully balanced power for well over sixty years. In comparison with the previous century or with the absolutist governments of the continent, England's institutional commitment to secure rights was far stronger. Evidence from capital markets provides a striking indication of this.

Recent research that has significantly upgraded France's economic performance before the French Revolution has led to an overhauling of traditional interpretations of British as well as French economic history.[56] If England and France were almost at parity in economic performance, the clear implication is that institutions per se—and in particular, the institutional changes we have described— were not so revolutionary after all. Similarly, the elaborate bureaucratic structure inherited from Louis XIV was not such a hindrance to economic growth. But that conclusion ignores the consequences that followed. It is clear that the institutional changes of the Glorious Revolution permitted the drive toward British hegemony and dominance of the world. England could not have beaten France without its financial revolution; and the funds made available by the growth in debt from 1688 to 1697 were surely a necessary condition for England's success in this war with France as well as the next one (1703–1714), from which England emerged the major power in the world.[57]

France, like England, had an ongoing fiscal crisis; and Louis XIV did come to terms with his constituents to gain more revenue early in his reign. But his success was temporary, not rooted in fundamental institutional change, and it was outdistanced by the magnitude of the English success. France's economy lived on borrowed time, and ultimately the unresolved institutional contradictions resulted in bankruptcy and revolution.[58]

The comparison of growth rates alone is therefore insufficient to judge economic parity. While in 1690 France was the major European power, it declined in power and stature relative to England over the next century. More wars followed those at the turn of the eighteenth century, so that in 1765—at the end of the Seven Years War, in which France suffered a humiliating defeat—it had lost its New World colonies (Canada and Louisiana) and was in financial peril from which it did not recover until after the revolution. The contrast between the two economies in mid-century is striking: in 1765 France was on the verge of bankruptcy while England was on the verge of the Industrial Revolution.[59]

It is always tempting to claim too much. Would Britain really have followed the path of continental countries if the Stuarts had won? Would there have been a first Industrial Revolution in England? One could tell a plausible counterfactual story that put more weight on the fundamental strength of English property rights and the common law that had evolved from the Magna Carta and which would have circumscribed royal behavior and ultimately forced "responsible government." One could point to the robust economy (particularly at the local level) that existed in seventeenth-century England despite the uncertainties we have described. There exists neither a definitive theory of economic growth which would define for us the necessary and sufficient conditions nor the evidence to reconstruct the necessary counterfactual story. But we are convinced from the widespread contemporary Third World and historical evidence that *one* necessary condition for the creation of modern economies dependent on specialization and division of labor (and hence impersonal exchange) is the ability to engage in secure contracting across time and space. That entails low transaction costs per exchange. The creation of impersonal capital markets is the single most important piece of evidence that such a necessary condition has been fulfilled. And we have told a story of how these institutions *did* come about in England.

As evidence against the counterfactual thesis, we again point to the financial revolution. A change of this magnitude in such a short period clearly hinged on the underlying constitutional reorganization. Because the financial revolution played a critical role in England's long-run success, the implication is that even if other forces would ultimately have led England to success under the Stuarts, they would have done so more slowly and probably less decisively.

We have thus shown how institutions played a necessary role in making possible economic growth and political freedom. Furthermore, it appears from our survey of seventeenth-century England, from the historical performance of other economies, and from performance records of current Third World economies, that the circumstances fostering secure rights and hence economic growth are relatively rare and deserve further exploration.

*The authors gratefully acknowledge the helpful comments of Robert Bates, Gary Cox, Paul David, Aaron Director, John Ferejohn, Jack Goldstone, Max Hartwell, Derek Hirst, Leonard Hochberg, Paul Milgrom, Glenn Nichols, Roger Noll, Alvin Rabushka, Thomas Sargent, Kenneth Shepsle, Gordon Tullock, and David Weir. They also thank Elisabeth Case for her editorial assistance. Barry Weingast thanks the National Science Foundation (grant no SES-8617516) for partial support.

Notes

1 Our discussion of the events prior to the Glorious Revolution (1603 to 1688) simply characterizes this period; it does not model or explain it. Moreover, since our history emphasizes the problems the winners (the Whigs) sought to solve, it necessarily contains strong elements of "Whig" history.

2 Throughout late medieval and early modern times, if rulers did not maintain a comparative advantage in coercion, they soon failed to be rulers. See William McNeill, *Pursuit of Power* (Chicago, 1983); Douglass North, *Structure and Change in Economic History* (New York, 1981); and Gordon Tullock, *Autocracy* (Dordrecht; 1987).

3 Oliver Williamson, *Economic Institutions of Capitalism* (New York, 1985), pp. 48–49.

4 Our formulation of the problem draws on the "new economics of organization." Application of this approach to political problems—and especially to the problem of providing institutions to enforce bargains over time—is just beginning. See, however, Barry R. Weingast and William Marshall, "The Industrial Organization of Congress; or Why Legislatures, Like Firms, Are Not Organized as Markets," *Journal of Political Economy*, 96 (Feb. 1988), pp. 132–63; and Terry Moe, "The New Economics of Organization," *American Journal of Political Science*, 28 (Aug. 1984), pp. 739–77.

5 Paul R. Milgrom, Douglass C. North, and Barry R. Weingast, "The Role of Institutions in the Revival of Trade, Part I: The Medieval Law Merchant," Mimeo., Hoover Institution, Stanford University, 1989. Jeremy Bullow and Kenneth Rogoff, "A Constant Recontracting Model of Sovereign Debt," *Journal of Political Economy*, 97 (Feb. 1989), pp. 155–78; John M. Veitch, "Repudiations and Confiscations by the Medieval State" this JOURNAL, 46 (Mar. 1986), pp. 31–36.

6 Joseph Schumpeter, "Fiscal Crises and the Tax State," in Richard A. Musgrave and Alan T. Peacock, eds., *Classics in the Theory of Public Finance* (London, 1962). John Hicks, *A Theory of Economic History* (Oxford, 1969). North, *Structure and Change*, and Veitch, "Repudiations and Confiscations." This is not to say that the sovereign will *never* honor commitments, only that he will not *always* do so.

7 Weingast and Marshall, "Industrial Organization of Congress"; Milgrom, North, and Weingast, "The Role of Institutions."

8 Vertical integration is the standard example: because of potential transactions problems due to "asset specificity" or "appropriable quasi-rents," firms that internalize the problem via vertical integration outperform those which do not. See Williamson, *Economic Institutions.*

9 In this sense our argument parallels that of James Buchanan and Geoffrey Brennan, who argue that the "recognition of the temporal dimensionality of choice provides one 'reason for rules'— rules that will impose binding constraints on choice options after the rules themselves have been established." James Buchanan and Geoffrey Brennan, *Reason of Rules* (Cambridge, 1981), p. 67.

10 See, for example, Derek Hirst, *Authority and Conflict: England, 1603–1658* (Cambridge, MA, 1986), chap. 4, and Lawrence Stone, *The Crisis of the Aristocracy, 1558–1641* (Oxford, 1965).

11 Robert Ashton, *The Crown and the Money Market, 1603–1640* (Oxford, 1960), p. 35.

12 Ashton, *Crown and the Money Market*, p. 36. Richard Cust, in his recent study of the 1626 forced loan, provides several instances of sanctions imposed on individuals refusing to provide funds: leading refusers were "either committed to prison or pressed in readiness for service abroad." Richard Cust, *The Forced Loans and English Politics* (Oxford, 1987), p. 3.

13 Robert B. Ekelund, and Robert D. Tollison, *Mercantilism as a Rent-Seeking Society* (College Station, 1981).

14 W. Price, *English Patents of Monopoly* (Boston, 1906). Examples include soap, tobacco, and starch.

15 F. W. Maitland, *Constitutional History of England* (Cambridge, 1908); Wallace Notestein, *The Winning of the Initiative by the House of Commons* (London, 1924); and Stone, *Crisis of the Aristocracy.*

16 There were two separate reasons for this: the total number of voters was increasing, and the expansion added new members whose views systematically differed from those of existing nobles. The exchange that brought new nobles to the Lords undoubtedly entailed a commitment of support for the king.

17 Hirst, *Authority and Conflict*, p. 103; and C. Hill, *Century of Revolution, 1603–1714* (2nd edn., New York, 1980), chap 4. See also John Kenyon, *Stuart England* (2nd edn., New York, 1985).

18 Hirst, *Authority and Conflict*, pp. 113–14.

19 Ibid., p. 103.

20 C. Hill, *Century of Revolution*, p. 103.

21 For details, see Notestein, *The Winning of the Initiative.*

22 Part of the Crown's motivation appears to have been a desire to move toward the absolutism prevalent on the continent, notably in France and Spain. As Kenyon observes, at the onset of the seventeenth century, "any further adjustments [in the balance of power between Parliament and the Crown] were likely to be at the expense of Parliament" (Kenyon, *Stuart England*, p. 43). It almost succeeded. Hirst describes debates in Parliament in which the participants were explicitly concerned with this possibility (Hirst, *Authority and Conflict*, chap. 3).

23 Dispensations for individuals, like most powers under the Stuarts, were put up for sale (Maitland, *Constitutional History*, pt. IV).

24 The Star Chamber, in which the most egregious examples of arbitrary power occurred, became a regular feature of Stuart England. See Maitland, *Constitutional History*, and Friedrich A. Hayek, *Constitution of Liberty* (Chicago, 1960), chap. 11.

25 Coke's dismissal, "the first of a judge in over thirty years, ushered in a period of increasing royal pressure on the bench: in Charles's reign two other chief justices, Crew and Heath, and one chief baron of the exchequer court, Walter, were to follow Coke" (Hirst, *Authority and Conflict*, p. 121). See also Hayek's excellent and extensive discussion, in *Constitution of Liberty*, chap. 11.

26 See H. J. Perkins, "The Social Causes of the British Industrial Revolution," *Transactions of the Royal Historical Society*, 18 (1968). Hill, discussing the 1660 Act confirming the abolition of feudal tenures, notes that in the eighteenth century Blackstone called this Act a greater boon to property owners than the Magna Carta itself *(Century of Revolution*, p. 127).

27 Jones, *Revolution of 1688*, pp. 47, 50. As B. W. Hill observes, James's efforts to repack the constituencies "came near to success in every respect but one: they alarmed landed society, Tory as well as Whig." See B. W. Hill, *The Growth of Parliamentary Parties: 1689–1742* (Hamden, 1976).

28 P. G. M. Dickson, *The Financial Revolution in England* (New York, 1967).

29 See, for example, Maitland, *Constitutional History*, pp. 298–301, or David Keir, *The Constitutional History of Modern Britain Since 1485* (London, 1966).

30 Jones, on p. 6 of the *Revolution of 1688*, concludes: "None of its architects could have predicted its effectiveness in securing the liberties, religion, property and independence of the nation after so many previous attempts had failed."

31 Ekelund and Tollison, *Mercantilism*, p. 149.

32 We emphasize, however, that this division of powers was not a clear-cut system of checks and balances. Nor can it be considered a true separation of powers. The designers of the new institutions were far more worried about constraints on the Crown than on protecting the Crown from encroachments by Parliament. Thus in the latter half of the eighteenth century, the power of the Crown diminished, and with it the constraints (or checks) on Parliament. See A. F. Pollard, *The Evolution of Parliament* (London, 1926).

33 Erskin May, *Parliamentary Practice* (17th edn., London, 1966; 1st edn., 1844). Further investigation of the procedures devised at this time is called for.

34 R. Braun, "Taxation, Sociopolitical Structure, and State-Building: Great Britain and Brandenburg-Prussia," in Charles Tilly, ed., *Formation of Nation States in Western Europe* (Princeton, 1975).

35 Ashton, *Crown and the Money Market*, p. 113.

36 Ashton reports only two such loans, the second of which (£58,400 in 1616) was still outstanding in 1636. Here too the Stuarts failed to develop a reputation for honoring agreements. By the 1630s the Crown was unable to borrow at all from either international sources or London.

37 See Glenn O. Nichols, "English Government Borrowing Before the Financial Revolution," manuscript, Anderson College, 1988. For details about the stop of the exchequer, see Dickson, *Financial Revolution*. In exchange for its short-term notes, the Crown gave new long-term loans. Much of the interest from the latter was still unpaid at the time of the Glorious Revolution, however.

38 Lord Macaulay, *The History of England,* (London, 1914), vol. V, p. 2438.

39 As David Ogg explains: "Thenceforth, the investor knew that, in lending money on a specified tax, he had parliamentary guarantee for the security of this investment, based not only on the particular fund, but on the whole of the national revenue." David Ogg, *England in the Reigns of James II and William III* (Oxford, 1955), p. 413. Regarding the second, see pp. 422–25.

40 C. D. Chandaman, *The English Public Revenue: 1660–88* (Oxford, 1975).

41 For figures on government debt and GNP estimates, see B. R. Mitchell, *British Historical Statistics* (Cambridge, 1988). On interest rates, see Sidney Homer, *A History of Interest Rates* (New Brunswick, 1963), p. 149.

42 Prices rose a little over 20 percent between 1690 and 1710 (and then fell again between 1710 and 1730). But the enormous increase in debt during this period suggests that the government did not attempt to meet its debt obligations through inflationary finance. The modern view of inflation suggests two further inferences (see, for example,

Thomas Sargent, *Rational Expectations and Inflation* [New York, 1986]). Since inflation in part reflects expectations about future governmental finance of deficits, the lack
of major increases in prices suggests that the market did not expect inflationary finance.
Since this pattern was maintained for several decades, it indicates that these expectations were "confirmed" in the sense that new information about current governmental
behavior did not change expectations. Robert Barro provides evidence that budget deficits had almost no effect on prices from 1700 until the Napoleonic campaigns. Robert
Barro, "Government Spending, Interest Rates, Prices, and Budget Deficits in the UK,
1701–1918," *Journal of Monetary Economics*, 20 (Sept. 1987), pp. 221–48.

43 This section summarizes the conclusions of the literature on the early eighteenth cen-
tury. See, for example, T. S. Ashton, *An Economic History of England* (London, 1955);
John Clapham, *The Bank of England* (New York, 1945); Phyllis Deane, *The First
Industrial Revolution* (2nd edn., Cambridge, 1979); Dickson, *Financial Revolution*;
Peter Mathias, *The First Industrial Nation* (2nd edn., London, 1983); and E. Powell,
The Evolution of the Money Market: 1385–1915 (London, 1966).

44 Ashton, *Economic History*, p. 178.

45 "The essence of the financial revolution of the early 18th century was the development
of a wide range of securities in which new mercantile and financial companies—the
chartered trading companies, the partnership banks, the insurance companies, etc.—
could flexibly and safely invest and disinvest" (Deane, *Industrial Revolution*, p. 185).

46 Ibid., pp. 184–85.

47 Clapham, *Bank of England*, L. S. Pressnell, "The Rate of Interest in the 18th Century,"
in L. S. Pressnell, ed., *Studies in the Industrial Revolution* (London, 1960), p. 181; and
Homer, *A History of Interest Rates*.

48 Pressnell, "Rate of Interest," p. 181.

49 As Dickson notes, "The development of a market in securities in London in the period
1688–1756 was one of the more important aspects of the Financial Revolution."
Dickson, *Financial Revolution*, p. 457.

50 See Charles P. Kindleberger, *Financial History of Western Europe* (London, 1984), p.
74; and Mathias, *Industrialized Nation*. The earliest provincial bank cited by Mathias
was in Bristol (1716), and there were not more than a dozen in 1750. By 1784, however, there were 120, and by 1800, 370 (Mathias, p. 151).

51 Ashton, *Economic History*, p. 185. Ashton's claim is also supported by the study of credit
instruments other than those provided by banks. B. L. Anderson, discussing the rise of
inland bills, notes that their legal status was markedly improved in the first years of the
eighteenth century. "This recognition of the bill as a transferable means of payment was a
decisive turning point in the development of the English credit system. . . . [The] English
practice made it an instrument of credit in a system of accommodation paper that was
highly responsive to the community's demand for money." B. L. Anderson, "Money and
the Structure of Credit in the 18th Century," *Business History*, 85 (No. 1, 1970), p. 90.

52 Clapham, *Bank of England*, p. 126.

53 While other banks issued notes, by far the largest source for most of the period we are
studying are those of the Bank of England. Throughout this period, these notes were
convertible to gold. See D. M. Joslin, "London Private Bankers, 1720–1785," in E. M.
Carus-Wilson, ed., *Essays in Economic History*, vol. 2, pp. 340–59.

54 The only year before 1720 reported by Clapham is 1698.

55 An additional piece of evidence concerns investment in transportation infrastructure,
which also increased at this time. By 1724 there were over 1,160 miles of river open to
navigation, double that of a century earlier. See Ashton, *Economic H*, p. 73; Mathias,
Industrial Nation, p. 100. While the "canal age" is usually dated at mid-century, it "did
not spring to life in 1750" but was the "conclusion of a mounting momentum of effort";
Mathias, *Industrial Nation*, p. 100. Both Ashton and Mathias noted that there were two

big booms in improving rivers during this period, one at the turn of the century and one between 1718 and 1720.

56 See, for example, F. Crouzet, "England and France in the Eighteenth Century," in Max Hartwell, ed., *Causes of the Industrial Revolution in England* (London, 1967).

57 Dickson, *Financial Revolution.*

58 See David Bien, "Offices, Corps, and a System of State Credit: The Uses of Privilege under the Ancient Regime," in K. Baker, ed., *The French Revolution and the Creation of Modern Political Culture* (New York, 1987), vol. 1, pp. 89–114; Philip Hoffman, "Taxes, Fiscal Crises, and Representative Institutions: The Case of Early Modern France," manuscript, California Institute of Technology, 1988; and Hilton Root and Daniel Ingberman,"Tying the King's Hands," manuscript, University of Pennsylvania, 1987.

59 Jeffrey Williamson's recent, if controversial, work provides further support for this thesis. It suggests that British growth rates rose substantially once the long series of wars with France, ending with the Napoleonic campaign, were over. If during this period England's growth rates were not substantially larger than France's, its ability to spend more on war without bringing financial peril meant at most lower domestic consumption and investment, and hence came at the expense of growth. France's near bankruptcy shows that, in comparison, it was living on borrowed time. See Jeffrey G. Williamson, "Why Was British Growth so Slow During the Industrial Revolution?" this JOURNAL, 64 (Sept. 1983), pp. 687–712.

6

THE FINANCIAL CRISIS OF 1825 AND THE RESTRUCTURING OF THE BRITISH FINANCIAL SYSTEM*

Larry Neal

Source: *Federal Reserve Bank of St. Louis Review*, 80, 3 (May/June), 1998, 53–76.

Today's financial press reports regularly on evidence of systemic risks, financial fragility, banking failures, stock market collapses, and exchange rate attacks throughout the global financial network of the 1990s. To a financial historian, these reports simply reprise similar concerns and risks in numerous episodes of financial innovation and regime change in the past. True, the 1990s have the peculiar feature of emerging markets among newly independent states that are trying to market either their government debt or securities issued by their former state enterprises. But this situation does not eliminate the relevance of past episodes; it merely limits it to fewer periods. The period after World War I had many of the same problems, for example, although policymakers then subsumed them largely under the issues of whether, when, and how to return to the pre-war gold standard that had created a much more benign financial system worldwide. Policymakers of that time were much more interested than their modern counterparts in exploring lessons from the past.

For example, William Acworth's classic study, *Financial Reconstruction in England, 1815-1822,* was published in 1925. He argued convincingly that the severe deflationary policy followed by the government and the Bank of England after peace in 1815 had prolonged and deepened unnecessarily the economic troubles accompanying the transition from a wartime to a peacetime economy. Nevertheless, the British government and the Bank of England pursued much the same strategy after World War I, again taking six years after the peace treaty to resume convertibility—and at the prewar standard. Again, monetary ease that followed resumption led to a surge of prosperity, speculative ventures in the capital markets, and eventual collapse of the financial system. The difference was that in 1825-26, there was a systemic stoppage of the banking system, followed by widespread bankruptcies and unemployment, while in 1931 there was abandonment of the gold standard, followed by imperial preference and worldwide movements toward autarky. So much for the lessons of history!

119

As pessimistic as Acworth was in assessing the consequences of Britain's first return to the gold standard in 1821, the consequences of the ensuing monetary expansion and speculative boom that ended in the spectacular collapse at the end of 1825 proved to be not so dire in the long run for the British economy. The policy changes that affected the monetary regime—the exchange rates, the structure of the banking sector, the role of the Bank of England and the management of the government's debt—while minor in each particular and slow to take effect, were cumulatively effective in laying the basis for Britain's dominance in the world financial system until the outbreak of World War I. This outcome contrasts sufficiently with the disappointing pattern of British economic progress during the twentieth century after both World War I and World War II that perhaps we should take a fresh look at the economic and financial transition after the Napoleonic Wars. What caused the problems identified by Acworth that culminated in the stock market crash of 1825 and the English banking system's failure to withstand its impact? More important, why did the British government's relatively modest reforms prove to be so effective in the long run? Perhaps we can glean more useful lessons for today's policymakers than previous historians have been able to provide.

The argument developed in this paper is that the common element in all the problems of Britain's first return to gold arose from the pressures of coping with vastly increased informational uncertainties within the existing structure of English institutions.[1] These problems started with the Treasury itself, confronted by the difficulties of servicing the huge government debt accumulated during the Napoleonic Wars and deprived of its primary source of revenue, the income tax. They continued within the Bank of England, forced now to take on new responsibilities while searching for new sources of revenue to replace its wartime profits. They were compounded by the response of the London capital market, which produced a bewildering array of new financial assets to its customers to replace the high-yielding government debt now being retired. All this left the London private banks and their corresponding country banks—as well as their customers in agriculture, trade, and manufacturing—floundering in the resulting confusion. The government's piecemeal reforms, introduced during the crisis of 1825 and its immediate aftermath, provided smoother patterns of tax collections and interest disbursements, established Bank of England branches throughout England, stimulated country bank competition with joint-stock companies outside of London, and eliminated the Bubble Act of 1720. Even the bankruptcy laws began to be rewritten in 1831.[2]

These disparate reforms made marginal improvements in the efficiency of information gathering and processing by the government, the central bank, the banking system, and the stock market while preserving the separation of functions among them. Maintaining these "firewalls" among the types of institutions making up the financial sector of the British economy diminished the immediate impact of the reforms, but it enabled them to become increasingly effective over time. True, crises continued to arise throughout the rest of the century as the British economy was subjected to repeated shocks of wars, famines, frauds, and foreign defaults. But the evolving financial sector of the British economy surmounted each crisis with increasing confidence, and all the while these firewalls were pre-served. The firewalls meant that relationships among financial intermediaries and financial markets had to be maintained by short-term contracts in a competitive market environment rather than by regulations imposed by centralized authority with long-term rigidity.

The focal point for these new market relationships was the market for dis-counted commercial bills that arose rapidly in importance after the crisis of 1825.[3] Once again, as in earlier crises and in those that were to follow until World War I, the British financial sector was able to find a market solution to the problems created by its relatively inefficient and disparate financial institutions. In the longer run, the flexibility of response provided by the combination of markets and financial intermediaries coexisting in the British financial system enabled it to withstand exogenous shocks and to finance expansion of the real economy. To elucidate and elaborate this argument, I analyze, in turn, the shock to the financial system of shifting from wartime to peacetime finance in 1821, the financial crisis that occurred at the end of 1825, the Bank of England's efforts to pick up the pieces, and, finally, the rise of a market in discounted commercial bills that put things right again—for a while. The lessons of each episode highlight the impor-tance of appraising the financial system as a whole, rather than focusing on what appears to be its weakest link. In retrospect, it seems critical to allow information to flow freely among the various parts of the system in order that markets may form to price and intermediate risk. At the time, the Bank of England refused to divulge important information and remained aloof from market activity until it was forced to act, usually too late. Only gradually were these lessons learned; now is not the time to forget them.

THE SHOCK: FROM WARTIME TO PEACETIME FINANCE IN 1821

In the expansion of war finance that the Napoleonic Wars induced in Britain, all parts of the British financial system prospered. At the top, the Treasury benefited from increased taxes, especially the income tax, as well as the expanded mar-ket for its debt, both long-term, funded debt and short-term, unfunded debt. The Bank of England profited throughout the Napoleonic Wars as the government's agent for fiscal transfers both at home and abroad throughout the most expensive war fought in history to that time. It increased its annual dividend to 12 percent from 7 percent in 1805 (reduced back to 10 percent in 1807), greatly enlarged its staff, built new facilities at its location on Threadneedle Street, and expanded its note issue as well as its advances to merchants and manufacturers in London.[4] The business of the London private banks expanded at the same time that for-eign merchants fleeing the extortions of Napoleon's troops brought their affairs to London.[5] Country banks multiplied in great number and profited by issuing small-denomination banknotes to replace metal coinage in the domestic circula-tion after the Bank of England suspended convertibility in February 1797, and the restrictions against issuing small-denomination notes were suspended in March 1797.[6] In short, the entire British financial sector enjoyed prosperity on the basis of war finance.

True, the commercial crisis of 1810 brought the Bank of England's prosperity— and arrogance—under close scrutiny by its enemies and led to the Bullion Report of 1810. By undermining the intellectual authority of the Bank's directors, the Bullion Report provided the courage needed for subsequent governments to constrain the Bank's power and to overrule its recommendations on monetary matters if that became politically popular. The Bank's practical autonomy, however, remained intact as the government still relied on it for managing its remittances and, especially, its recurrent issues of debt—both long-term, funded debt (perpetual annuities comprised mainly of 3 percent consols) and short-term, unfunded debt (one-year Exchequer bills bearing daily interest). The Treasury at this point was the Bank's strongest defender against the criticisms of the Bullionists, arguing that the needs of war finance justified the fall in the exchange rate of the paper pound.

As a result, for three years after the signing of the peace treaty in Paris in 1815, the government acquiesced to the Bank's various arguments that resumption of cash payments should be delayed— whether until the exchanges had stabilized, or the bond market had strengthened, or foreign trade had picked up, or its gold reserves were increased. Finally, in 1819, the government initiated a bill to force the Bank to resume convertibility, after initial experiments in 1817 at limited convertibility of Bank notes had succeeded without any harmful consequences. Even so, the Bank managed to make the transition as difficult as possible, first by amassing a large stock of gold, which helped keep up the price of gold in the markets, and then by withdrawing the notes from circulation that the government used to repay £10,000,000 of Exchequer bills that had been held by the Bank. Further, it refused to lower its rate of discount on bills and notes even as its loan business to the private sector declined. The resulting price deflation intensified both agricultural and manufacturing distress but enabled the Bank to resume full convertibility of notes into coin in May 1821 and to skip almost entirely the intermediate step of limiting convertibility to ingots of 60 ounces, as proposed by Ricardo. While, at the time, Ricardo criticized the Bank's directors as "indeed a very ignorant set,"[7] it appears to later historians that the Bank was responding angrily to the government's efforts to use the Bank to support its short-term debt financing while taking away the Bank's power to control the level of its own liabilities.[8]

The elimination of the income tax in 1816 brought an end to the mutually agreeable arrangements between the Treasury and the Bank that had existed during the war. The fall in tax revenues meant a sharp rise in the ratio of tax revenues that the government had to devote to servicing the huge debt accumulated during the war. Figures 1 and 2 show clearly the rise in government debt during the war, the ease with which the mounting debt was serviced while the income tax existed, and then the constraint upon the government's peacetime budget created by the continuing debt service. In the absence of an emerging revenue source, it was

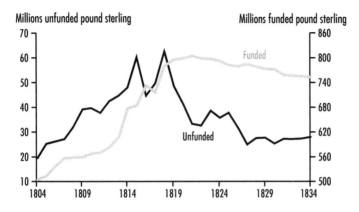

Figure 1 National Debt of the United Kingdom. Nominal amounts, funded and unfunded.
SOURCE: Mitchell (1988), p. 601.

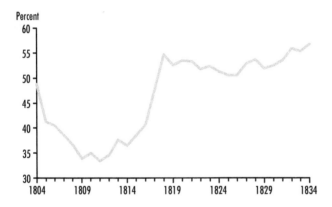

Figure 2 British Debt Service/Revenue. SOURCE: Mitchell (1988), pp. 581, 587.

a serious shock to the Treasury to lose an income stream that had amounted to nearly 20 percent of its total gross income in 1816 (£14.6 million) and had virtually vanished by 1818.[9] This was the shock that forced readjustment throughout the entire British financial system, from the Treasury right down to the country banks.

The Treasury confronted this situation with a variety of ploys. One was to raise the price of its long-term bonds in the London Stock Exchange so that new debt at lower interest rates could be issued in order to reduce its expenditures on debt service. It preferred to reduce this form of expenditure rather than cut back on traditional sinecures of the royal family and the landed aristocracy or reduce further the army and navy. Expenditures had to be cut not only because the repeal of the income tax had reduced revenue, but also because of the fear of further losses of revenue that might follow from reductions in various customs duties and excises. Counterarguments that both foreign trade and domestic commerce would increase in response to lower tax rates enough to generate the same revenues as before failed to persuade a timorous government. A few experiments were tried, some of which proved successful, but in the prevailing disturbed monetary conditions, any reductions in protection levels were vehemently opposed by manufacturing interests. The government was forced to find its budget balance in reduced debt service. By 1821, it became increasingly possible to do this.

Figure 3 shows the course of prices for the major government "stocks," namely the price of 3 percent consols, Bank of England stock, and East India Company stock, over the period 1811-31. The price of consols, with their constant £3 interest payment each year, reflects inversely the default risk-free yield on long-term debt. Its pattern shows clearly the increasing pressures of war finance during the Napoleonic Wars and the rocky road traversed by the British debt overhang in the decade-and-a-half following Waterloo. In the period encompassing the resumption of specie payments, from late summer 1820 to late 1822, the price of all three securities rose. With their dividend rates maintained at wartime levels, this meant the market yields on each fell for first-time investors. The actual market yields available to investors in "the funds," as they were known at the time, are shown in Figure 4. There was clearly a period of marked recovery from the trade crisis of 1819, when it was finally determined that Bank of England notes would again be convertible into gold at the pre-suspension mint par. A check occurred, however, at the end of 1822 that lasted until the spring of 1823. Then the upward course in price (and fall in yields) resumed for a year, leveling off from March to September 1824. The government's success in managing its debt service problem after resumption led to unusually low interest rates, especially in 1824, the year preceding the boom and bust of 1825.

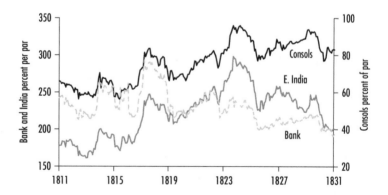

Figure 3 Price Levels of "The Funds". London Stock Exchange. SOURCE: Neal (1990), data appendix.

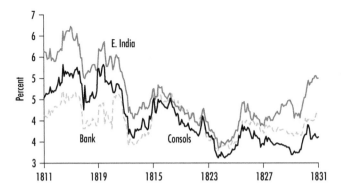

Figure 4 Yields on "The Funds". End of month. SOURCE: Derived data from Figure 3.

The charts of prices and yields for "the funds" illustrate nicely the problems created by the transition from wartime to peacetime finance. The price patterns of the three major securities available to risk-averse British investors changed their relationship from moving in synchrony to diverging unpredictably. The capital stock of both the East India Company and the Bank of England was invested in permanent government debt, on which the government paid regular interest. Typically, the two chartered monopolies passed this interest payment through to their shareholders along with some part of the profits obtained from their business activities. The dividends declared by the two had increased over the eighteenth century but rose to all-time highs during the Napoleonic Wars. The Bank's business as the remitting agent for the government's war finance has already been mentioned. The East India Company gained from absorbing all the Asian trade previously serviced by the French and Dutch East India companies while the hostilities lasted. However, it was assessed a huge annual sum by the government, purportedly as compensation for the naval and military services the government provided for the protection of the East India Company's trade.

A crossover in the prices of Bank of England and East India Company stock emerged clearly at the beginning of 1823 and widened through 1824. Part of the decline in the Bank's stock was certainly due to its decision in 1823 to drop its semi-annual dividend from £5 per £100, which had remained constant from 1807 through 1822, to £4 per £100. It remained there through 1838 before dropping again.[10] The Bank was steadily withdrawing from its discount business, husbanding reserves, and fending off Parliamentary pressures to resume convertibility. The East India Company, meanwhile, was in its final phases as a trading company in the period 1813-33 and faced with a mounting problem of encroachment by noncompany English traders in the exports of Indian goods to Britain. To counter this, the company was allowed to maintain its monopoly on all British trade with China. It was in the 1820s that the company's import of trade goods from India began to feel the pressure of competition—in 1826-27, they imported no goods whatsoever from India.[11] So it was the prospects of the continued China monopoly, and the earnings on monopoly pricing of tea for British consumers, that raised its market value in the early 1820s and the decline in Indian trade that lowered it in the mid-1820s.

In the early period from 1811 until 1819, by contrast, the London stock market had established a stable price relationship among the three securities. The market yield on East India Company stock was always the highest of the three. Presumably, this situation reflected the higher risk associated with the stock. The directors succeeded in keeping the dividend rate high at a steady 10 percent per annum throughout this period, but there was always a high risk that the government would either increase its charges on the company or reduce its source of profits, say by returning Ceylon and Indonesia to the Dutch. The much lower market yield on Bank stock reflected the perception that the Bank's business with the government was assured and even less risky than the government's financial affairs. The Bank stock's market yields were always lower than those available from the 3 percent consols, at least until 1819. This is not as counterintuitive as it may first appear, because the amount of Bank stock was fixed by terms of its most recent charter, while the supply of "Three Per Cents" kept changing unpredictably with the shocks to the government's finances.

All this changed, however, with the Resumption Act of 1819. The Bank's stock was assessed by the market to be then as risky as that of the East India Company. The success of actual resumption in full in 1821 appears to have reassured the market that it was less risky than the stock of the East India Company, whose fate was still a matter of intense discussion and dispute.

At times, Bank stock even appeared less risky than consols. The crisis of 1825 disrupted further the price and yield patterns. Thereafter, consols were clearly judged the safest security, East India Company stock became priced with a higher risk premium yet, and Bank stock was priced with a risk premium that seems to have risen steadily toward the fateful year of 1833, when its charter was up for renewal.

It may be helpful to put this argument, derived from visual inspection of the price and yield charts, in terms more familiar to modern financial analysts. The visual evidence is that the three major components of "the funds" were co-integrated in the period up to 1819 and presumably for a number of years before 1811. At some point in the period of conflict between the Bank and the government over the timing and terms of resumption of cash payments, from 1819 to 1821, the co-integrating relationship was broken. Table 1 presents the results of some formal testing of the statistical hypotheses implied by this argument.[12] The top panel demonstrates that the prices of all three securities probably followed random walks, both during the period 1811-20 and the period 1821-30. This is reassuring evidence that the market was at least weakly efficient in pricing each security. That is, there was no obvious trading rule that investors could use to make consistent profits by knowing when prices would rise or fall.

The second panel shows the results of Dickey-Fuller tests to see if there existed cointegrating relationships between each pair of securities in each subperiod.

Table 1 Co-Integration of the Funds and Market Index on the London Stock Exchange: 1811-20 and 1821-30

Panel A. Integration Diagnostics

1811-20	*D-F Test*	*ADF*	*1821-30*	*D-F Test*	*ADF*
Bank of England	−2.01	2.08	Bank	−1.35	−1.26
EIC	−1.02	−1.11	EIC	−1.40	−1.50
Threes	−1.68	−1.54	Threes	−2.30	−2.20

Panel B. Dickey-Fuller Tests for Co-Integrating Regressions

1811-20	*D-F Test*	*1821-30*	*D-F Test*
Bank of England vs. EIC	−2.15	Bank vs. EIC	−1.80
Threes vs. Bank of England	−2.65*	Threes vs. Bank	−2.18
Threes vs. EIC	−4.27***	Threes vs. EIC	−2.01

Panel C. Johansen Tests for Co-Integrating Vectors

1811-20	$^\lambda MAX$	$^\lambda TRACE$	*1821-30*	$^\lambda MAX$	$^\lambda TRACE$
Bank of England vs. EIC	5.33	7.08	Bank vs. EIC	5.02	7.09
Threes vs. Bank of England	19.27**	26.70***	Threes vs. Bank	5.59	8.10
Threes vs. EIC	15.35*	26.93***	Threes vs. EIC	5.09	6.81

NOTE: The Dickey-Fuller statistics reported under the integrating diagnostics and the co-integrating regressions are the t-statistics to test if the residuals are stationary. Critical values are based on James Hamilton (1994), *Time Series Analysis*, Princeton University Press, Table B-6, Case 2, p. 763.

Critical values for the Johansen statistics are taken from Osterwald-Lenum (1992).

* denotes 0.10 or less probability that there was a unit root,
** a 0.05 or less probability, and
*** a 0.01 or less probability.

These indicate that co-integration did exist between 3 percent consols and both Bank of England stock and East India Company (EIC) stock in the first subperiod, 1811-20. This is sensible, as the dividends for both the Bank and the EIC rested in large part on passing through the interest payments each company received from the government. However, no co-integration existed between Bank of England and East India Company stock. This is also reasonable, because each company's additional earnings above the interest payments received from the government were determined independently of each other. But even the co-integration of each company's stock with consols disappeared in the second subperiod, 1821-30.

Because the length of each time period is relatively short by the standards of time series statistics, and the Dickey-Fuller statistics are relatively inefficient for small samples, the third panel uses the Johansen technique for testing for the existence of a co-integrating vector for each pair of securities. Again, it shows that such vectors likely did exist in the first subperiod between consols and both Bank of England and East India stock, but not between Bank of England stock and East India stock, while no co-integration among any of the funds is evident in the second period. This reaffirms my argument that the transition from war finance to peace finance disrupted all the relationships within the entire structure of the British financial system, especially from 1821 on.

THE CRASH: FROM LATIN AMERICAN
BONDS TO COUNTRY BANKNOTES

Eventually, the government managed to bring the government budget back into balance and even run a small surplus, thanks mainly to reductions in the armed forces, especially the withdrawal of occupation forces from France after 1818. But in the period immediately following resumption of the gold standard, the government continued to make payments into the Sinking Fund, which was used to make periodic purchases of long-term debt at market prices and retire it. In effect, the Treasury was running open-market operations that increased liquidity in the economy. It did this by issuing Exchequer bills to the Bank and then using its credits with the Bank to retire some of the funded, long-term debt, mainly consols. Encouraged by the possibilities of retiring high-interest debt and reducing expenditures in this way, the government overreached in 1823. At the end of that year, the government converted £135 million of its 5 percent bonds to 4 percent bonds. It then continued to take advantage of monetary ease early in 1824 by converting £80 million of the 4 percent bonds to 3½ percent.[13]

This had a double-barreled effect, according to traditional accounts. On the one hand, British investors were disappointed to be receiving lower yields on their holdings in "the funds." "Even in that day 'John Bull could not stand two per cent.'"[14] On the other hand, the Bank of England was now obliged to buy back the "deadweight" part of the annuity yielding 3½ percent that the government had issued to cover its expenditure on naval and military pensions but had failed to sell to the public. The Bank had ample reserves to accomplish this, having accumulated bullion for minting into coins to replace the £1 and £2 notes it had issued during the paper pound period (1797-1821). In fact, as late as October 1824 the Bank's reserves amounted to fully one-third of its liabilities, and by February 1825 it had increased its holdings of public securities by 50 percent from the low of February 1822.[15]

This increase meant the Bank was also conducting open-market operations, inadvertently and unwillingly, that added to the monetary ease by placing cash in the public's hands in exchange for the government securities they previously held. This was done at the same time the Bank was drawing down its excessive gold reserves, a process that also increased public liquidity. John Easthope, a member of Parliament and a stockbroker, in his testimony to the Committee on the Bank of England Charter in 1832, argued that while the increase in the Bank's note issue before 1825 was not so large, it should have been decreased in light of falling gold reserves.[16] The episode he referred to was very likely the operations of Nathan Rothschild, who took advantage of the falling price of gold in Britain to borrow a large amount from the Bank to sell in France in November 1824.[17] Later, in mid-1825, when the Bank became concerned about its falling reserves and the fall of stock prices, Rothschild agreed to repay the loan, restoring the gold in installments spread over the months of June, July, August, and September.[18] The result was exceptional monetary ease in 1824 and into 1825, and then contraction in mid-1825, helping to bring on a payments crisis for country banks.

As Easthope argued, this was not the behavior one would want from a bank devoted to public service, although it was understandable behavior for a bank more concerned about the dividends it could pay to its stockholders than the general state of the monetary regime. On this point, the Bank's defense was that the exchanges had turned against Britain in 1825, so it was necessary then to contract its note issue and restore its gold reserves. Yet the evidence produced by the Bank itself for the committee indicates that the exchange rate was never seriously threatened (see Figure 5), at least no more than in earlier and later fluctuations that were not accompanied by financial panics. Indeed, such fluctuations as occurred may have created profit opportunities for the House of Rothschild, which the Bank was only too happy to share in part without taking the risks incurred by Rothschild.

The dysfunction of the financial system created at the top by the separation of operations and objectives between the Bank and the Treasury spread even further, affecting the country banks. Confronted by the distress caused by severe and unanticipated deflation in 1819-21, the Treasury did not wish to renew its reliance upon the Bank for buying Exchequer bills, as it had done in 1817 in order to finance public works projects in the manufacturing districts and Ireland.[19] Instead, it allowed the country banks to continue to issue notes of small denominations, deferring their elimination from circulation for 10 years. Instead of disappearing from the money supply in 1823, as previously provided in legislation of 1816 (which mandated their termination within two years after the Bank resumed cash payments), such notes were allowed to continue circulating until 1833.

The country banks, already providing necessary finance to manufacturing districts throughout England by the second half of the eighteenth century, found their business prospects greatly enhanced during the Napoleonic Wars.[20] Part of the reason was the expansion of heavy manufacturing in the Midlands and South Wales, part was the growth of foreign trade from outports other than London, and much was due to the role of country banks in remitting to London the government's

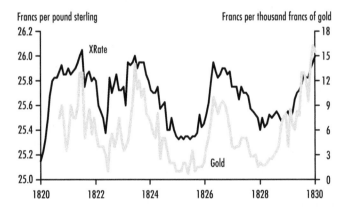

Figure 5 London's Exchange on Paris and Premium on Gold at Paris. SOURCE: Great Britain (1968), Appendix 97, pp. 110–11.

revenues from the land tax, the stamp tax, and the income tax while it was in effect. The end of the war reduced the basis for all these activities and eliminated the income tax. Moreover, the continuing threat of cash resumption by the Bank of England meant that the profitable note-issue business would have to be wound up and replaced by some other form of revenue.

Into the breach stepped the stockjobbers and brokers operating in the London stock exchange. Their business, too, was greatly enhanced by the incredible increase in government debt issued during the wars of 1793-1815. It was interrupted briefly by the crisis of 1810, which foretold the difficulties the stock exchange traders would face when the war ended. In 1811, the response of stock traders was to enlarge greatly the list of securities available for investors in the London stock exchange. Canal stocks were especially favored, although a few other joint-stock companies were listed—iron-tracked railways, docks, waterworks, and a few gasworks. Trading in most of these public-utility stocks was quite limited, however, as most shareholders preferred to hold them for their value as long-term assets and for their voting power. The various forms of government debt remained the most lucrative source of commission and speculative income for traders.

Latin American Securities

The withdrawal of foreigners from the British national debt after the war, however, removed one class of customers that had been most active in trading, while the rise in the price of government bonds reduced their attractiveness as sources of interest income to the *rentier* classes. The traders on the stock exchange began to develop a variety of new assets to maintain their customer base and their personal incomes. New government issues that mimicked in form the British 3 percent consol were offered by the peacetime governments in France, Prussia, Spain, Denmark, Russia, and Austria. The military successes of the revolting Spanish American colonies stimulated offerings of government bonds from the new Latin American states as well, followed by stocks in newly privatized mines. Many more gasworks were listed as every community in England rushed to provide its residents and businesses the gas lighting that was proving so successful in London. A number of insurance companies were created when entrepreneurs saw that the existing companies seemed especially able to profit from the ease of credit and the lack of attractive alternative assets to government debt.

But the most attractive assets offered were those from Latin America, following the success of the French 5 percent *rentes*. Following the final defeat of Napoleon at Waterloo in 1815, capital flowed back to the Continent from Great Britain. Foreign holdings of British debt diminished rapidly, the price of consols rose as the supply diminished, and prices of Bank and East India stock rose in tandem. British investors used to safe returns ranging between 4 and 6 percent for the past 20 years now found their options limited to yields between 3.5 and 4.5 percent. The opportunities for investment in new issues of French 5 percent *rentes* were

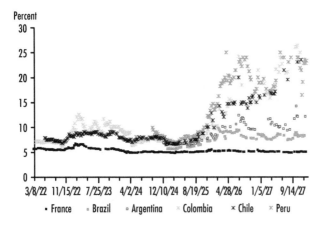

Figure 6 Yields of Latin Bonds. SOURCE: Course of the Exchange, Friday quotes.

more attractive than continuing their holdings in consols. Figure 6 shows that the *rentes* maintained a steady return over 5 percent throughout the crisis period and offered a stable alternative to the British funds. Baring Brothers and Co., by its successful finance of Wellington's army in 1815, had established itself as the dominant merchant bank in England. By undertaking the flotation of the first two issues of French *rentes* sold to pay the reparations and support Wellington's occupation forces, Barings became the "Sixth Power" in Europe, according to the Duc de Richelieu.[21] From February to July 1817, Barings disposed of three loans, the first two at a net price of 53 percent of par for 100 million francs each and the third at 65 percent of par, which raised 115 million francs. Yet, according to the historian of the Baring firm, no disturbance in the British trade balance or in French reserves seems to have occurred—the inflow of capital to France from Britain resulting from the issue of *rentes* seems to have been offset by indemnity payments and army contracts from France to Britain.[22] (What the historian has missed, of course, is the fall in the exchange rate of the British pound that occurred at the time; the pound was still floating after the suspension of convertibility in February 1797.) From this success for British investors in foreign investment with the French *rentes*, it has traditionally been argued, came increased enthusiasm for other forms of investment, first in the bonds issued by the new government of Spain established in 1820, and then in the bonds issued by the new states emerging in Latin America.[23]

The collapse of Spanish control over its American empire during the Napoleonic Wars led to a variety of independent states being formed out of the former colonies by 1820. Battling one another for control over strategic transport routes, mainly rivers and ports, and over state enterprises, mainly mines, each appealed to foreign investors as a source of government finance and as a means to substitute foreign expertise and technology for the vanquished Spanish. Their government bonds and their mining shares found a ready market in the London Stock Exchange, which had become the dominant marketplace for finance capital in the world during the Napoleonic Wars. The loan bubble of 1822-25 ensued, eventually giving British foreign-bond holders their first experience with defaults by sovereign states. None of the new Latin American states emerging from the remains of the Spanish empire (Brazil remained part of the Portuguese empire) found the means, whether by exports or taxes, to service the debts they had incurred in London. Meanwhile, the net proceeds they had received after the bonds were sold at discount—and after they had paid large commissions up front—to the London investment houses were dissipated rapidly in military conflicts with neighboring states.[24]

From 1822, when both Chile and Colombia floated bond issues with London agents, an increasing number of Latin American governments tried to find the means for financing their transition to independence from the flush pockets of British investors. The bonds they issued, in terms of the amounts actually paid up, as distinguished from the amounts actually received by the governments, were the largest single category of new investment in the London capital market in this period.[25] It is true, even so, that the amount was small relative to the remaining sum of the British government's funded debt—£43 million compared with £820 million.[26]

Figure 6 compares the prices of several bond issues of the emerging South American states, as given in James Wetenhall's semiweekly *Course of the Exchange.*[27] At the peak of the stock market boom, there was surprising convergence in the prices of all the Latin American bonds. It was only in the ensuing two years that information on the fiscal capacity of the individual governments and their respective economic bases enabled the London market to distinguish among them. Mexico and the Andean countries were clearly marked to be disaster cases by the end of 1828, while already Argentina and Brazil were demonstrating their attractiveness to British investors, an allure that would increase until the Baring crisis of 1890.

The pricing pattern of foreign government bonds displayed in Figure 6 is a classic illustration of the so-called "lemons" problem that can occur in emerging financial markets. In this case, it appears that investors in the London market priced the Latin American bonds at a substantial discount so that the typical 5 percent or 6 percent yield on par value could provide a substantial risk premium compared with both the British funds and the now-seasoned and solid French government debt. Until further information came in from newspapers or merchants' letters from the respective countries concerning their fiscal situation and credit arrangements, however, they all looked much alike, and all were priced at punitively low levels. This discouraged higher-quality governments, perhaps Brazil, from issuing debt until the House of Rothschild had assured itself that adequate provision was forthcoming for servicing it. But it also encouraged lower-quality governments, perhaps Peru, to issue debt early on. Indeed, at one point in October 1822, it induced the Scottish adventurer, Gregor McGregor, to issue bonds from an imaginary government of Poyais, presumably located around Honduras. On October 29, 1822, the official *Course of the Exchange* quoted Poyais scrip for 6 percent bonds at 81½ percent of par, compared with Peru's 6 percent bonds at 86¾, Chile's at 84, and Colombia's at 86!

Only as more information came in or as investors began to pull out of higher-risk investments and seek safer, better-quality assets did price differences begin to show up. This change began to occur in the fall of 1825 for the new government issues from Latin America; it did not affect the now-seasoned and secure French *rentes* at all. While the history of the various bond issues is extremely colorful, it appears that Leland Jenks' assessment of many years ago is still fundamentally correct—their main effect was to enrich some issuing agents and impoverish or imperil others, including the redoutable Barings. Jenks notes that the typical arrangement mimicked that devised by the Goldschmidts for the Colombian loan of 1824, whereby "[t]hey received a commission for raising the money, a commission for spending it, and a commission for paying it back."[28] On the other hand, the most recent historian of Barings argues that they lost money on the Argentina loan by buying back large amounts of it in a futile effort to maintain the market price of the bonds and lost even more on the ill-advised investments in Mexico of Francis Baring, the second son of Alexander Baring.[29] In the case of both the Rothschilds and the Barings, however, it appears that the sums risked were relatively small and the risks generally appreciated even by an inexperienced British public. We have to look elsewhere for an explanation of the 1825 speculative bubble and collapse, perhaps in the new domestic companies that were formed.

Domestic Securities

As the London stock market had proved attractive for the new issues of debt by the restored European governments and the revolutionary Latin American governments, by 1824 a much wider variety of newly formed joint-stock corporations offered their shares to London investors. In the words of a contemporary observer, "bubble schemes came out in shoals like herring from the Polar Seas."[30] The success of three companies floated to exploit the mineral resources of Mexico—the Real del Monte Association, the United Mexican Company, and the Anglo-American Company led to flotations of domestic projects in early 1824. In February 1824, the Barings and Rothschilds cooperated to found the Alliance British and Foreign Life & Fire Insurance Company. It enjoyed an immediate, enormous success.[31] In March there were 30 bills before Parliament to establish some kind of joint-stock enterprise, whether a private undertaking for issuing insurance or opening a mine, or a public utility such as gas or waterworks, or a canal, dock, or bridge. In April there were 250 such bills.[32]

The limitation of joint-stock enterprises to these fields arose from the limitations, first, of the Bubble Act of 1720, which forbade joint-stock corporations from engaging in activities other than those specifically stated in their charters; second, of common law, which made stockholders in co-partnerships with transferable shares (i.e., unincorporated joint-stock enterprises) liable in unlimited amount, proportional to their shares in the equity of the company; and, third, of the limited liability and ease of transfer for shareholders in mines created on the "cost-book" system.[33] They were subject only to calls up to the capitalization authorized by the cost-book, which required neither deed, charter, nor act of Parliament to establish. Despite the resistance of Parliament to incorporating new companies with limited liability, the speculative mania continued with new projects floated daily. Speculation was encouraged on the possibility that an enterprise might receive a charter, based on the connections in Parliament of its board of directors.

The extent of the speculative fervor and its lack of permanent effect was spelled out by a contemporary stockbroker, Henry English, and his analysis has remained authoritative to this day. Briefly, English listed 624 companies that were floated in the years 1824 and 1825. They had a capitalization of £372,173,100. By 1827, only 127 of these existed with a capitalization of £102,781,600, of which only £15,185,950 had been paid in, but the market value had sunk even lower to only £9,303,950.[34] But even at the height of the enthusiasm for new issues, the total capital paid in had amounted to no more than £49 million.[35] Compared with the stock of government debt available (£820 million), this amount was still almost as limited in scale as the investments in Latin American securities. Perhaps we have to look still further for an explanation of the events of 1825. The role of the country banks, in particular, needs to be examined.

The Country Banks

The expansion of the economy continued through 1823 and 1824. By April 1825 at the latest, the stock market boom reached its peak (Figure 7),[36] and the resulting drop in collateral values, combined with a contraction by the Bank of England in its note issue, began to create jitters in the money market. By July, city

Figure 7 London Stock Price Index. SOURCE: Compiled by author from quotes for 50 companies in the *Course of the Exchange*.

bankers were beginning to be more cautious. In September, reports of difficulties by country banks in Devon and Cornwall began to appear. All country banks were then faced with the seasonal strain that occurred each autumn. Government tax revenues were required to be remitted to London in the autumn before interest payments on government debt were made in December. This caused more country banks to fail in October and November in 1825. When the major London banks of Wentworth, Chaloner, & Rishworth and Pole, Thornton & Co. failed on December 8 and 13, respectively, and forced dozens of correspondent country banks to suspend payments, a general run began on country banks. These banks, in turn, came to their London banks for cash, and the London banks turned to the Bank of England. Finally, the directors of the Bank woke up to the crisis and began to discount bills and notes for their customers as fast as they could with diminished staff and resources. The pressure on the Bank lasted for the rest of December, depleted their bullion reserves, and forced them to issue small £1 and £2 notes again but did not force them to suspend payments as they had feared.

The credit collapse led to widespread bank failures (73 out of the 770 banks in England and even three out of the 36 in Scotland)[37] and a massive wave of bankruptcies in the rest of the economy, reaching an unprecedented peak in April 1826.[38] The Bank of England and the London private banks joined forces for once by blaming both the speculative boom and the subsequent credit collapse on excessive note issue by the country banks. They argued that the ease of note issue had encouraged the more careless or unscrupulous partners in country banks to invest in high-risk, high-return financial ventures such as the Poyais scrip that were being offered on the London capital market. The historian of British country banks, L.S. Pressnell, discounts this factor as the driving force both in the boom and in the timing of the collapse. Relying on evidence supplied by Henry Burgess, secretary of the Committee of Country Bankers, to the Bank Charter Committee of 1832, Pressnell notes that many country banks did increase their note issue substantially between July 1824 and July 1825. Burgess' unweighted index of the indexes of note issues provided to him by 122 country banks for the month of July in each year from 1818 through 1825 gave an overall average increase of 6.7 percent in the final year before the crisis, while 50 of the banks showed increases of more than 10 percent.[39]

Figure 8 shows, however, that the final level, reached in July 1825, was barely above the initial level of July 1818, which had fallen sharply until 1822. No doubt the country banks expanded their note issue in the years immediately preceding the crash. But much of this expansion was simply restoring note issue that had been reduced in response to Parliament's acts of 1816 and 1819. What is missing, of course, is evidence on the extent to which the initial withdrawal of notes was compensated for by an increase in demand deposits. If there was a one-to-one compensation (which is highly unlikely), then the expansion of note issues in 1824 and 1825 may have helped fuel the speculative fires burning on the London stock exchange. However, the expansion may also have been compensated by a reduction of deposits. Burgess' figures were collected from banks operating in

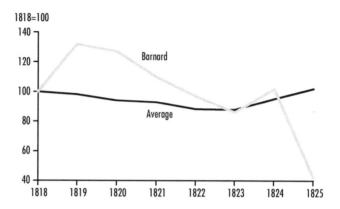

Figure 8 Average Issues of 122 Country Banks and of Barnard & Co. of Bedford.
SOURCE: Great Britain (1968), pp. 414–16 and Pressnell, pp. 512–13.

1830, which clearly had not been among the unfortunate firms that disappeared in the aftermath of the crisis. If those firms were much more aggressive than the survivors that appear in Burgess' large sample, then the country banks may remain indicted as a major contributing cause of the crisis of 1825.

Pressnell gives balance sheets from a handful of country banks that were operating in this period and whose records have survived. The bank Barnard & Co. of Bedford had an unusually rich set of accounts covering the entire period from 1800 to 1845. On the asset side of the balance sheet, this bank increased its cash holding substantially in 1821-23, and then greatly in 1824. By the end of 1825, however, its holdings had fallen from £106,559 to only £31,201, the lowest level since the crisis year of 1810. While the bank had begun to place surplus funds with a London bill-broker in 1823, this account remained quite small until the 1830s. Total assets fell sharply in 1825, from £152,585 to £109,079, but they fell less than the cash account. The difference came primarily in a doubling of the bank's balance with its London correspondent, from £33,877 to £66,256.[40] Apparently, this bank was one of the solvent banks whose surplus funds could be channeled to others through the intermediation of its London bank.

On the liability side of the Barnard & Co. bank, the note issues followed much the same path as the average shown by Burgess for his sample of 122 country banks (see Figure 8). The most striking difference occurs in 1825, but this is mostly explained by the fall that must have occurred in the note issue of all the country banks between July, for the average of the 122 banks, and December, for Barnard & Co. As far as Barnard's deposits are concerned, they fell as well from 1818 through 1823, but not as much as note issues. Deposits rose in 1824 more than note issues, and although they fell in 1825 as well, they ended the year of 1825 at a higher level than note issues. This was a bank that stayed clear of the speculative frenzy going on in London, weathered the storm and survived to prosper afterwards. Its good fortune was due, no doubt, to the large loss sustained by the founder, Joseph Barnard, the one time he did place funds in speculative issues available in London. That loss occurred in the crisis of 1810, and Barnard's "warning to those who may succeed me" from that incident was apparently heeded in 1825.[41]

If the record of accomplishment of Barnard & Co. may be dismissed as unrepresentative of the "problem" country banks, we can also examine the accounts of a country bank that did most of its business by note issue and that failed in the wave of bankruptcies occurring in December 1825. Figure 9 shows the gross level of £1 notes issued over the period 1817-25 of one of the unfortunates—the country bank of Sarah Crickett in Chelmsford, Essex County.[42] These do not take account of notes that may have been retired, but by plotting the highest number found for each date (notes were issued weekly) on a semilogarithmic scale, we can get a sense of how this bank, which seemed to rely more on note issue than deposit accounts, responded to the vagaries caused by the Bank of England's return to the gold standard in 1821.

At first glance, this bank shows quite a different pattern of note issuing from that of the successful banks shown in Figure 8. At the outset of business in 1817, it increased its issue of £1 notes very rapidly (it's interesting that these were still outstanding in 1826 when the holders turned them in to the Bankruptcy Commission), as a startup bank might be expected to do. But then it increased issues rapidly again in 1819, when it made sense for country banks to start withdrawing their notes, given that the Bank of England had resumed cash payments, and the Act of 1816 mandated that country banknotes under £5 should cease entirely two years later. The steady rise of notes in the early 1820s does not show any similar acceleration until the end of 1825, when the crisis was breaking.

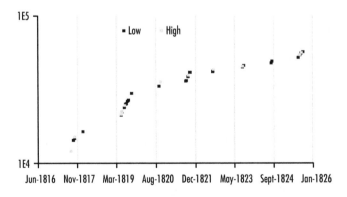

Figure 9 Chelmsford Country Bank One Pound Notes Issued. SOURCE: Public Record Office, B/3/1029. Sample figures extracted by author.

137

Given the bank's location in one of the richest agricultural districts of England, and the prevalence of small tradesmen and farmers among its noteholders, it may be that the note surges shown in 1817 and 1819 reflect local harvest conditions more than responses to the changes occurring in the London money market. They do occur in the fall of those years. It must be emphasized that these totals are cumulative and take no account of notes that may have been withdrawn when presented to the bank, so they are not comparable to the net issues outstanding, shown in Figure 8.

By the end of the Bankruptcy Commission for Crickett's Bank in the mid-1830s, 18 shillings in the pound (i.e., 90 percent) of the claims had been deposited in the assignee's account. Given the small sums claimed by most creditors, the length of time taken by the Bankruptcy Commission, and the location of the assignee's account at the Bank of England in London, much of the funds available for payment were not disbursed—a situation that was convenient for the commissioners and the assignee, who could then cover their charges very easily from the account. But for our purposes, the apparent willingness of so many note holders to retain their notes for long periods of time, plus the bank's basic soundness when its claims and assets were finally realized by the Bankruptcy Commission, indicates that this particular failure was an unfortunate victim of circumstances, not a contributor to the crisis.

The Bank of England

To understand the internal causes of the crisis of 1825, therefore, we must turn back to the role of the Bank of England—in particular, the relationship between its activities as a potential lender of last resort and the wave of bankruptcies that disrupted English commerical life for years following the crisis of 1825. This ground was covered many years ago by Norman Silberling (1923). He simply counted the number of bankruptcy commissions opened as recorded in the London *Gazette.* These have some weaknesses as discussed in Mitchell (1976, pp. 245–46), Duffy (1985, pp. 331–35), and Marriner (1989), but they are still useful as general indicators of the incidence and timing of bankruptcy over regions and industries. The problems arise from British bankruptcy law, which confined the possibility of bankruptcy to firms engaged in trade, excluding farms, factories, and the other professions. The latter were covered by the much harsher law of insolvency, but in case of difficulty they did what they could to come under bankruptcy law. To do this, they had to be engaged to a significant extent in trade, stop payment on debts amounting to over £100, and refuse in front of witnesses to pay a legitimate creditor. The creditor would then petition with other major creditors to open a commission; this was "striking a docket." If the Bankruptcy Court judged that the creditors had a legitimate case, they would "seal a commission," which would authorize a trio of commissioners to begin collecting evidence of the bankrupt's assets and liabilities. As this was an expensive procedure, which could last for years and eat up the remaining assets of the bankrupt in commissioners' fees, mutual efforts were often made to settle the dispute before the proceedings began. Once they began, the "commission opened." Figure 10, from Duffy (1985), shows the annual numbers of dockets struck, commissions sealed, and commissions opened. Regardless of which measure of financial distress is taken, the crash of the London stock market at the end of 1825 resulted in record numbers of business failures.

The 1825 spike is all the more anomalous for coming at the end of a period of declining numbers of bankruptcies, with no major changes in trade direction or policy evident, much less any sign of renewed warfare. From 1794 on, Silberling constructed quarterly totals of the advances made by the Bank of England to its private customers and the government. From his comparison of the pattern of advances with that of banknote issue, prices, and bankruptcies, he concluded that advances were a much better barometer of prices and business conditions than banknote issues and, moreover, that in general the claim of the Bank's officers that they followed a real-bills doctrine—responding passively to the demands of business for credit on realized trade contracts—was justified. The exceptional decrease in advances after 1819, driven by the Bank's determination to accumulate sufficient bullion to validate the resumption of convertibility of its banknotes into specie at the pre-war par in terms of gold, did not show up in bankruptcies.[43]

Closer examination of the relationship between advances and bankruptcies from 1819 through 1830, shown in Figure 11, shows possible encouragement of speculative movements in 1823 and 1824 but moderation in 1825 until the Bank responded to the crisis at the end of the year by increasing the total of advances enormously in the first quarter of 1826. Afterwards, Silberling's figures show a distinctive inverse pattern, which is so short in duration that it could again be consistent with the real-bills story, especially if we allow a lag of six months to a year from the actual credit restriction to the recorded opening of a bankruptcy commission.

Parliament collected evidence in the years afterward to determine the pattern of bankruptcies. Table 2 distinguishes town and country bankruptcies opened within

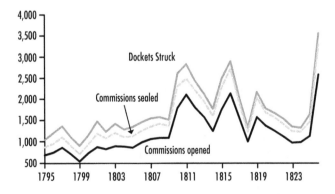

Figure 10 Bankruptcy Records Compared. SOURCE: Duffy (1985), p. 399.

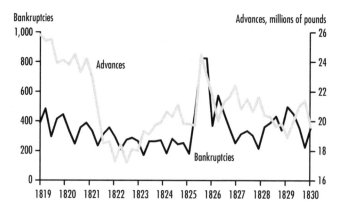

Figure 11 Bankruptcies and Bank of England Advances. SOURCE: Silberling (1923).

Table 2 Bankruptcy Commissions Sealed (total) and Opened (town and country): 1822-32

Year	Commissions Sealed	Town Commissions Opened	Country Commissions Opened
1822	1,419	468	534
1823	1,250	532	396
1824	1,240	574	396
1825	1,475	683	448
1826	3,307	1,229	1,220
1827	1,688	671	742
1828	1,519	601	620
1829	2,150	809	910
1830	1,720	661	748
1831	1,886	692	770
1832	1,772	643	740

SOURCE: British Parliamentary Papers, 1833, XXXI, p. 342.

the total of commissions sealed from 1822 through 1833. Again, 1826 shows up as the crisis year, but what is striking here is the much more dramatic jump in the country bankruptcies, a situation that continued afterwards with a consistently higher number of bankruptcies for country banks. Moreover, bankruptcies of banks located within 65 miles of London totaled only 38 from February 7, 1824, to March 22, 1832, compared to a total of 116 for banks located outside the 65-mile radius from London. Only 12 of the London banks failed in the crisis period from December 13, 1825, to March 11, 1826, while 52 of the country banks failed from December 12, 1825, to March 11, 1826. These bankruptcy records indicate further that the financial panic was transmitted through the credit channels of Great Britain, radiating out from the London capital market, and had its final impact in the trade and industry of the countryside through the liquidity crunch exerted upon the country banks.

Picking up the Pieces

The question naturally arises: Could the Bank of England have prevented this financial disaster, say, by acting earlier and as a monopoly bank bearing more responsibility to the public than to its stockholders? It must bear part of the blame for the expansion of the money supply that apparently arose in 1823-24 and especially for failing to offset the monetary expansion occurring elsewhere. But if, as Duffy suggests, it was the Bank's drawing account activity rather than its note issue that played the strongest role in easing or constraining the credit conditions in the London money market, then the Bank of England can be no more culpable than the country banks. The sums advanced from the Drawing Office plummeted after resumption of cash payments in 1821, and the Bank of England restricted drawings through most of 1825, never rising to the pre-resumption level until the first quarter of 1826. But this analysis simply casts the Bank of England in the role of just another bank, albeit much larger and more influential. If it was supposed, through its ability, to combine up-to-date, authoritative information from the worlds of finance, commerce, and government policy, it might be expected to have played an earlier, more constructive role. In fact, the evidence from the minutes of the Court of Directors of the Bank indicate that the Bank was taken by surprise and responded with much too little, much too late.

The Bank of England

The first mention of the crisis occurs on December 8, 1825, when "The Governor [Cornelius Buller] acquainted the Court that he had with the concurrence of the Deputy Governor [John Baker Richards] and several of the Committee of Treasury afforded assistance to the banking house of Sir Peter Pole, etc."[44] This episode is described in vivid detail by the sister of Henry Thornton Jr., the active partner of Pole, Thornton & Co. at the time. On the previous Saturday, the governor and deputy governor counted out £400,000 in bills personally to Henry Thornton, Jr., at the Bank without any clerks present.[45] All this was done to keep it secret so that other large London banks would not press their claims as well. A responsible lender of last resort would have publicized the cash infusion to reassure the public in general. Instead, the run on Pole & Thornton continued unabated, causing the company to fail by the end of the week. Then the deluge of demands for advances by other banks overwhelmed the Bank's Drawing Office.

Table 3 shows the breakdown of the Bank of England's discounts by branch of trade. I have ordered them by the largest amounts disbursed in the quarter ending in December 1825, when "Bankers" dominate. However, as late as November, the

Table 3 Amount of Each Branch of Trade in Discounts (thousands of pounds sterling)

Branch	Mar	Jun	Sept	Nov	Dec
Bankers	273	595	608	699	3,408
Hamburg, Fr., Sp., Port, S. Amer., Baltic and general merchants	411	1,809	1,094	1,238	2,955
Tea dealers, grocers, and sugar refiners	275	334	324	470	959
Russian merchants and dealers in hemp and tallow	46	95	154	243	733
Blackwell Hall factors and warehousemen woolen drapers	188	337	400	441	701
Linen drapers and Manchester warehousemen	220	300	363	413	594
West India merchants	120	156	196	242	559
Irish merchants, factors, dealers	114	191	201	272	551
Hop merchants	113	130	144	145	503
North American merchants	55	65	164	184	308
Silk men, mfrs. gauze weavers	137	185	226	247	297
Wine and brandy merchants	147	229	158	200	290
Corn factors	137	195	135	135	293
Dry salters	75	118	167	122	234
EI agents and merchants	19	93	13	68	226
Leather sellers, factors, tanners	177	254	259	190	224
Stationers	110	141	182	162	210
Timber merchants	81	85	148	160	200
Scotch factors and merchants	58	67	67	51	154
Totals (42 branches in all)	3,080	5,865	5,588	6,324	14,430

SOURCE: Bank of England. C 36/16 TVF 3/25 "Account of the Principal Amounts Discounted in Bills and Note per month for the years 1825 and 1826."

bankers were not unusually present in the Bank of England's offices. Indeed, it appears that the merchants engaged in the trades with "Hamburg, France, Spain, Portugal, South America, the Baltic, and General Merchants" were especially pressing in their demands upon the Bank in the quarter ending in June 1825. No other branch of trade showed unusual demands until the final month of 1825. But this alone should have warned the Bank of repercussions that would follow. If it was the South American merchants who accounted for the bulk of the increased demands for accommodation in June, this gave the Bank much better warning than could have been available to any country banker that remittances from South America were in disarray. This would affect the disbursement of dividends upon mining stocks as well as interest on government bonds. Instead of reacting to this information in a constructive way, however, the Bank decided it would be risky to advance funds on some categories of collateral, kept its rate of discount high compared with the rest of the market, and raised its rate of discount back to 5 percent in early December 1825, when demands became increasingly urgent. In the interim, the Bank chose to respond to the lack of discounting business by cutting costs. The number of clerks in the Drawing Office had fallen from 17 to

11 by February 1825, and of these 11, four were regularly sent to serve in other departments.[46]

The Bank of England's first proactive response at the level of the Court of Directors did not appear until January 12, 1826. At that meeting the court appointed a committee to report on the practicality and expediency of establishing branch banks. The very next week, the committee reported "Branch banks would be highly expedient." The reasons it gave, however, were quite revealing of the ruling mentality among Bank of England leaders at the time. The benefits were listed first for the Bank of England and then for the general public (see Table 4). The practicality was not an issue, given Scotland's experience for 80 years, not to mention the success of the Bank of the United States, the Bank of Ireland, and the recently established Provincial Bank of Ireland.

In this report, the Bank of England was clearly responding belatedly to the government's decision to force it to open branches and to promote large, joint-stock banks. The week after the report was laid before the court, the governor presented to the directors the letter he had received from Lord Liverpool, First Lord of the Treasury, and Mr. Frederick Robinson, Chancellor of the Exchequer. The arguments laid out in the letter show that the government, in this instance, was determined to work around the Bank rather than through it. The Liverpool-Robinson letter began with the assertion, "there can be no doubt that the Principal Source of it [the recent distress] is to be found in the rash spirit of Speculation which has pervaded the Country for some time, supported, fostered, and encouraged by the Country Banks."[47] So, the letter continued, it seemed advisable to repeal the authority of the country banks to issue small notes and return to a gold circulation. This action would spread pressure on the exchanges over a wider

Table 4 Report of the Bank of England's Committee on Branch Banking

---

Benefits to the Bank of England:
1) Increase circulation of Bank of England notes.
2) Increase Bank's control of whole paper circulation "and enable it to prevent a recurrence of such a convulsion as we have lately seen."
3) Provide large deposits.
4) Protect the Bank against competition of "large Banking Companies" if the government should encourage them.

Benefits to the General Public:
1) Provide more secure provincial circulation.
2) "Disasters arising from the sudden expansion and contraction of the currency would not so often occur."
3) Increase security and facility of transmission of money.
4) Provide secure places of deposit "in every quarter of the Kingdom."

SOURCE: Bank of England. TVC3/11 G4/48 "April 13, 1825, to 6th April, 1826, Minutes of the Court of Directors," folio 194.

surface and make it felt earlier—a clear reference to the Bank's negligence in 1825. But this alone would not suffice; after all, a similar convulsion had occurred in 1793 when there were no small notes and Scotland had "escaped all the convulsions which have occurred in the Money Market of England for the last thirty-five years, though Scotland during the whole of that time has had a circulation of One-Pound Notes." In the past, the Bank of England "may have been in Itself and by Itself fully equal to all the important Duties & Operations confided to it," but "the rise of country banks alone shows it is no longer up to the tasks required from the increased wealth and new wants of the Country."[48]

The government proposed two remedies: The Bank should establish branches of its own, and it should give up its exclusive privilege to issue notes within a certain distance from the Metropolis. The first suggestion was impracticable, in the government's view, and it was obvious that Parliament would never agree to an extension of the Bank's privileges in London. All in all, the government's proposed legislation would remove pressure from the Bank, and it would still have the government's business and be the only establishment at which the dividends on the national debt would be paid. With this condescending argument, the letter concluded, "so we hope the Bank will make no difficulty in giving up their privileges, in respect of the number of Partners in Banking as to any District [left blank] Miles from the Metropolis."[49]

Clearly, the Bank had failed to meet the recent challenges adequately, and the government was determined to create competitive banks that might better serve the public and, presumably, the government. The Bank's response was understandably churlish, which Liverpool informed them on January 25 he regretted, but he was determined to move ahead, merely asking if the government had any amendments to propose to the bill pending in Parliament to permit joint-stock banking. He did then accede to encouraging them to set up their own branches as well. Thus, the Bank went ahead with establishing branches, gradually dispersing seven of them into the industrial cities of Manchester, Gloucester, Swansea, Birmingham, Liverpool, Bristol, and Leeds, starting in 1828, and adding Exeter, Newcastle, Hull, and Norwich in 1829, when small note issues by the remaining country banks ceased. By the time of the Bank Charter Committee in 1832, the branches at Manchester and Birmingham were clearly the most dominant in terms of note issues and bills discounted.[50]

The Commercial Bill Market

Wilfred T. C. King, in his classic study of the London discount market, identified the crisis of 1825 as bringing about "changes in the banking structure which were responsible for every major influence upon market evolution in the succeeding twenty years."[51] His analysis of the crisis follows very much the lines above, adding only the additional factor that a series of good harvests had made the country banks in agricultural districts especially flush with funds. In terms of the conditions in the money market, however, the effects were limited in duration. By June of 1826, the money market rate had fallen well below 5 percent, and the Bank of England was no longer besieged with requests for re-discounting of bills. Of more interest to King were the implications for the development of the bill market in London from four changes in the financial structure that occurred in response to the crisis. These were: 1) the beginnings of joint-stock banking, 2) the establishment of Bank of England branches, 3) the cessation of re-discounting by the London private banks, and 4) the assumption of some central banking functions by the Bank of England.[52]

The new joint-stock banks had to function outside London (thanks to the resistance of the Bank of England) and they had to compete with existing country banks by attracting deposits rather than issuing notes. King does not explain why this was so, noting only that those joint-stock banks that began business by issuing notes gave them up after a few years. It appears that this development arose in large part because the Bank of England branches refused to do business with joint-stock banks that did issue notes.[53] Given that their business was necessarily local and that they had no notes to redeem, the new joint-stock banks kept minimum reserves, relying upon re-discounting bills of exchange to obtain cash when needed to meet withdrawals of deposits. They also had a strong preference for short-term loans in the form of bills, rather than government securities, as had been the case earlier.[54] As the country banks wound up their small-note business, they also turned increasingly toward deposits and the behavior of joint-stock banks, as described by King. King concludes that it was the period from roughly 1830 until the 1860s or 1870s that the bill market became the most important way in which domestic credit was distributed within Great Britain.[55]

The second change identified by King, the establishment of branches by the Bank of England, also promoted the rise of the bill market. While initially the Bank's branches would seem to be serious competitors to the local banks, they limited their lending activities strictly to commercial bills and then only to very short-term and highest-quality bills, as approved in London. This limitation effectively kept business intact for the existing local banks, save that their commissions on discounting bills were reduced by the knowledge among their customers that the Bank of England branches did not charge commissions. But the facility of making remittances to London and receiving credits back from London through the Bank's branches helped local bankers use the London bill market more cheaply. A bill drawn locally could now be sent directly to a bill broker in London, who would be instructed to pay the proceeds into the Bank of England for the credit of the local bank at the branch bank. Moreover, a trader in Leeds could pay or receive money in Birmingham through the medium of the Bank's branches, for the "simple charge of postage of a letter."[56] In short, the branches of the Bank of England greatly improved the payment mechanism that underlay the smooth functioning of the bill market.

The third change noted by King was the withdrawal of London private banks from re-discounting after the 1825 crisis. The run upon the Bank of England—as well as its obvious reluctance to hold too much reserves in gold, which was not earning income for its stockholders—convinced the London banks they should not rely on the Bank of England exclusively for cash in times of pressure. Instead, they turned to providing call loans to bill brokers, who could, in turn, increasingly become bill dealers. Instead of delaying discounting of bills in London until a matching buyer had been found for the bills offered for sale, larger firms could now purchase the bills immediately, using funds on deposit with them by the London private banks.[57] Only a few firms were as yet large enough to be able to risk this next step, moving from brokering to dealing in bills. Even those like Gurney's probably would not have done it then had not the market rate of discount fallen below the usury limit of 5 percent. Had it been at or above the usury limit, there would have been no possibility of making a profit from strict dealing.

The final step in completing the new structure did not occur until 1830, when the Bank of England opened its re-discount facilities to the bill brokers. Even this was not sufficient to overcome the informational asymmetries that could still arise in the market and that lay at the heart of later crises when the emerging bill market was abused opportunistically. The remaining problem was the Bank's continued refusal to discount at market rates, meaning that it was unaware of emerging imbalances in the demand and supply of bills of exchange until a large excess demand for cash showed up at the Drawing Office, as in December 1825. Only when the practice of maintaining fixed discount rates at the Bank was foresaken in the crisis of 1847 did the role of the "Bank Rate" come to play its key regulating role in the British financial system. But the information flows that had arisen through the medium of the bill market enabled the London banks to keep closer tabs on the conditions of the country banks, whether they were in agricultural or industrial districts, essentially through the intermediation of the London discount houses. Further improvements in the management of information flows within the entire financial structure were elicited in response to later financial crises, caused by new, unanticipated shocks encountered as the global economy of the nineteenth century was created.

POLICY LESSONS?

The evidence of the bankruptcies certainly suggest that problems of adverse selection in the London credit markets arose in intensified form during the 1824-25 bubble on the London stock market. Combined with the evidence on changing yield spreads for East India Company stock compared with Bank of England stock, and especially with the evidence of the initial bundling and then wide dispersion of yields on the various Latin American government bonds, it lends support to the hypothesis that the problem of information aysmmetry, always present in financial markets, became especially severe in the London markets in the years leading to the crash of 1825.

Asymmetric information is the term applied to the usual situation in which borrowers know more about the actual investment projects they are carrying out than do the lenders. Lenders, knowing this, charge a premium proportional to the uncertainty they feel about the borrowers in question. This situation, in turn, creates an adverse selection problem, in which higher-quality borrowers are reluctant to pay the high interest rates imposed by the market, while lower-quality borrowers are willing to accept the rates and to default if their ventures fail. In an expanding market, which the London stock exchange certainly was in the boom years of 1806 to 1807 and again in the early 1820s, the availability of loanable funds at premium rates will attract lemons to the market (say, Mexican mines) and discourage borrowing by sound enterprises (say, Brazilian diamonds). Borrowers turn back to internal sources of funds or to a compressed circle of lenders who know their superior quality and are willing to extend credit at lower rates.

In the case of British firms in the 1820s, the compressed circle of knowledgeable, low-interest lenders was the web of country banks that had arisen in the past three decades. The continued credit access of high-quality firms, however, depends in each case upon the continued liquidity of the small, local financial intermediaries. Their willingness to continue lending at preferential rates is limited increasingly by the risk of withdrawals by depositors who wish to participate in the high-interest, high-risk investments available in the national financial market. A financial boom of the kind normally experienced before financial crises can discourage real investment, therefore, and intensify the lemons problem as high-quality borrowers withdraw from the loanable funds market.[58] It can also place increasing pressure on local financial intermediaries that specialize in monitoring credit to local enterprises. It cannot be mere coincidence that the collapse of the bubble of 1825, according to one account, was set off by the refusal of a country bank in Bristol to honor the request of a Mr. Jones to redeem in gold its notes that he presented.[59] The *coup de grâce* occurs when higher-risk borrowers are asked to provide collateral for additional loans, and the financial collapse decreases the value of their collateral. The outcome is a general wave of bankruptcies.

Under public pressure, the Bubble Act was repealed in June 1825. In July 1826, joint-stock banks were allowed to establish beyond a 65-mile radius of London without limitation on the number of partners (the previous limit had been six). Both actions were counterproductive, if we take as given the traditional story that the entire episode was yet another example of irrational speculative bubbles derived from crowd behavior in which investors acted first too optimistically and then too pessimistically in response to fragments of information. On the basis of the information-processing story told above, however, we can conclude that both actions were constructive. Repeal of the Bubble Act sped up the Parliamentary process of granting corporate charters, limiting the speculative period during which uncertainty over the prospects of passage of the proposed charter dominated price movements in the initial share offerings. Moreover, repeal did not mean that shareholders were granted limited liability in the new joint-stock enterprises; unlimited liability remained in principle. Supplementary legislation in 1826 specified, moreover, that Parliament could determine for each charter the extent of liability of the shareholders. With these changes, Parliament both encouraged the continuation of the corporate charter business, which must have been profitable to large number of the members of Parliament, and discouraged overpricing of the subscription shares while the incorporation bill was in progress.

The collapse of country banks was one of the last examples of a banking panic in the British banking system. As Mishkin (1991) argues for U.S. banking panics, bank failures removed from the capital markets the principal monitors who could effectively distinguish borrowers by their quality without resorting to credit rationing or arbitrarily high prices for credit. Bank failures worsened the informational problems in the British capital markets. Creating joint-stock banks within which the country banks would become branches instead of correspondents helped restore this critical monitoring function to the British system. In the peculiarities of the 1826 Act, this was done by linking the various country banks within the structure of a joint-stock bank headquartered in London. But the London headquarters performed no banking function. Its role was to process and diffuse information to the various branch offices located beyond the 65-mile radius from London.

The results of the financial crisis of 1825 were beneficial for the British government. The funded debt continued to decline, after a small rise in 1827, throughout the remainder of the century. The government's gross income remained high and comfortably above gross expenditures, save for the years 1827 and 1828, when it dropped slightly below.[60] The comfortable financial situation gave Britain the lowest interest rates on its debt of any European government throughout the nineteenth century—a great advantage whenever it became necessary to mobilize resources for armed conflict anywhere in the world.[61] It also laid the basis for continuing political reform, culminating in 1834, and economic reform, culminating with the repeal of the Corn Laws and the Navigation Acts in the 1840s, and the promotion of limited liability joint-stock corporations in the 1850s and 1860s.[62]

*The author acknowledges with gratitude the support of the University of Illinois during his sabbatical leave of 1996-97 as well as the Guggenheim Foundation and the British Fulbright Commission, for research efforts on this project. This version of the paper has benefited not only from the comments of the discussant, Michael Bordo, and participants at the conference, but also from comments and suggestions made during seminars at the University of Illinois (especially Lee Alston and Salim Rashid), Indiana University (especially George von Furstenberg and Elmus Wicker), and the Research Triangle in North Carolina (especially Douglas Fisher, Judith Klein, and Gianni Toniolo). Remaining shortcomings and misinterpretations of the facts are, of course, the sole responsibility of the author.

Notes

1 Note the emphasis on English, rather than British, institutions. The Scottish and Irish banks avoided the Panic of 1825 almost entirely, a fact that caused much soul-searching among the English at the time.

2 Duffy (1985), ch. 1.

3   King (1936), ch. 2.
4   Clapham (1945), vol. 2, ch. 1.
5   Chapman (1984), p. 4.
6   Pressnell (1956), pp. 142–44.
7   Letter to Malthus of July 19, 1821, in Works, IX, p. 15 as cited in Fetter (1965), p. 98, n. 11.
8   Hilton (1977), p. 54.
9   Mitchell (1988), p. 581.
10 Clapham (1945), v. II, p. 428.
11 Clapham (1967), p. 487.
12 1 am grateful to Marc Weidenmier for his expertise in carrying out this analysis for me.
13 Gayer, Rostow, Schwartz (1975), vol. I, p. 185.
14 Gayer, Rostow, Schwartz (1975), vol. I, p. 185.
15 Pressnell (1956), p. 480.
16 Great Britain (1968), p. 469, item 5790.
17 Bank of England, Committee of the Treasury Minute Book, Oct. 29, 1823, to April 12, 1826, fo. 117. Rothschild on Nov. 30, 1824, requested a loan of £300 or £500,000 of bar gold at 77/10 1/2 per oz. and paid 3 1/2 percent per annum with collateral of stock. "As I may require about £225,000 value of Bar gold tomorrow, I beg to mention it to you, in order to facilitate the delivery." The Bank's Court of the Treasury complied with this application.
18 Bank of England, Committee of the Treasury Minute Book, May 26, 1825, fo. 161.
19 Hilton (1977) pp. 82,87.
20 Pressnell's classic study (1956) remains the standard work on English country banks.
21 Jenks (1927), p. 36. See also Ziegler (1988), pp. 100–11.
22 Jenks (1927), p. 37.
23 While the focus for foreign loans was mostly on Spain and Spanish America, Greece received a loan and much-needed publicity for its then-premature efforts to break away from Turkish rule. More than 50 years later, when the Greek government was attempting to assure the international community it would go on a gold standard, part of its commitment was to resume payment on these initial bonds!
24 Dawson (1990) provides a readable account of this episode, but Marichal (1989) puts it into a longer-run Latin American perspective. Brazilian bonds never went into default, which is why their prices remained the highest among the Latin American bonds in the late 1820s. They were, in fact, the only ones issued by the Rothschilds. None of their government bond issues for Austria, Belgium, Naples, Prussia, or Russia defaulted in this period (Doubleday, p. 281).
25 Gayer, Rostow, and Schwartz (1975), vol. I, p. 189.
26 Gayer, Rostow, and Schwartz (1975), vol. I, p. 408, fn. 8, and Mitchell (1976), p. 402. These are nominal values in each case, but government debt was then trading at close to par, so its market value was roughly the same.
27 Beginning probably in January 1825, Wetenhall apparently also began publishing a daily stock price list (No. 171 was for July 8, 1825), with slightly different coverage than that provided in his officially sanctioned, twice-weekly price sheet (which was No. 11,131 for July 8, 1825)—a bit of circumstantial evidence for the information-asymmetry theory, but I have located only one issue of the daily list for this period.
28 Jenks (1927), p. 49.
29 Ziegler (1988), pp. 102–07.
30 Hunt (1936), p. 30, quoting a letter to The Times, April 20, 1826.
31 Hunt (1936), p. 32.
32 Hunt (1936), p. 32.
33 Burt (1984), pp. 74–81 describes the cost-book system and its advantages for investors at this time.

34 As reproduced in Hunt (1936), p. 46.
35 Gayer, Rostow, and Schwartz (1975), vol. I, p. 414.
36 According to my own value-weighted index of 50 of the most important stocks traded on the London Stock Exchange, the peak occurs in March. Gayer, Rostow, and Schwartz (1975), using different weights for the same stocks, put the peak in April, although the actual peak if mine stocks are included occurs in January 1825.
37 Kindleberger (1984), p. 83.
38 Gayer, Rostow and Schwartz (1975), vol. 1, p. 205.
39 Pressnell (1956), pp. 480–81.
40 Pressnell (1956), pp. 512–13.
41 Pressnell (1956), pp. 433–34.
42 Public Record Office, B3/1008 and B3/1010-1029 contains the files of the Bankruptcy Commission for Sarah Crickett and her bank.
43 Doubleday rants about the widespread distress created from passage of Peel's Act in 1819 until its final full effect in May 1823, "but, in fact, his prime example of distress … calculated to tear in pieces, almost, the heart of every just and sensible man that reads it," deals with the loss of a country estate purchased with wartime profits by the son of a trader who went bankrupt in 1822. Clearly, this was not a general condition.
44 Bank of England, TVC3/11 G4/48, fo. 150.
45 Forster (1956), p. 117.
46 Bank of England, C 35/2 4783/2, No. 2, "Special Discount Committee from 12 Feb. 1811 to 26 Jan. 1830 inclusive," fo. 159. Later, the committee recommended a further reduction in the number of clerks (fos. 164-65).
47 Bank of England, TVC3/11 G4/48, fos. 201-2.
48 Bank of England, TVC3/11 G4/48, fo. 204.
49 Bank of England, TVC3/11 G4/48, fo. 215.
50 Bank Charter Committee Report, Appendix No. 46, p. 47.
51 King (1936), p. 35.
52 King (1936), p. 38.
53 "Testimony by Henry Burgess, the Secretary of the Association of Country Banks to the Committee on Bank of England Charter, 5324-26, in Great Britain (1968), pp. 427–28.
54 Pressnell (1956) later confirmed this tendency, even for country banks, pp. 415–34.
55 King (1936), p. 41.
56 "Testimony of William Beckett to the Committee on Charter of Bank of England, 1436-38, in Great Britain (1968), p. 101.
57 King (1936), p. 64.
58 Mishkin (1991), pp. 70–75, gives a detailed exposition of the various routes by which increases in asymmetric information may exacerbate adverse selection, monitoring, and moral hazard problems, especially if a banking panic limits the ability of financial intermediaries to serve a monitoring function.
59 Doubleday, pp. 288–89.
60 Mitchell (1976), pp. 392, 396, and 402.
61 See Neal (1992a), pp. 84–96, for a comparison of the British interest rates with the rest of the world.
62 See Neal (1992b).

References

Acworth, Angus Whiteford. *Financial Reconstruction in England, 1815-1822*, London: P.S. King and Son Ltd., 1925.

Burt, Roger. *The British Lead Mining Industry*, Cornwall: Dyllansow Truran, 1984.

Clapham, John Harold. *The Bank of England, A History,* Vol. II, "1797-1914," Cambridge: University Press, 1945.

_____. *An Economic History of Modern Britain,* Vol. I, "The Early Railway Age, 1820-1850," 2nd ed., Cambridge: University Press, 1967.

Dawson, Frank Griffith. *The First Latin American Debt Crisis. The City of London and the 1822-25 Loan Bubble,* Yale University Press, 1990.

Doubleday, Thomas. *A Financial, Monetary and Statistical History of England, from the Revolution of 1688 to the Present,* 2nd ed., London: Effingham Wilson, 1858-59.

Duffy, Ian P.H. *Bankruptcy and Insolvency in London During the Industrial Revolution,* Garland Publishing Co., 1985.

Evans, George Heberton. *British Corporation Finance, 1775-1850: A Study of Preference Shares,* Johns Hopkins Press, 1936.

Fetter, Frank W. *Development of British Monetary Orthodoxy, 1797-1875,* Harvard University Press, 1965.

Forster, Edward M. *Marianne Thornton, A Domestic Biography, 1797-1887,* Harcourt, Brace and Company, 1956.

Gayer, Arthur D., *W. W.* Rostow, and Anna Jacobson Schwartz. *The Growth and Fluctuation of the British Economy, 1790-1850,* 2 vols., Irish University Press Series of Harper & Row, 1975.

Great Britain. *British Parliamentary Papers, Monetary Policy, General,* Vol. 4, "Session 1831-32," "Report from the Committee of Secrecy on the Bank of England Charter," Shannon Ireland: Irish University Press, 1968.

Great Britain. Public Record Office, Bankruptcy Commissions, B/3.

Hamilton, James. *Time Series Analysis,* Princeton University Press, Table B-6, Case 2, p. 763.

Hilton, Boyd. *Corn, Cash, Commerce: The Economic Policies of the Tory Governments 1815-1830,* Oxford University Press, 1977.

Hubbard, R. Glenn, ed. *Financial Markets and Financial Crises,* University of Chicago Press, 1991.

Hunt, Bishop Carleton. *The Development of the Business Corporation in England, 1800-1867,* Harvard University Press, 1936.

Jenks, Leland H. *The Migration of British Capital to 1875,* Barnes and Noble, 1927.

Kindleberger, Charles P. *A Financial History of Western Europe,* George Allen & Unwin, 1984.

_____. "British Financial Reconstruction, 1815-22 and 1918-25," *Economics in the Long View,* Charles P. Kindleberger and Guido di Tella, eds., *Essays in Honour of W.W. Rostow,* Vol. 3, "Applications and Cases, Part II," New York University Press, 1982, pp. 105–20.

_____. *Manias, Panics, and Crashes. A History of Financial Crises,* Basic Books, 1978.

King, Wilfred T.C. *History of the London Discount Market,* George Routledge & Sons, 1936.

Kynaston, David, and Richard Roberts, eds. *The Bank of England: Money, Power & Influence 1694-1994,* Oxford: Clarendon Press, 1995.

Marichal, Carlos. *A Century of Debt Crises in Latin America: From Independence to the Great Depression, 1820-1930,* Princeton University Press, 1989.

Marriner, Sheila. "English Bankruptcy Records and Statistics before 1850," *Economic History* Review (August 1980), pp. 351–66.

Mishkin, Frederic S. "Asymmetric Information and Financial Crises: A Historical Perspective," *Financial Markets and Financial Crises,* R. Glenn Hubbard, ed., University of Chicago Press, 1991, pp. 69–108.

Mitchell, Brian R. *Abstract of Bristish Historical Statistics,* Cambridge: Cambridge University Press, 1976.

_____. *British Historical Statistics,* Cambridge: Cambridge University Press, 1988.

Morgan, E. Victor, and W.A. Thomas. *The Stock Exchange, Its History and Functions,* London: Elek Books, 1962.

Neal, Larry. "The Disintegration and Re-integration of International Capital Markets in the 19th Century," *Business and Economic History* 21, 1992a, pp. 84–96.

_____. "Commandite System," *The New Palgrave Dictionary of Money and Finance,* Murray Milgate and John Eatwell, eds., London: Macmillan, 1992b.

_____. *The Rise of Financial Capitalism: International Capitol Markets in the Age of Reason,* Cambridge: Cambridge University Press, 1990.

Osterwald-Lenum, Michael. "A Note with Quantiles of the Asymptotic Distribution of the Maximum Likelihood Cointegration Rank Test Statistics," *Oxford Bulletin of Economics and Statistics* (August 1992), pp. 461–72.

Pressnell, Leslie S. *Country Banking in the Industrial Revolution,* Oxford: Clarendon Press, 1956.

Silberling, Norman J. "British Prices and Business Cycles, 1779-1850," *Review of Economics and Statistics,* V, Suppl. 2 (October 1923), pp. 223–61.

Smart, William. *Economic Annals of the Nineteenth Century, 1821-1830,* Vol. II., Augustus M. Kelley, 1911, reprinted 1964.

Ziegler, Philip. *The Sixth Great Power: A History of One of the Greatest of All Banking Families, the House of Barings,* 1762-1929, Alfred A. Knopf, 1988.

7

STOCK MARKETS, BANKS, AND ECONOMIC GROWTH

Ross Levine and Sara Zervos*

Source: *American Economic Review* 88, 3, 1998, 537–558.

Do well-functioning stock markets and banks promote long-run economic growth? This paper shows that stock market liquidity and banking development both positively predict growth, capital accumulation, and productivity improvements when entered together in regressions, even after controlling for economic and political factors. The results are consistent with the views that financial markets provide important services for growth, and that stock markets provide different services from banks. The paper also finds that stock market size, volatility, and international integration are not robustly linked with growth, and that none of the financial indicators is closely associated with private saving rates.

Considerable debate exists on the relationships between the financial system and economic growth. Historically, economists have focused on banks. Walter Bagehot (1873) and Joseph A. Schumpeter (1912) emphasize the critical importance of the banking system in economic growth and highlight circumstances when banks can actively spur innovation and future growth by identifying and funding productive investments. In contrast, Robert E. Lucas, Jr. (1988) states that economists "badly over-stress" the role of the financial system, and Joan Robinson (1952) argues that banks respond passively to economic growth. Empirically, Robert G. King and Levine (1993a) show that the level of financial intermediation is a good predictor of long-run rates of economic growth, capital accumulation, and productivity improvements.

Besides the historical focus on banking, there is an expanding theoretical literature on the links between stock markets and long-run growth, but very little empirical evidence. Levine (1991) and Valerie R. Bencivenga et al. (1995) derive models where more liquid stock markets—markets where it is less expensive to trade equities—reduce the disincentives to investing in long-duration projects because investors can easily sell their stake in the project if they need their savings before the project matures. Enhanced liquidity, therefore, facilitates investment in longer-run, higher-return projects that boost productivity growth. Similarly, Michael B. Devereux and Gregor W. Smith (1994) and Maurice Obstfeld (1994) show that greater international risk sharing through internationally integrated stock markets induces a portfolio shift from safe, low-return investments to high-return investments, thereby accelerating productivity growth. These liquidity and risk models, however, also imply that greater liquidity and international capital market integration ambiguously affect saving rates. In fact, higher returns and better risk sharing may induce saving rates to fall enough such that overall growth slows with more liquid and internationally integrated financial markets. Moreover, theoretical debate exists about whether greater stock market liquidity actually encourages a shift to higher-return projects that stimulate productivity growth. Since more liquidity makes it easier to sell shares, some argue that more liquidity reduces the incentives of shareholders to undertake the costly task of monitoring managers (Andrei Shleifer and Robert W. Vishny, 1986; Amar Bhide, 1993). In turn, weaker corporate governance impedes effective resource allocation and slows productivity growth. Thus, theoretical debate persists over the links between economic growth and the functioning of stock markets.[1]

This paper empirically investigates whether measures of stock market liquidity, size, volatility, and integration with world capital markets are robustly correlated with current and future rates of economic growth, capital accumulation, productivity improvements, and saving rates using data on 47 countries from 1976 through 1993. This investigation provides empirical evidence on the major theoretical debates regarding the linkages between stock markets and long-run economic growth. Moreover, we integrate this study into recent cross-country research on financial intermediation and growth by extending the King and Levine (1993a) analysis of banking and growth to include measures of the functioning of stock markets. Specifically, we evaluate whether banking and stock market indicators are *both* robustly correlated with current and future rates of economic growth, capital accumulation, productivity growth, and private saving. If they are, then this suggests that both banks and stock markets have an independent empirical connection with contemporaneous and future long-run growth rates.

We find that stock market liquidity—*as measured both by the value of stock trading relative to the size of the market and by the value of trading relative to the size of the economy*—is positively and significantly correlated with current and future rates of economic growth, capital accumulation, and productivity growth. Stock market liquidity is a robust predictor of real per capita gross domestic product (GDP) growth, physical capital growth, and productivity growth after controlling for initial income, initial investment in education, political stability, fiscal policy, openness to trade, macroeconomic stability, and the forwardlooking nature of stock prices. Moreover, the level of banking development—*as measured by bank loans to private enterprises divided by GDP*—also enters these regressions significantly. Banking development and stock market liquidity are both good predictors of economic growth, capital accumulation, and productivity

154

growth. The other stock market indicators do not have a robust link with long-run growth. Volatility is insignificantly correlated with growth in most specifications. Similarly, market size and international integration are not robustly linked with growth, capital accumulation, and productivity improvements. Finally, none of the financial indicators is robustly related to private saving rates.

The results have implications for a variety of theoretical models. The strong, positive connections between stock market liquidity and faster rates of growth, productivity improvements, and capital accumulation confirm Levine's (1991) and Bencivenga et al.'s (1995) theoretical predictions. We do not find any support, however, for theories that more liquid or more internationally integrated capital markets negatively affect saving and growth rates or that greater liquidity retards productivity growth.[2] Further, the evidence does not support the belief that stock return volatility hinders investment and resource allocation (J. Bradford DeLong et al., 1989). Finally, the data also suggest that banks provide different services from those of stock markets. Measures of both banking development and stock market liquidity enter the growth regression significantly. Thus, to understand the relationship between financial systems and economic growth, we need theories in which stock markets and banks arise simultaneously to provide different bundles of financial services.

A few points are worth emphasizing in interpreting the results. First, since Levine and David Renelt (1992) show that past researchers have been unable to identify empirical links between growth and macroeconomic indicators that are robust to small changes in the conditioning information set, we check the sensitivity of the results to changes in a large conditioning information set. Stock market liquidity and banking development are positively and robustly correlated with current and future rates of economic growth even after controlling for many other factors associated with economic growth. Second, almost all previous cross-country studies of growth focus on data where both the dependent and explanatory variables are averaged over the entire sample period. Besides examining this contemporaneous relationship, we study whether stock market and banking development measured at the beginning of the period robustly predict future rates of economic growth, capital accumulation, productivity growth, and private saving rates. We find that stock market liquidity and banking development both predict long-run growth, capital accumulation, and productivity improvements. Although this investigation does not establish the direction of causality between financial-sector development and growth, the results show that the strong link between financial development and growth does not merely reflect contemporaneous shocks to both, that stock market and banking development do not simply follow economic growth, and that the predictive content of the financial development indicators does not just represent the forward-looking nature of stock prices. This paper's results are certainly consistent with the view that the services provided by financial institutions and markets are important for long-run growth. Finally, this paper's aggregate cross-country analyses complement recent microeconomic evidence. Asli Demirgüç-Kunt and Vojislav Maksimovic (1996) show that firms in countries with better-functioning banks and equity markets grow faster than predicted by individual firm characteristics, and Raghuram G. Rajan and Luigi Zingales (1998) show that industries that rely more on external finance prosper more in countries with better-developed financial markets.

Raymond Atje and Jovanovic (1993) present a cross-country study of stock markets and economic growth. They find a significant correlation between growth over the period 1980–1988 and the value of stock market trading divided by GDP for 40 countries. We make several contributions. Besides increasing the number of countries by almost 20 percent and almost doubling the number of years in the sample, we construct additional measures of stock market liquidity, a measure of stock return volatility, and two measures of stock market integration in world capital markets and incorporate these measures into our study of stock markets, banks, and economic growth. Furthermore, we control for economic and political factors that may influence growth to gauge the sensitivity of the results to changes in the conditioning information set. Moreover, we control for the potential forward-looking nature of financial prices since we want to gauge whether the functioning of stock markets and banks is tied to economic performance, not whether agents anticipate faster growth. Also, we use the standard cross-country growth regression framework of Robert J. Barro (1991) to make comparisons with other work easier, systematically test for the importance of influential observations, and correct for heteroskedasticity. Finally, besides the direct link with growth, we also study the empirical connections between stock market development and physical capital accumulation, productivity improvements, and private saving rates.

The next section presents measures of stock market and banking development, as well as four *growth indicators*—measures of the rate of economic growth, capital accumulation, productivity growth, and private saving. Section II examines the relationship between the four growth indicators and stock market liquidity, size, volatility, international capital market integration, as well as the level of banking development. Section III concludes.

I. Measuring Stock Market and Banking Development and the Growth Indicators

To assess the relationship between economic growth and both stock market and banking development, we need: (1) empirical indicators of stock market liquidity, size, volatility, and integration with world capital markets; (2) a measure of banking development; and (3) measures of economic growth and its components. This section first defines six stock market development indicators: one measure of stock market size, two measures of stock market liquidity, a measure of stock market volatility, and two measures of stock market integration with world capital markets. Although each of these indicators has shortcomings, using a variety of measures provides a richer picture of the ties between stock market development and economic growth than if we used only a single indicator. Second, we describe the empirical indicator of banking development. The third subsection defines the growth indicators: real per capita GDP growth, real per capita physical capital stock growth, productivity growth, and the ratio of private savings to GDP. Finally, we present summary statistics on these variables. The Appendix lists data sources, sample periods, and countries.

A. Stock Market Development Indicators

1. *Size—Capitalization* measures the size of the stock market and equals the value of listed domestic shares on domestic exchanges divided by GDP. Although large markets do not necessarily function effectively and taxes may distort incentives to list on the exchange, many observers use Capitalization as an indicator of market development.
2. *Liquidity indicators*—We use two related measures of market liquidity. First, *Turnover* equals the value of the trades of domestic shares on domestic exchanges divided by the value of listed domestic shares. Turnover measures the volume of domestic equities traded on domestic exchanges relative to the size of the market. High Turnover is often used as an indicator of low transactions costs. Importantly, a large stock market is not necessarily a liquid market: a large but inactive market will have large Capitalization but small Turnover.

The second measure of market liquidity is *Value Traded,* which equals the value of the trades of domestic shares on domestic exchanges divided by GDP. While not a direct measure of trading costs or the uncertainty associated with trading on a particular exchange, theoretical models of stock market liquidity and economic growth directly motivate Value Traded (Levine, 1991; Bencivenga et al., 1995). Value Traded measures trading volume as a share of national output and should therefore positively reflect liquidity on an economywide basis. Value Traded may be importantly different from Turnover as shown by Demirgüç-Kunt and Levine (1996). While Value Traded captures trading relative to the size of the economy, Turnover measures trading relative to the size of the stock market. Thus, a small, liquid market will have high Turnover but small Value Traded.

Since financial markets are forward looking, Value Traded has one potential pitfall. If markets anticipate large corporate profits, stock prices will rise today. This price rise would increase the value of stock transactions and therefore raise Value Traded. Problematically, the liquidity indicator would rise without a rise in the number of transactions or a fall in transaction costs. This price effect plagues Capitalization too. One way to gauge the influence of the price effect is to look at Capitalization and Value Traded together. The price effect influences both indicators, but only Value Traded is directly related to trading. Therefore, we include both Capitalization and Value Traded indicators together in our regressions. If Value Traded remains significantly correlated with growth while controlling for Capitalization, then the price effect is not dominating the relationship between Value Traded and growth. A second way to gauge the importance of the price effect is to examine Turnover. The price effect does not influence Turnover because stock prices enter the numerator and denominator of Turnover.

If Turnover is positively and robustly associated with economic growth, then this implies that the price effect is not dominating the relationship between liquidity and long-run economic growth.

3. *International integration measures*— Besides liquidity and size, we use two indicators of the degree of integration with world financial markets to provide evidence on theories that link market integration with economic growth. In perfectly integrated markets, capital flows across international borders to equate the price of risk. If capital controls or other barriers impede capital movements, then the price of risk may differ internationally. To compute measures of integration, we use the international capital asset pricing model (CAPM) and international arbitrage pricing theory (APT).

Since these models are well known, we only cursorily outline the estimation procedures. Both asset pricing models imply that the expected return on each asset is linearly related to a benchmark portfolio or linear combination of a group of benchmark portfolios. Following Robert A. Korajczyk and Claude J. Viallet (1989 p. 562–64), let P denote the vector of excess returns on a benchmark portfolio. For the CAPM, P is the excess return on a value-weighted portfolio of common stocks. For the APT, P represents the estimated common factors based on the excess returns of an international portfolio of assets using the asymptotic principal components technique of Gregory Connor and Korajczyk (1986). Firm-level stock returns from 24 national markets are used to form the value-weighted portfolio for the CAPM and to estimate the common factors for the APT. Given m assets and T periods, consider the following regression:

$$R_{i,t} = \alpha_i + b_i \mathbf{P}_t + \varepsilon_{i,t},$$

$$i = 1, 2, \ldots, m; \quad t = 1, 2, \ldots, T,$$

(1)

where $R_{i,t}$ is the excess return on asset i in period t, i.e., the return above the return on a risk-free asset or zero-beta asset (an asset with zero correlation with the benchmark portfolio). The $R_{i,t}$'s are based on monthly, firm-level stock returns that have been adjusted for dividends and stock splits. For an average month, there are 6,851 firms with return data from the 24 markets. If stock markets are perfectly integrated, then the intercept in a regression of any asset's excess return on the appropriate benchmark portfolio, $\mathbf{P}$, should be zero:

$$\alpha_1 = \alpha_2 = \cdots = \alpha_m = 0.$$

(2)

Rejection of the restrictions defined by (2) may be interpreted as rejection of the underlying asset pricing model or rejection of market integration.

Under the assumption that the CAPM and APT are reasonable models of asset pricing, we interpret the monthly estimates of the absolute value of the intercept terms from the multivariate regression (1) as measures of market integration. To compute monthly estimates of stock market integration for each national market, we compute the average of the absolute value of α_i across all stocks in each country each month. Then, we multiply this final value by negative one. Thus, these *CAPM Integration* and *APT Integration* measures are designed to be positively correlated with integration. Moreover, Korajczyk (1996) shows that international integration measures will be negatively correlated with higher official barriers and taxes to international asset trading, bigger transaction costs, and larger impediments to the flow of information about firms.[3]

4. *Volatility*—We measure the volatility of stock returns, *Volatility*, as a 12-month rolling standard deviation estimate that is based on market returns. We cleanse the return series of monthly means and 12 months of autocorrelations using the procedure defined by G. William Schwert (1989). Specifically, we estimate a 12th-order autoregression of monthly returns, R_t, including dummy variables, D_{jt}, to allow for different monthly mean returns:

$$R_t = \sum_{j=1}^{12} a_j D_{jt} + \sum_{k=1}^{12} b_k R_{t-k} + v_r. \tag{3}$$

We collect the absolute value of the residuals from equation (3), and then estimate a 12th-order autoregression of the absolute value of the residuals including dummy variables for each month to allow for different monthly standard deviations of returns:

$$|\hat{v}| = \sum_{j=1}^{12} c_j D_{jt} + \sum_{k=1}^{12} d_k |\hat{v}_{t-k}| + \mu_r. \tag{4}$$

The fitted values from this last equation give estimates of the conditional standard deviation of returns.[4] We include this measure because of the intense interest in market volatility by academics, practitioners, and policy makers.

B. Banking Development

An extensive theoretical literature examines the ties between banks and economic activity. Ideally, researchers would construct crosscountry measures of how well banks identify profitable activities, exert corporate governance, mobilize resources, manage risk, and facilitate transactions. Economists, however, have not been able to accurately measure these financial services for a broad cross section of countries. Consequently, researchers traditionally use measures of the overall size of the banking sector to proxy for "financial depth" (e.g., Raymond W. Goldsmith, 1969; Ronald I. McKinnon, 1973). Thus, researchers often divide the stock of broad money (M2) by GDP to measure financial depth. As noted by King and Levine (1993a), however, this type of financial depth indicator does not measure whether the liabilities are those of banks, the central bank, or other financial intermediaries, nor does this financial depth measure identify where the financial system allocates capital. Thus, we use the value of loans made by commercial banks and other deposit-taking banks to the private sector divided by GDP, and call this measure *Bank Credit.* Bank Credit improves upon traditional financial depth measures of banking development by isolating credit issued by banks, as opposed to credit issued by the central bank or other intermediaries, and by identifying credit to the private sector, as opposed to credit issued to governments. In our empirical work, we also used traditional measures of financial depth and discuss some of these results below. We focus almost exclusively on the results with Bank Credit.

C. Channels to Growth

Besides examining the relationship between these financial development indicators and long-run real per capita GDP growth, *Output Growth,* we also study two channels through which banks and stock markets may be linked to growth: the rate of real per capita physical capital stock growth, *Capital Stock Growth,* and everything else, *Productivity Growth.* Specifically, let Output Growth equal κ*(Capital Stock Growth) + Productivity Growth. To obtain empirical estimates, we: (a) obtain Output Growth from national accounts data; (b) use Capital Stock Growth from King and Levine (1994); (c) select a value for κ ($\kappa = 0.3$), and then compute Productivity Growth as a residual.[5] If Capital Stock Growth accurately reflects changes in physical capital and if capacity utilization remains stable when averaged over 18 years, then Productivity Growth should provide a reasonable conglomerate indicator of technological change, quality advances, and resource allocation enhancements.[6]

The last growth indicator we consider, *Savings,* equals gross private savings from Paul Masson et al. (1995). Measuring private saving rates is subject to considerable measurement error, and data on gross private savings are available for many fewer countries in our sample (32) than, for example, Output Growth data (47). Nevertheless, these data offer a unique opportunity to shed some empirical light on important theoretical issues: what is the relationship between private saving rates and stock market liquidity, international risk sharing through integrated capital markets, and the level of banking development?

We term the four variables — Output Growth, Capital Stock Growth, Productivity Growth, and Savings — growth indicators. Thus, this paper evaluates the empirical relationship between the four growth indicators and the six stock market indicators (Turnover, Value Traded, Capitalization, Volatility, CAPM Integration, and APT Integration) plus the banking development indicator (Bank Credit).

D. Summary Statistics and Correlations

Table 1 presents summary statistics on the six stock market development indicators, the bank development indicator, and four growth indicators. We have data for a maximum of 47 countries over the 1976–1993 period. Table 1 shows substantial variance among the countries in the growth and financial development indicators. For example, Korea averaged 9.7 percent annual growth over the 1976–1993 period and had a private savings rate of almost 30 percent of GDP, while Cote d'Ivoire grew at −2.5 percent in real per capita terms over the same period and Bangladesh's savings rate was 9 percent of GDP; Taiwan had Value Traded equal to almost 1.2, while Nigeria's Value Traded averaged 0.0002 from 1976–1993.

Table 2 presents correlations. Data permitting, we average the data over the 1976–1993 period so that each country has one observation per variable. We compute the correlations for Capital Stock Growth and Productivity Growth using data averaged over the 1976–1990 period. Three correlations are worth highlighting. First, Bank Credit is highly correlated with the growth indicators and all of the stock market indicators. Second, Bank Credit is very highly correlated with Capitalization (0.65), which suggests that it will be difficult to distinguish between measures of the overall size of the equity market and the measure of bank credit to private enterprises divided by GDP. Third, the liquidity measures are positively and significantly correlated with Output Growth, Capital Stock Growth, and Productivity Growth at the 0.05-percent level.

II. Stock Markets, Banks, and Economic Growth

This section evaluates whether measures of banking development and stock market liquidity, size, volatility, and integration with world capital markets are robustly correlated with economic growth, capital accumulation, productivity growth, and private saving rates. The first two subsections use least-squares regressions to study the ties between the growth indicators and measures of banking development, stock market liquidity, market size, and stock return volatility. The next subsection uses instrumental variables to examine the links between the growth indicators, banking development, and measures of capital market integration. We use instrumental variables because the international integration measures are estimated regressors. The final subsection conducts a number of sensitivity checks on the robustness of the results.

A. Framework: Banking, Liquidity, Size, and Volatility

This subsection uses cross-country regressions to gauge the strength of the partial correlation between each of the four growth indicators and measures of banking and stock market development. The growth indicators are averaged over the 1976–1993 period. The banking and stock market development indicators are computed at the beginning of the period 1976 (data permitting). There is one observation per country.

Table 1 SUMMARY STATISTICS: ANNUAL AVERAGES 1976–1993

	Mean	Median	Maximum	Minimum	Standard deviation	Observations
Output Growth	0.021	0.019	0.097	-0.025	0.022	47
Capital Stock Growth	0.028	0.024	0.095	-0.023	0.026	46
Productivity Growth	0.016	0.014	0.079	-0.019	0.017	46
Savings	20.0	20.8	29.7	9.1	5.1	32
Capitalization	0.32	0.17	2.45	0.01	0.43	46
Value Traded	0.11	0.04	1.16	0.00	0.19	47
Turnover	0.30	0.23	2.05	0.01	0.33	46
Volatility	0.07	0.05	0.31	0.03	0.06	36
Bank Credit	0.80	0.75	2.27	0.12	0.50	47
APT Integration	-4.30	-3.95	-2.17	-6.67	1.48	24
CAPM Integration	-4.08	-3.65	-2.00	-9.98	1.86	24

Notes: Output Growth = real per capita GDP growth; Capital Stock Growth = real per capita capital stock growth; Productivity Growth = Output Growth–(0.3) (Capital Stock Growth); Savings = private savings as a percent of GDP; Capitalization = value of domestic shares as a share of GDP; Value Traded = value of the trades of domestic shares as a share of GDP; Turnover = value of the trades of domestic shares as a share of market capitalization; Volatility — measure of stock return volatility; Bank Credit = bank credit to the private sector as a share of GDP; APT Integration — the arbitrage pricing theory measure of stock market integration; CAPM Integration = the international capital asset pricing model measure of stock market integration.

Table 2 Correlations

	Capital Stock Growth	Productivity Growth	Savings	Capitalization	Value Traded	Turnover	CAPM Integration	APT Integration	Volatility	Bank Credit
Output Growth	0.773 (0.001)	0.957 (0.001)	0.4466 (0.008)	0.037 (0.037)	0.522 (0.001)	0.487 (0.001)	0.343 (0.101)	0.28 (0.186)	-0.08 (0.644)	0.347 (0.013)
Capital Stock Growth	—	0.557 (0.001)	0.5300 (0.001)	0.203 (0.171)	0.425 (0.003)	0.356 (0.014)	0.228 (0.296)	0.182 (0.407)	-0.104 (0.547)	0.324 (0.023)
Productivity Growth	—	—	0.4191 (0.014)	0.222 (0.134)	0.417 (0.003)	0.444 (0.002)	0.277 (0.200)	0.209 (0.339)	-0.169 (0.325)	0.372 (0.008)
Savings	—	—	—	-0.0792 (0.656)	0.1601 (0.366)	0.4470 (0.008)	-0.1394 (0.620)	-0.3504 (0.200)	0.1189 (0.555)	0.1189 (0.168)
Capitalization	—	—	—	—	0.331 (0.022)	0.05 (0.735)	0.476 (0.019)	0.36 (0.084)	-0.261 (0.124)	0.647 (0.001)
Value Traded	—	—	—	—	—	0.831 (0.001)	0.188 (0.380)	0.068 (0.752)	0.085 (0.622)	0.449 (0.001)
Turnover	—	—	—	—	—	—	0.074 (0.730)	-0.003 (0.991)	0.186 (0.278)	0.328 (0.023)
CAPM Integration	—	—	—	—	—	—	—	0.78 (0.001)	-0.838 (0.001)	0.45 (0.027)
ATP Integration	—	—	—	—	—	—	—	—	0.573 (0.005)	0.454 (0.026)
Volatility	—	—	—	—	—	—	—	—	—	-0.404 (0.014)

Notes: p-values in parentheses. Output Growth = real per capital GDP growth; Capital Stock Growth = real per capita capital stock growth; Productivity Growth = Output Growth–(0.3) (Capital Stock Growth); Savings = private savings divided by GDP; Capitalization = value of domestic shares as a share of GDP; Value Traded = value of the trades of domestic shares as a share of GDP; Turnover = value of the trades of domestic shares as a share market capitalization; Volatility = measure of stock return volatility; Bank Credit = bank credit to the private sector as a share of GDP; APT Integration = the arbitrage pricing theory measure of stock market integration; CAPM Integration = the international capital asset pricing model measure of stock market integration.

163

We organize the investigation around the four stock market development indicators and always control for the level of banking development. Thus, we run 16 basic regressions, where the dependent variable is either Output Growth, Capital Stock Growth, Productivity Growth, or Savings averaged over the 1976–1993 period. The four stock market variables are either Turnover, Value Traded, Capitalization, or Volatility measured at the beginning of the sample period.

Traditionally, the growth literature uses growth and explanatory variables averaged over long periods. This approach, however, is frequently criticized because: (i) a common shock to the dependent and explanatory variables during the sample period may be driving the empirical findings; and (ii) *contemporaneous regressions*—regressions using dependent and explanatory variables averaged over the same period—do not account for the potential endogenous determination of growth and the explanatory variables. Besides conducting the contemporaneous regressions, we focus on the "initial value" regressions, where we use the values of the banking and stock market indicators in 1976. While this analysis does not resolve the issue of causality, the initial value regressions show that the strong relationship between financial development and the growth indicators does not merely reflect contemporaneous shocks to both, and that stock market and banking development do not simply follow economic development.

To assess the strength of the independent relationship between the initial levels of stock market and banking development and the growth variables, we include a wide array of control variables, *X*. Specifically, we include the logarithm of initial real per capital GDP, *Initial Output,* and the logarithm of the initial secondary-school enrollment rate, *Enrollment,* because theory and evidence suggest an important link between long-run growth and initial income and investment in human capital accumulation (Robert M. Solow, 1956; Lucas, 1988; N. Gregory Mankiw et al., 1992; Barro and Xavier Sala-i-Martin, 1995). The number of revolutions and coups, *Revolutions and Coups,* is included since many authors find that political instability is negatively associated with economic growth (see Barro and Sala-i-Martin [1995] for evidence and citations). We also include a variety of macroeconomic indicators in the conditioning information set. The initial values of government consumption expenditures to GDP, *Government*, and the rate of inflation, *Inflation,* are included because theory and some evidence suggests a negative relationship between macroeconomic instability and economic activity (William Easterly and Sergio Rebelo, 1993; Stanley Fischer, 1993; Michael Bruno and Easterly, 1998). Similarly, the initial value of the black market exchange rate premium, *Black Market Premium*, is part of the *X* variables since international price distortions may impede efficient investment decisions and economic growth (David Dollar, 1992). Moreover, the black market premium is a general indicator of policy, price, and trade distortions and therefore is a useful variable to use in assessing the independent relationship between the growth indicators and measures of financial sector development. As discussed below, alternative control variables and combinations of *X* variables do not materially affect the results on the relationship between financial development and economic growth.

B. Results: Banking, Liquidity, Size, and Volatility

First, consider the results on stock market liquidity and banking development. Table 3 presents four regressions, where the dependent variable is Output Growth, Capital Stock Growth, Productivity Growth, and Savings, respectively, and the liquidity measure is initial Turnover. White's heteroskedasticity-consistent standard errors are reported in parentheses. *Both* the stock market liquidity and banking development indicators enter the Output Growth, Capital Stock Growth, and Productivity Growth regressions significantly at the 0.05-percent significance level. To economize on space, we only present the coefficient estimates for the stock market and bank indicators. The full regression results for Table 3 are given in the Appendix [see Table A1]. The other explanatory variables generally enter the regressions as expected. Initial income enters with a significantly negative coefficient and the size of the convergence coefficient is very similar to other studies (Barro and Sala-i-Martin, 1995). Secondary-school enrollment enters the growth regression positively, while political instability enters with a significantly negative coefficient. Although the values of government consumption expenditures divided by GDP and inflation in 1976 enter the growth regression with negative coefficients, they are statistically insignificant, though inflation has a strong negative relationship with capital accumulation and private saving rates. In this sample of countries and with the extensive set of control variables, the black market exchange rate premium does not enter the Output Growth regression significantly, which confirms Levine and Renelt (1992). The growth regression R^2 of 0.50 is consistent with other cross-country growth studies (e.g., Barro and Sala-i-Martin, 1995).

In sum, we find that both the initial level of banking development and the initial level of stock market liquidity have statistically significant relationships with

Table 3 Initial Turnover, Banks and Growth, 1976–1993

Independent variables	Dependent variables			
	Output Growth	*Capital Stock Growth*	*Productivity Growth*	*Savings*
Bank Credit	0.0131 (0.0055)	0.0148 (0.0063)	0.0111 (0.0046)	3.8376 (2.3069)
Turnover	0.0269 (0.0090)	0.0222 (0.0094)	0.0201 (0.0088)	7.7643 (5.6864)
R^2	0.5038	0.5075	0.4027	0.4429
Observations	42	41	41	29

Notes: Heteroskedasticity-consistent standard errors in parentheses. Output Growth = real per capita GDP growth; Capital Stock Growth = real per capita capital stock growth; Productivity Growth = Output Growth-(0.3) (Capital Stock Growth); Savings = private savings divided by GDP; Bank Credit = initial bank credit to the private sector as a share of GDP; Turnover = initial value of the trades of domestic shares as a share of market capitalization. Other explanatory variables included in each of the regressions: Initial Output, Enrollment, Revolutions and Coups, Government, Inflation, and Black Market Premium.

future values of Output Growth, Capital Stock Growth, and Productivity Growth even after controlling for many other factors associated with long-run economic performance. These results are consistent with the view that stock market liquidity and banks facilitate long-run growth (Levine, 1991; Bengt Holmstrom and Jean Tirole, 1993; Bencivenga et al., 1995). The results are not supportive of models that emphasize the negative implications of stock market liquidity (Shleifer and Vishny, 1986; Shleifer and Lawrence Summers, 1988).

We do not find a statistically significant link between private saving rates and either stock market liquidity or banking development. Although the saving results should be viewed very skeptically because there are only 29 observations in the regressions, Catherine Bonser-Neal and Kathryn Dewenter (1996) find similar results using annual data with 174 observations: there is not a systematic association between stock market liquidity and private saving rates. It is also worth noting that these results do not contradict Tullio Jappelli and Marco Pagano's (1994) findings that countries where households are liquidity constrained tend to have higher saving rates. In Jappelli and Pagano (1994), "liquidity constrained" means that households find it relatively difficult to obtain mortgages or consumer credit. In contrast, this paper uses the term liquidity to refer to the ease with which agents can trade equities. Taken together, the two sets of findings imply that countries with large impediments to obtaining mortgage and consumer credit tend to have higher saving rates, while the level of activity on a country's stock exchange is unrelated to saving rates.[7] Furthermore, our finding that stock market liquidity is unrelated to private saving rates is not inconsistent with our finding that stock market liquidity is positively related to physical capital accumulation: (a) Capital Stock Growth is generated by private-sector, public-sector, and foreign investment, while Savings only measures gross private savings of domestic residents; and (b) the savings analysis is based on a much smaller sample of countries.[8] Moreover, while financial development is significantly associated with future Capital Stock Growth, economically, the major channel through which growth is linked to stock markets and banks is through Productivity Growth, not Capital Stock Growth, as we discuss below. Finally, the lack of a strong link between financial-sector development and private savings has implications for Mankiw et al.'s (1992) evaluation of the neoclassical growth model. One weakness in their analysis is that savings rates may be endogenous or proxying for some other country-specific factor. This paper's results suggest that saving rates are not proxying for financial-sector development.

Besides being statistically significant, the estimated coefficients suggest that the relationships between financial-sector development and future rates of long-run growth, capital accumulation, and productivity improvements are economically large. For example, the estimated coefficient implies that a one-standard-deviation increase in initial stock market liquidity (0.3) would increase per capita growth by 0.8 percentage points per year (0.027*0.3) over this period. Accumulating over 18 years, this implies that real GDP per capita would have been over 15 percent higher by 1994 (exp {18* 0.008}). The estimated coefficient on Bank Credit also suggests a similarly large economic relationship between banking development and growth. Specifically, a one-standard-deviation increase in initial banking development (0.5) would increase Output Growth by 0.7 percentage points per year (0.013*0.5). Taken together, the results imply that if a county had increased both stock market and banking development in 1976 by one standard deviation, then by 1994 real per capita GDP would have been 31 percent larger, the capital stock per person would have been 29 percent higher, and productivity would have been 24 percent greater. These conceptual experiments do not consider the question of causality nor how to change the financial sector. Nonetheless, the examples illustrate the potentially large economic consequences of stock market liquidity and banking development and the potentially large economic costs of impediments to financial-sector development.

The Value Traded measure of stock market liquidity confirms these findings. Table 4 presents the same type of regressions as in Table 3 except we replace Turnover with Value Traded. Again, the initial liquidity and banking development indicators are significantly and robustly correlated with future rates of economic growth, capital accumulation, and productivity growth. Again, the estimated coefficients suggest an economically large relationship between initial financial development and future long-run growth rates. For example, the results imply that if in 1976 Mexico had had the sample mean value of Value Traded (0.046) instead of its actual value of (0.004), annual per capita growth would have been almost 0.4 percentage points faster (0.095*0.04) over the sample period, such that GDP per capita would have been 7.5 percent higher by 1994 (exp{18*0.004}). The economic implications of a symmetric change in banking are even larger. If Mexico had had the sample mean value of banking development in 1976 (0.65) instead of its actual value of (0.13), growth would have been 0.8 percentage points faster per year (0.015*0.52). Combined, these improvements in stock market liquidity

Table 4 Initial Value traded, Banks and Growth, 1976–1993

Independent variables	Dependent variables			
	Output Growth	Capital Stock Growth	Productivity Growth	Savings
Bank Credit	0.0146 (0.0056)	0.0148 (0.0061)	0.0125 (0.0047)	3.4917 (2.1920)
Value Traded	0.0954 (0.0315)	0.0927 (0.0324)	0.0736 (0.0220)	15.8456 (14.0757)
R^2	0.4655	0.5224	0.3726	0.4278
Observations	43	42	42	29

Notes: Heteroskedasticity-consistent standard errors in parentheses. Output Growth = real per capita GDP growth; Capital Stock Growth = real per capita capital stock growth; Productivity Growth = Output Growth-(0.3) (Capital Stock Growth); Savings = private savings divided by GDP; Bank Credit = initial bank credit to the private sector as a share of GDP; Value Traded = initial value of the trades of domestic shares as a share of GDP. Other explanatory variables included in each of the regressions: Initial Output, Enrollment, Revolutions and Coups, Government, Inflation, and Black Market Premium.

and banking development in 1976 are consistent with Mexico enjoying almost 23-percent higher GDP per capita by 1994.

The findings in Tables 3 and 4 also provide some information on the relative importance of the Capital Stock Growth and Productivity Growth channels. For example, the estimated parameter values imply that a one-standard-deviation increase in Value Traded in 1976 (0.2) would increase Output Growth and Capital Stock Growth by about 1.9 percentage points per year. Since growth accounting exercises generally give Productivity Growth a weight that is about two times the weight on physical capital accumulation (i.e., κ - 1/3), this implies that Productivity Growth accounts for about 1.3 percentage points (1.9 - (1/3)* 1.9) of the 1.9-percentage-point increase in Output Growth generated by the increase in Value Traded. Thus, the main channel linking financial development with growth runs through Productivity Growth rather than Capital Stock Growth, which is consistent with the findings in Jose DeGregorio and Pablo E. Guidotti (1995).[9] As noted above, the estimated coefficients should not be viewed as exploitable elasticities. Rather, these conceptual experiments are meant to illustrate the economic size of the coefficients.

The forward-looking nature of stockprices— the "price-effect"—is not driving the strong link between market liquidity and the growth indicators. This can be deduced from two results. First, the price effect does not influence Turnover, and Turnover is robustly linked with future rates of economic growth, capital accumulation, and productivity growth. Second, we include Capitalization and Value Traded together in the same regression to test whether the price-effect is producing the strong empirical links between Value Traded and the growth indicators. The price-effect influences both Capitalization and Value Traded. If the price-effect is driving the empirical association between Value Traded and the growth indicators reported in Table 4, then Value Traded should not remain significantly correlated with the growth indicators when we simultaneously include Capitalization and Value Traded. This is not the case. As reported in Table 5, Value Traded in 1976 remains significantly correlated with future rates of economic growth, capital accumulation, and productivity growth even when controlling for market capitalization (with little change in the estimated coefficients). Thus, the evidence is inconsistent with the view that expectations of future growth, which are reflected in current stock prices, are driving the strong empirical relationship between stock market liquidity and growth. The evidence is consistent with the view that the ability to trade ownership of an economy's productive technologies easily promotes more efficient resource allocation, capital formation, and faster growth.[10]

Importantly, initial stock market size and stock return volatility are not generally robust predictors of the growth indicators. Although the coefficients presented in Table 6 indicate a positive association between Capitalization and both Output Growth and Capital Stock Growth, this relationship is strongly influenced by a few countries. Specifically, if Jamaica, Korea, and Singapore are removed from the regression, Capitalization no longer enters the regression significantly.[11]

Table 5 Initial Value traded, Capitalization, Banks and Growth, 1976–1993

Independent variables	Dependent variables			
	Output Growth	Capital Stock Growth	Productivity Growth	Savings
Bank Credit	0.0083 (0.0054)	0.0111 (0.0055)	0.0086 (0.0046)	2.9614 (2.0960)
Capitalization	0.0148 (0.0068)	0.0088 (0.0092)	0.0070 (0.0056)	−7.5606 (7.0266)
Value Traded	0.0700 (0.0322)	0.0780 (0.0382)	0.0592 (0.0227)	23.5929 (15.7283)
R^2	0.5186	0.5297	0.4083	0.4499
Observations	42	41	41	29

Notes: Heteroskedasticity-consistent standard errors in parentheses. Output Growth = real per capita GDP growth; Capital Stock Growth = real per capita capital stock growth; Productivity Growth = Output Growth-(0.3) (Capital Stock Growth); Savings = private savings divided by GDP; Bank Credit = initial bank credit to the private sector as a share of GDP; Value Traded = initial value of the trades of domestic shares as a share of GDP; Capitalization = initial value of domestic shares as a share of GDP. Other explanatory variables included in each of the regressions: Initial Output, Enrollment, Revolutions and Coups, Government, Inflation, and Black Market Premium.

Table 6 Initial Capitalization, Banks and Growth, 1976–1993

Independent variables	Dependent variables			
	Output Growth	Capital Stock Growth	Productivity Growth	Savings
Bank Credit	0.0089 (0.0061)	0.0090 (0.0078)	0.0094 (0.0050)	5.1226 (2.0927)
Capitalization	0.0230 (0.0065)	0.0207 (0.0081)	0.0135 (0.0055)	−0.7291 (7.1411)
R^2	0.4577	0.3754	0.3423	0.3189
Observations	45	44	44	31

Notes: Heteroskedasticity-consistent standard errors in parentheses. Output Growth = real per capita GDP growth; Capital Stock Growth = real per capita capital stock growth; Productivity Growth = Output Growth-(0.3) (Capital Stock Growth); Savings = private savings divided by GDP; Bank Credit = initial bank credit to the private sector as a share of GDP; Capitalization = initial value of domestic shares as a share of GDP. Other explanatory variables included in each of the regressions: Initial Output, Enrollment, Revolutions and Coups, Government, Inflation, and Black Market Premium.

Similarly, the results on market volatility do not suggest a reliable link to the growth indicators. As shown in Table 7, stock return volatility is not closely linked with future growth, productivity improvements, or private saving rates, and Volatility is positively correlated with capital accumulation. As discussed below, the results on market liquidity are much more robust to the removal of outliers. More importantly, the relationship between stock market size and the growth indicators vanishes when controlling for stock market liquidity (Table 5). Thus, it is not just listing securities on an exchange; it is the ability to trade those securities that is closely tied to economic performance.

Table 7 Initial Volatility Banks and Growth, 1976–1993

Independent variables	Dependent variables			
	Output Growth	Capital Stock Growth	Productivity Growth	Savings
Bank Credit	0.0150 (0.0074)	0.0140 (0.0085)	0.0130 (0.0066)	3.5945 (1.9631)
Volatility	0.0150 (0.0074)	0.4998 (0.1580)	0.0211 (0.2146)	115.0991 (99.4063)
R^2	0.4183	0.6817	0.2938	0.7708
Observations	32	32	32	23

Notes: Heteroskedasticity-consistent standard errors in parentheses. Output Growth = real per capita GDP growth; Capital Stock Growth = real per capita capital stock growth; Productivity Growth = Output Growth-(0.3) (Capital Stock Growth); Savings = private savings divided by GDP; Bank Credit = initial bank credit to the private sector as a share of GDP; Volatility = initial measure of stock return volatility. Other explanatory variables included in each of the regressions: Initial Output, Enrollment, Revolutions and Coups, Government, Inflation, and Black Market Premium.

C. International Capital Market Integration, Banking, and the Growth Indicators

To investigate the relationship between the growth indicators and international capital market integration, we slightly revise the analytical framework in two ways. First, we only have data on capital market integration for 24 countries. Thus, we use pooled cross-section time-series data averaged over the periods 1976–1985 and 1986–1993, so that each country has potentially two observations for a maximum of 48 observations.[12] Second, CAPM Integration and APT Integration are estimated regressors. Therefore, we use two-stage least squares to derive consistent standard errors as suggested by Adrian Pagan (1984).[13]

Tables 8 and 9 report the results on capital market integration. The CAPM and APT Integration measures enter the growth equations with a positive coefficient suggesting that greater capital market integration is positively related to economic performance. Furthermore, the point estimates imply a potentially large effect. For example, a one-standard-deviation increase in CAPM Integration (1.86) would increase Output Growth by about 1.2 percentage points per year (1.86*0.0065). Nonetheless, the data do not suggest a statistically strong link between capital market integration and the growth indicators. The CAPM and APT Integration measures are not significantly correlated with Output Growth at the 0.10 level. Moreover, the reported regressions exclude Inflation, which is very highly correlated with stock market integration. With inflation included, the *t*-statistics on CAPM Integration and APT Integration become even smaller. While the very small sample may lower confidence in these results, the findings do not support the hypothesis that greater risk sharing through internationally integrated markets affect growth, capital accumulation, productivity growth, or private saving rates.

Table 8 Stock Market Integration (CAPM), Banks, and Growth, 1976–1993, Pooled, Instrumental Variables

Independent variables	Dependent variables			
	Output Growth	Capital Stock Growth	Productivity Growth	Savings
Bank Credit	0.0096 (0.0134)	0.0143 (0.0172)	0.0032 (0.0136)	−4.3598 (2.9495)
CAPM Integration	0.0065 (0.0043)	0.0014 (0.0045)	0.0085 (0.0048)	2.0167 (2.0609)
Observations	38	38	38	25

Notes: First-stage R^2 for CAPM Integration: 0.73. Heteroskedasticity-consistent standard errors in parentheses. Output Growth = real per capita GDP growth; Capital Stock Growth = real per capita capital stock growth; Productivity Growth = Output Growth-(0.3) (Capital Stock Growth); Savings = private savings divided by GDP; Bank Credit = initial bank credit to the private sector as a share of GDP; CAPM Integration = the international capital asset pricing model measure of stock market integration. Instruments: a constant, Initial Output, Enrollment, Revolutions and Coups, and initial values of Government, Black Market Premium, Trade, Capitalization, Value Traded, Turnover, and Bank Credit.

Table 9 Stock Market Integration (APT), Banks, and Growth, 1976–1993, Pooled, Instrumental Variables

Independent variables	Dependent variables			
	Output Growth	Capital Stock Growth	Productivity Growth	Savings
Bank Credit	0.0148 (0.0143)	0.0186 (0.0166)	0.0117 (0.0150)	−3.8182 (2.3952)
APT Integration	0.0075 (0.0074)	−0.0008 (0.0076)	0.0086 (0.0073)	2.8466 (1.7108)
Observations	38	38	38	25

Notes: First-stage R^2 for APT Integration: 0.52. Heteroskedasticity-consistent standard errors in parentheses. Output Growth = real per capita GDP growth; Capital Stock Growth = real per capita capital stock growth; Productivity Growth - Output Growth-(0.3) (Capital Stock Growth); Savings = private savings divided by GDP; Bank Credit = initial bank credit to the private sector as a share of GDP; APT Integration = the arbitrage pricing theory measure of stock market integration. Instruments: a constant, Initial Output, Enrollment, Revolutions and Coups, and initial values of Government, Black Market Premium, Trade, Capitalization, Value Traded, Turnover, and Bank Credit.

D. Sensitivity Analyses

We conducted a wide array of sensitivity analyses to check the robustness of these results.[14] As mentioned above, regressions using values of the dependent and explanatory variables averaged over the entire sample period yield similar results. Furthermore, changing the conditioning information set did not materially affect our results.[15] For example, altering the set of explanatory variables included in the regression, adding measures of legal efficiency or institutional development, as defined in Paulo Mauro (1995), or using the King and Levine (1993a) measure of financial depth did not affect the strong link between stock market liquidity and growth.[16] We also experimented with an alternative measure of stock market liquidity that gauges trading relative to stock price movements. Specifically, we divide Value Traded by Volatility. All things equal, more liquid markets should be able to support more trading with less price volatility. This alternative measure produced similar results.

We test for the potential influence of outliers in two ways. First, we use the procedure for analyzing the influence of particular observations described in William Greene (1993 pp. 287–88). This procedure identifies countries that exert a large effect on each equation's residuals. Using a critical value of 2.5, we find that removing particularly influential observations does not affect our conclusions. Second, we use a more subjective method for identifying influential observations; we use scatterplots of the partial relationship between each of the growth indicators and the individual stock market indicators to identify outliers that may be excessively influencing the slope and significance of the estimated regression line.[17] Removing influential observations importantly weakens the relationship between the growth indicators and market size, as noted above. The other results do not change. In particular, stock market liquidity remains robustly correlated with growth, capital accumulation, and productivity growth after removing potential outliers.

We were also concerned about a potential sample selection problem: we only include countries with sufficient stock market activity to warrant inclusion in data bases. We have data on all the non-stock market data for an additional 31 countries. Although we do not have explicit observations on stock transactions in these economies, anecdotal information and a review of official documents suggest that stock market activity in these countries was inconsequential in 1976.

Table 10 Initial Stock Market Development, Banks, and Growth, 78-Country Sample

Dependent variable: Output Growth				
Stock market indicator (SMI):	*78-country sample*		*Original sample*	
	Bank Credit	*SMI*	*Bank Credit*	*SMI*
Turnover	0.015 (2.753)	0.022 (2.448)	0.013 (2.753)	0.027 (2.448)
Value Traded	0.013 (2.630)	0.111 (4.242)	0.015 (2.536)	0.095 (3.854)
Capitalization	0.012 (2.047)	0.018 (2.826)	0.009 (1.866)	0.023 (2.672)

Notes: Heteroskedasticity-consistent *t*-statistics in parentheses. Output Growth = real per capita GDP growth; Bank Credit = initial bank credit to the private sector as a share of GDP; Turnover = initial value of trades of domestic shares as a share of market capitalization; Capitalization = initial value of domestic shares as a share of GDP; Value Traded = initial value of trades of domestic shares as a share of GDP; Other explanatory variables included in each of the regressions: Initial Output, Enrollment, Revolutions and Coups, Government, Inflation, and Black Market Premium.

Thus, for these 31 countries, we enter values of zero for Capitalization, Value Traded, and Turnover.[18] Zero is not an extreme guess. Recall from Table 1 that the minimum values for Capitalization, Value Traded, and Turnover are 0.01, 0.0002, and 0.006 with standard deviations of 0.43, 0.19, and 0.33, respectively. As shown in Table 10, the link between economic growth and the initial levels of both stock market liquidity and banking development remains strong even when including data on these additional 31 countries.[19]

III. Conclusion

This paper studied the empirical relationship between various measures of stock market development, banking development, and long-run economic growth. We find that, even after controlling for many factors associated with growth, stock market liquidity and banking development are both positively and robustly correlated with contemporaneous and future rates of economic growth, capital accumulation, and productivity growth. This result is consistent with the view that a greater ability to trade ownership of an economy's productive technologies facilitates efficient resource allocation, physical capital formation, and faster economic growth. Furthermore, since measures of stock market liquidity and banking development both enter the growth regressions significantly, the findings suggest that banks provided different financial services from those provided by stock markets. Thus, to understand the relationship between the financial system and long-run growth more comprehensively, we need theories in which both stock markets and banks arise and develop simultaneously while providing different bundles of financial services to the economy. We find no support for the contentions that stock market liquidity, international capital market integration, or stock return volatility reduce private saving rates or hinder long-run growth. This paper finds a strong, positive link between financial development and economic growth and the results suggest that financial factors are an integral part of the growth process.

Data Appendix

A. Variables and Sources

Data are available at the web site http://www.worldbank.org/html/prdmg/grthweb /growth_t.htm.

CAPM Integration and *APT Integration:* Measure of each stock market's integration with world equity markets based on the capital asset pricing model and arbitrage pricing theory, respectively. (Sources: Korajczyk, 1994, 1996.)

Bank Credit: Stock of credit by commercial and deposit-taking banks to the private sector divided by GDP. (Source: International Monetary Fund's (IMF's) *International Financial Statistics.*)

Black Market Premium: Black market exchange rate premium. (Sources: *Picks Currency Yearbook through 1989 and World Currency Yearbook.*)

Capital Stock Growth: Growth rate in capital stock per person, available through 1990. (Sources: King and Levine, 1994.)

Capitalization: Average value of listed domestic shares on domestic exchanges in a year divided by GDP that year. (Sources: International Finance Corporation's (IFC's) *Emerging Markets Data Base* (electronic version) and the IMF's *International Financial Statistics.*)

Government: Government consumption share of GDP. (Sources: IMF's *International Financial Statistics* and World Bank's *World Development Indicators.*)

Inflation: Rate of change in the GDP deflator; if unavailable, consumer price index is used. (Sources: IMF's *International Financial Statistics* and World Bank's *World Development Indicators.*)

Initial Output: Logarithm of real per capita GDP in 1976. (Source: IMF's *International Financial Statistics.*)

Enrollment: Logarithm of the secondary-school enrollment rate in 1976. (Sources: IMF's *International Financial Statistics* and World Bank's *World Development Indicators.*)

Output Growth: Growth of real per capita gross domestic product. (Source: IMF's *International Financial Statistics.*)

Productivity Growth: Output Growth minus 0.3 times Capital Stock Growth, available through 1990. (Source: King and Levine, 1994.)

Revolutions and Coups: Number of revolutions and coups per year, averaged over the 1980's. (Source: Arthur S. Banks, 1994.)

Savings: Gross private saving as a percent of GDP, available from 1982 onward for countries classified as [4] 'developing' ' by the IMF and for the entire sample period for industrial countries. (Source: Masson et al., 1995.)

Trade: Exports plus imports divided by GDP. (Sources: IMF's *International Financial Statistics* and World Bank's *World Development Indicators.*)

Turnover: Value of the trades of domestic shares on domestic exchanges over the year divided by the average value of domestic shares listed on domestic exchanges in that year. (Sources: IFC's *Emerging Markets Data Base* (electronic version) and the IMF's *International Financial Statistics.)*

Value Traded: Value of the trades of domestic shares on domestic exchanges over the year divided by GDP. (Sources: IFC's *Emerging Markets Data Base* (electronic version) and the IMF's *International Financial Statistics.*) *Volatility:* Measure of the volatility of stock returns, based on the stock market index value. (Sources: IFC's *Emerging Markets Data Base* (electronic version) and the IMF's *International Financial Statistics.*)

B. Countries Coverage and Sample Period

The following countries were used in the analyses: Argentina (i, v), Australia (i, s, v), Austria (s, v), Bangladesh (s), Belgium (s, v), Brazil (i, v), Canada (s, v), Chile (i, s, v), Colombia (i, s, v), Cote d'Ivoire, Germany (s, v), Denmark (s, v), Egypt

Table A1 Complete Table 3 Results—Initial Turnover, Banks, and Growth, 1976–1993

Independent variables	Dependent variables			
	Output Growth	Capital Stock Growth	Productivity Growth	Savings
Constant	0.0464 (0.0246)	0.1049 (0.0341)	0.0324 (0.0150)	29.2948 (6.0756)
Initial Output	−0.0139 (0.0049)	−0.0120 (0.0073)	−0.0078 (0.0042)	−0.5831 (1.8875)
Enrollment	0.0230 (0.0125)	0.0049 (0.0152)	0.0118 (0.0097)	−0.3602 (4.7179)
Revolutions and Coups	−0.0346 (0.0108)	−0.0306 (0.0113)	−0.0227 (0.0083)	−13.0141 (4.3871)
Government	−0.0619 (0.0379)	−0.0021 (0.0532)	−0.0407 (0.0031)	−21.5703 (20.6724)
Inflation	−0.0071 (0.0065)	−0.0296 (0.0107)	−0.0085 (0.0082)	−11.3403 (5.9731)
Black Market Premium	0.000 (0.0000)	−0.0002 (0.0001)	0.0000 (0.0000)	−0.0036 (0.0204)
Bank Credit	0.0131 (0.0055)	0.0148 (0.0063)	0.0111 (0.0046)	3.8376 (2.3069)
Turnover	0.0269 (0.0090)	0.0222 (0.0094)	0.0201 (0.0088)	7.7643 (5.6864)
R^2	0.5038	0.5075	0.4027	0.4429
Observations	42	41	41	29

Notes: Heteroskedasticity-consistent standard errors in parentheses. Output Growth = real per capita GDP growth; Capital Stock Growth = real per capita capital stock growth; Productivity Growth = Output Growth-(0.3) (Capital Stock Growth); Savings = private savings divided by GDP; Initial Output = logarithm of initial real per capita GDP; Enrollment = logarithm of initial secondary school enrollment; Revolutions and Coups = number of revolutions and coups per year; Government = initial government consumption expenditures divided by GDP; Inflation = initial inflation rate; Black Market Premium = initial black market exchange rate premium; Bank Credit = initial bank credit to the private sector as a share of GDP; Turnover = initial value of the trades of domestic shares as a share of market capitalization.

(s), Spain (s, v), Finland (s, v), France (s, v), United Kingdom (i, s, v), Greece (i, s, v), Hong Kong, Indonesia (i, s), India (i, s, v), Israel (v), Italy (i, s, v), Jamaica (s), Jordan (i, v), Japan (i, s, v), Korea (i, s, v), Luxembourg, Mexico (i, v), Malaysia (i, s, v), Morocco (s), Nigeria (i, s), The Netherlands (s, v), Norway (s, v), New Zealand (s, v), Pakistan (i, v), Peru, Philippines (i, v), Portugal (i, s, v), Singapore, Sweden (s, v), Thailand (i, v), Turkey (s, v), Taiwan (i, v), United States (i, s, v), Venezuela (i, v), and Zimbabwe (i, s, v).

The "v" in parentheses indicates that this country is one of the 36 countries for which we computed Volatility from monthly stock returns. The "i" in parentheses indicates that this country is one of the 24 with CAPM and APT Integration data in Korajczyk (1994, 1996). The "s" in parentheses indicates that this country is one of the 32 countries with private savings data in Masson et al. (1995). Unless indicated otherwise, the data are averages over the period 1976–1993.

*Levine: Department of Economics, University of Virginia, Charlottesville, VA 22903; Zervos: Barclay's Capital Canary Wharf, London, U.K. We thank Mark Baird, Valerie Bencivenga, John Boyd, Jerry Caprio, Asli Demirgüç-Kunt, Doug Diamond, Bill Easterly, Michael Gavin, Bruce Smith, two anonymous referees, and seminar participants at Arizona State University, Cornell University,

Dartmouth College, Harvard Institute for International Development, the University of Virginia, and the University of Washington for helpful comments. We received excellent research assistance from Michelle Barnes and Ti Caudron. Much of the work on this paper was done while the authors were employed by the World Bank. Opinions expressed are those of the authors and do not necessarily reflect those of the World Bank, its staff, or member countries.

Notes

1 In terms of banks, Douglas W. Diamond (1984), John H. Boyd and Edward C. Prescott (1986), and Stephen D. Williamson (1986) develop models where financial intermediaries—coalitions of agents—lower the costs of obtaining information about firms from what those costs would be in atomistic capital markets where each investor must acquire information individually. Based on these core models, King and Levine (1993b) show that, by lowering information costs, financial intermediaries foster more efficient resource allocation and thereby accelerate technological innovation and long-run growth. Jeremy Greenwood and Boyan Jovanovic (1990) develop a model in which financial intermediaries affect, and are affected by, economic growth. See the review by Levine (1997).

2 See Bencivenga and Smith (1991) and Obstfeld (1994) for parameter values that lead to lower saving and growth rates with greater liquidity or risk sharing, respectively. The data are inconsistent with these parameter values. Note, however, that these models have parameter values that are consistent with our empirical findings that: (a) liquidity is positively associated with economic growth; and (b) neither liquidity nor international capital market integration is associated with private saving rates.

3 The CAPM and APT Integration measures rely on asset pricing models that the data frequently rejected as good representations of the pricing of risk. For this paper, however, we seek a numerical index of, for example, how much more the United States is integrated into world capital markets than is Nigeria. We are not concerned with whether the index is based at zero. Thus, even if the integration measures include a constant bias, the CAPM and APT Integration measures still provide information on cross-country differences in market integration.

4 As in Schwert (1989), we use iterated weighted least-squares estimates, iterating three times between (3) and (4), to obtain more efficient estimates.

5 To compute capital stocks, King and Levine (1994) estimate the capital-output ratio for over 100 countries in 1950, data permitting, and then iterate forward using Robert Summers and Alan Heston (1991) real investment data and a depreciation rate of 0.07. We update these estimates through 1990 using Summers and Heston (1993) data. Estimates of the capital share parameter, κ, typically range between 0.25 and 0.40 (see King and Levine [1994] for citations). We experimented with values in this range, and since the results do not importantly change, we report the results with $\kappa = 0.3$.

6 In the regressions, we include a term for investment in human capital.

7 More generally, Jappelli and Pagano (1994 p. 102) note that the finding that financial development is positively linked with economic growth does not contradict their findings, because they focus on "... the effect of imperfections in the mortgage and consumer credit markets, which have no necessary correlation with the development of lending to firms."

8 It is also true that in the regression analyses, Savings is only available for about 70 percent of the countries for which we have Capital Stock Growth data. However, the Bonser-Neal and Dewenter (1996) findings suggest that this smaller sample is not driving the results. Moreover, we restricted the Capital Stock Growth regressions to

those countries with Savings data. While the *t*-statistics on the financial indicators fall, financial development generally remains a significant predictor of Capital Stock Growth even in this smaller sample.

9　The Productivity Growth channel is also the main link between Bank Credit Output Growth in the Table 3 and 4 results.

10　The strong link between liquidity and capital accumulation suggests an area for future research. Specifically, three empirical findings need to be reconciled: (1) stock market liquidity is positively tied to capital formation, but (2) equity sales do not finance much of this capital formation (Colin Mayer, 1988), and (3) stock market liquidity is *positively* associated with corporate debt-equity ratios in developing countries (Demirgüç-Kunt and Maksimovic, 1996). These findings imply interactions between stock markets, banks, corporate finance, and corporate investment decisions that many existing theories do not fully capture (though, see Boyd and Smith [1996] and Elisabeth Huybens and Smith [1998]).

11　That is, the *p*-value on the coefficient on Capitalization rises above 0.10.

12　We choose this asymmetric dividing point because the data for some countries start in 1978.

13　For instruments, we use Initial Output, Enrollment, Revolutions and Coups, initial Capitalization, initial Value Traded, initial Turnover, initial Inflation, initial ratio of international trade to GDP (*Trade*), initial Government, and initial Black Market Premium. The first-stage R^2's are 0.73 for the CAPM Integration measure and 0.52 for the APT Integration measure and the F-statistic for both rejects the null hypothesis that none of the cross-sectional variation in capital market integration is explained by the explanatory variables. Furthermore, the simple OLS regressions yield virtually identical results to the instrumental variable results presented in Tables 8 and 9.

14　Unpublished appendices with numerous additional sensitivity analyses are available at http://www.worldbank.org/html/prdmg/grth web/growth_t.htm.

15　Furthermore, we used Summers and Heston (1993) data, instead of own currency prices, to compute Government and Output Growth. This did not affect the results.

16　When the legal efficiency and institutional development indicators are included with enough additional explanatory variables, the sample size falls dramatically, such that the Bank Credit becomes insignificant at the 0.05-percent level in some specifications.

17　Specifically, in the multivariate regression of $G(i)$ on X, Bank Credit, and $S(k)$, where $S(k)$ represents each particular stock market indicator taken in turn, the partial scatterplot is computed as follows: regress $G(i)$ on X and Bank Credit and collect the residuals, $U(G(i))$. Regress $S(k)$ on X and Bank Credit and collect the residuals, $U(S(k))$. Then plot $U(G(i))$ against $U(S(k))$. This gives a two-dimensional graph of the relationship between $G(i)$ and $S(k)$ controlling for X and Bank Credit. This helps identify particularly influential observations.

18　These 31 countries are Bolivia, Botswana, Cameroon, Central African Republic, Costa Rica, Dominican Republic, Ecuador, Ethiopia, Ghana, Guatemala, Guyana, Haiti, Kenya, Lesotho, Liberia, Madagascar, Malawi, Mali, Mauritania, Mauritius, Nicaragua, Niger, Paraguay, Rwanda, Senegal, Somalia, Sri Lanka, Tunisia, Uruguay, Zaire, and Zambia.

19　Using these additional 31 countries does not alter the conclusions about the robust links between the financial indicators and Capital Stock Growth and Productivity Growth.

References

Atje, Raymond and Jovanovic, Boyan. "Stock Markets and Development." *European Economic Review*, April 1993, 37(2/3), pp. 632–40.

Bagehot, Walter. *Lombard Street.* Homewood, IL: Irwin, 1873.

Banks, Arthur S. "Cross-National Time Series Data Archive." Center for Social Analysis, State University of New York, Binghamton, 1994.

Barro, Robert J. "Economic Growth in a Cross Section of Countries." *Quarterly Journal of Economics*, May 1991, 56(2), pp. 407–43.

Barro, Robert J. and Sala-i-Martin, Xavier. *Economic growth.* New York: McGraw-Hill, 1995.

Bencivenga, Valerie R. and Smith, Bruce D. "Financial Intermediation and Endogenous Growth." *Review of Economic Studies*, April 1991, 53(2), pp. 195–209.

Bencivenga, Valerie R.; Smith, Bruce D. and Starr, Ross M. "Transactions Costs, Technological Choice, and Endogenous Growth." *Journal of Economic Theory*, October 1995, 67(1), pp. 53–177.

Bhide, Amar. "The Hidden Costs of Stock Market Liquidity." *Journal of Financial Economics*, August 1993, *34*(2), pp. 3151.

Bonser-Neal, Catherine and Dewenter, Kathryn. "Does Financial Market Development Stimulate Savings? Evidence From Emerging Market Stock Markets." Mimeo, University of Indiana, 1996.

Boyd, John H. and Prescott, Edward C. "Financial Intermediary-Coalitions." *Journal of Economics Theory*, April 1986, *38*(2), pp. 211–32.

Boyd, John H. and Smith, Bruce D. "The Coevolution of the Real and Financial Sectors in the Growth Process." *World Bank Economic Review*, May 1996,*10*(2), pp. 37196.

Bruno, Michael and Easterly, William. "Inflation Crises and Long-Run Growth." *Journal of Monetary Economics*, March 1998, *41*(1), pp. 3–26.

Connor, Gregory and Korajczyk, Robert A. "Performance Measurement with the Arbitrage Pricing Theory: A New Framework for Analysis." *Journal of Financial Economics*, March 1986, *15*(3), pp. 373–94.

DeGregorio, Jose and Guidotti, Pablo E. "Financial Development and Economic Growth." *World Development*, March 1995, 23(3), pp. 433–48.

De Long, J. Bradford; Shleifer, Andrei; Summers, Lawrence H. and Waldmann, Robert J. "The Size and Incidence of the Losses from Noise Trading." *Journal of Finance*, July 1989, *44*(3), *pp.* 681–96.

Demirgüç-Kunt, Asli and Levine, Ross. "Stock Market Development and Financial Intermediaries: Stylized Facts." *World Bank Economic Review*, May 1996, *19*(2), 291–322.

Demirgüç-Kunt, Asli and Maksimovic, Vojislav. "Financial Constraints, Uses of Funds, and Firm Growth: An International Comparison." Mimeo, World Bank, 1996.

Devereux, Michael B. and Smith, Gregor W. "International Risk Sharing and Economic Growth." *International Economic Review*, August 1994, 55(4), pp. 535–50.

Diamond, Douglas W. "Financial Intermediation and Delegated Monitoring." *Review of Economic Studies*, July 1984, 57(3), pp. 393–414.

Dollar, David. "Outward-Oriented Developing Economies Really Do Grow More Rapidly: Evidence from 95 LDCs, 1976–1985." *Economic Development and Cultural Change*, April 1992, *40*(3), pp. 523–44.

Easterly, William and Rebelo, Sergio. "Fiscal Policy and Economic Growth: An Empirical Investigation." *Journal of Monetary Economics*, December 1993, 32(3), pp. 41758.

Fischer, Stanley. "The Role of Macroeconomic Factors in Growth." *Journal of Monetary Economics*, December 1993, 32(3), pp. 485–511.

Goldsmith, Raymond W. *Financial structure and development.* New Haven, CT: Yale University Press, 1969.

Greene, William H. *Economic analysis.* Englewood Cliffs, NJ: Prentice Hall, 1993.

Greenwood, Jeremy and Jovanovic, Boyan. "Financial Development, Growth, and the Distribution of Income." *Journal of Political Economy*, October 1990, Pt. 1, *98*(5), pp. 1076–107.

Holmstrom, Bengt and Tirole, Jean. "Market Liquidity and Performance Monitoring." *Journal of Political Economy*, August 1993, *101*(4), pp. 678–709.

Huybens, Elisabeth and Smith, Bruce D. "Inflation, Financial Markets, and Long-Run Growth." *Journal of Monetary Economics*, 1998 (forthcoming).

International Finance Corporation. *Emerging markets data base.* Washington, DC: International Finance Corporation, various issues.

International Monetary Fund. *International financial statistics.* Washington, DC: International Monetary Fund, various issues.

Jappelli, Tullio and Pagano, Marco. "Saving, Growth, and Liquidity Constraints. " *Quarterly Journal of Economics*, February 1994, *109*(1), pp. 93–109.

King, Robert G. and Levine, Ross. "Finance and Growth: Schumpeter Might Be Right." *Quarterly Journal of Economics*, August 1993a, *108*(3), pp. 717–38.

_____. "Finance, Entrepreneurship, and Growth: Theory and Evidence." *Journal of Monetary Economics*, December 1993b, 32(3), pp. 513–42.

_____"Capital Fundamentalism, Economic Development, and Economic Growth." *Camegie-Rochester Series on Public Policy*, June 1994, *40*, pp. 259–92.

Korajczyk, Robert A. "Measuring Integration of Developed and Emerging Markets." Mimeo, Northwestern University, 1994.

_____. "A Measure of Stock Market Integration for Developed and Emerging Markets." *World Bank Economic Review*, May 1996, *10*(2), pp. 267–89.

Korajczyk, Robert A. and Viallet, Claude J. "An Empirical Investigation of International Asset Pricing." *Review of Financial Studies*, September 1989, 2(4), pp. 553–85.

Levine, Ross. "Stock Markets, Growth, and Tax Policy." *Journal of Finance*, September 1991, *46*(4), pp. 1445–65.

_____. "Financial Development and Economic Growth: Views and Agenda." *Journal of Economic Literature*, June 1997, 35(2), pp. 688–726.

Levine, Ross and Renelt, David. "A Sensitivity Analysis of Cross-Country Growth Regressions." *American Economic Review*, September 1992, *82*(4), pp. 942–63.

Lucas, Robert E., Jr. "On the Mechanics of Economic Development." *Journal of Monetary Economics*, July 1988, 22(1), pp. 342.

Mankiw, N. Gregory; Romer, David and Weil, David. "A Contribution to the Empirics of Economic Growth." *Quarterly Journal of Economics*, May 1992, *107*(2), pp. 40737.

Masson, Paul; Bayoumi, Tamim and Samiei, Hossein. "Saving Behavior in Industrial and Developing Countries." International Monetary Fund Staff Studies for the World Economic Outlook, September 1995.

Mauro, Paulo. "Corruption and Growth." *Quarterly Journal of Economics*, August 1995, 770(3), pp. 681–712.

Mayer, Colin. "New Issues in Corporate Finance." *European Economic Review*, June 1988, 52(5), pp. 1167–88.

McKinnon, Ronald I. *Money and capital in economic development.* Washington, DC: Brookings Institution, 1973.

Obstfeld, Maurice. "Risk-Taking, Global Diversification, and Growth." *American Economic Review*, December 1994, 84(5), pp. 1310–29.

Pagan, Adrian. "Econometric Issues in the Analysis of Regressions with Generated Regressors." *International Economic Review*, February 1984, 25(1), pp. 221–47.

Picks Currency Yearbook. New York: Picks, various issues.

Rajan, Raghuram G. and Zingales, Luigi. "Financial Dependence and Growth." *American Economic Review*, June 1998, 88(3), pp. 559–86.

Robinson, Joan. "The Generalization of the General Theory." *The rate of interest and other essays.* London: Macmillan, 1952, pp. 67–146.

Schumpeter, Joseph A. *Theorie der wirt-schaftlichen entwicklung.* Leipzig, Germany: Dunker & Humblot, 1912.

Schwert, G. William. "Why Does Stock Market Volatility Change Over Time?" *Journal of Finance*, December 1989, 49(5), pp. 1115–53.

Shleifer, Andrei and Summers, Lawrence. "Breach of Trust in Hostile Takeovers," in A. Auerbach, ed., *Corporate takeovers: Causes and consequences.* Chicago: University of Chicago Press, 1988, pp. 33–56.

Shleifer, Andrei and Vishy, Robert W. "Large Shareholders and Corporate Control." *Journal of Political Economy*, June 1986, 96(3), pp. 461–88.

Solow, Robert M. "A Contribution to the Theory of Economic Growth." *Quarterly Journal of Economics*, February 1956, 70(1), pp. 65–94.

Summers, Robert and Heston, Allan. "The Penn World Table (Mark 5): An Expanded Set of International Comparisons, 19501988." *Quarterly Journal of Economics*, May 1991, 706(2), pp. 327–68.

_____ "Penn World Tables, Version 5.5," available on diskette from the National Bureau of Economic Research, Cambridge MA, 1993.

Williamson, Stephen D. "Costly Monitoring, Financial Intermediation, and Equilibrium Credit Rationing." *Journal of Monetary Economics*, September 1986, 78(2), pp. 159–79.

World Bank. *World development indicators.* Washington, DC: World Bank, various issues.

World Currency Yearbook. New York: International Currency Analysis, Inc., various issues.

8

CONTAGION AND CAPITAL MARKET INTEGRATION IN ASIA

Historical and Contemporary Evidence

Nathan Sussman and Yishay Yafeh*

Source: *Seoul Journal of Economics* 12, 4, 1999, 391–417.

We compare sovereign debt yields in the nineteenth century and today. Using data on nineteenth century Japanese government bonds, and on Korean sovereign debt today we show that foreign investors both then and now use summary indicators to evaluate country risk (the Gold Standard then, IMF packages today). However, "contagion" today is more common than in the past. Events in nineteenth century China hardly caused fluctuations in Japanese yields although capital markets were highly integrated. By contrast, minor events in Asia or Latin America had significant effects on Korean yields in recent years. (*JEL* Classification: F21, G15, N20)

I. Introduction

Reforms and institutional changes can make a country appealing to foreign investors, thereby attracting capital inflows and alleviating constraints on investment imposed by domestic savings. Yet a country's image in the eyes of foreign investors may be strongly affected by events taking place in neighboring countries. In this paper we examine these issues by investigating the determinants of country risk using two very different data sets on sovereign debt. The first data set contains monthly information on Japanese (and other developing countries') sovereign debt traded in London between 1870 and World War I. The second data set contains contemporary daily information on Korean (and other developing countries') sovereign debt traded in New York between late 1996 and mid 1999. The comparison is interesting because the last part of the nineteenth century is very often described as the "golden age" of high international financial integration with unparalleled capital flows (e.g. Bordo *et al.* 1998). The comparison is also interesting because of the dramatic reforms and institutional changes that took place in Japan during that period, as well as the structural changes that are taking place in present-day Korea.

The analysis of the two data sets yields two main results. The first is that, much like investors in the nineteenth century, foreign investors today rely on "summary indicators" to evaluate a country's credit risk, so that "nothing has changed" in this respect. In the nineteenth century the Gold Standard was the most important indicator of a country's stability and the soundness of its economic policies. We show both in this paper and, in more detail in Sussman and Yafeh (1999a), that the adoption of the Gold Standard was *the* major turning point in Japan's ability to access foreign capital markets, leading to lower interest payments and high capital inflows. By contrast, institutional changes and reforms in Japan were perhaps hard to evaluate and did not help British investors update their views. This is despite the fact that reforms in Japan during the Meiji period were unprecedented in scope and included major changes such as the abolition of feudalism, the formation of a modern central bank, the promulgation of a modern constitution, and the establishment of an elected parliament. Other authors (cited below) also argue that the Gold Standard was instrumental for many developing countries' access to global capital markets. Today, IMF-backed loans, as well as international credit rating agencies perform a role for Korean debt that is similar to that of the Gold Standard a hundred years ago. Much like in Meiji Japan, reforms and domestic events in present-day Korea have little effect on the country's risk premium until they are "certified" by a credible signal, such as an agreement with the IMF, or an upgrade by S&P or Moody's. This similarity exists even though investors today have access to state of the art information technology, and despite the fact our historical data cover over forty years of Japanese debt, whereas our modern data cover only two and a half years of Korean debt.

Our second result is that while capital flows between 1870 and World War I were of very large magnitudes, "contagion" was less prevalent in the past than it is today. We show that although the Japanese and Chinese risk premium series were correlated even in the nineteenth century major events in China, a developing country close to Japan, had a negligible immediate impact on the risk premium on Japanese government bonds in the Meiji period. On the other hand, we find that some of the most dramatic changes in the risk premium on Korean debt in recent years were driven by events in Thailand, Indonesia, or even Russia and Brazil. These events caused sharp changes in Korea's cost of capital, even though they had little to do with the risk of Korean default. These findings are very much in line with Kaminsky and Schmukler (1999) who argue that events in neighboring countries are crucial for understanding "jitters" in East Asian stock markets. There are a number of possible explanations for this result. One could simply be the data: we have long-term monthly series for the nineteenth century and a much shorter daily series for modern country risk. However, we will argue later that when our modern data set is converted into monthly frequency, the results become even more pronounced than they are when using daily data. Another possible explanation is that product markets today are better integrated so that "contagion" is spread across countries that trade a lot with each other (e.g. Glick and Rose 1998). We will argue that this explanation too cannot account for our findings because (as a fraction of total trade) Meiji Japan traded with China far more than Korea does with Indonesia or Thailand. It is, of course, possible that nineteenth century investors were more sophisticated than today's but there is another explanation which we find more plausible: Investors in the past had to incur more costs in order to re-balance their portfolio and consequently did so less frequently. Stated differently, the technology available a hundred years ago forced investors to "take a breath" before acting and thus led to less volatility and fewer imported shocks.

The paper is part of a growing literature that investigates capital flows and financial markets in the nineteenth century and that of today (e.g. Bordo *et al.* 1998). Our interest in the Gold Standard is in line with the literature on the impact of this institution on borrowing constraints (e.g. Gregory 1979; Bordo and Rockoff 1996; and Eichengreeen and Flandreau 1996). The paper is also related to the literature on modern country risk (e.g. Edwards 1986; and Izvorski 1998) as well as to the on-going discussion about "herd behavior" and "contagion" during Asia's recent crisis (e.g. Corsetti *et al.* 1999; and Radelet and Sachs 1998). Finally, this paper extends our previous work on this issue. In Sussman and Yafeh (1999a) we examine in detail the effects of institutional reforms on the risk premium on Japanese government bonds in the Meiji period. There we present detailed evidence showing that the adoption of the Gold Standard was the major turning point in Japan's "credit rating" between 1870 and 1914 (some of the results from that paper are reproduced here). In Sussman and Yafeh (1999b) we argue that, in addition to affecting the risk premium, the Gold Standard had a major impact on Japan's integration into world capital markets.

The rest of the paper is organized as follows: Section II provides some background on the Meiji period reforms in Japan and on the recent financial crisis in Korea. In Section III we describe the two data sets used for this study and present our empirical approach. Section IV presents the main findings. The interpretation of the results and some concluding remarks are in Section V.

II. A Brief Historical Overview

In this section we briefly survey some key facts about capital markets in the late nineteenth century, about Japan during the same period, and about Korea during the recent crisis. These facts will serve as background for the analysis that follows. This survey is by no means exhaustive, as each of the subjects covered is discussed in detail in a large number of publications and books.

A. International Capital Markets, 1870-1914

The period between 1870 and World War I is often described as an era of global finance in which capital markets were probably as integrated as they are today. Capital outflows from Britain to contemporary developing economies were extremely high and barriers to movements of capital (and labor) were virtually absent. For a more detailed discussion of this period, see, for example, Bordo *et al.* (1998) or O'Rourke and Williamson (1998).

B. Japanese Institutional Reforms in the Meiji Period (1868-1912)

In general, the Meiji era was a period of dramatic change in Japan. Within less than forty years, a backward, feudal society was transformed into an industrial and military power with a well established modern state structure. At the time, the pace and scope of the Meiji period reforms had no parallel in the world. At first, the old feudal system was abolished and major agrarian and tax reforms were introduced in 1873. The government began importing "model" textile plants at around the same time. The early 1880s witnessed the consolidation of the banking system, the establishment of a modern central bank, the Bank of Japan (1882), and the privatization of the industrial plants introduced by the government earlier. Also during the 1880s, a modern cabinet system replaced the traditional form of government. Possibly the most important institutional reform, the Meiji Constitution, was promulgated in 1889, after nine years of deliberations and attempts to incorporate the best features of contemporary European constitutions. The Meiji Constitution, which remained unchanged through the end of Word War II, guaranteed the rule of law, property rights, some freedom of speech, as well as occupational freedom for citizens. It also established an independent legal system and set the ground for a two-house parliamentary system in existence until today. The first parliament convened in 1890 following the first elections. The Meiji period was also a period of political turmoil including, among others, Japanese military victories over China (1894-5) and Russia (1904-5).

C. Korea, 1996-1999

There are so many chronologies of the recent financial crisis in Asia (e.g. Roubini 1999) that it should suffice to simply list briefly the major events that took place in Korea during this period. In October 1996 Korea gained the official status of a developed country when it joined the OECD. 1997, however, brought about a deep crisis. The change began with the collapse of the *Hanbo* conglomerate in early 1997, and was followed by trouble in two other *chaebols (Sammi* and *Jinro)* in the spring of the same year. By June 1997, *Kia,* a larger group, defaulted on its debt, and in September the Bank of Korea was forced to intervene to prevent massive bankruptcies of commercial banks. The Asian crisis reached Korea in October 1997 a few months after it hit Thailand and Indonesia. The collapse of the *won,* the flight of foreign investors, and the large amount of short term debt (both sovereign and private) forced the Korean government to seek assistance from the IMF in November of that year, after a government reform package failed to calm financial and currency markets. Korea received $57 billion from the IMF, as well as assistance from Japan and other lenders in December 1997. In February 1998, Kim Dae-Jung took office as the new president and began his tenure with attempts to reform the economy. In particular, President Kim sought to introduce market reforms that would limit the influence of the major *chaebol* conglomerates. Naturally, the government's attempts to limit their scope of activities were faced by *chaebol* opposition. In addition to reforming the conglomerates and the financial system, attempts were made to relax the existing strict labor laws so as to enable companies to fire at will. These attempts led to severe labor disputes in the spring and summer of 1998. Another source of conflict during the same period was the publication of a "hit list" of companies liable to be liquidated (because banks were forced to cut off their lines of credit). Despite these difficulties, by fall 1998 there were signs that reforms were on their way (some of the major conglomerates agreed to "focus;" labor disputes were settled) and the economy began to show signs of recovery in early 1999.

III. The Data and Methodology

A. Historical Japanese Data

Our data set includes *monthly* data on sovereign bond yields between 1870 and 1914 for Japan, China (and a number of other contemporary developing economies, which are not considered here). The data are drawn from the *London Times* and from the *Economist's Investor's Monthly Manual.* We define the yield difference between Japanese bonds and British consol yields as the risk premium (British consol yields are drawn from the NBER *Macroeconomic History* data set). Japanese bond coupons were payable in pounds in London, and therefore did not involve any exchange rate risk.

We supplement the statistical information by recording each time in which political or economic events in Japan or China are reported either in the *London Times* or in the *Economist* between 1870 and 1899. These data, as well as articles from the *Economist,* will be used to evaluate the nature of information British investors had on reforms in Japan and on events in China that could affect the risk associated with Japanese government bonds.

B. Modern Data: Korean and Other Sovereign Debt, Fall 1996 - Spring 1999

Our contemporary data set includes *daily* data on Korean quasi-sovereign debt (KDB bonds with a coupon of 7.25% and maturity in May 2006)[1] between October 1996 and May 1999. In addition, we have information on sovereign debt yields of Thailand, Indonesia and Malaysia, as well as Brazil and Argentina.[2] The risk premium on Korean debt is defined as the "spread," namely the yield differences relative to a similar US Treasury bond.

We construct a list of events in Korea and neighboring countries from a large number of newspapers and other sources. These include, among others, *The New York Times, The Financial Times, The International Herald Tribune, The Economist,* and *The Korea Herald.*

C. Empirical Approach

There are a number of possible (albeit imperfect) methods that can be used to identify the dates in which a dramatic change in a time series ("structural break") takes place. We apply these methods to the analysis of both the Japanese and the Korean risk premium series.

a) An iterative search for breaks

This method assumes no *a priori* knowledge of potential break dates. Instead, it is based on using all the available data for repeated estimations of the following equation:

$$\log\left(\text{Risk Premium}\right)_t = \beta_0 + \beta_1 \log\left(\text{Risk Premium}\right)_{t-1}$$

$$+ \beta_2 \Delta\log\left(\text{Risk Premium}\right)_{t-1} + \beta_3 \Delta\log\left(\text{Risk Premium}\right)_{t-2} \qquad (1)$$

$$+ \beta_4 \text{ Trend} + \beta_5 \text{ Event}_{\text{long}} + \beta_6 \text{ Event}_{\text{short}},$$

where $EVENT_{long}$ is a dummy variable that takes the value zero at all times prior to the proposed break and the value one from the time of the break onwards, and $EVENT_{short}$ takes the value one at the time of the event and zero at all other times. If an event had a long-term impact on yields then the "long" dummy variable should be different from zero (assuming the series in not unit root). A significant "short" dummy implies that an event created only short-term "blip."[3] The method involves repeated estimation of equation (1) while moving the break date and the corresponding $EVENT$ dummy variables one observation at a time and recording their statistical significance. The sample is then split in two at the point where the statistical significance of the $EVENT_{long}$ dummy is highest, and the process is repeated within each half of the sample until no statistically significant break points are detected in any sub-sample. We use this method to search for breaks in *both* the Japanese and the Korean risk premium series.

b) Search for breaks around major historical events

This alternative approach is based on using all the available institutional and historical background, rather than on searching the data without using any prior knowledge. This amounts to testing the hypothesis that a particular event that took place at a known date caused a break in the risk premium series. The disadvantage of this approach is that it is not always clear when an event should make an impact (some events are expected in advance, while others are understood only with some delay), and also raises a number of econometric difficulties (discussed in detail in Sussman and Yafeh 1999a). Here we apply this approach to the historical

Japanese data only because it is relatively easy to identify "important" events (in Japan or in neighboring China) with the hindsight of a full century. We do not, however, attempt to apply this method to the recent (short) Korean risk premium series where it is more difficult to determine which events "should have made an impact." In practice, the use of this method means that we construct an eighteen month *"window"* around events that we suspect may have influenced the risk premium and then estimate equation (1) within each "window." The "window" is constructed so as to include one major event only. Obviously, this imposes a constraint on the length of the "window" and consequently also on the statistical power of the test.

c) Listing "good" and "bad" days

For the Korean risk premium series (which is not only shorter but also of higher frequency) we choose to list the "worst twenty days" in which the risk premium increased by the largest percentage, and the "best twenty days" in which the risk premium sharply declined. This approach resembles the iterative search for breaks in that it assumes no prior knowledge about the nature of events that may have been important. Instead, it is an attempt to identify dates at which major changes in the risk premium took place and then examine what events took place on these dates and how they may have caused the observed market response. In the case of Korea, this is done by searching news articles and media reports for events that occurred on or around these days, either in Korea or in neighboring countries. Thus, we can evaluate the types of domestic events that affected the Korean risk premium, as well as the influence of events in neighboring economies ("contagion"). Naturally, this approach too raises several problems, most notably it does not provide a means to evaluate the statistical significance of the identified dates, and may tend to emphasize short-term "jitters." We return to these issues later.

d) A word of caution

All three methods listed here are far from perfect. The iterative search does not make use of any historical and institutional knowledge. The search for breaks around historical events is subject to several econometric critiques, assumes break dates correspond perfectly to dates of historical events, and is of limited statistical power. The listing of "good" and "bad" days does not enable an evaluation of their statistical significance or of the duration of their impact. Moreover, none of the three methods can measure cumulative effects of a sequence of events. Nevertheless, given the shortcomings of the available techniques, we use all three to draw some basic conclusions about the nature of events that affected financial markets in the nineteenth century and today. Our main findings seem clear enough regardless of the statistical approach used.

IV. Results and Discussion

In Section A, we discuss the events and reforms that determined the Japanese risk premium in the Meiji period. We then proceed to examine the impact of events in China (and elsewhere) on the Japanese risk premium. In Section B, we turn to modern Korea and identify (domestic and foreign) events that caused the most pronounced changes in the risk premium. A discussion of the results and their implications appear in Section V.

A. Japan, 1870-1914

Table 1 displays the dates, volume, and coupon interest rates for Japanese government debt issued in London. From 1870 to the early twentieth century coupon interest rates on newly issued Japanese government bonds declined from 9 percent (or about 200 percent higher than Consol yields at the time) to about 4 percent. Clearly the volume of debt issued in London (as well as in other markets) increased dramatically around the turn of the century, after the adoption of the Gold Standard. Figure 1 portrays the risk premium on Japanese government debt from 1870 to August 1914.[4]

Yields on Japanese government debt decreased from about 6 percentage points above British Consol yields in the early 1870s to slightly more than 2 percentage points above consol yields toward the end of the nineteenth century. It is important to note that this trend was not common to all developing countries of the time (e.g. yields on Russian and Turkish bonds did not fall during the period). Most important for the purpose of this paper is the fact that the decline in Japanese yields was not smooth. While yields fell in the 1870s (for reasons we discuss in detail in Sussman and Yafeh 1999a), they remained flat (or increased moderately) from the early 1880s until the mid-1890s. In particular, the dramatic reforms of

Table 1 Japanese Bond Issues in London

Year	Issue (pounds)	Interest Rate	Maturity (years)	Use of Proceeds
1870	1,000,000	9%	13	railways
1873	2,400,000	7%	25	misc.
1897	4,390,000	5%	53	military
1899	10,000,000	4%	55	railways, telephone
1902	5,104,000	5%	55	military, telephone
1904	22,000,000*	6%	7	military
1905	60,000,000*	4.5%	25	military
1905	25,000,000	4%	25	misc.
1907	23,000,000	5%	40	misc.
1910	11,000,000	4%	60	misc.

Note: * denotes total proceeds raised in two separate issues of similar terms. Source: Reproduced from Sussman and Yafeh (1999a), based on Suzuki (1994)

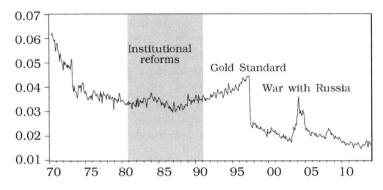

Figure 1 The Japanese Risk Premium, 1870–1914

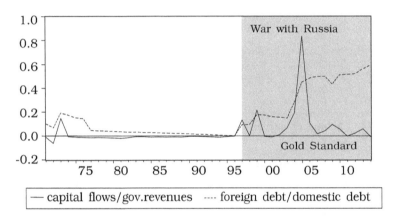

Figure 2 Japanese Foreign Borrowing, 1870–1914

1880s (the establishment of the Bank of Japan, the Meiji Constitution, and more) produced no discernible impact on the London capital market. Clearly, the most conspicuous change in Japan's risk premium took place in 1897 with the adoption of the Gold Standard. In its aftermath, the yield differential between Japanese and British bonds declined from over four percentage points to a two percent premium. A similar picture appears in the data on the volume of foreign borrowing and the composition of the Japanese government debt, see Figure 2. Capital inflows were miniscule until the adoption of the Gold Standard in 1897, when the trend was reversed.

We supplement the "ocular econometrics" presented so far with a more formal search for breaks in the Japanese risk premium series. This is done by using *both* the *iterative search for breaks* (where no breaks are assumed *a priori*) as well as the *search for breaks around major historical events*. The main result (reproduced from Sussman and Yafeh 1999a) is that the Gold Standard appears to be *the* major turning point in the Japanese risk premium series. It is found to be the most significant break point in the *iterative search for breaks* whereas no major breaks can be detected during the reform period of the 1880s (not shown). A similar picture emerges from the "windows" constructed around major historical events. Table 2 indicates that none of the major institutional reforms in Japan had any discernible impact on the Japanese risk premium, despite that this methodology has been criticized as likely to identify breaks "too easily" (e.g. Christiano 1992).[5] What we wish to emphasize here is not the relatively small number of events that

Table 2 Tests for Structural Breaks around Major Historical Events Japan, 1870-1914

Date	Event	Long-term break	Short-term "blip"
June 1873	Agrarian reform	−0.35*	None
Dec. 1877	Suppression of the Satsuma Rebellion	None	None
Nov. 1880	Privatization of government plants	None	None
Oct. 1882	Establishment of the Bank of Japan	None	None
June 1885	Introduction of convertible to silver yen notes	−0.05*	None
Feb. 1889	The Meiji Constitution	None	None
July 1890	First Parliamentary elections	None	None
July 1894	Outbreak of the Sino-Japanese war	None	+0.10*
April 1895	End of the Sino-Japanese war	None	None
June 1897	Adoption of the Gold Standard[1]	−0.50	Not available
June 1902	Anglo-Japanese treaty	−0.07*	None
Feb. 1904	Declaration of war on Russia[2]	None	+0.17*
Jan. 1905	Russian surrender in Lushon	−0.09*	None
Aug. 1910	Annexation of Korea	None	None
July 1912	Death of Emperor Meiji	None	None

Note: Using an eighteen month "window" around each event, we regress (the natural logarithm of) the risk premium, that is, the difference between Japanese bond yields and the yield on British Consols, on (a constant), the logarithm of the risk premium lagged one year, increments in the risk premium lagged one and two years, a trend (if significant), and two dummy variables for each event. The first dummy variable ("long") takes the value zero until the event, and the value one starting in the month in which the event took place and in every month thereafter through to the end of the "window." The second dummy variable ("pulse") takes the value one in the month of the event, and zero in all other months. If an event had a long-term impact on Japanese bond yields, we would expect the "long" dummy variable to be different from zero. A significant "pulse" dummy implies that an event created a short-term "blip." Yields are calculated as the ratio of interest payment to market price. For the wars with China and with Russia, the "long" dummy variable takes the value one starting in the month in which the war ended, and the "pulse" dummy variable equals one when in the month in which the war broke. We report the coefficient of the event dummy variables, both long-term and temporary, if their impact is statistically significant. Coefficients should be interpreted as percent change in existing yields. * denotes statistic significance at the five percent level.

1) Because the entire stock of outstanding bonds was redeemed, we do not apply the test to this event. The estimated impact is based on the issue of new 5 percent bonds instead of the outstanding 7 percent debt. See text for further details.

2) The "window" around the war with Russia is two years long.

Source: Reproduced from Sussman and Yafeh (1999a)

caused a break, but rather the kind of events that did influence the image of Japan in the eyes of foreign investors, and the kind of events that did not. Apparently, foreign investors found the institutional changes of the 1880s hard to evaluate. By contrast, the Gold Standard (and some political events, most notably the victory over Russia in 1905) played an important role in changing the image of Japan in the eyes of British investors.[6] Historical reports cited in Sussman and Yafeh (1999a) suggest that the Japanese government was well aware of the symbolic value of the Gold Standard and adopted it deliberately so as to improve the terms of Japanese foreign debt. Indeed, once "on" the Gold Standard, British investors showed great interest in Japanese government bonds, which could now be issued with far longer maturity (Table 1), with virtually no collateral, and with lower underwriting commissions (see Suzuki 1994). The evidence on the Gold Standard-induced improvement in Japan's "credit rating" fits the view that the Gold Standard was viewed as a commitment to a modern stable macro- economic policy. Eichengreen (1985) and Bordo and Rockoff (1996) also corroborate this hypothesis. They show that countries that were committed to the Gold Standard "as a good housekeeping seal of approval" (e.g. Canada and Australia) enjoyed lower risk premia in the period 1870-1914 relative to countries that went "on" and "off" the Gold (e.g. Brazil).

a) Contagion in Nineteenth Century Asia: Events in China and Japan's Risk Premium

In Table 3 we construct a "window" around several important events that took place in China, and using equation (1), examine their impact on the Japanese risk premium. We find that none of the major political and economic events that took place in China during the period (other than ones in which Japan was directly involved) had any impact on the risk British investors associated with Japanese sovereign debt. The dramatic Boxer Rebellion, in the suppression of which Japan took part, had only a small and marginally significant impact on Japan's country

Table 3 Contagion in Nineteenth Century Asia: The Impact of Events in China on the Japanese Risk Premium, Japan, **1870-1914**

Date	Event	Long-term break	Short-term "blip"
Dec. 1883	Outbreak of the Chinese-French War over Vietnam (Annam)	None	None
June 1896	Chinese-Russian military alliance	None	None
June 1900	Outbreak of the Boxer Rebellion	None	+0.05
May 1907	Instability and revolts in several regions of China	None	None
Sep. 1911	The Chinese Revolution	None	None

Note: The method used here is similar to that of Table 2.

risk, and the impact was short-lived for the duration of the rebellion (i.e. a "blip"). The Japan-China war (described in Table 2) affected Japan directly, but it too only caused a short-term "blip." Other "shocks" in China were not immediately transmitted to Japan's cost of foreign debt. This is despite the fact that the Japanese and Chinese risk premium series were highly correlated during the period. Moreover, this absence of short-run "contagion" is certainly not due to the fact that information about events in Asia was incomplete. Tables 4A and 4B clearly show that the *London Times* reported events in Asia regularly and in detail, as did the *Economist*.

Unlike "contagion" in Asia today, the perceived effect of events in China on Japanese debt was only due to the possibility that Japan would incur costs as

Table 4A Articles on Japan in the *London Times*

Year	Internal instability and wars	Commerce and economics	Foreign relations	Institutions and reforms
1871	3	5	2	1
1872	4	14	4	1
1873	5	8	6	3
1874	20	11	3	0
1875	1	6	6	3
1876	0	4	13	0
1877	23	3	2	0
1878	6	16	6	1
1879	4	14	2	5
1880	4	10	6	5
1881	1	3	5	0
1882	3	5	4	0
1883	0	4	3	0
1884	0	2	3	0
1885	0	2	3	2
1886	0	1	5	3
1887	2	2	9	3
1888	3	9	3	3
1889	15	12	10	9
1890	4	13	10	6
1891	7	5	3	2
1892	2	8	3	7
1893	1	4	1	1
1894	19	5	3	2
1895	18	9	12	0
1896	3	8	1	0
1897	1	10	11	1
1898	1	4	7	0
1899	0	5	6	1

Note: The table displays a classification of Japan-related articles in the *London Times* between 1871 and 1899. The classification is based on our own reading of the articles. Articles which could not be classified into the four categories (e.g. articles dealing with miscellaneous news on Japan or with Japanese culture) are not included.

Table 4B Articles on China in the *London Times*

Year	Internal instability and wars	Commerce and economics	Foreign relations	Institutions and reforms
1870	64	55	85	0
1871	14	33	21	2
1872	1	42	7	2
1873	6	75	27	0
1874	12	72	30	1
1875	24	71	74	2
1876	21	21	41	3
1877	6	34	29	4
1878	8	48	43	2
1879	17	17	30	2
1880	4	10	30	0
1881	1	21	18	0
1882	3	21	11	0
1883	29	16	67	1
1884	66	24	74	2
1885	18	10	43	3
1886	8	19	57	4
1887	7	20	35	5
1888	11	26	28	2
1889	13	86	15	4
1890	4	33	17	1
1891	77	11	142	0
1892	16	15	38	0
1893	14	17	15	0
1894	*	3		0
1895	*			
1896	2	21	70	1
1897	1	27	15	0
1898	17	12	37	6
1899	13	29	56	2
1900	55	18	76	1

Note: This table is similar to Table 4A, but displays a classification of China-related articles in the *London Times* between 1870 and 1900. * denotes a very large number of articles related to the Japan-China War of 1894-5.

a result of its direct involvement in China. The *Economist* expressed concern, for example, about the commercial implications on Japan of the 1911 Chinese Revolution, and on the possibility of Japanese military intervention in China (December 23, 1911). But in other cases, there was no reason for Chinese "shocks" to affect Japan's credit worthiness.[7] Finally, we examine if the one documented episode of "contagion" in the nineteenth century, namely the Baring Crisis (and Argentina's default) of 1890, had an impact on Japan's cost of capital.[8] Using a "window" around the crisis peak (November 1890), we find that the Baring Crisis did not have *any* impact on the Japanese risk premium. If anything, there was a slight increase in the price of Japanese bonds, which suggests that investors shifted some of their money into Japanese bonds, rather than run away and spread the crisis. As we will see in the next section, this is in sharp contrast with the experience of the recent Asian crisis.[9]

Before moving to examine present-day Korea, it is perhaps interesting to note that in both Table 2 and Table 3 very few events are significant (despite the claim mentioned above according to which this method should result in too many breaks). Perhaps this is due to the limited statistical power of the search for breaks using relatively short "windows." The important point, however, is not the actual magnitude of the effect, but the finding that most reforms caused little response until incorporated in a well understood signal, namely the Gold Standard. As for events in China, our basic claim is that (unlike the contagion observed in Asia today) these have been of limited importance in comparison with both the Gold Standard and political events concerning Japan itself (e.g. the 1905 victory over Russia or the 1902 alliance with Britain).

B. Present-Day Korea

The risk premium on Korean bonds is displayed in Figure 3. Unlike the Japanese bonds in the Meiji period there is no declining trend in the data, which obviously cover a much shorter time period. Yet there is quite a bit of variance in the series. The "spread" ranges between a minimum of about 50 basis points (above a comparable US Treasury bond) in October 1996 after Korea joined the OECD, and a maximum of about 1,000 which is reached during the financial crisis in fall 1997 and during the Russian debt crisis in summer 1998. In addition, the figure displays several "spikes" which represent days in which the risk premium increased (or declined) by up to thirty percent! Before investigating what happened on these dates, it is interesting to note another important feature of the Korean risk premium: The correlation between the Korean risk premium series and the premium on sovereign bonds of neighboring Asian countries is exceptionally high, in spite of the fact that the series cover a fairly short time span. In

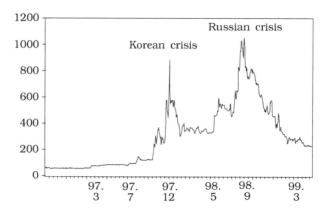

Figure 3 The Korean Risk Premium, 1996–1999

particular, the correlation between the Korean and Thai risk premia is close to 0.97. The comparable figure for the Indonesian and Malaysian premia is about 0.8, whereas the correlation with the premium on Latin American (Argentine and Brazilian) bonds is about 0.5 and 0.3, respectively.[10]

a) The best and the worst days

Table 5A lists the twenty days in which the risk premium on Korean sovereign bonds increased by the highest percentage (the "worst twenty days"), and Table 5B displays the "best twenty days." Of course, many of these days represent only short-term pulses, which do not amount to major "breaks" (that is, long-term changes in trends or levels). Such pulses should probably be compared in magnitude with

Table 5A The Largest Increases in the Korean Risk Premium (The Worst Twenty Days)

	Date	Event	% increase in premium	Effect on other countries
(1)	27/10/97	Bad economic news from Hong Kong*	27.53	Th, Indon
(2)	30/10/97	Bad economic news from Hong Kong	25.59	Th, Indon
(3)	02/06/98	Labor disputes*	24.90	No
(4)	23/10/97	Bad economic news from Hong Kong	24.37	Th, Indon
(5)	10/12/97	Government suspends five cash strapped companies	23.48	Indon
(6)	23/12/97	Credit agencies downgrade Korean sovereign debt	22.95	No
(7)	21/08/98	Russian default*	21.59	Mal, Indon
(8)	19/03/97	?	21.26	Indon
(9)	22/12/97	Moody's lowers ranking of Korean sovereign debt to junk	20.18	Th, Indon
(10)	11/12/97	Moody's lowers ranking of Korean sovereign debt	19.79	Th, Indon
(11)	19/12/97	Korea Investors Service downgrades *chaebol* affiliates	17.97	No
(12)	16/06/98	55 firms about to fail	17.64	No
(13)	02/09/97	Trouble selling Kia*	14.78	No
(14)	10/09/98	Bad economic news from Brazil	14.29	Lat Am
(15)	09/12/97	Stocks and won plunge - "investor worries"	13.77	No
(16)	25/08/97	S&P may cut Thailand's rating	13.70	No
(17)	25/11/97	Non-performing loans bigger than expected	13.19	No
(18)	27/08/98	Russian default	13.16	Th, Lat Am
(19)	13/01/99	Bad day in the stock market	13.12	Lat Am, Th, Indon, Mal
(20)	12/12/97	Suharto's health problems	12.73	Th, Indon

Note: Th, Indon, Mal, and Lat Am denote events that had a large impact (above 10 percent change) on the risk premium on Thai, Indonesian, Malaysian, and both Argentine and Brazilian bonds, respectively. * denotes events that are found significant in the iterative search for structural breaks. ? denotes a date in which no major event is reported.

195

Table 5B The Largest Decreases in the Korean Risk Premium (The Best Twenty Days)

	Date	Event	% decrease in premium	Effect on other countries
(1)	24/12/97	Overshooting the day before?*	−30.09	Th
(2)	21/11/97	Government to turn to the IMF for assistance	−24.17	No
(3)	21/12/98	Talk of debt upgrading	−24.09	No
(4)	10/10/96	Korea joins OECD	−20.99	No
(5)	19/01/99	Fitch upgrades Korean sovereign debt	−20.40	No
(6)	18/02/98	Conglomerates reach accord with foreign banks*	−19.10	No
(7)	04/11/97	Thai (and Korean) stocks rally	−18.40	Th
(8)	16/12/97	All three presidential candidates will abide by IMF deal	−18.35	Th, Indon
(9)	04/01/99	S&P upgrades Korean sovereign debt	−17.92	Th
(10)	29/07/98	Agreement with the IMF on revised economic goals	−17.52	No
(ID	26/12/97	Financial markets fully open to foreigners	−12.46	No
(12)	09/09/97	KDB issues $750 million bonds in US	−12.31	No
(13)	15/01/99	?	−11.45	Lat Am
(14)	23/01/98	?	−11.14	No
(15)	16/02/99	Successful negotiations with foreign creditors	−10.94	No
(16)	13/08/98	?	−10.66	Argentina
(17)	13/01/98	Government takes steps to ease cash crunch	−10.05	No
(18)	18/12/97	Reforms and approval of 2nd part of IMF loan	−9.77	No
(19)	25/01/99	?	−9.74	No
(20)	15/09/98	Government to acquire 2 ailing banks	−9.72	Lat Am

Note: Th, Indon, Mal, and Lat Am denote events that had a large impact (above 10 percent change) on the risk premium on Thai, Indonesian, Malaysian, and both Argentine and Brazilian bonds, respectively. * denotes events that are found significant in the iterative search for structural breaks. ? denotes dates in which no major event is reported.

short-term fluctuations in the historical data. Six of the forty days listed in Tables 5A and 5B are identified by the *iterative search for breaks* as significant (and relatively) long-term breaks in the Korean risk premium series. October 27, 1997 is the first and most significant break; December 24, 1997 is the second most significant; June 2, 1998 and September 7, 1997 are found in the third iteration; and February 18, 1998 and August 21, 1998 are the fourth iteration breaks.

V. Interpreting the Results and Their Implications

Our findings imply that there are interesting similarities and differences between Asian sovereign bonds in the nineteenth century and today. First, in both nineteenth century Japan and present day Korea, foreign investors relied on "summary statistics" and did not pay attention to interim news reports on domestic changes. For example, British investors though well informed about the Meiji Constitution did not update their beliefs about Japan as a borrower until she adopted the macroeconomic symbol of developed economies, namely the Gold Standard. In the case of Korea, investors seem to be very sensitive to agreements with the IMF (and possibly the implied commitment to reform), as well as to the opinion of well-known credit rating agencies. Korea's acceptance to the OECD and its successful negotiations with foreign creditors were two other "summary statistics." As noted above, these events need not be long-term break points, but they are nevertheless interpreted as "news" whereas other domestic events and attempted reforms with potentially equally important implications go unnoticed, at least until they are incorporated in a credit rating agency's assessment of credit worthiness.[11] Evidently, such "summary events" convey information beyond what investors can learn from other events. This would explain the "jump" in Japan's risk premium with the adoption of the Gold Standard which apparently contained new information beyond what was provided by the establishment of the Bank of Japan and the accumulation of gold reserves, both prerequisites for Japan to go "on" the Gold. Similarly, Moody's changes in Korea's credit rating must have conveyed information that was not available to market participants by observing earlier events. Again, note that our point here is not to gauge the number of events that make the Korean risk premium fluctuate, but rather to point out what kind of events matter a lot and what kind of events matter only a little.

Another evident feature in Tables 5A and 5B is that many of domestic events that are noticed by foreign investors are related to instability (e.g. labor disputes), much like the "pulses" of the nineteenth century (e.g. the outbreak of the wars with China or Russia, see Table 2). Other events are noticed apparently because they involve a foreign party (e.g. the accord between some of the Korean conglomerates and foreign banks and the relaxation of restrictions on foreign investment). A plethora of media reports about (for example) the relations with North Korea or attempted reforms in labor markets do not seem to have a big impact on the risk premium. The reason is probably the inability of investors to follow in detail all the events that take place in a large number of countries where they invest some of their portfolio. Another possible explanation is that foreign investors (both today and a hundred years ago) cannot evaluate the credibility and significance of domestic reforms. This creates the "Gold Standard symptom:" Reforms are not credible until they are "certified" by well- understood Western institutions.[12] It should be noted, however, that the magnitude (and frequency) of market responses seems much higher in the modern data than it was a hundred years ago.

Our results on "contagion" are, perhaps, more interesting. Even though British investors in the nineteenth century had fewer sources of information about Asia than investors today, the distinction between events in different Asian countries seems to have been clearer in the past than it is now. Instability in China was not immediately transmitted to the Japanese risk premium. By contrast, the panic and contagion of the recent Asian crisis are very clear in our modern data. Rumors about Indonesia's

President Suharto's health problems had a strong impact on the risk associated with Korean sovereign debt, as did economic news from Thailand, Hong Kong, and far away countries such as Brazil. The threat of Russian default in summer 1998 (and perhaps the LTCM fiasco as well) pushed the risk premium on Korean sovereign debt to unprecedented levels. These results on "imported shocks" are corroborated by the findings of Kaminsky and Schmukler (1999) who show that stock market "jitters" in East Asia are often caused by unrelated events in neighboring countries. Izvorski (1999) reports similarly that prices and yields on Brady bonds seem to move together, despite the issuing countries' different economic fundamentals.

One explanation for this phenomenon is that foreign investors "re-balance" their portfolio in favor of safer assets in view of information that reveals a risk greater than previously perceived with respect to their emerging market bonds. But the logic of this argument should apply also to nineteenth century bond markets, although it was probably more difficult and time consuming for investors at that time to shift large amounts of capital as swiftly as they can now. Moreover, it is not clear why the optimal response to bad news from Indonesia should be a sale of Korean bonds. Perhaps it is the case that regional funds today (e.g. Asia funds) lump together assets from neighboring countries, and are therefore forced to liquidate positions in all countries included in their portfolio if investors wish to withdraw money in view of a crisis in one emerging market. But if this is the reason for the impact of Suharto's health on the price of Korean bonds, it does not seem to be efficient either from the individual investor's point of view or from the point of view of the countries involved.

Another possible reason for the fact that shocks today are transferred more easily to neighboring countries may be that the world today, and particularly East Asia, are better integrated in terms of trade flows. This means that shocks are easily transmitted from a country to its trading partners (Glick and Rose 1999). Our results could then be explained if trade relations between Korea and Indonesia today were more important than Chinese-Japanese trade around the turn of the century, but this hardly seems to be the case.[13]

A third explanation for increased influence of events in neighboring countries could be the nature of the data. For example, the high-frequency (daily) modern Korean data may reveal short-term shocks that are hidden in the low frequency (monthly) historical data. To examine this issue we transform the Korean series from daily into monthly data by using only one observation at the end of each month. The transformed Korean risk premium series (not shown) is less volatile than the daily risk premium series but still appears to be quite different from the historical Japanese series. It is much less smooth, and foreign shocks do not seem to disappear in the transformed series. On the contrary, the events of August 1998 in Russia, for example, appear to be very dramatic in the monthly data as well, causing a 126 percent increase in the risk premium relative to the previous month. The events of fall 1997 are clearly evident too. Thus, it is unlikely that the increased magnitude and frequency of imported shocks are simply an artifact of the frequency of the data.

Before suggesting a more plausible explanation for the regularities we observe, it is interesting to note another feature that is common to our study of Korean sovereign debt and to Kaminsky and Schmukler's (1999) study of Asian stock markets. There are some days in which markets are highly volatile although there is no event or news report that can clearly account for the negative or positive "jump." This leads us to the following conclusion. The extreme degree of capital market integration today, combined with the large number of market participants and the easiness of trade, facilitates the flow of capital to developing economies. Yet huge and swift capital flows come with the cost of high volatility in financial markets with no apparent reason. Moreover, capital inflows are accompanied by shocks that are imported from neighboring countries ("contagion"), even though some of these shocks need not directly affect the economic wellbeing of the country whose markets they affect. This does not mean to suggest that international capital flows should be taxed or controlled, since such measures may have significant negative consequences. But it does mean that just like some stock markets impose trading halts to enable investors to "take a breath" and think twice when stock price movements are extreme, some mechanism that slows down transactions in sovereign bonds when there is very high volatility may also be beneficial. Similarly, investment funds that lump together assets from neighboring countries may be convenient, but they may also be one of the reasons why shocks cross borders from one country to the next even when fundamentals are quite different.

*This paper was prepared for presentation at the SJE-KIF International Symposium on "Structural Adjustments after the Asian Financial Crisis," Seoul, August 1999. We thank Lilach Weiss for excellent research assistance and the Department of East Asian Studies at the Hebrew University for financial support. We are also grateful to Jeffrey Wichmann from Deutsche Bank (New York) for kindly providing us with the data on contemporary sovereign bonds. Keunkwan Ryu and participants of a CEPR conference held in Oxford provided helpful comments and suggestions.

Notes

1   Information is available on other types of Korean government and quasi-government bonds. The correlation between the various series is very close to one. We choose this KDB bond because it provides the longest data series.

2   Included in the analysis are the following sovereign bonds: Thailand, coupon rate 7.75%, maturity date April 2007; Indonesia, coupon rate 7.75%, maturity date August 2006; Malaysia, coupon rate 7.75%, maturity date August 2006; Brazil, coupon rate 8%, maturity date April 2014; and Argentina, coupon rate 6.18%, maturity date March 2005.

3   When the time series is unit root, the $EVENT_{short}$ dummy variable identifies one-time breaks that have a permanent effect on the series, see Sussman and Yafeh (1999a).

4   There are a number of technical issues related to the calculation of the risk premium, which are discussed in Sussman and Yafeh (1999a). Figure 1 presents a naive calculation, based on the ratio of the bond's interest payments to market price. Other possible calculations are, for example, yield to maturity, or the *Economist's* risk premium series,

which is calculated according to a different formula. These calculations do not materially affect the results.

5 The declining risk premium of the 1870s occurs early in our period of observation, and may be due to a number of factors which are discussed in detail in Sussman and Yafeh (1999a).

6 In Table 2 we choose not to report the impact of the Gold Standard on yields using a "window" similar to that constructed around other events. This is because the decline in yields that accompanied the adoption of the Gold Standard was due to the complete withdrawal of the 1873 seven percent bonds and the issuance of new five percent bonds of longer maturity. When the entire stock of old bonds was about to be redeemed, yields approached the short-term risk-free interest rate (or prices approached the coupon redemption value). Therefore, the observed decline in interest rates from seven to five percent is likely to be an overestimate of the impact of the Gold Standard. A more conservative estimate can be inferred by using market yields in the early 1890s (before the approaching redemption began to drive them upwards) which were around six percent. The implied decline in the risk premium following the adoption of the Gold Standard according to this estimate is a third (rather than a half).

7 These findings are in line with Sussman and Yafeh (1999b): Although in the long run, sovereign debt yields of countries "on" the Gold Standard moved together, short-term idiosyncratic fluctuations were not always transmitted across the borders.

8 According to Eichengreen (1997), this crisis affected interest rates in many countries in Latin America and elsewhere.

9 The effect of the Baring Crisis on Japanese bond prices remains positive albeit statistically insignificant even when we examine *daily* data around the peak of the crisis.

10 Cointegration tests confirm that the Korean and Thai series are cointegrated with a coefficient that is close to 0.9.

11 Nevertheless, it appears that Korea's agreements with the IMF did not prove to be major turning points with an effect similar in magnitude to that of the Gold Standard in Meiji Japan. Note, however, that in general, short-term fluctuations in the Korean data are much larger than the "blips" identified in our historical Japanese data set.

12 In Sussman and Yafeh (1999a) we argue that a military victory over an *ex-ante* stronger rival (e.g. Japan's victory over Russia) can also "certify" a country's domestic progress and development.

13 For example, according to the *Historical Statistics of Japan* (published by the Japan Statistical Association) China accounted for about one eighth of Japan's foreign trade in 1900, whereas the *Economist's* Country Report for Korea does not rank Indonesia, Malaysia, or Thailand among Korea's major trading partners in 1996. Malaysia accounted for only 3 percent of Korea's exports and two percent of her imports. Indonesia accounted for about two and a half percent of Korea's imports and was not one of the major export destinations for Korean goods. Trade with Thailand was even smaller. Moreover, the volume of external trade of Meiji Japan (in relation to GNP) was substantial (see again the *Historical Statistics of Japan*) so that it is not possible to argue that trade with Indonesia today "matters more" to Korea than trade with China did for Japan a hundred years ago.

References

Bordo, M., Eichengreen, B., and Kim, J. "Was There Really an Earlier Period of International Financial Integration Comparable to Today?" NBER Working Paper No. 6738, 1998.

Bordo, M., and Rockoff, H. "The Gold Standard as a Good Housekeeping Seal of Approval." *Journal of Economic History* 56 (No. 2 1996): 389-428.

Christiano, Lawrence. "Searching for a Break in GNP." *Journal of Business and Economic Statistics* 10 (1992): 237-50.

Corsetti, G., Pesenti, P., and Roubini, N. "What Caused the Asian Financial Crisis?" *Japan and the World Economy* 11 (No. 3 1999): 305-73.

Edwards, S. "The Pricing of Bonds and Bank Loans in International Markets: An Empirical Analysis of Developing Countries' Foreign Borrowing." *European Economic Review* 30 (No. 3 1986): 565-89.

Eichengreen, B. *The Gold Standard in Theory and History.* New York: Methuen Press, 1985.

_____. "The Baring Crisis in a Mexican Mirror." In N. Lustig (ed.), *Essays in Honor of Albert Fishlow.* Ann Arbor, Michigan: University of Michigan Press, Forthcoming, Draft Dated 1997.

_____, and Flandreau, M. "The Geography of the Gold Standard." In J. Braga de Macedo, B. Eichengreen, and J. Reis (eds.), *Currency Convertibility: The Gold Standard and Beyond.* New York: Routledge Press, 1996.

Glick, R., and Rose, A. "Contagion and Trade: Why Are Currency Crises Regional?" *Journal of International Money and Finance* 18 (No. 4 1999): 603-17.

Gregory, P. "The Russian Balance of Payments, the Gold Standard, and Monetary Policy: A Historical Example of Foreign Capital Movements." *Journal of Economic History* 39 (No. 2 1979): 379-99.

Izvorski, I. "Brady Bonds and Default Probabilities." IMF Working Paper WP/98/16, 1998.

Kaminsky, G., and Schmukler, S. "What Triggers Market Jitters: A Chronicle of the Asian Crisis." *Journal of International Money and Finance* 18 (No. 4 1999): 537-60.

O'Rourke, K., and Williamson, J. *Globalization and History: The Evolution of a Nineteenth Century Atlantic Economy.* Cambridge: MIT Press, 1998.

Radelet, S., and Sachs, J. "The Onset of the Asian Financial Crisis." Mimeograph, Harvard University, 1998.

Roubini, N. "Chronology of the Asian Crisis and Global Contagion." http://www.stern.nyu.edu/nroubini-/asia/AsiaHomepage.html, 1999.

Sussman, N., and Yafeh, Y. "Institutions, Reforms, and Country Risk: Lessons from Japanese Government Debt in the Meiji Period." *Journal of Economic History.* Forthcoming, 1999a.

_____. "The Gold Standard, the Cost of Foreign Debt, and Capital Market Integration: Historical Evidence from Japanese Government Debt." *Economie Internationale 78* (No. 2 1999b): 85-105.

Suzuki, Toshio. *Japanese Government Loans on the London Capital Market, 1870-1913.* London: Athlone Press, 1994.

9

CAVEAT EMPTOR

Coping with Sovereign Risk Under the International Gold Standard, 1871–1913

Marc Flandreau

Source: *International Financial History in the Twentieth Century: System and Anarchy* (Cambridge: Cambridge University Press, 2003), pp. 17–50.

Caveat emptor: To those who forget the maxim, each new financial crisis brings an opportunity to relearn their lesson. The turmoil that swept Southeast Asian countries in the late 1990s is no exception: Once again, it has produced classic tales about late investors buying out of ignorance. According to some economists, rating agencies should take their share of the blame: They failed to provide appropriate signals to the market through early downgrades and then followed the market mood as it spiraled down.[1] In self-defense, rating agencies emphasize that their grades are not (and have never been) meant to establish any kind of standard on which one could base investment decisions: The availability of formal ratings should not discourage investors from devoting time and effort to get their own opinion. Why look for someone to blame? It is after all in the nature of risk to bring its crop of regrets.

At a deeper level, these recurrent complaints may be seen as illustrating the complexities of the economics of economic intelligence: The supply and demand of information are nested into an institutional setting from which they cannot be separated. This setting in turn provides incentives that contribute to more or less risk-taking on behalf of agents. For instance, the expectation of an eventual bailout by some public body (national or multilateral) reduces investors' incentives to collect data and process it in original ways: Less attention is paid to discussing economic developments in borrowing countries, fewer analyses are supplied, and they are of lesser quality.

Hence, the organization of economic intelligence should be a research topic in its own right. Yet problems of identification line the way. While a theoretical case can be made that the expectation of a rescue amplifies the magnitude of risk-taking, it is an altogether different and more difficult matter to prove it empirically. History on the other hand provides a way to ask that question in reverse: One only needs to look for occurrences when the market mechanism is "bailout free."

One such episode is the years before World War I. True, some authors have tried to argue that a measure of central bank cooperation existed between 1890 and 1914 and that it did work, on occasion, as a partial substitute for international lender of last resort facilities.[2] But such schemes (which in any case were not outright bailouts) were very occasional, often failed, and depended on a set of complex factors on which it was dangerous to bank.[3] The concern about moral hazard was a close companion of late nineteenth-century laissez-faire. The boldest proposal for an international mechanism to prevent crises from spreading was met with the belief that irresponsible behavior – not contagion – was the real danger.

Of course, it could still be that, even if they did not anticipate being bailed out by domestic monetary authorities, nineteenth-century investors expected their governments to help them "bail in" foreign debtors. Lending countries used in cases military expedients that mitigated the meaning of "sovereignty." The inclusion in sovereign debt contracts of collateral clauses provided a legal justification for military intervention. International control, as in Turkey and Greece, could ensue.[4] But muscle flexing is not without costs and, to be effective, requires a fair amount of lender coordination. Coordination was far from natural in the explosive political climate of the years before World War I, when global providers of capital were also global rivals.[5] Defaults did take place, and military intervention, when it occurred, did not result in complete recovery of lost funds. Banks thus had to watch their steps: In France, an early Crédit agricole went under in 1876 as a result of the Ottoman default. In England, Baring had to pay a high price for its way out of Argentinean losses.

This makes the pre-1914 experience of globalization "without the multilaterals" fascinating. A large number of classic studies have demonstrated that capital did move across borders, either through the agency of financial markets or, increasingly, through direct foreign investment or other arrangements such as "free standing companies."[6] These studies have paid much attention to the geographical distribution of international investment, to its contribution to economic growth, and to the trends and cycles of international finance. Yet the question of determining how investment priorities were set remains obscure. In what is perhaps the only study that has explicitly tackled the issue, Herbert Feis maintained that "politics" had been the overarching factor in allocating (or misallocating) capital.[7] To date, no full-fledged alternative has been provided. We know very little about the nineteenth-century devices to screen potential borrowers, balance risks, and "rate" sovereigns. This may explain the resilience of the popular myth of nineteenth-century investors lured by politicians.[8] Didn't sovereign rating begin only after World War I when U.S. capital arrived in the Old World?[9] To many, this is prima facie evidence of the lack of economic literacy among European bankers before World War I.

This chapter challenges that view. It argues that the type of analyses that are at the heart of formal rating had in fact developed in Europe at least a quarter of a century before World War I. I take a look at one French bank: France was the second largest international investor in the late nineteenth and early twentieth centuries.

It specialized in lending to the "risky" regions of the European Continent, such as the Mediterranean or Russia, where public debts were large and sovereign default a potentially huge problem. I focus on the Crédit Lyonnais. The choice, which in view of some recent developments may sound ironic, is not fortuitous: The Lyonnais, a private commercial bank created in 1863, grew patiently and prudently from being a financial underdog to becoming the largest European institution at the turn of the century.[10] At that point, it established itself as a prominent actor in foreign lending, even displacing traditional players of the Rothschild kind from this market to some extent.

The chapter's first lesson is that in the absence of international agencies, private risk analysis played an essential role in bringing about financial integration before World War I. In addition, I show that the lack of official provision of international statistics and rating led the Lyonnais to integrate the collection and analysis of data: Its financial studies unit, the Service des Etudes Financières (SEF), constructed a series that permitted direct comparisons between the macroeconomic health of various borrowers. The second lesson is that the lack of multilateral agencies, while providing incentives for private investment in information gathering, does not necessarily lead to an efficient provision thereof. The externalities in the supply of information can lead to monopolization. In this instance, I show how the Lyonnais sought to become a kind of mood-setter in the Paris market.

The remainder of the chapter is organized as follows: The first section is mostly descriptive. We start at the most microeconomic level and survey the background in which the SEF emerged and developed. The second section focuses on the Lyonnais's methods of assessing public finances and sovereign risk. I show that these methods led to a straightforward way of rating countries in risk categories. The conclusion, finally, discusses the lessons of the nineteenth-century experience.

The service des etudes financières, 1871–1914

The Founding of the SEF: Speculations

The SEF was set up in 1871 on request from Henri Germain, director and creator of Crédit Lyonnais. Its proclaimed objective was to provide facts and figures that would assist investment decisions. Over time, the SEF grew into a large research unit with a reputation.[11] Eugène d'Eichtal, in the short hagiographic obituary he wrote on Germain, makes special reference to the SEF.[12] Its creation, he explained, resulted from the great man's "passion for political economy." I suggest, instead, that one needs to relate the founding of the SEF to the general background of the market for economic information around 1870.[13]

The 1850s and 1860s were years of an "information revolution." This revolution had its technical side, with the installation of the cable between London and the Continent (1852) and later between Europe and America (1866). The cable brought national financial markets closer together, shortened drastically transmission lags from market to market, and reduced crossborder uncertainties. This revolution had, of course, an important economic side: The technical possibilities for channeling funds from market to market improved at the same time that both the supply and demand of funds were growing more competitive. The period after 1840 displayed a massive expansion of the key financial markets as global centers. The capitalization of both London and Paris accelerated, and cumulated securitized foreign lending amounted to a large share of both England and France's GDP.[14] Other industrialized countries, such as Belgium and Switzerland, also contributed to the process, exporting their own capital through the pipes of the leading financial centers.[15] The networking of railways across the Continent and the need to finance new nations in both their military and industrial enterprises also multiplied the number of possible outlets.

For lenders, this called for increased screening capacities. More information was required on more projects. With the growth of the number of markets, geopolitical coverage had to expand. The move that had begun in England with the creation of *The Economist* in 1844 extended to the Continent. *La Semaine financière*, the most comprehensive and well-informed French-language weekly, began in the 1850s in Brussels. The quality of its information was enhanced by a freedom of tone provided by its ability to escape from French political censorship. Progressively, the success of *The Economist* led to a multiplication of continental offspring: In 1873, at about the same time the SEF was launched, Paul Leroy-Beaulieu created *L'Economiste français.* Other clones followed.

The multiplication of sources of economic data also created a need for reference. Financial handbooks listing quoted bonds and collecting official information in a systematic way came much in vogue. From 1863, for instance, *The Economist* started issuing the *Investor's Monthly Manual.*[16] In France, Alphonse Courtois published the first edition of his *Manuel des fonds publics et des sociétés par actions* in 1856.[17] The volume described systematically all public and private bonds listed in Paris. The book was a hit and would be republished several times. It would later have an official competitor, the *Annuaire officiel des agents de change* issued by the association of Parisian brokers.

Such publications, however, were mere compilations of official pamphlets that borrowing institutions circulated when new loans were floated. The need to provide background information relating to the general macroeconomic, institutional, and political outlook thus remained. Macmillan seized the opportunity in the 1860s, when it started issuing *The Statesman's Yearbook.* Another slightly later attempt at improving the statistical background was that of the Société Internationale de Statistique, an international network of statisticians created in the 1880s that held conferences every four years. The meetings, which drew both official and independent statisticians, sought to define statistical "best practices." Proceedings were published. In some cases, the Société Internationale also lobbied to obtain changes in the way official returns were either collected or presented.[18] However, political resistance turned the odds against the feasibility of such "multilateral" endeavors, suggesting that more solitary investigations were better equipped to succeed. This may explain the large supply of individual statistical compilations, impressive by modern standards yet often redundant, and among which Michael G. Mulhall's stand out prominently.[19]

In contrast, the expansion in the competition for foreign credit implied that borrowers had growing incentives to become more transparent. Bilateral relations were increasingly replaced by broader multilateral underwriting syndicates that then turned to a large crowd of customers. This meant that borrowing governments could shop around for lower prices. But this also meant that they had to find some way to communicate with the rich public of the lending countries. The practice thus developed among borrowing governments to publish, on an annual basis, detailed financial accounts. Whereas in Western Europe, transparency of public accounts had been a companion of the rise of parliamentarism (the lenders to national governments were the domestic bourgeoisie), financial accountability developed in other countries with international lending. Fiscal returns were often bilingual: Russian accounts were published in Russian and French, the Hungarian ones also used French, while Japanese returns (after 1900) used both English and French. Thus, every year from the 1860s and 1870s onward, a huge crop of government documents flooded the marketplace.

This information "overflow" was both a challenge and an opportunity: If exploited intelligently, information could give an edge to newcomers. For years, international finance had been the private hunting ground of the traditional investment bankers. The Haute banque, with its high-profile customers and correspondents, collected money and information almost in the same move. By its extensive political and economic networks, the Haute banque had a first-hand knowledge of the risks involved and, through its political clout, even a degree of command on the risks themselves.[20] The limited extent of democracy in several borrowing countries also implied that fewer levels of government were involved. Personal contacts had a premium over "macroeconomic" analysis. This sort of intelligence clearly outsmarted any attempt at putting together figures that in most cases just did not exist. But the expanding supply of statistical returns meant that the time of bankers who kept your account in the back of their mind was passing. It is thus no wonder that the SEF was created in the middle of the early 1870s boom in foreign lending. As a newcomer on the financial scene, the Lyonnais did not have as strong political connections as the establishment. Being an outsider, it was excluded from the safest bets and had to take calculated risks.

The First Years of the Service, 1871–1889

The link between the expansion of financial press and the creation of the SEF is a direct one: While Desseilligny (a board member) was responsible for general supervision, Courtois (the author of the famous *Manuel des fonds publics et des sociétés par actions* to which I referred earlier) was appointed head of the service. An archetypal self-taught financial journalist, Courtois had, according to some sources, worked for the Lyonnais since the 1860s.[21] He was well acquainted with financial techniques and had authored a famous *Traité des opérations de bourse*

(1855). He had also been a pioneer in data collection: His *Tableaux des cours des principales valeurs* provided time series for bonds and stocks on the Paris bourse since 1797.[22] An opponent of government intervention and a member since 1851 of the Société Economique Politique, the French laissez-faire lobby, he had argued forcefully in his books that governments should not tamper with the stock market. In short, the Lyonnais had appointed a specialist of the French Bourse well acquainted with the tout Paris of economics.

The correspondence surrounding the creation of the SEF suggests that the whole process took place under much pressure from the top management. Abundant space and resources were devoted to the project. Two kinds of information were sought. First, Germain wanted the SEF to provide "insider" information that would fuel profitable trading. Second, he wanted it to perform "modern" economic analysis, which derives value from the intelligent use of publicly available information. This multiplicity of purposes was reflected in duality of names: The SEF was alternatively referred to as the "information office" (*bureau des renseignements*) or the "research bureau" (*bureau des etudes*). This caused much confusion for both Courtois and later historians.[23] Although both roles initially coexisted, the latter would gradually dominate.

The search for insider information involved spying on other banks and governments: The service hired foreign "agents" (in French, *correspondants*) working in competing finance houses. One of the first agents in Vienna was an employee at Rothschild's. Agents were paid for their tips, and in some cases valuable information was given in return. To maximize the flow of information and avoid the risk of being deceived by its own correspondents, the Lyonnais arranged redundancies: Two agents were hired in a single market, without their knowing.[24] Of course, insider information was not limited to foreign markets: Some SEF employees in Paris (*employés sédentaires* or resident employees) were hired because they were thought to be "well acquainted" or for their abilities "at finding [their] ways in ministries."[25] To conduct its economic studies, the SEF had to collect statistics. For this, it was equipped right away with a reference library that started purchasing books, newspapers, periodicals, and official reports. The library was meant to be comprehensive. This was to some extent similar to what the Library and Record Department of the Council of the Corporation of Foreign Bond Holders was doing at about the same time, although the library of the Lyonnais (which was substantially larger than CFB's) was meant for private use only.[26]

The output of the SEF was of two kinds. First, the service had to produce a daily "bulletin." The bulletin contained financial information of general interest made out of clippings from the international press. The daily bulletin's circulation was restricted to top management use: Only the heads of both the Paris and Lyons offices and of the main branches received it. Second, and more importantly, the service had to produce specific reports made on request from the executive office. Reports could cover a wide variety of topics, ranging from the prospects of PLM railways to Austrian finances.

Courtois had been asked to find the appropriate people. His correspondence is an echo of the obstacles he encountered. In 1871, political economy (not to mention applied macroeconomics) was not widely taught in France.[27] Courtois hired people from the Bourse (stock exchange) or the financial press. The results were disappointing.[28] Germain suggested recruiting from the offices of the Ministry of Finance, where one could find "hard working, intelligent, and moreover low paid, young men."[29] Germain must have been referring to services such as the Bureau de statistique et de législation comparée, which statistician Alfred de Foville headed since 1867.[30] But potential employees did not turn out to be as bright as Germain had hoped.[31] Courtois then sought to recruit economists through recommendations from members of the Société d'Economie Politique, of which he was a member. He used social events such as the dinner of the society to carry on his investigation and paid personal visits to some economists, again, with limited success.[32] He then turned to second-best solutions. Reasonably appropriate applicants, whose background showed their adaptability, could be tried. One of the first employees was a graduate from Saint Cyr (the French Military Academy) who had left the army and had become a merchant, then a broker, in various towns. This ensured that he was both numerate and flexible; the rest would have to be learned on site.

Looking through the Lyonnais files, one gets the feeling that the search was also impaired by the bank's own position. At that time, the Lyonnais was still a relatively recent institution and a career there implied a measure of risk taking. As a matter of fact, one civil servant from top government engineer schools which the Lyonnais was lucky to hire turned out to be a second-order type whom the administration was happy to part with.[33] The difficulty of actually attracting people is also evident from Germain's suggestion to recruit females.[34] It is probable that Germain had realized that top male graduates would not consider work at the SEF sufficiently attractive. Yet even this did not succeed.

To what extent did these obstacles hamper the initial development of the SEF? From its projected twelve employees in 1871, the staff rose to about twenty in 1881. This was quite large by the standards of the time, but in a sense fell rather short of the original ambitions. Moreover, the size of the staff did not increase much during the first twenty years. While it kept accumulating books, statistics, and studies, the SEF did not realize the grand scheme that had been initially envisioned. Ultimately, it would take the development of the teaching of economics in France, the rise of Lyonnais as a major bank, and the international banking crisis that climaxed in 1890 for the SEF to meet its initial goals.

The Rise of the SEF, 1889–1914

During the board meeting of November 5, 1889, Germain announced that he wanted to increase the size of the SEF. "Time has come," he said, "to give to the operations of the SEF maximum scope and efficiency."[35] René Brice, a member of the council of administration, was asked to head the service. He had no special skills in political economy: His appointment really reflected the increased control which Germain took at that point over the SEF, and, from that date on, the service expanded.

One factor explaining this evolution was the removal of bottlenecks on the supply of human capital. The Lyonnais's initial dissatisfaction with the general background of graduates had been a widely shared feeling in French commercial circles. The defeat of 1871 and the ensuing concern about economic decline provided the impetus for the creation of a number of institutions devoted to the teaching of business and economics.[36] At the Ecole Libre des Sciences Politiques, which was set up in 1871, Leroy-Beaulieu initiated a course on public finances in 1872. Although Leroy-Beaulieu stopped teaching in 1880, the number of courses in "macroeconomics" (political economy, money, finance) kept increasing. In 1883, these courses were organized within a formal curriculum in economics and finance – the "section économique et financière." In 1891, students of this program could major in either private or public finance. Those two majors became separate curricula in 1909–10. Lecturers at Ecole Libre (or "Sciences-Po" as it was already known at the time) were recruited from among the top echelon of statistics and economics.[37]

The Paris business school, known as Hautes Etudes Commerciales or HEC, was created in 1881. Garnier (1881–3) and, later, Courcelle-Seneuil (1883–8), both leaders of the French lobby for political economy, taught there. According to Levan-Lemesle, when Octave Noël took over the course in 1888, he gave it a practical twist that was most welcome.[38] Noël was a prolific writer who had published extensively on railways, money, and central banking. His lectures were intended to make the case for laissez-faire on the basis of practical examples. For instance, in an 1888 book, Noël explored the economic and institutional record of a number of European central banks in an attempt to show the advantages of central bank independence from government intervention – a view that would later become the conventional wisdom during the Belle Epoque.[39] This approach reflected Noël's special concern about the relevance of his teaching for the four hundred students he taught each year.

Taken together, graduates from HEC and Sciences-Po's "section économique et financière" represented a total of about five hundred students with degrees in economics. Moreover, the rising prestige of Crédit Lyonnais (it was by now no longer an eight-year-old outsider as in 1871, but an over twenty-five-year-old bank that often led major syndicates and had successfully resisted the 1881 stock market crash in Paris) had implications on its ability to attract first-class graduates from all schools. In addition to economists from HEC or Sciences-Po, the Lyonnais hired engineers from Ponts et Chaussées, Mines, Arts et Métiers, Polytechnique. This was especially important given that investment opportunities generally included a technical aspect for which "pure" economists were inadequate.

Whereas the availability of graduates with the appropriate background was probably a necessary condition for the growth of the SEF, it nevertheless did not prompt the November 1889 decision to expand. Rather, Germain's decision must be related to the increasing risks in international banking that developed as a result of the lending spree of the late 1880s.[40] The escalating tensions precipitated

209

the collapse of Comptoir d'escompte in 1889 and of Baring in 1890. The Banque de Paris et des Pays-Bas recorded heavy losses in Argentinean railways in 1890–1 and, in general, many banks suffered. Contagion ensued and the bonds of weaker governments depreciated. The exchange rates of a number of South American and Mediterranean countries declined. Several suspensions of interest payments followed. In this context, and given the Lyonnais's compulsive concern about liquidity and mismatches (an attitude that was Germain's trademark), the decision to expand the SEF seems quite understandable. The Lyonnais had probably realized that those who would survive would be the most careful students of international finance.

Recruiting thus resumed after 1890. The move, first gradual (there were still twenty employees in 1893), quickly accelerated: Eighty people worked in the service at the turn of the century. Increased budgets followed: Before 1889 the annual budget of the service had oscillated between 100,000 and 200,000 francs.[41] Returns for the period 1890–1905 show a take-off: The SEF's expenses trebled over the 1890s.[42] Drastic increases brought budgets near 800,000 francs per year after 1900. Indeed, budgets were mostly driven by trends in the work force (Figure 1.1): General office expenses, despite the 1890 introduction of the typewriter as well as of a number of computing Grand Total machines and massive purchases of books for the library, amounted to little in comparison to employees' earnings.[43]

The increase in the number of SEF employees also outpaced the growth of labor inputs for the bank at large. The gross wage of the SEF represented about 1.5 percent of the total wage burden in 1894.[44] This proportion almost doubled, rising to 2.5 percent in 1900. Similarly, the number of SEF employees rose during the same period from 0.5 percent of the overall Lyonnais work force to about

Figure 1.1 SEF expenses (Frenchfrancs, leftscale) and number of employees (right scale).
Source: Archives DEEF, "Boulevard des Italiens," sans cote.

210

0.8 percent. The average wage in the SEF (which came to about 6,300 francs per year) was roughly three times higher than the average at the Lyonnais (about 2,100 francs per year). This reflected the greater share of highly skilled employees in the service. The share of graduates was somewhere between 40 percent and 60 percent, while at the same time these represented only 10 percent of the Lyonnais at large.[45] After 1905, however, the growth of the service stalled. Budgets and probably staff stopped expanding. Yet with about a hundred employees and an annual budget between 500,000 and 600,000 francs, the SEF stood on the eve of the war unparalleled by contemporary or even modern standards.[46]

The growth of the SEF also led to a rationalization of its organization. During the 1890s, work was gradually divided among a number of research groups called "sections." Each section was headed by a *chef de section* who worked under the authority of the *directeur du Service des Etudes* (head of the SEF). Twelve formal sections emerged. Among the administrative sections, one finds the *section du bulletin*, which collected clippings from the press and edited the daily house magazine that was circulated to the managers. The *section des notes* wrote briefs to answer the queries of individual customers or official bodies (for example, ministries). The total number of replies generated per annum rose from 5,710 in 1893 to 11,297 in 1896, from 17,110 in 1899 to 20,057 in 1902, with a growing portion going to public administrations.[47] The *section des notes* could rely on the help of the *section des archives*, which kept and stored records, as well as of the *section du repertoire*, which maintained a huge database of facts and figures on companies, banks, and so forth.[48] Secretarial aid was provided by the *section de copie*, which typed memoranda, drew charts, and performed other such tasks.

Moreover, there were five research sections. These sections had the largest staffs and were fully separate from the rest of the bank. They were never directly involved in investment decisions, and their reports could not be communicated to other departments without management approval.[49] One section dealt with industries and mines (*section des mines et de l'industrie*), one with railways and navigation (*section des transports*), one with banks (*section des banques*), and one with public finances (*section des fonds d'états*).[50] In addition, the *section de statistique* collected macroeconomic data (for example, on agricultural and industrial products, money, and population). Over time, the *section de statistique* also developed expertise on fiscal issues, which gave birth after World War I to separate *section de législation fiscale*. Finally, two sections provided technical support: The *section des cotes* recorded exchange rates and stock prices; the *section des calculs financiers* used or constructed logarithmic tables to make actuarial computations.[51]

The SEF's operations were not limited to the Paris facilities. The creation of agencies or branches in leading financial centers provided the Lyonnais with a ready infrastructure for collecting and double-checking information. The former policy of paying for tips was progressively abandoned, or at least did not feature as prominently as in the past. Offices were opened within the Lyonnais's foreign branches. In 1905, there were permanent representatives in Berlin, Johannesburg,

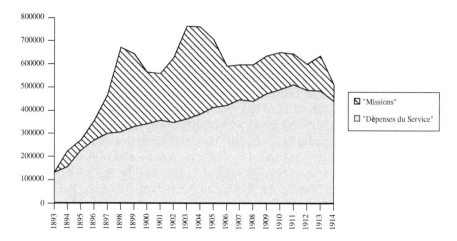

Figure 1.2 SEF expenses (French francs): Paris and Missions. *Source: Archives DEEF, "Boue-vard des Italiens," sans cote.*

London, New York, and Saint Petersburg. These outposts were run by civil engineers from the SEF who conducted audits of local companies.[52] In Saint Petersburg, for instance, there was a *bureau de l'ingénieur chargé des études industrielles et financiers* (office of the engineer in charge of industrial and financial studies).[53] In general, foreign facilities also served as mediators between the SEF and local officials, bankers, and entrepreneurs. A fascinating letter of 1898 from the Lisbon branch, for instance, recalls the visit of a Portuguese official who was offered a position in the Ministry of Finance and wanted to look at the Lyonnais figures on Portugal before accepting the position.[54] Finally, extensive expeditions were sent abroad to prospective markets. These included Australia, China, Mexico, South America, and the Danubian states. Most of these missions took place between 1897 and 1905 and feature prominently in SEF expenses (Figure 1.2).

The Public Debts Unit

We have quite detailed records on the personnel from *section des fonds d'états*, which formalized as a specific unit in the late 1890s.[55] From 1896, the number of *chargés d'études* monitoring sovereign debts increased steadily. A first surge took place between 1899 and 1906, when the section reached nine *chargés d'études*. This puts the section at 20 percent of the SEF (including clerks and *auxiliaires*). A second surge occurred after 1905. Between 1908 and 1912, there were twelve to sixteen *chargés d'études* in the section, or a total of about thirty employees, one-third of the SEF. This evolution ran counter the general trend of the SEF in the ten years preceding the war, which was one of relative stagnation: The prewar growth

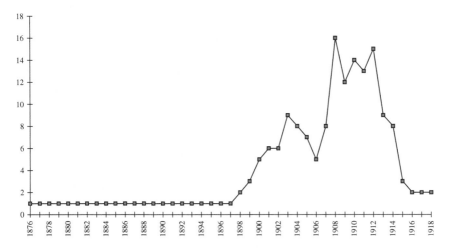

Figure 1.3 Number of employees in the *Section des Fonds d'Etats*. *Source*: *Author's computation, Archives du Crédit Lyonnais, Historique DEEF.*

of the section thus took place at the expense of other sections.[56] This suggests tremendous activity in *section des fonds d'etats*.[57] The movement stalled in 1912 (see Figure 1.3).[58] The interruption of French foreign lending with the outbreak of World War I was a final blow to the section that was nonetheless revived after the war with the resumption of international capital flows.

All *chargés d'études* from the *section de fonds d'etats* came from either HEC or Sciences-Po. The right candidates had strong skills in accounting, high performance at school, and a command of foreign languages. Fonds d'Etats produced a kind of elite. One, Dujardin, a major (prize winner) from HEC later became head of the Paris offices. Another, Escarra became head of the SEF and later CEO of Crédit Lyonnais. Most departures from the *section de fonds d'états* on which we have information were really promotions. Those who left the Lyonnais received attractive offers to head or create small research departments in other financial institutions. One, Hennequin, a graduate from HEC who had worked for the *section des fonds d'états* between 1900 and 1911, became chief economist at the Banque française de commerce et d'industrie. One, Laroche, became *chef des études* at the Banque de la Seine. One, Droz, moved to Union parisienne. Over time, the SEF had been able to overcome the initial human capital shortages to the extent that it could now export employees it had trained.

The Glory and the Power: SEF Propaganda During the Belle Epoque

The Belle Epoque was the heyday of the SEF. With its impressive library of more than 30,000 volumes, its 45,000 files on countries, industries, railways, and banks, its catalog of firm-specific data, and its hundreds of employees, it clearly surpassed anything that existed at the time, either in France or abroad. Kaufman argued that in France only the Comptoir national d'escompte had a somewhat analogous service.[59] But this service, created only a few years before World War I, was of much more limited scope. As for Europe, Kaufman believed, no other bank, British, German, or other, could stand comparison.[60]

Having heavily and steadily invested in the SEF, the Lyonnais was fully aware of its superiority.[61] This unique position had many advantages that could be exploited in various ways. One possibility would have been to sell its "ratings" to the market place. In effect, however, the bank never abandoned a strict policy of secrecy: It never disclosed more than limited parts of its reports. It is striking that, although contemporary economists were aware of the existence of the service, they apparently never received access to the figures it collected, nor to the precise way the SEF combined them.[62]

There were two mutually reinforcing advantages for this policy. The first had to do with the notes that the SEF wrote for customers. Without disclosing complete returns, the Lyonnais could provide depositors with topical memoranda on specific issues. This was a way to attract more depositors and increase market share. Second, the expertise of the SEF could become a resource to foster the bank's influence as a market mood setter. The Lyonnais thus took great care to make sure the general public realized that the bank had access to valuable information. Prestigious foreign guests were thus invariably brought to the SEF when they visited the Lyonnais.

One high point of this campaign was the April 1904 visit that the Lyonnais organized for the international press. The occasion was to show the bank's new facilities on the Boulevard des Italiens. A crowd of journalists gathered at the SEF, and during the following days, long articles appeared in the French, English, Spanish, German, Italian, and American press.[63] From the striking similarities between the various articles, it is obvious that the Lyonnais had provided journalists with a document on which they could canvass, perhaps monetary incentives as well. The articles praised the SEF in forceful words. For instance, A. Johnson, from the *New York Herald*, wrote:

> From a financial point of view [the SEF] is a "veritable practical university." I have never heard of a similar organization either in France or abroad. Figures taken from official documents, accounts of sovereign states and reports of limited liability companies are tabulated methodically by employees chosen in the majority of cases from prize winners at the Polytechnic, the Ecole Centrale, the Ecole des Mines, and the Ecole des Hautes Etudes Commerciales. The most rigid impartiality presides at the making up of these tabulated records, without the employees, who do not know about the conclusion of the affairs studied by the bank, having other care than the finding out of the truth. The clientele of the Crédit Lyonnais is greatly benefited by this department, which acts as its secretary, and which, upon a request to that effect,

214

addressed to the branch office with which the client transacts business, will go through all the documents published upon any commercial, industrial or other affair.[64]

Virtually identical accounts with carbon copy wording (including the reference to the "practical university" which also features in Germain's obituary) were found in other newspapers.[65] They reflected the attempt at presenting the Lyonnais as a standard of informational reliability. The claim was everywhere the same: The Lyonnais had paid a high price to have a huge database that you could not bank against. So you were better advised to bank with the Lyonnais. As one French journalist wrote: "We got the message: the Lyonnais is well informed."[66]

Sovereign "rating" at the Lyonnais

Fiscal Concerns, Statistical Doubts, and the Making of a Framework of Analysis

Whereas the need to attract foreign capital had created pressures on borrowers to release financial information, efforts at increasing formal resemblance between national returns remained nonetheless inconclusive: The definition of "revenue" and "expenditure," the units in which outstanding debts were denominated, or even the comprehensiveness of public accounts varied significantly among countries. This was not always disingenuous, but in some cases, concerns about the implications of deficits on borrowing costs led governments to creative accounting: As one Portuguese official confessed to the Crédit Lyonnais in 1898, the annual abstract of Portuguese finances was "filled with intended errors."[67]

One reason for this was the lack of national (let alone international) consensus on the appropriate framework. This problem was widely recognized at the time, because fierce battles were fought over figures in almost every country.[68] Such disputes were not clear-cut bouts that pitted fudging governments against benevolent opponents. Rather, information was retained, released, corrupted, and criticized according to the interests of the various groups involved. The press (domestic and foreign) was often bought. Perhaps the most famous illustration of this was the debates within the Russian Imperial Council in the late 1890s and early 1900s, where statistical accuracy became a political issue.[69] The Russian case was not exceptional. As SEF economists concluded: "If one were to judge from the disputes surrounding the yearly vote of the budget, it would seem that it is absolutely impossible to assess the financial situation of any given state with enough precision. Except in rare instances, those who participate in those discussions do not seem to be prepared to agree on the calculus that serve as a basis of their discussion. Concerned more than anything else with the need to free themselves from any kind of controls, they oppose unfounded rebuttal to unfounded assertions, and if by chance, debate develops, the general tone of the discussion quickly deteriorates without bringing any clarity."[70]

This situation was discouraging in view of the kind of systematic quantified comparisons that investors were looking for. Yet one could dream of a "rationalist" alternative, which would require designing a framework in which itemized public accounts could be split and then reconstructed. This framework, by fixing the methodological problems, would in turn help to focus more specifically on accuracy. Such was the ambitious route that the Lyonnais adopted. It is possible to identify the main stages in the development of the Lyonnais's method. Economists had long been aware of the relations between public finances and the price of debt instruments. For instance, in his *Traité des opérations de bourse*, Courtois claimed that the financial situation of a given government determined the likelihood of an increase in its demand for funds. The greater that probability, the lower the price of its bonds.[71]

These views were echoed by those of Germain, who displayed an early interest in the empirical assessment of the way public finances would behave in the wake of given shocks. In 1871, he asked SEF economists to perform some "stress analyses" in their fiscal reports in order to determine, for instance, how public finances would react to a one-time increase in spending: Given the inertia of some expenses (such as interest service), he reasoned, one could get an idea of the amount of free resources that would be available. He further argued that this could be used to extrapolate the borrowing capacity of any government given alternative scenarios on the evolution of its revenues.[72] Such analyses, however, remained fairly rudimentary, at least until the early 1890s.[73]

The crisis of 1890 was a watershed. In 1891, as the Argentinean crisis was spreading, Germain received several reports among which were memoranda on Spain, Portugal, and Italy, with whom the Lyonnais had business relations and whose bonds had been seriously shaken. Germain was perceptibly anxious about financial developments in these nations, and he wanted to better understand each country's macroeconomic prospects. In particular, he wanted to disentangle permanent weaknesses from transitory difficulties and to understand whether there were structural differences between the countries under study. This led him to write a detailed technical memorandum.[74]

Germain's blueprint for public finance research combined four main directions. First was the concern about accuracy. All government accounts (general and special) had to be investigated in detail. To track inconsistencies, Germain recommended constructing separate "capital" and "operating" accounts, and to decide whether they matched: Variations in public indebtedness had to be mirrored into government deficits. Government borrowing accounts, he emphasized, should include short-term obligations on top of the long-term debt. These included government bills, overdrafts from both private and "central" banking institutions, and foreign loans. The importance of short-term debt was of special concern because it could be more easily concealed. Moreover, short-term debts, facing a rollover risk, were inherently riskier.

The second direction was to use a "historical approach" that would serve "to characterize with more certainty the country's performance."[75] A country's tendency to run persistent deficits could escape the scrutiny of an observer focusing on short frequencies but would come to the crudest light when extended time periods would be considered. The historical approach also served as a guide to extrapolate current trends, as it would give some clues on what should be considered as "permanent" versus "transitory." Finally, the historical approach permitted checking the consistency of returns, revealed hidden items, and provided indications on each country's propensity to turn to short-term debt in case of fiscal needs. In practice, Germain asked for a twenty-year period.[76]

Third was the concern about the dynamics of government assets. Germain advised that one should provide a breakdown of government revenue between "taxes" and "income from government assets" (railways, forests, state monopolies, state properties, and so forth) in order to underline the element of enterprise in the fiscal machinery. Similarly, spending should have to be differentiated to highlight its nature. Government investment was not the same as consumption. The former would eventually bring an increase in government revenue. This view was quite pervasive at the time: The nature of government spending was a frequent theme of the annual reports of the Council of Foreign Bondholders (from 1873). Similarly, Mulhall's estimates of public debts sought to disentangle "consumption debt," from "railway debt," although his estimates only focused on railways.[77]

The last direction was to require that the new accounts be tabulated along with background information regarding the country under study: imports, exports, exchange rates, interest rates, and population. Space was saved for comments; this could be used to mention specific events with fiscal relevance. Germain asked that three studies be made right away according to the new principles. The first would focus on Russia, the second on France, and the third on Italy. Dozens of others would follow. Whereas a substantial share of these studies have been lost, those surviving are rather impressive: huge spreadsheets, spanning three feet by five feet with extra columns pasted or pinned, listed for time periods of about fifteen to twenty years scores of statistical series.

"Une méthode rationnelle"

The actual method that the SEF developed was a response both to Germain's requests and to the practical challenges encountered along the way. In line with Germain's emphasis on the entrepreneurial functions of the state, the SEF tables were organized around "revenues and expenditure accounts," on the one hand, and states' "balance sheets" on the other. These accounts were constructed though an investigation of all government records, which involved careful corrections.

The next step was the construction of what the SEF called *comptes d'ordre*. In an attempt to measure the net income from specific taxes as well as the net cost of given expenditures, these recorded either expenditures implied by revenue collection or revenues associated with given expenses. On the revenue side, one had, for instance, to pay the taxman: The net return from taxation was the difference between taxes and tax collection expenses. On the spending side, a government that subsidized education could nonetheless collect some tuition fee that partly covered expenses – net subsidies to education were the difference between the two items. *Comptes d'ordre* were handled with special care when it came to state business. National accounting techniques created spurious fluctuations in official revenue and expenditures: One example was the Spanish tobacco monopoly, which, until 1887, was state run. Spending on personnel and the like was thus recorded among government expenditures, and gross income was recorded on the revenue side. The resulting net profit until 1887 was an annual income of about 70 million peseta. In 1887, however, the Spanish government farmed out its monopoly. The franchised company had to pay a 90-million peseta annual duty. These 90 million became the only item recorded on the revenue side. This represented a 20-million improvement on net revenues, but also implied that total government income was reduced. If one wanted to assess the "normal income" of the Spanish government, the Lyonnais reasoned, one would have to correct the pre-1887 returns in order to purge both the income and expenditure side from gross expenses. This way returns would display a 20-million increase in government revenue in 1887. By contrast, measures based on gross revenue would display a spurious weakening of government income.

The Lyonnais method had the effect of making accounts leaner: Revised revenues and expenditures (called *recettes et dépenses normales*) were constructed by netting out items. This implied a seemingly smaller burden of government in economic activity and was thus in contrast with the more familiar concept of government share in the economy, where aggregate income and expenditures are compared to national products.[78] In fact, this comparison with modern practices underlines the Lyonnais's view of states as investors and its corollary concern about efficiency, as opposed to the Keynesian view of states as spenders and the corollary concern about weight. The *comptes d'ordre* allowed one to focus on the net income from government activities, thus getting closer to a concept of comparative profitability.[79] As a lender to governments, the Lyonnais wanted to trace what governments had done with private monies.

Moreover, *comptes d'ordre* were an intermediary step in the construction of state balance sheets, which compared public debts and public assets. Indeed, while constructing debt estimates merely required care and patience, the asset side involved much greater challenges. Official assets accounts were poorly maintained if at all. Only some countries such as Scandinavia, Switzerland, and a number of German states published such returns.[80] Existing accounts overlooked amortization, recorded assets at their nominal purchasing price, and gave a positive price to loss-making enterprises.[81]

Comptes d'ordre, by contrast, provided a way to circumvent these shortcomings: The itemized accounts of government activities yielded a direct measure of "dividends" (net of maintenance, reparation, and so forth) from public assets. One way to look at net indebtedness was thus to capitalize net dividends at an interest rate equal to the government marginal borrowing rate. A 100-franc debt bearing a 5 percent interest and issued to finance the construction of a railway whose net return was 4 francs per year implied a corresponding asset of 80 francs – a 20-franc net debt. Another way to look at net indebtedness was to focus on flows. The SEF suggested comparing state dividends to the annual flow of interest payments on the public debt. As the SEF reckoned, each way to assess net indebtedness had weaknesses of its own. The stock approach raised the question of which interest rate should be used to capitalize dividends; it compared a known expense to an uncertain income. On the other hand, the flow approach was unable to handle non-interest-bearing assets or debts: Two governments that were similar in all respects but an interest-free debt (for example, an overdraft at the central bank) would feature in a similar way in the flow approach and yet would be in a different situation. Taken together, however, these measures were much superior to anything existing at the time and could in addition allow more rigorous comparisons of real indebtedness.

Toward Quasi-Cardinal "Ratings"

The measures of net indebtedness that the SEF constructed opened the door to recommendations for investment strategy. The trick was to find a denominator to which indebtedness could be compared in order to provide a measure of "debt sustainability." The hierarchy of risk that would emerge from this could then be compared to hierarchies of prices and signal profitable portfolio reallocations. Modern approaches to sovereign debt sustainability typically use the ratio of public debts to national income, measures of openness, and so forth. Nineteenth-century economists believed in stocks more than in flows, and the consensus view was that national wealth, not national income, was what mattered. Public obligations would have to be serviced out of taxing private agents: A sovereign's ability to pay was thus best measured by comparing its current stock of debt to the present value of private wealth owned by the agents it could tax.

This conceptual clarity contrasted sharply with a dearth of data. One exception was Mulhall, who computed wealth estimates for 1895 and provided point-wise debt-to-wealth ratios for Europe, the United States, Canada, and Australia (Figure 1.4). However, Mulhall's estimates had serious limitations. He used fixed coefficients (calibrated on the basis of estimates for countries for which he had returns) to capitalize national earnings: Land was capitalized at 30 times the annual agricultural production, houses at 16.5 times the gross rental, and so forth.[82] Contemporaries were critical, especially when it came to late developers whose economic structure was likely to differ from the countries upon which coefficients had been calibrated. Tito Canovai, a leading Italian economist, thought that Mulhall's figures "lacked scientific basis."[83] The whole issue was further complicated by matters of national pride, as well as by international politics: Because political alliances had a financial side, official statisticians were under much pressure. On top of it all, Mulhall's returns were only comprehensive for 1895 and were never updated: The 1909 edition of Mulhall's *Dictionary of Statistics* still relied on estimates for 1895.[84]

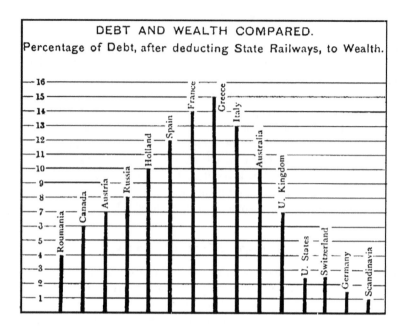

Figure 1.4 Mulhal's debt-to-wealth ratios. *Source*: Mulhall (1896), p. 55.

Contemporaries thus used proxies that would serve to monitor financial evolutions over shorter frequencies. National income figures were as scarce as wealth estimates. A frequent denominator was population: *Faute de mieux*, this was seen as a crude substitute for wealth.[85] Such ratios, however, were not computed out of candor: Readers were immediately warned against the deficiencies of such measurement. Different levels of economic development meant very different income per head. For instance, dividing both Russia's and Britain's debts by their respective populations gave a fictitious advantage to the former.[86] Poor countries such as India or China had the largest populations.

Like everybody else, the SEF thus had to rely on its own tools. But contrary to others, its way of reorganizing government accounts yielded an almost straightforward way to compare debt burdens. The flow approach to net indebtedness led to a natural choice of the denominator: Dividing the annual flow of interest payments net of dividends from government assets, by "normal revenues" (that is, the SEF-corrected gross government revenues minus *dépenses d'ordre*) produced an index of sustainability. Indeed, this ratio measured the proportion of government income that was earmarked for debt servicing: The smaller this ratio, the less likely was the government to meet servicing problems. In turn, this could be thought of as an index of "sovereign riskiness."

Rating agencies are explicitly concerned with providing assessments of sovereign risks. As a result, their output is highly formalized. Grades are given to each country, and the significance of each grade is explained. But because the SEF analyses were homemade and home-consumed, they did not need to be summarized through explicit grades. This, of course, is an obstacle for modern researchers. Yet in one instance, the SEF did provide a formal classification of countries: We found three spreadsheets, constructed in 1898, which ranked foreign sovereigns in three groups.[87] Each document displayed a list of countries belonging to a given "risk group" and provided an estimate of the ratio of net interest service to "normal revenues" in 1897–8 (plus a reference to the level of that ratio ten years earlier). The first list included countries "whose financial management is of first order" ("Pays dont la gestion financière est de premier ordre" in Lyonnais's words).[88] The second group included intermediary nations, whose "financial management is of second order." Finally, a third list included nations "of third order."[89] The lists also included brief comments on each country and an indication of whether a default or repudiation had occurred in the recent past.

These tables were not comprehensive, and the exercise was never made again.[90] Yet they can help us to demonstrate that the SEF's measure of debt sustainability loomed large in shaping its perceptions of sovereign risks. Consider that the SEF operated on the basis of some implicit function (the Lyonnais formula), which related each given country's diagnostic statistics (for example, the ratio of net interest service to normal revenues) to a score. Depending on the score that a given country obtains, the SEF then decided to put it either in the first (low risk), second (average risk), or third (high risk) group. The Lyonnais formula is unknown to the modern researcher, and the score is unobservable, but we do observe the final allocation. Assuming that the Lyonnais formula was linear, it is possible to implement an econometric technique (described in the appendix) that yields both the parameters of the Lyonnais formula and the thresholds at which countries switched from one category to the other one.

The explanatory variables that we use are the SEF's estimates of the net burden of interest service as a share of normal revenue and a "dummy" variable that captures the recent occurrence of sovereign default. Defaults or debt repudiations, while they lowered the interest service, also signaled a higher risk, and this balanced the seemingly "good" performance which interest service alone implied. Results are presented in Table 1.1 (groups of countries are listed in Table 1.2). Figure 1.5 displays the estimated score (a low score means a low risk). Countries whose scores are less than zero were put in the top category (group I). Countries between zero and 5.6 were put in the intermediate category (group II). Finally, countries whose score is above 5.6 are put in the high-risk group (group III). The best scores (equal to α_0 or -3.06) were obtained by countries with essentially no net interest service and no recent default: Sweden, Finland, Switzerland (Federal state), Denmark, and the Transvaal. In general, category I includes countries with a low net-debt service and no payment problems. One such country was Russia, which was featured within group I. This resulted from Russia's policies of public investment: The large involvement of the Russian state in the domestic economy implied that substantial net dividends accrued to the government.

Table 1.1 Estimating the Lyonnais grading formula: $q_i = \alpha_0 + \alpha_1 \cdot I_i + \alpha_2 \cdot \text{Fault}_i + \omega_i$

Parameter	Estimate	Standard-Error	t-statistic
α_0	−3.06*	0.69	−4.42
α_1	0.21*	0.046	4.58
α_2	13.57*	1.23	11.03
$\sqrt{q_1}$	2.37*	0.35	6.69

n-obs = 24; standard errors computed from analytic first and second derivatives (Eicker-White).
* : significant at 5%. q_1 = 5.6.

Table 1.2 The Lyonnais risk tables

Group 1: Pays dont les finances sont de premier ordre	Group 2: Pays dont les finances sont de second ordre	Group 3: Pays dont les finances sont de troisieme ordre
Germany (imperial gov.), United Kingdom, United States (federal gov.), Russia, Sweden, Finland, Denmark, Belgium, Norway, Transvaal, Switzerland (federal gov.)	Holland, Egypt, Japan, Austria, Hungary, Romania, Italy, [Chile, Dutch Indies, British India]	Brazil, Argentina, Spain, Portugal, Greece, Serbia, [Bulgaria, 'Roumélie']

Note: No figures reported for countries within brackets. These countries were excluded from the regression.
Source: Archives du Crédit Lyonnais, DEEF 72879/1.

These compensated the annual flow of interest payments, bringing it (as a share of government income) below 10 percent. No default countries, on the other hand, were downgraded to the second category when they reached a net interest service around 15 percent of normal revenues. This was true in the case of Holland, a nation with otherwise sound finances. The switch to the third category occurred when the interest service moved beyond 40 percent (again, with no default).[91] Recent defaults, finally, automatically put a country (whatever its interest service burden) in the third category.

One way to assess the performance of the model is to examine its ability to replicate the Lyonnais's actual groupings as presented in Table 1.2: Most countries (20 out of 24, or 83 percent) are adequately allocated by the model. Misallocated countries obtain scores that are borderline and thus in fact very close to the group where they "should" have been put. The model, despite its simplicity, is extremely close to perfection, suggesting that the explicit scoring formula that we have reconstructed is a very good approximation of the Lyonnais's perceptions of sovereign risks. The important conclusion is obviously that the SEF's sustainability measures played an overarching role in deciding relative risks.[92]

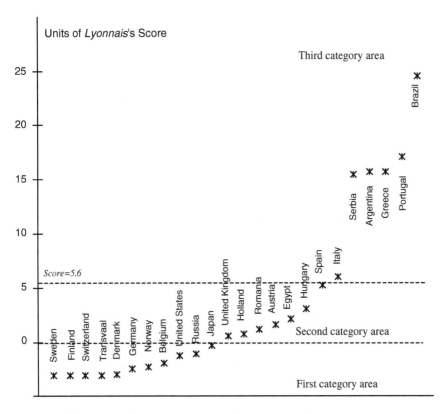

Figure 1.5 The Lyonnais's scoring formula: predicted grades and implied category. *Source*: *Author's computations*.

However, the small discrepancies between the Lyonnais's predicted scores and the observed allocation of sovereign debtors suggest some qualifications regarding the attitude of the SEF toward its own measures. First, it seems that the ratings had not been constructed in a mechanistic way. A naive implementation of the net debt burden measure, for instance, would have implied putting the United Kingdom in the second category. Yet it is obvious that the "richest and most developed economy in the world" – as was written on the margin of the document – had to be put in the lowest risk category despite a net interest service at 16.8 percent of revenues.[93] Similarly, the inverted ordering of Spain and Italy (respectively, just below and above the switching line, and yet placed by SEF economists in the third and second category) reveals an awareness of current developments. Italy, while being the most heavily burdened European nation, had stabilized its public debt by 1898 and reorganized its fiscal process, without default, thus paving the way for a successful debt conversion a few years later.[94] Spain, in contrast, was in 1898 in the midst of a military conflict that could push it to the verge of bankruptcy (as a matter of fact, a note on the margin of the document recognized that partial repudiation was an option). Finally, the allocation of Japan to the second category – despite a debt burden that should have had it mechanistically in the first one – might have been related to the monetary system of the country: Indeed, SEF economists argued that while stabilization on the gold standard was under way in Japan, the nature of the monetary regime was not yet fully established.[95]

Thus, a number of factors balanced the lessons from the SEF's sustainability measure. As emphasized in the 1903 memorandum, the SEF fulfilled a "purely scientific" role and had no ability to determine the incidence of some complex facts on creditworthiness.[96] The SEF's task rested mainly in providing information to the Conseil d'Administration, where responsibilities remained. This may explain why formal "ratings" were never performed again after 1898. Instead, SEF country studies came to be accompanied by a number of qualitative notes, economic, political, or financial.[97] Such were the elements that, along with the more general policy orientations of the bank, drove investment decisions. Yet it remains that the statistical exercises performed by the Lyonnais were undoubtedly, by their clarity and "objectivity," an essential piece of information and thus an essential aspect of decision making. It is possible to claim, on the basis of existing evidence, that they loomed large in orienting the direction of French foreign investments: How to resist relating the surprisingly good grade obtained by Russia, or the excellent mark which Scandinavia received, to the well-known attraction that these countries' public debts had on French monies, especially from the 1890s? Although more evidence and further research are needed, we believe that our finding is a first hint that, contrary to the conventional wisdom, economics, not politics, was a key factor in allocating French exports of capital. At least, we hope to have convinced readers that the Lyonnais's sustainability accounts, for what they were worth, made a decisive contribution in shaping the opinion of French financiers regarding foreign investment opportunities.

Conclusions: market opinion and willingness to lend

This chapter has described the evolution of the Crédit Lyonnais sovereign risk analysis department, the *section des fonds d'etat*, a subunit of the SEF, the Lyonnais's research department, over the period from 1871 to 1914. I described how the SEF grew into a large research center with numerous and ample means. I also studied the making of its "ratings" system. Several lessons can be drawn. First and foremost, this episode sheds light on how late nineteenth-century investors reacted to the absence of official data, formal ratings, and international bailouts. Both the enlargement of the SEF and the design of a systematic framework of financial analysis were prompted by the collapses of the Comptoir d'escompte and Baring. The process accelerated during the severe international financial crisis of the early 1890s, when the Lyonnais realized that it needed to determine which, among the various sovereigns of the gold standard periphery, deserved support. The decision to internalize a number of methods for monitoring sovereign risk is thus evidence of the key contribution of the market mechanism to pre–World War I "globalization."

A second lesson is the considerable importance of investors' perceptions in shaping the market mechanism itself. While a large literature has studied the determinants of debtors' willingness to pay, I found that cognitive aspects of the assessment of public finances played a crucial role for what I suggest calling investors' willingness to lend. In particular, I demonstrated that the favor in which investment finance (as opposed to consumption finance) was held proved decisive in comparing sovereign risks. This belief was pushed to its logical conclusion in the SEF's measure of debt sustainability, which discounted from interest service the net dividends from government "assets" and was responsible for a grading formula that most characteristically featured Russia as a "blue chip" country. Because most loans to the Russian government were used for industrial investments and because these investments provided a revenue, Russia's "indebtedness" remained moderate in the eyes of Crédit Lyonnais economists. This finding is obviously important in view of the well-known attraction that Russia had for French capital. Inasmuch as the SEF's ratings mattered (and I suggested they did), they provide a strong case for arguing that economics, not politics, drove French capital in Saint Petersburg.

Finally, my last conclusion has to do with the economics of financial information. I began this chapter with a reference to the challenges of sovereign risk assessment by rating agencies. My discussion of nineteenth-century experience suggests that privately collected information is not without faults. Indeed, the SEF was not a research department picked at random in a large population of competitors. It was not an individual voice in a broad market of opinions. Rather, the SEF was the research unit of one bank that took a prominent position in French and international finance. While the Lyonnais's willingness to retain its credibility certainly encouraged it to do its homework, it is likely that this also led other banks to pay much less attention. The absence of other serious domestic competing opinion and the secretive attitude that the Lyonnais took toward the SEF output probably induced other banks to get on board of Lyonnais-led syndicates without due caution. The issue is thus not to question the sincerity of the SEF – it genuinely believed in its reports. But finance is a game where one makes money because one's view becomes the market view, not because one is right: The externalities of being a market leader cannot be ignored.

Appendix: estimating the lyonnais grading formula

We use a three states ordered probit model. The intuition is the following: The SEF was observing a vector of (exogenous) variables (X) which it then sought to relate to a given country "score" (q). The score (known in qualitative variables econometrics as a "latent variable") is not observable, but we assume that it was a linear function (vector α) of the exogenous observations. ω is an error term. We have:

$$q = X\alpha + \omega$$

There are three "states" (risk categories) available. They are mutually exclusive. Category 1 is the group of countries whose financial management is of first order, and so on. Let's call γ the state variable. We have:

$$\gamma = 1, 2, 3$$

If the score obtained by multiplying the performance variables by their corresponding weight is below 0, the country under study will be assigned to category I (first-order country). If the score obtained is between 0 and q_1, the country will be assigned to category II (second-order country). Finally, if the score is above q_1, the country will be assigned to category III (third-order country):

$$\gamma = 1 \quad \text{for } q \leq 0 \text{ i.e. } \omega \leq -X\alpha$$

$$\gamma = 2 \quad \text{for } 0 < q < q_1 \text{ i.e. } -X\alpha < \omega \leq q_1 - X\alpha$$

$$\gamma = 2 \quad \text{for } q_1 < q_2 \text{ i.e. } q_1 - X\alpha < \omega$$

The exogenous variables are: I_i (the net burden of interest service as a share of Lyonnais measured revenues) and Fault_i (which takes value 1 if a default has recently occurred and zero otherwise). We have the Lyonnais grading formula:

$$q_i = \alpha + \alpha_1 I_i + \alpha_2 \text{ Fault}_i + \omega_i$$

The estimation procedure uses the maximum likelihood formula, assuming that ω_i are i.i.d. Results are shown in Table 1.1.

*The comments of the conference participants are gratefully acknowledged. The author wishes to thank Roger Nougaret, Conservateur des archives historiques du Crédit Lyonnais, for his kind, patient, and friendly help. Thanks to Lucette Levan-Lemesle and Luc Marco for their information on the Parisian political economists of the nineteenth century, and to participants of the OFCE/EHESS "Convergences en Histoire Economique" Seminar as well as of the Warwick Conference on Globalization for their suggestions. Thanks are also due to Valérie Richard for her help with the manuscript.

Notes

1 G. Larrain, H. Reisen, and J. von Maltzan, "Emerging Market Risk and Sovereign Credit Ratings," OECD Development Centre, Technical Paper, no. 124.

2 Barry Eichengreen and Marc Flandreau, "The Geography of the Gold Standard," in J. Braga de Macedo et al., eds., *Currency Convertibility, the Gold Standard, and Beyond* (London, 1996).

3 Marc Flandreau, "Central Bank Cooperation in Historical Perspective: A Sceptical View," *Economic History Review* (1997).

4 N. Herbault, "Le contrôle international en Egypte, Turquie et Grèce," Congrés International des Valeurs Mobilières, 4 fascicule, no. 166 (1901): 1–51.

5 On these "debt games," see V. Aggarwal, *Debt Games* (Cambridge, 1996). Charles Lipson provides an overview of the interactions between debt crises and international politics before World War I (Charles Lipson, "International and National Debt: Comparing Victorian Britain and Postwar America," in Barry Eichengreen and P. Lindert, eds., *The International Debt Crisis in International Perspective* (Cambridge, Mass., 1989)). The classic reference on the topic remains Herbert Feis, *Europe, The World's Banker, 1870–1914* (New Haven, Conn., 1930).

6 L. H. Jenks, *The Migration of British Capital to 1875* (London, 1927); Albert H. Imlah, *Economic Elements in the Pax Britannica* (Cambridge, Mass., 1958); Rondo Cameron, *France and the Economic Development of Europe, 1800–1914* (Princeton, N.J., 1961); Maurice Lévy-Leboyer, *Les banques européennes et l'industrialisation internationale dans la première moitié du XIXème siècle* (Paris, 1964); Mira Wilkins, *The History of Foreign Investment in the United States to 1914* (Cambridge, Mass., 1989). See also Mira Wilkin's chapter in this book.

7 Feis, *Europe, the World's Banker*.

8 Ignorance and herding behavior play an important role in the boom and bust approaches to international lending. See Charles P. Kindleberger, "International Propagation of Financial Crises: The Experience of 1888–93," in Charles P. Kindleberger, *Keynesianism vs. Monetarism and Other Essays in Financial History* (London, 1985).

9 The first edition of Moody's *Government and Municipals Manual* appeared in 1919.

10 Jean Bouvier, *Le Crédit Lyonnais, de 1863 à 1882: Les années de formation d'une grande banque de depots*, 2 vols. (Paris, 1961).

11 It was to the SEF that the Bank of France turned when it was asked by the U.S. National Monetary Commission to provide data on the French Monetary System. And it would be to the SEF that French officials would turn when they sought to assess the German reparations after World War I.

12 Eugène d'Eichtal, *Notice sur la vie et les travaux de M. Henri Germain* (Paris, 1905).

13 Bouvier (1961), p. 289ff. provides a somewhat different narrative of the evolution of the SEF between 1871 and 1873 but concurs with our view of the "information revolution."

14 For instance, cumulated foreign issues in Paris amounted to about 8 billion in 1865 while French Net National product was about 18 billion.

15 Lévy-Leboyer, *Les banque européenes et l'industrialisation internationale*.

16 See also W. T. C. King, *History of the London Discount Market* (London, 1936), 266.

17 Alphonse Courtois, *Manuel des fonds publics et des sociétés par actions*, 8th ed. (Paris, 1883).

18 Lucette Levan-Lemesle, "L'enseignement de l'économie politique en France 1860–1939," 6 vols., Ph.D. diss., University of Paris I, Panthéon-Sorbonne, 1995.

19 Michael G. Mulhall, *Industries and Wealth of Nations* (London, 1896); Michael G. Mulhall, *The Dictionary of Statistics*, 4th ed. (London, 1909).

20 Karl Polanyi, *The Great Transformation* (Boston, 1944); Bertrand Gille, *Les Rothschild*, 2 vols. (Geneva, 1967).

21 See *Dictionnaire de biographie française*, 9:1036. G. Vapereau, *Dictionnaire universel des contemporains*, 6th ed. (Paris, 1893), 386, concurs, albeit in looser terms. We could not check the accuracy of this information. Documents from the Crédit Lyonnais writ-

ten at the time of the creation of the SEF refer to Courtois as a "publiciste," suggesting that he was really a journalist at the time.

22 Alphonse Courtois, *Tableaux des cours des principales valeurs négociées et cotées en bourse des effets publics de Paris* (Lyon, 1873).

23 This tension is, in my opinion, the origin of the alleged formal distinction which Bouvier is thought to have identified between "renseignements" and "etudes" (Bouvier [1963]). Bouvier's claim is swept away by a letter from Courtois, who lost patience: "We are called Etudes financières!" (letter of Oct. 13, 1871, Archives historique du Crédit Lyonnais, Historique DEEF (hereafter Historiques DEEF)). Clearly, the "bureau des renseignements" was a subsection of Service des Etudes Financières, not a separate unit. This interpretation is fostered by the eventual use of the expression *bureaux* as a substitute for SEF *sections* (DEEF 62694).

24 Key financial centers included New York, Rio de Janeiro, Buenos Aires, Berlin, Frankfurt, Vienna, Saint Petersburg, Constantinople, Florence, Madrid, Lisbon, Brussels, Alexandria. The Lyonnais had a branch in London.

25 Letter of Nov. 3, 1871.

26 See the CFB, Annual Report, 1899.

27 The only business school in Paris, the Ecole Supérieure de Commerce de Paris was described by one of its former graduates as being at the time a "school where there were indeed a few lectures on trade, but whose main occupation was to teach French to young men from Latin America, who came to study these things which one learns so well in Paris" (Levan-Lemesle, "L'enseignement de l'économie politique," vol. 2, chap. 10).

28 Archives historiques du Crédit Lyonnais, 62AH 20, Letter from Mazerat to Letourneur.

29 Letter of Oct. 4, 1871.

30 Levan-Lemesle, "L'enseignement de l'économie politique."

31 One potential candidate who was approached turned out to be a typical "rond-de-cuir" (lazy bureaucrat): He asked whether he could work at home.

32 Showing up at Cernuschi's mansion, he was told that the famous bimetallist was touring silver standard Asia.

33 Information provided by Cécile Omnes, "La gestion du personnel au credit Lyonnais (1863–1939)," 2 vols., Ph.D. diss., University of Paris I, 1997.

34 Germain encouraged Courtois to hire Félicité Guillaumin. Félicité, twenty-five at the time, was the elder of two daughters of the famous publisher of *Political Economy.*

35 Minutes of the Conseil d'administration, Nov. 5, 1889.

36 Levan-Lemesle, "L'enseignement de l'économie politique."

37 They included Levasseur, Juglar, Foville, Aupetit (a student of Walras), and Cheysson (a founder of modern econometrics). See Levan-Lemesle, "L'enseignement de l'économie politique."

38 Levan-Lemesle, "L'enseignement de l'économie politique," 472.

39 Octave Noël, *Les banques d'émission en Europe* (Paris, 1888). Marc Flandreau, Jacques le Cacheux, and Frédéric Zumer, "Stability Without a Pact? Lessons from the European Gold Standard," *Economic Policy* (1998): 27.

40 Kindleberger, "International Propagation of Financial Crises."

41 Bouvier, *Le Crédit Lyonnais*, 294.

42 Archives du Crédit Lyonnais, DEEF, Bd des Italiens.

43 Nonwage costs were limited to journal or periodical subscriptions, purchase of books, paper, pencils, and travel expenses for missions. A breakdown of these expenses is found in Archives du Crédit Lyonnais, DEEF, sans cote, Bd des Italiens.

44 See author's computation on the basis of the SEF archives and Omnes, "La gestion du personnel au crédit Lyonnais."

45 For the Lyonnais at large, the estimate is provided by Omnes. For the SEF, the estimation is made as follows: Kaufman claims that there were before the war about fifty

white collar employees (economists, lawyers, accountants) working in the service. Given the figures we have for the overall SEF work force, this implies that there were about as many clerks without university degrees. E. Kaufman, *La banque en France* (Paris, 1914).

46 For budgets, Kaufmann quotes even higher figures (between 600,000 and 800,000) but it is not clear to what period he refers. The slowdown in the growth of the SEF was both absolute and relative. By 1913, the SEF had returned to about 1.5 percent of total wages and 0.5 percent of the Lyonnais total work force. Kaufman, *La banque en France.*

47 3,554 in 1901, 6,875 in 1902. Archives du Crédit Lyonnais, DEEF, sans cote, Bd des Italiens. In a later document of July 10, 1916, the section des notes is called "section de renseignement" (DEEF 62694).

48 We are told (Archives du Crédit Lyonnais DEEF 62694) that in 1904 the *répertoire* contained 117,000 referenced items; 243 volumes listed information on governments, municipals, and 51,000 joint stock companies. The *répertoire* has been lost.

49 Archives du Crédit Lyonnais, DEEF 62694. This is reminiscent of the "Chinese wall" that exists between commercial and research departments in modern banks.

50 See also Kaufman, *La banque en France*, who finds only 8 sections.

51 DEEF 62694.

52 DEEF 62694.

53 Historique DEEF.

54 Archives du Crédit Lyonnais, "Visite de M. Figueira."

55 "Fonds d'états, composition de la section," Historique DEEF, Archives du Crédit Lyonnais.

56 Mostly from the section de statistique, the section des banques, and the section du bulletin.

57 The number of governments (local and central) covered rose from 182 in 1905 to 206 in 1907. At that time, there were 2,519 tables, 436 notes, 30 maps, 2,182 budgetary returns, and 817 memoranda on individual loans. DEEF 62694.

58 This reduction took place to the benefit of the rest of the SEF. There were eight departures to other sections between 1910 and 1914 against four arrivals from other sections. See DEEF, "Fonds d'états, composition de la section"

59 Kaufman, *La banque en France.*

60 Kaufman, *La banque en France*, 353. According to my colleague Richard Roberts, the Lyonnais's example was also unparalleled in the UK before the war. Knut Borchardt told me during the Princeton conference that he could not think of a German equivalent.

61 The scathing description of the Bank of France research department made by an employee from the SEF in 1894 is one example. The Lyonnais ridiculed the meager resources, three-employee staff, and six square meters of the bureau des études économiques. Des Essarts, the chief economist, was reportedly "completely left to himself, working at random, without any method, any guide, any compass." He had been hired as a reward for the "numerous services" he had rendered to the Bank of France, not for his skills. His role was merely to produce, "once or twice per year, the situation of the reserve of Banks of Issue," Archives du Crédit Lyonnais Historique DEEF.

62 Historique DEEF. With the departure of a number of SEF economists to other banks around 1910, it is probable that the Lyonnais's methods became widely known. But by the time this took place, the huge volume of past studies was the bank's best protection. There were probably cases where specific individuals were shown original returns. One such instance was the conversion of Luzzatti to favorable views toward Russian

finances, a conversion which reportedly occurred after an extensive stay at the SEF (see L'Economista d'Italia, 1908, n.d. clipping found in DEEF 73316/1).

63 Une journée au Crédit Lyonnais. Paris, 1904.

64 *New York Herald*, European ed., Paris, Saturday, Apr. 23, 1904.

65 Whole parts of the *Herald* article can be found in the *Daily Telegraph* dated May 2, under a different name. D'Eichtal, *Notice sur la vie et les travaux.*

66 Crédit Lyonnais, *Une visite au credit lyonnais, ses nouvelles installations, opinion de lapresse étrangère* (Paris, 1904).

67 Archives du Crédit Lyonnais, "Visite de M. Figueira," AH.

68 See the various issues of *The Statesman's Yearbook* or the *Bulletin de la Société Internationale de Statistique* (1886–). In fact the contemporaries' reluctance to swallow official figures is in contrast with the gullibility that rating agencies would display during the interwar period. In its general introduction, *Moody's Government and Municipal Manual*, 1926 ed., plainly stated: "The information furnished on foreign governments and their securities is derived from original sources [i.e., official documents]. We have taken great pains to gather facts and figures directly from the governments and municipalities of the whole world. And the prompt and very satisfactory replies were indeed most gratifying." One may doubt that statistical honesty had much changed over the war to warrant such trust.

69 The more recent controversies between Theodore H. Von Laue ["The High Cost and the Gamble of the Witte System: A Chapter in the Industrialization of Russia," *The Journal of Economic History* 13 (1953): 424–48] and Arcadius Kahan ["Government Policies and the Industrialization of Russia," *The Journal of Economic History* 27 (1967): 460–77] illustrate how partisan views on the topic have transpired until more recent debates.

70 Etudes financières, "Comment faut-il?" p. 1, Historique DEEF.

71 Alphonse Courtois, *Traité des operations de bourse, un Manuel des fonds publics français et étrangers et des actions et obligations de sociétés françaises et érangères négociés à Paris, précédé d'une appréciation des opérations de bourses dites dejeu, et des rapports de la bourse avec le crédit public et les finances de l'État* (Paris, 1855).

72 Letter dated October 19, 1871, Archives du Crédit Lyonnais AH 9–58.

73 Henri Germain, *La situation financière de la France en 1886* (Paris, 1886).

74 Historique DEEF. The idea of ascertaining "scientifically" the economic situtation of economic entities was emerging at the time. E. Cheysson, "La statistique géométrique ou méthode pour la solution des problèmes commerciaux et industriels," in *Oeuvres Choisies* (Paris, 1887/1991), vol. 1.

75 Henri Germain, 1891, note "Finances portugaises," Historique DEEF.

76 Germain's memorandum, 1891, historique DEEF. This lag, not accidentally, coincided with the creation of the SEF.

77 Mulhall, *Industries and Wealth of Nations*, 54. In a recent article, Trish Kelly found that in the 1890s, the nature of government spending had favorable consequences on sovereign debtors' willingness to pay (Trish Kelly, "Ability and Willingness to Pay in the Age of Pax Britannica, 1890–1914," *Explorations in Economic History* 35, no. 1 [1998]: 31–58). The difference between investment finance and consumption finance was also emphasized by Albert Fishlow in "International Capital Flows: Lessons from the 1890s and 1980s," *International Organization* (1985).

78 See, e.g., L. Schuknecht and V Tanzi, "The Growth of Government and the Reform of the State in Industrial Countries," IMF Working Paper, WP/95/130, Dec. 1995.

79 For instance, it was well known that the corrupted Russian Internal Revenue Service brought a lower return than other nations' revenue services. See Jean de Block, *Les finances de la Russie au XIXe siècle*, 2 vols. (Paris, 1899).

80 See *The Statesman's Yearbook, various issues.*

81 Mulhall's net debt estimates were flawed by this very problem. Mulhall, *Industries and Wealth of Nations.*

82 Ibid.

83 Tito Canovai, "Del Problema Finanziaro in Italia," *Nuova Antologia*, 4th ser., 78 (1898): 344.

84 These dilemmas proved quite resilient: They were still present a quarter century later when formal sovereign rating developed. For instance, the 1926 introduction of *Moody's Government and Municipal Manual* sought to provide debt-to-wealth tables in order to document comparative debt burdens: "The best single index to the credit or standing of foreign governments undoubtedly is the wealth per capita. . . . In the past unfortunately, estimates of wealth have been too much biased by national prejudice. Even learned economists have placed high estimates upon the wealth of their own and related peoples, and low estimates upon that of unrelated and disliked peoples. Besides this, even now, there is a great dearth of data regarding both total wealth and per capita wealth" (*Moody's Government and Municipals Manual*, 1926 ed., xiii).

85 See, for example: R. Dudley Baxter, *National Debts* (London, 1871); NAME Canovai, "Del Problema Finannziario in Italia," *Nuova Antologia*, 4th ser., 78, 340–52; Ottomar Haupt, Arbitrages et parités (Paris, 1894); Edm.ond-Amédée Théry, *Europe et Etats-Unis d'Amerique* (Paris, 1899).

86 The use of population as a proxy for GDP was customary up to the 1870s, for instance in international treaties. It had the advantage of being a well-known figure, and thus one which it was easy to agree upon. When the Latin union was created in 1865, for instance, national quotas for issued of debased coins were expressed in percentage of the population.

87 DEEF, 72879/1, "Généralités, 6, Classification des Etats d'après les résultats de leur gestion financière." The tables included, along with pure sovereigns, a number of borrowers that belonged to federal or confederated states countries (Prussia, the Swiss cantons), and colonies (the British and Dutch Indies).

88 Moreover, the SEF hinted that the way countries were listed in the category had to be interpreted as formal intra-category ratings: Some cursory comments explained the position of a given country in the list of well-behaved countries. No intra-group ratings were provided for the second and third categories.

89 Extensive footnotes described first- and second-order countries in some detail. Third-order countries, by contrast, did not receive any mention, apart from records of the net interest service before and after the default.

90 It is not fully clear what led the SEF to include or exclude given borrowers from the list. Note that in terms of volume the list included most of the outstanding bonds, although some substantial sovereigns, such as Mexico or France, were excluded. Data limitation cannot explain this, as the SEF had files on virtually every country.

91 Interestingly, this echoes a mention in the SEF's files that "no trouble has been observed in countries whose net interest service was below 40 percent" (Archives Crédit Lyonnais, Historique DEEF).

92 It is in fact very hard to improve on the model given the almost perfect allocation provided by the net debt service measure alone. Adding additional explanatory variables, such as a dummy for each misallocated country or a measure of deficits, creates a situation which is equivalent to the well-known "complete separation" problem in a binary probit model. Provided that the extra variables are able to capture the little variance that's left out in the original model, the data fits the new model perfectly. In this case, the coefficients want to become infinitely large although preserving their relative magnitude.

93 The same would probably also hold for France, which was not included in the risk tables but which would have probably featured in group one despite a net flow of inter-

est service of 39.4 percent in 1887 and 30.4 percent in 1897 (see "Etude de la situation financière de la France," 42, table "Comparaison du produit net de l'actif de l'Etat et du service de la dette").

94 Canovai, "Del Problema Finanziaro in Italia."

95 See Eichengreen and Flandreau, "Geography of the Gold Standard."

96 "Note sur la méthode," 12.

97 These included a list of comments on macroeconomic outlook, a general assessment of financial policy, information on specific questions (monetary or fiscal reforms, and so forth), a note on the evolution of the public debt, a note on the political regime and bureaucracy, and a political chronology since 1875. Interestingly, this is exactly the type of information on which credit agencies would rely twenty years later. *Moody's Government and Municipal Manual*, 1929 ed., recommended to enquire on "Geography, ethnology [by which it meant "culture"], history, type and stability of government, actual and potential wealth, enterprise, international position [creditor vs. debtor and underlying trend], fiscal, monetary and banking systems, government budget, taxation and debt, and finally an assessment of the "vitality of civilization." "A knowledge of all the foregoing subjects," Moody's concluded, "will enable the investor to determine intelligently the question of credit in a broad, general way."

10

LDC FOREIGN BORROWING AND DEFAULT RISK

An Empirical Investigation, 1976–80

*Sebastian Edwards**

Source: *American Economic Review* 74, 4, 1984, 726–734.

The recent foreign debt crisis faced by some less developed countries *(LDCs)* (Mexico, Brazil, Argentina, among others) has generated concern among economists, bankers, and politicians. In particular, the ability of the international banks to distinguish between "good" and "bad" risks has been questioned. It has even been suggested that the inability to restrict credit to countries with low "credit worthiness" has resulted in the overextension of some major banks and that, as a consequence, this has increased the probability of a global international financial collapse.[1]

The purpose of this paper is to investigate to what extent the international financial community has taken into account the risk characteristics of *LDCs* when granting loans. Specifically, this study analyzes the determinants of the spread between the interest rate charged to a particular country and the London Interbank Borrowing Rate *(LIBOR)*. If the financial community distinguishes between countries with different probabilities of default, these perceptions will be reflected in the spreads over *LIBOR*, with riskier countries (i.e., countries with a higher probability of default) being charged a higher risk premium or spread. However, when the perceived probability of default exceeds a given level, a "credit-ceiling" will be reached, and that particular country will be completely excluded from the credit market (Jonathan Eaton and Mark Gersovitz, 1980, 1981a, b; Jeffrey Sachs and Daniel Cohen, 1982; Sachs, 1983). This paper also tries to determine if the international financial community anticipated, as late as 1980, the international debt crisis of 1982–83. This is done by computing the implicit subjective probabilities of default from the econometric analysis of the spreads over *LIBOR*.

The empirical analysis of the determinants of the default risk premium is important for several reasons. First, an understanding of the factors that influence lending behavior is useful for borrowing countries. With this knowledge *LDCs* can take positive steps towards managing their economies in a way such that the perceived default risk is kept at a level compatible with what lenders think is prudent. Second, additional information on how the market assesses default risk will be helpful for determining the probability that the present repayment difficulties faced by some *LDC*s can be transformed into a major global crisis. And third, empirical information on the relationship between the level of the foreign debt and its cost is useful for the analysis of optimal borrowing strategies and of the social rate of discount in an open economy (see Arnold Harberger, 1983.)

A number of papers have recently analyzed the theoretical determinants of default country risk.[2] Recent work has focused on a number of aspects of the problem. First, the existence of credit ceilings, above which countries cannot borrow, has been explicitly introduced into the analysis (Eaton and Gersovitz, 1980, 1981a, b; Sachs and Cohen, 1982; Sachs, 1983; David Folkerts-Landau, 1982.) Second, variables other than the level of foreign debt, like international reserves, the propensity to invest and the current account deficit have been explicitly considered as affecting the default risk premium (Gershon Feder and Richard Just, 1979; Eaton and Gersovitz, 1980, 1981a; Sachs and Cohen, 1982; Sachs, 1983; myself, 1983). Recent theoretical analyses have also made a distinction between bond and bank foreign financing, and have explicitly introduced the possibility of rescheduling debt payments (Sachs and Cohen, 1982; Sachs, 1982). Finally, it has beeen argued that if borrowers and lenders have different perceptions with respect to the probability of default, the analysis of optimal borrowing strategies would be substantially affected (Harberger, 1976, 1980).

The empirical work on the subject has investigated several aspects of the problem, including the probability of a country rescheduling its payments (Charles Frank and William Cline, 1971; Nicholas Sargen, 1977), and the probability that a particular *LDC* borrower has reached its credit ceiling (Eaton and Gersovitz, 1980, 1981a, b). Generally, those studies that have analyzed lending behavior in international financial markets have found that lenders tend to take into account the riskiness of borrowers in making their lending decisions (Frank and Cline, 1971; Feder and Just, 1977a,b; Feder and Knud Ross, 1982; Sachs, 1981). Some studies, however (Feder and Just, 1977b; Sachs, 1981), have only found a weak and insignificant relationship between the spread and the debt-output ratio. In their paper Feder and Ross used data from the *Institutional Investor* creditworthiness ranking to show that lenders risk perceptions are systematically reflected in the spreads charged in Euromarkets.

The analysis presented in the present paper uses data for several years (1976–80) to investigate the determinants of the subjective probability of default.[3] The sample considered in this paper only includes loans denominated in Eurodollars, thus avoiding the problem of different currency composition of loans, mentioned by Donogh McDonald (p. 630). Also this paper only includes public and publicly guaranteed loans, thus restricting the analysis to the determinants of country risk, as distinct from financial risk. Finally, the present study has considered a larger set of possible determinants of the probability of default than previous work.

234

I. Empirical Analysis

Assume that, as postulated by Feder and Just (1977b), Eaton and Gersovitz (1980), and Sachs (1981) among others, the spread over *LIBOR* charged on Eurodollar loans reflects the probability of default of a particular country. Then, observed data on the spread can be used to formally analyze the way in which variables like the debt-output ratio, the propensity to invest, the level of international reserves, and others affect the level of this perceived probability. However, before empirically analyzing the determinants of the spread, three important questions should be addressed: What is the exact form of the relationship between the spread and the probability of default? What is the functional form of the probability of default? What are the determinants of this probability?

With respect to the first question—the relationship between the spread and the probability of default—in this paper I assume that the spread can be written in the following form:

$$s = \left[p / (1-p) \right] \gamma, \tag{1}$$

where s is the spread over *LIBOR* charged on a particular loan, p is the (subjective) default probability during the life of the loan, and γ is a variable that captures other elements affecting s. There are several ways to justify the choice of equation (1). For example, this expression can be directly derived from the assumption of risk neutral banks and perfect competition.[4]

Regarding the functional form of p, I follow the standard convention and assume that p has a logistic form:

$$p = \frac{\exp \Sigma \alpha_i y_i}{1 + \exp \Sigma \alpha_i y_i} \tag{2}$$

where the y_is refer to the determinants of the perceived probability of default (i.e., the debt-service ratio, the propensity to invest) and the α_is are the corresponding coefficients. Combining equations (1) and (2) the log of the spread can be written in the following form:

$$\log s = \alpha_0 + \Sigma \alpha_i y_i + \log \gamma \tag{3}$$

In this section the results obtained from the estimation of an equation of the type of (3) using data on 727 public and publicly guaranteed loans granted to 19 *LDC*s during 1976–80 are reported.[5] The spread variable for each country in a particular year was constructed as a weighted average of spreads actually charged for the individual public and publicly guaranteed loans granted to that particular country, where the weights were given by the value of each loan.[6] The basic data were obtained from various issues of the World Bank's *Borrowing in International Capital Markets*, and are presented in my earlier paper.

Several variables were considered as possible determinants of the spread, including those suggested by a number of models that have recently appeared in the literature. (See Feder and Just, 1977b; Sachs and Cohen, 1982; Sachs, 1983; Eaton and Gersovitz, 1980; my earlier paper) Specifically, the following variables—some of which have also been included in previous empirical work on the subject—were considered as possibly affecting s in the empirical analysis.

1) The debt-output ratio. As has been argued by Sachs and Cohen (1982) and others, it is expected that this variable will have a positive coefficient in the regression analysis. This variable can be considered to be an indicator of the degree of solvency of a particular country. The data on this variable refers to public and publicly guaranteed debt and was obtained from the World Bank *World Debt Tables.*

2) The ratio of debt service to exports. This indicator measures possible liquidity (as opposite to solvency) problems faced by a particular country. It is expected that its coefficient will be positive. Data on this ratio was obtained from the *World Debt Tables.*

3) Ratio of international reserves to *GNP.* This indicator measures the level of international liquidity held by a country and as suggested in my earlier paper, it is expected that its coefficient will be negative. This variable was constructed from data obtained from the IMF's *International Financial Statistics.*

4) Loan duration. This variable is measured in years, and measures the (weighted) average maturity of loans granted to a particular country. As has been shown by Feder and Ross (1982) its a priori sign in the regression analysis is ambiguous. The weighted average was constructed from data reported in *Borrowing in International Capital Markets.*

5) Loan volume. This variable shows the average value of each loan, and was obtained from *Borrowing in International Capital Markets.* Also, a priori, its sign is ambiguous.

6) Propensity to invest. This variable was constructed as the ratio of gross domestic investment of *GDP*, and will tend to capture the country's prospectives for future growth. As is shown in Sachs and Cohen (1982), and in my earlier paper, it should be negatively related to the spread. This indicator was obtained from data reported in the *World Tables* and in *World Development Report* (various issues).

7) Ratio of the current account to *GDP.* Sachs (1981) has argued that this variable will be negatively related to the probability of default. The data on this variable was obtained from various issues of the *World Tables* and *World Development Report.*

8) Average propensity to import. This indicator was constructed as the ratio of imports to *GNP,* and measures the degree of openness of a country. To the extent that a more open country is more vulnerable to foreign shocks (Jacob Frenkel, 1983), it is expected that it will be positively related to the

probability of default. This variable was constructed from data obtained from the *International Financial Statistics*.

9) Growth of per capita *GDP*. It has been argued that a higher rate of growth of output will result in a lower probability of default (see Feder and Just, 1977b). Data on this indicator was obtained from *World Tables* and the *World Development Report*.

10) *GNP* per capita. This variable measures the relative economic size of a country. Some authors have argued (i.e., Feder and Just, 1977b) that this variable should have a negative coefficient in equation (3). This variable was obtained from various issues of the World Bank's World Tables and World Development Report.

11) Rate of inflation. It is possible to argue that, with other things given, a higher rate of inflation indicates a larger probability of a balance of payments crisis, and consequently a higher probability of default (McDonald). This variable was taken from the *International Financial Statistics*.

12) Variability of International Reserves. According to the literature on the demand for international reserves (for example, Frenkel) the more variable are the flows of foreign funds faced by a country, the higher the probability of a balance of payments crisis. Consequently, it is expected that the coefficient of this variable will be positive. This indicator was constructed from data obtained from the *International Financial Statistics*.

13) Rate of Devaluation. This variable summarizes the exchange rate policy followed by a particular country. For a given level of the other variables (in particular inflation and reserves), a higher rate of devaluation will tend to indicate a higher willingness to use exchange rate adjustments to avoid balance of payments crises.[7] It is expected that it will have a negative coefficient in the regression analysis. The data was obtained from *International Financial Statistics*.

14) Government expenditure over *GNP*. It has been suggested that the larger the size of the government sector in a developing country, the higher the probability of a balance of payments crisis.[8] It is then expected that the coefficient of this variable will be positive. The data was obtained from *World Tables* and *World Development Report*.

Other variables were also considered as possible determinants of the probability of default (oil exporters dummy variables, for example). However, due to space considerations, and since their inclusion did not affect the results in any significant way, the estimates obtained when they were included are not reported here.

Equation (3) was estimated using pooled cross-section time-series data for 19 countries during five years (1976–80). For estimation purposes it was assumed that $\log \gamma_{nt}$ was equal to a constant k plus a random element u_{nt} ($\log \gamma_{nt} = k + u_{nt}$). Following the usual convention in pooled time-series cross-section estimation, it was assumed that this random term u_{nt} was formed of a country-specific random error s_n, with zero mean and variance σ_v^2; a time-specific random element w_t with zero mean and variance σ_w^2; and an independently distributed random term

ε_{nt}, with zero mean and variance σ_ε^2 (see Theodore Anderson and Cheng Hsiao, 1981). Then the equation to be estimated can be written as

$$\log s_{nt} = \alpha_0 + k + \sum_{i=1}^{m} \alpha_i y_{int} + v_n + w_t + \varepsilon_{nt}, \tag{4}$$

where

$$E\left(v_n^2\right) = \sigma_v^2; \ E\left(w_t^2\right) = \sigma_w^2; \ E\left(\varepsilon_{nt}^2\right) = \sigma_\varepsilon^2,$$

and

$$E\left(v_n w_t\right) = E\left(v_n \varepsilon_{nt}\right) = E\left(w_t \varepsilon_{nt}\right) = 0$$

$$E\left(v_n v_m\right) = 0 \quad \text{for } n \neq m$$

$$E\left(w_t w_s\right) = 0 \quad \text{for } t \neq s$$

$$E\left(\varepsilon_{nt} \varepsilon_{ns}\right) = E\left(\varepsilon_{mt} \varepsilon_{nt}\right) = E\left(\varepsilon_{nt} \varepsilon_{ms}\right) = 0.$$

Expression (4) is a typical random-effect error components equation. The results presented in this paper were obtained using the technique suggested by Wayne Fuller and George Batesse (1974). In the estimation ($\alpha_0 + k$) was combined into a constant β_0. A possible problem with the estimation of (4) is that, to the extent that banks determine the spread and loan duration at the same time, use of Fuller-Batesse's technique would be subject to a simultaneity bias. However, following Feder and Ross, and David Beim (1977) it was assumed that the duration of the loan is determined by banks *prior* to the determination of the spread. This indeed appears to be the case in the Eurocurrency credit markets (see *Euromoney*, September 1978).

Table 1 contains the results obtained from the estimation of equation (1) using Fuller- Batesse's technique. These results are quite satisfactory, both from the point of view of the mean square errors of the regressions, and from the perspective of the signs and level of significance of the coefficients. Broadly speaking, the empirical evidence shows that international lending behavior to *LDC*s tends to take into account some of the economic characteristics of the specific borrowing countries. As may be seen, in all regressions the debt-output ratio is significantly positive, and smaller than one. This result suggests that a higher level of indebtedness will be associated with a higher probability of default and thus, a higher

Table 1 Estimation of Equation (4): Fuller-Batesse Procedure, 1976–80

Independent Variable	Equations					
	(4.1)	(4.2)	(4.3)	(4.4)	(4.5)	(4.6)
Constant	0.329 (1.422)	0.141 (0.726)	0.305 (1.216)	0.285 (1.225)	0.345 (1.062)	0.314 (1.424)
Debt/GNP	0.622 (2.512)	0.544 (2.251)	0.634 (2.461)	0.545 (2.107)	0.613 (2.120)	0.633 (2.453)
Reserves/GNP	−1.155 (−2.164)	−1.211 (−2.253)	−1.079 (−1.632)	−1.282 (−2.345)	−0.995 (−1.412)	−1.152 (−2.142)
Debt Service/Exports	0.426 (1.688)	0.567 (2.344)	0.440 (1.797)	0.441 (1.749)	0.386 (1.400)	0.353 (1.458)
Loan Duration	−0.012 (−0.648)	−0.011 (−0.581)	−0.013 (−1.719)	−0.014 (−0.753)	−0.018 (−0.953)	—
Loan Value	−0.001 (−1.340)	−0.001 (−1.658)	−0.001 (−1.269)	−0.001 (−1.131)	−0.001 (−1.500)	—
Investment/GNP	−0.681 (−1.991)	—	−0.756 (−1.324)	−0.757 (−1.318)	−0.624 (−0.972)	−1.186 (−2.266)
Current Account/GNP	0.435 (1.966)	—	0.387 (0.970)	0.487 (2.131)	0.365 (0.863)	—
Growth	—	—	0.007 (0.377)	—	0.008 (0.337)	—
Imports/GNP	—	—	−0.004 (−0.105)	—	0.007 (0.176)	—
Government Expenditure/GNP	—	—	—	0.708 (1.316)	—	—
Income per Capita	—	—	—	—	−0.208 (−0.532)	—
Inflation	—	—	—	—	−0.008 (−0.127)	—
Reserves Variability	—	—	—	—	0.085 (0.974)	—
Rate of Devaluation	—	—	—	—	0.178 (0.888)	—
MSE	0.021	0.023	0.021	0.021	0.023	0.028

Note: Asymptotic *t*-statistics are shown in parentheses. *MSE* is the mean square error of the transformed regression.

spread over *LIBOR*. This contrasts with results previously obtained by Feder and Just (1977b), using data for eight quarters in 1973–74, and by Sachs (1981) where the coefficient of the debt-output ratio was always insignificant and very low. With respect to the debt-service ratio—that measures potential liquidity problems—its coefficients are also positive, as expected, and in most cases significant either at the 5 or 10 percent level.

The coefficient of the reserves to *GNP* ratio is, as expected, consistently negative, and in most equations it is significant at the 5 percent level. Also, the estimated values of these coefficients are high, indicating that the behavior of the reserves ratio has played an important role in the determination of the perceived probability of default. The main importance of this result is that from a policy point of view, countries that want to reduce the probability of being excluded from the international financial market, due to an increase in the perceived probability of default, should be particularly careful in managing their international reserves. Also, these results suggest that the analysis of the demand for international reserves should incorporate the level of foreign indebtedness as an additional determinant of the desired level of international liquidity (see Eaton and Gersovitz, 1980). It is also interesting to note that the coefficient of the reserves ratio is quite high in absolute terms, exceeding in all cases the estimated value of the coefficient of the debt to *GNP* ratio.[9]

The coefficients of loan duration and loan value are negative, but insignificant. The coefficients of the imports-output ratio, growth, *GNP* per capita, variability of reserves, inflation, the government expenditure ratio, and the rate of devaluation are also insignificant.

In all regressions the estimated coefficient of the gross investment-*GDP* ratio was negative, as expected. Also in two of the five regressions where it was included, it was significant, suggesting that as has been indicated by Sachs (1981), Sachs and Cohen (1982) and my earlier paper, a higher propensity to invest will tend to be associated with a lower perceived probability of default. The coefficient of the current account ratio is positive in the three regressions where it was included, being significant in two of the cases. This is a somewhat puzzling result, since it indicates that a lower deficit (or higher surplus) will result in a higher perceived probability of default and spread. The problem with this is that, with other things given—especially the investment ratio—a higher current account deficit means that the *same* investment is being financed with a higher proportion of foreign savings, and one would generally expect that in this case (i.e., lower domestic savings ratio) the perceived probability of default would be higher.

In all cases the estimated variance of the time-specific element $\hat{\sigma}_w^2$ exceeded the estimated country-specific variance $\hat{\sigma}_v^2$, indicating that during the period under consideration, differences across time in the country risk premium were more important than differences across country. This result is capturing the fact that throughout the period under consideration (1976–80) the level of world liquidity varied significantly (see my earlier paper). On the whole, however, the low value of the mean square error of the regressions (*MSE*) show a quite satisfactory fit.

In sum, the evidence presented in this section shows that during the recent past, lending behavior by international banks in Eurocurrency markets has taken into account (some of) the economic characteristics of borrowers. Even though some of the coefficients were sensitive to the specification of the estimated equations and were not always significant at the conventional levels, the general results regarding some of the most important variables are consistent with what was expected. Particularly important is the result of a significantly positive relation between the debt-*GNP* ratio and the spread. These results which contradict previous findings (i.e., Feder and Just, 1977b; Sachs, 1981) indicate that, as has been suggested by Harberger (1983), there are "externalities" in the process of *LDC* borrowing and that these could be dealt with by imposing an optimal tax on foreign borrowing in developing countries.

II. The Perceived Probabilities of Default

The econometric estimates reported in Table 1 can be used to compute the estimated banks' perceived probabilities of default as

$$
p_{nt} = \frac{\exp\left\{ \tilde{\alpha}_{0n} + \sum_{i=1}^{k} \hat{\alpha}_{in} y_{nti} \right\}}{1 + \exp\left\{ \tilde{\alpha}_{0n} + \sum_{i=1}^{k} \hat{\alpha}_{in} y_{nti} \right\}},
\tag{5}
$$

Where $\tilde{\alpha}_0 = \hat{\beta}_0 - k$ is the imputed value for α_0 in equation (4) (for $\hat{\beta}_0$ the estimated value of the constant in the regression analysis). Table 2 presents estimated probabilities of default for each country and each year, obtained from Table 1, equation (4.1).[10] A number of interesting characteristics of these probabilities can be observed. First, it can be seen that, within each year, there is a fairly wide variation in the perceived probability across countries. Second, for each country, these probabilities of default show some variation through time. For example, for the case of Venezuela the probability increases steadily between 1977 and 1980. While in 1976 Venezuela has the lowest estimated perceived probability of default, in 1980 this probability is around the middle of the distribution. For the case of Brazil, one of the countries that eventually ran into serious foreign debt problems, there is an increase in the perceived probability of default of approximately one full percentage point. Surprisingly, however, for Argentina, a country which in 1982 encountered serious financial difficulties, Table 2 estimates indicate that the perceived probability of default *declined* throughout the period. Also for the case of Mexico, these results show a decline in the probability of default in 1980.

In sum, the computations presented in Tables 1 and 2 suggest that even as late as 1980 the international financial market had not predicted in any important way the future payment difficulties faced by Argentina, Mexico, and Uruguay.

241

Table 2 Estimated Perceived Probabilities of Default from Table 1, Equation (4.1) (Shown in Percent)

	1976	1977	1978	1979	1980
Greece	8.0	8.0	7.7	7.2	7.9
Portugal	8.4	8.3	8.5	8.9	8.6
Spain	7.8	8.1	8.1	7.8	7.9
Yugoslavia	7.6	7.6	7.8	7.0	7.4
Argentina	8.4	8.7	8.8	7.2	6.1
Brazil	8.9	8.8	8.9	9.1	9.6
Colombia	8.7	8.3	7.8	7.5	7.3
Ecuador	7.8	8.0	8.4	8.6	8.6
Mexico	9.9	10.1	10.5	10.5	9.2
Panama	10.4	11.6	11.9	11.3	11.5
Uruguay	10.6	10.2	10.5	8.6	8.5
Venezuela	5.9	5.8	6.3	7.1	7.9
Indonesia	9.6	9.6	9.3	8.4	8.7
Korea	8.9	8.5	7.7	7.7	8.5
Malaysia	7.0	7.4	7.0	7.1	6.3
Phillipines	7.4	7.9	7.7	7.7	7.7
Thailand	7.4	7.4	7.4	7.6	7.8
Ivory Coast	9.9	10.0	9.4	9.9	10.0
Morocco	8.0	8.1	9.4	9.2	10.3

III. Concluding Remarks

This paper has analyzed the relationship between foreign debt and default country risk in developing countries. The empirical analysis has used data on 727 public and publicly guaranteed loans granted to 19 *LDC*s during 1976 and 1980. The results obtained suggest that banks lending behavior has tended to consider (some of) the economic characteristics of countries when determining the spread they charge. However, the results also suggest that, at least during this period, banks might have overlooked some aspects of the developing countries' economies. One of the most interesting results obtained is the robust and significant positive relation (with a coefficient of approximately 0.6) between the log of the spread over *LIBOR* and the debt-output ratio. This relationship suggests that, as has been recently indicated by Harberger (1983), there are externalities in the process of *LDC* borrowing. These externalities could be dealt with by imposing an optimal external borrowing tax in these countries (Harberger, 1983).

*Financial support from UCLA's Council on International and Comparative Studies is gratefully acknowledged. I have benefited from helpful discussions with John Bilson and Carlos Rodriguez, and from comments by two anonymous referees, Michael Darby, Susan Woodward, and the participants in seminars at the University of Chicago, UCLA, and the World Bank. Steve Feinstein and Evan Tanner provided able research assistance. The research reported here is part of the NBER's Research Studies in International Studies. Any opinions expressed here are my own and not those of the NBER.

Notes

1 See, for example, the *Wall Street Journal* editorial, March 9, 1983. On the recent international debt crisis, see the comprehensive discussion in William Cline (1983). In particular, see his ch. 5 for a discussion on bank's responsibility in the present crisis. See also *Time* magazine (January 10, 1983), *The Economist*, (March 5, 1983), Martin Feldstein (1983), David Folkerts-Landau (1982). The indebtedness situation is particularly critical regarding Latin American debtors. For example, U.S. private banks have "extended credit of more than U.S. $50 billion to Mexico, Brazil and Argentina, an amount that exceeds 80 percent of the banks equity" (Feldstein, p. 2). The extent of the indebtedness crisis is reflected by the fact that in 1982, twenty countries undertook debt renegotiations, while in the second half of the 1970's, an average of only four countries per year renegotiated their debts.

2 See Donogh McDonald (1982) for an excellent and exhaustive survey on the subject.

3 Most previous work has used cross-section data for a particular year or quarter. Feder and Just (1977b) used loans data for 8 quarters during 1973–74. The present paper uses the most recent data available, since in 1981 the World Bank stopped the publication of *Borrowing in International Capital Markets* from where the data on the spreads was obtained.

4 This can be illustrated by assuming the simple case of a one-period loan. Consider that the risk-free interest rate is given by $LIBOR(i*)$, and that the interest rate charged to a particular country (i) is equal to $LIBOR$ plus the spread (5). Assume also that in case of default the principal and interest are completely lost (this is a nonessential assumption). Then, the following equilibrium condition will hold: $(1 - p)(1 + i) = (1 + i*)$. From here it follows that $s = [p/(1 - p)]\gamma$, for $\gamma = (1 + i*)$. Alternatively, more complicated models, like the one in Feder and Just (1977b), can be used to develop expressions similar to (1).

5 Countries included in the empirical analysis are Argentina, Brazil, Colombia, Ecuador, Greece, Indonesia, Ivory Coast, Korea, Malaysia, Mexico, Morocco, Panama, Philippines, Portugal, Spain, Thailand, Uruguay, Venezuela, and Yugoslavia.

6 It is important to notice that there are some problems with the quality of this data. The most serious problem is that the interest rate is not the only component of a loan's cost. In particular in the present study —as in those by Feder and Just (1977b) and Sachs (1981), for example— it has not been possible (due to lack of information) to incorporate data on fees and commissions. It should be noted, however, that these fees are typically low compared to the interest rate component of the costs (see, for example, the discussion in Cline, pp. 82–83).

7 Cline (ch. 1) has indicated that the mismanagement of the exchange rate policy is one of the main causes of the international debt crisis. Deviations of Purchasing Power Parity were included instead of the rate of devaluation as an indicator of exchange rate policy. The results obtained, however, were not different.

8 See, for example, the discussion in Harberger's and my article (1982). Cline argues that the increase in the Mexican fiscal deficit was one of the main causes for the 1982 debt crisis in that country.

9 An interesting question is what will happen to the perceived probability of default if a country increases its foreign debt to finance the accumulation of international reserves. In this case the change in the (log of the) spread will be given by

$$d\log s = \left[\hat{\alpha}_1 + \hat{\alpha}_2 + \hat{\alpha}_3(\psi + i)/XR\right]d(DR),$$

where $\hat{\alpha}_1$, $\hat{\alpha}_2$ and $\hat{\alpha}_3$ are estimated regression coefficients of debt-*GNP*, reserves-*GNP*, and debt service- exports ratios, respectively; ψ is the fraction of the debt's principal that has to be amortized every year; i is the interest rate actually charged; XR is the exports-*GNP* ratio; and DR is the debt-*GNP* ratio. Computations reported in my earlier paper suggest that an increase in DR coupled with an equiproportional accumulation of reserves will tend to leave the spread unaffected.

10 Each equation's estimates will generate different sets of perceived probabilities. However, the overall picture presented in Table 2 is not affected by the equation used to generate these probabilities. For further details on this and on the computation of these perceived probabilities of default, see my earlier paper.

References

Anderson, Theodore W. and Hsiao, Cheng, "Estimation of Dynamic Models with Error Component," *Journal of the American Statistical Association,* September 1981, 76, 598–606.

Beim, David, "Rescuing the *LDC*'s," *Foreign Affairs*, July 1977, 55, 717–31.

Cline, William, *International Debt and the Stability of the World Economy*, Washington: Institute for International Economics, 1983.

Eaton, Jonathan, and Gersovitz, Mark, "*LDC* Participation in International Financial Markets: Debt and Reserves," *Journal of Development Economics*, March 1980, 7, 3–21.

_____ and _____, (1981a) "Debt With Potential Repudiation: Theoretical and Empirical Analysis," *Review of Economic Studies*, April 1981, *48,* 289–309.

_____ and _____, *(1981b) Poor-Country Borrowing in Private Financial Markets and the Repudiation Issue*, Princeton Studies in International Finance, No. 47, International Finance Section, Princeton University, June 1981.

Edwards, Sebastian, "*LDC*'s Foreign Borrowing and Default Risk: An Empirical Investigation, 1976–1980," Working Paper No. 1172, National Bureau of Economic Research, July 1983.

Feder, Gershon and Just, Richard E., (1977a) "A Study of Debt Servicing Capacity Applying Logit Analysis," *Journal of Development Economics*, March 1977, 4, 25–38.

_____ and _____, (1977b) "An Analysis of Credit Terms in the Eurodollar Market," *European Economic Review*, May 1977, 9, 221–43.

_____ and _____, "Optimal International Borrowing, Capital Allocation and Creditworthiness Control," *Kredit and Kapital,* No. 2, 1979, 12, 207–20.

_____ and _____, "A Model for Analyzing Lender's Perceived Risk," *Applied Economics*, June 1980, 12, 125–44.

_____ and Ross, Knud, "Risk Assessments and Risk Premiums in the Eurodollar Market," *Journal of Finance*, June 1982, 37, 679–91.

Feldstein, Martin, "Coping with the International Debt Problem," unpublished manuscript, March 1983.

Folkerts-Landau, David F. I., "Credit Rationing and Debt Rescheduling in the International Bank Loan Market," unpublished paper, IMF, December 1982.

Frank, Charles R., Jr. and Cline, William R., "Measurement of Debt Servicing Capacity: An Application of Discriminant Analysis," *Journal of International Economics*, August 1971, 1, 327–44.

Frenkel, Jacob, "International Liquidity and Monetary Control," Working Paper No. 1118, National Bureau of Economic Research, May 1983.

Fuller, Wayne and Batesse, George, " Estimation of Linear Models With Crossed Error Structure," *Journal of Econometrics*, February 1974, 2, 67–78.

Harberger, Arnold C., "On Country Risk and the Social Cost of Foreign Borrowing by Developing Countries," unpublished manuscript, University of Chicago, 1976.

_____, "Vignettes on the World Capital Market, *American Economic Review Proceedings*, May 1980, 70, 331–37.

_____, "Welfare Consequences of Capital Inflows," paper presented at World Bank Conference, Washington, October 1983.

_____ **and Edwards, Sebastian,** "Lessons of Experience with Fixed Exchange Rates," in M. Gersovitz et al., eds., *The Theory and Experience of Economic Development*, London: Allen and Unwin, 1982, 183–93.

Kapur, Ishan, "An Analysis of the Supply of Eurocurrency Finance to Developing Countries," *Oxford Bulletin of Economics and Statistics*, August 1977, 37, 171–88.

McDonald, Donogh C., "Debt Capacity and Developing Country Borrowing," *IMF Staff Papers*, December 1982, 29, 603–46.

Sachs, Jeffrey D., "The Current Account and Macroeconomic Adjustment in the 1970s," *Brookings Papers on Economic Activity*, 1: 1981, 201–68.

_____, "*LDC* Debt in the 1980s: Risk and Reforms," in Paul Wachtel, ed., *Crises in the Economic and Financial Structure*, Lexington: D. C. Heath, 1982, 197–243.

_____, "Theoretical Issues in International Borrowing," National Bureau of Economics Research, Working Paper No. 1189, August 1983.

_____ **and Cohen, Daniel, "*LDC* Borrowing** with Default Risk," Working Paper No. 925, National Bureau of Economic Research, July 1982.

Sargen, Nicholas, "Economic Indicators and Country Risk Appraisal," *Federal Reserve Bank of San Francisco Economic Review*, Fall 1977, 19–35.

Economist, March 5, 1983.

Euromoney, September 1978.

International Monetary Fund, *International Financial Statistics*, Washington, various issues.

Time, January 10, 1983.

Wall Street Journal, March 9, 1983.

World Bank, *Borrowing in International Capital Markets, Washington, various issues.*

_____, *World Debt Tables, Washington,* various issues.

_____, *World Development Report 1982,* New York: Oxford University Press, 1982.

_____, *World Tables*, Baltimore: Johns Hopkins University Press, 1980.

11

THE FRENCH CRIME OF 1873

An Essay on the Emergence of the International Gold Standard, 1870–1880

Marc Flandreau

Source: *Journal of Economic History* 56, 4, 1996, 862–897.

This article attempts to provide a new view of how the bimetallic standard was maintained before 1873 and how it came to change into a monometallic gold standard between 1870 and 1880. The conventional view that the gold standard emerged out of the contradictions of bimetallism is not persuasive. Instead, this article claims that bimetallism might have survived and provides an alternative explanation of the emergence of the gold standard. Political and historical factors proved essential in precipitating the uncoordinated emergence of the international gold standard.

The 1870s was a decade of dramatic changes in the organization of the international monetary system. Before 1870 nations were roughly divided into three categories. The members of the first group (United Kingdom, Portugal, Turkey, Brazil, Australia) were on the gold standard. The members of the second (German states, Austria, Holland, Scandinavia, Mexico, Asian countries) were on some form of silver standard. The members of the third (the United States, France, Switzerland, Italy, Belgium) were on a dual standard, called at the time the "double standard," and eventually known as "bimetallism." In these countries, a fixed ratio (implicitly defined by stating the number of grams of gold or silver one had to give up in order to settle a debt) was set between the two metals. By 1880 however, most industrialized nations had moved to gold: the monetary role of silver declined. Its price (which had been virtually fixed until the early 1870s) began an irreversible fall. Central banks started to peg the value of their notes in terms of gold. The international gold standard was born.[1]

The causes of these phenomena have been variously assessed. So far, four arguments have dominated the literature. The fundamentals theory emphasizes the importance of rising silver production in the late 1860s and 1870s. This would have led to silver depreciation and thus forced nations to abandon that metal.[2] Alternatively, the strategical theory posits that the forces of rising silver production were supplemented by Germany's demonetization of silver. Germany's move from silver to gold in the early 1870s would have inevitably led to silver depreciation and thus triggered a general flight away from silver, thereby reinforcing the depreciation itself.[3] The third type of argument, the technological theory, stresses the role of micromotives. Silver, it is said, was bulkier than gold and hence more costly for international payments. A gold standard was a necessarily superior regime, and its introduction was only delayed by technical reasons.[4] Finally the political economy interpretation emphasizes the respective properties of a gold, a silver, and a bimetallic standard in terms of price stability and argues that it was the actions of the creditors' class (the dominant bourgeoisie) that favored a stable standard of value that produced the convergence to gold in the 1870s.[5]

Although analytically distinct, these four main arguments often concur in standard analyses of the emergence of the classical gold standard (see in particular Jacques Mertens's authoritative account, which probably remains the best—yet often underrated—source for the period). What differentiates the various descriptions is mainly the weight they attach to each cause. But they all assume that the making of the gold standard was inevitable. This research started as an attempt to disentangle these theories in order to provide a clearer understanding of their relative explicative power. However, it became increasingly clear that these interpretations were incomplete and generally unsound. Indeed, far from being preordained for structural, technological, or political reasons, the making of the gold standard was an accident of history.

Conventional interpretations suffer a number of flaws. First, it is not clear how rising silver production in the late 1860s could really threaten bimetallism, since this rise was proportionately much smaller than the one that had affected gold after 1848 without determining dramatic changes. Second, France would have been able to buffer the impact of Germany's move to gold so that Germany's reform could not by itself trigger the flight away from silver. Third, contrary to popular beliefs, it is not true that gold strongly dominated silver as an instrument for international transactions. Fourth, before 1873 the political support in favor of gold was much less homogeneous than what is commonly believed: as a creditor-debtor opposition, it developed after the emergence of the gold standard, not before.

The policy shifts of the 1870s are better understood as being based on the interaction between network externalities and switching costs.[6] During the 1860s growing trade led commercial interests (especially in Europe) to be attracted by the advantages of having a common standard. Given the predominance of gold or partly gold-based nations in world trade, a gold standard appeared to be a natural choice. On the other hand, the practical implementation of such a reform implied discarding silver. This involved considerable difficulties, especially for silver-standard nations such as Germany. These countries had to find the means to purchase gold, and they had to be able to get rid of demonetized silver on the best possible terms. Until the late 1860s, the difficulty of the exercise deterred many countries from actually moving to gold. However, after 1870, the Franco-Prussian war gave Germany the resources necessary to carry on its adoption of the gold standard. It also planned to get rid of its demonetized silver through the agency of France's bimetallic system, which had so far acted as a stabilizer of the international monetary system. The French retaliated in suspending silver coinage, in an attempt to block Germany's move to gold. But the bulk of legislation adopted in Germany in the early 1870s prohibited such a reversal, and France's decision only provoked the world's flight away from silver. In other words, the emergence of the gold standard was a blatant failure of international cooperation.

The first section of the article documents the operation of the international monetary system prior to 1870 and develops a framework in which conventional theories of the making of the gold standard will be conveniently discussed. The second section reviews and criticizes conventional explanations. The last section presents an alternative view.[7]

THE OPERATION OF THE INTERNATIONAL
MONETARY SYSTEM BEFORE 1870

Despite its monetary heterogeneity, the pregold standard regime was one of quasi-fixed exchange rates. From 1820 until the 1870s, the gold-silver ratio modestly fluctuated around the 15.5 to 1 legal ratio defined by the French bimetallic system (Figure 1). As a result, exchange-rate stability between monies based on different

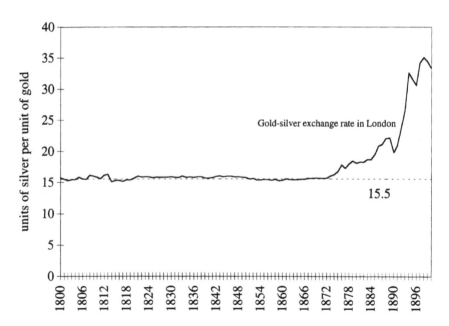

Figure 1 GOLD-SILVER EXCHANGE RATE, 1800–1900. *Source*: Warren and Pearson, *Prices.*

metals was quite amazing.[8] In fact, this stability is something of a puzzle: after all, gold and silver are both commodities, and their relative price should fluctuate. How is it that their exchange rate remained so stable? To answer that question, a number of authors have assumed that it was the active policy of some monetary institution (such as central banks) that provided the pre-1873 stability of the gold-silver exchange rate. In case of excess supply of (for instance) gold, those institutions would buy the surplus against their silver reserves. According to Barry Eichengreen, for instance, France "attempted to operate a commodity price stabilization scheme, using reserves of gold and silver to stabilize the relative price of the two metals."[9]

This hypothesis, however, was rejected by historical research on the actual behavior of central banks and treasuries in bimetallic nations. Separate accounts for the United States, Belgium, Italy, and France consistently support the view that central institutions were never committed to exchange one metal for the other.[10] For instance, the Bank of France, a private institution, had, as any other private agent, the option to redeem its notes in whatever metal it wished. This leaves open the question of how the gold-silver exchange rate was stabilized.

In fact, the answer lies in an argument that was initially developed by Jean-Baptiste Say but the implications of which have never been fully understood, even by its own author. In a bimetallic regime, agents (not only central banks) have the option to pay their debts using the metal of their choice. They thus look for the less expensive currency (per unit of purchasing power). This tends to increase their demand for the relatively depreciated metal and feeds back onto its price, which is eventually stabilized at a level that has to be close to the legal ratio. Moreover, since agents realize that the equilibrium gold-silver exchange rate is the legal ratio, they compete to wipe out any discrepancy between the two relative prices. And indeed, between 1850 and 1870 (the period of focus in this section), the gold-silver exchange rate was pegged within an interval reflecting the costs associated with melting one metal and minting the other one.[11] These arbitrages implied that in the bimetallic bloc, monetary holdings adjusted endogenously to buffer shocks on bullion markets. Holdings tended to become relatively more intensive in the metal that was relatively more abundant.

What constitutes probably the most important conclusion of the previous analysis is that the operation of the pregold standard international monetary regime relied on the existence of some particular national monetary system that adjusted to preserve the worldwide stability of the gold-silver exchange rate. Those countries' commitment to bimetallism enforced the credibility of the ratio that in turn led to stabilizing interventions by private agents. The bimetallic bloc acted as an arbitrageur of last resort for the world monetary system at large, absorbing disequilibria originating on the international bullion markets.

A priori, this buffer role was likely to depend upon the size of the bimetallic block, where France, with a huge specie circulation, played a dominant role. In 1850 France held about 2.3 billion French francs in silver, and the annual gold production was just about 360 million. The system was thus likely to cushion many gold supply shocks.[12] However, speculating upon the durability of this scheme certainly

FLANDREAU

Table 1 CORRELATION BETWEEN INFLATION RATES: VARIOUS COUNTRIES, 1848–1870

	Gold (U.K.)	Bimetallic (France)	Silver (Germany)	Silver (Asia)
Gold (U.K.)	1			
Bimetallic (France)	0.60	1		
Silver (Germany)	0.67	0.77	1	
Silver (Asia)	0.84	0.63	0.44	1

Note: Asia is represented by a bundle of oriental goods (Soetbeer, *Matériaux*).
Source: Flandreau, *L'or du monde*.

requires a more careful analysis. To do so, I constructed a model of the international economy that focuses on the interactions between various monetary blocs.

The model pictures a unified world economy that is formed by three regions being respectively on a gold, a silver, and a bimetallic standard. The gold-silver exchange rate (p_G) is given by the legal ratio of the bimetallic bloc. The price of silver is set equal to one. There is one consumption good that is traded, and its price p (the world price level) is uniform across regions. The relative harmlessness of this assumption is supported by Table 1, which illustrates the tendency of prices in various areas to move together.[13] Indeed, Table 1 shows that intra-bloc correlations (such as those between Asia and Germany, which were on a silver standard) were not larger than interbloc correlation (such as those between Germany and the United Kingdom), suggesting that there is no rationale for discriminating between blocs on the basis of prices.

The model can be shown to derive from a general equilibrium (static) framework, in which money demand is introduced through cash in advance constraints. However, for the sake of simplicity, I will focus on its semireduced form that distinguishes between monetary and nonmonetary demand for bullion in the various blocs.[14] Furthermore, as in any static model, this framework may be interpreted as representing the steady state of some more complex dynamic system.

Money demand in the gold, silver, and bimetallic blocs are respectively given by the following equations where Y^i represents exogenously given real wealth, defined as beginning of period stock of consumption goods, monetary and nonmonetary metal, M_j^i is the monetary demand for metal j by country i, K^i is bloc i's Cambridge coefficient, i equals g for gold, s for silver, and b for bimetallism:[15]

$$M_G^g p_G = k^g p Y^g \tag{1}$$

$$M_S^s = k^s p Y^s \tag{2}$$

$$M_G^b p_G + M_S^b = k^b p Y^b \tag{3}$$

250

The demand for nonmonetary gold and silver in the three blocs is given by:

$$D_G^i = \mu_G^i \frac{p}{p_G} Y^i \text{ and } D_S^i = \mu_S^i p Y^i$$

$$\text{with } i = g, s, b \tag{4}$$

Finally, we consider that the various blocs have stable relative sizes, and time independent monetization rules.[16]

$$Y^g = \beta_g Y^b \text{ and } Y^s = \beta_s Y^b \tag{5}$$

Where β_g and β_s are parameters reflecting relative sizes. The model is closed by equating gold and silver resources. In equilibrium, the outstanding world gold resources (or supply) must equal the aggregate uses for monetary and nonmonetary gold (or demand). Calling G (respectively S) the world stock of gold (respectively silver), we have:

$$G = M_G^g + M_G^b + \sum_i D_G^i \text{ and } S = M_S^s + M_S^b + \sum_i D_S^i \tag{6}$$

As shown in the appendix, this set of equations can be solved for equilibrium prices (p and p_G). This in turn can be used to solve for the bimetallic bloc gold and silver holdings. We finally get equations 7 and 8, which describe the equilibrium effect of a marginal increase in the stock of either metal and thus allows to sort out relations between stocks and flows (m_G and m_s are functions of the parameters of bullion demand for both monetary and nonmonetary uses). In this system, left-hand side variables (endogenous bimetallic specie holdings) are determined by right-hand side variables (exogenous world stocks of gold and silver). These equations show how the structure of the bimetallic bloc's circulation adjusts to exogenous shocks on bullion markets:

$$p_G M_G^b = p_G G \cdot (1 - m_G) - S \cdot m_G \tag{7}$$

$$M_S^b = -p_G G \cdot m_S + S \cdot (1 - m_S) \tag{8}$$

This system may be thought of as capturing the economics of Gresham's Law in a bimetallic regime. If the world stock of gold increases by one franc, the gold holdings of the bimetallic bloc will increase by $(1 - m_G)$ franc, while its silver holdings will decrease by m_s franc. In other words, the relatively more abundant metal drives the other one out of the bimetallic bloc. However, the increase in the outstanding stock of gold will not necessarily result in a one for one substitution of one metal for the other one. To clarify this point, consider the following thought experiment. Assume that new gold outlets are discovered in some gold-standard country. The newly extracted bullion is partly monetized. This tends to produce a rise in the price level of that country. But both commodity and bimetallic arbitrages insure price uniformity across the world, implying that demand for money in the other nations has to rise in order to rebuild eroding real balances. In particular, there is an increased demand for monetary silver in silver-standard countries. With a fixed exchange rate between gold and silver, this requires substituting gold for silver in the bimetallic bloc, where gold holdings increase, and silver holdings decrease. But since nominal balances have to rise everywhere in the world, gold inflows in bimetallic countries must outweigh silver outflows.

Consider now the statistical assessment of bimetallism, focusing on the period from 1850 to 1870. This will allow us to capture the "normal" mechanics of bimetallism, before the gold standard emerged. Two ingredients are necessary in order to estimate equations 7 and 8. We must first use a series for the annual world production of gold and silver. These are quite well documented, and although some competing series do exist, they are good substitutes for econometric purposes.[17] The second ingredient is the series for gold and silver specie holdings of the bimetallic bloc. Obviously, given France's enormous weight within bimetallic nations (it held about nine-tenths of the bimetallic bloc's aggregate stock of specie) it is sufficient to have the series for France's gold and silver holdings.[18] These were constructed in earlier work on the basis of a monetary census conducted in 1878.[19]

The estimation procedure is presented in the appendix. Equations 7 and 8 describe long-run equilibrium relations between nonstationary variables.

This allows implementation of least squares techniques that are known to produce estimates that are super-consistent. The results are presented in Table 2. Although the model is simplicity itself, it does perform very well: the R^2s are quite high, and Figure 2 shows that the fit between actual and predicted series is good. This is rather remarkable, given the extreme paucity in the number of series used and the fact that we have in addition one linear restriction.[20]

The interpretation of these results is straightforward. If we round off m_G and m_s to 0.4, we get the following: an exogenous increase of one franc in the world stock of one given metal led to a long-run absorption of approximately 0.6 franc of this metal within the French economy, which then exported about 0.4 franc of

Table 2 ESTIMATION OF THE COINTEGRATION EQUATIONS

Variables	Equation 7	Equation 8
Estimated coefficients	$m_G = 0.37$	$m_s = 0.39$
Constant	$A = 603$	$B = 2,528$
R^2	0.97	0.92

Note: *t*-statistics are not reported because they cannot be used for statistical inference.

Source: See the text for author's computations.

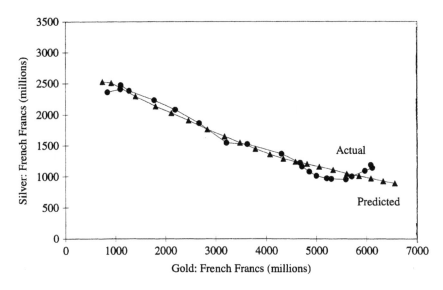

Figure 2 ACTUAL AND PREDICTED SPECIE HOLDINGS IN FRANCE, 1850–1870.
Source: Actual series, Flandreau, "Coin Memories." For the predicted series, see text.

the other metal. The estimated marginal rate of substitution was of two-thirds: two francs evicted for three francs absorbed). However, as illustrated in Figure 2, the ex-post structural rate of substitution over the period 1850 to 1870 (roughly corresponding to the slope of the actual holdings curve in Figure 2) was only about one-third: 5.2 billion worth of gold was gained, and 1.8 billion worth of silver was lost. The reason for this smaller structural effect is that the buffer role of the French economy only had to play on net disequilibria. This is why bimetallism was so flexible. Even when submitted to massive shocks on one side of the bullion market, France's pivotal role could always rely on additional help from the supply of the other metal.

To what forces was this unilateral scheme vulnerable? This is the question to which the article now turns.

TRADITIONAL THEORIES: A CRITIQUE

The Fundamentals Theory

The fundamentals theory emphasizes the role of rising silver output after discoveries of new outlets in Nevada and Mexico and improvements in silver production. This was, according to C. P. Kindleberger, a serious blow for bimetallism. France would not have possessed sufficient gold resources to stabilize the gold-silver ratio and would thus have been forced to end bimetallism by limiting silver coinage in 1873. However, the silver shock of the late 1860s and 1870s was far more limited than the gold shock of the 1850s—in fact it was about half as large. And since bimetallism had resisted the California glut, it could as well have survived the Comstock Lode.[21]

It is possible to discuss this thesis more rigorously by using the model developed in the previous section. That framework offers a simple way to test the fundamentals theory by determining what I. Fisher called the "structural limits" of bimetallism. As long as there remain gold and silver coins available for arbitrage purposes (joint circulation of gold and silver in France), the commercial ratio can be pegged to the legal ratio. Consistently, a necessary and sufficient condition for France's stabilizing influence to be effective is that it retain positive holdings of both currencies.[22] But this condition can be translated into a constraint upon the relative amounts of precious metals existing in the world. Formally:

$$\left(p_G M_G^b \geq 0 \ \& \ M_S^b \geq 0\right) \Leftrightarrow \frac{m_G}{\left(1-m_G\right)} \leq \frac{p_G G}{S} \leq \frac{\left(1-m_S\right)}{m_S} \tag{9}$$

Hence, to test bimetallism sustainability in the wake of changing fundamentals, one has to look at the evolution of the relative gold and silver resources after 1870 under the counterfactual assumption that the gold-silver ratio was pegged at 15.5. If the relative gold and silver resources remain within the estimated structural limits, one has to reject the fundamentals theory. Since m_G and m_s were estimated in the previous section, direct evaluation of the structural limits is straightforward. The test is performed in Figure 3. Not only would have

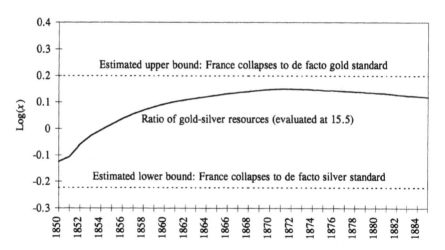

Figure 3 RISING SILVER PRODUCTION VERSUS STRUCTURAL LIMITS. *Source*: See the text. All variables are in logarithms.

France been able to buffer rising silver production but, in addition, the proportion of gold in its circulation would have remained dominant. Bimetallism was not doomed by fundamentals.

The Monetary Consequences of Bismarck

The previous conclusion however was obtained under the assumption that monetary geography would remain unchanged. The strategical theory, by contrast, takes into account the consequences of political moves such as regime changes in other countries. This in turn raises the question of the consequences of Germany's monetary reform.

In 1871 Germany had imposed on a defeated France an enormous indemnity of five billion francs, about one-third of France's GNP. The transfer took place in the years 1871 to 1873. In the meantime, Germany decided that its monetary unification would be implemented on the basis of gold. About two billion francs in silver waited to be exchanged against gold on world bullion markets.[23] This provides the background for the strategical theory of the emergence of the gold standard.[24] According to this view, Germany's 1871 decision to switch to gold increased the supply of silver and thus drove down its price, triggering a flight away from that metal, because "countries on a silver or bimetallic standard faced the possibility of substantial monetary inflation. As a result, the demonetization of silver became general after the mid-seventies." The theoretical nature of this view is recognizable. It *can* be characterized as a free-rider argument. As Henry Russell put it, "States were afraid of employing silver on account of the depreciation, and the depreciation continued because the states refused to employ it."[25]

From a logical point of view, this reasoning implies that given Germany's decision to move to gold other countries had no option but to abandon silver or face dramatic depreciation of their currency. This might have been true for smaller countries that were unable to influence the rest of the world, but what about France? Was French bimetallism strong enough to buffer Germany's reform? The implicit assumption of the strategical theory is that the transfer of five billion francs in gold from France to Germany combined with the sale on international markets of about two billion francs in silver would have forced the French economy on a de facto silver standard.

This view, however, is flawed by a number of historical and analytical inaccuracies. Contrary to a common belief, the French indemnity was not paid in specie.[26] The French government issued a perpetual bond—the so-called *Rente Thiers*—which was subscribed not only by French investors, but by foreigners as well. With the proceeds of that operation, it obtained short-term bills on various places (London, Hamburg, Amsterdam, and so on). The bills were then transferred to Germany. A mere 500 million French francs were paid in specie (of which 250 million was in silver). The German government, on the other hand, used a fraction of the bills (less than one-fifth) to obtain gold.[27] Germany was counting on sales of its silver holdings to complete its move to gold. Hence the monetary consequences of the indemnity as a shock on bullion markets were likely to be far more limited than usually suggested.

Clearly, Germany's policies (which amounted to the defection of a member of the silver bloc) would have had no effect on the gold-silver exchange rate nor on the silver-bloc price level, provided that France held a larger stock of gold than the stock of silver that Germany was about to sell. Intuitively, since there existed in 1870 an international equilibrium in which the gold-silver exchange rate was pegged around 15.5, where France held six billion French francs in gold and 1.2 billion in silver, and where Germany held two billion French francs in silver, there existed as well an international equilibrium in which the gold-silver exchange rate would still be pegged around 15.5, where France would hold 6 − 2 = 4 billion (FF) in gold and 1.2 + 2 = 3.2 billion (FF) in silver, and where Germany would hold two billion (FF) in gold.[28]

However, in order to assess more rigorously the net drain from the indemnity, one needs to go beyond the simple accounting developed above. In terms of the framework sketched out in the previous section, Germany's adoption of the gold standard would not merely cause a substitution in France's specie holdings. It would also provoke a permanent shift in the structural limits of bimetallism, for Germany's reform increased the aggregate (monetary) demand for gold at the expense of the aggregate (monetary) demand for silver. Yet Figure 4 (which contrasts the evolution of the world stocks of gold and silver to the new structural limits) shows that despite rising silver production and despite changing structural limits, France's circulation was strong enough to accommodate the shock. Although it is true that France would have ended up with a smaller proportion

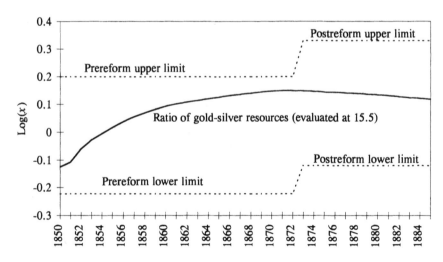

Figure 4 GERMANY'S REFORM: SHIFTING STRUCTURAL LIMITS. *Source:* See the text.

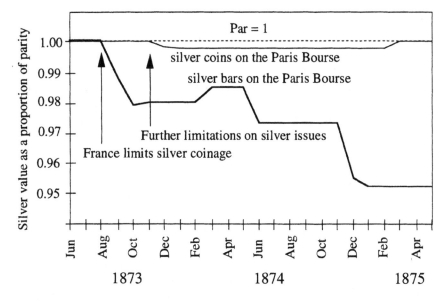

Figure 5 PRICE OF SLIVER ON THE PARIS STOCK EXCHANGE. *Source*: France, Archives de la Monnaiede Paris, *Cours Authentidues des Matières d'Or et d'Argent.*

of gold in its circulation (about 60 percent in 1880 against 85 percent in 1870), Germany's reform could not destroy bimetallism.

A final proof is given by looking at the price of silver on the Paris market. Despite intensifying sales of demonetized silver Thalers by the German government after July 1873, the quote for silver in Paris remained during the whole summer at or above the level at which it was becoming profitable to buy bars and pay the coinage charge. However, on the morrow of the very day when the coinage of silver had been limited, the price of silver fell through its floor (Figure 5). Obviously, it was the French decision that had produced the fall in the price of silver—not the other way around.

Transaction Costs Arguments

The transaction costs approach to the emergence of the gold standard was developed by Angela Redish. It is based on a ranking of the various possible monetary systems in terms of their advantage and constraints for payment purposes.[29] The underlying prejudice is that gold dominated silver as a mean of payment, implying that the question is not so much why the gold standard emerged but when it emerged. In this perspective, silver only fitted smaller transactions for which it dominated token monies, as long as token coins could be easily counterfeited. Silver coins by contrast had an intrinsic value equal to their nominal price, thus ruling out profitable counterfeiting. However, if some hard-to-copy substitute for silver coins could be designed, one would be able to reap the advantages associated with adopting a gold standard and give up silver. Moreover, Redish argued that since bimetallism required gold and silver holdings to adjust endogenously to shocks on international bullion markets, bimetallic economies could find themselves with inadequate silver circulation to meet their needs. This was an additional reason for preferring a gold standard with token coins for smaller change to a bimetallic system.

This led Redish to argue that the emergence of the gold standard was related to technological changes, and in particular, to the adoption of the steam press, which was able to produce high-quality token coins, thus preparing the ground for silver demonetization. As a result, the earlier adoption of the steam press in Britain caused an earlier introduction of the gold standard in Britain.[30]

This perspective has two flaws. If technological constraints had mattered that much, then France should have moved to gold in 1832 (when the Le Thonnelier steam press was designed), or in 1845 (when the Paris Mint adopted it) not in 1873.[31] Indeed, as Redish herself acknowledges, her explanation at most refers to the preconditions of the emergence of the gold standard. To obtain an interpretation of the timing of the emergence of the gold standard, one is thus bound to rely on a set of events that would have produced a 40-year delay after the technological problem was solved.

Second, it is incorrect to assert that the endogeneity of the supply of smaller silver currency was an inescapable consequence of the operation of bimetallism. The two questions could be easily separated by debasing the smaller silver coins (say up to two francs) and keeping the larger denominations (mainly the five-franc coin or ecu, worth about one silver dollar) in an unaltered state. This type of institutional change—which was introduced in the United States in the 1850s and in Italy, Switzerland, and Belgium in the early 1860s—meant that one could very well insulate transactions from arbitrages. This was done in France in 1864, and yet the gold standard waited until 1873.

Finally, the question boils down to determining whether gold was or was not a superior mean of payment relative to silver for international transactions. In fact, the seemingly intuitive claim that gold dominated silver turns out to be based on the incorrect assumption that shipping expenses depended on the weight of the shipment. Instead, as illustrated by Figure 6 (which gives a few figures for international shipments circa 1868 as reported by Ernest Seyd) the fees charged for international exports of *numeraire* were assessed on the value of the shipment. From this perspective the two metals were essentially perfect substitutes. In other words, there was no strong reason for preferring gold to silver for international transactions. An international silver standard would have done almost as well as an international gold standard.[32]

The Political Economy Approach

According to Giulio Gallarotti, the events of the 1870s have to be related to the growing progold agitation of the 1850s and 1860s when the urban-capitalist

SHIPPING OF BULLION.

RATES OF FREIGHT and INSURANCE
for BULLION from or to LONDON.

		Freight.	Insurance.
PARIS . By S. E. Railway or Messageries Impériales			
For sums between £800 and			
£4000—for every £100		4s 7d	
For sums above £4000		4s	$\frac{1}{16}$ o/o
BOULOGNE ⎫ By General Steam Navigation			
CALAIS . ⎪ Company			
ANTWERP ⎬ For sums up to £5000		$\frac{1}{8}$ o/o	
ROTTERDAM ⎪ ,, above ,,		$\frac{1}{16}$,,	$\frac{1}{16}$,,
HAMBURG ⎭			
ST. PETERSBURG By Steamer		$\frac{1}{4}$,,	$\frac{1}{4}$,,
MADRAS . ⎫ By Peninsular and Oriental			
BOMBAY . ⎬ Steamships .		2 o/o	$\frac{1}{4}$,,
CALCUTTA ⎭			
HONG KONG .	Do.	2$\frac{1}{4}$,,	$\frac{3}{4}$,,
SHANGHAI .	Do.	2$\frac{1}{2}$,,	1 ,,
AUSTRALIA .	Do.	2	1
	By Sailing Vessel	2d a 2$\frac{1}{2}$d per oz.	
NEW YORK Per Cunard Steamers, up to 10,000		$\frac{1}{4}$,,	
,, ,, 30,000		$\frac{1}{4}$,,	$\frac{1}{4}$ o/o in summer
,, ,, 50,000		$\frac{3}{16}$,,	
Above 50,000		$\frac{1}{8}$,,	$\frac{1}{2}$,, in winter
Other Steamers may charge lower rates.			
CALIFORNIA* . By Pacific Mail Steamers to			
Panama $\frac{1}{2}$ o/o		1$\frac{1}{2}$,,	1 ,,
,, Royal Mail Steamers from			
Panama to England $\frac{1}{2}$ o/o			
PANAMA . By Royal Mail Steamers			
For Gold		1$\frac{1}{4}$,,	
,, Silver		1$\frac{3}{8}$,,	$\frac{3}{4}$,,
VALPARAISO . By Pacific Steamers and			
Royal Mail			
For Gold		2$\frac{1}{4}$,,	1 ,,
,, Silver		2$\frac{1}{2}$	
RIO JANEIRO . Per Steamers to Southampton		1 ,,	
Delivered in London		1$\frac{1}{4}$,,	$\frac{3}{4}$,,
CAPE of GOOD ⎫ Per Union Steamship Com-			
HOPE . ⎭ pany from Southampton		1$\frac{1}{4}$ a 2 o/o	$\frac{3}{4}$ a $\frac{3}{4}$ o/o
MAURITIUS .	Do.	2 a 2$\frac{1}{2}$,,	$\frac{3}{4}$ a $\frac{3}{4}$ o/o

The rates of freight are exclusive of the usual Primages; the rates of Insurance
include discount and commission.

* The competition between rival Steamer Lines sometimes reduces the rates
of freight on the Pacific side to $\frac{1}{4}$ o/o.

Figure 6 ERNEST SEYD FIGURES FOR RATES OF FREIGHT AND INSURANCE
FOR BULLION. *Source*: The table is reprinted from Seyd, *Bullion*, p. 257.
The table shows that in general no distinction was made between gold and
silver. Quotes for bullion were given as a fraction of the value of the shipment.
Distinctions between gold and silver were only made for Panama and Valparaiso.
But they show *a contrario* how small differences could be.

interests (businessmen, bankers, creditors, and other proponents of stable money) were opposed to inflationary agrarian interests (farmers and landowners).[33] In this view, silver is identified with inflation and gold with stable prices. Once more, however, this analysis has to be qualified.

First, it is not quite rigorous to aggregate bankers and businessmen into one single progold category. Indeed, it is well known that during the 1860s and beyond bankers usually offered strong support for the bimetallic system. During the French Commissions Monétaires a majority of financiers consistently opposed moves to gold monometallism. For instance, during the *Enquete* of 1870 a large delegation of bankers came to support bimetallism. Bimetallism provided for the stability of the gold-silver exchange rate thus reducing the risk premium attached to lending money to nations on different standards. Besides, as pointed out by Henry Parker Willis, the operation of the dual standard offered constant arbitrage opportunities to international bankers.[34] Thus some important creditors supported bimetallism, and their support extended well beyond the demise of bimetallism. After 1876, Alphonse de Rothschild in France and Gerson von Bleichröder in Germany—both prominent bankers—offered material help to bimetallist campaigns.

Second, although it is true—as demonstrated by Richard S. Sayers—that nineteenth-century debates about the question of the standard may to some extent be interpreted as a debtor-creditor conflict, it was only after 1876 that the connection between bimetallism and easy-money interests was achieved.[35] This was in large part related to the observed decline in world prices that started after 1873 and was more pronounced for agricultural than for industrial goods. Hence gradually, across developed nations, silver men and agricultural interests met, and the various bimetallic leagues created in the 1880s received strong help from indebted farmers. In France for instance, the agrarian Méline was an open supporter of the reintroduction of the double standard. Similarly, as demonstrated by Eichengreen, votes for William Jennings Bryan's bimetallic ticket were substantially higher in agricultural districts. But this was well after the collapse of bimetallism.[36]

During the 1850s and 1860s by contrast, it was gold, not silver, that was seen as the inflationary metal. The flows of gold that poured on European markets after the Gold Rush led several economists to advocate gold demonetization to foster price stability.[37] Hence the 1850s and 1860s agitation in favor of gold and the subsequent demise of bimetallism in the early 1870s cannot be the mere result of a conservative agenda. Had the concern about price behavior been the main cause of the emergence of the gold standard, it should have worked earlier and produced in the late 1840s or early 1850s the emergence of the international silver standard. As a matter of fact, a number of countries, such as Belgium or Holland, had (temporarily or permanently) moved to silver for fear of gold inflation—and yet bimetallism had survived. What was the new ingredient of the 1870s?

A NEW VIEW ON THE EMERGENCE OF THE
INTERNATIONAL GOLD STANDARD: THE
STRATEGICAL THEORY RECONSIDERED

Externalities versus Switching Costs: Stable Bimetallism, 1850–1870

Having demonstrated that bimetallism was viable, we must explain the causes of its demise. It has often been observed that the 1860s—which began with the Anglo-French Trade Treaty—were years of considerable expansion in world trade, and of growing European integration. Between 1860 and 1870, European intratrade grew from about 59.5 percent to 65 percent.[38] This wave of free-trade brought into focus the advantages of improving communications. Import duties had to be reduced and transactions had to be facilitated. Economic interests generally favored a world currency. As John Stuart Mill had put it, "So much of barbarism, however, still remains in the transactions of most civilized nations, that almost all independent countries choose to assert their nationality by having, to their own inconvenience and that of their neighbours, a peculiar currency of their own."[39] Consistently, the period was characterized by a growing agitation in favor of currency uniformization, which was motivated by the desire to reduce transaction costs.

The logic underlying these movements can be clarified by analyzing the results of a survey that was conducted in France in 1868.[40] A number of chambers of commerce were asked to state their opinion about a possible move to gold as opposed to maintaining the status quo. Although everybody favored the notion that France should adjust its monetary system to that of its main trading partners, there was a good deal of controversy among the chambers of commerce as to what was the most suitable metal. The main source of disagreement was that every region tended to favor the currency of its main trading partner, which of course varied substantially. Regions trading with gold nations tended to vote for gold, whereas regions trading with silver nations voted for silver. Figure 7 reveals a number of telling contrasts. Atlantic or Mediterranean ports, which had extensive trade with South America or Asia, as well as some Eastern industrial centers, such as Strasbourg, which traded with Germany, Austria, or Holland, opposed silver demonetization arguing that bimetallism offered a convenient way to settle balances with silver- standard nations.[41] On the other hand, towns located along the Seine River (Paris, Elbeuf, and Rouen) or in northern France (Amiens, Saint-Quentin, Arras, or Abbeville) usually favored the gold standard, for gold was the only thing they needed to trade with England or Belgium. In each case, the degree of trade integration—often linked to geographic proximity— motivated preferences for one metal over the other. Of course, given that France was realizing about half of its aggregate trade with England, those who favored gold clearly outnumbered those who favored silver.

A similar pattern can be discerned in other countries, although we lack the detailed source of information that we have for France. In Germany, for instance,

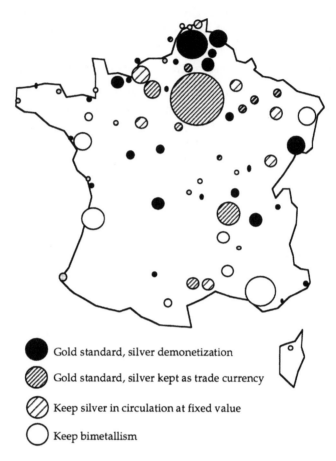

Gold standard, silver demonetization

Gold standard, silver kept as trade currency

Keep silver in circulation at fixed value

Keep bimetallism

Figure 11.7 VOTES OF THE CHAMBRES DE COMMERCE (1868). *Notes*: The map was constructed on the basis of the information provided by the various chambers of commerce regarding how they felt about a possible move to gold. For each chamber, answers reflect the opinion of the majority. Four reactions were observed: oppose any kind of alteration of bimetallism; oppose any kind of modification that would raise doubts about the value of silver écus; support a reform to gold with silver becoming a trade currency (no fixed exchange rate with gold); and support a full adoption of the gold standard. One chamber (Cherbourg) reported that no majority emerged, and is not represented on the map. The size of the various chambers is approximated on the basis of the aggregate discount business of the Bank of France's subsidiaries in each town, constructed on the basis of Levasseur, *Histoire*, p. 285–86. *Source*: Bibliothèque Nationale, Documents Relatifs à la Question Monétaire.

campaigns for the introduction of a gold currency developed through *Handelstage* meetings in 1861 and 1865. In these gatherings, a large number of leaders of the commercial and industrial communities recommended the adoption of a gold standard in order to facilitate foreign transactions.[42] Some, however, opposed these moves on the ground that it was preferable for Germany to stick to the silver-related Austrian system since Austria was the main trading partner of several German states.[43] In 1868 a third *Handelstag* convened in Berlin. A majority vote decided that in addition to moving to a gold standard, Germany should base its coins on the French unit. That a majority of Germans wanted to adopt a franc-related unit at a time when French trading with Germany opposed silver demonetization illustrates very well the mechanism at work. In fact, even the British favored a partial debasement of the pound, that would bring it down to match a proposed 25-franc gold coin.[44]

The forces at work may be described as resulting from strategic externalities. One tends to favor the currency that is used by one's main trading partner. As a result, the utility of using one given currency is an increasing function of the number of agents that have adopted it. There is thus a trend towards the adoption of one single currency. Of course, by themselves, these externalities were not liable to produce any specific system. A silver standard might have emerged as well: strategic externalities imply that everything is ruled by path dependency. In the 1860s, the odds were favorable for gold. Britain—the main trading nation—was on gold, and thanks to the Gold Rush, several important continental traders (France, Belgium, Switzerland, and Italy) had a large proportion of their circulation in gold. This logic culminated in the votes of the 1867 International Monetary Conference held in Paris, which had opted for a gold franc and the 25-franc gold coin as being the most natural basis for world monetary unification.

Is it to say that the emergence of the international gold standard in the 1870s was a pure result of network externalities? Not quite. The nonbinding agreement reached in 1867 revealed deeper questions, the importance of which became obvious when the technical aspects of the reform came under discussion. The advantages of having one common standard were offset by substantial switching costs and feasibility constraints.[45] When faced with the expenses of the reform, several large countries were much less inclined to move to gold. In France, demonetizing silver would require getting rid of at least one billion francs in écus.[46] Since the reform meant that France would renounce its role as an arbitrageur of last resort for the gold-silver exchange rate, it was not clear how the écus could be sold. Losses were to be expected. Alternatively, some institutional scheme for pegging the value of the écus might be designed, but it was not clear how. Besides, the government was warned that if the reform went amok, this would be a cause of blame against the regime—a serious problem in a period of extension of the franchise.[47] Why change a system that had delivered exchange-rate stability with all kinds of trading partners that had performed quite well so far and whose alteration was opposed by a significant portion of the population? Thus, the various Ministers of Finances of the late 1860s resisted the reform.[48]

Germany's situation was even trickier, as acknowledged by the Prussian delegate to the 1867 international conference.[49] Germany's strong reliance on imports of raw products made it especially concerned about having a convenient means of payment to purchase through London (if not from England) the goods it required.[50] Moreover, Germany's exchange stability against gold nations was only indirectly achieved through the agency of the French system. This meant that the fate of German exchange-rate stability in terms of the pound was to a certain extent under French control. Finally, the northern German states that were regrouped since 1866 in a German confederacy were contemplating the possibility of a unification of their currencies, and had accordingly transferred the power to rule over monetary questions to a protofederal parliament. It was propitious to take advantage of a possible recoinage to change more radically Germany's monetary system.

On the other hand, Germany's already substantial silver circulation (an estimated two billion of French francs) designated it as the country that was the least likely to operate an easy reform. A move from one standard to the other one could not be achieved overnight. It was not possible to throw on international bullion markets two billion in silver and wake up to a gold standard. Instead, gold reserves had to be accumulated in advance. The only option was to first purchase a certain amount of gold, then implement gold convertibility, and eventually complete the reform by gradually exchanging silver Thalers for gold on world markets. Hence, two difficulties had to be faced. First, Germany had to solve the financial problem, (find the resources to purchase gold). Second it had to solve the liquidation problem, (be able to exchange silver against gold on good terms).[51]

Both problems were enormous. The amount of gold that had to be accumulated to start up the reform can be estimated at about one billion Reichsmarks. This is indeed what Germany would coin between 1871 and 1873 before it launched its transition to gold.[52] But the average income that the federal government would collect after 1875 was only about 600 million Reichsmarks.[53] The reform thus did cost more than future annual receipts of the federal government, and in the late 1860s unification prospects were far from obvious. There was no way that before 1870 a nonunified Germany could easily obtain such funds. It is well known that in the late 1860s Prussia, which was leading the unification movement, was desperately short of cash. Worse still, borrowing to move to gold had to be achieved with the help of the banking elite, which as argued above, opposed any move away from bimetallism.[54]

Germany's liquidation problem was in no way smaller. One possibility was to obtain France's passive cooperation, that is, sell silver and hope that French arbitrageurs would not be disrupted by French monetary authorities in their buying of demonetized Thalers and selling of French gold coins. Given the huge size of Germany's circulation, it was unlikely that the French could be taken by surprise. J. Prince-Smith (later a leader of the bimetallist party in Germany) had very neatly exposed the dilemma: "France may not passively attend German reform . . . but instead may change its monetary system as soon as we would decide to throw our silver on international markets."[55]

Finally, our conclusion is that the 1860s debates about the adoption of the gold standard reveal that two key factors shaped the controversies. The microeconomic element of strategic externalities and economies of scale that pushed towards currency uniformization was counteracted by the constraints associated with moving from one standard to the other one. And this difficulty, which was even larger for Germany than for France, in turn stabilized the policies of smaller nations, whose monetary system was tied to that of their larger partners.

The War and the Indemnity: Bimetallism Destabilized

The war was to change this situation. The huge indemnity that Germany imposed on France solved the financial problem. The five billion of French francs represented more than what was needed to purchase gold. Moreover, the German government apparently felt that the liquidation problem was fixed as well, perhaps because it seemed unlikely that a crippled France could oppose Germany's transition. Between 1871 and 1873, a series of votes in the German parliament prepared the introduction of the gold standard.[56] Massive gold coinage was undertaken and as mentioned earlier, the Germans started silver sales during the summer of 1873. Despite some opposition by people like Adolf Soetbeer and Ludwig Bamberger who urged that silver sales be started without delay, German officials had decided to wait until France's financial situation was sound enough so that the old bimetallic machine once more could be put into action. This way officials believed that they would be able to dispose conveniently of the old Thalers.

At first, the French government did not react, for it was busy completing the payment of the indemnity. However, on September 5, 1873, the last portion of the indemnity was transferred. The next day France limited silver coinage to 280,000 francs per day, a decision that, as argued above, triggered the fall in the price of silver. Three elements appear to have determined the French decision. First, it must be emphasized that there was no panicking on behalf of the French monetary authorities. An inspection of the government archives (and in particular of the mint archives) provides evidence of France's confidence in its monetary system. They show conclusively that the minister of finance was to a large extent thinking in terms of the model described above. It was understood that Germany's reform would have mostly a substitution effect, silver driving out a limited portion of the gold circulation. For instance, in a memo addressed to his representatives for the January 1874 Latin Union meeting that convened in order to deal with the effects of Germany's adoption of the gold standard, Minister Pierre Magne (a strong supporter of the dual standard) wrote: "Under the influence of silver demonetization in Germany, this metal tends to be coined here in uncommon quantities ... . This however is a *purely transitory phenomenon.*"[57]

In fact the immediate instinct behind the limitation of silver coinage was anti-German. That this decision took place on the very day after the last part of the indemnity was paid is more than a hint. For the French, the indemnity had already been a large enough tribute. Moreover, the French perceived that removing the ladder that the Germans were using to reach for the gold standard, could lead to a change in Germany's policy. Indeed, during the January 1874 meeting of the Latin Union members, the French delegates emphasized that the Germans had not yet succeeded in disposing of their silver and that a reversal of their actions was still possible. France's position was simple. As long as Germany would not complete (or renounce) its reform, France would not re-establish free-silver coinage. This conditional strategy would later be known as the *attitude expectante* (wait and see policy).

The second reason that prompted France's decision was more domestic by nature. Paying the indemnity had put France's financial system under considerable stress, and Germany's selling of silver and buying of gold was likely to renew the pressures. Indeed, in periods of intense arbitrage activity, the sensitivity of the Paris market to foreign shocks usually increased. This had already been the case in the 1850s, when France had to buffer the effects of the Gold Rush.[58] Moreover, given that a large number of foreign investors had purchased the French indemnity bonds, the administration could think that it was wise to send a signal of commitment to fixed exchange rates with gold nations. Although the French were generally confident in the sustainability of bimetallism, they had to persuade foreigners as well.

Finally, and most importantly, the limitation of silver coinage was a precautionary and transitory decision, which was not perceived by government officials as a challenge to France's bimetallism. As mentioned by the Minister of Finance, "the only goal of [the limitation of silver coinage was] to protect [France's] circulation against foreign influences, and to *maintain it in an unaltered state.*"[59] A year later, the Directeur du Mouvement Général des Fonds would again insist that "there must not be any doubt as to what are the reasons that guided the French administration when it decided to limit silver coinage. This decision did not imply *any desire to move towards a single standard system.* Having observed that the normal conditions of circulation were threatened by exterior and incidental moves, it was decided to take a *precautionary and revocable decision.*"[60] Hence in early 1874, neither France nor Germany was properly speaking on a gold standard. While Germany had only one foot on gold, France had only one foot off bimetallism. However, France's decision to limit silver coinage— like the pebble that causes the avalanche—triggered the emergence of the international gold standard.

In Germany, the law of 1873 had specified that the demonetization would have to take into account the capacity of the market.[61] In practice, there was a threshold price under which no sales would take place. Germany waited for the price of silver to go up before it could get rid of its old Thalers. The markets waited for the German government to get rid of its holdings before they would consider bidding up the price of silver. And of course the outcome of this game between speculators and the German government was one in which only limited sales could occur.[62] Between 1873 and 1879—when German sales were officially suspended—a mere third of the initial stock of Thalers had been sold. France's policy had thus been successful in effectively forcing Germany to keep most of its silver holdings. However, given the bulk of the legislation that had been voted in the early 1870s, it had failed to produce an immediate reversal of Germany's policies. Instead, the Reichsbank was compelled to carry on the transition not by selling silver (as initially planned) but by attracting gold through discount rate increases. This way, gold was taken from European markets (chiefly from London), thus leading to retaliatory increases in the Bank of England discount rate.[63]

But German difficulties were mirrored by a corresponding problem that France had created for itself; it now held a large amount of écus, whose intrinsic value was smaller than their nominal price. One could not have it both ways. Either the market was allowed to arbitrage deviations in the gold-silver ratio, in which case the gold-silver exchange rate would be pegged by market interventions around the legal ratio, and the quantity of écus in France's circulation would endogenously adjust to disequilibria on world bullion markets; or the monetary demand for silver was rationed, in which case increased supply of this metal would inevitably produce a fall in its market price, thus rising doubts about overvalued écus. In other words, the view that France's commitment to bimetallism could be credibly maintained while silver coinage was limited relied on a misconception. Indeed, the administration's decision to introduce quotas on silver coinage—although reassuring to foreign investors—was interpreted by arbitrageurs as bad news for bimetallism. The Rothschild Archives illustrate the growing anxiety as bankers sought to obtain insider information about the government's next move.[64]

Two courses were possible. A first possibility was a speculative attack outcome—a run where the public would try to give up the écus. Of course, this would result in a fall in the price of the écus, a corresponding loss for their holders, and possibly a monetary contraction (since part of the nominal value of the money stock would be destroyed).[65] Alternatively, this could be avoided if some agent was ready to step in and guarantee the value of silver coins. This is where the Bank of France entered the picture.

On November 19, 1873, silver coinage was further reduced to 150,000 francs per day, and a small discount of one-thousandth appeared on the silver écus (Figure 5). It was reported that one would accept silver coins only to the extent that he could transfer them to the Bank of France.[66] Since the Bank was bound to accept écus in payment, the discount at which the écus were trading could not be larger than the transaction cost associated with purchasing them on the market and exchanging them at the Bank against notes. Although modest, the discount meant that the écus were no longer taken at their face value. As a result the silver écus flowed into the reserves of the Bank of France. In a matter of months (between November 1873 and March 1874), the proportion of silver in the Bank's reserves in Paris jumped from 25 percent to 50 percent. Similarly, whereas in 1873 the Bank held about 10 percent of the gold and silver circulation, its share in the aggregate silver holdings rose to almost 60 percent (contrasted with 15 percent for gold). The fear of demonetization was keeping more than one-half of the total stock of silver in the vaults. The market was using the Bank of France to insure itself against silver demonetization. If such an event did occur, the Bank would have to pay for it.

Thus the problem was now with the Bank of France and, not surprisingly, it started to worry about the amounts of silver coinage that would be authorized.[67] It knew indeed that those issues would eventually end up in its reserves, potentially displacing an equivalent amount of gold. As the Minister Léon Say would declare a few years later, "any increase of the bank silver holdings only makes the whole reserve more uncertain."[68] Hence the Bank of France found appropriate to sterilize the addition to its silver reserves. Only increases in the gold component could lead it to lower its discount rate.[69] The Bank then started to lobby actively in favor of low limits on the annual silver issues. As long as free-silver coinage would not be reintroduced (allowing the market to stabilize the gold-silver ratio), the Bank would oppose large quotas. Finally, in 1876, the Bank succeeded in imposing a bill that fully suspended silver coinage in France.[70]

France was gradually abandoning the silver arena. The overtures of the American government in favor of a coordinated reintroduction of bimetallism (the so-called American Conference that was held in Paris in 1878) were met by reluctance on behalf of the French authorities, for Germany had refused to participate and had made clear that it was definitely not ready to renege on its adoption of the gold standard. But without a change in Germany's policies, France did not want to modify its attitude. And without France's participation, the conference was to fail, only leading the Latin Union to align on France's 1876 decision, and thus reinforcing the drift away from bimetallism.[71]

When it became clear that the industrialized world had irremediably abandoned silver, Germany finally reconsidered its policies. It had now to come to terms with the fact that it would never be able to sell its silver at the 15.5 par value, or even near it. Some advocated a move to bimetallism, and there is evidence that Bismarck was not unfavorable to it. But the fierce opposition of parliament, which reflected the bourgeoisie consensus for stable prices—silver was by then clearly identified with inflation— succeeded in forcing Bismarck to retreat. The most Bismarck could do—under wild attacks that he was preparing the reintroduction of bimetallism—was to decide the official suspension of silver sales in 1879, a measure that he presented as beneficial to both Germany and mankind.[72] At that date, France and Germany found themselves in a very analogous situation. Although they had both stabilized their exchange rate in terms of gold, neither was fully on gold, both had a substantial silver circulation that was still legal tender, neither could sell overvalued silver holdings without making huge losses, and both needed an active commitment of their central bank to peg the value of their silver coins. This situation would come to be known as "limping bimetallism."

Finally, in the wake of the noncooperative game that the two continental powers had played between 1871 and 1879, most European nations had switched to gold, thus rendering a move back to bimetallism increasingly more difficult to implement. Ironically, smaller nations such as Denmark, Norway, and Sweden— which had adopted gold in the wake of Franco- German trap-thy-neighbor policies—swiftly completed their reform by rapidly selling their limited silver holdings on world markets.

CONCLUSION

This article argued that the four most popular explanations of the emergence of the international gold standard were probably too naive. Instead, the transformations of the 1870s reflected shifts in the constraints and benefits from deviating from the previous regime. Until 1870, Germany had believed that moving to gold was impractical, and France found it costly and not very rewarding. After all, bimetallism had performed well, and it was simpler to amend it mildly (by debasing smaller coins) than to discard it. This situation was modified by the Franco-Prussian War. Thanks to the war indemnity, Germany was now able to loosen its budget constraint. France, on the other hand, was not prepared to help Germany and limited silver coinage. This left that metal without the backing of arbitrages, a crucial feature in a bimetallic regime. At that point bimetallism (as a unilateral stabilization scheme) was virtually dead. The central banks of France and Germany were then forced to step in and provide a backing to silver coins. Hence, the international gold standard did not emerge from the structural contradictions of bimetallism, nor did it result from the adoption of fully fledged gold-standard constitutions. Rather, it was introduced through a change in central banks' policies, with monetary authorities pegging the value of both notes and silver coins in terms of gold.

Clearly, failure to cooperate had been an important ingredient of this great transformation. On the surface, this conclusion seems to give some credence to the strategic view. However, contrary to the crudest version of this analysis, this article demonstrated that the collapse of bimetallism after Germany moved to gold was avoidable provided that France be induced to maintain unlimited silver coinage. Does that mean that there was a French crime of 1873, of much more dramatic consequences than the American one?[73] Indeed, French policymakers seemed to underrate the fact that their actions would undermine the credibility of their commitment to bimetallism. Likewise, they clearly overlooked that their moves, by leading to the demise of silver as a monetary metal, would have deflationary consequences. However, this was not perceived by the Germans either.

For had German authorities realized it, they should have stepped back, instead of going further.[74] But in the fight for gold that developed in the early 1870s, staying pegged to gold became a matter of national pride. Thus there was a French crime of 1873, but there was a German crime, too.

All this has a familiar ring. Discussions of the international gold standard usually oppose its golden age (1880 to 1914) to its gloomy age (1920s and 1930s). During the latter period, it is said, failure of international cooperation was responsible for the depth of the depression. By symmetry, some authors have claimed that international cooperation was an essential element of the period 1880 to 1914.[75] The interpretation of the emergence of the gold standard advanced here casts serious doubts on this view. Indeed, most of the evils at work during the interwar years (competition among nations to attract gold, inability to enforce a coordinated outcome, neglect of the international effects of national monetary policies, and the Franco-German rivalry) were already operating during the 1870s. Not only did these forces contribute to the long deflation initiated in 1873, but they also led to the emergence and shaping—at least in continental Europe—of the international gold standard. It was in 1873, not in the 1920s, that the "Golden Fetters" were tied.

Appendices

APPENDIX 1: DERIVATION OF THE LONG-RUN EQUILIBRIUM RELATIONS

The strategy followed in the first part of the article was to obtain explicit long-run equilibrium relations between world bullion stocks and specie holdings in the bimetallic bloc. There are several advantages associated with this approach. In particular, modeling equilibrium relations allows to circumvent the well-known simultaneous equations bias that usually characterizes separate estimation of demand and supply equations.

While the model allows for considering as many countries as wanted, it is convenient to aggregate the demand for monetary silver in the silver bloc with the demand for nonmonetary silver in the three blocs. This new demand schedule is labeled the "pseudo silver-bloc monetary demand function" (hereafter S_n). Given the proportionality hypothesis, this new variable only depends on prices, real income, and a set of exogenous parameters. The same procedure is applied to gold, thus defining a "pseudo gold-bloc monetary demand function" (hereafter G_n). This gives the new parameters of the new pseudo-money demand functions:

$$m_G^m = \left(k^g + \mu_G^g\right)\beta_G + \mu_G^s\beta_S + \mu_G^b \tag{10}$$

$$m_S^m = \mu_S^g\beta_G + \left(k^s + \mu_G^s\right)\beta_S + \mu_S^b \tag{11}$$

Finally, setting $k^b = k$, $Y^b = Y$, and calling G_m (respectively S_m) the demand for monetary gold (silver) in the bimetallic bloc, gives (G and S being the outstanding quantities of gold and silver; on the exogeneity of bullion supply, see Eichengreen and McLean, "Supply"):

$$G_n = m_G^m\left(p/p_G\right)Y \qquad S_n = m_S^m pY \tag{12}$$

$$kpY = p_G G_M + S_M \tag{13}$$

$$G_M + G_n = G \qquad S_M + S_n = S \tag{14}$$

This model can be easily solved, giving the following equations:

$$p_G G_M = p_G G \cdot (1 - m_G) - S \cdot m_G \tag{15}$$

$$S_M = -p_G G \cdot m_S + S \cdot (1 - m_S) \tag{16}$$

where

$$m_G = \frac{m_G^m}{k + m_G^m + m_S^m} \quad \text{and} \quad m_S = \frac{m_S^m}{k + m_G^m + m_S^m}$$

APPENDIX 2: ASSESSING SUSTAINABILITY: ESTIMATING THE STRUCTURAL LIMITS OF BIMETALLISM AND THE RATIO OF RELATIVE RESOURCES IN GOLD AND SILVER.

Methodology

Since the overall stocks of gold and silver typically exhibit a unit root (indeed they are the sum of random annual production), so are by construction the holdings of gold and silver in the French economy (they are a linear combination of integrated variables). This can be checked by performing Dickey-Fuller tests (Appendix Table 1). For bullion stocks, these tests were implemented for the period 1849 to 1885 (corresponding to the period for which we make the counterfactual assessment). For French specie holdings, the tests were limited to the period 1849 to 1873. Indeed, only in a bimetallic regime does nonstationarity of both specie stocks in France hold. The tests lead to reject stationarity for the four series.

It is now clear that equations 15 and 16 may be interpreted as long-run equilibrium relations between nonstationary variables. That these nonstationary variables are integrated can be checked by running regressions for G_m and S_m on gold and silver stocks. These (unrestricted) regressions give Durbin-Watson statistics equal to 0.69 for equation 15 and 0.5 for equation 16, leading to the rejection of the null that residuals are nonstationary (the 5 percent critical value is 0.38). This suggests applying the cointegration methodology (Hendry, "Econometric

Appendix Table 1 TESTING FOR NONSTATIONARITY

Series	G	S	G_m	S_m
Dickey-Fuller	2.50*	3.30*	1.5*	0.7*

* = significant at the 5 percent level.

Source: See the text for author's computations. Entries show the result of the ordinary Dickey-Fuller test.

Modelling"; and Engle and Granger, "Cointegration"). From an econometric point of view, $(1, 1 - m_G, -m_G)$ and $(1, - m_s, 1 - m_s)$ can be interpreted as being the (restricted) cointegrating vectors of each equation. Least squares techniques provide super-consistent estimates of these cointegrating vectors.

Data

The following series were used. Specie holdings in France are from Flandreau, "Coin Memories"; annual gold and silver production are from Hay, "Stock." Hay's estimates would be later used in the Reports of the Director of the U.S. Mint. These figures (which start in 1849) allow the construction of a series for the world stock of gold and silver, up to a constant representing the stocks of bullion in 1849. For those latter, it is safer not to rely on the estimates that may be found in the literature (for instance Soetbeer's *Matériaux*). Indeed these figures have been strongly criticized by Alexander Del Mar who joked on Soetbeer's "fertile imagination" (*History*, pp. 401–02).

This problem can nonetheless be circumvented by rewriting the world stock of gold (respectively silver) as the sum of the series of annual production of gold (silver) during year i, called $\Delta G(i)$ ($\Delta S(i)$) and of the initial gold (silver) holdings, as of 1849:

$$G(t) = \sum_{i=1850}^{t} \Delta G(i) + G(1849) \tag{17}$$

$$S(t) = \sum_{i=1850}^{t} \Delta S(i) + S(1849) \tag{18}$$

Substituting these relations into equation 15, we get the new equations:

$$p_G G_M(t) = (1 - m_G) p_G \left\{ \sum_{i=1850}^{t} \Delta G(i) + G(1849) \right\}$$
$$- m_G \left\{ \sum_{i=1850}^{t} \Delta S(i) + S(1849) \right\} \tag{19}$$

$$S_M(t) = -m_S p_G \left\{ \sum_{i=1850}^{t} \Delta G(i) + G(1849) \right\}$$
$$+ (1 - m_S) \left\{ \sum_{i=1850}^{t} \Delta S(i) + S(1849) \right\} \tag{20}$$

These equations may be rewritten as:

$$p_G G_M(t) = (1 - m_G) p_G \left\{ \sum_{i=1850}^{t} \Delta G(i) \right\} - m_G \left\{ \sum_{i=1850}^{t} \Delta S(i) \right\} + A \tag{21}$$

$$S_M(t) = -m_S p_G \left\{ \sum_{i=1850}^{t} \Delta G(i) \right\} + (1 - m_S) \left\{ \sum_{i=1850}^{t} \Delta S(i) \right\} + B \tag{22}$$

where $A = p_G(1 - m_G)G(1849) - m_G S(1849)$ and $B = -m_S p_G G(1849) + (1 - m_S) S(1849)$.

Hence estimation of equations 15 and 16 as transformed in equations 21 and 22 gives not only estimates of the cointegrating vector but estimates for A and B as well. These can be used to solve for $S(1849)$ and $G(1849)$.

APPENDIX 3: THE MONETARY CONSEQUENCES OF BISMARCK

In light of the equations presented in Appendix 1, it is easy to interpret the consequences of a change in the monetary standard of a given country. In the case of Germany, the operation may be described as a defection from the silver bloc to the gold bloc. This affects the parameters of the pseudo-money demand functions for both gold and silver. For a given level of prices, the pseudo-money demand for gold shifts upwards while the pseudo-money demand for silver moves downwards. The impact of this change on the sustainability of bimetallism depends on the size of the defecting economy. The larger it is the harder it will be to accommodate the resulting shift.

A natural way to model the consequences of Germany's reform is thus to follow its implications on m_G and m_s. The postreform parameter of the pseudo-money demand for gold is increased by a coefficient corresponding to Germany's monetary needs. On the other hand, the postreform parameter of the pseudo-money demand for silver is reduced by that very same coefficient. Formally, we have:

$$\bar{m}_G^m = m_G^m + k^g \beta_g \tag{23}$$

$$\bar{m}_S^m = m_S^m + k^s \beta_S \tag{24}$$

Defining α as the coefficient of proportionality between the demand for money in the bimetallic bloc and the demand for money in the defecting country (the larger k, the smaller α) yields

$$\alpha = k^s \beta_S / k \tag{25}$$

Finally using equations 23, 24, and 25 and substituting into the formula for m_G and m_S gives the postreform parameters:

$$\bar{m}_G = m_G + \alpha\left(1 - m_G - m_S\right) \tag{26}$$

$$\bar{m}_S = m_S - \alpha\left(1 - m_G - m_S\right) \tag{27}$$

Since the prereform parameters are known, estimating the postreform parameters only requires evaluating α, the size of Germany's money demand schedule with respect to France's money demand schedule. This can be easily done by computing the average relative size of Germany's to France's specie holdings during the period 1870 to 1878 (on the basis of Flandreau, "Coin Memories"; and Flelfferich, *Reform*). This gives 0.27, implying that Germany's holdings represented between one-third and one-fourth of France's holdings. Substituting this into equations 26 and 27 yields

$$\bar{m}_G = 0.43$$

$$\bar{m}_S = 0.32$$

from which the new structural limits can be derived. To conclude, it is important to note that these estimates of the new structural limits are extremely robust. Assuming for instance that the evaluation of a has a bias as large as 50 percent either way would not change the conclusion.

*The author owes an enormous debt to Barry Eichengreen who asked several of the questions that motivated this article. Thanks are also due to J.-C. Asselain, Forrest Capie, Milton Friedman, Peter Garber, Avner Greif, Pierre-Cyrille Hautcoeur, John James, Charles Kindleberger, D. Lacoue- Labarthe, Maurice Lévy-Leboyer, Ian McLean, Alan Milward, Gilles Postel-Vinay, Massimo Roccas, Jean-Laurent Rosenthal, Pierre Sicsic, participants to seminars at Berkeley, Stanford, the OFCE (the Convergences en Histoire Economique Seminar), the Institut Universitaire des Hautes Etudes Internationales at Geneva, and the University of Bordeaux, as well as to participants to the 1995 ASSA meetings in Washington, for their suggestions. The careful and extensive comments and criticisms of Joel Mokyr as well as of two anonymous referees proved extremely helpful. Of course none of them should be held responsible for the views expressed in this article.

Notes

1 For a description of the evolution of nineteenth-century monetary geography, see Eichengreen and Flandreau "Geography."

2 Kindleberger, *Financial History*, pp. 67–68.

3 Kenwood and Lougheed, *Growth*, chap. 7.

4 Redish, "Persistence."

5 Gallarotti, "Scramble" and *Anatomy.*

6 For a formal analysis of the interaction between network externalities and switching costs, see Dowd and Greenaway, "Currency Competition." In this model, the advantage of using one given currency depends positively on the number of people who use it. On the other hand moving to a new currency entails expenses. As a result, instead of tending to converge towards a single currency world, one converges towards a regime in which several currency areas may coexist.

7 The counterfactual assessment of the effects of not suspending silver coinage in the 1870s has a long tradition in the U.S. context. See for instance Hütter, *L'incidence économique*; Drake, "Reconstruction"; and Friedman, "Crime." Studies of the same issue in the French context include Mertens *Naissance*; and recently Oppers "Was the Worldwide Shift." Both tend to reject the conventional view, as I do here. This article, however, is the first to rely on a sound time series. (Flandreau, "Coin Memories"). In addition, it provides an alternative explanation of the emergence of the gold standard. Milward, "Origins," contains a good survey of the historiography on the emergence of the gold standard.

8 For instance, Collins ("Sterling Exchange Rates") reports that between 1846 and 1880 coefficients of the variation of exchange rates between gold, silver, and bimetallic countries are usually smaller than 2 percent.

9 Eichengreen, *Gold Standard.* See also Roccas, "L'italia."

10 For the United States, see Laughlin, *History*; for Belgium, see Kauch, *Banque*; for Italy, see Luzzatti, "Delle Attinenze"; and for France, see Flandreau, "Les règles."

11 Flandreau, "As Good." For a dissenting view see Oppers, "Arbitrage," which does not estimate arbitrage costs, however. For a concurring view, see Friedman, "Bimetallism."

12 At the same date, France held one billion French francs in gold while annual silver production was of about 250 million.

13 Correlations reported in Table 1 are at least as strong as those reported for the gold-standard period by McCloskey and Zecher, "Success."

14 As a result of Walras's Law we can drop one market, for instance, the commodity market. My model may be shown to derive from an explicit general equilibrium system, with Cobb-Douglas utility function and cash in advance constaints. The Cobb-Douglas specification (although admitedly not general) has the convenient implication that demand for each commodity is dependent only on own price and endowments. This renders the model tractable and allows straight-forward estimation.

15 A "proper" bimetallic equilibrium must have $M_G^b > 0$ and $M_S^b > 0$, that is strictly positive holdings of both metals.

16 Note that the model allows for different monetization behaviors in different blocs: the only requirement is that the relative monetization behavior be stable across time.

17 To see this compare Hay, "Stock"; Soetbeer, *Matériaux*; and Mertens, *Naissance.* Note that in equations 7 and 8, the stock of gold and silver (not the annual production) is the relevant concept. Hence, one also needs an estimate for the stocks of bullion in 1849. The trouble is that, as argued by Hay, the figures for 1849 are nothing more than "vague assumptions" (Hay, "Stocks," p. 172). Fortunately, equations 7 and 8 allow for direct estimation of the stocks of gold and silver in 1849 (see the appendices). World bullion holdings are estimated to be of about 5.6 billion francs (for gold) and 7.5 billion francs for silver. "Vague assumption" may be found in Soetbeer, *Matériaux*, p. 10.

18 The U.S. economy—which made a much more extensive use of notes than the French did—held at most one-tenth of the bimetallic bloc stock of specie. Other bimetallic countries (Belgium, Switzerland, and Italy) relied heavily on French currency as part of

the Latin Union (see Willis, *History*). Moreover, during most of the period under study, the United States and Italy experienced episodes of inconvertible paper, which probably further reduced their stock of specie and hence their weight in the bimetallic bloc.

19 This survey was used by the French statistician Foville to construct an estimate of the stock of specie in 1878: His estimate, however (see Sicsic, "Estimation"), was biased. Flandreau "Coin Memories," offers a method to clear the bias and retropolate the series back to 1840. Oppers, "Was the Worldwide Shift," by contrast, uses Foville's biased estimate directly and retropolates the series by merely subtracting from Foville's figure the data for annual coinage. This approach omits losses from exports, thus weakening any inference about bimetallism's sustainability.

20 The super-consistency property provides a way to test the validity of the restriction that coefficients in each equation sum to unity. Indeed, suppose that the restriction does not hold. This means that we are not picking the correct cointegration vector. As a result, residuals must be nonstationary. A CRDW test performed for equations 7 and 8 gives statistics at 0.5 and 0.51, respectively, which are above the 0.34 criterion for nonstationarity. Hence, residuals are stationary, and the restriction does hold.

21 The rising-silver-production argument is often coupled with another theory that emphasizes the "additional" effect of decreasing demand for silver resulting from reduced trade surpluses in silver-standard countries (de Cecco, *Money*; and Gallarotti, "Scramble"). There is no reason to distinguish between both phenomena because they were the two sides of the same coin. Indeed, we have shown in the previous section that the adjustment of rising gold production during the 1850s and 1860s required that silver be displaced from bimetallic countries to silver-standard countries and thus created a transitory trade surplus in the silver bloc. This was known as the "Eastern drain" (Cairnes, *Essays*). Consistently, rising silver production after 1865 reduced the trade surplus of silver-standard countries against nonsilver countries.

22 Fisher, "Mechanics." Note that if ones introduces uncertainty, the necessary and sufficient condition represented in (equation 9) becomes a necessary condition. The distinction, however, is not very meaningful as long as annual bullion production remains small relative to world bullion holdings (a situation that is confirmed by the data). In this case the boundaries associated with equation (9) virtually coincide with the boundaries that would be derived from a stochastic version of the model.

23 Mertens, *Naissance*; and Helfferich, *Money*.

24 This explanation was originally suggested by Russell, *International Monetary Conferences*, and has permeated most accounts of the period: Willis, *History*; Mertens, *Naissance*; Kenwood and Lougheed, *Growth*; Yeager, *International Monetary Relations*; de Cecco, *Money*; and Gallarotti, "Scramble."

25 Kenwood and Lougheed, *Growth*, p. 121; and Russell, *International Monetary Conferences*, p. 215.

26 Say, *Rapport*.

27 The rest of the indemnity was used to improve the public finances of the new Empire and was evenly spent both at home and abroad.

28 The estimates for the stock of specie in France and Germany are from Flandreau "Coin Memories"; and Helfferich, *Money*, respectively. Of course, through wealth effects, France may have wanted to reduce a bit its specie holdings (its government was now 5 billions more indebted, which meant higher taxes in the future), while Germany would want to increase them (its government was 5 billion richer). However, given that the 5 billions indemnity represented perhaps 10 percent of the wealth of Frenchmen measured as the sum of bonds and stocks, the reduction in specie holdings was likely to be quite moderate. Indeed the net specie outflow that occured between 1870 and 1873 was of 200 millions, representing a loss of about 350 millions in gold and a gain of about 150 million in silver.

29 See Redish, "Evolution of the Gold Standard in France" and "Evolution of the Gold Standard in England" and "Persistence."

30 Trying to generalize Redish's case to a larger sample of countries would only weaken her thesis. Germany, for instance, did develop a high-quality minting technology well before 1873 and yet remained on a silver standard until that date.

31 See Darnis, *La Monnaie*; and Flandreau, *L'or du monde*.

32 Besides, it is quite naive to assume that there is a one-for-one relation between the intrinsic properties of a given metal and the efficiency of the payment system at large. A more costly medium of payment is likely to push towards institutional improvement that eventually may lead to greater efficiency. Ricardo himself argued: "The only objection to the use of silver is its bulk ... but this objection is entirely removed by the substituting of paper money as a general circulation medium." (quoted in Sayers, "Question of the Standard, 1815–1844," p. 91.

33 Gallarotti, *Scramble*. In a similar vein, see Baas, "Doppelwährungspolitik." In the U.S. context, albeit for a somewhat later period, see Frieden, "Dynamics."

34 Willis, *History*; Conseil Supérieur du Commerce, *Enquete Relative à la Question Monétaire*, p. 100 ff.; Flandreau, *L'or du monde*; and de Cecco, "Gold Standard."

35 Sayers, "Question of the Standard, 1815–1844" and "Question of the Standard in the 1850s." The change in 1876 coincided with Senator Jones's (of Nevada) speech about the silver causes of the fall in prices. Describing the period from 1873 to 1896, Friedman and Schwartz (*Monetary History*) observe: "The decline and subsequent rise in world prices in terms of gold were naturally reflected in U.S. prices, and the different price trends in turn were reflected in domestic politics." See also Mertens, *Naissance*.

36 Eichengreen, "Endogeneity."

37 Sayers, "Question of the Standard, 1815–1844" and "Question of the Standard in the 1850s."

38 These figures represent the proportion of European nations' foreign trade that was directed to other European nations. Figures are computed on the basis of Bairoch, "Geographical Structure."

39 Quoted by Mundell, "Theory," p. 662.

40 The results are published in *Documents*.

41 An exception was Besançon, which mostly traded with franc-based Switzerland. As part of the Latin Union, Switzerland's monetary stock was predominantly made of gold.

42 Mertens made a similar claim, although he combined it with more ideological reasons: "For the convenience of commerce, it was thus necessary to obtain a gold currency. This is what the *Handelstage* wanted. ... But from contemporary literature, one gets the impression that a gold currency was not only an economic necessity, but that it also corresponded to sentimental motives: commercial interest thought that Germany's prestige required her to have a gold currency as its British rival" (Mertens, *Naissance*, pp. 112–23).

43 French Consul in Germany, France, Archives du Ministère des Affaires Etrangères, Série F[A]29 600bis. Note that Austria was at the time struggling with inconvertible paper currency; this weakened the gulden's potential as a basis of the German system.

44 This coin (which would never be issued) had been chosen by the 1867 conference to materialize a system of correspondence between national units. See the *Report of the Royal Commission on International Coinage*, where a majority of people (including Jevons) supported the pound debasement scheme.

45 Dowd and Greenaway, "Currency Competition."

46 Flandreau, *L'or du monde*; contemporaries often quoted higher figures, ranging between 1.5 and 2 billion.

47 *See* Documents.

48 See Flandreau, "Was the Latin Union."

49 See *Conférence Monétaire Internationale de 1867*. The Bibliothèque de la Faculté de Droit (Cujas) holds these and other members of the Conférence Monétaire Internationale. The Prussian delegate Meinecke had indeed declared that although his country was "satisfied with the silver standard" (p. 16), his government did favor the adoption of the gold standard, pointing out that "the difficulty of such a reform was much bigger for Germany than for any other nation" (p. 33).

50 As mentioned by Milward and Saul (*Economic Development* p. 428), in 1870, "there were obvious weaknesses in Germany's economic position in 1870 ... . Sources of supply [for the major industries] were more unsure for Germany did not have the world empire of her European rivals and the domestic raw material base was already inadequate to sustain the developments which had taken place. Raw materials accounted for 62.5 per cent of all imports in 1869 and raw materials for the textile industries alone accounted for 31 per cent."

51 The analysis of transitional dynamics in terms of the "financial" and "liquidation" problems was pioneered by Taussig (*International Trade*, p. 269).

52 See for example, Helfferich, *Reform*, t. 2, p. 393. Of course, such a figure does not include the numerous expenses associated with collecting old coins, coining new ones, paying intermediaries.

53 See *Statesman's Yearbook*, various issues (1870–1880). The figures we have for the early 1870s overestimate actual receipts because they include the indemnity payments.

54 Stern, *Gold*. In chapter 3, Stern describes the general opposition of Western European finance to Prussia's schemes. To a certain extent this led Bismarck to his policy of short-term borrowing to finance his military projects followed by indemnity imposed to the defeated. And ironically, Bleichröder (Bismarck s main financier) was a supporter of bimetallism.

55 Parieu, "Les conferences." See also Prince-Smith, *Währung*. As Mertens argued, "although the gold standard did certainly enjoy some popularity in a large fraction of the public opinion, which included people like Soetbeer, Bamberger, Delbrück, governmental circles both before and after 1871, were certainly not ready to implement a reform." Mertens, *Naissance*, p. 124.

56 See Nothomb, *Rapport sur la loi monétaire allemande du 4 décembre 1871* and *Rapport sur la deuxième loi monétaire allemande du 9 juillet 1873*.

57 Italics are mine. France, Archives de la Monnaie de Paris [hereafter AMP], Série K. The memo continued: "La limitation de la frappe de l'argent est une mesure de pure prévoyance, qui n'implique à aucun degré un changement du système monétaire lui-même; elle a pour objet au contraire de le préserver contre les conséquences d'un fait accidentel et de e maintenir intact dans ses conditions normales." See also Soubeyran, the French delegate at the January 1874 meeting of the Latin Union: the official view was that the substitution of silver to gold was "the transitory consequence of the momentary perturbation caused ... by the new monetary law in Germany."

58 Cottrell, "London"; and Flandreau, "Adjusting to the Gold Rush."

59 Memo to the French representatives for the 1874 Latin Union Conference, AMP, Série K. The "Directeur du Mouvement Général des Fonds" (head of treasury) summarized this opinion by saying that "it is recognized that the possibility of a demonetization of silver in Germany is the main source of difficulty" *Conférence Monétaire Internationale de 1874*, p. 23.

60 *Conférence Monétaire Internationale de 1875*, p. 60.

61 Mertens, *Naissance*, p. 132.

62 See for instance, the declarations of Camphausen, the German Minister of Finances (4 April 1874) "I do not want to contribute to the propagation of the belief that Germany is about to get rid of a large sum of silver. This opinion has done us much harm, since it

has persuaded others that their silver would never be sold quickly enough, and since it has led the British markets to believe that Germany would be in any case bound to sell its silver. ... I strongly wish that the markets will understand this and, when the Empire will have to sell silver, that they will pay a good price for it" (Quoted by Mertens, *Naissance*, p. 142). That markets remained unconvinced is at least understandable. One century later, the U.S. government would face a similar problem when it attempted to dispose of its gold reserves (see Henderson and Salant, "Market Anticipations").

63 In England contemporaries such as Disraeli blamed the monetary conferences of the 1860s as the "sirens" being responsible for an increased demand for gold that in turn led the Bank of England to raise its discount rate close to 10 percent in 1873. See *The Economist*, 31 January 1874.

64 Flandreau, *L'or du monde*, p. 276.

65 The extent of the contraction however would of course depend on a set of other factors relating to post attack monetary-creation behavior.

66 France, Archives Nationales, Archives Rothschild, 132 AQ 891 ff (Copie de lettres "Matieres": letters on bullion trade, 1873).

67 Besides, up to 1873, the Bank used to make advances using gold or silver deposits as collateral, with 1 percent discount on the mint price. But the fall in the price of silver meant that agents had now an incentive to default, leaving the Bank with depreciated silver in its hands. Thus the Bank suspended loans on silver, a decision that further weakened the market for that metal.

68 *Conférence Monétaire Internationale de 1878*, p. 40.

69 Say: "Today the discount rate is only determined by changes in the gold reserve. Changes in the silver reserve, by contrast have no consequence." Ibid., p. 40.

70 AMP contain a document showing that the decision had been prepared through negotiations between the Governor of the Bank (Rouland), and the Minister of Finances (Say). Conventions Monétaires Internationales, Série K.

71 The Bank's dilemma was heightened by France's participation in the Latin Union, which induced the Bank—the largest institution of the monetary union—to back foreign silver as well. The Bank of France used this situation of "backer of last resort" to force other countries of the Latin Union to limit silver coinage as well (Flandreau "On the Inflationary Bias").

72 Helfferich, *Money*.

73 For a survey of the literature on the U.S. crime, see Friedman, "Crime."

74 As early as 1869, Seyd had warned that a transition to gold would provoke a monetary contraction with deflationary consequences (Seyd, *Depreciation*). Seyd however stood alone in this view, as a useless Cassandra.

75 Eichengreen, *Golden Fetters*.

References

Baas, N. W. J. "Die Doppelwährungspolitik Frankreichs 1850–1885." Ph.D. diss., European University Institute, Florence, 1984.

Bairoch, Paul. "The Geographical Structure and Trade Balance of European Foreign Trade from 1800 to 1974." *The Journal of European Economic History* 3, no. 3 (1974): 557–608.

Cairnes, John Elliot. *Essays in Political Economy.* London: Macmillan and Co., 1873; New York: A. M. Kelley, 1965.

Collins, Michael. "Sterling Exchange Rates, 1847–1880." *Journal of European Economic History*, 15, no. 3. (1986): 511–33.

Conférence Monétaire Internationale de 1867. Paris: Imprimerie Impériale, 1867.
Conférence Monétaire Internationale de 1874. Paris: Imprimerie Nationale, 1874.
Conférence Monétaire Internationale de 1875. Paris: Imprimerie Nationale, 1875.
Conférence Monétaire Internationale de 1876. Paris: Imprimerie Nationale, 1876.
Conférence Monétaire Internationale de 1878. Paris: Imprimerie Nationale, 1878.
Conseil Supérieur du Commerce, de L'Agriculture et de l'Industrie. *Enquête sur la Question Monétaire.* Paris: Imprimerie Nationale, 1872.
Cottrell, P. L. "London, Paris and Silver 1848–1867." In *Business, Banking and Urban History,* edited by A. Slaven and D. H. Aldcroft, 129–45. Edinburgh: John Donald, 1982.
Darnis, Jean-Marie. *La Monnaie de Paris, Sa Création et son Histoire du Consulat et de l'Empire à la Restauration (1795–1828).* Paris: Centre d'Etudes Napoléonniennes, 1988.
Drake, L. S. "Reconstruction of a Bimetallic Price Level." *Explorations in Economic History* 22 (1985): 194–219.
de Cecco, Marcello. *Money and Empire.* Oxford: Blackwell, 1974.
____. "Gold Standard." In *The New Palgrave: A Dictionary of Economics,* vol. 2, edited by John Eatwell, Murray Milgate, Peter Newman, 539–44. London: Macmillian, 1987.
Del Mar, Alexander. *A History of Precious Metals.* New York: Cambridge Encyclopedia Co., 1902.
Documents relatifs à la Question Monétaire. Paris: Imprimerie Impériale, 1868.
Dowd, Kevin, and David Greenaway. "Currency Competition, Network Externalities and Switching Costs: Towards an Alternative View of Optimum Currency Areas." *The Economic Journal* 103 (1993): 1180–89.
Eichengreen, Barry, ed. *The Gold Standard in Theory and History.* London: Methuen, 1985.
____. *Golden Fetters: The Gold Standard & the Great Depression, 1919–1939.* Oxford: Oxford University Press, 1992.
____. "The Endogeneity of Exchange Rate Regimes." Mimeo. University of California, Berkeley, 1993.
Eichengreen, Barry, and Marc Flandreau. "The Geography of the Gold Standard." In *Currency Convertibility,* edited by Barry Eichengreen, Jaime Reis, and Jorge Braga De Macedo, 113–43. London: Routledge, 1996.
Eichengreen, Barry, and Ian McLean. "The Supply of Gold Under the Pre-1914 Gold Standard." *Economic History Review* 67 (1994): 288–309.
Engle, Robert F., and C. W. J. Granger. "Cointegration and Error Correction: Representation, Estimation and Testing." *Econometrica* 55 (1987): 251–76.
Fisher, Irving. "The Mechanics of Bimetallism." *Economic Journal* 4 (1894): 527–37.
Flandreau, Marc. "On the Inflationary Bias of Common Currencies: The Latin Union Puzzle." *European Economic Review* 37 (1993): 501–06.
____. "Was the Latin Union a Franc-Zone?" In *International Monetary Systems in Historical Perspective,* edited by Jaime Reis, 71–89. London: Macmillan, 1994.
____. "Coin Memories: Estimates of the French Metallic Currency, 1840–1878." *Journal of European Economic History 24, no. 2 (1995): 271–310.*
____. "Les règies de la pratique: La Banque de France, le marché des métaux précieux, et la naissance de l'étalon or, 1848–1876." *Annales: Histoire, Sciences Sociales* no. 4 (1996): 849–72.

280

____. *L'or du monde: la France et la stabilité du système monétaire international.* Paris: L'Harmattan, 1995.

____. "Adjusting to the Gold Rush: Endogenous Bullion Points and the French Balance of Payments 1846–1870." *Explorations in Economic History* 33 (1996): 1–24.

____. "As Good as Gold? Bimetallism in Equilibrium 1848–1873." In *Monetary Standards in History,* edited by Lawrence Officer. London: Routledge, forthcoming.

France. Archives de la Monnaie de Paris. (AMP).

France. Archives Nationales. Archives Rothschild.

France. Archives du Ministère des Affaires Etrangères.

Frieden, J. "The Dynamics of International Monetary Systems: International and Domestic Factors in the Rise, Reign and Demise of the Classical Gold Standard." In *Coping with Complexity in the International System,* edited by J. Snyder and R. Jervis, 137–62. Boulder, CO: Westview Press, 1993.

Friedman, Milton, and Anna Schwartz. *A Monetary History of the United States.* Princeton: Princeton University Press, 1963.

Friedman, Milton. "Bimetallism Revisited." *Journal of Economic Perspectives* 4, no. 4 (1990): 85–104.

____. "The Crime of 1873." *Journal of Political Economy* 98, no. 6 (1990): 1154–94.

Gallarotti, Giulio M. "The Scramble for Gold: Monetary Regimes Transformation in the 1870s." In *Monetary Regimes in Transition,* edited by Michael D. Bordo and Forrest Capie, 85–104. Cambridge: Cambridge University Press, 1993.

____. *The Anatomy of an International Monetary Regime: The Classical Gold Standard, 1880–1914.* Oxford: Oxford University Press, 1995.

Flay, Sir Hector. "Stock of Gold and Silver in the World." *Journal of the Institute of Bankers* (1886): 172–76.

Helfferich, Karl. *Die Reform des deutschen Geldwesens nach Gründung des Reiches.* Leipzig: Duncker, 1898.

____. *Money.* 2 vols. New York: Adelphi Company, 1927.

Henderson, D. W., and S. W. Salant. "Market Anticipations of Government Policies and the Price of Gold." *Journal of Political Economy* 86, no. 4 (1978): 627–48.

Hendry, David. "Econometric Modelling with Cointegrated Variables: An Overview." *Oxford Bulletin of Economics and Statistics* 48, no. 3, (1986): 201–12.

Hütter, Jean-Paul. *L'incidence économique de la frappe de monnaie d'argent aux Etats-Unis de 1878 à 1893, interprétations contemporaines et essai d'évaluation quantitative.* Paris: Presses Modernes, 1938.

Kauch P. *La Banque Nationale de Belgique, 1850–1918.* Brussels: Banque Nationale de Belgique, 1950.

Kenwood, A. G. and A. L. Lougheed. *The Growth of the International Economy 1820–1960: An Introductory Text.* London: Allen & Unwin, 1971.

Kindleberger, Charles P. *A Financial History of Western Europe.* 2d ed. Oxford: Oxford University Press, 1993.

Laughlin, J. Laurence. *The History of Bimetallism in the United States.* New York: D. Appleton, 1885.

Levasseur, Emile. *Histoire du commerce de la France, de 1789 à nos jours.* Paris: Rousseau, 1912.

Luzatti, L. "Delle Attinenze dei Biglietti di Banca col Bimetallismo." *Nuova Antologia di Scienze, Lettere, ed Arti.* Rome, (1883): 524–45.

McCloskey, Donald N., and J. Richard Zecher. "The Success of Purchasing Power Parity." In *A Retrospective on the Classical Gold Standard*, edited by Michael D. Bordo and Anna J. Schwartz, 121–72. Chicago: University of Chicago Press, 1984.

Mertens, Jacques. *La naissance et le développement de l'etalon or; 1696–1922.* Paris: Presses Universitaires de France, 1944.

Milward, Alan, and S. B. Saul. *The Economic Development of Continental Europe, 1780–1870.* London: Allen & Unwin, 1973.

____. "The Origins of the Gold Standard." In *Currency Convertibility*, edited by Barry Eichengreen, Jaime Reis, and Jorge Braga de Macedo, 87–101. London: Routledge, 1996.

Mundell, Robert. "A Theory of Optimal Currency Areas." *American Economic Review* 51 (1961): 657–65.

Nothomb, Eugene. *Rapport sur la loi monétaire allemande du 4 décembre 1871.* Bruxelles, 1871.

____. *Rapport sur la deuxième loi monétaire allemande du 4 juillet 1873.* Bruxelles, 1873.

Oppers, Stefan. "Arbitrage in Bimetallic Money Supplies: Evidence from the Exchange Rate." Mimeo, University of Michigan, 1994.

____. "Was the Worldwide Shift to Gold Inevitable?" Mimeo, University of Michigan, 1994.

Parieu. "Les Conférences monétaires internationales de 1865 et 1867 et leurs résultats." *Journal des Economistes* 1 (1869): 243–66.

Prince-Smith, John. *Währung und Münze.* Annalen des deutschen Reichs, Hirth, 1869.

Redish, Angela. "The Evolution of the Gold Standard in England." this JOURNAL 50, no. 4 (1990): 789–806.

____. "The Evolution of the Gold Standard in France." Mimeo, University of British Columbia, 1992.

____. "The Persistence of Bimetallism in Nineteenth-Century France." *Economic History Review* 68, no. 4 (1995): 717–36.

Report from the Royal Commission on International Coinage. London: Her Majesty Stationery Office, 1868.

Roccas, Massimo. "L'italia e il sistema monetario internazionale dagli anni '60 agli anni '90 del seccolo scorso." Banca d'Italia. Temi di Discussione, No. 92, 1987.

Russell, Henry B. *International Monetary Conferences.* New York: Harper & Brothers, 1898.

Say, Léon. *Rapport sur le payement de l'indemnité de guerre et sur les opérations de change qui en ont été la conséquence.* Paris: Guillaumin, 1874.

Sayers, R. S. "The Question of the Standard in the 1850s." *Economic History, Economic Journal Supplement*, 2, no. 8 (1933): 575–601.

____. "The Question of the Standard, 1815–1844." *Economic History, Economic Journal Supplement*, 3, no. 10 (1935): 79–102.

Seyd, Ernest. *Bullion and Foreign Exchanges.* London: Effingham Wilson, 1869.

____. *The Depreciation of Labour and Property Which Would Follow the Demonetization of Silver.* London: Effingham Wilson, 1869.

Sicsic, Pierre. "Estimation du stock de monnaie métallique en France à la fin du XIXème siècle." *Revue Economique* (1989): 709–35.

Soetbeer, Adolphe. *Matériaux pour faciliter l'intelligence et l'examen des rapports economiques des métaux précieux et de la Question Monétaire.* Paris and Nancy: Berger Levrault, 1889.

Statesman's Yearbook. London: Macmillan, 1870–1880.

Stern, F. *Gold and Iron, Bismarck, Bleichröder, and the Building of the German Empire.* New York: Alfred A. Knopf, 1977.

Taussig, F. W. *International Trade.* New York: Macmillan, 1927.

The Economist, 31 January 1874.

Warren, G. F. and F. Pearson. *Prices.* New York: Wiley, 1933.

Willis, H. P. *A History of the Latin Monetary Union: A Study of International Monetary Action.* Chicago: University of Chicago Press, 1901.

Yeager, L. B. *International Monetary Relations: Theory, History and Policy.* New York: Harper and Row, 1976.

12

THE GOLD STANDARD AS A "GOOD HOUSEKEEPING SEAL OF APPROVAL"

Michael D. Bordo and Hugh Rockoff

Source: *Journal of Economic History*, 56, 2, 1996, 389–428.

In this article we argue that during the period from 1870 to 1914 adherence to the gold standard was a signal of financial rectitude, a "good housekeeping seal of approval," that facilitated access by peripheral countries to capital from the core countries of western Europe. Examination of data from nine widely different capital-importing countries, using a model inspired by the Capital Asset Pricing Model, reveals that countries with poor records of adherence were charged considerably more than those with good records, enough to explain the determined effort to stay on gold made by a number of capital-importing countries.

The global economy in its present form emerged in the half century before World War I. That "golden age" was characterized by massive interregional flows of capital, labor, and goods. It was also an era when most nations adhered to (or attempted to adhere to) the gold standard rule of convertibility of national currencies into a fixed weight of gold. Common adherence to gold convertibility in turn linked the world together through fixed exchange rates. In this article we argue that adherence to the gold standard also served as "a good housekeeping seal of approval" that facilitated access by peripheral countries to capital vital to their development from the core countries of western Europe.

We view the gold standard as a contingent rule or a rule with escape clauses. Members were expected to adhere to convertibility except in the event of a well-understood emergency such as a war, a financial crisis, or a shock to the terms of trade. Under these circumstances, temporary departures from the rule would be tolerated on the assumption that once the emergency passed, convertibility at the original parity would resume.[1]

It is well known that a number of core countries (England, France, and Germany as well as several other developed western European countries) adhered to this rule before 1914. Even a number of developing peripheral countries also did so

(Canada, Australia, and the United States), or attempted to do so (Argentina, Brazil, and Chile), or "shadowed" the performance of the gold standard (Italy, Spain, and Portugal).[2] One possible reason for faithful adherence to the rule is that adherence provided improved access to capital vital to development.[3] This point, we believe, has been strangely neglected.[4] It explains why countries were so determined to adhere to gold even when doing so involved substantial costs: faithful adherence significantly lowered the cost of loans from metropolitan Europe. Thus, "the good housekeeping seal" provides an alternative to traditional explanations for the popularity of the gold standard that turn on internal differences between creditors and debtors or even on irrational prejudices in favor of gold. If adherence to the rule was evidence of financial rectitude—like "the good housekeeping seal of approval"—it would signal that a country followed prudent fiscal and monetary policies and would only temporarily run large fiscal deficits in well-understood emergencies. Monetary authorities then could be depended on to avoid defaulting on externally held debt.

In many cases loans were made with gold clauses or were sterling denominated, to minimize currency risk. But there still would be risk of abrogation of the gold clauses or of total default on the debt, which would be reflected in a country risk premium on the loan.[5] Moreover, in a world of asymmetric information, a credible commitment to the gold-standard rule would provide a signal to lenders of the costs borrowers would be willing to bear to avoid default and hence would circumvent the aversion to lending imposed by asymmetric information.[6]

In this article, we first define the concept of the gold standard as a contingent rule and as a credible commitment mechanism to serve as "the good housekeeping seal of approval." Then we survey the historical background of gold-standard adherence in the period from 1870 to 1914 by nine important peripheral countries. We next discuss the data and methodology for a test of "the good housekeeping seal of approval" hypothesis. We then present the results for the nine countries. The evidence suggests that in most cases successful adherence to gold significantly improved the terms at which peripheral countries could borrow from the core countries. Finally, we conclude with some lessons from history.

THE GOLD STANDARD AS A COMMITMENT MECHANISM

Traditionally, a monetary rule such as the gold standard (or other specie standards such as silver or bimetallism) by causing a nation's money supply to vary automatically with the balance of payments, was deemed to be superior to entrusting policy to the discretion of well-meaning monetary authorities.[7] In contrast to this view, which stresses both impersonality and automaticity, we adopt the approach to rules in the recent literature on the time inconsistency of monetary and fiscal policy.[8] A rule then serves as a credible commitment mechanism binding policy actions over time.

In the simplest sense, government policy is said to be time inconsistent when a policy plan, calculated as optimal based on the government's objectives and expected to hold indefinitely into the future, is subsequently revised. Discretion, in this context, means setting policy sequentially. This could then lead to policies and outcomes that are very different from the optimal plan as market agents rationally incorporate government actions into their planning. For that reason, society would benefit from the government having access to a commitment mechanism to keep it from changing planned future policy.

According to this approach, adherence to the fixed price of gold served as a credible commitment mechanism to prevent governments from following the otherwise time-inconsistent policies of creating surprise fiduciary money issues in order to capture seigniorage revenue or defaulting on outstanding debt.[9] On this basis, adherence to the gold-standard rule before 1914 enabled many countries to avoid the problems of high inflation and stagflation that troubled the late twentieth century.

The simplest example of how a commitment mechanism operates is in a modern closed economy where monetary authorities attempt to maintain full employment and zero inflation. Assume the monetary authority has announced at the beginning of the year a rate of monetary growth consistent with zero inflation. Assume further that the public believes the announcement, and it is incorporated into wage bargaining and other contracts that are binding over the year. In this circumstance, the authorities, in the absence of precommitment, have an incentive to create a monetary surprise (follow an expansionary monetary policy), to reduce unemployment (stimulate the economy), or to capture seignorage revenue. However, the public, with rational expectations, will incorporate the government's actions into their behavior and in the next year, when new contracts are formed, will demand higher wages and prices. This will in turn lead to higher inflation and a return to the original level of employment and economic activity. In addition, desired real cash balances will decline reducing the tax base for seigniorage. A credible precommitment mechanism, such as a rule that prevents the authorities from altering monetary growth from its preannounced path, by preventing the government from cheating, can preserve long-run price stability.[10]

A second example is in the use of fiscal policy. Governments use debt finance to smooth tax revenues over time. When faced with unusual government expenditures such as in wartime, it is more efficient to sell bonds than to impose higher taxes that can reduce work effort. The debt is issued on the assumption that taxes will be raised once the emergency is passed in order to service and reduce the debt. In this context, a time-inconsistent fiscal policy would be to impose a capital levy or to default on the debt, once the public has purchased it. Following such a policy would capture additional resources for the government in the *present* but in the event of *a future* emergency would make it very difficult for the government to sell its bonds at favorable prices. A credible commitment mechanism can force the government to honor its outstanding debt.

The pledge to fix the price of a country's currency in terms of gold was just such a rule or commitment mechanism to prevent governments from following the previously mentioned practices. The rule defined a gold coin as a fixed weight of gold called, for example, one dollar. The monetary authority was then committed to keep the mint price of gold fixed through the purchase and sale of gold in unlimited amounts. Under the bimetallic system based on gold and silver that prevailed in most countries until the third quarter of the nineteenth century, the monetary authorities would define the weight of both gold and silver coins. Maintaining the bimetallic ratio fixed is a variant of the basic convertibility rule, since it is the fixed value of the unit of account that is the essence of the rule.[11] The gold-standard rule in the century before World War I can be viewed as a contingent rule, or a rule with escape clauses.[12] The monetary authority maintains the standard—keeps the price of the currency in terms of gold fixed—except in the event of a well-understood emergency such as a major war. In wartime it may suspend gold convertibility and issue paper money to finance its expenditures, and it can sell debt issues in terms of the nominal value of its currency on the understanding that debt will eventually be paid off in gold. The rule is contingent in the sense that the public understands that the suspension will last only for the duration of the wartime emergency plus some period of adjustment and that after-wards the government will adopt the deflationary policies necessary to resume payments at the original parity.[13] Observing such a rule will allow the government to smooth its revenue from different sources of finance: taxation, borrowing, and seigniorage.[14]

Examples of discretion—breaches of the rule—include postponement of resumption after the war and reasonable delay period had passed and pegging to specie at a devalued parity. As a result, in the event of another war within memory of the previous one, the public would be less willing to absorb government debt, even if the situation were otherwise similar, and the government proposed a rea-sonable delay.

It is crucial that the rule be transparent and simple and that only a limited num-ber of contingencies be included. Transparency and simplicity avoided the prob-lems of moral hazard and incomplete information, which prevented the monetary authority from engaging in discretionary policy under the guise of following the contingent rule.[15] In this respect a second contingency—a temporary suspension in the face of a financial crisis, which in turn was not the result of the monetary authority's own actions—might also have been part of the rule. However, because of the greater difficulty of verifying the source of the contingency than in the case of war, invoking the escape clause under conditions of financial crisis (or in the case of a shock to the terms of trade, a third possible contingency) would be more likely to create suspicion that discretion was the order of the day.

The gold-standard contingent rule worked successfully for three core countries (in the traditional sense) of the classical gold standard: Britain, France, and the United States.[16] In all these countries the monetary authorities adhered faithfully to the fixed price of gold except during major wars. During the Napoleonic War and World War I for England, the Civil War for the United States, and the Franco-Prussian War for France, specie payments were suspended and paper money and debt were issued. But in each case, after the wartime emergency had passed, poli-cies leading to resumption at the prewar parity were adopted.[17] Indeed, successful adherence to the pre-World War I rule may have enabled the belligerents to obtain access to debt finance more easily in subsequent wars. In the case of Germany, the fourth core country, no occasions arose for application of the contingent aspect of the rule before 1914. Otherwise, its record of adherence to gold convertibility was similar to that of the other three countries.

A number of other countries also followed the rule. These included the British Dominions of Canada and Australia; the western European countries of Sweden, The Netherlands, and Switzerland; and Japan. In marked contrast to this group are the countries of southern Europe and Latin America (see Table 1 for a chronology of adherence). For the southern European countries, adherence to the gold standard was an important objective but, for most of them, difficult to achieve. Their experience of low money growth, of low fiscal deficits (with the principal exception of Italy), and of exchange rates that never drifted far from parity suggests that the rule was important. The Latin American countries suspended convertibility in wartime and also in the face of financial crises and terms-of-trade shocks. They usually returned to gold at a depreciated parity. Their experience was characterized by higher money growth rates, higher fiscal deficits, and higher inflation rates than the other countries. For them gold convertibility was the exception rather than the rule.[18]

The gold-standard rule originally evolved as a domestic commitment mechanism, but its enduring fame is as an international rule. The classical gold standard emerged as a true international standard by 1880 following the switch by the majority of countries from bimetallism, silver monometallism, and paper to gold as the basis of their currencies.[19] As an international standard, the key rule was maintenance of gold convertibility at the established par. Maintenance of a fixed price of gold by its adherents in turn ensured fixed exchange rates. The fixed price of domestic currency in terms of gold provided a nominal anchor to the international monetary system.

Recent evidence suggests that, indeed, exchange rates throughout the 1880 to 1914 period exhibited a high degree of fixity in the principal countries. Although exchange rates frequently deviated from par, violations of the gold points were rare, as were devaluations.[20]

According to the game theoretic literature, for an international monetary arrangement to be effective, both between countries and within them, a time-consistent credible-commitment mechanism is required. In other words each member must adhere to a credible rule.[21] Adherence to the gold convertibility rule provided such a mechanism. Indeed, Giovannini finds the variation of both exchange rates and short-term interest rates within the limits set by the gold points in the period from 1899 to 1909 consistent with market agents' expectations of a credible commitment by the core countries to the gold-standard rule in the sense of this article.[22] In addition to the reputation of the domestic gold standard and constitutional provisions that ensured domestic commitment, adherence to the international gold-standard rule may have been enforced by other mechanisms.[23] These include the operation of the rules of the game, the hegemonic power of

England, central-bank cooperation, and improved access to international capital markets, the subject of this article.

One of the enforcement mechanisms of the gold-standard rule for peripheral countries was presumably access to capital obtainable from the core countries.[24] To the extent that adherence to the gold standard served as a signal of good behavior we would expect to see countries that always adhered to gold convertibility to pay lower interest rates on loans contracted in London and other metropolitan centers than others with less consistent performance.

Our approach suggests that adherence to gold would affect the volume of capital attracted as well as the terms. However, we have been unable to assemble enough high-quality data to tell us how much more capital flowed to good adherents because of their reputation for financial rectitude relative to others.[25] An extensive earlier literature on capital flows focused on the determinants of long-term capital flows.[26] Those scholars attempted to ascertain whether "pull factors" (higher expected rates of return) in the periphery or "push factors" (poor investment prospects and higher savings rates) in the core predominated. Our approach builds upon this earlier literature to the extent that we grant that the key determinants of capital flows are the traditional variables they utilized: the expected real rates of return in both countries, the levels of real activity, the terms of trade, and the phase of the business cycle. But in addition we posit that adherence to the gold-standard rule would have an incremental and significant impact.

THE RECORD OF ADHERENCE TO THE GOLD STANDARD

To assess evidence for the "good housekeeping seal of approval" we examine the behavior of long-term bond yields for nine peripheral countries in the classical gold-standard period from 1870 to 1914. Our choice of countries was dictated partly by availability of the data and to give us a diverse sample reflecting four groups of countries. The groups include countries that always adhered to gold (Canada and Australia); countries that followed the contingent rule and temporarily suspended payments but returned to gold at the original parity (the United States and Italy for part of the period); countries that, for the period with data available to us, did not adhere to gold but may have shadowed it (Portugal, Spain, and Italy for part of the period); and countries that broke the gold-standard rule by intermittently suspending payments and devaluing their currencies (Argentina, Brazil, and Chile).

The chronology in Table 1 summarizes the adherence record until 1914 for each of the countries mentioned. In addition it shows the reasons for a change in monetary standard and an indication as to whether a country changed its parity when it returned to gold. A brief convertibility history of the nine countries follows. Also, Figure 1 shows each country's exchange rate in terms of sterling relative to gold parity at the beginning of the period (with the exception of Australia and Canada, which never depart from parity).

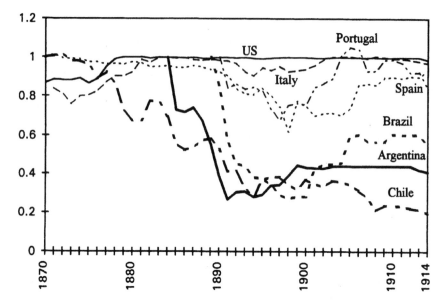

Figure 1 NORMALIZED EXCHANGE RATES FOR SEVEN COUNTRIES. *Note*: Australia and Canada are omitted because their currencies remained at par during the period. *Sources*: See the exchange rates (EXRT) for each country in the Appendix.

Canada adopted the gold standard in 1853. Although it experienced a sharp cyclical downturn in the years 1907 to 1908, Canada did not suspend convertibility until 1914.

Australia adopted the gold standard in 1852. Despite severe banking problems in the 1890s, Australia did not suspend convertibility until July 1915 during World War I.

The United States Coinage Act of 1792 defined a bimetallic standard at a mint ratio of 15 to 1. In 1834 and again in 1837 the mint ratio was altered, remaining unchanged thereafter at 16 to 1. This ratio overvalued gold at the mint so that by 1849 the United States was on a defacto gold standard. The Civil War led to suspension of specie payments from 1862 through 1878. Despite contentious political opposition to deflation that resumption enforced, resumption to gold was achieved at the prewar parity on January 1, 1879, in line with the declaration of the Resumption Act of 1875. Apart from the silver threat to gold convertibility in the mid 1890s stemming from Populist agitation, convertibility in the United States was never in doubt from 1879 to 1914. It was preserved even during two banking panics in 1893 and 1907 when banks restricted payments.

In 1862 Italy adopted the bimetallic standard, although in fact the standard was gold. In 1865 Italy joined the Latin Monetary Union. Fiscal improvidence and war against Austria in 1866, however, ended convertibility.[27] Fiscal and monetary discipline was achieved by 1874, and exchange-rate parity was restored. The government announced on March 1, 1883, that it would restore convertibility on April 12, 1884, but convertibility took place only in silver because silver was overvalued at the mint. Public finances then deteriorated, and unlawful bank issues indicated an absence of monetary discipline. By 1894 Italy was back on a paper standard. Inconvertibility lasted until 1913. After a period of laxity ending by 1903, the government embraced fiscal and monetary rectitude as if it were on a gold standard but did not formally resume (see Figure 1).[28]

Although Spain adopted a bimetallic regime in April 1848, with a ratio of 16 to 1, only after the currency reform of 1868 that established the peseta as the monetary unit was the regime fully operative. In 1868, following six reductions in the ratio, it was set at 15.5 to 1, as in the Latin Monetary Union (which Spain, however, did not join). With the fall in the market price of silver in the 1870s, the 15.5 to 1 ratio undervalued gold. Gold was driven out of circulation, and the gold reserves of the Bank of Spain declined. A declining trade balance and capital outflows from 1881 to 1883 led Spain to end convertibility to avoid deflation. Between 1888 and 1900 the peseta exchange rate depreciated, a budget deficit arose in every year but three from 1884 to 1899, money creation largely financed the war with Cuba in 1898 and 1899, and Spanish prices until 1905 fell much less than world prices. All of these factors proved hostile to resumption. After 1900 these factors mainly turned favorable to resumption, but it did not take place. Efforts by finance ministers to restore convertibility and adopt the gold standard before World War I foundered on the opposition of the Bank of Spain. Nevertheless, the behavior of the exchange rate and of both monetary and fiscal variables in this period suggest that Spain shadowed the gold parity rule (Figure 1).[29]

Portugal had been on a bimetallic standard since the 1680s with de facto gold predominance alternating with de facto silver predominance. The decision to shift to a gold standard in 1854 was made because gold circulation was ample.[30] The parity with the pound was unchanged from 1854 until 1891, a period during which there were no convertibility crises. Furthermore, the mint ratio the law established favored gold. All this came to a halt after an increase in the ratio of debt service payments to revenues, and government support of failing domestic enterprises clouded Portugal's reputation as a creditworthy nation. Suspension of convertibility in 1891 lasted until after World War I. However, from 1895 to 1914 Portugal pursued conservative fiscal and monetary policies as if it were shadowing the gold standard (see Figure 1).[31]

Gold convertibility in Argentina began in February 1867 after a failed attempt in 1863.[32] Convertibility was suspended in May 1876 after several years of political unrest and rising government deficits. Although the exchange rate reached parity by 1881, resumption that year failed. Convertibility was restored in 1883 but lasted only until January 1885, at a time of financial crisis in Europe and following a period of expansionary fiscal policy. Inconvertibility thereafter until 1899 was associated with a lax fiscal policy leading to debt default in 1890 in the infamous Baring crisis.[33] In 1899 convertibility was restored at the original parity of 5 gold pesos to the pound with the return to fiscal orthodoxy in 1896 and the establishment of a currency board. However, paper pesos that had been circulating since 1885 at a large discount relative to gold were frozen at 2.27 per gold peso, giving the effect of a substantial devaluation (see Figure 1). Argentina suspended convertibility in 1914 on the outbreak of war.

From 1808 onwards Brazil was on a bimetallic standard at the colonial ratio of 16 to 1. From then until 1846, when it was altered to favor gold, the ratio was changed three times. Gold convertibility was suspended in November 1857 in the wake of a banking crisis and resumed in 1858. It was subsequently abandoned on several succeeding occasions, notably during the war with Paraguay.[34] Suspension lasted for slightly more than a year in 1888 and 1889. A republican revolution in November 1889 coincided with the ending of convertibility.[35] In 1906 Brazil restored convertibility to prevent continued appreciation of the milreis exchange rate that was harmful to coffee and rubber exporters. In addition it created a Conversion Office with a limit set to its issue of convertible notes at a newly established parity. Convertibility ended at the outbreak of World War I.

Chile was on a bimetallic standard from 1818 to 1851; it then made a technical change in the mint ratio but maintained the bimetallic standard until 1866. Although it resumed in 1870, by the end of 1874 with the fall in the price of silver, it was on a de facto silver standard. After bank runs in 1878 the authorities made bank notes inconvertible.[36] For the next 17 years, Chile remained on a paper standard. The War of the Pacific (1879 to 1883) was financed by government note issues. The first attempt to return to a metallic standard was made in 1887, but it failed. An eight-month civil war from January to August 1891 resulted in further monetary expansion and exchange-rate depreciation, A second conversion law in November 1892 was strictly implemented, and the exchange rate appreciated, but again the government responded to political discontent by issuing notes. The exchange rate thereupon depreciated. A new conversion law of February 11, 1895, set June 1 as the day for redemption of government notes, devalued the gold content of the peso, and authorized loans and sales of nitrate fields to accumulate a gold reserve. Following rumors of war with Argentina and a run on the banks in July 1898, the legislature ended convertibility and, to deal with the panic, bank notes were declared government obligations.

Thus our survey suggests a wide variance in adherence to the gold standard rule by peripheral countries. If the "good housekeeping seal of approval" hypothesis has validity we would expect, other things equal, that the country-risk premium on long-term bond yields would be lowest for Canada and Australia, followed by the United States and Italy, then by Spain and Portugal, and then by Argentina, Brazil, and Chile. The next section considers the evidence.

DATA, MODELS, AND ECONOMETRIC METHODOLOGY

Data

Our data consist of annual interest rate observations (typically government bond rates) and related variables, including exchange rates, real income, fiscal deficits, and the money supply for nine countries during the classical gold-standard era.[37] The nine countries, as noted above, were chosen with one eye on the availability of the data and the other on the variety of experiences with the gold standard. The sample is divided into four groups of countries. The first group includes two countries that were always on gold, Australia and Canada. The second group includes the United States and Italy, two countries that observed the gold-standard contingent rule in the sense that they abandoned convertibility in the face of an emergency such as a war but returned to the original parity afterwards. Although, unlike the U.S. experience, Italy, after its second suspension in 1894, did not restore convertibility at the original parity, but its exchange rate shadowed it (see Figure 1). The countries also differed on the reasons for departure (see Table 1). For the United States it was a wartime emergency; for Italy it was lax fiscal policy. The third group consists of Spain and Portugal, which in the period before our data begin adhered to convertibility but during our sample period did not do so. However, the performance of their exchange rates (see Figure 1), and their inflation, money growth rates, and fiscal deficits suggest that their policies shadowed gold.[38] The final group includes Argentina, Brazil, and Chile, which intermittently adhered to gold convertibility but at altered parities. The appendix gives full descriptions of the data and sources.

The interest rates are plotted in Figures 2 through 7. The panels in each figure show the rate of return on representative long-term bonds for a particular country (or, to save space, two comparable countries) and, for comparison, the return on British consols. The periods when a country was on the gold standard are indicated by boxes within the figures.

Interest rates for Canada and Australia, the only countries that stayed on the gold standard throughout the period from 1870 to 1914, were generally quite close to the consol rate, especially after 1900, when a general convergence of foreign rates with the consol rate took place (Figure 2).[39]

Of the two interest rates for the United States over the period 1870 to 1914, the higher rate from 1870 to 1878 is for gold bonds (bonds that promised interest and principal in gold before the United States returned to gold), and the lower rate is for bonds that promised interest and principal in paper, the famous greenbacks (Figure 3).[40] At first glance it may seem strange that the gold rate is above the paper rate during a time of flexible exchange rates. The explanation is that gold was the depreciating currency. At the end of the Civil War the price of gold dollars in terms of greenback dollars was well above one, but this price was expected to fall, as it in fact did, until resumption of convertibility in 1879 at the rate of one greenback dollar per one gold dollar. The gold interest rate, in other words, had to be higher before redemption to compensate for the expected future loss on the

Table 1 A CHRONOLOGY OF ADHERENCE TO THE GOLD STANDARD FOR
NINE COUNTRIES: CIRCA, 1870–1914

Country	Period	Standard	Reason for Change	Change in Parity?
Canada	1853–1914	Gold	War	No
Australia	1852–1915	Gold	War	No
United states	1792–1861	Bimetallic (de facto gold after 1834)		No
	1862–1878	Paper (greenbacks)	War	
	1879–1917[a]	Gold	War	No
Italy	1862–1866	Bimetallic	Lax fiscal policy, war	No
	1866–1884	Paper		
	1884–1894	Gold	Lax fiscal policy	Yes
	1894–1914	Paper		
Spain	1868–1883	Silver	Crisis	Yes
	1883–1914	Paper		
Portugal	1854–1891	Gold	Crisis	Yes
	1891–1914	Paper		
Argentina	1867–1876	Gold		No
	1876–1883[b]	Paper	Lax fiscal policy	
	1883–1885	Gold		Yes
	1885–1899	Paper	Lax fiscal policy	
	1899–1914	Gold	War	Yes
Brazil	1857–1888	Paper		
	1888–1889	Gold		Yes
	1889–1906	Paper	Revolution	
	1906–1914	Gold	War	Yes
Chile	1870–1878	Bimetallic	Crisis	Yes
	1878–1895[c]	Paper		
	1895–1898	Gold	War threat	Yes
	1898–1925	Paper		

[a] Gold Embargo 1917–1919, Standard not suspended.
[b] Failed attempt to restore convertibility in 1881.
[c] Failed attempt to restore convertibility in 1887.

Source: Bordo and Schwartz, "Operation."

conversion of gold into greenbacks. As can clearly be seen in Figure 3 both the
gold and paper rates lay well above the U.K. consol rate before resumption and
converged quite markedly thereafter.

Two rates for Italy, a gold rate and a paper rate, were somewhat higher than
the rates for Australia, Canada, and the United States (Figure 4).[41] Also note that
there is no decisive downward movement during the brief period in which Italy
was officially on the gold standard. If anything, there is an upward trend during
this interval.

Paper rates for Spain (beginning in 1883) and Portugal (beginning in 1891),
after both countries had abandoned convertibility, appear to have been declining

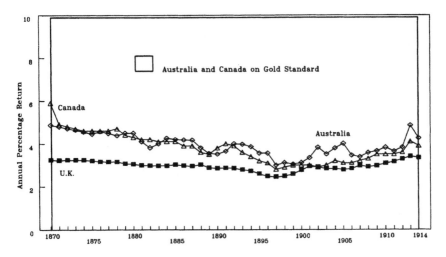

Figure 2 LONG-TERM RATES FOR AUSTRALIA AND CANADA. *Sources*: See LTIR.UK, LTIR.AUS, and LTIR.CAN in the Appendix.

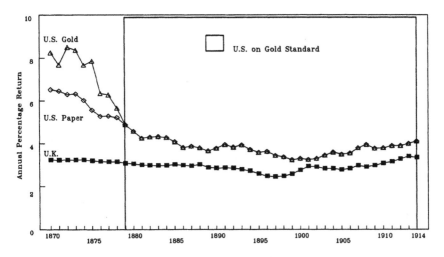

Figure 3 LONG-TERM RATES FOR THE UNITED STATES. *Sources*: See LTIR.UK, LTIR.US, and LTIR.USGC in the Appendix.

(Figure 5). The Spanish rate, in particular, closes in on the consol rate after 1900 in much the same way as the Australian, Canadian, Italian, and U.S. rates.

The gold rate for Argentina (beginning in 1885) peaks with the 1890 Baring crisis. Brazil's rate begins in 1892. Both rates fell after 1900 as both countries returned to the gold standard (Figure 6). But it is difficult to determine whether

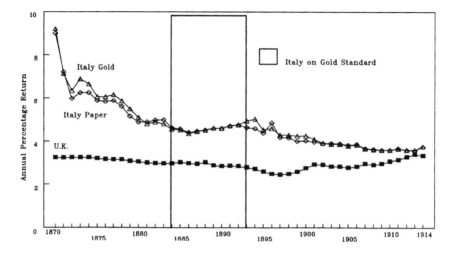

Figure 4 LONG-TERM RATES FOR ITALY. *Sources*: See LTIR.UK, LTIR.IT, and LTIR.ITG in the Appendix.

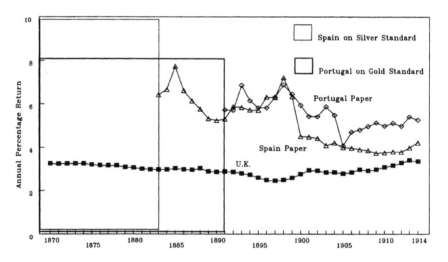

Figure 5 LONG-TERM RATES FOR PORTUGAL AND SPAIN. *Sources*: See LTIR. UK, LTIR.POR, and LTIR.SP in the Appendix.

it was the result of adherence to gold or of some other factor that produced the general convergence of rates after 1900.

For Chile, Figure 7, the relationship between the London rate payable in gold and a domestic rate payable in paper differs from the U.S. case. The paper rate is well above the gold rate, confirming our intuition that paper rates are higher

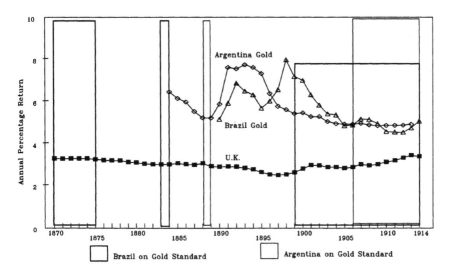

Figure 6 LONG-TERM RATES FOR ARGENTINA AND BRAZIL. *Sources*: See LTIR.
UK, LTIR.ARG, and LTIR.BRZ in the Appendix.

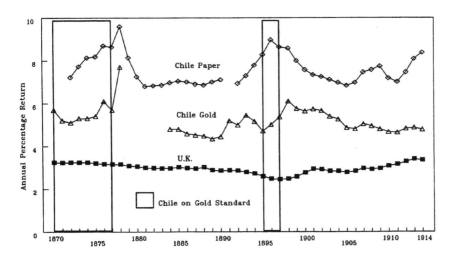

Figure 7 LONG-TERM RATES FOR CHILE. *Sources*: See LTIR.UK, and LTIR.CH in
the Appendix.

because of the risk of a fall in the gold value of the currency. More telling is that
the gold rate, although lower than the paper rate, is substantially higher than are
the Australian, Canadian, U.S., and Italian gold rates. Simply promising to pay in
gold was not enough to achieve the lowest international rates; country risk mattered even for gold bonds.

One phenomenon apparent in all the figures is convergence after 1900 of the long-term yields with the U.K. consol yield. One explanation is growing confidence in the safety of international investments (a decline in the market price of risk), produced in part by the general acceptance of the gold standard.[42] But there may also have been other factors at work such as factor-price equalization reflecting the high degree of mobility of capital as well as labor during the "golden age" before 1914.[43] Thus, a preliminary inspection of the long-term yields suggests that long-term commitment to the gold standard mattered, even when bonds were denominated in gold. Countries that remained on gold throughout the classical era were charged lower rates than countries that had a mixed record of adherence. The evidence on the effect of short-term attachments to or departures from the gold standard, however, is less clear.

The Model

To explore these issues further we estimated regressions of the following form.

$$R_{it} - R_{UKt} = a_i + b_{i1}\left(\bar{R}_t - R_{UKt}\right) + b_{i2}dum_{it} + b_{i3}M_{i,t-1} + b_{i4}D_{i,t-1} + \epsilon_{it} \tag{1}$$

$$\epsilon_{it} = \rho_i\,\epsilon_{it-1} + \mu_{it}, \quad i = 1, 2, \ldots 9$$

where R_{it} equals the interest rate of country i in year t; R_{UKt} equals the interest rate of the United Kingdom in year t; $\bar{R}_t$ equals the average of all rates in the sample at time t; dum_{it} equals a dummy variable that takes the value 1 if country i is on the gold standard in year t; $M_{i,t-1}$ equals the rate of growth of money less the rate of growth of real GNP in country i between $t-2$ and $t-1$, (Monetary Policy); and $D_{i,t-1}$ equals the level of government expenditures less taxes divided by nominal GNP in country i in year $t-1$, (Fiscal Policy).[44]

We use the average spread $(\bar{R}_t - R_{UKt})$ as our benchmark because our preliminary inspection of the data suggested that some sort of benchmark was needed to account for market-wide rate fluctuations. One possible rationale for this benchmark is the Capital Assets Pricing Model (CAPM).[45] On this analogy, $\bar{R}_t$ is a proxy for the return on the efficient market portfolio (although, obviously, it is far removed from the variable prescribed by the theory) and R_{UKt} is a proxy for the risk free rate (perhaps not a bad proxy given the reputation of British consols). Thus, b_{i1} can be viewed as an analogue of beta, the measure of systematic risk in CAPM. Below we report results for an unweighted average $\bar{R}_t$ and for an average weighted by a country's share of debt in the total issued by the sample countries and held by Britain in 1914.[46] We also experimented with a GNP weighted average, but the results were unsatisfactory because the average was completely dominated by the United States.

To test directly whether adherence to gold influences rates paid we include a dummy variable that takes the value one when a country is on the gold standard and zero when it is off. An on-off dummy is the simplest way to estimate the effects of adherence to gold, but it may miss subtler, long-run effects. For a country on the gold standard, but subject to political and economic upheaval, long-term interest rates might not be unusually low. For a country off the gold standard because of a war but expected shortly to resume, long-term interest rates might not be unusually high. In both cases a country's beta (b_{i1}) may yield as much or more information as the gold dummy because the beta reflects, we conjecture, long-term commitment.

The model also includes monetary and fiscal policy variables to test whether investors looked beyond adherence to gold to fundamentals that would determine the probability that a country would be unable to pay its debts or could do so only in a depreciated currency. Rapid growth of the stock of money relative to output, we presumed, would raise the probability of a devaluation and raise interest rates. (Although alternatively, in the short run, it would lower interest rates via the liquidity effect.) A large government deficit relative to national income, we conjectured, would raise interest. (Alternatively, a country charged a low interest rate might be encouraged to borrow more, creating a negative correlation.)[47]

Econometrics Methods

We first estimated separate regressions for each bond in our sample using only the data for the country that issued the bond. These results are reported below. However, there are two problems with estimating separate equations for each country. First, the gold dummy cannot be included for those countries that were always on gold (Australia and Canada) or that were always off during our sample period (Portugal and Spain). With no change in the country's status, the effects of being on or off gold cannot be separated from the constant term in equation 1. Second, innovations in interest rates may be correlated across countries. Although estimates of equation 1 are consistent, even when each country is treated separately, a seemingly unrelated-regressions (SUR) model that pools data for a number of countries increases the efficiency of our procedure.

We use a restricted SUR model that allows for autocorrelation and unequal numbers of observations. Our assumptions for the innovations are as follows.

$$\epsilon_{it} = \rho_i \epsilon_{it-1} + \mu_{it}, \mu_{it} \sim \left(0, \sigma_i^2\right), \text{ for } i = 1, 2 \ldots 9 \tag{2}$$

$$E\left(\mu_{it}\, \mu_{jt^*}\right) = \sigma_{ij}, \quad \text{if } t = t^*$$

$$E\left(\mu_{it}\, \mu_{jt^*}\right) = 0, \quad \text{if } t \neq t^*$$

That is, innovations in country i's interest rate are first-order autocorrelated, and the innovations in the interest rates of country i and j are also correlated, provided there is an observation for both countries in that year.

We applied the SUR model separately to a sample including only gold bonds (seven countries) and only paper bonds (five countries) because we expected them to react differently to a country's commitment to gold. We checked this division of the sample by applying the SUR model to two pooled samples that combined gold and paper bonds. One included one rate from each country, choosing the gold rate when it was available (seven gold rates and two paper rates); the other was a paper-weighted sample that included four gold rates and five paper rates. The results for these pooled regressions were similar to those reported below.

The coefficients on the gold dummy are restricted to be the same across countries. This allows information for those countries that are always on or off gold to be used. The coefficients on the fundamentals are also restricted to be the same across countries.

We used the following procedure to estimate the model. We ran OLS regressions for the nine countries. The original data were transformed using the Cochrane-Orcutt method.[48] We ran OLS regressions on the transformed data and used the residuals to estimate the contemporaneous covariance, σ_{ij} The transformed data were then used in a SUR model to produce final estimates of the coefficients of equation 1. We created an R^2 that is analogous to the one used with ordinary least square regressions, but the statistical properties of our analogue is unknown.

THE RESULTS

Tables 2 and 3 show individual country regressions with the sample divided into gold bonds and paper bonds.[49] For each country we show two regressions: a pure CAPM regression and a CAPM-plus-policy-variables regression. In most cases the improvement in the equations from adding the policy variables was marginal at best.

The results for the gold dummy for the gold bonds (Table 2) offer some support for our story. The coefficient is negative for four of the five countries and statistically significant in the case of Chile and the case of Italy when the CAPM-plus-policy-variables model is used. The gold dummy is marginally significant in the case of the United States. These bonds, we should note, were payable in gold even when the ordinary currency of the country was not convertible into gold at a fixed rate. The higher price of gold bonds when the domestic currency was convertible presumably reflected the lower probability of some kind of national bankruptcy.

A stronger confirmation is provided by the beta coefficients. Almost all of the betas are highly statistically significant, except for one regression each in the cases of Brazil and Chile. The betas are substantially less than one for Canada and Australia, two countries that demonstrated considerable commitment to gold. For the United States, also a strong gold adherent, the beta equals one in the simple CAPM regression and was less than one in the augmented regression. At the other extreme, two countries with poor records of adherence, Argentina and Brazil, had very high betas as expected. In the case of Italy, which for a few years followed

Table 2 INDIVIDUAL COUNTRY REGRESSIONS DEPENDENT VARIABLES: YIELDS ON GOLD BONDS

Country	Intercept	Beta	On Gold?	Monetary Policy	Fiscal Policy	AR(1)	Adj R^2	DW	N
Canada	-0.17 (0.91)	0.63*** (4.84)	—	—	—	0.79*** (11.0)	0.91	1.08	44
	-0.03 (0.12)	0.57*** (5.02)	—	-0.19 (-1.07)	0.46 (0.29)	0.93*** (14.9)	0.94	1.62	42
Australia	0.21 (1.05)	0.53*** (3.99)	—	—	—	0.53*** (3.82)	0.60	1.89	44
	-0.58 (1.22)	0.72** (3.70)	—	-0.40 (1.08)	3.83 (1.53)	0.70*** (5.41)	0.56	1.95	42
United states	0.047 (0.08)	1.00** (4.01)	-0.42 (1.46)	—	—	0.90*** (17.2)	0.96	2.24	44
	0.34 (0.71)	0.72** (3.10)	-0.41 (1.60)	-0.48 (0.95)	2.20 (0.18)	0.83*** (18.6)	0.96	2.62	42
Italy	0.12 (0.40)	1.04*** (4.56)	-0.17 (0.92)	—	—	0.61*** (6.99)	0.91	1.27	44
	-0.51 (0.16)	0.39* (1.90)	-0.34** (2.04)	0.37 (0.91)	-0.74 (0.37)	0.97*** (20.5)	0.94	1.77	42
Argentina	0.13 (0.23)	2.06*** (5.04)	0.004 (0.02)	—	—	0.81*** (5.47)	0.91	1.81	29
	-0.29 (0.43)	2.57*** (5.86)	-0.19 (0.62)	-0.53 (0.80)	0.50 (0.10)	0.47*** (1.96)	0.90	1.63	27
Brazil	0.87 (0.74)	1.67** (2.17)	-0.11 (0.19)	—	—	0.82*** (5.97)	0.80	1.45	24
	1.19 (0.88)	1.41 (1.63)	-0.08 (0.13)	0.18 (0.39)	-3.21 (0.96)	0.86*** (6.15)	0.79	1.20	24
Chile	2.35 (38.3)	0.44 (1.22)	-0.99*** (4.67)	—	—	0.93*** (7.54)	0.38	2.05	38
	1.40*** (10.3)	0.89** (2.28)	-0.89*** (3.62)	0.04 (0.11)	1.59 (0.68)	0.76*** (5.35)	0.30	2.00	36

* means significant at the 10 percent level.
** means significant at the 5 percent level.
*** means significant at the 1 percent level.

Notes: The coefficients in each row were estimated from the data for the country named on the left by ordinary least squares with an adjustment for first order autocorrelation. The "On Gold?" dummy was omitted for countries that were at par throughout the period. The Monetary and Fiscal variables were excluded in the top regression for each country. Absolute values of t-statistics are in parentheses.

301

Table 3 INDIVIDUAL COUNTRY REGRESSIONS DEPENDENT VARIABLES: YIELDS ON PAPER BONDS

Country	Intercept	Beta	On Gold?	Monetary Policy	Fiscal Policy	AR(1)	Adj R²	DW	N
United states	0.35 (1.08)	0.42*** (3.50)	-0.11 (0.78)	—	—	0.91*** (25.2)	0.97	1.77	44
	0.26 (1.02)	0.49*** (4.16)	-0.07 (0.53)	-0.45* (1.83)	-11.3* (1.87)	0.88*** (21.2)	0.97	1.78	42
Italy	0.41 (1.29)	0.75*** (3.16)	-0.09 (0.51)	—	—	0.64*** (8.15)	0.89	1.38	44
	-0.30 (0.10)	0.36* (1.75)	-0.27 (1.58)	0.14 (0.34)	0.23 (0.11)	0.97*** (17.8)	0.92	2.18	42
Spain	0.32 (0.31)	1.22*** (2.12)	—	—	—	0.86*** (9.09)	0.83	1.79	31
	0.16 (0.25)	0.49 (0.88)	—	-0.04 (0.04)	19.3 (1.51)	0.84*** (5.53)	0.72	1.61	11
Portugal	0.56 (0.74)	1.81*** (2.87)	—	—	—	0.60*** (3.44)	0.68	1.95	23
	-0.33 (0.35)	2.30*** (3.43)	—	1.30 (0.66)	24.2 (0.81)	0.53*** (3.10)	0.69	1.75	22
Chile	3.59*** (20.0)	0.79*** (2.33)	0.23 (0.84)	—	—	0.62*** (5.43)	0.11	1.29	42
	3.62*** (18.5)	0.78*** (2.26)	0.29 (1.02)	0.23 (0.52)	-1.31 (0.51)	0.58*** (4.84)	0.09	1.27	42

* means significant at the 10 percent level.
** means significant at the 5 percent level.
*** means significant at the 1 percent level.

Notes: The coefficients in each row were estimated from the data for the country named on the left by ordinary least squares with an adjustment for first order autocorrelation. The "On Gold?" dummy was omitted for countries that were at par throughout the period. The Monetary and Fiscal variables were excluded in the top regression for each country. Absolute values of t-statistics are in parentheses.

the gold standard contingent rule and for a longer period shadowed gold, the beta in the simple regression was close to that of the United States. However, when the policy variables were added the beta was somewhat lower than we would have expected. This was also the case for Chile, although these equations were the least well estimated in the gold sample.[50]

For the paper bonds (Table 3) none of the coefficients on the gold dummy are statistically significant at conventional levels. Again, however, the betas confirm the importance of long-term commitment. In this subsample the U.S. beta is well below one, a result consistent with its relatively high commitment. Italy, Spain, and Portugal, which shadowed gold, in general had higher betas, although the results were not uniform across specifications and countries. In the case of Chile, as with the gold bonds, the beta was somewhat lower than expected.

In general the OLS results are consistent with the "good housekeeping" hypothesis, although there are some anomalies. Part of the problem may be the inefficiency of the OLS approach, and there is some evidence for this in the insignificant coefficients and low R^2 in some of the regressions. The pooled seemingly unrelated regressions presented in Tables 4 and 5, we believe, address these issues.

Turning to the results for the unweighted gold-bond sample, the gold dummy is negative and highly significant in both regressions. Moreover, the betas line up for the most part as expected. And most supportive of our hypothesis is that the betas for the three countries with poor adherence records were considerably higher than the others. The results for the sample in which the average rate was weighted by the shares in British overseas investment were quite similar to the regressions that use unweighted averages. The main exceptions are that the monetary policy variable is significant and the U.S. beta is somewhat higher than expected. The latter result may reflect the heavy weight of the United States in the weighted average.

Table 5 shows the pooled seemingly unrelated regressions for the paper-bond sample. The gold dummy is insignificant in the regressions that use the unweighted average interest rate and significant in the regressions that use an average interest rate weighted by the shares of British overseas investment. However, the coefficients are half the size of those in the gold-bond sample.

One explanation is that the paper sample includes more temporary departures and returns to the gold standard that the market ignored, whereas the gold sample includes more cases of long-term commitment. It is also possible that paper and gold bonds appealed to different classes of investors and that the more risk-averse investors who insisted on gold bonds were more sensitive to whether a country was currently adhering to gold. Alternatively, the explanation may be that borrowers could effectively price discriminate between domestic and foreign lenders.[51]

As in the case of the gold-bond sample the betas in both unweighted cases lined up as expected. The only anomaly is Spain in the British-overseas-investment weighted-policy-variables regression where the beta is unusually low and insignificant.[52]

Table 4 POOLED REGRESSIONS DEPENDENT VARIABLES: YIELDS ON GOLD BONDS

	Average Interest Differential: Unweighted		Average Interest Differential: Weighted by Share in British Overseas Investment	
	(1)	(2)	(3)	(4)
Intercept	0.15 (1.30)	0.30** (2.24)	0.41*** (4.44)	0.37*** (4.01)
Canada	0.47*** (5.67)	0.37*** (4.41)	0.53*** (5.65)	0.62*** (6.03)
Australia	0.54*** (6.96)	0.49*** (5.66)	0.73*** (7.19)	0.66*** (7.15)
United states	0.42*** (2.79)	0.49*** (5.10)	0.90*** (4.61)	0.80*** (5.76)
Italy	0.72*** (8.07)	0.50*** (4.08)	0.79*** (5.89)	0.60** (2.62)
Argentina	1.49*** (14.2)	1.42*** (11.1)	1.99*** (14.2)	1.95*** (13.0)
Brazil	1.49*** (13.0)	1.43*** (13.6)	2.06*** (7.58)	2.06*** (8.34)
Chile	1.26*** (9.05)	1.22*** (8.34)	1.16*** (3.08)	1.43*** (4.45)
On gold?	−0.34*** (4.15)	−0.38*** (4.70)	−0.41*** (5.51)	−0.41*** (6.02)
Monetary policy	—	−0.08 (0.74)	—	−0.22*** (3.10)
Fiscal policy	—	−0.17	—	0.88*
Simulated R^2	0.57	0.24 (0.63)	0.70	(1.72) 0.66
DW	1.87	1.98	1.81	1.87
N	267	255	267	255

* means significant at the 10 percent level.
** means significant at the 5 percent level.
*** means significant at the 1 percent level.

Notes: The coefficients in each column were estimated from the pooled sample of gold bonds by seemingly unrelated regression with adjustments for autocorrelation and the unequal number of observations for each country. The coefficient for each country is its "beta," the relationship between its interest rate differential with London and an average differential. Absolute values of *t*-statistics are in parentheses.

In sum the pooled results provide strong support for the "good housekeeping seal." In both the pooled-gold and pooled-paper samples we find a similar correspondence between gold standard adherence (including shadowing) and low country risk as measured by the betas. In addition, the gold adherence dummy that may capture the impact of adherence not accounted for by the betas was negative and significant as predicted. Indeed, if we were to single out one number to represent our findings with respect to the significance of the gold-adherence dummy it would be 40 basis points, approximately the coefficient of the gold dummy in the British-overseas-investment weighted regression (or in the current parlance the "haircut" charged for not being on gold.) In other words, all other things equal, the rate on a gold bond would be 40 basis points lower if the country were on the gold standard. Other factors, perhaps related to regional preferences, undoubtedly also played a role in determining the country-risk premia. But our analysis suggests that a willingness to commit to the discipline of the gold standard was an important determinant of the risk premia established in the London capital market.

Table 5 POOLED REGRESSIONS DEPENDENT VARIABLES: YIELDS ON PAPER BONDS

	Average Interest Differential: Unweighted		*Average Interest Differential: Weighted by Share in British Overseas Investment*	
	(1)	*(2)*	*(3)*	*(4)*
Intercept	0.09 (0.68)	0.28** (2.02)	0.78*** (3.80)	0.88*** (4.48)
United States	0.39*** (5.21)	0.36*** (5.54)	0.44*** (3.39)	0.31** (2.36)
Italy	0.64*** (7.57)	0.42*** (3.24)	0.45*** (2.88)	0.38** (2.12)
Spain	1.35*** (5.44)	0.55*** (4.40)	1.17*** (2.87)	0.18 (0.85)
Portugal	1.41*** (16.7)	1.38*** (15.6)	1.66*** (6.73)	1.64*** (6.36)
Chile	2.10*** (10.6)	2.13*** (14.4)	2.34*** (7.40)	2.50*** (9.24)
On gold?	0.06 (0.71)	−0.01 (0.16)	−0.24** (2.27)	−0.18** (2.05)
Monetary policy	—	−0.19 (1.31)	— (0.49)	−0.08
Fiscal policy	—	−0.42 (0.38)	— (0.62)	−0.78
Simulated R^2	0.74	0.81	0.66	0.76
DW	1.61	1.44	1.60	1.54
N	184	159	184	159

* means significant at the 10 percent level.
** means significant at the 5 percent level.
*** means significant at the 1 percent level.

Notes: The coefficients in each column were estimated from the pooled sample of paper bonds by seemingly unrelated regression with adjustments for autocorrelation and the unequal number of observations for each country. The coefficient for each country is its "beta," the relationship between its interest rate differential with London and an average differential. Absolute values of *t*-statistics are in parentheses.

The Bottom Line

Was it worthwhile for a country to adopt the gold standard to gain the seal of good (financial) housekeeping? Figures 8 and 9 illustrate the benefits. On the left in each figure, for comparison, is the average British consol rate over the years 1870 to 1914, our proxy for the risk-free rate. Next to it are predicted rates for each country measured in percentage. The countries are ranked from left to right in descending order according to their adherence to gold. Figure 8 shows the gold bonds, which were especially important because they were a major vehicle for the transmission of capital from the core to the periphery, and Figure 9 shows the paper bonds. In each case we computed the predicted rate from the betas and gold dummy that we estimated and the average price of risk (the average return for the sample less the average consol rate) for the entire period. In this way we were able to compare countries even when the underlying interest series were not available for the same periods.

It is clear from Figure 8 that the benefits of committing to gold were significant in economic as well as statistical terms. Where commitment was high, rates were low; where commitment was low, rates were high. Over the whole period the risk-free

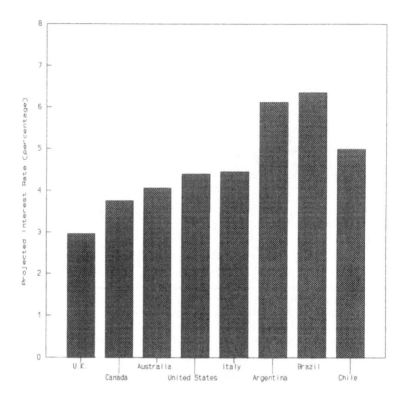

Figure 8 THE VALUE OF ADHERING TO GOLD: GOLD BONDS, 1870–1914. *Note*: Data were computed by using the coefficients of regression 3 in Table 4

rate averaged about 3 percent. Canada, Australia, and the United States, countries with strong commitments, paid about one percentage point more. Italy, which had a decidedly worse formal adherence record, paid only a fraction more. Presumably the markets attached nearly as much weight to close shadowing the gold standard as actual adherence. Argentina, Brazil, and Chile, which adhered intermittently at altered parities, paid two to three percentage points more.[53] Figure 9 for the paper bonds tells a similar story. In this sample the United States and Italy paid a little more than one percentage point above the U.K. rate (125 and 140 basis points respectively). The Chilean rate, on the other hand, was over four percentage points higher. The Spanish and Portuguese rates lie between these extremes.

Both figures underscore the point that the difference in rates was substantial for countries that were attempting to raise large amounts of capital on international markets. Or to put it somewhat differently, the numbers make it easy to see why there were strong economic pressures on countries that were off the gold standard to resume and strong pressures on countries that were on the gold standard to stay on.

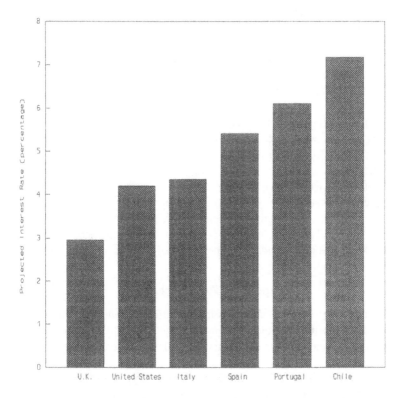

Figure 9 THE VALUE OF ADHERING TO GOLD: PAPER BONDS, 1870–1914. *Note*:
Data were computed by using the coefficients of regression 3 in Table 5

CONCLUSIONS

Our principal findings are that the interest rates charged on long-term bonds in
core capital markets during the era of the classical gold standard differed substantially from country to country and that these differences were correlated with
a country's long-term commitment to the gold standard. Countries that adhered
faithfully to the standard were charged rates only slightly above the British consol
rate; countries that made only sporadic attempts to maintain convertibility and
that altered their parities were charged much higher rates. Countries that did not
formally adhere but that followed policies that shadowed gold fell in between. We
interpret these findings to mean that adhering to gold was like the "good housekeeping seal of approval."

It should be emphasized that adherence to the gold standard rule, although a
simple and transparent test, implied a far more complex set of institutions and
economic policies. Indeed, those countries that adhered to the gold standard rule
generally had lower fiscal deficits, more stable money growth, and lower inflation

rates than those that did not.[54] But those countries that adhered to gold also paid a price for doing so because they gave up the flexibility to react to adverse supply shocks by following expansionary financial policies and altering the exchange rate. Those countries that did not adhere to the rule in fact faced greater supply shocks than those that did.[55] In responding to those shocks, and thereby sacrificing the rule, this group of countries, through the substantial risk premia they had to pay, may have reduced their long-run growth prospects. However, countries may have abandoned the rule not in response to adverse supply shocks but in response to other (possible political economy) factors. Whether in particular cases sacrificing the rule was worth it or not is an empirical question and a subject for future research.

Although the world today is very different from the world before 1914, the same issues are at stake. Many emerging countries have tried to recreate the "good housekeeping seals" by pegging their currency to a stronger one or by establishing currency boards. However, whether a "good housekeeping seal" as transparent and durable as the gold standard can be recreated today is an open question.

Appendix: Data Description

In this study we use annual data for nine countries: Argentina, Australia, Brazil, Canada, Italy, Portugal, Spain, the United Kingdom, and the United States. Our goal was to include data for each country for the entire era of the classical gold standard, 1870 to 1914, but in a number of cases we were able to find data for only part of the period. The series are arranged by country. In each case we give our variable name (which identifies the series in a spreadsheet file on disk available on request), the definition of the variable, and a parenthetical reference. In some cases we include notes that describe special features of the series.

Cross-country studies of this sort are inevitably a community effort. In a number of cases variables were supplied to us by scholars from their personal files, for which we are very grateful. These series may not be available in published sources. Users of this data set should consult these scholars directly for permission to use their data.

Argentina

CCAL.ARG($m): Total Capital Calls of Argentina, 1865–1914. *Sources*: Figures provided by Lance Davis, California Institute of Technology and Robert Gallman, University of North Carolina, Chapel Hill.

FB.ARG($M): Foreign Borrowing of Argentina, 1884–1900. *Source*: Ford, *Gold Standard*, table 14, p. 139.

CUK.ARG($M): U.K. issues for Argentina, 1881–1914. *Source*: Ford, *Gold Standard*, table 25, p. 195.

LNCI.ARG($M): Net Capital Inflow of Argentina, 1884–1914. *Source*: Ford, *Gold Standard*, derived from table 25, p. 195.

DFT.ARG: GDP Deflator of Argentina, 1884–1914. 1913 = 1. *Source*: Della Paolera, "How the Argentine Economy," table 37, p. 186.

EXRT.ARG(Arg / $): Exchange Rate of Argentina (5 gold pesos = 1 pound), 1884–1914. *Source*: Della Paolera, "How the Argentine Economy," table 37, p. 186.

GDP.ARG (millions of paper pesos): Nominal GDP of Argentina, 1884–1914. *Source*: Della Paolera, "How the Argentine Economy," table 37, p. 186.

RGDP.ARG (millions of paper pesos): Real GDP of Argentina, 1884–1914. *Source*: Della Paolera, "How the Argentine Economy," table 37, p. 186.

G.ARG (millions of paper pesos): Government Expenditure of Argentina, 1883–1914. *Source*: Della Paolera, "How the Argentine Economy," table 36, p. 183.

T.ARG (millions of paper pesos): Government Revenue of Argentina, 1883–1914. *Source*: Della Paolera, "How the Argentine Economy," table 36, p. 183.

LTIR.ARG: Argentina Average Annual Yield on External Bond, 1884–1913. *Source*: Della Paolera, "How the Argentine Economy," table 33, p. 178.

M.ARG: (millions of paper pesos) Argentina Money Supply, 1883–1913. *Source*: Della Paolera, "How the Argentine Economy," table 37, p. 186.

POP.ARG (millions): Argentina Population. *Source:* Mitchell, *International Historical Statistics: The Americas.*

TOT.ARG: Argentina Terms of Trade, 1884–1913. 1913 = 100. *Source*: Della Paolera, "How the Argentine Economy," table 37, p. 186.

Australia

CCAL.AUS(U.S. $m): Total Capital Calls of Australia in millions of U.S. dollars, 1865–1914. *Sources*: Figures provided by Lance Davis, California Institute of Technology and Robert Gallman, University of North Carolina, Chapel Hill.

LNCI.AUS($M): Net Apparent Capital Inflow of Australia. *Source*: Pope, "Australia's Payments," appendix 2, pp. 231–32.

CPI.AUS: Consumer Price Index of Australia, 1913 = 100. *Source*: Pope, "Australia's Payments," appendix 2, pp. 231–32.

DFT.AUS: GDP Deflator of Australia. 1913 = 1. *Source*: Pope, "Australia's Payments," appendix 2, pp. 231–32.

EXRT.AUS($A/U.S. $): Exchange Rates of Australia. *Source*: Pope, "Australia's Payments," appendix 2, pp. 231–32.

G.AUS($m): Government Expenditures of Australia. (1870–1971 as 1870). *Source*: Pope, "Australia's Payments," appendix 2, pp. 231–32.

GDP.AUS($m): Nominal GDP of Australia, 1861–1900. *Sources*: Pope, "Australia's Payments," appendix 2, pp. 231–32. The original was in £m; we converted to $m. Figures after 1900 are from Butlin, "Our 200 Years," pp. 229–30.

RGDP.AUS($m): Real GDP of Australia. RGDP.AUS = GDP.AUS / (GDP Deflator).

LTIR.AUS: Long-term Interest Rates of Australia. Government bonds. *Source*: Vamplew, *Australians*, p. 2.

STIR.AUS Short-term Interest Rates of Australia. Savings bank deposit rates. *Source*: Vamplew, *Australians*, p. 2. PF1, p. 240.

M2.AUS($m): Australian Money Stock. M2. M2.AUS = M1.AUS + public's saving banks deposits, where M1.AUS is currency held by the public + trading banks current deposits. *Source*: Vamplew, *Australians*, p. 247, PF 57–63, column 61 (original in calendar years), and p. 248, PF 64–71, column 69 (converted to calendar years).

POP.AUS(millions): Population of Australia. *Source:* Mitchell, *International Historical Statistics: The Americas.*

T.AUS($m): Government Revenue of Australia. *Source*: Pope, "Australia's Payments," appendix 2, pp. 231–32.

TOT.AUS: Australian Terms of Trade. TOT.AUS = (Export price index) / (Import price index). *Source*: Pope, "Australia's Payments," appendix 2, pp. 231–32. The base year is 1913. The 1914 figure was obtained by averaging the 1913 estimate (1.163) and the 1914 to 1915 estimate (1.210).

Brazil

DFT.BRZ: GDP Deflator of Brazil, 1880–1914. *Source*: Bordo and Jonung, "Monetary Regimes," data appendix.

EXRT.BRZ (cruzeiros / $): Exchange Rate of Brazil, 1889–1914. *Source*: Bordo and Jonung, "Monetary Regimes," data appendix.

GDP.BRZ (millions of cruzeiros): Nominal GDP of Brazil, 1880–1914. *Source*: Bordo and Jonung, "Monetary Regimes," data appendix.

RGDP.BRZ (millions of cruzeiros): Real GDP of Brazil. The base year is 1913. *Source*: Bordo and Jonung, "Monetary Regimes," data appendix.

G.BRZ (millions of cruzeiros): Government Expenditure of Brazil, 1880–1914. *Source*: Bordo and Jonung, "Monetary Regimes," data appendix.

T.BRZ (millions of cruzeiros): Government Tax Revenue of Brazil, 1880–1914. *Source*: Bordo and Jonung, "Monetary Regimes," data appendix.

LTIR.BRZ: Long-Term Interest Rates of Brazil, 1890–1914. *Sources*: Figures provided by Eliana A. Cardoso, World Bank, and Rudiger Dornbusch, Massachusetts Institute of Technology; and *Commercial and Financial Chronicle*. A graph of the price of the bonds is presented in Cardoso and Dornbusch, "Brazilian Debt Crises." We use the current yield: the coupon divided by the price of the bond. We also calculated yields to maturity because there were deep discounts on Brazilian bonds, the case in which current yields and yields to maturity will differ the most. But the yield to maturity produced almost identical results in the regressions. In our results we report only regressions on current yields to maintain comparability with the other series.

M.BRZ (millions of cruzeiros): Money Supply of Brazil, 1880–1914. *Source*: Bordo and Jonung, "Monetary Regimes," data appendix.

POP.BRZ: Population of Brazil, 1880–1914. *Source*: Bordo and Jonung, "Monetary Regimes," data appendix.

TOT.BRZ: Terms of Trade of Brazil, 1870–1914. *Estatisticas historicas do Brasil*, p. 597.

Canada

CCAL.CAN(U.S. $million): Total Capital Calls of Canada, 1865–1914. *Sources*: Figures provided by Lance Davis, California Institute of Technology and Robert Gallman, University of North Carolina, Chapel Hill.

LNCI.CAN: Long-Term Net Capital Inflow, 1871–1913. *Source*: Dick and Floyd, *Canada*, table B1, pp. 190–91.

CPI.CAN: Consumer Price Index of Canada, 1870–1914. 1913 = 100. *Source*: Maddison, *Dynamic Forces*, table E2, pp. 296–97.

DFT.CAN: Price Deflator of Canada. 1913 = 1. *Source*: Urquhart, "New Estimates," pp. 30–31.

EXRT.CAN: Exchange Rate of Canada, 1870–1914. *Source*: Bordo and Jonung, "Monetary Regimes," data appendix.

G.CAN(in millions of $): Government Expenditure of Canada, 1870–1914. *Source*: Mitchell, *International Historical Statistics: The Americas*, pp. 654–56.

T.CAN (in millions of $): Government Revenue of Canada, 1870–1914. *Source*: Mitchell, *International Historical Statistics: The Americas*.

LTIR.CAN: Long-term Interest Rates of Canada. *Sources*: Bordo and Jonung, *Long-Run Behavior*, p. 160; and Neufeld, *Financial System*, table 15.

M.CAN: Money Supply of Canada. (M2). *Source*: Bordo and Jonung, *Long-Run Behavior*, p. 160.

GNP.CAN($mm): Nominal GNP of Canada, 1870–1914. *Source*: Urquhart, "New Estimates of GNP," pp. 30–31.

RGNP.CAN($mm): Real GNP of Canada, 1870–1914. *Source*: Urquhart, "New Estimates of GNP," pp. 30–31.

TOT.CAN: Terms of Trade of Canada. 1913 = 1. *Source*: Social Science Federation of Canada, *Historical Statistics*, pp. 299–300.

POP.CAN(millions): Canada Population, 1870–1914. *Source*: Mitchell, *International Historical Statistics: The Americas*.

Chile

DFT.CH: GDP deflator of Chile. Derived from GDP.CH and RGDP.CH.

EXRT.CH (peso/$): Exchange Rate of Chile, 1880–1914. *Source*: Bordo and Jonung, "Monetary Regimes," data appendix.

RGDP.CH (millions of paper pesos): Real GDP of Chile, 1870–1914. The base year is 1913. *Source*: Llona-Rodriguez, "Chilean Monetary Policy." RGDP in 1913 gold pesos (table 8, p. 37), was converted to 1913 pesos using the exchange rate in table 65 (p. 285).

GDP.CH (millions of paper pesos): Nominal GDP of Chile, 1870–1914. *Source*: Llona-Rodriguez, "Chilean Monetary Policy." Nominal GDP is constructed from RGDP in 1913 gold peso and Conversion Factor II in table 64 (pp. 284–85).

G.CH (millions of paper pesos): Government Expenditures of Chile, 1870–1914. *Source*: Llona-Rodriguez, "Chilean Monetary Policy," table 8, p. 37. The original is in 1913 gold pesos. Conversion Factor II (table 64, p. 284) was used to convert to current pesos.

T.CH (millions of paper pesos): Tax Revenue of Chile, 1870–1914. See G.CH.

LTIR.CH: Long-Term Interest Rate of Chile, 1870–1914. We have two long-term rates for Chile: 4.5 percent external Sterling bonds and 7 percent internal peso bonds. *Source*: Mamalakis, *Historical Statistics*, table 8.2, p. 365; table 8.5, p. 387.

M.CH (millions of paper pesos): Money Supply of Chile, M1, 1870–1914. *Source*: Mamalakis, *Historical Statistics*, p. 36.

POP.CH (millions): Population of Chile, 1870–1914. *Source*: Mitchell, *International Historical Statistics: The Americas*, pp. 62–63.

Italy

CPI.IT: Consumer Price Index of Italy, 1870–1914. 1913 = 100. *Source*: Fratianni and Spinelli, "Italy."

DFT.IT: GNP Deflator of Italy, 1870–1914. 1913 = 1. *Source*: Fratianni and Spinelli, "Italy."

EXRT.IT (lire / $): Exchange Rate of Italy, 1880–1914. *Source*: Fratianni and Spinelli, "Italy."

GNP.IT (millions of lires): Nominal GNP of Italy, 1870–1914. Derived from RGNP.IT and DFT.IT.

RGNP.IT (millions of lires): Real GNP of Italy, 1870–1914. 1913 = 1. *Source*: Fratianni and Spinelli, "Italy."

G.IT (millions of lires): Government Expenditure of Italy, 1870–1914. *Source*: Mitchell, *International Historical Statistics: Europe*, p. 797.

T.IT (millions of lires): Government Tax Revenue of Italy, 1870–1914. *Source*: Mitchell, *International Historical Statistics: Europe*, p. 812.

LTIR.IT: Long-Term Interest Rates of Italy (long-term government bond rates), 1870–1914. *Source*: Figures provided by Franco Spinelli, Universita Degli Studi Brescia.

LTIR.ITG: Yields of Long-Term Government Bonds sold in Paris, net of taxes. *Source*: Figures provided by Franco Spinelli, Universita Degli Studi Brescia, from ISTAT, *Annuario Statistica Italiano.* The coupon was 4 lire net of taxes until 1906 when a conversion lowered the coupon to 3.75 lire. Payments made abroad by the Italian Treasury were made in gold.

M.IT (millions of lires): Money Supply of Italy, M1, 1870–1914. *Source*: Fratianni and Spinelli, "Italy."

POP.IT (million): Population of Italy, 1870–1914. *Source*: Spinelli, "Demand."

TOT.IT: Terms of Trade of Italy, 1870–1914. 1913 = 1. *Source*: Spinelli and Fratianni, *Storia Monetaria*, pp. 69–70.

Portugal

DFT.POR: GDP Deflator of Portugal, 1880–1914. *Source*: Bordo and Schwartz, "Operation," data appendix.

EXRT.POR (escudo / $): Exchange Rate of Portugal, 1890–1914. *Source*: Bordo and Schwartz, "Operation," data appendix.

GDP.POR (millions of escudos): Nominal GDP of Portugal, 1880–1914. *Source*: Bordo and Schwartz, "Operation," data appendix.

RGDP.POR: Real GDP of Portugal, 1880–1914. *Source*: Bordo and Schwartz, "Operation," data appendix.

G.POR: Government Expenditure of Portugal, 1890–1914. *Sources*: Figures provided by Fernando Teixeria dos Santos, Porto University; and Bordo and Santos, "Portugal," data appendix.

T.POR: Tax Revenue of Portugal, 1890–1914. *Sources*: Figures provided by Fernando Teixeria dos Santos; and Bordo and Santos, "Portugal," data appendix.

LTIR.POR: Long-Term Interest Rates of Portugal, 1891–1914. *Sources*: Figures provided by Fernando Teixeria dos Santos; and Bordo and Santos, "Portugal," data appendix.

M.POR (millions of escudos): Money Supply of Portugal, M1, 1890–1911. *Source*: Bordo and Schwartz, "Operation," data appendix.

POP.POR: Population of Portugal, 1880–1914. *Source*: Bordo and Schwartz, "Operation," data appendix.

TOT.POR: Terms of Trade of Portugal, 1870–1914. 1913 = 1. *Source*: Lains, "Economia Portuguesa."

Spain

CPI.SP: Consumer Price Index of Spain, 1870–1914.

DFT.SP: GDP Deflator of Spain, 1901–1914. *Sources*: Bordo and Schwartz, "Operation," data appendix; and *Estadisticas historicas de Espana.*

EXRT.SP(peseta / $): Exchange Rate of Spain, 1870–1914. *Sources*: Bordo and Schwartz, "Operation," data appendix; and *Estadisticas historicas de Espana.*

GDP.SP (millions of pesetas): Nominal GDP of Spain, 1901–1914. GDP.SP (millions of pesetas) = RGDP.SP × DFT.SP.

RGDP.SP (millions of pesetas): Real GDP of Spain, 1901–1914. *Estadisticas historicas de Espana*, p. 554.

G.SP (millions of pesetas): Government Expenditure of Spain, 1870–1914. *Source*: Mitchell, *International Historical Statistics: Europe*, p. 798.

T.SP (millions of pesetas): Tax Revenue of Spain, 1870–1914. *Source*: Mitchell, *International Historical Statistics: The Americas*, p. 814.

LTIR.SP: Long-Term Interest Rates of Spain, 1883–1914. *Source*: Martin-Acena, "Spain," p. 163.

M.SP (millions of pesetas): Money Supply of Spain, M1, 1874–1914. *Source: Estadisticas historicas de Espana*, pp. 385–86.

POP.SP (million): Population of Spain, 1870–1914. *Source: Estadisticas historicas de Espana*, p. 70.

TOT.SP: Terms of Trade of Spain, 1870–1914. *Source: Estadisticas historicas de Espana*, p. 352.

United Kingdom

CPI.U.K.: Consumer Price Index of U.K., 1870–1914. 1913 = 100. *Source*: Capie and Webber, *Monetary History*, p. 535.

DFT.U.K.: GNP Deflator of U.K. 1913 = 1. *Source*: Capie and Webber, *Monetary History*, p. 535.

EXRT.U.K. (pound / $): Exchange Rate of the U.K., 1870–1914. Friedman and Schwartz, *Monetary Trends*, table 4.9, pp. 130–31.

GNP.U.K. (£m): Nominal GNP of U.K. *Source*: Capie and Webber, *Monetary History*, p. 535.

RGNP.U.K. (£m): Real GNP of U.K. RGNP.U.K. = GNP.U.K. / DFT.U.K.

G.U.K. (millions): Government Expenditures of the U.K., 1870–1914. *Source*: Mitchell, *International Historical Statistics: Europe*, pp. 798–99.

T.U.K. (millions): Revenue of the U.K. government, 1870–1914. *Source*: Mitchell, *International Historical Statistics: Europe*, pp. 815–16.

M.U.K. (£m): Money Stock of the U.K. *Source*: Friedman and Schwartz, *Monetary Trends*, table 4.9, pp. 130–31. M.U.K. is "the sum of gross deposits at London and country joint stock and private banks (later London clearing banks and other domestic deposit banks,) and at Scottish and Irish banks, less interbank and transit items, plus private deposits at Bank of England and currency held by public" (Friedman and Schwartz, *Monetary Trends*, p. 134).

LTIR.U.K: The U.K. Long-term Interest Rates. (Yields on Consols). *Sources*: Bordo and Jonung, *Long-Run Behavior*, and *Annual Abstract.*

STIR.U.K.: The U.K. Short-term Interest Rates. (Rates on Three-month Bills). *Sources*: Bordo and Jonung, *Long-Run Behavior*, p. 162; and *Annual Abstract.*

POP.U.K. (millions): The U.K. Population. *Source*: Mitchell, *International Historical Statistics: Europe.*

TOT.U.K.: Terms of Trade of the U.K., 1870–1913. 1913 = 1. *Source*: Mitchell, *Abstract.*

United States

CCAL.U.S. ($million): Total Capital Calls of the United States, 1865–1914. *Sources*: Figures provided by Lance Davis, California Institute of Technology and Robert Gallman, University of North Carolina, Chapel Hill.

CCAL.USH ($Million): Capital Net Inflow derived from the balance of payments. U.S. Bureau of Census, *Historical Statistics*, pp. 564–65.

CCAL.USW ($million): Long-Term Capital Imports of the United States. *Source*: Williamson, *American Growth*, table 36, p. 151.

CPI.US: Consumer Price Index of the United States, 1870–1914. 1913 = 100. *Source*: U.S. Bureau of the Census, *Historical Statistics*, pp. 210–11.

DFT.US: Implicit Price Deflator. 1913 = 1. *Source*: Friedman and Schwartz, *Monetary Trends*, table 4.8, pp. 122–23.

EXRT.US (Pound / $): Exchange Rate in the United States. *Source*: Friedman and Schwartz, *Monetary Trends*, table 4.9, pp. 130–31.

GNP.U.S. ($million): Nominal Income of the United States. *Source*: Friedman and Schwartz, *Monetary Trends*, table 4.9, pp. 130–31.

RGNP.US ($million): Real Income of the United States. *Source*: Friedman and Schwartz, *Monetary Trends*, table 4.9, pp. 130–31.

G.US (millions): Government Expenditures of the United States, 1870–1914. *Source*: Mitchell, *International Historical Statistics: Americas*, pp. 654–56.

T.US (millions): Revenue of the U.S. Government, 1870–1914. *Source*: Mitchell, *International Historical Statistics: Americas*, pp. 671–74.

M.US ($million): Money Stock of United States. *Source*: Friedman and Schwartz, *Monetary Trends*, table 4.8, pp. 122–23. M.US is the sum of currency held by the public plus adjusted deposits at all commercial banks: M2.

LTIR.US: Long-term Interest Rates of the United States, 1870–1914. (Yields on High-Grade Corporate Bonds). *Source*: Friedman and Schwartz, *Monetary Trends*, table 4.8, pp. 122–23. Unfortunately, there do not appear to be enough long-term federal government bond quotes to construct a long-term government yield series. Partly this was because most government bonds were held by banks as security for bank notes. The rate we use is the usual substitute.

LR.USGC: Long-Term Interest Rate of the United States, Gold Rate Computed by Charles Calomiris. *Source*: Calomiris, "Historical Perspectives."

LR.USGM: Long-Term Interest Rate of the United States, Gold Rate Computed by Frederick Macaulay. *Source*: Macaulay, *Movements*, table 19, pp. 217–18.

STIR.US: The Short-term Interest Rates of the United States. (Commercial Paper Rate). *Source*: Friedman and Schwartz, *Monetary Trends*, table 4.8, pp. 122–23.

POP.US (millions): The U.S. Population. *Source:* Mitchell, *International Historical Statistics: The Americas.*

TOT.US: Terms of Trade of the United States. 1913 = 1. *Source*: Williamson, *American Growth*, table B4, pp. 261–62.

*We owe an immense debt to our research assistant Zhongjian Xia who went beyond the usual duties to make valuable contributions to the analysis in the paper. For helpful suggestions we would like to thank Ehsan Choudhri, Michael Edelstein, Richard Grossman, Peter Kenen, Bruce Mizrach, Lawrence Officer, Gerardo Della Paolera, Angela Redish, Anna Schwartz, Hiroki Tsurumi and participants at the International Economics Seminar at Princeton University. For providing us with data we are also indebted to Eliana Cordoso, Rudiger Dornbusch, Jaime Reis, Fernando Santos, and Franco Spinelli.

Notes

1 Bordo and Kydland, "Gold Standard."
2 Eichengreen, *Golden Fetters*; Giovannini, "Bretton Woods"; Grilli, "Managing Exchange Rate Crises"; Bordo and Schwartz, "Operation"; and Morgenstern, *International Financial Transactions.*
3 There is a debate about whether the United States should be treated as a core or peripheral country. Those who view it as a peripheral country do so for two reasons: first, because it was a net capital importer and hence more like Australia and Canada than the core countries that provided the capital; second, because the silver agitation and legislation of 1878 and 1890 threatened the convertibility of U.S. currency into gold. See Eichengreen, *Golden Fetters*; Giovanni, "Bretton Woods"; and Grilli, "Managing Exchange Rate Crises." The view that the United States was a core country stresses three reasons: first, the United States was wealthier and more populous than the United Kingdom and certainly than France or Germany; second, the United States was a capital exporter as well as an importer in the late nineteenth century, and by 1914 it was a net capital exporter; and third, the silver threat was temporary, and convertibility was never suspended. Therefore, the United States by the end of the nineteenth century, a colossus on the world stage, belongs in the core. See Bordo and Schwartz, "Operation"; and Morgenstern, *International Financial Transactions.* For purposes of this article, because we are focusing on the determinants of capital flows from the mature economies of western Europe to countries of new settlement (as well as other developing countries), we include the United States with the other peripheral countries. Nevertheless, in terms of its role as a player in the international monetary system, we view it as part of the core.
4 With the exception of Gallarotti, *Anatomy,* p. 39.
5 Frankel, *On Exchange Rates,* pp. 41–69; and Frankel and Okungwu, "Liberalized Portfolio," decompose interest differentials between emerging and developed countries into a country-risk premium and a currency-risk premium. In our empirical work, in the absence of data suitable to measure expectations of change in exchange rates and hence to account for the currency-risk premium, we use to the extent available to us, gold denominated securities to account for the country-risk premium.
6 Stiglitz and Weiss, "Credit Rationing."
7 Simons, "Rules." The Currency School in England in the early nineteenth century made the case for the Bank of England's fiduciary note issue to vary automatically with the level of the Bank's gold reserve ("The currency principle"). Such a rule was preferable (for providing price-level stability) to allowing the note issue to be altered at the discretion of the directors of the Bank (the position taken by the opposing Banking School). For a discussion of the Currency Banking School debate, see Viner, *Studies*; Fetter, *Development*; and Schwartz, "Banking School."
8 Kydland and Prescott, "Rules."

9 Bordo and Kydland, "Gold Standard"; and Giovannini, "Bretton Woods."

10 Barro and Gordon, "Rules."

11 As a rule in the traditional sense—as an automatic mechanism to ensure price stability— bimetallism may have had greater scope for automaticity than the gold standard because of the possibility of a switch from one metal to the other. See Friedman, "Bimetallism."

12 Grossman and Van Huyck, "Sovereign Debt"; DeKock and Grilli, "Endogenous Exchange"; Flood and Isard, "Simple Rules"; and Bordo and Kydland, "Gold Standard."

13 This description is consistent with a result from a model of Lucas and Stokey, "Optimal Fiscal and Monetary Policy," in which financing of wars is an optimal contingency rule. In their example, where the occurrence and duration of the war are uncertain, the optimal plan for the debt is not to service it during the war. Under this policy, people realize when they purchase the debt that it will be defaulted on in the event the war continues longer than expected.

14 See Lucas and Stokey, "Optimal Fiscal and Monetary Policy"; and Mankiw, "Optimal Collection." A case study comparing British and French finances during the Napoleonic Wars shows that Britain was able to finance its wartime expenditures by a combination of taxes, debt, and paper money issue to smooth revenue; whereas France relied primarily on taxation. France relied on a less efficient mix of finance than Britain because it had used up its credibility by defaulting on outstanding debt at the end of the American War of Independence and by hyperinflating during the French Revolution. Napoleon ultimately returned France to the bimetallic standard in 1803 as part of a policy to restore fiscal probity, but because of the previous loss of reputation France was unable to take advantage of the contingent aspect of the bimetallic standard rule. See Bordo and White, "British and French Finances."

15 Canzoneri, "Monetary Policy Games"; and Obstfeld, "Destabilizing Effects."

16 Bordo and Schwartz, "Operation."

17 The behavior of asset prices (exchange rates and interest rates) during suspension periods suggests that market agents regarded the commitment to gold as credible. For the United States, see Roll, "Interest Rates"; and Calomiris, "Price," who present evidence of expected appreciation of the greenback during the American Civil War based on a negative interest differential between bonds that were paid in greenbacks and those paid in gold. Also, see Smith and Smith, "Wesley Mitchell," who demonstrate that movements in the premium on gold from the Resumption Act of 1875 until resumption was established in 1879 were driven by a credible belief that resumption would occur. For the case of Britain's return to gold in 1925, see Smith and Smith, "Stochastic Process Switching"; and Miller and Sutherland, "Britain's Return" and "Speculative Anticipations." An application of the literature on stochastic process switching suggests that the increasing likelihood that resumption would occur at the original parity gradually altered the path of the dollar-pound exchange rate towards the new ceiling, several months in advance of resumption.

18 Bordo and Schwartz, "Operation."

19 Eichengreen, "Editor's Introduction."

20 Officer, "Efficiency;" and Eichengreen, "Editor's Introduction."

21 Canzoneri and Henderson, *Monetary Policy.*

22 Giovannini, "Bretton Woods." Also see Officer, "Gold-Point Arbitrage." His calculations of speculative bands (bands within which uncovered interest arbitrage prevails consistent with gold-point arbitrage efficiency) for the interwar dollar-sterling exchange rate show serious violations only in 1931, at the very end of the gold-exchange standard.

23 Bordo and Kydland, "Gold Standard."

24 In addition to developing countries seeking long-term capital, countries also sought short-term loans, such as Japan, which financed the Russo-Japanese War of 1905 to 1906 with foreign loans seven years after adopting the gold standard. See Hayashi, "Japan's Saving Rate."

25 Virtually all of the available data on long-term capital flows for the countries we consider (if it exists) is calculated as the difference between the current account and changes in international reserves. Little attempt is made to distinguish between invisible items, errors, and omissions or to adequately separate short-term from long-term capital movements. An alternative measure is capital calls on new issues in London; see Davis and Cull, *International Capital Markets.* Preliminary investigation for a subset of our sample of the connection between capital calls, on the one hand, and a number of fundamental determinants and gold standard adherence, on the other, however, did not yield meaningful results.

26 Ford, *Gold Standard*; Bloomfield, *Patterns*; Abramovitz, "Monetary Side"; Davis and Cull, *International Capital Markets*; and Edelstein, *Overseas Investment.*

27 Fratianni and Spinelli, "Italy."

28 Tonniolo, *Economic History.*

29 Acena, "Spain."

30 Reis, "Gold Standard."

31 Macedo, "Convertibility."

32 Cortés Condé, *Dinero.*

33 Full service on the Argentine external national debt was postponed for three years by a moratorium arranged by a consortium of London creditor banks. Marichal, *Century*, p. 160. The provincial bonds were in default until 1898. We thank Gerardo Della Paolera for pointing this out.

34 Pelaez and Suzigan, *Historia.*

35 Fritsch and Franco, "Aspects."

36 Llona-Rodriguez, "Chile."

37 All the series used except for the United States were yields on national or federal government debt. For the United States we used a long-term corporate bond rate. Here we follow Friedman and Schwartz, *Monetary Trends,* p. 120, who prefer this series because some U.S. long-term governments bore the circulation privilege and because none were outstanding in some years.

38 Bordo and Schwartz, "Operation."

39 One possible explanation for the similarity between the U.K. consol rate and the Australian and Canadian rates, in addition to our maintained hypothesis, is that after 1893 Dominion government securities were endowed with the status of "trustee investments" by the British government. This could be construed as a strong signal of their quality. See Havinden and Meredith, *Colonialism*, pp. 88–90. We thank Shizuyu Nishimura for bringing this to our attention.

40 The attempt to estimate gold rates and paper rates for the United States has a long history, going back at least to Fisher, *Theory of Interest*, pp. 401–03. Here we use recent estimates by Calomiris, "Historical Perspectives," pp. 137–43, although we also tried the estimates computed by Macaulay, *Movements*, table 19, pp. 217–18, in our regressions to see if it made a difference.

41 The gold rate for Italy is the rate for long-term government bonds quoted in Paris. The rates for other countries in our sample were quoted in London.

42 Friedman and Schwartz, *Monetary Trends,* pp. 515–16, concluded that the decline in the difference between short-term interest rates in the United States and the United Kingdom after 1896 was the result of the resolution of concerns about the free-silver movement in the United States.

43 O'Rourke and Williamson, "Were Hechsher and Ohlin Right?"

44 Durbin-Watson tests on OLS regressions for equation 1 always show significant positive autocorrelation in error terms. We assume that the error terms follow an AR(1) process.
45 The CAPM was first developed in classic papers by Sharpe, "Capital Asset Prices"; and Lintner, "Valuation." Since then an enormous literature has grown up describing limitations, variants, and alternatives. Brennan, "Capital Asset Pricing Model," is an accessible recent survey.
46 The weights in percentages were Canada 22.8, Australia 18.5, the United States 33.5, Italy 0.6, Spain 0.8, Portugal 0.4, Argentina 14.2, Brazil 6.6, and Chile 2.7; Feis, *Europe*, p. 23. Feis's estimates have been subject to considerable criticism. It is not clear, however, that there are superior alternatives for our purposes. Moreover, although London was the principal capital market during the era of the classical gold standard, Paris was not far behind. In our sample the three southern European countries borrowed more in Paris than in London so the weights we use understate their role as borrowers in the world capital market.
47 The level of national debt, a variable we did not have, might have been a better measure of the creditworthiness of a country. But the interest payments on a burdensome debt should be reflected eventually in the fiscal deficit.
48 The first observations were dropped because alternative procedures became extremely complicated.
49 We include Australia and Canada with the countries issuing gold bonds because their currencies were convertible throughout the period.
50 This may reflect missing observations in a number of crisis periods.
51 Calomiris, "Motives," shows that the United States tailored its debt in the nineteenth century on the assumption that the long-term bond market was more sensitive to default risk.
52 This may reflect the small number of observations for Spain.
53 Although Chile had a worse gold-standard-adherence record than Argentina and its exchange rate depreciated more, the fact that Argentina defaulted on its gold debt in 1890 while Chile did not, may explain why its projected interest rate was over 100 basis points lower.
54 Bordo and Schwartz, "Operation."
55 Bordo and Jonung, "Monetary Regimes," and Bordo and Schwartz, "Operation."

References

Abramovitz, Moses. "The Monetary Side of Long Swings in U.S. Economic Growth." Stanford University Center for Research on Economic Growth. Memorandum No. 146, Mimeo 1973.

Acena, Pablo Martin. "Spain During the Classical Gold Standard Years, 1880–1914." In *Monetary Regimes in Transition*, edited by Michael D. Bordo and Forrest Capie, 135–72. Cambridge: Cambridge University Press, 1993.

Annual Abstract of Statistics. Central Statistics Office, London.

Barro, Robert J. and David B. Gordon. "Rules, Discretion, and Reputation in a Model of Monetary Policy." *Journal of Monetary Economics* 12 (1983): 101–21.

Bordo, Michael D. "The Bretton Woods International Monetary System: An Historical Overview." In *A Retrospective on the Bretton Woods System: Lessons for Monetary Reform*, edited by Michael D. Bordo and Barry Eichengreen, 3–98. Chicago: University of Chicago Press, 1993.

Bordo, Michael D. and Lars Jonung. *The Long-Run Behavior of the Velocity of Circulation: The International Evidence*. Cambridge: Cambridge University Press, 1987.

_____. "Monetary Regimes, Inflation, and Monetary Reform: An Essay in Honor of Axel Leijonhufvud." In *Inflation, Institutions, and Information: Essays in Honor of Axel Leijonhujvud*, edited by D.F. Vaz and K. Vellapillai. London: MacMillan Press, 1996.

Bordo, Michael D. and Anna J. Schwartz. "The Operation of the Specie Standard: Evidence for Core and Peripheral Countries, 1880–1990." In *Historical Perspectives on the Gold Standard: Portugal and the World*, edited by Barry Eichengreen and Jorge Braga de Macedo. London: Routledge, 1996.

Bordo, Michael D. and Fernando Santos. "Portugal and the Bretton Woods International System." In *The History of International Monetary Arrangements*, edited by Jaime Reis, 181–208. London: Macmillan, 1995.

Bordo, Michael D. and Eugene N. White. "British and French Finances During the Napoleonic Wars." In *Monetary Regimes in Transition*, edited by Michael D. Bordo and Forrest Capie, 241–73. Cambridge: Cambridge University Press, 1993.

Bloomfield, Arthur. *Patterns of Fluctuations in International Investment before 1914.* Princeton Studies in International Finance, No. 21. Princeton: Princeton University Press, 1968.

Brennan, M. J. "Capital Asset Pricing Model." In *The New Palgrave Dictionary of Money & Finance*, edited by Peter Newman, Murray Milgate, and John Eatwell, s.v., 287–91. London: The Macmillan Press, Ltd., 1992.

Butlin, Noel G. *Australian Domestic Product, Investment and Foreign Borrowing, 1860–1938/39.* Cambridge: Cambridge University Press, 1962.

_____. "Our 200 Years: Australian Wealth and Progress Since 1788, A Statistical Picture." In *Commemorative Bicentenary Diary.* Brisbane, Australia: Sunshine Diaries, 1987.

Calomiris, Charles W. "Historical Perspectives on The Tax-Based Theory of Money." Ph.D. diss., Stanford University, 1985.

_____. "Price and Exchange Rate Determination During the Greenback Suspension." *Oxford Economic Papers* 40, no. 4 (1988): 719–50.

_____. "The Motives of U.S. Debt-Management Policy, 1790–1880: Efficient Discrimination and Time Consistency." *Research in Economic History* 13 (1991): 67–105.

Canzoneri, Matthew. "Monetary Policy Games and the Role of Private Information." *American Economic Review* 75(1985): 1056–70.

Canzoneri, Matthew B. and Dale W. Henderson. *Monetary Policy in Interdependent Economies.* Cambridge, MA: MIT Press, 1991.

Capie, Forrest and A. Webber. *A Monetary History of The UK 1870–1982.* London: George Allan & Unwin, 1985.

Cardoso, Eliana A. and Rudiger Dornbusch. "Brazilian Debt Crises: Past and Present." In *The International Debt Crisis in Historical Perspective*, edited by Barry Eichengreen and Peter H. Lindert, 106–39. Cambridge: MIT Press, 1989.

Commercial and Financial Chronicle, various dates.

Cortés Condé, Roberto. *Dinero, deuda y crisis: Evolución fiscal y monetaria en la Argentina.* Buenos Aires: Editorial Sudamericana, Instituto Torcuato Di Tella, 1989.

Davis, Lance and Robert Cull. *International Capital Markets and American Economic Growth.* Cambridge: Cambridge University Press, 1994.

DeKock, Gabriel and Vittorio Grilli. "Endogenous Exchange Rate Regime Switches." NBER Working Paper No. 3066, Cambridge, MA, 1989.

Della Paolera, Gerardo. "How the Argentine Economy Performed during the International Gold Standard: A Reexamination." Ph.D. diss., University of Chicago, 1988.

De Mattia, Renato. *Storia del capitale della Banc d'Italia e degli istitute predecessori.* Rome: Banca d'Italia, 1977.

Dick, Trevor J. O. and John E. Floyd. *Canada and the Gold Standard.* New York: Cambridge University Press, 1992.

Edelstein, Michael. *Overseas Investment in the Age of High Imperialism: The United Kingdom, 1850–1914.* New York: Columbia University Press, 1982.

Eichengreen, Barry. *Golden Fetters: The Gold Standard and the Great Depression, 1919–1939.* Oxford: Oxford University Press, 1992.

Eichengreen, Barry and Peter H. Lindert, eds. *The International Debt Crisis in Historical Perspective.* Cambridge, MA: MIT Press, 1989.

Eichengreen, Barry. "Editor's Introduction." In *The Gold Standard in Theory and History*, edited by Barry Eichengreen, 1–35. London: Methuen, 1985.

Estatisticas historicas do Brasil: Series economicas, demograficas e sociais de 1550 a 1988. Rio de Janeiro: Brasilia. 1990.

Estadisticas historicas de Espana, Siglos xix-xx Madrid: Fundacion Banco Exterior 1989.

Feis, Herbert. *Europe: The World's Banker; 1870–1914: An Account of European Foreign Investment and the Connection of World Finance with Diplomacy before the War.* New York: Council on Foreign Relations. Reprinted by Augustus M. Kelley, 1974.

Fetter, F. *Development of British Monetary Orthodoxy, 1797–1875.* Cambridge: Harvard University Press, 1965.

Fisher, Irving. *The Theory of Interest: As Determined by Impatience to Spend Income and Opportunity to Invest It.* New York: The Macmillan Company, 1930.

Flood, Robert P. and Peter Isard. "Simple Rules, Discretion and Monetary Policy." NBER Working Paper No. 2934, Cambridge, MA, 1989.

Ford, A. G. *The Gold Standard 1880–1914: Britain and Argentina.* Oxford: Clarendon Press, 1962.

Frankel, Jeffrey A. *On Exchange Rates.* Cambridge, MA: Cambridge University Press, 1993.

Frankel, Jeffrey A. and Chudozie Okongwu. "Liberalized Portfolio Capital Inflows in Emerging Markets: Sterilization, Expectations, and the Incompleteness of Interest Rate Convergence." NBER Working Paper No. 5156, Cambridge, MA, 1995.

Fratianni, M. and F. Spinelli. "Italy in the Gold Standard Period, 1861–1914." In *A Retrospective on the Classical Gold Standard, 1921–1931*, edited by Michael D. Bordo and Anna J. Schwartz, 405–41. Chicago: University of Chicago Press, 1984.

Friedman, Milton. "Bimetallism Revisited." *Journal of Economic Perspectives* 4, no. 4 (1990): 85–104.

Friedman, Milton and Anna J. Schwartz. *Monetary Trends in the United States and the United Kingdom: Their Relation to Income, Prices, and Interest Rates, 1867–1975.* Chicago: University of Chicago Press for the NBER, 1982.

Fritsch, Winston and Gustavo H. B. Franco. "Aspects of the Brazilian Experience Under the Gold Standard." PUC Rio de Janeiro. Mimeo, 1992.

Gallarotti, Giulio M. *The Anatomy of an International Monetary Regime: the Classical Gold Standard 1880–1914.* New York: Oxford University Press, 1995.

Giovannini, Alberto. "Bretton Woods and Its Precursors: Rules Versus Discretion in the History of International Monetary Regimes." In *A Retrospective on the Bretton Woods System*, edited by Michael D. Bordo and Barry Eichengreen, 109–47. Chicago: University of Chicago Press, 1993.

Grilli, Vittorio. "Managing Exchange Rate Crises: Evidence from the 1890s." *Journal of International Money and Finance 9* (1990): 258–75.

Grossman, Herschel J. and John B. Van Huyck. "Sovereign Debt as a Contingent Claim: Excusable Default, Repudiation, and Reputation." *American Economic Review* 78 (1988): 1088–97.

Havinden, Michael and David Meredith. *Colonialism and Development: Britain and its Tropical Colonies, 1850–1960.* London: Routledge, 1993.

Hayashi, Fumio. "Japan's Saving Rate: New Data and Reflections." NBER Working Paper No. 3205, Cambridge, MA, 1989.

ISTAT Annuario Statistica Italiano, Rome, various years.

Kydland, Finn E. and Edward Prescott. "Rules Rather than Discretion: The Inconsistency of Optimal Plans." *Journal of Political Economy* 85 (1977): 473–91.

Lains, Pedro. "A economia Portuguesa no seculo XIX: Crescimento economico ecomercio externo, 1850–1913." Unpublished Manuscript, 1995.

Lintner, J. "The Valuation of Risk Assets and the Selection of Risky Investments in Stock Portfolios and Capital Budgets." *Review of Economics and Statistics* 47 (1965): 13–37.

Llona-Augustin. "Chilean Monetary Policy: 1860–1925." Ph.D. Diss., Boston University, 1990.

Llona-Rodriguez, Augustine. "Chile During the Gold Standard: A Successful Paper Money Experience." Mimeo. Instituto Torcuato Di Tella, 1993.

Lucas, Robert E. Jr. and Nancy L. Stokey. "Optimal Fiscal and Monetary Policy in an Economy Without Capital." *Journal of Monetary Economics* 1 (1983): 55–93.

Macedo, Jorge Braga de. "Convertibility and Stability 1834–1994: Portuguese Currency Experience Revisited." Mimeo. Nova University, Lisbon, 1995.

Macaulay, Frederic. R. *The Movements of Interest Rates, Bond Yields and Stock Prices in The United States Since 1856.* New York: NBER, 1938.

Maddison, Angus. *Dynamic Forces in Capitalist Development.* Oxford: Oxford University Press, 1991.

Mankiw, Gregory. "The Optimal Collection of Seigniorage: Theory and Evidence." *Journal of Monetary Economics* 20, no. 2 (1987): 327–41.

Mamalakis, Markos J. *Historical Statistics of Chile.* Vol. 5. New York: Greenwood, 1989.

Marichal, Carlos. *A Century of Debt Crisis in Latin America: From Independence to the Great Depression 1820–1930.* Princeton: Princeton University Press, 1989.

Miller, Marcus and Alan Sutherland. "Britain's Return to Gold and Entry into the ERM." In *Exchange Rate Targets and Currency Banks*, edited by Paul Krugman and Marcus Miller, 82–106. Cambridge: Cambridge University Press, 1992.

Miller, Marcus and Alan Sutherland. "Speculative Anticipations of Sterling's Return to Gold: Was Keynes Wrong?" *Economic Journal*, 1994.

Mitchell, Brian R. *Abstract of British Historical Statistics.* Cambridge: Cambridge University Press, 1962.

_____. *International Historical Statistics: Europe, 1750–1988.* New York: Stockton Press, 1992.

_____. *International Historical Statistics: The Americas, 1750–1988.* 2d ed. New York: Stockton Press, 1993. (This volume includes data on Australia).

Morgenstern, Oskar. *International Financial Transactions and Business Cycles.* Princeton: Princeton University Press, 1959.

Neufeld, Edward P. *The Financial System of Canada.* Toronto: Macmillan, 1972.

Obstfeld, Maurice. "Destabilizing Effects of Exchange Rate Escape Clauses." NBER Working Paper No. 3606, Cambridge, MA, 1992.

Officer, Lawrence. "The Efficiency of the Dollar-Sterling Gold Standard, 1980–1908." *Journal of Political Economy* 94 (1986): 1038–073.

_____. "Gold-Point Arbitrage and Uncovered Interest Arbitrage Under the 1925–1931 Dollar-Sterling Gold Standard." *Explorations in Economic History* 30, no. 1 (1993): 98–127.

O'Rourke, Kevin and Jeffrey Williamson. "Were Hechsher and Ohlin Right? Putting the Factor Price Equalization Theorem Back Into History? *NBER Working Papers on Historical Factors in Long-Run Growth*, No. 37, Cambridge, MA, 1992.

Pelaez, Carlos M. and Wilson Suzigan. *Historia monetaria do Brazil.* Editoria Universidade de Brazilia, 1976.

Pope, David. "Australia's Payments Adjustments and Capital Flows Under the International Gold Standard, 1870–1913." In *Monetary Regimes in Transition*, edited by Michael D. Bordo and Forrest Capie, 201–37. Cambridge: Cambridge University Press, 1993.

Reis, Jaime. "The Gold Standard in Portugal, 1854–1891." Mimeo. Universidale Nova de Lisbon, 1992.

Roll, Richard. "Interest Rates and Price Expectations During the Civil War." This JOURNAL 32, no. X (1972): 476–98.

Schwartz, Anna. J. "Banking School, Currency School, Free Banking School." In *New Palgrave Dictionary of Economics*,148–521. London: Macmillan, 1987.

Sharpe, W. F. "Capital Asset Prices: A Theory of Market Equilibrium Under Conditions of Risk." *Journal of Finance* 19(1964): 425—42.

Simons, Henry C. "Rules Versus Authorities in Monetary Policy." In A.E.A. *Readings in Monetary Theory* edited by Friedrich A. Lutz and Lloyd W. Mintz, 337–68. Homewood, Illinois: Richard D. Irwin, 1951.

Smith, Gregor and Todd Smith. "Wesley Mitchell and Irving Fisher and the Greenback Gold Reforms, 1865–1879." Mimeo. Queens University, 1993.

Smith, W. S. and Smith, R. T. "Stochastic Process Switching and the Return to Gold." *Economic Journal* 100(1990): 164–75.

Social Science Federation of Canada. *Historical Statistics of Canada.* 2d ed. Ottawa: Statistics Canada in joint sponsorship with the Social Science Federation of Canada, 1983.

Spinelli, Franco and Michele Fratianni. *Storia monetaria D'Italia: I'Evoluzione del sistema monetario e bancario.* Milano: A. Mondadori, 1991.

Spinelli, Franco. "The Demand For Money In The Italian Economy: 1867–1965," Research Report. Department of Economics, University of Western Ontario, 1978.

Stiglitz, Joseph and Andrew Weiss. "Credit Rationing in Markets with Imperfect Information." American *Economic Review* 71, no. 8 (1981): 393–410.

Tonniolo, G. *An Economic History of Liberal Italy:1850–1918.* New York: Routledge, 1990.

Unger, I. *The Greenback Era: A Social and Political History of American Finance, 1865–1879.* Princeton: Princeton University Press, 1964.

Urquhart, Malcolm C. "New Estimates of GNP, Canada, 1870–1926." In *Long-Term Factors in American Economic Growth*, NBER Studies in Income and Wealth, vol. 51, edited by Stanley L. Engerman and Robert E. Gallman, 9–94. Chicago: University of Chicago Press, 1986.

U.S. Bureau of Census. *Historical Statistics of the United States: Colonial Times to 1957.* Washington, DC: GPO, 1960.

_____. *Historical Statistics of the United States, Colonial Times to 1970, Bicentennial Edition.* Washington, DC: GPO, 1975.

Vamplew, Wray. *Australians, Historical Statistics.* Broadway, N.S.W. Australia: Fairfax, Syme, and Weldon Associates, 1987.

Viner, J. *Studies in the Theory of International Trade.* Chicago: University of Chicago Press, 1937.

Williamson, Jeffrey G. *American Growth and the Balance of Payments.* Chapel Hill: The University of North Carolina Press, 1964.

Wilson, Roland. *Capital Imports and the Terms of Trade.* Melbourne: Melbourne University Press in association with Macmillan & Co., 1931.

13

THE EMPIRE EFFECT

The Determinants of Country Risk in the First Age of Globalization, 1880–1913

Niall Ferguson and Moritz Schularick

Source: *Journal of Economic History* 66, 2, 2006, 283–312.

This article reassesses the importance of colonial status to investors before 1914 by means of multivariable regression analysis of the data available to contemporaries. We show that British colonies were able to borrow in London at significantly lower rates of interest than noncolonies precisely because of their colonial status, which mattered more than either gold standard adherence or the sustainability of fiscal policies. The "empire effect" was, on average, a discount of around 100 basis points, rising to around 175 basis points for the underdeveloped African and Asian colonies. Colonial status significantly reduced the default risk perceived by investors.

It was obvious to contemporaries—among them John Maynard Keynes—that membership in the British Empire gave poor countries access to the British capital market at lower interest rates than would have been required had they been politically independent. For liberal critics of the empire, this "empire effect" seemed detrimental to the economic health of the British Isles, which might otherwise have attracted a higher proportion of aggregate investment. Later historians agreed that this was one of the ways in which, by the later nineteenth century, the empire had become a drain on British resources. From the point of view of the colonies, on the other hand, the ability to raise funds in London at relatively low interest rates must surely have been a benefit—a point seldom acknowledged by critics of imperialism.

But did the empire effect actually exist other than in contemporary imaginations? Recent econometric studies of financial markets before the First World War have pointed instead to the gold standard as conferring a "good housekeeping seal of approval," which lowered the borrowing costs of the governments of poorer countries regardless of whether they were colonies or not. An alternative hypothesis that has been advanced is that the sustainability of a country's fiscal policy was the prime determinant of market assessments of creditworthiness. Were institutions and investors in the City of London primarily interested in a country's monetary and fiscal policy, regardless of its degree of political dependence? Or did colonial status have an additional effect on market confidence?

It will be seen at once that these things are not easily disentangled because British rule generally implied both currency stability and balanced budgets, among other things. This article therefore seeks to reassess the importance of colonial status in the eyes of investors before the First World War by means of multivariable regression analysis. We use a new and substantially larger sample of data than previous scholars have used. At the same time, we give priority to variables that we know were available to and heeded by contemporary investors. We show that even when monetary, fiscal, and trade policies are controlled for, there was still a marked difference between the spreads on colonial bonds and those on the bonds issued by independent countries. The main inference we draw is that the empire effect reflected the confidence of investors that British-governed countries would *maintain* sound fiscal, monetary, and trade policies. We also suggest that British rule may have reduced the endemic contract enforcement problems associated with crossborder lending. Investing in Calcutta was not so different from investing in Liverpool, because both transactions took place within a common legal and political framework that served to protect investors' rights. Sovereign states, by contrast (and indeed by definition), could not be held to account under English law. This has important implications in the context of the emerging consensus among economists that defective political and legal institutions are one of the major barriers to large, sustained, and productive capital flows from rich to poor countries.[1]

BRITISH IMPERIALISM AND FINANCIAL
GLOBALIZATION BEFORE 1914

Between 1865 and 1914 more than £4 billion flowed from Britain to the rest of the world, giving the country a historically unprecedented and since unequalled position as a global net creditor—"the world's banker" indeed; or, to be exact, the world's bond market. By 1914 total British assets overseas amounted to somewhere between £3.1 and £4.5 billion, as against British GDP of £2.5 billion.[2] This portfolio was authentically global: around 45 percent of British investment went to the United States and the colonies of white settlement, 20 percent to Latin America, 16 percent to Asia and 13 percent to Africa, compared with just 6 percent to the rest of Europe.[3] Adding together all British capital raised through public issues of securities, as much went to Africa, Asia, and Latin America between 1865 and 1914 as to the United Kingdom itself.[4]

It has been claimed by Michael Clemens and Jeffrey Williamson that there was something of a "Lucas effect" in the period between 1880 and 1914, in other words that British capital tended to gravitate towards wealthy countries rather than relatively poor countries.[5] Yet the bias in favor of rich countries was much less pronounced than it has been in more recent times. In 1997 only around 5 percent of the world's stock of international capital was invested in countries with per capita incomes of a fifth or less of U.S. per capita GDP. In 1913, according to Maurice Obstfeld and Alan Taylor, the proportion was 25 percent.[6] Very nearly half of all international capital stocks in 1914 were invested in countries with per capita incomes a third or less of Britain's, and Britain accounted for nearly two-fifths of the total sum invested in these poor economies.[7] The contrast between the past and the present is striking. Whereas today's rich economies prefer to "swap" capital with one another, largely bypassing poor countries, a century ago the rich economies had very large, positive net balances with the less well-off countries of the world.[8]

How important was the empire as a destination for British capital? According to the best available estimates, more than two-fifths (42 percent) of the cumulative flows of portfolio investment from Britain to the rest of the world went to British possessions.[9] An alternative measure— the imperial proportion of stocks of overseas investment on the eve of the First World War—was even higher: 46 percent. And about half of this amount went to relatively poor British colonies, not to the much more prosperous areas of white settlement. An obvious hypothesis might therefore be that investors a century ago were more willing to invest money in relatively poor countries because a high proportion of these countries were not sovereign states but were under the political control of the investors' own country.

Did membership of the British Empire give countries access to the British capital market at lower interest rates than they would have paid as independent states? Contemporaries and an older historical literature had little doubt that it did. Writing in 1924, Keynes noted that "Southern Rhodesia—a place in the middle of Africa with a few thousand white inhabitants and less than a million black ones—can place an unguaranteed loan on terms not very different from our own [British] War Loan." It seemed equally "strange" to him that "there should be investors who prefer[ed] … Nigeria stock (which has no British Government guarantee) [to] … London and North-Eastern Railway debentures."[10] More recently, Michael Edelstein has argued "that the British capital market treated empire borrowers differently from foreign borrowers."[11] An obvious explanation for an "imperial discount" on bonds issued by British colonies is that they were in some way guaranteed by the British government and therefore in a legal sense indistinguishable from British bonds in terms of default risk.[12] However, Edelstein rejects this explanation:

> Even when London backing and oversight were absent from colonial government issues … the British capital market charged lower interest rates than comparable securities from independent nations at similar levels of economic development. … The strong inference is that colonial status, apart from the direct guarantees, lowered whatever risk there was in an overseas investment and that investors were therefore willing to accept a lower return.[13]

Another explanation may lie in the effect of legislation specifically calculated to encourage investors to buy colonial bonds. At the turn of the century, two laws were passed, the Colonial Loans Act (1899) and the Colonial Stock Act (1900), which gave colonial bonds the same "trustee status" as the benchmark British government perpetual bond, the "consol."[14] At a time when a rising proportion of the national debt was being held by Trustee Savings Banks, this was an important stimulus to the market for colonial securities.[15] However, the importance of this legislation should not be exaggerated. The average difference between noncolonial and colonial yields was above 250 basis points between 1880 and 1898 and about 180 basis points between 1899 and 1913—in other words the premium on noncolonial bonds was actually higher before the Colonial Loans Act and Colonial Stock Act came into force. Prior to the First World War, these acts were the only formal encouragements to investors to favor colonial bonds.[16]

There are, however, other, less formal reasons why prewar investors may have incorporated an imperial discount when pricing bonds. The Victorians imposed a distinctive set of institutions on their colonies that very likely enhanced their appeal to investors. These extended beyond the Gladstonian trinity of sound money, balanced budgets, and free trade to include the rule of law (specifically, British style property rights) and relatively noncorrupt administration—among the most important "public goods" of late-nineteenth-century liberal imperialism.[17] Debt contracts with colonial borrowers were more likely to be enforceable than those with independent states. It would be rather puzzling if investors had regarded Australia as no more creditworthy than Argentina, or Canada as no more creditworthy than Chile.

For a number of reasons, then, it is possible that the imposition of British rule practically amounted to a "no default" guarantee; the only uncertainty investors had to face concerned the expected duration of British rule. Before 1914, despite the growth of nationalist movements in possessions as different as Ireland and India, political independence still seemed a fairly remote prospect for most subject peoples. At this point even the major colonies of white settlement had been granted only a limited political autonomy. Thus, in the words of P. J. Cain and A. G. Hopkins: "One of the key reasons why the colonies could borrow cheaply [was that] they offered almost complete safety."[18]

DETERMINANTS OF BOND SPREADS

The possibility exists, nevertheless, that other considerations mattered more to investors than the extent to which a country's sovereignty had been reduced by imperialism. The recent literature on the determinants of risk premia has centered on these other factors.

An alternative approach focuses on monetary policy rather than colonial status. Michael Bordo and Hugh Rockoff argued that adherence to the gold standard worked as a credible "commitment mechanism," reassuring investors that governments would not pursue time-inconsistent fiscal and monetary policies.[19] Investors rewarded this binding policy commitment by charging—ceteris paribus—lower risk premia. The gold standard worked in this respect as a "Good Housekeeping seal of approval." A commitment to gold convertibility, they calculate, reduced the yield on a country's bonds by around 40 basis points.[20] Using a somewhat larger sample, Obstfeld and Taylor confirmed that gold standard membership lowered spreads.[21] In this analysis, therefore, it was membership of the informal and voluntary gold "club" rather than membership of the British Empire that lowered the yields paid by some emerging markets. As Obstfeld and Taylor conclude, "Membership in the British Empire was neither a necessary nor sufficient condition for preferential access to London's capital market before 1914."[22]

As a *contingent* commitment, however, membership in the gold standard was nothing more than a promise of self-restraint under certain circumstances. Independent countries on gold were not members of some kind of monetary union. They retained the right to suspend convertibility in the event of an emergency such as a war, revolution, or a sudden deterioration in the terms of trade. Such emergencies were in fact quite common before 1914. Argentina, Brazil, and Chile all experienced serious financial and monetary crises between 1880 and 1914. By 1895 the currencies of all three had depreciated by around 60 percent against sterling. This had serious implications for their ability to service their external debt, which was denominated in hard currency (usually sterling) rather than domestic currency.

A second hypothesis is that investors were primarily interested in the fiscal policies of borrowing countries. Marc Flandreau and Frédéric Zumer have recently suggested that the most important risk factors were public debts, the corresponding amount of debt service, and the relation between these burdens and tax revenues.[23] They find that, once differences in indebtedness are taken account of, gold standard adherence was insignificant. In addition, they present evidence that contemporary economic thinking about default risk centered on debt sustainability and the soundness of public finances.[24]

A third determinant of risk premia may simply have been political events. According to Ferguson, revolutions, governmental crises and wars were regarded by nineteenth-century investors as increasing the likelihood of defaults by the countries affected.[25] Finally, Clemens and Williamson have identified demographic characteristics, natural resource endowment, and education as significant determinants of yield spreads.[26]

To determine whether or not membership in the British Empire genuinely lowered borrowing costs, it is therefore imperative to control for these and other factors. British colonies may simply have been able to borrow at lower rates than other foreign countries because they were on the gold standard, had more sustainable fiscal policies, were less susceptible to political crises, or were simply better situated relative to trade routes and temperate climatic zones.

YIELD DATA AND ECONOMIC CONTROL VARIABLES

We constructed the largest possible sovereign bond database for the period 1880–1913. Price data for government bonds quoted and traded in the London market were copied by hand from the leading financial publication of the time, the *Investor's Monthly Manual*. Some additional quotations were taken from the *London Stock Exchange Weekly Intelligence*, the London Stock Exchange's official weekly gazette. The bonds chosen had to pass three strict criteria to qualify as benchmark issues. First, they had to be payable in London in either sterling or gold, enabling us to focus exclusively on country risk and to ignore the currency risk inherent in bonds denominated in other currencies.[27] Secondly, the selected bonds had to be issued in large volumes and actively traded. Finally, the bonds needed to be long-term, typically of a maturity of over ten years, and to have quotations for at least three consecutive years.

The resulting dataset includes securities from 57 independent countries, colonies, and self-governing parts of the British Empire: in other words, almost the entire universe of foreign borrowing in the London market, reaching not only "from the Cape to Cairo" but also from Boston to Buenos Aires and from Budapest to Beijing.[28] The rationale for constructing such a broad sample was to avoid the regional biases that characterized previous studies. Bordo and Rockoff used observations for just ten countries, all either European or American.[29] The two most recent investigations of pre-1914 bond yields by Obstfeld and Taylor and by Flandreau and Zumer were based on samples of around 20 countries. The samples in both cases were predominantly European and American. Quite clearly it is difficult to form robust conclusions about the significance of colonial status without including data for at least some Asian and African countries.

Table 1 shows the summary statistics for our current yield series.[30] In total, we count about 1,450 observations, roughly 900 for independent countries from Europe, America, Asia, and Africa and about 550 for issuers from the British Empire, drawn from these four continents as well as Australasia. Immediately obvious from the yield data is the significantly lower average yield of Empire borrowers (3.89 percent) compared with the yields of independent countries (6.30 percent).

Older research on financial investment in the age of high imperialism looked only at raw yield data, thus leaving open the possibility that lower colonial spreads were a function of better economic "fundamentals" rather than the explicit or implicit guarantees to investors stemming from empire membership.[31] The only way to say for sure that there was an empire effect is therefore to regress yield

Table 1 SUMMARY STATISTICS OF YIELD DATA, 1880–1913 (yield, percent per annum)

	Observations	*Mean*	*St. Dev.*	*Minimum*	*Maximum*
All borrowers	1,461	5.39	2.86	2.86	22.33
Independent countries	909	6.30	3.30	2.97	22.33
Empire borrowers	552	3.89	0.43	2.86	6.35

Sources: Data appendix at http://fas.harvard.edu/~history/facultyPage.cgi?fac=ferguson.

spreads against an appropriate range of additional control variables. The obvious question is which variables to include. In our view, there are powerful methodological objections to the inclusion of anachronistic indicators such as debt to GDP ratios.[32] Self-evidently, people usually do not base their actions upon concepts that have not yet been invented or upon figures nobody yet calculates.[33] Rather, if we want to determine how nineteenth-century investors made their decisions, we need to model their behavior deductively on the basis of the data that were available to them at that time.[34]

The economic data were collected from primary and secondary sources.[35] As anyone familiar with the financial press of the period knows, there was a plethora of publications available to investors. Standard reference publications such as *Fenn's Compendium*, the *Investor's Monthly Manual* (henceforth IMM), the *Stock Exchange Weekly Intelligence* and the *Corporation of Foreign Bondholders Annual Reports* collected and analyzed statistical data on government borrowers in a manner not unlike that of the handbooks on equity investments pioneered by Moody's in the United States. In addition to this dedicated financial press, there was a rapidly growing number of more general statistical publications.[36]

The subtitle of the 1898 edition of *Fenn's Compendium*, the self-proclaimed "doyen of all financial books of reference," neatly summarizes what economic indicators the City of London had access to: it was "a handbook of public debts containing details and histories of debts, budgets and foreign trade of all nations, together with statistics elucidating the financial and economic progress and position of various countries."[37] In many respects, the main problem for contemporaries was not so much the raw data in the numerator—whether public debts, debt service charges, or exports—but the denominator. In the absence of a direct measure of a nation's output such as gross national product, a concept then its infancy, it was far from easy to compare the fundamental resources of different countries. Population was generally acknowledged to be an unreliable choice, though it had the advantage of being readily available, thanks to fairly regular and accurate censuses, and was often used to denominate export capacity. However, in more sophisticated analyses of fiscal sustainability, the debt burden tended to be related to public revenues or to export earnings.[38] The same was true of budget and trade balances.

Drawing on the records of the *Service d'Études Financières* of the Crédit Lyonnais, Flandreau and Zumer have suggested that debt *service* to revenue was the contemporary indicator that best measured the creditworthiness of borrowers.[39] However, for a number of reasons we chose to stick to the more traditional debt to revenue ratio. First, in contemporary statistical publications, the overall debt burden was far more frequently given, and was also, it seems, less frequently subject to revisions. Secondly, as the debt service itself is determined by the interest rate, it is questionable whether it should be used as an independent variable to estimate the interest rate. Nevertheless, we can also work with debt service data for a far larger number of countries than previous studies and will show that our key findings do not depend on the choice of a particular fiscal measure.

Another indicator watched by contemporaries was the budget deficit to revenue ratio. As Cain and Hopkins have argued, the principles of "Gladstonian finance"—which aimed at budget surpluses during peacetime in order to repay existing public debt—were all but sacrosanct in the eyes of the "gentlemanly capitalists" of the City of London.[40] In addition, we collected information on those countries that breached the "London consensus" on good housekeeping by defaulting on their obligations; the *Annual Reports* of the Corporation of Foreign Bondholders contain detailed information on defaulters. Because default damages reputation, we constructed a control variable for default within the preceding ten years.[41]

Apart from public debt data, the second class of economic statistics readily available to late-nineteenth-century investors related to foreign trade. That there was a link between trade and creditworthiness was obvious to contemporaries because countries needed to earn foreign exchange in order to service their external debts. Export capacity was also seen as a proxy for wealth and the state of economic development. Because we wanted to capture the risks stemming from both large external deficits and low levels of international trade, we collected data for both the trade deficit and the sterling value of exports per capita. Modern studies of country risk tend to use GDP per capita as a proxy for risk-reducing factors such as more stable politics or better institutions. The City of London had to settle for something less than that before the First World War, but it was looking for analogous information.

Given the importance attributed by some scholars to gold standard adherence, we also wished to control for the positive effects of being on gold. The question of whether or not a country's currency was—*de facto* or *de jure*—convertible into gold is in itself a difficult issue; indeed, it is far from clear-cut even for well-researched economies such as Austria and Italy, both of which "shadowed" the gold standard without officially having fully convertible currencies.[42] Nonetheless, because considerable attention has been paid to the role of gold adherence in reducing country risk, our estimations include two dummies for gold standard adherence. Following Christopher Meissner as well as Obstfeld and Taylor, we use the "strict" gold coding.[43] We also take account of Obstfeld and Taylor's point that "the market's view of gold standard adherence [ought] to depend on whether a country [was] in full compliance with its debt contracts."[44] Finally, we took the idea seriously that internal or external political conflicts may have been important determinants of yield fluctuations.[45]

Table 2 summarizes the core economic control variables used in the statistical analyses. It will be seen that they are comparable, though not identical, to the variables used by Flandreau and Zumer.[46] By applying them to a much larger sample of countries, however, we are able to pose a question they did not consider: How far yield spreads reflected the fundamental differences in political status that distinguished independent borrowers from those that were members of the British Empire. The important point to be borne in mind is that our approach may tend to underestimate the empire effect by assuming that it is possible to separate colonial

Table 2 SUMMARY STATISTICS OF ECONOMIC VARIABLES

	Mean	St. Dev.	Minimum	Maximum
All borrowers				
Debt/revenue	4.95	3.45	0.05	23.70
Debt service/revenue	0.20	0.13	0.01	0.75
Budget deficit/revenue	0.12	0.36	−0.59	9.60
Trade balance/exports	−0.14	0.81	−14.12	0.79
Exports/population	4.72	7.34	0.05	66.64
Independent countries				
Debt/revenue	4.98	3.62	0.16	23.70
Debt service/revenue	0.21	0.14	0.01	0.75
Budget deficit/revenue	0.10	0.40	−0.49	9.60
Trade balance/exports	−0.05	0.39	−2.51	0.79
Exports/population	2.38	2.27	0.05	12.43
Empire borrowers				
Debt/revenue	4.92	3.16	0.05	20.48
Debt service/revenue	0.19	0.11	0.001	0.44
Budget deficit/revenue	0.14	0.26	−0.59	2.00
Trade balance/exports	−0.26	1.15	−14.12	0.69
Exports/population	8.45	10.57	0.16	66.64

Sources: Data appendix at http://fas.harvard.edu/~history/facultyPage.cgi?fac=ferguson.

status cleanly from "fundamentals" such as fiscal, monetary, and trade policy, or indeed political stability, all of which were almost by definition affected by the imposition of British rule. As Table 2 shows, empire borrowers were slightly less indebted than independent countries. They were more likely to be on the gold standard than independent states, though we still have enough cases of British possessions off gold to distinguish empire membership from gold standard membership. Exports per capita were markedly higher inside the empire than outside it (the dominions and colonies exported about four times more per capita than independent countries), which tends to confirm conventional wisdom about the relative openness of the imperial trade regime.[47]

ESTIMATING THE EMPIRE EFFECT

In order to gauge the size of the empire effect on country risk premia, we first investigated the relationship between the spread over consols, i.e., the difference between the yield on a country's bonds and the yield on consols, and the economic control variables discussed previously. We look to the coefficient of the empire dummy (coded 1 if a borrower was a British possession) for an estimate of the empire effect.

The estimation of panel or time-series cross-section data has become a standard method of exploring large datasets in economic history. Pooling enables us to increase the amount of informative data, through combining variation across countries with variation over time. It also makes it possible to control for exogenous events affecting all units at a point in time, thus to control for time effects—a crucial advantage here because we need to take account of global interest rate shocks affecting all countries in a specific year.[48] We borrow an estimation method that has become the standard for datasets like ours in quantitative research in comparative political economy: OLS with panel corrected standard errors (PCSE).[49] This method allows for the inclusion of a unit-specific AR1 term to correct for serial correlation, while retaining the unbiased OLS coefficient estimates and calculating reliable "panel-corrected standard errors."[50]

Our research agenda is complicated by the fact that we are interested in coefficient estimates for a largely time-invariant variable. There are only three borrowers in our sample which became *(de facto* or *de jure)* colonies within the period: Egypt in 1882, and the Transvaal and the Orange Free State after the Boer War in 1900. As case studies their experiences are instructive. Spreads on Egyptian bonds were as high as 500 basis points in 1880. After the imposition of British rule and the restructuring of public finances and public debts, they fell to 270 basis points in 1882 and declined further to about 130 by the end of the 1880s.[51] A similar story can be told for the southern tip of Africa, where the two Boer republics of Transvaal and Orange both had bonds quoted in London in the 1890s with yields of about 200 to 300 basis points above the British benchmark. After the war in 1900, the new colonies contracted large loans in London (with the blessing of Westminster), increasing their debt-to-revenue ratios from the low levels of the 1890s (about 100 percent of revenues) to more than 500 percent. At the same time, the yield spread fell to around 20 basis points over consols.

The main implication of this limited time-variation of empire membership is that there are two ways to get a reliable estimate of the financing advantage of colonial borrowers. In a standard fixed-effects model the empire effect would appear in the country fixed-effects. The estimated unit effects of the model would show whether or not empire issuers had on average lower overall spread levels than independent borrowers.[52] The drawback is that all time-invariant differences are included in the fixed effects. The alternative is to drop the fixed-effects and to run a pooled OLS regression. Yet this approach could suffer from omitted variable bias if cross-sectional heterogeneity were no longer captured by different intercepts.[53] However, if the unit effects are spanned (or accounted for) by a linear combination of the time-invariant regressors, then pooled OLS would still be the estimator of choice.[54] As will be seen, the pooled and the fixed-effects models yield very similar results.

THE EVIDENCE

The results of our benchmark regression, 1, lend strong support to the idea of an empire effect. All other things being equal, the yield on a bond would be about 100 basis points lower if the issuer came from the British Empire.[55] The finding is backed by the number of observations (1,294), which is more than double the number in previous investigations with a comparable number of controls.[56] In regression 2 we test whether or not it makes a difference to include country fixed-effects. We drop the empire dummy and include individual country dummies (but keep the year-dummies from our benchmark specification). For a summary comparison, we can now look at the mean fixed effect of the unit effects of the empire group and the mean of independent countries. The result is reassuring: a statistically significant (the null here is a mean of zero) group effect appears, and the difference between the empire and independent countries is both significant and large at more than 150 basis points. The other coefficients match closely those of our benchmark regression, 1. In regression 3 we limit our sample to "developing countries," in other words capital-poor countries.[57] Here, the empire effect reaches more than 180 basis points, suggesting that being part of the British Empire was particularly important for the borrowing of less-developed African and Asian colonies.

But can we be sure this is truly an empire effect? Could there be a third factor (correlated with, but independent of, colonial status) that increased market confidence? Obviously, it was not the geographic position, measured by distance from the core or climatic conditions. British colonies were spread over all continents and climate zones. Nor can empire be considered a proxy for the impact of European settlement or the introduction of liberal parliamentary institutions, because the extent of settlement and political representation varied greatly across the empire, yet the exceptionally low country-effects apply equally to the dependent empire and the more autonomous dominions.[58]

What about the macroeconomic control variables? Our results support Flandreau and Zumer's emphasis on public finance as a determinant of pre-1914 bond spreads: the debt to revenue ratio is correctly signed and significant in all regressions. As noted, Flandreau and Zumer have argued that contemporary investors paid more heed to the ratio of debt service to public revenues. It is obvious that, by virtue of their lower spreads, British colonies had to pay less interest on their debt than independent countries. We would therefore expect the empire effect to get weaker if one relies exclusively on the debt service ratio—but not to disappear. Regression 4 provides the corresponding empirical test. It demonstrates that the empire effect does not depend on the choice of the debt indicator. The empire effect remains highly significant. Only its size is, unsurprisingly, somewhat smaller if the debt service serves as the only debt control—about 82 basis points in this specification.[59] Clearly, empire mattered beyond the differences in debt burdens between borrowers, however scaled.[60]

As for gold standard adherence, our results provide mixed evidence and point to the need for further analysis. Although the gold standard variable (conditional on no default) is correctly signed and has the expected effect of a 15 to 40 basis point reduction in spreads, it passes the significance test only in some regressions. Moreover, we found that, unlike the debt to revenue ratio, the gold standard dummy is rather sensitive to changes in the estimation specification, to influential observations, and to differences in the coding criteria.[61]

As expected, both defaulters and previous defaulters were heavily penalized by the City, but the budget deficit seems to have had no significant effect on spreads. (One possible explanation is that investors did not regularly follow the budget balances of various countries, but concentrated on debt indicators instead as an excess of expenditure over revenues would show up in the debt figures.) The picture is different for the external trade indicators. Richer countries (measured by exports per capita) paid less interest and, other things being equal, a country that ran an export surplus would have lower borrowing costs. Our estimations also lend some support to the argument that current political factors were important spread determinants: any incidence of internal political conflict raised spreads by as much as 70 basis points (see Table 3).

Why do we find strong evidence for an empire effect of about 100 basis points, where Obstfeld and Taylor concluded it did not exist? Apart from the bigger sample, different controls for time-specific asset market shifts could drive the result. Such shifts can be controlled for by using time-dummies (or any other market-wide measure) that affect all borrowers in a given year, which is what we opted for in the benchmark regression. The time dummies from our regression show a clear downward trend over the period, briefly interrupted in the crisis years of the early 1890s (Figure 1). The picture mirrors the general trend towards spread convergence discussed by Obstfeld and Taylor as well as Flandreau and Zumer.

However, Bordo and Rockoff as well as Obstfeld and Taylor took a different track. They included a measure of systematic risk—a weighted "world spread" over consols in every year with country-specific slopes or "betas"—following the capital asset pricing model (CAPM) and its predictions about pricing of assets according to systematic risk.[62] The coefficient on this variable indicates how closely the spread of a country conformed to the variation in the "average" risk of foreign bonds as perceived by British investors. A coefficient greater than one would signal that a bond of a given country was more strongly affected by an increase in market risk than the average borrower. This could have an impact on our estimation of the empire effect, if colonies as a group experienced much less correlation with the market-wide risk than independent countries.

To test this, we constructed a debt-weighted world spread for any given year.[63] In estimation 5 we regress the spread on the usual controls plus the average world spread in a fixed-effects framework, and look again at the group effects. The difference between colonial borrowers and independent countries does indeed fall dramatically, and more importantly, it turns statistically insignificant at conventional thresholds.

Why does the empire effect fade once one switches to CAPM-style controls? Our large sample enables us to identify the underlying causes with great certainty: the key driver for the different findings is the much lower covariance of colonial interest rates with the average risk of foreign bonds (or significantly lower individual betas in CAPM-language).[64] The mean correlation of empire borrowers (0.24) with the market-wide average risk premium on foreign borrowing was close to zero (the risk-free rate) and far below the coeefficient of independent

Table 3 DETERMINANTS OF SOVEREIGN BOND SPREADS (dependent variable: spread over U.K. consols)

Regression	1	2	3	4	5
Sample	All	All Fixed Effects	LDCs	All	All Fixed Effects
Estimation	Pooled	Time Effects	Pooled	Pooled	Betas
Observations	1,294	1,294	879	1,147	1,294
Groups	57	57	40	54	57
R^2	0.66	0.74	0.69	0.55	0.85
Empire	−110.01 (4.71)***		−183.02 (9.34)***	−81.61 (3.19)***	
Debt/revenues	6.75 (2.13)**	11.74 (3.53)***	6.36 (1.84)*		10.02 (3.42)***
Debt service/revenues				311.24 (3.28)***	
Budget balance/revenues	−8.98 (0.62)	−10.85 (0.72)	−11.90 (0.72)	−9.79 (2.10)**	−11.13 (1.34)
Trade balance/exports	−1.94 (0.72)	−1.75 (1.53)	−1.07 (1.36)	−1.76 (1.96)	−1.37 (−1.50)
Exports/population (ln)	−28.43 (2.45)**	−31.76 (1.59)	−25.33 (2.46)**	2.02 (0.24)	−26.88 (2.69)**
Default	348.79 (6.84)***	320.67 (6.27)***	355.35 (7.08)***	267.71 (4.74)***	271.20 (5.61)***
Previous default	173.72 (3.58)***	141.71 (3.65)***	175.98 (4.48)***	117.79 (2.47)**	85.86 (2.58)***
GS x no default	−16.33 (0.74)	20.89 (0.97)	−17.06 (0.90)	−39.65 (2.05)**	−13.87 (0.89)
GS x default	67.14 (0.87)	92.26 (1.23)	59.36 (0.77)	0.78 (0.01)	6.06 (0.10)
International conflict	−4.48 (0.20)	−1.32 (0.06)	−11.03 (0.38)	27.07 (1.13)	−7.14 (0.31)
Civil conflict	64.23 (2.22)**	62.42 (2.05)**	64.59 (2.24)	1.93 (0.07)	113.75 (4.24)***
Group effects					
Empire		−101.33 (2.02)**			92.05 (5.07)***
Independent countries		55.44 (0.96)			85.23 (1.98)**
Difference		−156.78 (5.05)***			6.82 (0.16)
Betas (empire)					0.24 (2.63)***
Betas (independent)					1.34 (3.48)***
Difference					−1.10 (2.87)***

* = significant at the 10 percent level.
** = significant at the 5 percent level.
*** = significant at the 1 percent level.

Notes: Coefficients on time-dummies, regional dummies (in regressions 1, 3, 4) and country-specific rhos are not reported. Figures are available from the authors. Figures in parentheses are z-statistics. Group effects refer to the mean of the linear combination. The null is a zero mean (*t*-statistics in parentheses).

Sources: See text and appendix at http://fas.harvard.edu/~history/facultyPage.cgi?fac=ferguson.

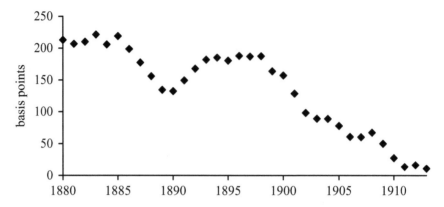

Figure 1 TIME EFFECTS, 1880–1913. *Note*: Time dummies are from benchmark regression 1.

countries (1.34). The difference is of considerable magnitude (1.10) and highly significant. Following the logic of the CAPM, colonial bonds were safe assets, whereas bonds of independent countries carried a high systematic risk. In other words, the country risk of colonies was much less sensitive to changes in the perception of the average riskiness of foreign investment. Even in times of crisis (during the Baring crisis) colonial risk premia remained low. The empire effect was therefore strongest during crisis periods; it was lower when the market sentiment towards foreign investment was more positive.

The lower sensitivity of colonial assets to market risk actually confirms the empire effect hypothesis. Investors treated colonial bonds differently, as reflected in the exceptionally low betas.[65] They were, in effect, slightly higher-yielding substitutes for risk-free British consols. In a specification with CAPM-style controls, however, the fundamentally different risk characteristics of colonial borrowers and independent economies are effectively swept away by the country-specific coefficients. It is not surprising, then, that the country dummies do not show a large empire effect anymore. This would seem to explain why previous studies considered the idea of an empire effect to be an optical illusion of contemporaries.

BOND SPREADS WITHIN THE BRITISH EMPIRE

The last part of our analysis of spread determinants is devoted to an equally old question in the study of the British Empire: Who profited most from preferential access to the London capital market—the dependent empire, the Dominions, or India? Ceteris paribus, which did investors see as the safest place to put their money? Looking in detail at loan issues in the period under investigation, Lance Davis and Robert Huttenback concluded that "within the British Empire, India consistently paid less for capital than either the dependent colonies or those with

Table 4 BOND SPREADS WITHIN THE BRITISH EMPIRE

Regression	6	7
Estimation	Pooled	Fixed Effects
Observations	517	517
Groups	24	24
R^2	0.68	0.72
Debt/revenue	1.88 (2.47)**	2.00 (2.43)**
Budget balance	0.91 (1.02)	3.81 (1.40)
Trade balance	−1.24 (1.25)	−3.23 (11.39)***
India	−35.60 (3.35)***	
Self-governing parts	−9.33 (1.30)	
Group effects		67.62 (8.52)***
Self-governing parts		
India		40.58 (3.29)***
Difference		−27.03 (2.50)**

* = significant at the 10 percent level.
** = significant at the 5 percent level.
*** = significant at the 1 percent level.

Notes: Linear regression, correlated panels and corrected standard errors (PCSE). Coefficients on time-dummies and country-specific rhos are not reported. Figures in parentheses are z-statistics. Group effects refer to the mean of the linear combination where the null is a zero mean (figures in parentheses are *t*-statistics).

Sources: Data appendix at http://fas.harvard.edu/~history/facultyPage.cgi?fac=ferguson.

responsible government."[66] Does this finding—based on groupings of yield data without further controls—stand up to the inclusion of economic controls for the level of debt, the external position, and the state of development?

Regressions 6 and 7 exploit our dataset to give a more comprehensive answer (see Table 4). They essentially confirm the conclusions of Davis and Huttenback; Indian bonds had a distinctly lower risk premium than either dependent or self-governing borrowers within the empire. In both estimations, we found India's financing advantage to have been worth about 30 basis points. This result is not surprising because, unlike some other colonial bonds, "Indian government bonds carried the backing of the British government and were listed in the official rosters of the London stock exchange with 'British funds'."[67]

COUNTRY RISK AND CAPITAL FLOWS

The City of London viewed British possessions as safe places to invest. As a result, distant colonies gained access to the London capital market at cheaper rates than comparable sovereign states. But what implications did this have for the *amounts* of capital that flowed from Britain to her empire? In other words, did the empire effect mean more capital as well as lower interest rates? Any answer to this question depends both on counterfactual argumentation and ceteris paribus assumptions and must therefore remain highly speculative. Nevertheless, such questions have been raised before and played an important role in the debate on the costs and benefits of British imperialism, and we cannot therefore ignore them.[68] Edelstein, for example, estimated that had they been independent, colonies would have paid twice the actual interest rate. As a consequence, they would have received only as much capital per capita as other comparably developed independent countries. He concluded on that basis "that the non-white-settler colonies would have had British investments one fifth their actual £140 and £480 million levels in 1870 and 1913."[69] By the same token, the self-governing parts of the empire would have received about 30 percent less capital.

Figure 2 allows a first visual impression of the patterns of international borrowing in the London capital market, and underlines the risk aversion of British financial investors. More than 60 percent of aggregate public borrowing in the boom years between 1900 and 1913 was concentrated in the low-risk segment of the market (spreads of less than 100 basis points), while another 30 percent went to public borrowers whose spreads were less than 200 basis points above the British consol. This tendency looks even more pronounced if borrowing is denominated by population. It therefore seems reasonable to assume that, if the colonies suddenly had gained their independence, capital flows would have fallen rather substantially. Higher default risks would have depressed the expected return for investors, rendering foreign investment less attractive and drying up the supply of capital.

To illustrate these considerations in an empirical framework, we can try to estimate the relationship between the amount of foreign borrowing in London and risk premia. We would expect to find that capital flows decreased with higher country risks, because investors tend to limit their exposure to high-risk assets.[70]

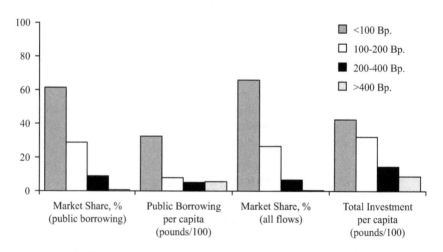

Figure 2 DISTRIBUTION OF BRITISH PORTFOLIO INVESTMENT, 1900–1913.
Note: Thirty-five countries, unweighted yearly averages over the entire period.
Sources: Data appendix at http://fas.harvard.edu/~history/facultyPage.cgi?fac =ferguson.

However, whereas risk premia are certainly an important determinant of capital flows, comparably important roles are played by investment opportunities, the institutional environment and many other country-specific fundamentals. Despite these complexities we try to derive some illustrative insights from estimating the determinants of capital flows in a simple cross-sectional model accounting for country-specific "pull" factors and global "push" factors.[71]

First, we use five-year averages to level out cyclical effects, reduce the impact of outliers, and get a reliable picture of the underlying factors. Second, we control for a number of other plausible determinants, regressing the yearly average capital inflows per capita not only on spreads, but also on population (to control for country size), the period average of population and export growth (for demographic and growth trends), and on the ratio of rail miles in operation to country size (as a proxy for opportunities for "reproductive investment"). Finally, we include U.K. interest rates as a "push" factor.

Regression 8 includes the full sample of British investment, while regression 9 limits the sample to independent countries and regression 10 to the less developed independent countries outside Western Europe and North America (see Table 5). The main finding that runs through all regressions is that higher risk premia were indeed associated with lower flows. The elasticity of flows to independent countries in relation to the risk premium, about 0.3 at average regressor values, was also substantial. For the less developed countries in our sample, the

Table 5 COUNTRY RISK AND CAPITAL FLOWS (dependent variable: capital inflow per capita, 1880–1913)

Regression	8	9	10
Estimation	All	Independent	Less-Developed Independent
Observations	189	150	98
R^2	0.23	0.16	0.18
Spread over consols	−0.0005 (4.17)***	−0.0002 (2.20)**	−0.0004 (2.93)***
ln(Population)	−0.20 (5.32)***	−0.12 (3.92)***	−0.18 (3.59)***
Population growth	0.04 (1.02)	0.05 (1.21)	0.03 (0.93)
Export growth	0.006 (0.73)	−0.002 (0.34)	−0.002 (0.36)
ln(Rail miles/ land area)	−0.07 (3.44)***	−0.04 (2.28)**	−0.06 (1.90)*
U.K. interest rate	0.32 (1.34)	0.13 (0.99)	0.04 (0.19)
Constant	1.09 (1.38)	0.74 (1.47)	1.70 (2.02)**

* = significant at the 10 percent level.
** = significant at the 5 percent level.
*** = significant at the 1 percent level.

Notes: Observations were averaged over five year periods (1880–1884, 1885–1889 ...) and one four year period (1910–1913). Pooled cross-section, estimation via least squares with heteroskedasticity consistent standard errors (GLS). The figures in parentheses are t-statistics.

Sources: Data appendix at http://fas.harvard.edu/~history/facultyPage.cgi?fac=ferguson.

impact was even greater. Other things being equal, a country received more than twice as much capital per capita if its risk premium was only half of the developing country average. And cutting risk premia by half is what empire membership probably implied for the poor African and Asian colonies. In view of the highly exploratory character of the estimation, we are inclined not to read too much into these results. However, the significance of market size and the positive sign on population growth are in line with previous studies.[72]

At the very least, it seems legitimate to conclude that the higher country risks that would have been consequent on an "Edwardian decolonization" would, in turn, have reduced capital flows to Britain's former possessions. For British investors did not place voluminous bets on risky governments; they extended relatively more credit to the low-risk segment of the market. Given this preference, the appeal of investing in the empire is obvious.

CONCLUSIONS

Our findings indicate that the empire effect observed by contemporaries a century ago was no optical illusion. Even when—using information that was available to contemporaries—we allow for differences in monetary and fiscal policy, openness to trade, political stability, as well as geographical location and level of economic development, we find that a country that was a part of the British Empire was still able to borrow at significantly lower interest rates than one that was not. Although this is true for all colonies, the main beneficiaries were the poor and underdeveloped parts of the British Empire. For these economies, the empire effect cut risk premia by more than 150 basis points, or by about 60 percent compared to the average spread charged to developing countries between 1890 and 1913.

As it turned out, the interwar period confirmed what pre-1914 investors had rightly suspected: it was indeed riskier to invest in sovereign foreign states than to lend to comparable colonial economies. There were defaults by numerous independent debtor countries including Argentina, Brazil, Chile, Mexico, Japan, Russia, and Turkey.[73] By contrast, all British colonial governments weathered the storms and stresses of the interwar period without resorting to default. The imperial relationship was thus based on a virtuous circle. Colonial administrators tended to favor sound money, balanced budgets, and openness to trade—precisely the things that reassured investors. In turn, the low risk premium paid by British colonies when they raised capital in London made it less likely that they would fall into the kind of debt traps that claimed other emerging markets, whose interest payments out to foreign creditors exceeded the amounts of money flowing in from new loans and being generated by the foreign-financed investments. Small wonder, then, that an increasing share of British overseas investment ended up going to the empire after the First World War. In the 1920s the empire accounted for around two-thirds of all new issues on the London market.[74]

When Keynes criticized the low yields on colonial loans in the 1920s, his point was that this state of affairs was not in the economic interests of Britain herself. With unemployment stubbornly stuck above prewar levels and mounting evidence of industrial stagnation, capital export seemed like a misallocation of resources. But Keynes did not consider the benefits reaped by colonial economies from cheap access to British savings. From an imperial rather than a narrowly national point of view, it was highly desirable that capital from the wealthy metropolis be encouraged to flow to the developing periphery. Besides ensuring that British investors got their interest paid regularly and their principal paid back, the imperial system was conducive to *global* economic growth—more so, certainly, than an alternative policy of the sort Keynes had in mind, which would have prioritized the industrial production and employment of the United Kingdom.

This conclusion has wider implications for historical debates about imperialism and modern debates about economic development. Whatever the impact on Britain of large-scale overseas investment, it can hardly have been disadvantageous to British colonies that they could raise capital in London at rates up to 60 percent lower than comparably endowed sovereign states, or that they were able to attract more British capital than otherwise comparably situated but independent countries. To be sure, indigenous peoples by and large had little say over the ways in which the capital so raised was invested. Conceivably, independent governments might have invested it in ways better calculated to foster economic growth. Yet the record of most postcolonial governments, especially in sub-Saharan Africa, strongly suggests otherwise. The inability of so many former colonies today to attract foreign investment— other than in the form of credits or aid from noncommercial lenders and donors—suggests that there may be a trade-off for poor countries between political sovereignty and creditworthiness.[75] The empire effect encapsulated that trade-off. For many poor countries struggling today to attract foreign investment at affordable rates of interest, the answer may not be a currency peg or even "structural adjustment," but the importation (or imposition) of less dysfunctional economic, legal, and political institutions.

*We are grateful to Nitin Malla for research assistance. We would also like to thank Michael Bordo, Michael Clemens, Warren Coats, Marc Flandreau, Carl-Ludwig Holtfrerich, Trish Kelly, Chris Meissner, Ronald Oaxaca, Thomas Pluemper, Hugh Rockoff, Martin Schueler, Irving Stone, Nathan Sussman, Alan Taylor, Adrian Tschoegl, Marc Weidenmier, and Jeffrey Williamson for comments or assistance with the construction of the dataset. Three anonymous referees provided helpful suggestions.

Notes

1 See, for example, World Bank, *World Development Report 2005.*
2 Cain and Hopkins, *British Imperialism*, pp. 161–63.
3 Maddison, *World Economy*, table 2–26a.

4 Davis and Huttenback, *Mammon*, p. 46.
5 According to Clemens and Williamson, "about two-thirds of British foreign invest-ment went to the labor-scarce New World where only a tenth of the world's popu-lation lived, and only about a quarter of it went to labor-abundant Asia and Africa where almost two-thirds of the world's population lived": Clemens and Williamson, "Wealth Bias," p. 305. However, see also the different findings in Schularick, "Two Globalizations."
6 Obstfeld and Taylor, "Globalization and Capital Markets," p. 60, figure 10.
7 Schularick, "Two Globalizations," table 3.
8 Similarly, Schularick and Steger, "Does Financial Integration," find that financial inte-gration had a positive impact on growth in developing countries before World War I, but not after 1990.
9 The authoritative source for the distribution of British capital exports is Stone, *Global Export*. See also Schularick, "Two Globalizations," table 3.
10 Keynes, "Advice," pp. 204f.
11 Edelstein, "Imperialism," p. 205.
12 Ibid., p. 206.
13 Ibid., pp. 206–07.
14 Cain and Hopkins, *British Imperialism*, pp. 439, 570. See for a detailed discussion, Keynes, "Foreign Investment," pp. 275–84.
15 MacDonald, *Free Nation*, p. 380.
16 It was only after the war that the Treasury and the Bank of England began systemati-cally to give preference to new bond issues by British possessions over new issues by independent foreign states: see Atkin, "Official Regulation," pp. 324–35.
17 Ferguson, *Empire*, especially chapter 4. A modern survey of 49 countries concluded that common-law countries offered "the strongest legal protections of investors." The fact that 18 of the countries in the sample have the common law system is, of course, almost entirely due to their having been at one time or another under British rule: La Porta et al., "Law and Finance." See Rostowski and Stacescu, "Wig."
18 Cain and Hopkins, *British Imperialism*, p. 240.
19 Bordo and Kydland, "Commitment Mechanism," p. 56; and Bordo and Schwartz, "Monetary Policy Regimes," p. 10.
20 Bordo and Rockoff, "Gold Standard," p. 327.
21 Obstfeld and Taylor, "Sovereign Risk," p. 253.
22 Obstfeld and Taylor, "Sovereign Risk," p. 265.
23 Flandreau and Zumer, *Making of Global Finance*; see also Flandreau et al., "Stability."
24 Unfortunately, it cannot be excluded that different gold coding is responsible for the incompatible results. Flandreau and Zumer, *Making of Global Finance*, used a *de facto* criterion, i.e., exchange rate stability over a couple of years, whereas Obstfeld and Taylor, "Sovereign Risk," looked both at *de jure* and *de facto* criteria, following Meissner, "New World Order."
25 See Ferguson, *Cash Nexus* and "Political Risk."
26 Clemens and Williamson, "Wealth Bias," table 7, p. 322. The authors see colonial status as significant but less important than these nonpolitical variables. Ibid., p. 319, regressions 6 to 8.
27 This forced us to eliminate France and Germany as well as some smaller European economies that issued debt in domestic currency only. The (in)ability of countries to borrow internationally in domestic currency has been explored in detail in the "origi-nal sin" literature; see Bordo, Meissner, and Redish, "Original Sin"; and Flandreau and Sussman, "Old Sins." For the United States we followed Bordo and Rockoff, "Gold Standard," by using gold equivalent yields instead of dollar yields. The terms of repayment of U.S. government debt were in doubt: after 1879, all government debt

was to be payable in coin—technically silver or gold, but in practice gold. It was not until 1910 that gold was legally declared the only medium of repayment in the United States.

28 The complete list of countries and colonies can be found in the data appendix. The countries that were excluded despite the availability of loan quotations fulfilling our criteria were Bolivia, Costa Rica, Paraguay, Honduras, and Cuba as well as some small island empire borrowers such as Barbados and Trinidad, mostly for lack of economic control variables.

29 Bordo and Rockoff, "Gold Standard."

30 We decided to exclude about 20 observations with yields of more than 20 percent, virtually all these refer to Latin American loans that had been in full default for many years. The *Annual Reports* of the Corporation of Foreign Bondholders indicated that investors reckoned that full repayment was most unlikely in these cases.

31 See Davis and Huttenback, *Mammon*; and Edelstein, *Overseas Investment* and "Imperialism."

32 Bordo and Rockoff, "Gold Standard"; and Obstfeld and Taylor, "Sovereign Risk."

33 This point was advanced in Ferguson and Batley, "Event Risk"; and in Ferguson, *Cash Nexus*, pp. 285f. For a more recent development of this theme, see Flandreau and Zumer, *Making of Global Finance*, pp. 30–35.

34 This is a practical as well as methodological issue. A lot of financial investment went to countries for which no modern GDP reconstructions exist. A more practical problem discussed in greater detail in Schularick, "Two Globalizations," is the limited comparability of the GDP reconstructions.

35 Special gratitude is due to Trish Kelly, Peabody College, Vanderbilt University, for sharing unpublished data collected from the Corporation of Foreign Bondholders' *Annual Reports*. Additional data were gathered from historical collections, mainly from the three volumes by Mitchell, *Historical Statistics*, if the figures were also available to historical investors. For some indicators, we made use of Arthur Banks's *Cross-National Time Series Database*. Professor Banks confirmed to us in mail correspondence that all pre-1913 indicators we used for our study were originally collected from *The Statesman's Yearbook*. For some countries, we were happy to rely on material collected by Michael Bordo, Chris Meissner, Maurice Obstfeld, Hugh Rockoff, Nathan Sussman, and Alan Taylor. Despite this collective effort, some gaps in the dataset remained.

36 Having spent considerable time on the collection of late-nineteenth and early-twentieth-century economic data, we found the quantity of indicators available to contemporary investors to be less of a problem than their mixed quality. Indeed, for most countries we found more than one series for the same indicator. Although it was rare that two series turned out to be completely incompatible, differences of the order of 10 percent were not uncommon. The story the sources tell is that of a market driven not so much by short-term economic information, but by knowledge of long-term structural trends supplemented by short-term political news from which investors apparently inferred fiscal and monetary policy changes.

37 *Fenn's Compendium* is probably the best overall source for country-risk indicators. Revised editions of *Fenn's Compendium* were published in 1883, 1889, 1893, and 1898. Unfortunately, the series was then discontinued, apparently because the main contributor, Robert Nash, emigrated to Australia.

38 For a further discussion of contemporary risk analysis see Flandreau and Zumer, *Making of Global Finance*.

39 Flandreau and Zumer, *Making of Global Finance*, p. 31.

40 Cain and Hopkins, "Gentlemanly Capitalism," p. 7.

41 For a detailed discussion see Flandreau and Zumer, *Making of Global Finance*, p. 38.

42 A more detailed account of the problems involved can be found in Bordo and Kydland, "Gold Standard as a Rule"; Obstfeld and Taylor, "Sovereign Risk"; and Meissner, "New World Order."

43 See Meissner, "New World Order"; and Obstfeld and Taylor, "Sovereign Risk": essentially, a combination of "de jure and de facto" criteria, as opposed to the some-what more flexible "de facto" test employed by Flandreau and Zumer, *Making of Global Finance*. For the countries not classified in prior studies, we coded only those countries on gold that passed both de facto and de jure test. Colonies without their own currencies, thus being in a currency union with the United Kingdom, were also coded on gold.

44 Obstfeld and Taylor, "Sovereign Risk," p. 249. In order to obtain comparable results, we followed their example by including two gold dummy variables, one for nonde-faulters and one for defaulters.

45 Ferguson, "Political Risk."

46 Flandreau and Zumer use the ratio of debt charges to tax revenue, the ratio of central bank reserves to banknote circulation, the ratio of exports to population, the ratio of the budget deficit to tax revenue, the record of default, the exchange rate (presence or absence of a peg to gold) as well as two political variables: the extent of the franchise and "political crises" (a selection of wars and revolutions). For a detailed critique of their methodology see Ferguson, "Political Risk."

47 See, on this point, Mitchener and Weidenmier, "Trade."

48 In our benchmark regressions we opted for simple time-dummies. As part of the sensi-tivity checks we also included country specific betas following the logic of the capital asset pricing model; see the discussion in what follows.

49 This method was made popular by Nathaniel Beck and Jonathan Katz: see Beck and Katz, "What to do (and not to do) with time-series." In a different article the same authors have shown that the PCSE method is not only better than FGLS but also superior to Kmenta's "cross- sectionally heteroskedastic and timewise autocorrelated model" in research applications such as ours; Beck and Katz, "Nuisance vs. Substance."

50 Also, clustered robust standard errors would be an alternative given the panel- heter-oskedastic setting. We experimented with this method, but the results were very simi-lar. See comments below.

51 See Ferguson, "City of London and British Imperialism." Spread reductions could also be observed in other countries as a consequence of the imposition of international financial control in the wake of a debt default, e.g., in the Ottoman Empire and in Greece. The reduction of financial sovereignty was typically associated with gains in market confidence, even in the absence of direct financial guarantees by the Powers.

52 This is what Obstfeld and Taylor, "Sovereign Risk," do in their "empire test." To check the robustness of our results we apply the same methodology. A random-effects model would technically work with time-invariant variables, but random-unit effects are not a plausible assumption.

53 Haussmann and Taylor have proposed identifying and consistently estimating the coef-ficients of the time-invariant variables through a two-stage procedure; see Haussmann and Taylor, "Panel Data."

54 Oaxaca and Geisler, "Fixed Effect Models." To test the proposition that the unit effects are accounted for by a linear combination of the time-invariant regressors, we first ran a fixed effects model and regressed the estimated unit effects on the time-invariant variables including the empire dummy. We found that about 75 percent of the variance of the fixed effects is accounted for by colonial status and the geographical controls. We also tested whether or not the coefficient of the time-variant variables from the fixed-effects model changes once the unit effects are taken as regressors in an identical specification without fixed effects, but the coefficients hardly changed.

55 It can be argued that the autocorrelation could also be forced to be the same across all groups. This would increase the empire effect to about 120 basis points in our benchmark regression.

56 Repeating our benchmark regression with a different estimator, namely feasible generalized least squares (FGLS), produced the expected overconfident test statistics, but the empire effect remained the same. We obtain virtually the same result—a 100 basis point reduction—if we estimate the model by OLS but use the clustered Huber-White-sandwich estimates of variance (and standard errors).

57 See the data appendix for the country list; we coded all economies of Africa, Asia, Latin America, and peripheral Europe as developing countries.

58 The inclusion of regional dummy variables or other geographical controls has become common in quantitative explorations of cross-country spreads in order to account for the various economic effects associated with geography such as common shocks, records of regional political stability, or culture (See Eichengreen and Mody, "Changing Spreads"; Clemens and Williamson, "Wealth Bias"; Kamin and Kleist, "Credit Spreads"; and Cline and Barnes, "Spreads"). If we omit geographical controls altogether, the empire effect actually grows even stronger, to more than 150 basis points. We obtain similar results if we substitute the regional dummies for a geographic constant—the pre-Panama canal shipping distance from London. The results are available from the authors on request.

59 In a FGLS regression and using clustered robust standard errors, the effect is again close to 100 basis points. In a PCSE fixed-effects model in which the debt service ratio is the only debt indicator, a statistically highly significant mean difference of 160 basis points appears between the fixed-effects of colonies and independent countries.

60 Further sensitivity tests involved the estimation of a log-linear model, the inclusion of lagged independent variables, debt and revenues per capita, the growth rate of exports and of the population, the terms of trade, the share of natural resource exports in total exports, and the regression of end-of-period spreads (in other words, spreads calculated at December closing prices). We also tested a dynamic panel specification and ran pure cross-sections for period averages. None of this changed our main finding on the size and significance of empire membership, which was worth about 100 basis points, often more, especially when we compared poor colonies with poor independent countries.

61 It is important to note that not all colonies were also on the gold standard. Some joined relatively late, some colonies never did adhere. The different effects of gold standard membership and colonial status can thus be econometrically separated. This was confirmed when we introduced a separate variable for noncolonial gold standard members. Arguably, endogeneity of the exchange rate regime could be a problem, but it is unlikely to influence the estimation of the empire effect. For a more detailed discussion see Obstfeld and Taylor, "Sovereign Risk," p. 244.

62 It is well known that the empirical support for the CAPM is rather weak. Flandreau and Zumer, *Making of Global Finance*, reject this approach and underline the dangers of anachronistic modelling, pointing out that CAPM had not been invented by 1913. However, on an "as- if" basis this approach could remain valuable. It should also be noted that many well-known contemporary studies do not employ country-specific betas, but control for asset market shifts and investor's risk aversion using a common control variable such as time-dummies or the spread between low and high risk assets. See Cantor and Packer "Determinants"; Eichengreen and Mody, "What Explains Changing Spreads"; and Kamin and Kleist, "Evolution."

63 We also tried an unweighted and a GDP-weighted world spread for a subsample, but none of this changed our findings.

64 We are especially indebted to Alan Taylor for helpful comments on this point.

65 Obstfeld and Taylor, "Sovereign Risk," p. 255 (footnote 13). They call it the "strong empire test."
66 Ibid., p. 174.
67 Edelstein, "Imperialism," p. 206.
68 See Davis and Huttenback, *Mammon*, p. 174; and Edelstein, "Imperialism," pp. 207–10.
69 Edelstein, "Imperialism," p. 209.
70 For theoretical aspects of international lending and sovereign risk, see Eaton et. al., "Theory"; and Hermalin and Rose, "Risks." An application is Taylor and Sarno, "Capital Flows."
71 A much more comprehensive attempt to estimate the determinants of capital flows from Great Britain was recently made by Clemens and Williamson, "Wealth Bias." The authors also report that country risk mattered for the amount of capital countries attracted. Detailed analysis of British financial investment is possible since the publication of the flow data in Stone, *Global Export.*
72 Clemens and Williamson, "Wealth Bias"; Kelly, "Ability"; and Fishlow, "Lessons."
73 Lindert and Morton, "Sovereign Debt."
74 Cain and Hopkins, *British Imperialism*, p. 439.
75 See Krasner, *Organized Hypocrisy.*

References

Primary Data Sources

Brachelli, H. F. von. *Statistische Skizzen der europäischen und amerikanischen Staaten nebst den auswärtigen Beziehungen der ersteren.* Leipzig: Hinrichs'sche Buchhandlung, 1887.

Corporation of Foreign Bondholders. *Annual General Report of the Council of the Corporation of Foreign Bondholders.* London: Council of the Corporation, 1880–1914.

Fenn, C. *Fenn's Compendium.* London: E. Wilson, 1893.

Fenn, C., and R. L. Nash. *Fenn's Compendium.* London: Effingham Wilson, 1883.

The Investor's Monthly Manual: A Newspaper for Investors. London: Investors Monthly Manual Office: 1880–1914.

Juraschek, F. von. *Otto Hübner's Geographisch-Statistische Tabellen aller Länder der Erde.* Frankfurt: Heinrich Keller, 1880–1914.

London Stock Exchange. *The Stock Exchange Weekly Official Intelligence: An Official Financial Gazette of Information Concerning All Classes of Securities.* London: 1900–1913.

Nash, R. L. *Fenn's Compendium.* London: Effingham Wilson, 1889.

Oss, S.F. van. *Fenn on the Funds.* London: Effingham, 1898.

Philip, George. *Philip's Mercantile Marine Atlas.* London: Geographical Institute, 1914.

Royal Statistical Office. *Statistical Abstract for the Several Colonial and Other Possessions of the United Kingdom (Statistical Abstract for the British Empire).* London: 1880f.

Royal Statistical Office. *Statistical Abstracts for the Principal and Other Foreign Countries.* London: 1880f.

The Statesman's Yearbook: The Politics, Cultures and Economies of the World / Statistical and Historical Annual of the States of the World. London: Macmillan/Basingstoke/Palgrave, 1880–1916.

The full data appendix is available from Niall Ferguson's webpage at Harvard: http://fas.harvard.edu/~history/facultyPage.cgi?fac=ferguson

Secondary Sources

Atkin, John. *British Overseas Investment, 1918–1931.* New York: Arno Press, 1977.

_____. "Official Regulation of British Overseas Investment, 1914–1931." *Economic History Review* 23, no. 2 (1970): 324–35.

Avramov, Roumen. *120 Years Bulgarian National Bank (1879–1999).* Sofia: Bulgarian National Bank, 1999.

Banks, Arthur. *Cross-National Time Series Database 1815–1973.* http://www.databanks .sitehosting.net/

Beck, Nathaniel, and Jonathan Katz. "Nuisance vs. Substance: Specifying and Estimating Time-Series Cross-Section Models." *Political Analysis* 6 (1995): 1–36.

_____. "What To Do (and Not To Do) with Time-series Cross-section Data." *American Political Science Review* 89, no. 3 (1995): 634–47.

Bordo, Michael, and Finn. E. Kydland. "The Gold Standard as a Rule: An Essay in Exploration." *Explorations in Economic History* 32, no. 4 (1995): 423–64.

_____. "The Gold Standard as a Commitment Mechanism." In *Modern Perspectives on the Gold Standard,* edited by Tamim Bayoumi, Barry Eichengreen, and Mark P. Taylor, 55–100. Cambridge: Cambridge University Press, 1996.

Bordo, Michael, Christopher M. Meissner, and Angela Redish. "How 'Original Sin' was Overcome." NBER Working Paper No. 9841, Cambridge, MA, July 2003.

Bordo, Michael, and Hugh Rockoff. "The Gold Standard as a 'Good Housekeeping Seal of Approval'." This JOURNAL 56, no. 2 (1996): 389–428.

Bordo, Michael, and Anna Schwartz. "Monetary Policy Regimes and Economic Performance: The Historical Record." NBER Working Paper No. 6201, Cambridge, MA, June 1997.

Cain, P. J., and A. G. Hopkins. *British Imperialism.* London: Longman, 1994.

Cantor, R., and F. Packer. "Determinants and Impacts of Sovereign Credit Ratings." *Federal Reserve Bank of New York Economic Policy Review,* October (1996): 37–53.

Clemens, Michael A., and Jeffrey Williamson. "Wealth Bias in the First Global Capital Market Boom, 1870–1913." *Economic Journal* 114, no. 2 (2004): 304–37.

Cline, W. R., and K. J. Barnes. "Spreads and Risk in Emerging Markets Lending." Institute of International Finance Research Papers No.97/1, Institute of International Finance, Washington, DC, 1997.

Couper, Alistair, ed. *The Times Atlas of the Oceans.* London: Times Books, 1983.

Davis, Lance, and Robert A. Huttenback. *Mammon and the Pursuit of Empire. The Political Economy of British Imperialism.* Cambridge: Cambridge University Press, 1986.

Denzel, Markus. "Finanzplätze, Wechselkurse und Währungsverhältnisse in Lateinamerika (1808–1914)." In *Währungen der Welt.* Vol.7, edited by Jürgen Schneider, 1–106. Stuttgart: Steiner, 1997.

Drazen, Allan. "Towards a Political-Economic Theory of Domestic Debt." In *The Debt Burden and Its Consequences for Monetary Policy,* edited by G. Calvo and M. King, 159–176, London: Palgrave Macmillan, 1998.

Eaton, Jonathan, Mark Gersovitz, and Joseph Stiglitz. "The Pure Theory of Country Risk." NBER Working Paper No. 1894, Cambridge, MA, December 1986.

Edelstein, Michael. "Imperialism: Cost and Benefit." In *The Economic History of Britain Vol. 2,* edited by Roderick Floud and Donald McCloskey, 197–216. Cambridge: Cambridge University Press, 1994.

_____. *Overseas Investment in the Age of High Imperialism.* New York: Columbia University Press, 1982.

Eichengreen, Barry, and Ashoka Mody. "What Explains Changing Spreads on Emerging Market Debt: Fundamentals or Market Sentiment?" NBER Working Paper No. 6408, Cambridge, MA, February 1998.

Eichengreen, Barry, and Marc Flandreau. "The Geography of the Gold Standard." Centre for Economic Policy Research Discussion Paper in International Macroeconomics No. 1050, London, 1994.

Ferguson, Niall. *The Cash Nexus.* London: Penguin Press, 2001.

_____. *Empire: How Britain Made the Modern World.* London: Allen Lane, 2003.

_____. *The World's Banker: The History of the House of Rothschild.* London: Weidenfeld and Nicolson, 1998.

_____. "The City of London and British Imperialism: New Light on an Old Question." In *London and Paris as International Financial Centres in the Twentieth Century*, edited by Yousef Cassis and Eric Bussière, 57–77. Oxford: Oxford University Press, 2004.

_____. "Political Risk and the International Bond Market between the 1848 Revolution and the Outbreak of the First World War." *Economic History Review* (forthcoming).

Ferguson, Niall, and Richard Batley. "Event Risk and the International Bond Market in the Era of the Classical Gold Standard." Unpublished Manuscript, Oxford University, Oxford, 2001.

Fieldhouse, David K. *The West and the Third World.* Oxford: Blackwell, 1999.

_____. *Economics and Empire 1830–1914.* London: Weidenfeld & Nicolson, 1973.

Fishlow, Albert. "Lessons From the Past: Capital Markets during the 19th Century and the Interwar period." *International Organization* 39 (1985): 383–439.

Flandreau, Marc, and Nathan Sussman. "Old Sins: Exchange Rate Clauses and European Foreign Lending in the Nineteenth Century." Centre for Economic Policy Research Discussion Paper 4248 (February 2004).

Flandreau, Marc, and Frédéric Zumer. *The Making of Global Finance. 1880–1913.* Paris: OECD, 2004.

Flandreau, Marc, Jacques Le Cacheux, and Frédéric Zumer. "Stability without a Pact? Lessons from the European Gold Standard, 1880–1914." *Economic Policy* 13, no. 26 (1998): 115–62.

Hale, David. "The British Empire In Default: Should Newfoundland Be a Role Model For Argentina?" Mimeo, 28 January 2003.

Hausmann, J. A., and W. E. Taylor. "Panel Data and Unobserved Individual Effects." *Econometrica* 49 (1981): 319–39.

Hermalin, Benjamin E., and Andrew K. Rose. "Risks to Lenders and Borrowers In International Capital Markets." NBER Working Paper No. 6886, Cambridge, MA, January 1999.

Kamin, Steven B., and Karsten von Kleist. "The Evolution and Determinants of Emerging Market Credit Spreads in the 1990's." International Finance Discussion Papers No. 653, Board of Governors of the Federal Reserve System, Washington, DC, 1999.

Kelly, Trish. "Ability and Willingness to Pay in the Age of the Pax Britannica 1890–1914." *Explorations in Economic History* 35, no. 1 (1998): 31–58.

Kennedy, Peter. *A Guide to Econometrics.* Oxford: Blackwell, 2003.

Keynes, John Maynard. "Foreign Investment and National Advantage." In *The Collected Writings of John Maynard Keynes, Vol. 19*, edited by Donald Moggridge, 275–84. London: Macmillan, 1981.

_____. "Advice to Trustee Investors." In *The Collected Writings of John Maynard Keynes. Vol. 19.* edited by Donald Moggridge, 202–06. London: Macmillan, 1981.

Krasner, Stephen. *Sovereignty: Organized Hypocrisy.* Princeton, NJ: Princeton University Press, 1999.

La Porta, Rafael, Florence Lopez-de-Silanes, Andrei Shleifer, et al. "Law and Finance." *Journal of Political Economy* 106, no. 6 (1998): 1113–55.

Levy, Maria Barbara. "The Brazilian Public Debt—Domestic and Foreign, 1824–1913." In *The Public Debt in Latin America in Historical Perspective*, edited by Reinhart Liehr, 209–54. Frankfurt: Vervuert, 1995.

Lindert, Peter H., and Peter Morton. "How Sovereign Debt Has Worked." In *Developing Country Debt and the World Economy*, edited by J. Sachs, 225–35. Chicago: University of Chicago Press, 1989.

Macdonald, James. *A Free Nation Deep in Debt.* New York: Farrar, Straus and Giroux, 2003.

Maddison, Angus. *The World Economy: A Millennial Perspective.* Paris: OECD, 2001.

Meissner, Christopher M. "A New World Order: Explaining the Emergence of the Classical Gold Standard." *Journal of International Economics* (forthcoming).

Mitchell, B. R. *International Historical Statistics: Africa, Asia & Oceania.* New York: Stockton Press, 1995.

_____. *International Historical Statistics: The Americas 1750–1988.* New York: Stockton Press, 1993.

_____. *International Historical Statistics: Europe 1750–1988.* New York: Stockton Press, 1992.

Mitchener, Kris James, and Marc Weidenmier. "Empire, Public Goods, and the Roosevelt Corollary." This JOURNAL 65, no. 3 (2005): 658–92.

_____. "Trade and Empire." Working Paper, Claremont McKenna College, March 2005.

Mody, Ashoka, and Mark P. Taylor. "International Capital Crunches: The Time-Varying Role of Information Asymmetries." International Monetary Fund Working Paper 02/43, Washington, DC, 2002.

Oaxaca, Ronald, and Iris Geisler. "Fixed Effect Models with Time Invariant Variables: A Theoretical Note." *Economic Letters* 80, no. 3 (2003): 373–77.

Obstfeld, Maurice, and Alan M. Taylor. "Sovereign Risk, Credibility and the Gold Standard: 1870–1913 vs. 1925–1931." *Economic Journal* 113, no. 2 (2003): 241–75.

_____. "Globalization and Capital Markets." In *Globalization in Historical Perspective*, edited by Michael D. Bordo, Alan M. Taylor, and Jeffrey G. Williamson, 121–87. Chicago: Chicago University Press, 2003.

Rostowski, Jacek, and Bogdan Stacescu. "The Wig and the Pith Helmet: The Impact of 'Legal School' versus Colonial Institutions on Economic Performance." Draft paper, April 2004.

Sarkees, Meredith Reid. "The Correlates of War Data on War: An Update to 1995." *Conflict Management and Peace Science* 18 (2000): 123–44.

Schneider, Jürgen, et al., eds. *Währungen der Welt, Vol. 1–8: Beiträge zur Wirtschafts- und Sozialgeschichte No. 44–57.* Stuttgart: Steiner, 1991–1997.

Schularick, Moritz. "A Tale of Two 'Globalizations': Capital Flows From Rich to Poor in Two Eras of Global Finance." *International Journal of Finance and Economics*, forthcoming.

Schularick, Moritz, and Thomas Steger. "Does International Financial Integration Spur Economic Growth? New Evidence from the First Era of Financial Globalization." ETH Zurich Working Paper 06/46.

Sédillot, René. *Toutes les monnaies du monde.* Paris: Sirey, 1955.

Siller, Javier Pérez. "Deuda y consolidacion del poder en México, 1867–1896." In *The Public Debt in Latin America in Historical Perspective*, edited by Reinhart Liehr, 293–336. Frankfurt: Vervuert, 1995.

Stone, Irving. *The Global Export of Capital from Great Britain 1865–1914.* London: Macmillan, 1999.

Taylor, Mark P., and Lucio Sarno. "Capital Flows to Developing Countries: Long-and Short-Term Determinants." *World Bank Economic Review* 11 (1997): 451–70.

Wooldridge, Jeffrey M. *Econometric Analysis of Cross-Section and Panel Data.* Cambridge, MA: MIT Press, 2002.

World Bank. *World Development Report 2005: A Better Investment Climate for Everyone.* Washington, DC: World Bank, 2004.

14

DISCIPLINING THE 'BLACK SHEEP OF THE BALKANS'

Financial Supervision and Sovereignty in Bulgaria, 1902–38[1]

Adam Tooze and Martin Ivanov

Source: *Economic History Review* 64, 1, 2011, 30–51.

Using the example of Bulgaria, we argue that familiar models of international political economy fail to capture the tension between national sovereignty and access to capital markets experienced by peripheral debtors in the late nineteenth and early twentieth centuries. Existing accounts exaggerate the significance of the gold standard as a good housekeeping seal of approval and underestimate the role of direct financial controls. Furthermore, they underestimate the linkage in zones of interimperial rivalry, such as the Balkans, between foreign borrowing and strategic alignment. We show how Bulgaria found its politics destabilized prior to 1914 by the demands of its creditors. After defeat in the First World War, Bulgaria was forced to submit to an even tighter system of creditor control. Though it obtained substantial debt relief during the 1930s, these concessions were gained not through an assertion of national sovereignty and default, but at the price of even closer supervision. This in turn casts new light on the conventional view of Bulgaria as a victim of Nazi 'informal imperialism'. In light of Bulgaria's previous experience, the more striking feature of its trade relations with Hitler's Germany is that they were conducted on a basis of sovereign equality.

Modern Bulgaria came into existence in 1878, in the heyday of late Victorian globalization. Not surprisingly, national economic development was from the outset a key priority of the country's fledgling political leadership.[2] This article is about the difficulty of reconciling Bulgaria's aspirations to sovereign self-government and economic development with its international context.[3] The Bulgarian case is of wider interest, we argue, because it exposes blind spots in three of the most influential narratives of global political economy in the period 1870–1939: the 'gold standard interpretation', Flandreau's structural account of the international currency system, and Ferguson's empire-centred model. Furthermore, we hope to reveal new facets of the interwar crisis by relating Bulgaria's trajectory in the 1930s to its earlier experience.

I

Bulgaria's trajectory might seem to fit neatly within the interpretation centred on the gold standard developed by Bordo, Rockoff, Eichengreen and others. The central theme of this narrative is the tension between the need of debtor countries to adopt the gold standard as a 'good housekeeping seal of approval' and the constraints which adherence to the gold standard imposed on the free exercise of national economic policy.[4] This tension became ever more acute in the course of the early twentieth century as economic aspirations began to be expressed through increasingly democratic political systems. In the 1890s Bulgaria was one of many countries whose political class aspired to the gold standard as a badge of financial respectability. Substantial international loans flowed to Bulgaria after 1900, which included among their conditions the retention of the lev's parity with the gold franc. However, when it entered the Great War in 1915 Bulgaria, like all the other combatants, was forced to abandon the metallic standard. In the war's aftermath, Bulgaria played out the paradoxical drama made familiar by Eichengreen's *Golden fetters*. The inflation and political turmoil of the early 1920s made the 'knave proof' gold-exchange standard irresistibly attractive as a totem of stability. Bulgaria returned to gold in 1928, but the changed political and financial conditions made the restored currency system unworkable. Within three years, in the autumn of 1931 the global crisis left Sofia with no option but to abandon free convertibility in favour of exchange controls. Thereafter Bulgaria might seem to be just one more instance of a country released from the constraints of gold and free to follow its own national economic trajectory. Eichengreen and Portes include Bulgaria in their class of 'heavy defaulters'.[5] Behind a shield of exchange controls, the Bulgarian government adopted an interventionist programme of agrarian price support and, true to the hypothesis of *Golden fetters*, the result appears to have been an unusually rapid recovery from the trough of the recession.

Nevertheless, as appealing as it may be to incorporate Bulgaria into this familiar narrative of the emancipation of national economic policy, this story pays insufficient attention to the hierarchical gradations within the international economy, which have recently been delineated by Flandreau and his collaborators.[6] Before 1914 Bulgaria was never a full member of the gold standard, let alone a core member. Its currency, the lev, was so obscure that it escapes even Flandreau's unprecedentedly wide-ranging network analysis of global currency trading.[7] It seems safe to assume, however, that Bulgaria belonged alongside its Balkan neighbours, such as Serbia, in Flandreau's third tier. For countries in this category, adherence to the gold standard may have been a necessary condition, but it was never sufficient to secure admission to international capital markets. As Flandreau has shown, in the 1880s and early 1890s borrowers whose 'governance' was suspect faced painfully high interest charges and discount rates. If a borrower were to gain access to credit on reasonable terms, lenders needed to be persuaded that its financial 'fundamentals' were truly sound.

The emphasis placed by Flandreau and his colleagues on the hierarchical structure of the gold standard is crucial to understanding Bulgaria's subordinate position. However, the plausibility of their analysis as far as the Bulgarian case is concerned is substantially weakened by their surprisingly optimistic interpretation of the system's operation. According to the Flandreau narrative, what drove the expansion of international lending and the considerable reduction in the interest premiums paid by low-grade borrowers was the underlying process of convergent economic growth. Yet evidence for sustained per capita income growth in the Balkans prior to 1914, let alone convergence, is surprisingly hard to come by.[8] Furthermore, the optimistic political conclusions of Flandreau's analysis are jarringly out of kilter with the actual experience of Bulgaria and its Balkan neighbours. Whereas Bordo and Eichengreen stress the tension between international monetary institutions and popular political aspirations, Flandreau et al. see no such conflict. Indeed they claim to have found a significant negative correlation across a large global data set between the expected probability of default and an index measuring the degree of enfranchisement.[9] They interpret this finding as suggesting that lenders trusted borrowers with more fully developed democratic institutions. This statistical result certainly needs further investigation, but as far as Bulgaria is concerned Flandreau et al.'s optimistic interpretation seems wide of the mark.

What analyses based on interest spreads leave undiscussed are three features of lending to third-tier borrowers, which yield a far less optimistic picture. Firstly, international creditors in dealing with borrowers such as Bulgaria went beyond either general badges of good housekeeping, such as gold standard membership, or the kind of arms-length monitoring described by Flandreau, to impose a variety of direct controls.[10] From the early 1880s onwards, a common arrangement was the hypothecation or 'mortgaging' of particular revenue streams. In more extreme cases European creditors took direct control of a debtor's fiscal apparatus, the most important examples being the Ottoman Public Debt Administration and the European-administered Chinese Maritime Customs Service. If such demands provoked nationalist resistance as in Egypt, creditor interests could be backed up, not merely by gunboats, but, if need be, by full-scale military invasion and the imposition of a quasi-colonial protectorate. Such methods were used in Persia and Morocco as well as Egypt.[11] Needless to say, credits accompanied by controls of this type were at odds with the full exercise of national sovereignty.

Not surprisingly, given the threat posed by such intrusive modes of creditor control, international borrowing was often highly controversial in the recipient countries, and international creditors exercised little restraint in picking sides in these arguments. They thus interfered not only externally but directly in the operation of their clients' political systems, often, as we will show with regard to Bulgaria, with ruinous consequences for the political culture of the debtor states.

This temptation to interfere in internal political affairs was all the more pressing when considerations beyond the merely financial were in play. From the 1890s onwards, lending by France, Russia, and Austria-Hungary to Balkan countries routinely came with strategic strings attached. Quite apart from the threat posed to national sovereignty by intrusive foreign financial regulation, the question of borrowing abroad thereby acquired an existential quality. Procuring a loan via Paris, for instance, meant not only submitting to the supervision of French bond-holders, but tying one's nation's destiny to the Franco-Russian alliance. Victory for one's Great Power patron promised the fulfilment of cherished national aspirations. Defeat spelled catastrophe. Not surprisingly, questions of this magnitude, in which financial decisions bearing on a country's long-term economic development were imbricated with life and death decisions about military alliances, had the potential to destabilize national politics explosively.

These entanglements of finance and imperial rivalry were once a staple of the scholarly literature, but they have lately slipped from view.[12] The author who in recent years has come closest to capturing this strategic dimension of international finance is Ferguson, with his celebration of the British Empire as the liberal nursery of global, capitalist modernity.[13] Much controversy surrounds the details of Ferguson's econometrics.[14] However, if we grant that there may be some truth in Ferguson's contention that the making of the modern world was inherently linked to the project of liberal empire, then we must also admit that the formation of peripheral regions beyond the secure boundaries of empire and the precarious existence of states caught in danger zones of inter-imperial rivalry, is as inherent to the general process of global development as the secure, upward progress of the imperial core. Born out of the collapse of one empire, and struggling to establish itself in a zone of intense inter-imperial rivalry, Bulgaria provides an interesting illustration of the darker side of the process through which empires, in Ferguson's words, 'made the modern world'.

II

In the 1880s newly independent Bulgaria obtained modest amounts of funds from London, Vienna, and Berlin.[15] However, these sources of finance dried up in the course of the 1890s as the Franco-Russian alliance began to assert its influence throughout the Balkans. Second only to London in the depth of its financial markets, Paris was in a position to provide funds, but on what terms? That Bulgaria would have to pay an interest premium was obvious. The real issue was not the price of the loan, but the extent of the supervision that Bulgaria's creditors might demand. In an effort to establish its credibility as a borrower, Bulgaria stabilized its largely silver-backed currency in relation to the gold franc in the 1890s and announced its intention of formally joining the gold standard in 1897.[16] However, no one imagined that this would be sufficient to secure funding. Even Romania

with its strong export balance and far more credible commitment to the gold standard was able to obtain credit only on condition of the hypothecation of key taxes.[17]
Serbia, whose economic potential was more comparable to that of Bulgaria, first
resorted to selling its tobacco monopoly to Viennese bankers. Then in 1895, as
it drifted into the orbit of France and Russia, Belgrade accepted creditor supervision of its Monopolies Administration.[18] Greece resisted any such control until
1898 when the disastrous war with Turkey over Crete precipitated a financial crisis so severe that Athens was forced to accept a tight regime of supervision exercised by an International Financial Commission, in this case with a major British
interest.[19] In the Balkans, however, even such controls were not enough. From the
1890s onwards the receipt of funding was tied quite explicitly to adherence to one
or other of the military blocs that were increasingly destabilizing European politics. In some cases, where creditors' and debtors' strategic interests were aligned,
one might speak as scholars of the twentieth-century Marshall Plan have done,
of a form of 'empire by invitation'.[20] Serbia, as the willing tool of Russia and
France against Austria-Hungary, was only too happy to use the stamp of approval
provided by the representative of French bondholders in Belgrade to tap a flow of
almost 500 million francs between 1896 and 1914.[21] Bulgaria illustrates a more
damaging possibility.

Sandwiched as it was between Turkey, Romania, Serbia, and Greece and
haunted by unresolved territorial questions, Bulgaria's strategic alignment was
ambiguous from birth. A firm commitment to either the Paris–St Petersburg or the
Berlin–Vienna axis might lead to national disaster. It also risked a damaging split
within the Bulgarian political class between the conservative pro-Russian and
the liberal pro-Austrian factions. Stability required a strategy of balance, or even
neutrality. Given the need for funds, that was not an option. An agrarian crisis in
1899, on top of a botched programme of railway construction, left Bulgaria in
desperate need of a consolidation loan. To clear the way, the pro-Austrian liberal
party were turfed out of office and in 1902 Sofia negotiated a credit with Paribas
bank. Under the terms of the loan Sofia committed itself to maintaining full convertibility on the gold standard. Additional security was provided by creditor control of the revenue from Bulgaria's tobacco tax, and the installation in Sofia of a
bondholders' representative endorsed by the French government.

Though this was by the standards of the Balkans a relatively modest level of
intrusion and though the financial terms of the loan were good, it coincided with an
unprecedented opening of Bulgarian politics. The election of January 1901 had seen
the return of 21 Agrarian deputies and eight Marxist Social Democrats.[22] Outraged
at the prospect of slipping into the kind of dependence exemplified by Greece and
Serbia, the Bulgarian Parliament, the Sobranje, twice refused to approve the loan.
To secure the foreign funds, Prince Ferdinand was forced to disband the assembly
and hold rigged elections that produced a sufficiently compliant majority.[23]

Having established this precedent, the French also absorbed Bulgarian bond
issues in 1904 and 1907 against further hypothecation of tax revenue (table 1).
However, Bulgaria's political class never reconciled itself to this intrusion into its

Table 1 Bulgarian foreign loans backed by collateralized revenues as of 1929–31 in leva (millions), 1929–31

Loans	Collateralized revenues	1929	1930	1931
5% 1902	Tobacco excise label	594.8	694.1	682.6
5% 1904	Stamp duty and surplus of tobacco excise label	309.9	390.2	335.8
4.5% 1907	Surplus of excise label and stamp duty			
7% 1926	Excise on ethylated spirit and alcohol	52.4	48.1	42.5
	Excise on salt and different other commodities	275.0	332.3	328.7
	Excise on boxes of matches	89.1	105.4	94.2
7.5% 1928	Import duties	1,080.0	774.2	869.9
	Export duties	53.7	16.8	5.5
	3% tax on export of commodities	3.6	0.4	0.1
	Storage, statistical tax, and other customs taxes	83.5	70.5	56.2
	Total	2,542	2,432	2,416
	As % of total budgeted revenues	37.2	41.3	45.5

Source: Mesechni izvestiya na Direktsiyata za darjavni dulgove [Quarterly Proceedings of Public Debts Agency], various issues.

sovereignty and at the end of 1908, following the declaration of full *de jure* independence in the wake of the Young Turk Revolution, Bulgaria approached France for a new loan, this time without special guarantees. Notwithstanding Bulgaria's continued commitment to maintaining the parity of the lev with the franc, the French response was immediate. Paribas withdrew and the Quai d'Orsay vetoed the participation of any other French lenders. Sensing an opportunity to prize Bulgaria loose from Paris and St Petersburg, Vienna responded by offering a long-term loan without onerous guarantees. Despite the pressure on its limited capital markets, the German government in the autumn of 1911 raised no objection to the listing of the loan in Hamburg. This in turn triggered a response from Russia, which demanded that Paris should resume lending to Sofia. The Balkans, however, were now abuzz with rumours of an imminent war. These rumours were confirmed in October 1912 when a coalition of Romania, Serbia, Greece, and Bulgaria inflicted a quick defeat on Turkey, followed within months by a Second Balkan War in which Bulgaria was in turn defeated by its former allies. To the frustration of St Petersburg, France halted long-term funding for the duration.[24] However, as soon as peace descended in the summer of 1913, the financial manoeuvring resumed and it now took on increasingly dangerous forms.[25]

All of the participants in the fighting in 1912–13 were on the edge of bankruptcy and desperate to rebuild their armies. With strong Russian backing, Serbia obtained a large French loan. Romania played the field, attracting offers both from Paris and Berlin. Sofia's options were more limited. As a condition for the resumption of lending, France demanded a definitive commitment to the Franco-Russian alliance, even if this meant overriding the will of the Sobranje and imposing a change of cabinet. In an extraordinary move, the Russians proposed side-stepping the formal structures of the Bulgarian state altogether, and providing a personal loan of no less than 100 million francs directly to the Tsar. As France's loan to Russia had done in 1906, this would have permitted the Bulgarian Tsar to dispense altogether with the Parliament. But both Tsar Ferdinand and the nationalist liberal Radoslavoff government were bent on only one thing: reversing the disastrous outcome of the Second Balkan War. Neither Russia nor France had any interest in sponsoring this revisionism. Vienna, on the other hand, was only too keen to encourage Bulgaria as a counterweight to Serbia, but Austria lacked the necessary funds and, though the German foreign office was keen to help, the Deutsche Bank insisted that any loan to Bulgaria should be backed by the revenue from a tobacco monopoly. Such a guarantee smacked of Serbian-style subservience and was hugely unpopular with the Bulgarian peasantry, whose voice in Sofia politics was growing with every election. Finally in June 1914, the Disconto Gesellschaft under pressure from the Wilhelmstrasse agreed to an advance of 120 million francs, backed not by a tobacco monopoly but by a contract placing Bulgaria's industrial development in German hands. Even this modest compromise was hugely controversial in the super-charged political environment of Sofia.

The opposition to creditor control, which had already been strong in 1902, was now compounded by the high drama of strategic choice. When the loan was put to the vote in the Sobranje, there was uproar. In their struggle to secure both the financial means for national development and their country's position within the increasingly dangerous international system, the once dignified Bulgarian political class were reduced to scenes that confirmed the worst stereotypes of 'Balkan disorder'. The Prime Minister, speaking in defence of the Disconto loan, was struck on the head by a book hurled at him by a furious opponent. In the mêlée the parliamentary clerks were unable to keep track of who was present in the Chamber, and it was never conclusively established whether the German loan had, in fact, gained the majority Radoslavoff's government later claimed for it.

Ironically, despite the strategic importance attached to the loan, the Disconto Gesellschaft had in the name of 'good governance' insisted that the funds be reserved for infrastructure development, rather than military spending, and in August 1914 Bulgaria stood aside from the conflagration triggered by the confrontation between Austria-Hungary and Serbia. Furthermore, given the demands of the war, Germany was in no position actually to make good on the loan. However, as far as Bulgaria was concerned this only meant that the game was not yet played out.[26] In retaliation against the disputed Sobranje vote, France and Russia called in Bulgaria's overdraft, forcing it into deeper dependence on Germany. Meanwhile, the French bondholders' representative in Sofia continued to lobby on behalf of the Entente, attempting to lure Bulgaria away from the Central Powers by promising to buy up the entire harvest of 1915.[27] This served only to compound the damage already done to Bulgarian political culture. First the Prime Minister had been tainted by association with Disconto. Now the Agrarian Party, rapidly emerging as the main party of democratic opposition, was denounced as being in the pockets of French capital. In any case, for the nationalist leadership the temptation to establish Bulgaria as a dominant regional power was too great and in the autumn of 1915 Sofia threw in its lot with the Central Powers, who immediately provided a large loan.

At first the Bulgarian armies fighting under German command went from success to success. In 1915 they crushed Serbia, in 1916 Romania. By 1917 Greece was reduced to near civil war, split between pro-German and pro-Entente camps. In the spring of 1918 at Brest Litovsk a Bulgarian delegation enjoyed a ringside seat at the dismantling of the mighty Russian Empire. When a no less draconian peace was imposed on Romania in May 1918, Bulgaria's bid for regional hegemony seemed on the brink of success, but everything now depended on the success of its German ally, and with the sudden collapse of the Central Powers in the autumn of 1918, Sofia faced its greatest crisis since independence.

III

Remarkably, the immediate effect of the war was not to disable the Bulgarian political system. The nationalist elite of the prewar period were discredited, but the effect was to reinforce the impulse towards democratization clearly evident before the war. The driving force was Stamboliiski's agrarian movement (Bulgarian Agrarian National Union, hereafter BANU), with a proud record of resistance to Bulgaria's three disastrous wars and deep roots in the peasantry, who made up at least 75 per cent of the population. With an agenda of progressive agrarian development, state welfare, and anti-militarism, Stamboliiski's government was determined to avoid confrontation with the victor powers. Despite the desperate shortage of foreign exchange and the deterioration in the lev, which by December 1918 was already reduced to one-tenth of its prewar value, in March 1919 Bulgaria resumed service of its prewar debts, owed mainly to France.[28]

However, such gestures of compliance were now beside the point. After the Treaty of Versailles, German nationalists denounced reparations as threatening their country with a regime of creditor control even more draconian than that which had been inflicted on the Ottoman Empire in the 1880s.[29] With British and French forces advancing out of their Salonika bridgehead and Serbia, Romania, and Greece resurgent, Bulgaria must have feared that it would be reduced to the more humiliating fate of Egypt. The Peace signed in the Paris suburb of Neuilly in the autumn of 1919 was a national disaster no less severe than Versailles. The treaty stripped Bulgaria of its Aegean territories, displacing hundreds of thousands of refugees, while imposing a reparations bill of 2.25 billion gold francs plus occupation expenses. As table 2 makes clear, this was a truly staggering burden in relation to Bulgaria's limited national resources. If Bulgaria failed to comply, it would now face military sanctions. The rough-and-tumble rules of prewar debt diplomacy had taken an even uglier turn.

When Stamboliiski's government was unable to make its first payment, a reparations commission headed by a French colonel was despatched to Sofia in February

Table 2 Bulgarian foreign debt ratios (%)

	1892	1911	1921	1925	1929	1933	1935	1939
Net debt and reparations/GNP	9.5	32.9	213.2	76.6	62.6	53.5	56.2	19.8
Debt service/Export	11.9	19.8	30.7	25	21	33.5	9.4	4.5
Interest/Export	6.1	16.2	22.2	15.8	17.7	30.1	4.3	3.8

Source: Authors' own calculations. Debt and export from *Statistical Yearbooks of Bulgarian Kingdom* (hereafter SYBK), various issues; GNP from Ivanov and Tooze, 'Convergence', pp. 699–700.

1921. Over the next 18 months on pain of sanctions it forced the BANU government to prioritize debt repayment and reparations and to abandon much of its domestic programme, including any investment in land reform, the highly controversial compulsory labour service programme, and a progressive programme of elementary education.[30] In June 1922, as negotiations over a further moratorium on reparations reached a critical stage, the commission imposed compulsory 'shock therapy' in the form of a law limiting government borrowing from the Bulgarian National Bank, requiring an immediate monetary and fiscal consolidation.[31]

Remarkably, the internal discipline of BANU was sufficient to enable its government to make these concessions without sacrificing the loyalty of its supporters or the hope of major reforms to come. In March 1923 Stamboliiski reaped the benefits of his concerted effort to foster good relations with Bulgaria's former enemies when, instead of imposing sanctions like those being applied to Germany, the reparations creditors agreed to cut the final sum of reparations to 550 million francs and to accept a more reasonable repayment schedule.[32] At the end of April 1923 BANU scored an overwhelming general election victory and, with the burden of reparations sharply reduced, it seemed as though Stamboliiski might now be free to embark on the realization of his programme of domestic transformation, at least within the tight fiscal limits set by the reparations commission. However, this prospect of a socially radical regime backed by a domestic majority, and a peaceful reconciliation with Yugoslavia, was deeply worrying for the nationalist right. The Bulgarian establishment had reason to fear Stamboliiski's disdain for Parliament and the privileges of nineteenth-century elite politics. Nor was BANU's consolidation of power welcomed by the Entente powers, who regarded the Agrarians, quite wrongly, as a stalking horse for Bolshevism. On 9 June 1923, Stamboliiski was overthrown and brutally murdered in a military coup. He was succeeded by Alexander Tsankov, a professor of political economy at Sofia University and head of a coalition euphemistically known as the Democratic Accord.[33] The lev, which under the impact of the stabilization plan had been strengthening since January 1923, leapt 26 per cent on news of the coup. The French ambassador, who was known for his hostility towards BANU, later boasted of having conspired with Tsankov.[34] The British too welcomed the new regime and Tsankov rewarded their confidence by pledging to honour Bulgaria's financial obligations under the Neuilly Treaty.

Long caricatured by the Communist historiography as 'fascist', Tsankov's ideological affinity for national socialism actually only developed once he was out of power. The substance of his economic policies consisted of a continuation of the conservative monetary and fiscal policies imposed by the Allied Commission, combined with the adaptation of certain key elements of BANU's economic and social policy in authoritarian guise.[35] In December 1923, following the suspension of free foreign exchange dealing, the lev was stabilized at the highly competitive rate of c. 137–9 to the dollar.[36] With prices stable and the balance of trade improving, Bulgaria's credit was certainly recovering. But the norms of international respectability in the 1920s demanded more than mere financial conformity. Images of Stamboliiski's mutilated corpse and the terrifying 'white terror' that followed the botched Communist bombing of Sofia Cathedral in April 1925 had irrevocably tarnished Tsakov's reputation. In January 1926 *Time* magazine awarded his regime the dubious accolade of 'the worst and most ruthless Government in Europe'.[37] When at the end of 1925 Tsankov applied for League of Nations support for the accommodation of Bulgaria's 300,000 postwar refugees, the League and other international creditors made it clear that the 'butcher of Sofia' would have to be replaced by a more moderate factional leader of his Democratic Accord, the respectable prewar Liberal Andrei Lyapchev.[38]

The League issued reconstruction loans to Bulgaria in 1926 and 1928. The loans were conditional on the mortgage of further major elements of the Bulgarian fiscal system, but as far as Bulgaria was concerned, that was merely a continuation of prewar practice. With League backing, a regime of fiscal austerity produced a balance budget in 1927–8. In December 1928 Bulgaria formally committed itself to the gold-exchange standard. On the face of it this might be seen as a return to the liberal respectability of the prewar era. However, this would be to ignore the fact that to gain readmission to the international financial community Bulgaria had accepted a radical reduction in its political options—foreswearing the nationalist ambitions of the prewar period, curbing the dangerous popular mobilization of the early 1920s, and removing from view the more distasteful extremes of counter-revolution.[39]

Within the tight confines of this settlement, the pluralism of Bulgaria's political culture underwent an ill-timed revival in June 1931, when, following the freest election in interwar Bulgarian history, the Democratic Accord was peacefully displaced from office by the so-called People's Bloc. This brought the domesticated Agrarian Party back into government, promising a clean break with the bloody spectre of Tsankov's regime.[40] The radical rhetoric of the Stamboliiski era had been replaced by talk of 'social reconciliation'. This was soon to be tested by the collapse of the international framework within which Bulgaria had been stabilized since the mid-1920s.

IV

A poor harvest in 1929, combined with the disastrous shift in the international terms of trade and the ongoing drain of debt service and capital flight, caused the

Bulgarian National Bank (BNB) to lose 60 per cent of its foreign exchange and gold holdings between the peak of December 1928 and the trough of September By the autumn of 1931 Bulgaria's reserves had fallen perilously close to the 33.3 per cent minimum backing requirement (figure 1).

By the end of 1931, 14 countries had already followed Britain off gold. In April 1932, urged on by British advisors, Greece too abandoned the fight.[41] The example was hardly encouraging to Mushanov's government, since the shock of leaving the gold standard was sufficient to shake the authority even of the redoubtable Greek Prime Minister Venizelos. In relation to Bulgaria, London in any case equivocated. In May 1932 Frederick Leith-Ross, the British representative in the League of Nations' Commission of Inquiry that monitored the economic performance of the League debtor countries, suggested that Bulgaria should adopt the desperate measures of selling its last remaining gold reserve to maintain its debt service. When news of this heretical suggestion leaked in the *Daily Telegraph* it created a panic in Sofia. With the backing of France and Italy, the Bulgarian authorities vigorously rejected the suggestion.[42] The British chose not to force the issue. Bulgaria was clearly outside their main sphere of interest. At the moment that Otto Niemeyer (Bank of England director and member of the League's Financial Committee) was urging Athens to abandon the gold-exchange standard, all Sofia was getting from him were instructions on how to balance the budget.[43] In September 1932 the British ambassador in Sofia advised the Bulgarian government that Britain 'has no good reason to take measures to save Bulgaria' in the event of a currency crisis.[44]

As in Germany, there were a handful of Bulgarian economists who favoured unorthodox solutions to the crisis.[45] In March 1932 the elitist, technocratic journal *Zveno* suggested a British-style 30 per cent devaluation and two years' moratorium on foreign debt service.[46] The *Slovo* newspaper of the conservative opposition

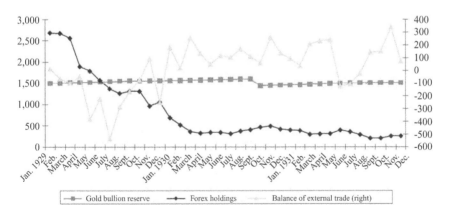

Figure 1 Bulgarian gold-exchange reserves and balance of trade in m. leva, Dec. 1929-Dec. 1931. Source: Proceedings of BNB and Supreme Statistical Office Monthly Bulletin (1929–31).

went as far as to demand a controlled devaluation of as much as 50 per cent.[47] The 'Czech model' of monetary expansion also found adherents.[48] By limiting the gold stock to backing only banknotes in circulation and excluding the sight liabilities of the BNB, it was suggested that the Bank could be enabled to emit an additional 1.2 billion leva in currency. The influential director of the Public Debt Agency (PDA) Nicola Stoyanov proposed a 1 billion leva zero interest credit from the BNB.[49] The cause of heterodoxy was not helped, however, by the fact that its best-known advocate was none other than the notorious Professor Tsankov.[50]

From the autumn of 1931 onwards, advocates of fiscal and monetary conservatism flooded the media with different catastrophic scenarios in case of devaluation. Rather than conformity to the gold standard being seen as a painful international constraint, the People's Bloc government chose to wrap the gold standard in the national flag, hailing the resistance of the lev when the storm of world recession had knocked down first sterling and then the dollar.[51] However, it was Todor Kalinov, director of the Commerce Department in the Ministry of Trade, Industry, and Labour, who put forward what was surely the decisive argument against devaluation, in the Bulgarian as in the German case. With the 'excessive external debts, payable only in gold … neither the exchequer, nor the national economy could benefit from a devaluation of our currency'.[52] A later estimate was to suggest that in case of a 25 per cent devaluation, the debt burden on the public exchequer would have doubled from a quarter to a half of all revenues.[53]

While Bulgaria did not go off gold, given the precarious state of its foreign reserves it had no option but to introduce exchange controls. On 15 October 1931 the BNB was granted full control over the foreign exchange (forex) market with a monopoly on all foreign currency exchange.[54] This was enough to stabilize the immediate situation, but, given Bulgaria's heavy indebtedness and the poor prospects for its exports, it also urgently needed to begin the delicate process of renegotiating its three tranches of foreign debt—the League Loans, reparations, and the pre-1914 loans. The golden fetters may have been loosening, but the coils of debt remained tight.

V

Politically speaking, the least difficult issue to broach in the wake of President Hoover's moratorium on political debts of June 1931 was the issue of reparations. Since the majority of these monies were owed to Greece, the League of Nations approved a bilateral approach to Athens. By the end of the year an accommodation had been agreed in which a moratorium on reparations payments was bartered against the cancellation of Greek payments to Bulgarian refugees.[55]

Far more difficult was the situation with regard to Bulgaria's prewar debts. As a comparison with Greece reveals, the institutional legacy of the pre-1914 debt regime continued to shape the range of options open to Balkan governments in the 1930s. Of Greece's prewar debts, the preponderant share had originated in London (49 per cent). Only 28 per cent came from France. By contrast, in the

Bulgarian case the annulment of prewar debts owing to Germany and Austria-Hungary, which had accounted for 39 per cent of its pre-1912 borrowing, left the French share, which even before 1914 had stood at 45 per cent, entirely dominant.[56] This difference was decisive, because whereas London was pragmatic in its approach, France was to prove fiercely protective of its bondholders.

As was only to be expected, the savage devaluation of the drachma that followed the Greek departure from gold immediately put at risk the service of Greece's foreign debts.[57] Having urged Athens to leave gold, the Treasury and Bank of England made clear that they would not back the British bondholders against the Greek government. A default was duly forthcoming.[58] The outraged protests of *The Times* on behalf of the jilted bondholders were a deep humiliation to Venizelos,[59] but the savings to the Greek economy were undeniable (table 3).

Bulgaria could expect nothing like the same kind of cover from Paris. In early 1932 French bondholders rebuffed an initial approach from the Bulgarian Finance Ministry.[60] Despite its desperate need for financial relief Mushanov's government was therefore forced to adopt a tactic of careful diplomatic manoeuvre. In January 1932 Bulgaria made its application for debt relief not to Paris, but to the League of Nations. The League's initial response was not encouraging, but after a tour of inspection in February the League Council approved a resolution calling for Bulgaria over the next six months (May–October 1932) to transfer only half the

Table 3 Foreign debt negotiations history: % of exchange transfer, 1932–9

Year	Bulgaria	Greece
1932	50% (May–Oct.)	Default, 1 April
	40% (Oct.–Dec.)	30% in forex and 35% in local currency (Aug.–Dec.), not implemented
1933	40% (Jan.–Oct.)	30% + 35% (Jan.–Aug.), not implemented
	25% (Oct.–Dec.)	July, Greece transferred 27.5% for 1933 and 1934
1934	25% (Jan.–July)	
	32.5% (25% + 10% buyback of the non-transferred amounts); (July–Dec.)	Negotiations 'bogged down'
1935	21.5% (15% + 10% buyback of the non-transferred amounts); (Jan.–Dec.)	No payments made, Greece offered 35%, not accepted
1936	29.35% (21.5% + 10% buyback of the non-transferred amounts); (Jan.–Dec.)	40% payment for Aug.–Dec.
1937	Additional transfer of 7.87% for 1935–6 and 5.5% for 1936–7	40% payment for Jan.–March
	32.5%	n.a.
1938	32.5%	No payments
1939	36.5% (Jan.–July)	n.a.
	40% (Aug.–Dec.)	n.a.

Source: Bulgaria: Ivanov, *Politicheskite igri.* Greece: Mazower, *Greece.*

amount due in foreign currency, the rest being held in a blocked account in the name of the foreign advisor to the BNB. Turning a blind eye to the sensitive issue of whether the League's recommendation applied equally to prewar and postwar debts, Sofia seized the opportunity to play one off against the other and rushed through a decree restricting all debt payments as of 20 April.

The British, whose chief concern was with Bulgaria's 1920s bonds, responded in moderate tones. The Corporation of Foreign Bondholders in London limited itself to an expression of 'deep concerns'. Moreover, when in May 1932 Bulgaria honoured the interest due on the postwar debts *The Times* commented that: 'Bulgarian action cannot fail to enhance her credit in the eyes of the investing public in these days when default is unfortunately all too common'.[61] The French, by contrast, were in no mood to be indulgent. The Quai d'Orsay chose to regard Bulgaria's suspension as the first step towards an outright default. It let it be known that it was considering recalling its ambassador from Sofia.[62] In a sharp declaration the Paris creditors committee insisted on a separate account for the non-transferred half of the prewar debts, on which interest should be paid at the normal treasury bill rate. Bulgaria was required to guarantee full payment in convertible currencies after the expiry of the moratorium period and to assure complete equality of treatment between prewar and postwar creditors. When Sofia replied by invoking the authority of the League resolutions, the French bondholders moved swiftly to impose the draconian sanctions provided by the prewar debt agreements. The bondholders instructed their delegate in Sofia to cease handing excise-labels and duty stamps to the government, thus depriving the exchequer of the means to finance its mounting deficit.[63] In extremis, Sofia threatened to print its own excise-labels, but this would have risked a total breach and by mid-July both sides had agreed to accept League of Nations arbitration, which resulted in a settlement not unfavourable to Bulgaria.[64] In the British media, Bulgaria even acquired a reputation as a model debtor.[65] By April 1934, *The Times* 'found it rather striking that a poor country like Bulgaria should feel itself able to increase her external debt payments at a time when richer countries like Germany should still be talking of reducing theirs'.[66]

Given its vastly less favourable starting position, as an impoverished former 'aggressor' in the First World War and given the stark contrast in the attitudes of London and Paris, the results of Bulgaria's debt diplomacy, as shown in table 4,

Table 4 The result of different behaviour: Greece vs. Bulgaria

	Bulgaria	Greece
Total savings, 1931–5 (1929 £ millions)	3.45	10.97
Savings as % of export, 1931–5	19.30%	18.10%
Savings as % of total government expenditures	11.10%	11.00%
Export earnings/total value of foreign debt, 1928–30	36.80%	21.30%

Source: Mazower, *Greece*, p. 315.

were impressive. Thanks to its appeals to the League of Nations, Bulgaria obtained a reduction in its debt burden which, though smaller in absolute terms, was, when measured as a proportion of its export earnings and government outlays, almost on a par with that obtained by Greece. However, these results were not the fruits of a straightforward assertion of national autonomy against the fetters of the international financial system. Rather, they were concessions purchased at the price of a yet further tightening of creditor control.

Following the negotiations of 1932, creditors gained the right to be informed in writing prior to all new economic legislation. Furthermore, any significant economic policy initiative had to carry the seal of approval of the newly constituted Committee of the Four, which from October 1932 acted as a supervisory agency on behalf of the League. The Committee included two prominent Bulgarians, but its powers were considerable, particularly its right to pre-approve treasury bill emissions and short-term advances to the government. When in 1933 the Sobranje failed to meet the agreed deadline for measures to deal with non-performing agricultural debts, the Committee blocked 150 million leva in tax revenue, delaying the payment of September's civil service salary bill.[67] Only with difficulty was Bulgaria able to avoid an even more drastic extension of foreign supervision in the form of the appointment of a financial advisor to exercise direct control over budgeting. The Mushanov government managed to convince Geneva that such a humiliating measure risked reigniting the nationalist passions of the pre-war period. Instead, a dedicated control unit was established within the Finance Ministry.[68]

Though this degree of international supervision certainly constituted a new level of intrusion into Bulgarian sovereignty, it also contributed to domestic efforts at state-building. As part of its campaign to avoid the imposition of a financial advisor, the Mushanov government pushed through a law extending tax administration powers in December 1933. The new Central Control Office in the Ministry of Finance exercised close surveillance over the process of setting and levying taxes. As a result, the gap between actual and forecast revenues closed from more than 35 per cent in fiscal year 1928/9 to virtually nothing by the mid-1930s.[69]

It was not merely budgetary practices that were tightened up. Though we lack the information necessary for a precise estimate of the full-employment budget position of the Bulgarian state, there can be no doubt that the People's Bloc governments, under the watchful eyes of the creditors, administered a severe deflationary shock to the Bulgarian economy. In the face of a rapidly shrinking tax base the deficit on regular account was cut from 605 million leva in the 1930/1 budget to as little as 191 million leva in 1933/4.[70] By the mid-1930s budget outlays were reduced to only two-thirds of the level of 1929/30. Expenditure cuts were reinforced by vigorous efforts to find additional revenues. Altogether, fiscal reform combined with the flow of funds from the non-transferred debt payments brought an additional 1.954 billion leva for the public purse.[71] As a share of disposable money income, taxes rose from 26 per cent in 1928 to 34.3 per cent in 1933.[72]

Table 5 Real effective exchange rates in south-east Europe, 1927–38 (1927 = 100)

	Bulgaria	Greece	Romania	Yugoslavia
1927	100.00	100.00	100.00	100.00
1928	99.47	100.99	102.35	100.72
1929	102.01	101.50	108.88	104.01
1930	105.56	102.73	110.13	110.19
1931	103.08	98.18	110.69	115.77
1932	98.17	134.32	118.63	115.36
1933	95.60	155.58	125.09	115.42
1934	86.14	145.21	127.49	117.19
1935	90.72	137.80	127.68	149.80
1936	99.95	139.69	110.61	145.62
1937	106.56	127.41	102.86	138.92
1938	108.28	128.23	92.69	144.37

Source: Ivanov/Morys south-east Europe data base (further details available from the second author on request).

In the Bulgarian case this deflationary strategy at least had some prospect of success, since even after 1931 more than 85 per cent of Bulgaria's exports went to non-devaluing countries, and because even relative to the deflationary norm of the gold bloc, the Bulgarian deflation was particularly severe. Certainly, Bulgaria's export competitiveness, as measured by the real effective exchange rate, improved considerably after 1930 especially if compared with the other south-east European countries (table 5).[73]

With prices falling so severely, the total money income of the rural population halved between 1929 and 1933.[74] To cushion this disaster, the Mushanov government extended the network of state intervention across the Bulgarian countryside. To absorb non-performing agricultural credits estimated at 10 billion leva or roughly 25 per cent of GNP, the government set up a national debt relief fund, which by the end of the 1930s had absorbed 6.6 billion leva in loans, providing relief to nearly 1.2 million debtors, the largest such operation in the Balkans.[75] The once autonomous agrarian cooperative movement was firmly tied to the state. To stabilize agricultural incomes, a grain purchasing board, the so-called Hranoiznos, was set up, modelled on the controversial grain consortium established by Stamboliiski's government, which had had to be scrapped on the orders of the reparations commission.[76] The new-model Hranoiznos of the 1930s was no more popular with the foreign supervisors of Bulgarian public finance. Niemeyer denounced the grain board as a 'black hole'.[77] However, for the centre-left People's Bloc government the political logic was simply overwhelming. As Finance Minster Stefanov put it in a report to the League, '[T]he losses incurred by the Agency were necessary to ... preserve the internal peace'.[78]

The Bulgarian state's growing managerial capacity was further revealed by the establishment of an elaborate export promotion system. By August 1934 all export commodities had been divided into four lists according to the level of

Table 6 Premium earned by private compensation deals, 1935–9 (%)

	1935	1936	1937	1938	1939
French francs	33.8	31.0	30.5	32.0	34.9
British pounds	—	—	30.5	34.0	35.0
German Reichsmarks	3.9	−1.5	−1.6	−2.0	−1.6
Czech crowns	21.8	18.5	29.9	25.1	20.3
Austrian Schillings	15.7	12.8	27.5	27.4	0.0
Free-traded currencies	35.7	31.9	32.9	33.0	—
Average premiums for all currencies	24.5	22.5	22.0	19.0	—

Source: SYBK (1935–9).

demand in world markets. Those struggling to export 'soft' commodities facing fierce competition in world markets (rose attar, dried tobacco, cattle, lard, meat, dairy products, and so on) were incentivized by being permitted to retain extra quotas of 'free' foreign currency up to a maximum of 50 per cent. This foreign currency could then be exchanged at advantageous rates with would-be importers, whose standard ration of foreign exchange was restricted to no more than 50 per cent of their imports of 1931 (table 6).[79]

VI

Since 1918 Sofia had struggled to come to terms with a unipolar power structure dominated by its former enemies, the Entente powers. The disintegration of the gold standard shook this structure, but Bulgaria remained enmeshed in overlapping regimes of creditor discipline, a discipline that France, the mainstay of the gold bloc, was clearly determined to enforce. Sofia certainly gained financial concessions, which were in fact comparable to those obtained by more aggressive defaulters such as Greece, but it paid the price of even tighter creditor control. By the early 1930s Bulgaria's sovereignty was too severely compromised and its political class too chastened for an outright 'heavy default' to have been a realistic option. This, in turn, throws fresh light on the significance of the rise of Hitler's Germany as Bulgaria's chief economic partner after 1933.

Given the conventional view of Bulgaria as a victim of Nazi 'informal imperialism', it is worth emphasizing that the resurgence of Hitler's Germany in fact offered Bulgaria the opportunity to dramatically expand its room for manoeuvre in economic as well as strategic terms.[80] This was even more the case when France responded to the German threat by moving towards a strategic alliance with the Soviet Union, a move that profoundly destabilized the loyalties of the former Entente partners, notably Romania. Taken together, the re-emergence of Germany and Russia as challengers undid the hegemony exercised since 1918 by the victors of the First World War. In 1933, Sofia followed with close attention as Hitler moved towards a debt moratorium and a break with the League of Nations. Negotiations for a clearing agreement began as early as the autumn of 1933. In early 1934 Tsar Boris was the first foreign head of state to receive an official welcome by the Führer. Whereas in Paris Prime Minister Mushanov had been fobbed off by French foreign minister Louis Barthou, Hitler found time amidst his busy birthday schedule for a personal interview. Field Marshall Hindenburg welcomed him as a former comrade in arms and the Bulgarian prime minister was treated to a working breakfast at the Siemens head office.[81] By the autumn of 1934 the Bulgarian–German clearing agreement was in effect and Germany was taking a large slice of the Bulgarian harvest. With efforts to secure alternative trade deals with France and Britain having met with repeated disappointment, Germany was the only major market open to Bulgaria.[82] Not surprisingly, Germany's share of Bulgarian exports rocketed from a depression low of 26 per cent in 1932 to reach almost 47 per cent in 1937 and to exceed that following the Anschluss in 1938.

The Bulgarians were fully aware of the dangers of over-concentration on Germany. As is clear from table 6, the export subsidy scheme was rigged to counteract this massive German dominance. Sofia never ceased its search for additional clearing arrangements, notably with Czechoslovakia.[83] However, despite the obvious risks, the unprecedented sales to Germany undoubtedly benefited the intensification efforts of the Bulgarian peasantry, particularly since commodity exports were reciprocated by considerable imports of German fertilizer and agricultural equipment.[84]

Nevertheless, the focus in the literature on Bulgaria's trade relations with the Third Reich and the workings of the clearing system has obscured an even more important point.[85] Whatever the precise terms of trade, Bulgaria's economic relations with Nazi Germany were conducted on an entirely different political basis to its fraught relations with France and its other creditors. Economic negotiations between Berlin and Sofia were conducted on terms of ostentatious, formal equality.[86] Bulgaria was not Germany's debtor, but an economic partner and potential strategic ally. By comparison with the western creditors who had sought so forcefully and so consistently to intervene in the inner workings of the Bulgarian state, Berlin appeared the very model of restraint. Unlike the League, Nazi Germany did not peremptorily demand access to Bulgaria's fiscal accounts. Unlike the reparations creditor or French bondholders, Hitler and Goering did not hold hostage Sofia's tax revenues, or insist that debt service should take priority over investment in primary schools. On the contrary, teams of German experts were tasked with drawing up a long-term vision of developmental partnership.[87] This was in large part illusory, of course, but neither Britain nor France had ever offered Bulgaria anything of the sort.

However, if the attractions of this partnership were obvious to Sofia, so were its dangers. It was not that the Nazi regime intervened directly in Bulgarian politics. The risks to Bulgaria arose from Germany's destabilizing effect on the entire balance of power. The danger was that the room for manoeuvre created by the rise of Hitler's Germany would trigger the same kind of all-or-nothing strategic debates that had destabilized Sofia in 1913–15, and though the struggle for power in central Europe gave Bulgaria additional bargaining power, when it came to an outright clash it would once more have to face a moment of existential decision.

By early 1934 Mushanov's government was clearly ailing. The liberal and agrarian wings were at odds. Beyond the government the signs of political polarization were ominous. The Communist party had scored a surprise victory in local elections. Tsankov announced a fascist march on Sofia for 20 May 1934 and there were voices in the Nazi party who advocated throwing their weight behind him, but the German foreign office promptly reined them in. There was to be no repeat of 1923. Instead, on 19 May Mushanov was displaced by a group of technocrats and junior officers. In domestic affairs they continued the state-building efforts of the Tsankov and Mushanov regimes, but in foreign policy they displayed a dangerous new freedom. In the space of a few months they managed both to upset Bulgaria's new German friends by attempting a rapprochement with the Soviet Union and at the same time to alienate Britain and France by reopening the debt question. On 26 October 1934 Bulgaria requested a fact-finding mission from the League of Nations to reconsider the payment schedule.[88] However, even before this could be discussed by the League, Sofia abruptly announced that it would cease payment on selected prewar debts. This was as close as Bulgaria ever came in the interwar period to an outright, unilateral default. The western creditors responded to it as an action quite out of keeping with Bulgaria's previous behaviour. Even at this point, however, Bulgaria did not break off contact with the League. As in 1932, a fact-finding mission was dispatched to Sofia. This time, however, it declared against the Bulgarian government, announcing in January 1935 that payment must continue at the agreed rate. In any case, the 19 May government's dalliance with the Soviets and its dangerous republican tendencies were enough. Within weeks of the League ruling, the king and senior military commanders had launched a counter-coup, installing a succession of conservative cabinets that ruled without relying on the Bulgarian Parliament.[89]

The overriding aim of this 'monarchical dictatorship' was to navigate safely the dangerous new international waters, balancing between the old and new power blocs. In economic policy this meant offsetting the heavy commitment of Bulgarian exports to Germany, against the continued dominance of western creditors on the capital account. In 1935, steering firmly away from the Soviet Union, the Tsar's reward was immediate. Desperate to ward off the German influence, the western creditors agreed to a further reduction in interest payments from 25 to 15 per cent.[90] By 1938 the French had not only agreed to Bulgaria's remilitarization, but were even offering armaments credits.[91] Britain suddenly interested itself in the Bulgarian mining industry. The German foreign office waved tanks and Messerschmitts. Bulgaria was enjoying a degree of external freedom it had not seen since before the First World War. However, this came at a price. Fearful of the polarization that had occurred over the 'alliance question' in the disastrous decade between 1913 and 1923, the Tsar effectively suspended the operation of the Bulgarian Parliament and suppressed both nationalist and left-wing extremes.

Furthermore, though the sums of foreign money on offer were small in the late 1930s relative to those discussed in 1913–14, the strategic linkage was no less explicit. Bulgaria was being asked to choose sides. Even with the lid firmly on domestic radicalism, the choice could be postponed only so long as the balance between the great power blocs was roughly preserved. When in the summer of 1940 Hitler and Stalin began forcibly reordering south-eastern Europe, Bulgaria had little alternative but to eat, or be eaten.

VII

In conclusion, the Bulgarian case suggests the need for a more complex understanding of the relationship between foreign debt and national sovereignty in the early twentieth century. Our case study suggests that the narrative of tension between national politics and the international financial regime articulated by Eichengreen, Bordo, et al. needs to be expanded, to take account of more overt encroachments upon sovereignty than those required by the general rules of the gold standard. Precisely because creditors were interested in issues of governance that went beyond membership in the gold standard, as Flandreau et al. have argued, international lenders developed systems of intrusive regulation. Of course, local elites might regard such restrictions on their freedom of action in pragmatic terms simply as the price that had to be paid for credit. They might regard them cynically as a useful alibi for necessary but unpopular policies, or they might embrace them as a form of developmental discipline, hastening their country along the road to modernization. However, as the Bulgarian Parliament had demonstrated already with regard to the first such loan in 1902, the most straightforward response was one of nationalist rejection. As the bitter experience of the Stamboliiski government suggests, there was no reason to expect creditors to welcome a government simply because it had a solid democratic mandate. Overshadowing these issues of financial governance is the issue of sovereignty in the wider sense of strategic alignment. Where strategic alignment was unproblematic or simply not a matter of choice, as within the safe confines of Ferguson's Pax Britannica, attachment to an external power might well serve as a productive conduit for foreign funds, which in turn might help to consolidate domestic stability and at least a modicum of political pluralism. Where, by contrast, strategic alignment was unclear and the subject of contestation, as was repeatedly the case in Bulgaria, the question of the choice of foreign economic partners and the management of those relationships could easily become too much for a country's fragile political institutions to handle.

Notes

1 We owe our title to Buxton, *Black sheep of the Balkans.*
2 *Crampton, Concise history; Lampe, Bulgarian economy.*
3 On the issue of sovereignty more generally, see Krasner, *Sovereignty.*

4   M. D. Bordo and H. Rockoff, 'The gold standard as a good housekeeping seal of approval', NBER working paper 5340 (1996); Eichengreen, *Golden fetters*; idem, *Globalizing.*

5   Eichengreen and Portes, 'Debt and default'; B. Eichengreen and R. Portes, 'Dealing with debt: the 1930s and the 1980s', CEPR discussion paper 300 (1989); Eichengreen, 'Historical research'.

6   Flandreau and Zumer, *Making.*

7   M. Flandreau and C. Jobst, 'The ties that divide. A network analysis of the International Monetary System', CEPR discussion paper 5129 (2005).

8   Ivanov and Tooze, 'Convergence'.

9   Flandreau and Zumer, *Making*, p. 44.

10 The classic Feis, *Europe*, remains indispensable.

11 The only recent paper fully to appreciate the extent of such sanctions is K. J. Mitchener and M. D. Weidenmier, 'Supersanctions and sovereign debt repayment', NBER working paper 11472 (2005). The effort to downplay their role in Tomz, *Reputation*, is vitiated by the formalistic treatment of his data set, which excludes many of the most important cases of coercive discipline.

12 Feis, *Europe*; Kindleberger, *World in depression*; and with regard to Bulgaria specifically, Friedrich, *Bulgarien.*

13 N. Ferguson and M. Schularick, 'The "thin film of gold": monetary rules and policy credibility in developing countries', NBER working paper 13918 (2008); Ferguson and Schularick, 'Empire effect'; Ferguson, *Empire.*

14 Accominotti, Flandreau, Rezzik, and Zumer, 'Black man's burden'.

15 Feis, *Europe*, p. 272.

16 Lampe and Jackson, *Balkan economic history*, pp. 207–20.

17 Feis, *Europe*, p. 272.

18 Ibid., pp. 263–8.

19 Ibid., pp. 284–92.

20 Lundestad, 'Empire by invitation?'.

21 Ibid., p. 268.

22 Crampton, *Concise history*, pp. 124–9.

23 Feis, *Europe*, pp. 283–4, Bell, *Peasants*, pp. 51–3.

24 Feis, *Europe*, p. 260.

25 For the following, see the extraordinarily illuminating discussion in Friedrich, *Bulgarien*, pp. 20–105.

26 Ibid., pp. 186–8.

27 Bell, *Peasants*, p. 118.

28 Ibid., p. 65; Stoyanov, *Reparatsii*, pp. 93–140; Vatchkov, 'Des essais', pp. 58–9.

29 Feldman, *Great disorder*, p. 434.

30 Petrova, 'Government'; Avramov, *Komunalniat capitalism*, vol. 1, pp. 374–380.

31 Lampe, *Bulgarian economy*, pp. 56–60; Crampton, *Concise history*, pp. 149–57; Petrova, *Samostoyatelnoto*; Vatchkov, 'Antiinfalcionnata politika'; idem, 'Des essais'.

32 Petrova, 'Government', p. 53.

33 Tankova, 'Das System', pp. 79, 90.

34 Bell, *Peasants*, pp. 239–40.

35 Kolev, 'Die Wohnungsfrage'; Tankova 'Das System'.

36 Nenovski and Dimitrova, 'Exchange rate', p. 67.

37 'Tsankov out', *Time*, 18 Jan. 1926.

38 Crampton, *Concise history*; Tankova, 'Das System', pp. 96–7.

39 Parvanova, 'Democratic accord'; idem, 'Stabilization loan'.

40 For a highly critical review, see Moser, *Dimitrov*, pp. 52–5. For a more balanced assessment, see Stojanova, 'Le Parti'.

41 Mazower, *Greece*, pp. 154–76.
42 Editorial, *Sofia*, 8 May 1932; editorial, *Vreme [Times]*, 9 May 1932.
43 Mazower, *Greece*, pp. 151–73; Arhiv na Ministerstvoto na vanshnite raboty (Archive of the Ministry of Foreign Affairs), Sofia, Bulgaria (hereafter Arhiv MVnR), f.176k, a.e. 1848, pp. 1–2.
44 TNA, PRO, FO, 421/318–323, 2 Sept. 1932.
45 Borchardt, 'Constraints'. Cf. also idem, 'Could and should'.
46 Bogomil, 'Anatemosanite sredstva. Moratorium i deflatsiya' ['The anathemized instruments: moratorium and deflation'], *Zveno [Link]*, 5 (1932), pp. 182–5.
47 D. Boshnakov, 'Inflatsiya. Otkazvaneto ot zlatniya standart vodi li kum inflaciya?' [Does abandoning the gold standard lead to inflation?], *Slovo [Word]*, 2979, 26 May 1932; anon., 'Nujdae li se Bulgaria ot zlatniya etalon?' ['Does Bulgaria need the gold standard?'], *Slovo [Word]*, 2982, 30 May 1932.
48 G. Toshev, 'Borba s ikonomicheskata kriza' ['Struggling with the economic crisis'], *Zname [Banner]*, 63, 65–6, 22, 24–5 May 1932; L. Leshtov, 'Banknotnoto obrashtenie' ['Money circulation'], *Vreme [Times]*, 175, 15 May 1932.
49 Tsentralen darjaven arhiv (Central State Archive), Sofia, Bulgaria (hereafter TDA), f. 176k, a. e. 1845, pp. 160–4.
50 A. S. Tsankov, 'Kum inflatsiya?' ['Towards inflation?'], *Izgrev [Dawn]*, 102, 11 May 1932.
51 Bogomil, 'Anatemosanite sredstva. Moratorium i deflatsiya' ['The anathemized instruments: moratorium and deflation'], *Zveno [Link]*, 5 (1932), pp. 182–5; Economist, 'Inflatsiya za nashiya Lev?' ['Inflation for our lev?'], *Targovsko-promishlen glas [Commercial and Industrial Voice]*, no. 1832, 27 May 1932; D. D., 'Pak za inflatsiyata' ['Again on the inflation problem'], *Slovo [Word]*, no. 2989, 7 June 1932.
52 Kalinov, 'Stopanska i kreditna kriza'.
53 M. Dimitrov, 'Nujna li e inflatsiya?' ['Do we need inflation?'], *Slovo [Word]*, 2986, 3 June 1932.
54 Ivanov, *Politicheskite igri*, pp. 106–12.
55 Ibid.
56 Lampe and Jackson, *Balkan economic history*, p. 231.
57 Mazower, *Greece*, pp. 179–202.
58 Nier, *La Politique*, pp. 158–66.
59 'The Greek debt proposal. Bondholders' protest to the editor of *The Times*', *The Times*, 26 April 1932.
60 Service des archives économiques et financiers (Archive of the French Ministry of Finance and Economics) (hereafter SAEF), 33651, report to the French Foreign Ministry, 26 Jan. 1932; Avramov, *Komunalniat kapitalism*, vol. I, pp. 503–6. On the Tardieu plan, see Kaiser, *Economic diplomacy*, pp. 76–8; Noël, 'La Bulgarie'.
61 'The credit of Bulgaria', *The Times*, 4 May 1932; Corporation of Foreign Bondholders, *30th annual report*.
62 SAEF 32804, 2 May 1932.
63 Avramov, *Komunalniat kapitalism*, vol. I, pp. 509–15; Ivanov, *Politicheskite igri*, pp. 80–6; Nier, *La Politique*, pp. 131–2.
64 TDA, f. 258k, a.e. 634, pp. 100–4, 143; Ivanov, *Politicheskite igri*, pp. 78–85; Avramov, *Komunalniat kapitalism*, vol. I, pp. 514–19.
65 'Bulgaria pays', *The Times*, 17 March 1932; 'The Bulgarian payments', *The Times*, 19 March 1932; 'Bulgarian League loans: settlement of unpaid interest', *The Times*, 4 May 1934.
66 'Bulgarian League loans: government's proposal', *The Times*, 20 April 1934.
67 TDA, f. 258k, a.e. 944, pp. 124–8; Ivanov, 'Mojehme li', p. 60.
68 TDA, f. 366b, a.e. 46, pp. 89–90.
69 Ivanov, 'Mojehme li', p. 77.

70 Nedkov, 'Razvitie', p. 213.
71 Ivanov, *Politicheskite igri*, pp. 61–144.
72 Tchakalov, *Nationalniat dohod*, p. 141.
73 Ivanov/Morys south-east Europe data base.
74 Tchakalov, *Nationalniat dohod*, p. 119.
75 Palazov, 'Problemata'; idem, 'Za oblekchavaneto', p. 19; Stojanova, 'Le Parti', pp. 194–7.
76 Lampe and Jackson, *Balkan economic history*, p. 450.
77 TNA, PRO, FO 421/318–323, pp. 76–9.
78 *13e Rapport du Ministre, p. 8.*
79 Bobchev, 'Vanshnata targovia', pp. 16–18; Ivanov, *Politicheskite igri*, pp. 131–2.
80 For an excellent review of the literature to date, see Ritschl, 'Nazi'. Our argument, by contrast, develops Hoppe, *Bulgarien.*
81 *Zname [Banner]*, 14 April 1934, 19 April 1934, editorial.
82 For a recent round of contrasting accounts of the Bulgarian-German clearing system, cf., respectively, Avramov, *Komunalniat kapitalism*, vol. II, pp. 250–1, and Zlatarsky, 'Raihat', pp. 248–9.
83 Hoppe, *Bulgarien*, p. 48.
84 Ivanov and Tooze, 'Convergence'; Zlatarsky, 'Raihat'; Momtchiloff, *Ten years.*
85 Asenova, *Money.*
86 Confirmed by Zlatarsky, 'Raihat'.
87 For instance, Leibrock, *Bulgarien*; Wagemann, *Der Neue*; Kalinov, ed., *Die bulgarische.*
88 For the following, see TDA, f. 393k, op. 1, a.e. 14, pp. 105–7; ibid., a.e. 15, pp. 13–14.
89 Crampton, *Concise history*, pp. 163–4.
90 Corporation of Foreign Bondholders, *32nd annual report.*
91 Hoppe, *Bulgarien*, pp. 53–62.

References

Accominotti, O., Flandreau, M., Rezzik, R., and Zumer, F., 'Black man's burden, white man's welfare: control, devolution and development in the British Empire 1880–1914', *European Review of Economic History*, 14 (2010), pp. 47–70.

Asenova, V., *Money and power in bilateral relations. German-Bulgarian relations in the interwar period* (Saarbruecken, 2008).

Avramov, R., *Komunalniat kapitalism [Communal capitalism], 3* vols. (Sofia, 2007).

Bell, J. D., *Peasants in power. Alexander Stamboliski and the Bulgarian agrarian national union, 1899–1923* (Princeton, N.J., 1977).

Bobchev, K., 'Vanshnata targovia na Bulgaria sled voinata' ['Bulgarian foreign trade after the Second World War'], *Trudove na stopanskiyat institute za socialny poruchvaniya pri Sofiiskya darjaven universitet [Working papers of the Economic Institute for Social Studies at Sofia State University]*, 4 (1938), pp. 1–48.

Borchardt, K., 'Constraints and room for manoeuvre in the Great Depression of the early thirties: towards a revision of the received historical picture', in K. Borchardt, ed., *Perspectives on modern German economic history and policy* (Cambridge, 1991), pp. 143–60.

Borchardt, K., 'Could and should Germany have followed Great Britain in leaving the gold standard?', *Journal of European Economic History*, 13 (1984), pp. 471–97.

Buxton, L., *The black sheep of the Balkans* (1920).

Corporation of Foreign Bondholders, *30th annual report* (1933).

Corporation of Foreign Bondholders, *32nd annual report* (1935).

Crampton, R. J., *A concise history of Bulgaria* (Cambridge, 2003).

13e rapport du Ministre des finances sur la situation budgétaire (Geneve, 16 Jan. 1932).

Eichengreen, B., *Golden fetters: the gold standard and the Great Depression, 1919–1939* (Oxford, 1989).

Eichengreen, B., 'Historical research on international lending and debt', *Journal of Economic Perspectives*, 5 (1991), pp. 149–69.

Eichengreen, B., *Globalizing capital: a history of the international monetary system* (2nd edn. Princeton, 2008).

Eichengreen, B. and Portes, R., 'Debt and default in the 1930s: causes and consequences', *European Economic Review*, 30 (1986), pp. 599–640.

Feis, H., *Europe the world's banker 1870–1914* (New Haven, Conn., 1930).

Feldman, G. D., *The great disorder. Politics, economics, and society in the German inflation 1914–1924* (Oxford, 1997).

Ferguson, N., *Empire. How Britain made the modern world* (2003).

Ferguson, N. and Schularick, M., 'The empire effect. The determinants of country risk in the first age of globalization, 1880–1913', *Journal of Economic History*, 66 (2006), pp. 283–312.

Flandreau, M. and Zumer, F., *The making of global finance 1880–1913* (Paris, 2004).

Friedrich, W.-U., *Bulgarien und die Mächte 1913–1915. Ein Beitrag zur Weltkrieg-s und Imperialismusgeschichte* (Stuttgart, 1985).

Hoppe, H.-J., *Bulgarien—Hitlers eigenwilliger Verbündeter* (Stuttgart, 1979).

Ivanov, M., *Politicheskite igri s vanshniya dalg. Blgaski siujheti na stopanski krizi i vazhod, 1929–1934 [Bulgarian foreign debt and foreign trade during the Great Depression]* (Sofia, 2001).

Ivanov, M., 'Mojehme li da devalvirame? Kakvo se krie zad ortodoksalnia bulgarski otgovor na Golyamata depresia?' ['Could we have devalued in 1930s? What hides behind Bulgarian orthodox policy during the Great Depression?'], *Istoricheski Pregled [Historical Review]*, 61 (2005), pp. 60–80.

Ivanov, M. and Tooze, A., 'Convergence or decline on Europe's southeastern periphery? Agriculture, population, and GNP in Bulgaria, 1892–1945', *Journal of Economic History*, 67 (2007), pp. 672–703.

Kaiser, D. E., *Economic diplomacy and the origins of the Second World War: Germany, Britain, France, and Eastern Europe, 1930–1939* (Princeton, N.J., 1981).

Kalinov, T., 'Stopanska i kreditna kriza' ['Economic and credit crisis'], *Spisanie na Bulgarskoto ikonomichesko druzhestvo [Journal of the Bulgarian Economic Society]*, 31 (1932), pp. 24–37.

Kalinov, T., ed., *Die bulgarische Landwirtschaft. Deutsch-bulgarische Gemeinschaftsarbeit* (Berlin, 1942).

Kindleberger, C. P., *The world in depression 1919–1939* (Berkeley, Calif., 1973).

Kolev, V., 'Die Wohnungsfrage unter der Regierung von Prof. Alexander Zankov (1923–1925)', *Bulgarian Historical Review*, 24 (1996), pp. 148–65.

Krasner, S. D., *Sovereignty. Organized hypocrisy* (Princeton, N.J., 1999).

Lampe, J. R., *The Bulgarian economy in the twentieth century* (London and Sydney, 1986).

Lampe, J. R. and Jackson, M. R., *Balkan economic history, 1550–1950: from imperial borderlands to developing nations* (Bloomington, Ind., 1982).

Leibrock, O., *Bulgarien Gestern und Heute* (Berlin, 1938).

Lundestad, G., 'Empire by invitation? The United States and western Europe, 1945–1952', *Journal of Peace Research*, 23 (1986), pp. 263–77.

Mazower, M., *Greece and the inter-war economic crisis* (Oxford, 1991).

Momtchiloff, N., *Ten years of controlled trade in south-eastern Europe* (Cambridge, 1944).

Moser, C. A., *Dimitrov of Bulgaria. A political biography of Dr Georgi M. Dimitrov* (Ottawa, Ill., 1979).

Nedkov, B., 'Razvitie na bulgarskata finansova sistema prez poslednoto desetiletie' ['The Bulgarian financial system during the last decade'], *Trudove na stopanskiyat institute za socialny poruchvaniya pri Sofiiskya darjaven universitet [Working papers of the Economic Institute for Social Studies at Sofia State University]*, 3 (1937), pp. 1–212.

Nenovski, N. and Dimitrova, K., 'Exchange rate and inflation: France and Bulgaria in the interwar period', in R. Avramov and S. Pamuk, eds., *Monetary and fiscal policies in south-east Europe: historical and comparative perspective* (Sofia, 2006), pp. 57–92.

Nier, H., *La Politique de Moratoire en matiere de fonds d'état dans les pays Balkaniques, 1932–1934* (Paris, 1934).

Noël, G., 'La Bulgarie entre les deux guerres: un pays agricole marginalisé', *Etudes Balkaniques*, 00 (1999), pp. 97–109.

Palazov, I., 'Problemata za oblekchavaneto na dlajnitsite' ['Debt relief problem'], *Spisanie na Bulgarskoto ikonom-ichesko druzhestvo [Journal of the Bulgarian Economic Society]*, 31 (1932), pp. 206–20.

Palazov, I., 'Za oblekchavaneto na dlajnitsite' ['Debt relief for the debtors'], *Spisanie Na Sajuza Na Popularnite Banki [Journal of the Union of Popular Banks]*, 17 (1938), pp. 18–24.

Parvanova, R., 'The democratic accord and the stabilization loan', *Bulgarian Historical Review*, 26 (1998), pp. 197–217.

Parvanova, R., 'The stabilization loan to Bulgaria of 1928', *Bulgarian Historical Review*, 27 (1999), pp. 72–96.

Petrova, D., *Samostoyatelnoto upravlenie na BZNS 1920–1923 [The government of the Bulgarian Agrarian People's Union 1920–1923]* (Sofia, 1988).

Petrova, D., 'The government of the Bulgarian Agrarian People's Union and the control exercised by the entente (1920–1923)', *Bulgarian Historical Review*, 18 (1990), pp. 36–55.

Ritschl, A. O., 'Nazi economic imperialism and the exploitation of the small: evidence from Germany's secret foreign exchange balances, 1938–1940', *Economic History Review*, LIV (2001), pp. 324–45.

Stojanova, R., 'Le parti democratique et la politique economique du bloc populaire (1931–1934)', *Bulgarian Historical Review*, 26 (1998), pp. 174–214.

Stoyanov, N., *Reparatsii i mejhdusajuzni dalgove. Balgarski darjavni dalgove [Reparations and sovereign debts. Bulgarian public debts]* (Sofia, 1933).

Tankova, W., 'Das System der wirtschaftlichen Verwaltung in Bulgarien zwischen den zweiWeltkriegen', *Bulgarian Historical Review*, 28 (2000), pp. 76–111.

Tchakalov, A., *Nationalniat dohod i razhod na Balgaria 1924–1945 [National income and outlay of Bulgaria 1924–1945]* (Sofia, 1946).

Tomz, M., *Reputation and international cooperation: sovereign debt across three centuries* (Princeton, N.J., 2007).

Vatchkov, D., 'Des essais de rétablissements financier et économique de la Bulgarie après la premier guerre mondiale (1920–1923)', *Bulgarian Historical Review*, 28 (2000), pp. 56–83.

Vatchkov, D., 'Antiinfalcionnata politika na BZNS v perioda na samostoyatelnoto mu upravlenie' ['Anti-inflation policy of the BANU government'], *Istoria [History]*, 11 (2003), pp. 102–9.

Wagemann, E., *Der Neue Balkan* (Hamburg, 1939).

Zlatarsky, V., 'Raihat i tsarstvoto. Germanskoto prisastvie v Bulgaria' ['The Reich and the Kingdom. German presence in Bulgaria'] (unpub. Ph.D. thesis, Bulgarian Academy of Sciences, 2008).

CPSIA information can be obtained
at www.ICGtesting.com
Printed in the USA
BVHW010442160222
628968BV00013B/27